INTERPRETING THE MMPI-2-RF

Interpreting the MMPI-2-RF

Yossef S. Ben-Porath

University of Minnesota Press
Minneapolis · London

Published by the University of Minnesota Press
111 Third Avenue South, Suite 290
Minneapolis, MN 55401–2520
http://www.upress.umn.edu

Library of Congress Cataloging-in-Publication Data

Ben-Porath, Yossef S.
  Interpreting the MMPI-2-RF / Yossef S. Ben-Porath.
  Includes bibliographical references and index.
    ISBN 978-0-8166-6966-0 (hc : alk. paper)
  I. Title.
  [DNLM: 1. MMPI. WM 145.5.M6]
  616.890076—dc23
                         2011031741

Printed in the United States of America on acid-free paper

The University of Minnesota is an equal-opportunity educator and employer.

19 18 17 16 15 14 13 12   10 9 8 7 6 5 4 3 2 1

To Auke Tellegen—
mentor, colleague, friend.

Contents

List of Tables   ix

List of Figures   xi

Preface   xv

Chapter 1   **Historical Foundations of the MMPI-2-RF: The MMPI and MMPI-2**   1
  The Original MMPI   1
  The MMPI-2   20
  Conclusions   36
  Toward the MMPI-2-RF   37

Chapter 2   **Transitioning to the MMPI-2-RF: The Restructured Clinical (RC) Scales**   39
  Why Restructure the Clinical Scales?   39
  Developing the Restructured Clinical Scales   43
  Delineating the Restructured Clinical Scale Constructs   52
  Appraisals of the Restructured Clinical Scales   92

Chapter 3   **Completing Development of the MMPI-2-RF: The Substantive Scales**   97
  Higher-Order Scales   98
  Specific Problems and Interest Scales   106
  Personality Psychopathology Five Scales   126
  Conclusion   131

Chapter 4   **Completing Development of the MMPI-2-RF: The Validity Scales**   133
  Threats to Protocol Validity   133
  Assessing Threats to Protocol Validity with the
    Original MMPI   137
  The MMPI-2 Validity Scales   148
  The MMPI-2-RF Validity Scales   159
  Conclusion   174

Chapter 5   **Administering and Scoring the MMPI-2-RF**   175
  Administering the MMPI-2-RF   175
  Scoring the MMPI-2-RF   181
  Computer-Generated Reports   191
  Conclusion   240

Chapter 6   **Interpreting the MMPI-2-RF Validity Scales**   241
            Guidelines for Interpreting the MMPI-2-RF Validity Scales   241
            Integrating MMPI-2-RF Validity Scale Findings   252

Chapter 7   **Interpreting the MMPI-2-RF Substantive Scales**   277
            Higher-Order Scales   279
            Restructured Clinical Scales   281
            Specific Problems Scales   292
            Interest Scales   310
            Personality Psychopathology Five Scales   313

Chapter 8   **Interpreting the MMPI-2-RF: Recommended Framework and Process**   319
            Using the MMPI-2-RF Interpretation Worksheet   319
            Case Example: Mr. I   341
            Conclusion   354

Chapter 9   **MMPI-2-RF Case Studies**   355
            Ms. G: Obsessive–Compulsive Symptoms   355
            Mr. P: A Chronic and Severe Disorder   366
            Ms. L: An Abusive Relationship Ends   378
            Mr. E: Substance-Induced Psychotic Symptoms   390
            Mr. D: Bariatric Surgery Candidate   401
            Ms. B: Spine Surgery Candidate   413
            Ms. X: A Case of Factitious Disorder   424
            Ms. R: A Case of Posttraumatic Stress Disorder   435
            Mr. M: Not Guilty by Reason of Insanity   446
            Mr. F: Law Enforcement Officer Candidate   459

Chapter 10 **Summary and Initial Appraisals of the MMPI-2-RF**   473
            Appraisals of the MMPI-2-RF   474
            Conclusion   476

Notes   479
References   483
Index of Subjects   513
Index of Names   529

Tables

5-1.	Percentile Equivalents of Uniform T Scores	191
5-2.	Demographic Characteristics of the Standard Comparison Groups	207
5-3.	Scales Considered in the Substantive Scale Interpretation Section	230
5-4.	Possible Diagnostic Considerations	231
6-1.	CNS (Cannot Say) Interpretation	242
6-2.	VRIN-r (Variable Response Inconsistency) Interpretation	243
6-3.	TRIN-r (True Response Inconsistency) Interpretation	244
6-4.	F-r (Infrequent Responses) Interpretation	245
6-5.	Fp-r (Infrequent Psychopathology Responses) Interpretation	247
6-6.	Fs (Infrequent Somatic Responses) Interpretation	248
6-7.	FBS-r (Symptom Validity) Interpretation	249
6-8.	RBS (Response Bias) Interpretation	250
6-9.	L-r (Uncommon Virtues) Interpretation	251
6-10.	K-r (Adjustment Validity) Interpretation	253
6-11.	MMPI-2-RF Validity Scales: Threats to Protocol Validity and Confounds	255
7-1.	EID (Emotional/Internalizing Dysfunction) Interpretation	280
7-2.	THD (Thought Dysfunction) Interpretation	280
7-3.	BXD (Behavioral/Externalizing Dysfunction) Interpretation	281
7-4.	RCd (Demoralization) Interpretation	283
7-5.	RC1 (Somatic Complaints) Interpretation	284
7-6.	RC2 (Low Positive Emotions) Interpretation	285
7-7.	RC3 (Cynicism) Interpretation	286
7-8.	RC4 (Antisocial Behavior) Interpretation	287
7-9.	RC6 (Ideas of Persecution) Interpretation	288
7-10.	RC7 (Dysfunctional Negative Emotions) Interpretation	289
7-11.	RC8 (Aberrant Experiences) Interpretation	290
7-12.	RC9 (Hypomanic Activation) Interpretation	291
7-13.	MLS (Malaise) Interpretation	293
7-14.	GIC (Gastrointestinal Complaints) Interpretation	294
7-15.	HPC (Head Pain Complaints) Interpretation	294
7-16.	NUC (Neurological Complaints) Interpretation	296
7-17.	COG (Cognitive Complaints) Interpretation	296
7-18.	SUI (Suicide/Death Ideation) Interpretation	298
7-19.	HLP (Helplessness/Hopelessness) Interpretation	298
7-20.	SFD (Self-Doubt) Interpretation	300
7-21.	NFC (Inefficacy) Interpretation	300
7-22.	STW (Stress/Worry) Interpretation	301
7-23.	AXY (Anxiety) Interpretation	301
7-24.	ANP (Anger-Proneness) Interpretation	303
7-25.	BRF (Behavior-Restricting Fears) Interpretation	303
7-26.	MSF (Multiple Specific Fears) Interpretation	304

7-27.   JCP (Juvenile Conduct Problems) Interpretation   305
7-28.   SUB (Substance Abuse) Interpretation   306
7-29.   AGG (Aggression) Interpretation   306
7-30.   ACT (Activation) Interpretation   308
7-31.   FML (Family Problems) Interpretation   308
7-32.   IPP (Interpersonal Passivity) Interpretation   309
7-33.   SAV (Social Avoidance) Interpretation   311
7-34.   SHY (Shyness) Interpretation   311
7-35.   DSF (Disaffiliativeness) Interpretation   312
7-36.   AES (Aesthetic–Literary Interests) Interpretation   312
7-37.   MEC (Mechanical–Physical Interests) Interpretation   313
7-38.   AGGr-r (Aggressiveness–Revised) Interpretation   315
7-39.   PSYC-r (Psychoticism–Revised) Interpretation   315
7-40.   DISC-r (Disconstraint–Revised) Interpretation   316
7-41.   NEGE-r (Negative Emotionality/Neuroticism–Revised)
         Interpretation   317
7-42.   INTR-r (Introversion/Low Positive Emotions) Interpretation   318
 8-1.   Recommended Framework and Sources of Information for
         MMPI-2-RF Interpretation   320

Figures

5-1. MMPI-2-RF Validity Scales: Normative sample mean T scores and associated standard deviations.   184

5-2. MMPI-2-RF Higher-Order (HOD) and Restructured Clinical (RC) Scales: Normative sample mean T scores and associated standard deviations.   185

5-3. MMPI-2-RF Somatic/Cognitive and Internalizing Scales: Normative sample mean T scores and associated standard deviations.   186

5-4. MMPI-2-RF Externalizing, Interpersonal, and Interest Scales: Normative sample mean T scores and associated standard deviations.   187

5-5. MMPI-2-RF Personality Psychopathology Five (PSY-5) Scales: Normative sample mean T scores and associated standard deviations.   188

5-6. Prototype distribution used as a target for deriving the Uniform T scores.   190

5-7. Mr. I's MMPI-2-RF Score Report, page 1.   193

5-8. Mr. I's MMPI-2-RF Score Report, page 2.   194

5-9. Mr. I's MMPI-2-RF Score Report, page 3.   195

5-10. Mr. I's MMPI-2-RF Score Report, page 4.   196

5-11. Mr. I's MMPI-2-RF Score Report, page 5.   197

5-12. Mr. I's MMPI-2-RF Score Report, page 6.   198

5-13. Mr. I's MMPI-2-RF Score Report, page 7.   199

5-14. Mr. I's MMPI-2-RF Score Report, page 8.   200

5-15. Mr. I's MMPI-2-RF Score Report, pages 9–10.   201

5-16. Mr. I's MMPI-2-RF Score Report with Comparison Group data, page 2.   209

5-17. Mr. I's MMPI-2-RF Score Report with Comparison Group data, page 3.   210

5-18. Mr. I's MMPI-2-RF Score Report with Comparison Group data, page 4.   211

5-19. Mr. I's MMPI-2-RF Score Report with Comparison Group data, page 5.   212

5-20. Mr. I's MMPI-2-RF Score Report with Comparison Group data, page 6.   213

5-21. Mr. I's MMPI-2-RF Score Report with item-level information, pages 8–10.   215

5-22. Mr. I's MMPI-2-RF Interpretive Report, pages 8–17.   220

5-23. An invalid MMPI-2-RF.   234

5-24. An invalid MMPI-2-RF Interpretive Report, page 8.   239

6-1. MMPI-2-RF Score Report Validity Scales profile showing nonresponding.   256

6-2.   MMPI-2-RF Score Report Validity Scales profile showing
         variable inconsistent responding.   258
6-3.   MMPI-2-RF Score Report Validity Scales profile showing
         fixed "false" responding.   260
6-4.   MMPI-2-RF Score Report Validity Scales profile showing
         fixed "true" responding.   261
6-5.   MMPI-2-RF Score Report Validity Scales profile showing
         variable and fixed responding.   262
6-6.   MMPI-2-RF Score Report Validity Scales profile showing
         a highly elevated F-r score reflecting overreporting.   264
6-7.   MMPI-2-RF Score Report Validity Scales profile showing
         an elevated F-r scale possibly reflecting genuine
         psychopathology.   265
6-8.   MMPI-2-RF Score Report Validity Scales profile showing
         an elevated Fp-r score reflecting overreporting of severe
         psychopathology.   266
6-9.   MMPI-2-RF Score Report Validity Scales profile showing
         an elevated Fs score very likely indicating overreporting
         of somatic symptoms.   267
6-10.   MMPI-2-RF Score Report Validity Scales profile showing
         scale elevations very likely reflecting overreporting of
         somatic, cognitive, and psychological symptoms.   269
6-11.   MMPI-2-RF Score Report Validity Scales profile showing
         an elevated RBS score very likely reflecting exaggerated
         cognitive complaints.   270
6-12.   MMPI-2-RF Score Report Validity Scales profile showing
         an elevated L-r score very likely reflecting underreporting.   272
6-13.   MMPI-2-RF Score Report H-O/RC Scales profile showing
         elevations on RC3 and RC6.   273
6-14.   MMPI-2-RF Score Report Validity Scales profile showing
         an elevated K-r score very likely reflecting underreporting.   275
6-15.   MMPI-2-RF Score Report Validity Scales profile showing
         elevated scores on L-r and K-r very likely reflecting
         underreporting.   276
8-1.   MMPI-2-RF interpretation worksheet.   321
8-2.   MMPI-2-RF interpretation worksheet with completed
         Validity Scales page.   326
8-3.   MMPI-2-RF Score Report Validity Scales profile.   327
8-4.   Mr. B's MMPI-2-RF Score Report.   329
8-5.   Mr. B's MMPI-2-RF completed interpretation worksheet.   335
8-6.   Mr. I's MMPI-2-RF Score Report.   342
8-7.   Mr. I's completed MMPI-2-RF interpretation worksheet.   348
9-1.   Ms. G's MMPI-2-RF Score Report.   356
9-2.   Mr. P's MMPI-2-RF Score Report.   368

9-3.	Ms. L's MMPI-2-RF Score Report.	380
9-4.	Mr. E's MMPI-2-RF Score Report.	392
9-5.	Mr. D's MMPI-2-RF Score Report.	403
9-6.	Ms. B's MMPI-2-RF Score Report.	414
9-7.	Ms. X's MMPI-2-RF Score Report.	426
9-8.	Ms. R's MMPI-2-RF Score Report.	437
9-9.	Mr. M's MMPI-2-RF Score Report.	448
9-10.	Mr. F's MMPI-2-RF Score Report.	460

Preface

The Fifth Annual Symposium on Recent Developments in the Use of the MMPI was convened in 1970 to honor the codeveloper of the MMPI, Starke Hathaway. The conference included a discussion of how to go about updating the then 30-year-old test, with leading authorities in personality assessment providing recommendations for its revision. Another decade was to pass before the research project that generated a revised inventory was launched, and almost two decades passed before the MMPI-2 was published. As a member of the committee charged with revising the inventory, Professor Auke Tellegen, of the University of Minnesota, advocated that the update include a comprehensive revision of the original MMPI Clinical Scales. However, to maintain continuity between the original and revised inventories, the committee chose to keep the Clinical Scales intact, thus not addressing in the MMPI-2 the problems with the scales identified during the 1970 symposium.

Following up on his proposal, Tellegen began work in the early 1990s on a project that eventually produced the MMPI-2 Restructured Clinical (RC) Scales. I joined the effort to revise the Clinical Scales at its conclusion in 1998. We spent the next four years studying the RC Scales, analyzing data from samples that represented a broad range of settings in which the MMPI-2 was used. We sought to evaluate the psychometric properties of the scales and to develop interpretive guidelines for them. Our findings and recommendations were incorporated into a monograph (Tellegen, Ben-Porath, McNulty, Arbisi, Graham & Kaemmer, 2003) published when the RC Scales were added to the MMPI-2. In the concluding chapter of the monograph, we noted that further research could eventually produce a completely restructured inventory, and Tellegen and I spent the next several years first exploring this possibility and then developing the MMPI-2 Restructured Form (MMPI-2-RF) and its supporting material and documentation. Publication of the MMPI-2-RF in 2008 was thus the culmination of a 10-year collaborative effort to modernize the MMPI.

Our objective in developing the MMPI-2-RF was to represent the clinically significant substance of the MMPI-2 item pool with a comprehensive set of psychometrically adequate measures. A central aspect of our approach was to link the test to contemporary concepts and models of personality and psychopathology. Our aim was to enhance the construct validity of the instrument, an intended feature of the original MMPI, which, as described in Chapter 1, had largely given way to criterion validity-focused interpretation. Although not necessary for the success of the revision, we assumed that assessment of the clinically significant substance represented by the item pool of the test could be accomplished with fewer than the 567 MMPI-2 items. A reduction of approximately 40% in the length of the instrument was a welcome confirmation of this expectation.

When developing the MMPI-2-RF materials, we were mindful that contrary to the availability of secondary sources (i.e., textbooks) to guide MMPI-2 interpretation, the test manual would initially be the only source available to MMPI-2-RF users. We therefore opted to provide comprehensive coverage of psychometric findings in the *MMPI-2-RF Technical Manual* (Tellegen & Ben-Porath, 2008/2011) and detailed guidelines for use of the test and, in particular, its interpretation in the *MMPI-2-RF Manual for Administration, Scoring, and Interpretation* (Ben-Porath & Tellegen, 2008/2011). The present volume is designed to complement these primary sources. In Chapters 1–4, the foundations of the MMPI-2-RF are described in detail, beginning with a comprehensive review of the development of the MMPI and MMPI-2, linking the current version of the test to its predecessors, followed by a detailed description of the restructuring of the Clinical Scales and the development of the remaining MMPI-2-RF Substantive Scales and validity indicators. The psychological constructs assessed by the MMPI-2-RF are described in detail, and empirical findings related to these constructs and the MMPI-2-RF Scales are reviewed. Chapters 5–8 provide detailed recommendations for administration, scoring, and interpretation of the MMPI-2-RF. These chapters build on material covered in the *Manual for Administration, Scoring, and Interpretation* and on several years of experience using and teaching the MMPI-2-RF. Chapter 9 provides 10 case studies designed to illustrate MMPI-2-RF use and interpretation in a broad range of settings in which the test is used. Chapter 10 includes a brief review of initial appraisals of the inventory.

Several individuals made important contributions to this book, for which I am very thankful. MMPI-2-RF coauthor Auke Tellegen and Krista Isakson, from Pearson, provided helpful recommendations during planning for the book. Karly Gritzan and Nicole Sanders provided extensive administrative assistance during its writing. Karen Perkins, from Pearson, provided instrumental assistance in developing the case material used to illustrate MMPI-2-RF interpretation. Andrew Block, Roger Gervais, and Manfred Greiffenstein each provided one of the cases used to illustrate MMPI-2-RF interpretation in Chapter 9. Neil Aronov, Paul Arbisi, Hope Goldberg, and Auke Tellegen provided very helpful reviews of an initial draft of the book. Beverly Kaemmer, associate director of the University of Minnesota Press, provided much-needed and appreciated support in all aspects of development and writing of *Interpreting the MMPI-2-RF*. Bev's steadfast leadership and skillful shepherding of the MMPI enterprise are gratefully acknowledged.

I would also like to acknowledge the support and encouragement of my wife, Denise, and children Adam, Johnathan, and Ella. Their patience and perseverance made completion of this project possible.

CHAPTER 1

Historical Foundations of the MMPI-2-RF: The MMPI and MMPI-2

The MMPI item pool, assembled by Hathaway and McKinley (1943) and augmented for the MMPI-2 by Butcher, Dahlstrom, Graham, Tellegen, and Kaemmer (1989), has been a mainstay of psychological assessment for seven decades, a testament to the richness and clinical utility of the MMPI instruments. However, the original MMPI Clinical Scales, constructed in the late 1930s using then state-of-the-art methods, do not conform to modern psychometric standards. To address this shortcoming, Professor Auke Tellegen, of the University of Minnesota, initiated a revision of the Clinical Scales shortly after the MMPI-2 was published. Tellegen's development of the MMPI-2 Restructured Clinical (RC) Scales (Tellegen, Ben-Porath, McNulty, Arbisi, Graham & Kaemmer, 2003) became the first phase of a project to revise the entire MMPI-2, which resulted in the MMPI-2-RF (Restructured Form).

To set the stage for chapters discussing the rationale for and methods used to develop the MMPI-2-RF, this chapter begins with a review of the original MMPI, outlining the conceptual and empirical foundations of the test, major milestones in its development and use as a clinical assessment device, and the role it played in some important developments in assessing personality and psychopathology. The MMPI Restandardization Project and its product, the MMPI-2, are described next, including discussion of both the major accomplishments and limitations of the revision.

THE ORIGINAL MMPI

As detailed by Dahlstrom (1992), the MMPI was published during a period of increasing skepticism concerning the utility of self-report personality inventories (e.g., Landis & Katz, 1934; Landis, Zubin & Katz, 1935). The two major instruments in use at the time, the Bernreuter Psychoneurotic Inventory (Bernreuter, 1933) and the Humm–Wadsworth Temperament Scales (Humm & Wadsworth, 1935), were viewed as overly transparent and, as a result, subject to manipulative distortion. They were also considered too narrow in scope to serve as omnibus measures of psychopathology. Thus, Hathaway and McKinley (1940) sought to "create a large reservoir of items from which various scales might be constructed in the hope of *evolving* a greater variety of valid personality descriptions than are available at the present time" (p. 249; emphasis added). It is noteworthy that as early as 1940, Hathaway and McKinley viewed their initial efforts at scale development as a starting point for what they hoped would be an evolving instrument.

Theoretical Foundations

The scale construction method that Hathaway and McKinley adopted was clearly empirical, but it is a mistake to view the development of the MMPI as atheoretical. The inventory was assembled in a medical setting, to be used as a screening instrument for the detection of psychopathology. The test authors relied on an existing model of psychopathology and were influenced by behavioral and psychodynamic thinking as well as by the psychometric knowledge and experience of their time.

When compiling the candidate test items, Hathaway and McKinley (1940) were guided by psychiatric practices of the 1930s:

> The individual items were formulated partly on the basis of previous clinical experience. Mainly, however, the items were supplied from several psychiatric examination direction forms, from various textbooks of psychiatry, from certain of the directions for case taking in medicine and neurology, and from the earlier published scales of personal and social attitudes. (p. 249)

In selecting targets for scale development, Hathaway and McKinley followed the diagnostic classification system of the 1930s, which was a derivative of the descriptive system developed by Kraepelin (1921). Kraepelinian nosology, which allowed for reliable diagnoses of disorders such as Hysteria, Schizophrenia, and Manic Depression, supplied the model for the initial designation of MMPI scales, and a combination of behavioral, psychodynamic, and psychometric thinking characterized early theoretical writings on the test. All three elements are found in Meehl's (1945a) article "The Dynamics of 'Structured' Personality Tests," written in response to a critique of self-report personality inventories that faulted them for relying on the assumption that test items must always have the same meaning for different individuals. While agreeing that this assumption was unsupported, Meehl asserted that it was also unnecessary for tests such as the MMPI:

> A "self-rating" constitutes an intrinsically interesting and significant bit of verbal behavior, the non-test correlates of which must be discovered by empirical means. Not only is this approach free from the restriction that the subject must be able to describe his own behavior accurately, but a careful study of structured personality tests built on this basis shows that such a restriction would falsify the actual relationships that hold between what a man says and what he *is*. (p. 297)

Thus, according to Meehl (1945a), the literal content of the stimulus (item) was unimportant, even irrelevant, and potentially misleading. The empirical correlates of scales composed of item responses should be the sole source for test interpretation. Moreover, Meehl provided examples of MMPI items scored in counterintuitive or nonintuitive directions, laying the foundation for psychodynamically based assumptions:

The complex defense mechanisms of projection, rationalization, reaction formation, etc., appear dynamically to the interviewer as soon as he begins to take what the client *says* as itself motivated by other needs than those of giving an accurate verbal report. There is no good a-priori reason for denying the possibility of similar processes in the highly structured "interview'" which is the question–answer personality test. (p. 298)

Here Meehl appears to equate ambiguous item content with the ambiguous stimuli used in projective testing, which, at that time, was the most common method used in clinical assessments of personality.

Although he provided a theoretical rationale for ignoring item content in test interpretation, Meehl (1945a) was well aware that those who completed the MMPI were attuned to the meaning of test items and might, for a variety of reasons, distort their self-presentation. He recognized that item subtlety could go only so far in preventing such distortions and that other means must also be employed to counter this possibility. The MMPI Validity Scales L and F and the later-added K scale (Meehl & Hathaway, 1946) provided additional psychometric means for detecting, and possibly correcting, the effects of distortion.

In sum, the theoretical foundations of the MMPI included the following:

1. initial development of items and designation of scales based on the then-contemporary Kraepelinian descriptive nosology
2. treatment of test items as stimuli for behavioral responses, the aggregates of which may have certain empirical correlates, including diagnostic group membership
3. rejection of content-based test interpretation as overly susceptible to the influences of overt (intentional) and covert (unconscious) distortion
4. recognition that, point 3 notwithstanding, test takers do attend to item content and may intentionally or unintentionally respond in a misleading manner

Construction of the MMPI

Hathaway and McKinley described the development of several of the original Clinical Scales in a series of articles (Hathaway & McKinley, 1940, 1942; McKinley & Hathaway, 1940, 1942, 1944) compiled in Welsh and Dahlstrom's (1956) *Basic Readings*. Applying a methodology analogous to the one used by Strong (1938) to construct his Vocational Interest Blank, they assembled the scales by contrasting responses of differentially diagnosed patient samples with the responses of a nonclinical sample and, for each of the Clinical Scales, selecting items judged satisfactorily to differentiate the former from the latter. Additional contrast groups were used in constructing some of the scales. The nonclinical sample consisted primarily of visitors to the University of Minnesota Hospital who volunteered to answer the broad list of experimental test items described earlier. They were mostly rural Minnesotans with an average of eight years of education, employed primarily as skilled and semi-skilled laborers and farmers. The individuals served as the normal contrast group for item selection, and their responses were used to develop norms for the MMPI.

Clinical Scale raw scores were calculated for each scale by counting how many items assigned to the scale in question an individual had answered in the keyed direction (true or false), that is, keyed in the direction more often answered by the targeted disorder group (e.g., hypochondriasis) than by the normative sample. These scores were converted into standardized T scores with a mean of 50 and a standard deviation of 10, corresponding to the raw score mean and standard deviation for the normative sample on each given scale.

Subsequent Developments

Despite the care and ingenuity that characterized Hathaway and McKinley's efforts, for a number of reasons the MMPI never worked as its authors had intended. Attempts to replicate the validity of the Clinical Scales as predictors of diagnostic group membership were only marginally successful for some scales and largely unsuccessful for others (Hathaway, 1960). However, rather than fading away, as had many of its predecessors, the MMPI underwent a substantial transformation. As quoted earlier, Hathaway and McKinley (1940) viewed the initial development of the MMPI as a start, not an end point. Led by Paul Meehl, Hathaway's students and colleagues reinvented the MMPI by directing its use away from the narrow task of differential diagnosis to a considerably broader application.

A Paradigm Shift: Code Types

Although no doubt disappointed by the failure of the test to meet its original goal, early users of the MMPI observed that certain *patterns* of scores tended to recur in the settings in which they practiced, and test takers who produced these combinations shared certain clinical characteristics. Researchers began to shift their focus from scores on individual scales to identifying replicable empirical correlates of these patterns of scale scores. MMPI researchers began to use the term *profile* to refer to the complete set of scores on the Clinical Scales, which now included two later additions, Masculinity/Femininity and Social Introversion, and profile types to identify certain patterns or combinations of scores. Gough (1946), Meehl (1946), and Schmidt (1945) published a series of articles on the utility of certain *profile types* in differential diagnoses. Hathaway (1947) and then Welsh (1948) developed numerical coding systems that provided convenient summaries of the pattern of scores on a profile. This led to adoption of the term *code type* to designate different classes of profiles.

Within a decade of its initial publication, the prevailing use of the MMPI had changed dramatically. The Kraepelinian nosological model was dropped in favor of a considerably broader and more ambitious goal of describing normal and abnormal personality characteristics. Code types rather than individual scales were viewed as the primary source of information provided by the test. Reflecting this change, the original scale names that corresponded to the Kraepelinian nosological system were modified by using either abbreviations (e.g., Hs for Hypochondriasis) or digits representing their order of appearance in the profile (e.g., Scale 1 for Hypochondriasis). Seeking to advance this transition, Meehl (1956), in his presidential address to the Midwestern Psychological Association, issued a call for an "MMPI cookbook." Researchers were implored to identify a new, clinically useful set of MMPI-based classes and establish their empirical correlates. With the development of an actuarial classification system, test interpretation would involve the simple clerical task of using the scores to identify the individual's type and looking up its empirical correlates in actuarial tables. Investigators responded with a number of comprehensive efforts to develop such systems (e.g., Gilberstadt & Duker, 1965; Marks & Seeman, 1963). Hathaway (1960) summarized this transformation as follows:

> The MMPI began with validity based upon the usefulness of the various diagnostic groups from which its scales were derived. Now the burden of its use rests upon construct validity. Only a small fraction of the published data relating clinical or experimental variables to its scales or profiles can be understood in terms of the original approach. If the validity views of 1941 were the only support for the inventory, it could not survive. What is happening is that the correlations being observed with other variables in normal and abnormal subjects are filling out personality constructs that emerge, to be in turn tested for their ability to survive. It is significant that constructs, in the general sense of construct validity [Cronbach & Meehl, 1955], can be the forerunners of diagnostic classes. (p. viii)

Further Scale Development

The codebook approach just described became the primary approach to MMPI interpretation. However, soon after the initial publication of the inventory, researchers began creating additional scales from the MMPI item pool. Most early efforts followed the methods of Hathaway and McKinley by using contrasted groups to select items for their scales (e.g., Cuadra, 1953; Gough, 1948, 1951; Gough, McClosky & Meehl, 1951; H. L. Williams, 1952). This early work was followed by a profusion of similar studies designed to construct empirically keyed scales for the MMPI. By 1975, volume 2 of the *MMPI Handbook* (Dahlstrom, Welsh & Dahlstrom, 1975) listed almost as many Supplementary Scales (455) as there were test items. Eventually, the number of Supplementary Scales exceeded the number of test items. In contrast with the 10 Clinical and 3 Validity Scales that were scored from only 383 of the 550 MMPI items, the Supplementary Scales made use of the entire item pool. Most, however, remained obscure and were rarely used in clinical practice.

Another Paradigm Shift: Content-Based Assessment

Although Hathaway and McKinley, for the most part, ignored item content in selecting items for the Clinical Scales, it was not assumed that individuals taking the test would do so. Subsequent scale development efforts sought to take advantage of opportunities (some only perceived, others real) to capitalize on this feature of self-report measures.

Wiener–Harmon Subscales

Recognizing that some MMPI Clinical Scale items appeared much more obviously related in content to the scale on which they were scored than were others, Wiener and Harmon (1946) sought to divide the scales into "obvious" subscales, composed of items the scoring of which on a given scale was intuitively clear, and "subtle" subscales, made up of items whose connection to the scale was either unclear or counterintuitive based on the content and/or scoring direction. Working in a Veterans Administration counseling center, Wiener and Harmon articulated two goals for their efforts: (1) "[to] detect symptoms of emotional disturbance in test-conscious veterans who did not want to indicate them" (p. 7) and (2) "[to distinguish] invalidity on the separate scales of the Multiphasic Inventory" (p. 7). Concealed problems would be indicated when a test taker's subtle subscale score was elevated but the full scale score was not. Scale-level invalid responding would be detected by contrasting the individual's score on the subtle and obvious subscales within each scale. A significant discrepancy between the two scores would signal either over-reporting, if the obvious subscale score was higher, or underreporting, if the subtle subscale score was higher. For these subscales to function as intended, the necessary implicit assumption was that the subtle subscales were no less valid than the obvious subscales and were not (or were less) susceptible to misleading responding.

Wiener (1948) conducted one of the first external validation studies of the subtle and obvious subscales. He compared the obvious and subtle T scores of 100 veterans, half of whom had been successful in school and in on-the-job training. Previous analyses of these data using the full scales indicated that "the MMPI showed consistent but generally insignificant differences favoring the emotional stability of the successful group" (Wiener, 1948, p. 168). In Wiener's new analyses, all five obvious subscales were significantly higher for the unsuccessful group than for the successful group, averaging a 6.5 T-score point difference. Foretelling subsequent findings, none of the subtle subscales discriminated significantly between the two groups. Wiener interpreted these findings as supporting the use of the subtle and obvious subscales because the obvious scales were able to discriminate between the two groups much more successfully than did the full scales. However, these findings failed to provide empirical support for the subtle subscales and should have raised questions from the beginning about the appropriateness of including the subtle items in the full Clinical Scales. On the other hand, they did demonstrate for the first time that using the MMPI item pool for content-based assessment (as represented by the rationally derived obvious subscales) could yield statistically and clinically significant findings.

Weish Factor Scales

Development of the Welsh factor scales, A and R, was another important landmark in the evolution of content-based MMPI interpretation. Welsh (1956) developed these scales to provide measures of two dimensions that appeared repeatedly in factor analyses of the MMPI Clinical Scales. How these scales were constructed is less important for the present discussion than is the manner in which Welsh analyzed them and recommended their use. Prominent among the analyses he reported was a detailed inspection of the item content of each scale; that is, Welsh's recommendations for interpreting scales A and R were guided, to a significant degree, by their psychodynamically interpreted content. This approach, advocated by one of the leading figures in MMPI research, marked a significant departure from the early doctrine of strict empirically based test interpretation.

Harris–Lingoes Subscales

Harris and Lingoes (1955) carried out an even more direct attempt to incorporate item content in MMPI interpretation. These authors developed another set of subscales designed to assist in interpreting Clinical Scale scores by indicating which of several diverse sources of content contributed to an elevated score on a given scale. Harris and Lingoes rationally assigned items on most of the Clinical Scales to content-based subscales. The utility of these subscales was predicated on the assumption that test takers respond in interpretable ways to MMPI item content.

Critical Item Lists

If interpretable item content is relevant to assessing personality and psychopathology, a logical extension is to examine responses to individual items. Grayson (1951) first proposed such an approach and devised a list of 38 items he believed to be indicative of severe psychopathology that should, if answered in the keyed direction, lead the test interpreter to pause and take notice. Grayson generated his list based on a rational inspection of item content. A similar list of 68 items was proposed later by Caldwell (1969). Two subsequent lists were developed by Koss and colleagues (Koss & Butcher, 1973; Koss, Butcher & Hoffman, 1976) and by Lachar and Wrobel (1979) based on empirical analyses of item sets nominated by groups of expert judges.

Critical item lists are, in some respects, the most radical of the content-based approaches to MMPI interpretation. The psychometric limitations of individual item responses are well known, chief among them being unreliability. However, developers of these lists did not propose that they be used as psychometric indicators; rather, they were viewed as a useful way for the test interpreter to get the flavor of some of the specific issues of concern to the test taker.

The Wiggins Content Scales

Wiggins (1966) set the standard for rigorous construction of Content Scales for the MMPI. In providing a rationale for his project, he noted the dearth of attempts to develop content-based scales for the test. He attributed this to the ambivalence, if not the opposition, of the authors of the MMPI toward any deviation from the strict external criteria–based "empirical" approach to scale construction and interpretation. Wiggins offered cogent arguments favoring development of content-based scales for the MMPI, citing research that had demonstrated equivalence, if not superiority, of content-based measures over empirically keyed ones and the desirability of developing psychometrically sound dimensional means of gauging the information conveyed by the test taker.

Wiggins (1966) began his study by examining the internal consistency of the 26 content-based groupings of the MMPI item pool presented originally (for descriptive purposes) by Hathaway and McKinley (1940). He found some content areas to be promising for further scale-development efforts, whereas others, for a variety of reasons, including a dearth of items, clearly were not. He then set about revising the content categories based on a rational-intuitive analysis followed by additional empirical analyses that yielded a set of 15 content dimensions promising enough to warrant further analyses. Empirical analyses involving the entire item pool of the MMPI eventually yielded a set of 13 internally consistent and relatively independent Content Scales.

The significance of Wiggins's (1966) efforts cannot be overstated. His methods served as the prototype for all subsequent efforts to develop content-based scales for the MMPI. The psychometric success of his endeavor provided much-needed empirical support for the still-fledgling content-based approach to MMPI interpretation in particular and to personality assessment more generally.

Validity Scales

The development of the MMPI Validity Scales, intended to measure how a test taker approached the instrument, also reflected early recognition that item content could not be ignored. In the same article in which he articulated the theoretical foundations for empirical interpretation of the MMPI, dubbed by Wiggins (1990) "the empiricists manifesto," Meehl (1945a) noted,

> While it is true of many of the MMPI items, for example, that even a psychologist cannot predict on which scale they will appear or in what direction different sorts of abnormals will tend to answer them, still the relative acceptability of defensive answering would seem to be greater than is possible in responding to a set of inkblots. (p. 302)

Picking up on this theme, Meehl and Hathaway (1946) commented later,

> One of the important failings of almost all structured personality tests is their susceptibility to "faking" or "lying" in one way or another, as well as their even greater susceptibility to unconscious self-deception and role-playing on the part of individuals who might consciously be quite honest and sincere in their responses. (p. 525)

The development and routine use of the MMPI Validity Scales (described in detail in Chapter 4) were thus predicated on the assumption that test takers respond to item content in meaningful ways.

In summary, although construction of the Clinical Scales was carried out with little or no attention paid to item content, and code type–based interpretation was devoid of any content considerations, MMPI interpreters were provided the means for assessing and considering test takers' content-based responses.

Appraisals of the MMPI and Thoughts about Its Revision

Various methods may be used to appraise the utility of a psychological assessment device, including an examination of how frequently it is used in practice and in research and taking into account scholarly reviews by experts in the field. Consideration of these criteria points to diverging views of the original MMPI.

Clinical Application and Research

Judged by these two criteria, the MMPI was clearly well received. In a survey of practicing psychologists in the late 1950s, Sundberg (1961) found that the inventory was by then the most widely used objective measure of personality and psychopathology and was among the most widely used psychological tests. Lubin, Wallis, and Paine (1971) reported similar findings based on a survey conducted in 1969. Welsh and Dahlstrom (1956) provided a list of 689 papers published through December 1954 that made "more than casual reference to the MMPI" (p. 619). Twenty years later, Dahlstrom et al. (1975) listed over 5,000 MMPI references compiled through the end of 1973. Together, these data show that by the end of the 1960s, the MMPI had become one of the more widely used and by far the most frequently studied psychological test.

During the 1940s through the 1960s, MMPI investigations contributed significantly to two lines of research: one involving the advance of applied personality assessment, the other consisting of basic studies of personality and psychopathology. Examples of the former are the introduction and elucidation of a construct validity approach to appraisals of psychological tests (Cronbach & Meehl, 1955), the formulation of and answers to questions about the merits of clinical versus statistical prediction (Meehl, 1954), examination of linear versus configural scoring and interpretation (e.g., Goldberg, 1965; Meehl & Dahlstrom, 1960), and studies of the putative influences of response styles on self-report measures of personality and psychopathology (e.g., Block, 1965; Edwards, 1964; Jackson & Messick, 1962). The psychopathology studies include research designed to identify the basic building blocks and structures of personality and psychopathology (e.g., Welsh, 1956), investigations of the role of personality in physical disease and in Somatoform Disorder (e.g., Hanvik, 1951; Wiener, 1952), studies of the association between personality and criminal conduct (e.g., Edwards, 1963), and identification of physiological correlates of psychopathology (e.g., Halevy, Moos & Soloman, 1965).

These dual tracks of basic and applied MMPI research fostered significant cross-fertilization. Test users were provided the means to incorporate findings of basic research into their clinical assessments, and researchers were given access to a wealth of clinical data enabling relevant research and encouraging theoretical developments that would otherwise have been very difficult to accomplish.

However, beginning in the 1960s, MMPI research became increasingly focused on the cookbook approach to test interpretation. As investigators compiled sizable data sets and identified clinically relevant empirical correlates of the code types, MMPI interpretation became focused almost exclusively on these correlates, that is, on criterion validity rather than more broadly on construct validity. Basic researchers, on the other hand, found limited value in the practically convenient but theoretically undeveloped code types and turned instead to alternative measures for studying personality and psychopathology. This schism had unfortunate consequences for both camps. MMPI research became increasingly divorced from developments in the fields of personality and psychopathology, and basic researchers lost access to rich sources of clinical data available on literally hundreds of thousands of individuals tested with the instrument in a broad array of mental health, medical, forensic, and various nonclinical settings.

Scholarly Appraisals

Hathaway's own appraisals of the MMPI might best be characterized as ambivalent. In a foreword to the first edition of Dahlstrom and Welsh's (1960) *MMPI Handbook*, he wrote (Hathaway, 1960),

> Our most optimistic expectation was that the methodology of the new test would be so clearly effective that there would soon be better devices with refinements of scales and of general validity. We rather hoped that we ourselves might, with five years' experience, greatly increase its validity and clinical usefulness, and perhaps even develop more solidly based constructs or theoretical variables for a new inventory. I doubt now that it is possible to improve the MMPI enough to repay the effort. I am not even sure that we could hold to what validity and usefulness we have. (p. vii)

Hathaway went on to explain that his skepticism stemmed from the absence of a sound alternative to the Kraepelinian nosological system, which was the basis for his work with McKinley in developing the original Clinical Scales. On a more optimistic note, he observed (Hathaway, 1960),

> That the MMPI will be a stepping stone to a higher level of validity I still sincerely hope; I hope too that the new level will soon loom in sight. In the meantime I see it as a stepping stone that permits useful communication at its own level even though the stone is rather wobbly. (p. viii)

Hathaway (1972a) revisited this topic in a brief foreword to the second edition of the *MMPI Handbook*. Writing 12 years after his previous comments were made, he stated,

> If another twelve years were to go by without our having gone on to a better instrument or better procedure for the practical needs, I fear that the MMPI, like some other tests, might have changed from a hopeful innovation to an

aged obstacle. Do not misunderstand me. I am not agreeing with a few critics who have already called for the funeral and written the epitaph. They have not yet identified what is better. We cannot lay down even a stone-age axe if we have no better one to hew with. (p. xiv)

In a paper titled "Where Have We Gone Wrong? The Mystery of the Missing Progress," Hathaway (1972b) elaborated on these observations and reiterated his view that to a large extent, the lack of progress in refining the MMPI Clinical Scales could be attributed to the absence of an improved (or, for that matter, equally useful) alternative to the Kraepelinian diagnostic system. Hathaway also discussed his disagreement with those who had already eulogized the MMPI, citing as an example a statement by Goldberg (1968, as cited by Hathaway, 1972b) that included the following:

Historically, the MMPI is of the greatest importance to those of us committed to personality assessment. At present, my own belief is that soon it will be little more than an historically interesting instrument. (p. 23)

Hathaway (1972b) responded,

I am not denying a place in history for the MMPI, but Dr. Goldberg's time schedule suggests that it will become historical sooner than I think is likely. Even if it has little more to offer us in research, I fear that the aged MMPI will be tolerated for some time by those concerned with practical problems in psychological evaluation. (p. 23)

Hathaway here conceded that the MMPI was likely to become of increasingly limited interest to basic personality researchers, and even to those investigating applied questions in personality assessment, but predicted that this would not deter practitioners from continuing to use the test until a viable alternative materialized. Hindsight shows that Hathaway's prediction was accurate on all counts.

Whether and How to Improve the MMPI

Hathaway's (1972b) paper was one of several presented at a conference convened in his honor in 1970 (the Fifth Annual Symposium on Recent Developments in the Use of the MMPI), devoted to consideration of whether the time had come for a revision of the MMPI and, if so, what form it should take. The conference produced an edited volume (Butcher, 1972a) that included most of the presentations and a detailed discussion of the topic by Meehl (1972). Among the most critical commentators were Jane Loevinger and Warren Norman. Although not a participant in this conference, Douglas Jackson, also a critic of the MMPI, had recently weighed in on this topic, and his recommendations are considered here as well.

Loevinger

Advocating the development of measures of theoretically promising constructs, Loevinger (1972) argued,

There is no substitution for having a psychologist in charge who has at least a first-approximation conception of the trait he wishes to measure, always open to revision, of course, as the data demand. (p. 56)

She rejected Hathaway's view that personality theory had yet to reach a point where it could meaningfully inform the writing and selection of items for a self-report measure of psychopathology. On a related note, and addressing a question raised by several conference contributors, Loevinger observed,

If a categorical diagnostic decision is the aim of the new test, then quantitative measures are inappropriate. If quantitative traits are to be measured, then discrimination of extreme groups is too crude and inappropriate a method for item selection. (p. 56)

Her own work clearly favored quantitative (i.e., continuous) traits and measures.

A third issue identified by Loevinger (1972) as a critical concern for any MMPI revision was the need to attend to what she saw as a ubiquitous feature of self-report measures: "Every test seems saturated with a method factor that outweighs other kinds of valid variance" (p. 49). Loevinger viewed the already well-established finding that a strong general factor contributed substantial variance to all the MMPI Clinical Scales as evidence of the influence of a nuisance variable. She characterized the K correction as a failed (presumably because even K-corrected scores remained heavily saturated with this variable) attempt to control for this factor and advocated that efforts to do so occur at the point of scale construction rather than ad hoc.

Norman

Norman (1972) focused on several conceptual and psychometric problems with the original MMPI Clinical Scales. Conceptually, he argued that the model that guided Hathaway and McKinley in constructing the MMPI was obsolete and no longer relevant to how the test was used:

Whether or not Kraepelinian nosology was an appropriate system on which to base a psychiatric diagnostic instrument in the early 1940s, its relevance for that purpose in the late 1960s has surely become tenuous at best. In one respect, the MMPI already reflects this shift away from classical terminology by the substitution of numerical designations for the old scale names and by the shift in interpretive emphasis from the original, single scales to profile code types. (p. 64)

Anticipating a possible retort that bootstrapping and the shift from single-scale to code-type interpretation had made it unnecessary to rely on the original model and thus rendered its inadequacies largely irrelevant, Norman (1972) went on to observe,

Whatever one thinks of the desirability of the original construction of the basic clinical scales (granting the purposes for which they were intended), it is abundantly clear that they are about as inappropriate and maladapted a set as one could imagine for their current uses in profile analysis and interpretation and typal classification system. (p. 64)

He singled out their heterogeneity and the excessively high intercorrelations among them (stemming, to a degree, from item overlap) as the most serious problems with use of the Clinical Scales as configural indicators of meaningful types:

> In brief, linear composites of items which are to be used as the component scales of a profile, the configural properties of which are of potential interest, must each be statistically homogeneous. It would also be desirable from the viewpoint of efficiency for the separate scales to be relatively uncorrelated with one another. And, of course, it would be nice if some interpretation of each component scale based on the content of its items could be given, although that would not be strictly necessary for purposes of diagnosis alone. There is no possible benefit or justification I can think of, however, for keying single responses on two or more of the component scales of such a profile set. (p. 66)

On a related note, Norman (1972) commented on the "general factor" of the MMPI, which Loevinger (1972) had viewed as a nuisance variable. Granting that it *might* instead reflect a substantive factor analogous to "g" in cognitive assessment devices, he noted that the MMPI

> displays a large first factor variously known as "alpha," "A," "ego strength," "social desirability," or "general pathology," depending upon one's predilections. But, in general, with adequate domain sampling of traits and with application to relevant populations a general personality factor seems less likely to appear or to be interpretable than is true in the ability or aptitude area. When such a factor is present, however, I would argue that clarity of interpretation and meaningfulness of the assessments are likely to be best served by dealing with such a component separately from the others implicit in the residual sources of variation. (p. 82)

Jackson

In contrast to Hathaway's (1960, 1972a, 1972b) pessimistic appraisal, Jackson (1971) argued that progress in the science of personality had been sufficient to allow the replacement of a descriptive model such as the Kraepelinian nosology with a conceptually richer set of targets for scale construction. He advocated that a modern approach to this task entail candidate items written by experts well versed in the science of personality and selection of those items that pass a succession of psychometric hurdles related to enhancing internal consistency and controlling for response styles.

Jackson (1971) argued that the bootstrapping method (described by Cronbach & Meehl, 1955) for enriching the construct validity of scales that were developed on the basis of fallible criteria (e.g., Kraepelinian diagnoses in the case of the MMPI Clinical Scales), though perhaps a necessary step owing to limitations of knowledge at the time the test was developed, was no longer needed or justified. In his words, "the ignorance about personality to which Meehl alluded a quarter of a century ago hardly seems a suitable defense at the present time" (Jackson, 1971, p. 232). He singled out the subtle items (discussed earlier) as an example of the detrimental impact of blind empiricism, noting, "Most subtle items have been shown to correlate negatively with the rest of the items contained in an MMPI scale, raising the suspicion that they did not belong there in the first place" (p. 234), and he speculated that these items were "present in MMPI scales due to errors in sampling items and subjects in the initial item-selection procedures" (p. 234).

Jackson (1971) was also critical of the nonlinear (categorical) measurement model underlying the MMPI code types, that is, of the notion that they represented true classes or types. He also noted the absence of evidence that configural scoring (e.g., code-type classification or other, even more complex models) improves on methods that rely on "a linear relationship between items and a single underlying latent continuum" (p. 239).

Finally, Jackson (1971) revisited the issue of "response styles" that he and others had raised earlier as a major criticism of the MMPI. Jackson and Messick (1962), building on the work of Edwards (1957), had proposed that much (if not all) of the variance in MMPI Clinical Scale scores was attributable to two response styles (rather than substantive sources), termed *social desirability* and *acquiescence*. These investigators factor analyzed MMPI scale scores in a broad range of samples and concluded that two factors accounted for much of the variance in the test. They attributed variance on these factors to the two response styles and cautioned that MMPI scale scores appeared primarily to reflect individual differences on these two dimensions. In an extensive and sophisticated series of analyses, Block (1965) later demonstrated that these two primary MMPI factors actually represented substantive personality dimensions, with meaningful, real-world correlates that could be understood within a theoretical framework rather than stylistic response tendencies.

Jackson (1971) was unconvinced by Block's (1965) analysis, contending that his finding of meaningful external correlates of the two broad dimensions was not sufficient to rule out that they are primarily nonsubstantive and should, at the very least, be measured separately rather than repeatedly and therefore redundantly. Ignoring Block's detailed theoretical framework for understanding the two dimensions as measures of the constructs *ego control* and *ego resiliency*, Jackson maintained that "if in the tradition of radical empiricism one eschews theoretical or substantive definitions and prefers to rest one's case solely with external correlates, there is, indeed, no basis for distinguishing content from stylistic variance" (p. 241).

Meehl

Responding to an invitation to comment on these and other observations regarding the need for a revision and the methods that might be used, Meehl (1972) revisited his earlier (Meehl, 1945a) justification for a strict empirical approach to MMPI construction and interpretation. He conceded some of Jackson's criticisms, while holding steadfast on others. Declaring his "'dustbowl empiricist' paper of 1945" (Meehl, 1972, p. 147) to be "half-right half-wrong" (p. 134), Meehl considered how, with the benefit of 30 years of accumulated knowledge and experience, one might go about revising the MMPI (and whether this would be worth doing). On the matter of the role of theory in test construction and interpretation, he stated,

> I now think that at all stages in personality test development, from the initial phase of item pool construction to a late-stage optimized clinical interpretive procedure for the fully developed and "validated" instrument, theory—and by this I mean all sorts of theory, including trait theory, developmental theory, learning theory, psychodynamics, and behavior genetics—should play an important role. (p. 150)

On the related topic of item subtlety, a key feature of Jackson's (1971) critique, Meehl (1972) indicated,

> I now believe (as I did not formerly) that an item ought to make theoretical sense, and without too much *ad hoc* explaining of its content or properties. But going in the other direction, I would still argue that if an item has really stable psychometric (internal and external) properties of such-and-such kinds, it is the business of a decent theory to "explain" its possession of those properties in light of its verbal content. (p. 155)

Meehl's position had evolved from the radical 1945 notion that understanding item content was of no consequence (or a distraction) to a view that allowed for exploratory analyses of a heterogeneous item pool, provided that the items finally selected could be understood within a developing theoretical framework. He thus rejected Jackson's (1971) stance that a fully developed theory must precede and guide all aspects of item writing and selection. However, although he did not state this directly, it is doubtful that Meehl saw much evidence to support the construct validity of the MMPI subtle items, and it is clear that he now rejected the use of items whose contribution to a scale could not be understood.

Responding to Loevinger's (1972) criticism of the use of continuous measures, such as the Clinical Scales, to assess or predict categorical class membership, Meehl (1972) commented,

> I do not see anything inherently absurd about employing quantitative fallible indicators for the probabilistic identification of a taxonic entity, as examples from the genetics of loose syndromes—or, for that matter, the numerous dimensional indicators employed in internal medicine—attest. . . . However, the test constructor ought to think through whether, when he constructs a "depression" key, he has in view primarily the assessment of degree (depth of depressed mood) cutting across nosological categories, or whether he wants instead to build an instrument that will classify individuals as belonging, say,

to the taxon "endogenous psychotic depression, unipolar type," where the aim is one of minimizing classification errors in a two-category population with specific base rates. In arguing that the investigator should have in mind his preferred substantive views as to the existence of a certain taxonomic entity when proceeding with his psychometric job, I do not deny that the behavior of the test items may itself contribute to the corroboration or falsification of that substantive position. (pp. 151–152)

Meehl's preference for taxonic variables is evident in his development of taxometric methods in a quest to identify psychopathology taxa. However, in his 1972 conjectures about future directions for the MMPI, he considered as open the ultimate question of whether certain psychopathologies were better understood as taxa or as continua (let alone whether one needed to adopt one model entirely to the exclusion of the other) but insisted that an MMPI revision should, at the very least, be guided by a position (subject to revision in response to empirical data) on this fundamental conceptual question.

In response to Norman's (1972) criticism of the continued reliance on the Kraepelinian nosology (an inherently taxonic system) as the basis for developing the Clinical Scales, Meehl (1972) stood firm:

I cannot refrain from a cautionary comment about Dr. Norman's (otherwise sound and helpful) contribution, where he permits himself the usual psychologist's dogma that the old Kraepelinian nosological categories are not worth anything. . . . A fair-minded reading of the literature should convince Dr. Norman that the prognostic and treatment-selective power of our major nosological rubrics is at least as good as any "psychodynamic" assessment (by clinical interview) or any existing psychometric device, structured or projective. (p. 157)

Commenting specifically on the assertion that a major problem with the Kraepelinian diagnostic classes is that they are "notoriously unreliable," Meehl (1972) first contended that the evidence in support of this assertion is tainted by methodologically flawed research and went on to observe that "psychologists have a tendency to be obsessed with reliability . . . and an insufficient concern for what might be called the intrinsic or qualitative validity, of a construct or judgment" (p. 159). Using an example from medicine that he recalled hearing as a student in Hathaway's class 30 years earlier, Meehl noted that although the test–retest reliability of blood pressure measurement (around .65) was substantially lower than that of measuring the width of a patient's wrist (.98), physicians find the former much more relevant to the task of assessment and management of medical conditions.

On the issue of scale heterogeneity and the related topic of the impact of a broad general factor on Clinical Scale interpretation, Meehl (1972) conceded that

one difficulty with an unqualified blind criterion keying is that it does not provide even a weak guarantee—unless done in the context of multiple exclusionary criteria along with the positive one—that it is "causally close" to the psychological variable of interest. Example: MMPI scale 4 (Pd = psycho-pathic deviate) is one of the better validated clinical keys; when its elevation is found together with an elevated 9 (Ma = Hypomania) and a relative absence of either neurotic or psychotic elevations—especially with a normal or super-normal pattern on the "neurotic triad"—it is a pretty powerful identifier of the broadly "sociopathoid" type. But every clinician experienced with the MMPI has learned that, taking the Pd scale alone, there are some important clinical differentiations which we would like to make better than we can. (p. 170)

Expanding on the source of this difficulty and prescribing a potential solution, Meehl (1972) went on to note,

Unfortunately one can achieve a moderate and sometimes rather high eleva-tion on scale 4 without being a sociopath—not surprising when we look at the items scored for this variable. . . . At an increment of two or three T-score points per raw score item shift, it takes less than ten items in the combined areas of family strife and "institution troubles" to achieve a score at T = 70. We all recognize today that this kind of thing happens, and is one source of error which we attempt to "correct for" mentally by taking the patient's situation into account as well as looking at the rest of his profile. But it would be nicer if such error were eliminated from the Pd key entirely. As a factor analyst once complained to me during a heated discussion on criterion keying, internal consistency, scale "purity," and related topics, "If you Minnesotans are going to eyeball the profile and do a subjective factor analysis in your head that way, why not let the computer do it better, at the stage of scale construction?" Not an easy argument to answer. (pp. 170–171)

Here Meehl (1972) proposed that criterion keying might be a good starting point for identifying a set of construct-relevant items, to be followed up with additional analyses designed to identify and develop separate measures of homogeneous components of the resulting item pool.

On the related topic of the impact of a general factor, Meehl (1972) noted,

That an item discriminates a criterion "significantly" does not tell us whether it might be discriminating something else even more. And if it happens further that the criterion of interest is correlated with a variable that runs through a whole batch of items, it is possible statistically that I should con-struct a key which, while admittedly "valid for the criterion," is even more valid for some nuisance variable that got dragged along in the process. (p. 172)

As a corrective, Meehl proposed that criterion keying be augmented by analyses designed to ensure that the items selected for a scale are adequately correlated with the relevant construct and minimally correlated with measures of nonrelevant constructs, including the general factor. To accomplish the former, and in a concession to Jackson (1971), he stated,

> It no longer seems sensible to me to oppose internal consistency approaches to empirical criterion keying approaches, especially in light of what I have said above about the necessity of having available an extended and qualitatively "good" network of interlocking "negative criterion" and other psychometric variables, even when we aim to measure only a single important clinical dimension. (p. 174)

Finally, in response to Goldberg's (1965, 1969) evidence against the utility of configural scoring, which Meehl (1972) now appeared to accept at the item level, he equivocated with regard to its implications for scale-level interpretation,

> I doubt that Professor Goldberg wants to maintain that a strong anticonfigural generalization can safely be made at this time, except in the cautious way in which he makes it, that is, there is no satisfactory positive evidence for significant configural effects. I will bravely record my prophecy that with (1) sufficiently large N and (2) adequate criteria, there will be found (3) some significant configural effects in accord with the clinical lore of experienced MMPI users. But it may well be that any such found (while statistically significant) will be so small that they are not worth the trouble. (p. 182)

Summary and Conclusions

The MMPI was developed to fulfill a practical need for an omnibus differential diagnostic instrument. Introducing the test to the medical community, McKinley and Hathaway (1943) stated (using the language of the time),

> Many a medical man has wished for an easily applicable measuring device which would identify and characterize the psychoneurotic patient with a minimum use of the time consuming interview technique that is conventional in the psychiatric approach. Realizing this problem and desiring to contribute to its solution, we began work in 1937 on the development of an objective personality test which was simple to use, easy to interpret, and conserving of time. (p. 161)

As just reviewed, from a practical perspective, Hathaway and McKinley's quest to develop a useful assessment device was clearly successful. Within a decade and a half of its release, the MMPI had become the most widely used self-report measure of psychopathology and personality and among the most widely used of all psychological tests. By the early 1970s, it had become by far the most widely studied assessment device. Hathaway was ambivalent about the instrument. Regretting the lack of further refinement of the MMPI Clinical Scales, which he attributed to the absence of progress in our understanding of psychopathology, he expressed his belief that the MMPI would continue to be used for the foreseeable future because the needs that prompted its development remained. He did not envision a clear path toward the construction of a successor.

Critics such as Goldberg, Jackson, Loevinger, and Norman found fundamental problems with the MMPI. Chief among these was the developers' reliance on dated Kraepelinian nosology. To a retort that this criticism was unwarranted owing to the paradigm shift toward code-type interpretation, these critics would undoubtedly have responded with concerns about the absence of evidence in support of configural scoring and interpretation (Goldberg, 1965, 1969), criticism of the code-type approach as (like the Clinical Scales) bereft of any theoretical foundation (Jackson, 1971; Loevinger, 1972), and problems with the Clinical Scales as components of the code types—excessive intercorrelations stemming from a strong general factor and item overlap and excessive heterogeneity represented most egregiously by the inclusion of invalid subtle items on the scales (Norman, 1972).

Meehl (1972) conceded that the radical empirical rationale outlined in his 1945 defense of the MMPI was overstated. In particular, he agreed that sound psychometric practice should include consideration of item content at the various stages of scale development. He also now advocated reliance on statistical analyses, including possibly factor analyses, to control for competing (with the targeted construct) sources of variance at the stage of scale development. Relatedly, he now viewed internal consistency of scales as desirable and heterogeneity as undesirable. In contrast, Meehl remained steadfast in his view that at least some of the constructs of interest in psychopathology were taxonic, and he staunchly defended the utility of the Kraepelinian nosological system as an exemplar of such a model. With respect to the latter, it is noteworthy that four subsequent revisions of the *Diagnostic and Statistical Manual for Mental Disorders* (*DSM-III*, American Psychiatric Association [APA], 1980; *DMS-III-R*, APA, 1987; *DMS-IV*, APA, 1994; *DSM-IV-TR*, APA, 2000) reflect (essentially) a neo-Kraepelinian descriptive model for the classification of psychopathology.

Toward the MMPI-2

The conference held to honor Hathaway's contributions was convened in 1970. In addition to the contributions just reviewed, papers by Butcher (1972b), Dahlstrom (1972), and Campbell (1972) discussed the mechanics of a possible revision of the test. Contributors to this conference, and to the subsequent volume in which these papers appeared (Butcher, 1972a), would likely have found it difficult to reach a consensus on how to go about revising the inventory, though all, for varying reasons, would likely have agreed with the statement that the MMPI needed to be revised.

Complicating matters further, a process or the means for undertaking a revision of the inventory did not exist. The owner of the MMPI, the University of Minnesota, had, through its press, licensed publication rights for the instrument to the Psychological Corporation and lacked a mechanism with which to plan, fund, and oversee any type of revision. However, in the early 1980s, under the leadership of Beverly Kaemmer, later to be appointed manager of the University of Minnesota Press's newly formed Test Division, a major change in the university's role in managing the MMPI made a revision feasible. In 1982, the press, as publisher of the MMPI, licensed National Computer Systems (now Pearson Assessments) to distribute the instrument. As part of this agreement, the university undertook the task of revising the test with funding generated by royalties made possible under the new arrangement. A committee consisting initially of James Butcher, Grant Dahlstrom, and John Graham, joined later by Auke Tellegen, and coordinated by Beverly Kaemmer, known as the MMPI Restandardization Committee, initiated and carried out a revision that produced the MMPI-2.

THE MMPI-2

The 1989 publication of a revised version of the MMPI, the MMPI-2 (Butcher et al., 1989), represented the culmination of nearly a decade of research. Among the main objectives for revising the test, reflected in the title, the MMPI Restandardization Project, was an update of the test norms, a task that had not been the focus of the 1970 conference just discussed. The MMPI normative sample was collected in the 1930s and, as reported earlier, consisted almost exclusively of Caucasian, working-class, rural Minnesotans possessing an average of eight years of education who happened to be visiting friends and relatives at the University Hospital at the time the test was developed. This sample represented well the initial target population for the test, patients receiving services at the hospital, but was no longer adequate as the MMPI became more widely used in a variety of settings throughout the United States.

A second focus of the revision was on problematic MMPI items. The item pool of the inventory had come under considerable criticism over the years. Foremost among these concerns was the inclusion of item content that was no longer (and, in some cases, had never been) clear, relevant, or appropriate for assessing personality and psychopathology (e.g., "drop the handkerchief"). A set of MMPI items singled out as particularly problematic addressed test takers' religious beliefs and practices. Other controversial items concerned excretory functions and sexual orientation.

In addition, a relatively large set of MMPI items was not scored on any of the Clinical, Validity, or widely used Supplementary Scales. These nonworking items were candidates for deletion and replacement. A final item-level issue was the absence of content dealing with matters relevant to contemporary clinical personality assessment (e.g., suicidal ideation, Type A Behavior, use of drugs such as marijuana, work-related difficulties, and treatment readiness). A trade-off between nonworking and new items was viewed as the appropriate strategy for confronting both problems. The revision of the test was an opportunity to eliminate objectionable items, rewrite others that were worded archaically or contained gender-specific references, and eliminate nonworking items and replace them with items addressing contemporary clinical concerns. In the next sections, the goals, methods, and outcome of the revision are described and then evaluated.

Goals for the Revision

In the 1989 MMPI-2 manual and the writings of the three original committee members (Butcher, Dahlstrom, and Graham), one finds little or no discussion of the proposals by Jackson (1971), Loevinger (1972), Meehl (1972), and Norman (1972) for addressing fundamental problems with the MMPI Clinical Scales. Early on, these committee members made a strategic decision to keep the Clinical Scales essentially intact to allow for continued and unchanged reliance on the reported empirical correlates of code types formed by these scales, which, as discussed previously, had become the primary focus of MMPI interpretation.

The Restandardization Committee thus assigned itself two goals: to improve the test and maintain as much continuity as possible with the original MMPI. Improvement was to be attained by updating the normative base and correcting the item-level deficiencies just noted. Continuity was to be accomplished by minimizing changes to the basic scales, making it possible for test interpreters to continue to rely on decades of accumulated research and clinical experience with these measures.

Methods of Revision

Instruments

The Restandardization Committee's first step was to develop an experimental booklet with which the new normative data would be collected and from which new items could be added to the test. The MMPI-AX was developed by retaining all 550 original MMPI items (although 82 were reworded slightly to correct for archaic or otherwise problematic language), dropping the 16 repeated items that had been added to the test for machine scoring, and writing 154 new, experimental items, candidates for replacing nonworking and objectionable items.

Additional instruments developed for the Restandardization Project included a biographical data form used to collect extensive demographic data on normative and other subjects as well as a life events form designed to identify subjects who had been experiencing extreme stress in the six months prior to participating in the project. A subset of subjects who participated in the normative data collection along with their spouses or live-in partners also completed a modified version of the Katz and Lyerly (1963) Adjustment Scale and Spanier's (1976) Dyadic Adjustment Scale. These were to be used as sources of validity and correlate data for new scales that might be developed.

Participants

The MMPI-2 normative sample (later also used as the normative sample for the MMPI-2-RF) was collected throughout the United States using a variety of procedures designed to sample the population of individuals with whom the test is used. Over

2,900 individuals completed the test battery. Of these, 2,600 (1,462 women and 1,138 men) produced valid and complete protocols and were included in the normative sample; 1,680 members of the normative sample who participated along with their spouses or live-in partners completed the two additional forms just mentioned. Individual subjects were paid $15 for their participation; couples received $40. Demographics of the normative sample subjects are reported in Chapter 5.

A number of additional clinical and nonclinical data sets were compiled and used in various scale development and validation studies. These included a sample of psychiatric inpatients (Graham & Butcher, 1988), individuals undergoing substance abuse treatment (McKenna & Butcher, 1987), patients at a pain treatment clinic (Keller & Butcher, 1991), college students (Ben-Porath & Butcher, 1989a, 1989b; Butcher, Graham, Dahlstrom & Bowman, 1990), military personnel (Butcher, Jeffrey et al., 1990), mothers at risk for child abuse (Egland, Erickson, Butcher & Ben-Porath, 1991), and participants in the Boston Normative Aging Study (Butcher, Aldwin, Levenson, Ben-Porath, Spiro & Bosse, 1991). Altogether, over 10,000 individuals were tested as part of the Restandardization Project.

Outcome of the Revision

From the 704 items in the AX experimental booklet, 567 were selected for inclusion in the MMPI-2 test booklet; 372 of the 383 items scored on the 13 basic Validity and Clinical Scales of the original MMPI were retained in the MMPI-2; 11 items were deleted owing to objectionable content, but no basic scale lost more than four items, and most scales did not lose any; 64 of the 82 reworded items were included on the MMPI-2. Ben-Porath and Butcher (1989a) found the revised items to have a negligible impact on the psychometric functioning of the scales on which they were scored. Thus, consistent with the goal of maintaining continuity, the basic Validity and Clinical Scales of the MMPI-2 were nearly identical to those of the MMPI. Improvements were made with the introduction of new norms, a new way of calculating MMPI-2 standard scores, new Validity Scales, and the MMPI-2 Content Scales (Butcher, Graham, Williams & Ben-Porath, 1990).

New Norms

As noted, the MMPI-2 norms were based on the national sample of 2,600 individuals tested for the Restandardization Project. For a number of reasons, members of the MMPI-2 normative sample produced higher raw scores on the test's Clinical Scales than did their 1930s counterparts. A change in the instructions given to MMPI test takers contributed significantly to this difference. At the time it was developed, the original MMPI was administered by presenting a test taker with each item printed on a separate index card and instructing her or him to sort them into three piles, representing statements that were true, statements that were false, or statements about which they "cannot say" whether the statement was true or false. These instructions, used when the original norms were collected, did not discourage the "cannot say" response option. When MMPI administration shifted from the card form to booklet, the instructions were altered, and item omission was explicitly discouraged. These revised instructions, which had become the standard for MMPI administration, were used in the normative data collection for the MMPI-2. As a result, members of the new normative sample responded to a larger number of the test items than did their counterparts who responded to the original MMPI, thus contributing to the increase in raw scores on the Clinical Scales.

Societal changes over the 40 plus years that separated the two normative data collections also contributed to higher Clinical Scale raw scores in the MMPI-2 normative sample. These included both real shifts in psychological functioning and a greater willingness to admit holding potentially unattractive beliefs and engaging in undesirable behaviors. A final factor potentially contributing to normative changes was the collection of a broader, much more diverse sample than the one used to derive the original MMPI norms.

Regardless of their cause, higher raw scores in the new normative sample resulted in lower T scores based on the new norms. This shift led the Restandardization Committee to lower the cutting point for determining clinically meaningful elevation from a T score of 70 on the MMPI to a T score of 65 on the MMPI-2.

Another potential source of change at the T-score level was the development of Uniform T scores for the MMPI-2 (Tellegen & Ben-Porath, 1992). Uniform T scores were developed to correct a fundamental problem with MMPI T scores. Because the raw- score distributions for the Clinical Scales were differentially skewed, when linear T scores were used (as was the case with the original MMPI norms), the same T-score value did not necessarily correspond to the same percentile for different scales. The lack of percentile equivalence across scales made direct comparisons of T scores on different Clinical Scales potentially misleading. The solution, developed by Tellegen and adopted by the Restandardization Committee, was to compute the average distribution of non-K-corrected raw scores on the eight original Clinical Scales for men and women in the normative sample and then adjust (in the transformation of raw score to T score) the distribution of each of the scales to fit this composite distribution. This approach yielded percentile-equivalent T scores while retaining the skewed nature of the distributions of the Clinical Scales (Tellegen & Ben-Porath, 1992). Uniform T scores have also been adopted for use with the MMPI-2-RF and are described in detail in Chapter 5.

New Scales

As discussed earlier, the Restandardization Project had two potentially conflicting goals: to improve the instrument and to maintain continuity with its empirical and experiential foundations. Continuity was fostered by leaving the 13 basic Validity and Clinical Scales of the MMPI largely intact. Improvement at the scale level was accomplished primarily through the introduction of 21 new measures, including three new Validity Scales, the MMPI-2 Content Scales (Butcher, Graham, Williams et al., 1990), and three Supplementary Scales, two designed to measure gender roles and one Posttraumatic Stress Disorder (PTSD) indicator.

Validity Scales

One of the three new Validity Scales, the Back F (F_B) Scale, was made up of items that appear in the latter portion of the test booklet that were endorsed infrequently by the MMPI-2 normative sample. The MMPI-2 scale was designed to detect changes in the test taker's pattern of responding to items that were placed after the first part of the booklet, where nearly all of the F Scale items were located. All of the items required to score the 13 basic MMPI-2 scales were placed among the first 370 items of the MMPI-2 test booklet to facilitate an abbreviated administration of the inventory to individuals deemed incapable of completing the 567-item MMPI-2.

The other two new MMPI Validity Scales were Response-Inconsistency Scales fashioned after similar measures developed by Tellegen for the Multidimensional Personality Questionnaire (MPQ; Tellegen, 1995/2003). Variable Response Inconsistency (VRIN) was designed to detect quasi-random responding by considering test takers' responses to pairs of MMPI-2 items selected through a series of statistical and semantic analyses designed to yield item pairs that were nearly identical or opposite in meaning. The second Inconsistency Scale, True Response Inconsistency (TRIN), was designed to detect patterns of indiscriminant fixed (true or false) responding by considering responses to pairs of items, all opposite in meaning, identified in a manner similar to the VRIN pairs. Construction of these scales is described in detail in Chapter 4.

The MMPI-2 Content Scales

As noted earlier, beginning in the 1950s, content-based considerations gained increasing acceptance as a supplement to the code type–based interpretation of scores on the MMPI Clinical Scales. The MMPI-2 Content Scales (Butcher, Graham, Williams et al., 1990) were developed through a series of rational-conceptual and empirical analyses fashioned after those used by Wiggins (1966) to develop the original MMPI Content Scales. Candidate items were assigned first to potential scales based on a consensus among judges, who conducted a rational examination of the content. Next, a series of statistical analyses was carried out to eliminate items that did not contribute to the internal consistency of a scale and to identify additional item candidates for inclusion that were missed in the first round of rational analyses. The latter were added if found by consensus to be related conceptually to the domain a scale was designed to measure. Final statistical analyses were conducted to eliminate items that contributed to excessively strong intercorrelations between the Content Scales.

This process yielded a set of 15 Content Scales. As might be expected, some of these scales were similar in composition to those developed by Wiggins (1966). Nearly all the scales included new MMPI-2 items, and some (e.g., Type A Behavior and Negative Treatment Indicators) were composed predominantly of new items.

Other Scales

Three additional scales introduced in 1989 with the MMPI-2 did not fare as well as the new Validity and Content Scales and therefore did not play a role in the development of the MMPI-2-RF. They included two gender role measures, Gender

Role–Masculine and Gender Role–Feminine, and a scale designed to assess symptoms of PTSD, the Schlenger PTSD Scale.

Subsequent Developments: The 2001 MMPI-2 Manual

During the decade following its publication, the MMPI-2 was the subject of over 800 journal articles, 70 book chapters, 20 books, and approximately 360 doctoral dissertations. Some research focused initially on comparing Clinical Scale scores based on the MMPI and MMPI-2 norms. Concerns about possible incongruence between the two sets of norms were resolved after it was determined that if code-type interpretation was limited to well-defined cases, where there was sufficient separation of the scales defining the code type from the remaining Clinical Scales, the two sets of norms yielded comparable Clinical Scale profiles (Graham, Timbrook, Ben-Porath & Butcher, 1991; McNulty, Ben-Porath & Graham, 1998; Tellegen & Ben-Porath, 1993). The focus then shifted to validating the new scales and exploring further scale development based (in part) on the new items in the inventory. The revised edition of the MMPI-2 manual (Butcher, Graham, Ben-Porath, Tellegen, Dahlstrom & Kaemmer, 2001) was designed to update interpretive guidelines for some scales, formalize the discontinuation of other scales, and provide guidelines for interpreting several new measures developed during the decade following the revision. The revised manual did not introduce any changes to the norms or item composition of the MMPI-2 scales included in the 1989 manual.

Discontinued Scales

Two years prior to publication of the 2001 manual, the MMPI-2 publisher, the University of Minnesota Press, decided to discontinue one set of MMPI subscales that had been included in the 1989 manual, the Wiener and Harmon (1946) Subtle and Obvious subscales. As discussed earlier, empirical support for the validity of the subtle subscales was scant from the beginning. Nonetheless, in the interest of continuity, the Restandardization Committee retained them in the official scoring materials for the test. This sparked renewed effort to study these measures (e.g., Timbrook, Graham, Keiller & Watts, 1993; Weed, Ben-Porath & Butcher, 1990), which continued to point toward invalidity of the subtle subscales. Given these disconfirmatory results, the Wiener–Harmon subscales were dropped from the MMPI-2. The Schlenger PTSD Scale was also dropped from the test and did not appear in the 2001 manual. During the decade following publication of the MMPI-2, it was found to be largely redundant with the Keane PTSD Scale, an original MMPI measure developed by Keane, Malloy, and Fairank (1984), which remained on the list of Supplementary Scales.

Revised Validity Scale Profile

The authors of the 2001 manual introduced a significant structural change to the Validity Scale profile. The four original Validity Scales (Cannot Say, L, F, and K) had been augmented, as described earlier, by the F_B, VRIN, and TRIN scales introduced with the 1989 publication of the MMPI-2. In the following decade, two additional Validity Scales, Infrequency Psychopathology (F_P; Arbisi & Ben-Porath, 1995) and

Superlative Self-Presentation (S; Butcher & Han, 1995), had been introduced and validated sufficiently to warrant inclusion among the MMPI-2 validity indicators. The 2001 revisions to the Validity Scale profile placed these scales within a conceptual framework for assessing test protocol validity and presented them in the order in which they were recommended for consideration. This framework also guided construction of the MMPI-2-RF Validity Scales and is described in detail in Chapter 4.

The Content Component Scales

Item analyses designed to maximize internal consistency ensured that the MMPI-2 Content Scales would be considerably more homogeneous than the Clinical Scales. Nonetheless, it was possible to parse some of the Content Scales into relatively independent subsets of items. Ben-Porath and Sherwood (1993) constructed the MMPI-2 Content Component Scales to clarify Content Scale interpretation, much as the Harris–Lingoes subscales were used with the Clinical Scales. The Content Component Scales were derived through a series of principal component and item analyses of each of the Content Scales separately, resulting in a total of 28 subscales for 12 of the 15 Content Scales. Most scales yielded only two component subscales.

Initial data reported by Ben-Porath and Sherwood (1993) indicated that the Content Component Scales had sufficient within-parent-scale discriminant validity to enable the test interpreter to develop a more refined picture of the test taker's self-portrayal. Subsequent studies (e.g., M. E. Clark, 1996; Englert, Weed & Watson, 2000) supported the utility of the Content Component Scales in clarifying the interpretation of scores on their parent Content Scales.

The Personality Psychopathology Five (PSY-5) Scales

The Personality Psychopathology Five (PSY-5) Scales were a major addition to the MMPI-2, incorporated into the 2001 manual. They had been introduced first by Harkness, McNulty, and Ben-Porath (1995) as measures of a personality psychopathology model developed and described in detail by Harkness and McNulty (1994). Harkness, McNulty, Ben-Porath, and Graham (2002) subsequently provided extensive analyses of the psychometric properties of the PSY-5 Scales. Revised versions of the MMPI-2 PSY-5 Scales have been incorporated into the MMPI-2-RF. A detailed description of the five constructs is presented in Chapter 3.

Additional Supplementary Scales

Three new and one existing scale were added to the MMPI-2 Supplementary Scale profile in the 2001 manual. The three new scales were the Marital Distress Scale (MDS), developed by Hjemboe, Almagor, and Butcher (1992), and two substance abuse measures: the Addiction Potential Scale (APS) and Addiction Acknowledgment Scale (AAS), developed by Weed, Butcher, McKenna, and Ben-Porath (1992). These authors reported initial data indicating that APS and AAS were incrementally valid with respect to the MacAndrew Alcoholism Scale–Revised (MAC-R), a revised version of the scale that was the primary source of information regarding risk for substance abuse on the original MMPI. Similar results were reported by Greene, Weed, Butcher, Arredondo, and Davis (1992). Follow-up studies (e.g., Aaronson,

Dent & Kline, 1996; Rouse, Butcher & Miller, 1999; Sawrie, Kabat, Dietz, Greene, Arredondo & Mann, 1996; Stein, Graham, Ben-Porath & McNulty, 1999; Svanum, Mcgrew & Ehrmann, 1994) supported the utility of AAS in particular as a predictor of substance abuse. Results for APS were more equivocal. Finally, an original MMPI scale that was not included in the 1989 manual, the Cook and Medley (1954) Hostility (Ho) Scale, was added to the Supplementary Scale profile following renewed interest in the scale (e.g., Han, Weed, Calhoun & Butcher, 1995), given the association between hostility and health problems largely cardiac in nature. This literature is reviewed in detail in Chapter 2 in the section on the restructured version of Clinical Scale 3 (Cynicism).

Appraisals of the MMPI-2

Practitioner surveys across a variety of settings found that the MMPI-2 was the most widely used self-report measure of personality and psychopathology (e.g., Archer, Buffington-Vollum, Stredny & Handel, 2006; Boccaccini & Brodsky, 1999; Camara, Nathan & Puente, 2000; Lally, 2003; Lees-Haley, Smith, Williams & Dunn, 1995; Sharland & Gfeller, 2007) and among the most frequently used of all psychological tests. As of January 2011, roughly 2,000 empirical studies that include MMPI-2 data have been published. Judged by the criteria of frequency of use and research utilized earlier to evaluate the MMPI, the MMPI-2 was similarly successful despite criticisms expressed initially by some MMPI users who were concerned that the test had changed too much as well as complaints by critics of the original MMPI who found that the test had not changed enough.

Initial Reactions

Although not without debate, four years after publication of the MMPI-2, the inventory had replaced the original MMPI in the vast majority of applied settings (Webb, Levitt & Rojdev, 1993). Initial reactions by some psychologists foresaw a different outcome. An article published in the *APA Monitor* under the title "Does the 'New' MMPI Beat the 'Classic'?" (Adler, 1990) began as follows:

> Psychologists have had nine months to scrutinize the new Minnesota Multiphasic Personality Inventory (MMPI) and some leaders in the field are likening the revised product to "New Coke." They like the classic version better, and they aren't ready to switch. (p. 18)

The article ended with the following prognostication:

> While the final outcome of the MMPI–MMPI-2 debate looks to be a long way off, Irving Gottesman, of the University of Virginia, was willing to hazard a guess: "The consumers will say they prefer the classic Coke," he said. (p. 19)

The primary concern expressed by those quoted in the article related to the representativeness of the new normative sample, triggered by data reported in the MMPI-2 manual indicating that members of the normative sample were better educated than the general population. Another concern raised about the new norms (and, in particular, the Uniform T scores) was that deflated T scores distorted the Clinical Scale code types and, as a result, compromised reliance on the original MMPI code-type literature when interpreting the MMPI-2.

Concerns about Norms

The Restandardization Committee was aware that the MMPI-2 T scores were lower than corresponding scores on the MMPI (for reasons discussed earlier) and, accordingly, lowered the threshold for clinically significant elevation from 70T to 65T. To address concerns about the relatively high socioeconomic status (SES) of the new normative sample, Pope, Butcher, and Seelen (1993) produced figures illustrating the absence of clinically meaningful differences between the profiles of various SES groups. Schinka and Lalone (1997) later recalculated the MMPI-2 norms based on a reduced sample designed to match national SES distributions and concluded that the altered norms were not meaningfully different from the MMPI-2 norms.

To address concerns that the Uniform T scores were responsible for the lower scores and, possibly, changed code types, Graham et al. (1991) compared profiles based on Uniform versus traditional linear T scores (both derived from the new normative sample) and found that Uniform T scores did not substantially alter the pattern or level of scores on the MMPI-2 Clinical Scale profile. Thus, empirical data showed that the relatively high SES standing of the MMPI-2 normative sample and the Uniform T scores did not affect the utility of the revised norms.

Code-Type Congruence

Initial concerns about inadequate congruence between code types resulting from the old and new norms were prompted by data reported in the 1989 MMPI-2 manual indicating that the same two-point code type was found in only two-thirds of cases when the same raw scores were transformed to T scores based on MMPI versus MMPI-2 norms. These concerns were not trivial. As noted earlier, the Restandardization Committee decided not to make meaningful changes to the Clinical Scales, given their goal of maintaining continuity with the original MMPI, in particular, with code type–based interpretation. If, as suggested by data in the MMPI-2 manual, in roughly one-third of the cases the two sets of norms yielded different code types, which set of empirical correlates (corresponding to which of the two code types) should be used in interpreting the profile? As it turned out, this concern was based on problematic data analyses, including those reported in the 1989 MMPI-2 manual.

The method used to define code types in the analyses reported in the 1989 manual (and later by Dahlstrom, 1992, a member of the Restandardization Committee) yielded highly unstable and thus unreliable code types. A change of one T-score point on two scales could lead to an entirely different code-type designation. Because none of the Clinical Scales is perfectly reliable, meaningful code-type classification cannot be sensitive to such unreliable changes; rather, a minimal degree of separation between the scales in the code type and the remaining scales on the profile must be present for the code type to be stable. Analyses conducted by Graham et al. (1991) indicated that scales in a code type needed to be at least five points higher than the remaining scales in a profile for the code type to be sufficiently stable. Such well-defined code types were also quite stable across the MMPI and MMPI-2 norms.

Helmes and Reddon (1993)

The strategic decision by the Restandardization Committee to keep the Clinical Scales intact was bound to disappoint those who had earlier called, or agreed with calls, for major changes to, if not a complete overhaul of, the inventory. Helmes and Reddon (1993), former students of Douglas Jackson (who had challenged Meehl's, 1945a, radical empirical justification for the MMPI; Jackson, 1971), and, later, Jackson himself weighed in with strenuous criticisms. They were critical of nearly all aspects of the revision but, in particular, objected to the decision to retain the Clinical Scales. Helmes and Reddon (1993) repeated (and cited) many of the criticisms of Jackson (1971), Loevinger (1972), and Norman (1972) discussed in detail earlier in the chapter. It is regrettable that Helmes and Reddon (1993) did not discuss Meehl's (1972) detailed responses to these critiques, in which he agreed with some of the earlier criticisms but offered cogent rebuttals to others.

Helmes and Reddon (1993) raised fundamental questions about the psychometric soundness of the MMPI and MMPI-2. Because these two tests served as the foundation for developing the MMPI-2-RF and some of Helmes and Reddon's criticisms could be thought to apply to the latter, these issues are addressed here in detail, beginning with an analysis of several mistaken claims and assertions, followed by a discussion of structural and conceptual problems with the Clinical Scales that were the focus of changes that shaped the MMPI-2-RF.

Erroneous Claims and Assertions

Helmes and Reddon's (1993) critique included several factual, logical, conceptual, and psychometric errors. Those that pertain to features of the MMPI-2 carried over to the MMPI-2-RF are discussed next.

Outdated Nosology

Under the heading "Major Theoretical Problems," Helmes and Reddon (1993) stated,

> Although an open role of theory was rejected in the development of the MMPI, an implicit theory filled the void. The implicit theory was that [i.e., was the one] underlying the diagnostic categories used to form the clinical scales . . . as well as the theoretical conceptions underlying the process that led to the selection of the MMPI item pool . . . many of the concepts used then are no longer used in modern theories of psychopathology. . . . The heavy reliance on diagnostic practices that are now outdated now [sic] makes the entire foundation of the clinical scales suspect. (p. 455)

In his response to the same arguments made previously by Loevinger (1972) and Norman (1972), Meehl (1972) observed that although it had become fashionable to criticize the Kraepelinian diagnostic system as outdated or, worse yet, obsolete, a viable alternative of equal prognostic or treatment-relevant powers had yet to materialize. Meehl's defense of this system, based, at the time, mainly on his own experience, was later affirmed by the adoption of the neo-Kraepelinian perspective underlying the *DSM-III* and its successors.

Moreover, soon after the test was published, the focus of MMPI interpretation shifted from differential diagnosis to code type–based identification of clinical and personological test correlates. Anticipating this response, Helmes and Reddon (1993) commented,

> Undoubtedly, many users of the MMPI would protest that diagnosis is not the use to which they put the MMPI. Many would say that they use it to describe an individual and that they base their interpretation on code types and the profile configuration. However the use of the Clinical Scales in a code type implicitly carries with it the diagnostic implications inherent in the construction of the Clinical Scales, as these underlie the shape of the profile. (p. 457)

This assertion is puzzling. It is one thing to question the psychometric wisdom of using heterogeneous and redundant measures as the building blocks for complex multivariate indicators (as did Norman, 1972) and quite another to assert that the code types were inextricably bound conceptually to the diagnostic scheme that informed the Clinical Scales. Hathaway (1960) had long before noted that in an early paradigm shift, MMPI interpretation was no longer predicated on the original diagnostic categories but rather on subsequently observed correlations of the MMPI with other variables.

On this point, Helmes and Reddon (1993) asserted that "one might conclude that demonstrating the construct validity of scales developed by the empirical-contrasted-groups method would be an illogical and impossible task" (p. 456). However, in introducing the concept of construct validity, Cronbach and Meehl (1955) explained that "even when a test is constructed on the basis of a specific criterion, it may ultimately be judged to have greater construct validity than the criterion" (p. 286). They termed the process of learning about a construct through the empirical correlates of its measure *bootstrapping* and used one of the original Clinical Scales, Pd, as an example of how the construct validity of a scale consolidates as empirical evidence is gathered.

Social Desirability

A second major shortcoming Helmes and Reddon (1993) attributed to the decision to retain the Clinical Scales was the problem of "Response Styles," which they asserted, "particularly in regard to *social desirability*, has never been resolved since the mid 1960s" (p. 461). Although they limited their criticism on this topic to the Clinical Scales, Jackson, Fraboni, and Helmes (1997) later extended it to the MMPI-2 Content Scales, which, they concluded, were extremely confounded with stylistic variance, leading the authors to "doubt that the MMPI-2 Content Scales would show acceptable discriminant properties in appropriate studies utilizing multitrait-multimethod designs" (p. 117). In fact, previously published findings (e.g., Ben-Porath, Butcher & Graham, 1991), actually cited by Helmes and Reddon (1993), had already demonstrated the discriminant properties of the Content Scales in reference to non-self-report criteria. Moreover, as discussed earlier, Block (1965) marshaled compelling evidence that the two broad sources of MMPI variance that Jackson and his colleagues attributed to construct-irrelevant response styles were actually substantive dimensions of direct relevance to the assessment of personality and psychopathology.

To understand the flaw in the "social desirability" critique of the MMPI and MMPI-2, it is necessary to consider the method on which Jackson and his colleagues relied to measure this presumably stylistic source of MMPI variance. Much of the early research on this topic was conducted with a scale developed by Edwards (1957) on the basis of college students' judgments regarding the "desirability" of MMPI items. The Edwards Social Desirability (Esd) Scale was made up of items describing various behaviors, attitudes, and experiences the students considered undesirable. On the basis of substantial (negative) correlations between this scale and the MMPI Clinical Scales, Edwards (1957) and, later, Jackson and Messick (1962) concluded that a sizable proportion of Clinical Scale variance was of stylistic rather than substantive origin; that is, an elevated score on a Clinical Scale was more likely to reflect the test taker's tendency to attribute undesirable features to himself or herself rather than the extent to which he or she actually possessed these attributes.

The basic problem with this approach is that psychopathology is undesirable; therefore, any item describing psychopathology symptoms will inevitably be judged undesirable. Helmes and Reddon (1993) conceded, "Indeed, it may not be possible to develop measures of psychopathology that are completely free of an evaluative bias" (p. 461) but went on to caution that

> the danger in this case, as with all confounds, is that one can never know which interpretation is correct, that of social desirability or that of overt item content. Thus, it is important to have an independent index of social desirability even in measures of psychopathology to determine its relative contribution in any particular individual. (p. 461)

Although they criticized the MMPI-2 for lacking such a measure, Helmes and Reddon (1993), as collaborators in the development of Jackson's own self-report measure of psychopathology, the Basic Personality Inventory (BPI; Jackson, 1989), which they recommended as an alternative to the MMPI-2, must have known that the BPI itself lacked such a measure or any other independent (from substantive measures) Validity Scales. In fact, as chronicled by Tellegen, Ben-Porath, Sellbom, Arbisi, McNulty, and Graham (2006), "the most important and sophisticated program of inventory development to have been predicated on the idea of a general and separately measurable social desirability dimension ended up abandoning that construct" (p. 150).

Unbalanced Scale Keying

Helmes and Reddon (1993) were critical of the unequal proportion of true and false keyed items on many MMPI and MMPI-2 scales. Advocating instead balanced scoring keys, they asserted that "the major reason for having balanced keying is to control for an acquiescent response style" (p. 462). However, balanced scoring keys do not provide protection from acquiescence or nonacquiescence and may actually mask such a test-taking approach if it occurs. Consider two 20-item scales, A and B. A is perfectly balanced, with 10 items keyed true and the other 10 keyed false. All 20 items on B are keyed true. If an extremely acquiescent test taker were to answer all 40 A and B items true irrespective of their content, both scale scores would be equally invalid. Moreover, while the resulting raw score of 20 on B would be extreme, and thus potentially alert the interpreter that an unlikely score was attained, a raw score of 10 on A, although equally invalid in this case, would more likely go unnoticed.

Helmes and Reddon (1993) also contended that "low scores on unbalanced scales reduce the amount of possible information that might be obtained if the scales were bipolar" (p. 462) and proposed that

> on a scale that has items keyed only in one direction, a low score implies the absence of the characteristics measured by the scale. In contrast, with a bipolar scale, a low score implies the opposite of the characteristics measured by the scale. (p. 462)

In fact, balanced scoring keys are neither necessary nor sufficient for developing bipolar measures or scales with informative low scores. Bipolarity is a property of constructs, not scales. Consider the example of two four-item scales: C, a measure of introversion, and D, a measure of persecutory thinking. C is made up of the following items, all keyed true:

- I prefer to be on my own.
- I rarely go to parties.
- I have very few friends.
- I avoid being the center of attention.

D is made up of the following items, alternatively keyed true and false:

- Someone is out to get me.
- The CIA has never tapped my phone.
- I am being followed.
- I have never been poisoned intentionally.

A test taker with a raw score of zero on C presents as outgoing and extraverted. On the other hand, a test taker with a raw score of zero on D presents as lacking persecutory beliefs. C is an unbalanced scale that assesses a bipolar construct, and D is a perfectly balanced scale that assesses a unipolar construct.

Unequal Scale Lengths

Helmes and Reddon (1993) were also critical of the unequal lengths of MMPI and MMPI-2 scales, asserting,

> Problems when scales within a test are of unequal length arise when one attempts to interpret a profile and to determine if scales are significantly different. It is commonly recognized that one must take into account the reliabilities of the scales in question when one is comparing scales of different lengths (Lord & Novick, 1968), but one should also adjust the reliabilities (using the Spearman–Brown formula) to equate the length of the scales before calculating standard errors or differences between scales. (pp. 462–463)

This assertion is patently incorrect. All that is necessary to calculate the standard error of the difference between two standardized scale scores are the standard errors of measurement of these two scores and the correlation between the two scales.

Moreover, the Spearman–Brown formula actually establishes a relation between scale length and scale reliability that can imply the desirability of *unequal* scale lengths if comparable reliabilities are desired.

Consider the following hypothetical example of two 20-item scales, E and F, with reliability estimates of .85 and .75, respectively. Applying the Spearman–Brown formula, if six items are deleted from E and six items are added to F, it is possible to achieve comparable reliabilities of approximately .80 for both scales with 14 and 26 items, respectively. Requiring equal scale lengths not only is unnecessary but can actually be counterproductive.

The MMPI-2 Norms

Helmes and Reddon (1993) also advanced several criticisms of the MMPI-2 norms. They characterized the use of the 704-item experimental booklet for the collection of norms as a "curious feature for the MMPI-2" (p. 465) and expressed concern that the resulting MMPI-2 norms may not be "truly appropriate for it" (p. 465), although they conceded that "it is probable that the true norms would be very similar" (p. 465). This issue is addressed directly by data reported in Appendix C of the *MMPI-2-RF Technical Manual* (Tellegen & Ben-Porath, 2008/2011), showing that the 567-item MMPI-2 booklet and 338-item MMPI-2-RF booklet yield comparable scores on the 51 scales of the MMPI-2-RF. Moreover, two cohorts tested 20 years apart, one with the 704-item MMPI-AX, the other with the 338-item MMPI-2-RF, produced comparable scores on the same scales.

Helmes and Reddon (1993) also erroneously criticized a dual use of MMPI-2 normative data for scale development and for scale norming purposes. In fact, MMPI-2 normative data were not used in any scale development. The developers of new MMPI-2 scales deliberately avoided using the normative data for anything but standardization. Finally, they cited concerns that MMPI-2 normative shifts had substantially altered the Clinical Scale code types. However, empirical data, some published subsequent to Helmes and Reddon's critique, demonstrated that in the relatively uncommon cases where the two sets of norms yielded reliably different code types, those based on the MMPI-2 norms showed evidence of improved validity (McNulty et al., 1998).

Uniform T Scores

Helmes and Reddon (1993) devoted a section of their critique to the Uniform T-score transformation that was adopted for the MMPI-2 Clinical and Content Scales and has been carried over to the MMPI-2-RF. Tellegen and Ben-Porath (1992) had already provided a detailed description of this transformation and the rationale for its use, discussed in detail in Chapter 5. The distinctive function of Uniform T scores is to preserve the generally positive skew of the raw-score (and original T-score) distributions of the scales in question, while producing distributions that are more similar across scales.

Helmes and Reddon (1993) proposed that

an argument might be made for normalized scores in that there is likely to be a certain number of individuals in a random sample who have some form of psychopathology, thus leading to a positive skew with samples not screened for abnormality. (p. 465)

This is precisely the feature of a representative population sample that calls for not using normalization but instead for using the kind of skewness-preserving transformation provided by the Uniform T scores. If we assume that the normative sample is indeed essentially a representative sample and not one made up of persons specifically selected for being in good mental health (i.e., a "normal" sample), then, arguably, the expectable occurrences of psychopathology would cause the normative underlying distribution to have a positive skew. In that case, only a skewness-maintaining standardization could preserve the basic metric of the latent dimension, while normalization would distort it (Tellegen & Ben-Porath, 1992).

Validity of the Content Scales

Helmes and Reddon (1993) expressed concern that "unlike the clinical scales" (p. 466), there is little evidence for the validity of the Content Scales. However, credible interpretation of structurally and substantively coherent Content Scales is not dependent solely on the availability of empirical correlates. Content Scales allow the test interpreter to make informative normative statements about what the test taker actually said in responding to the test items. An elevated score on a Fears Content Scale is by definition a content-valid indication that the test taker reported a larger than average number of fears, a finding of potential clinical significance. As the score increases further above the clinical cutoff point, the test interpreter can characterize the types of fears reported by the test taker (as reflected in the content of the scale) with greater specificity.

Structural and Conceptual Problems with the Clinical Scales

Although large segments of their critique were marred by errors and unsound reasoning, Helmes and Reddon (1993) also discussed some actual structural problems and conceptual difficulties with the Clinical Scales.

Structural Problems

Helmes and Reddon (1993) revisited a number of structural problems with the Clinical Scales that had been the focus of criticisms raised at the 1970 conference on revising the MMPI. Chief among these, and related to all, was the heterogeneous content of the Clinical Scales, which significantly limited their convergent validities, and the overlap and redundancy among the scales, which significantly restricted their discriminant properties. Related to heterogeneity, Helmes and Reddon raised questions about the lack of cross-validation in the initial item selection process and the role this played in the inclusion of invalid subtle items on the scales. They correctly identified the problem of redundancy as stemming from the way in which the criterion-keying approach to item selection was applied by Hathaway and McKinley, including the decision to allow substantial item overlap among the scales. However, they incorrectly concluded that adding the K correction to five of the Clinical Scales exacerbated this problem and further inflated the correlations between them. In fact, K-corrected scores are less highly intercorrelated than are non-K-corrected scores. On the other hand, Helmes and Reddon correctly questioned the utility of the K correction and observed the near absence of any empirical support for its application.

A Fundamental Conceptual Question

Citing Loevinger's (1972) critique, Helmes and Reddon (1993) also questioned the soundness of "mixing of categorical and dimensional measurement models" (p. 457) when using continuous measures such as the Clinical Scales to predict categorical variables such as diagnoses: "Strictly speaking the prediction of class membership requires the use of base rates and cutting points and the calculation of sensitivity and specificity, not T scores" (p. 457). As noted earlier, Meehl (1972) had already pointed out in response to Loevinger (1972) that there is nothing inherently wrong (in his wording, absurd) about using continuous measures such as the Clinical Scales to predict categorical class membership, a standard practice in the use of many medical tests. Moreover, Helmes and Reddon's (1993) assertion that interpretation of T scores somehow precludes the use of base rates, designation of cutting points, and calculation of sensitivity and specificity is, frankly, absurd. However, the fundamental conceptual question of whether the focus or orientation of a measure of psychopathology should be dimensional, categorical, or some combination of both, and the methodological questions that follow (i.e., what is the optimal measurement approach for assessing categorical vs. dimensional constructs), are matters that require careful consideration in the early stages of test development.

Following the Kraepelinian model, Hathaway and McKinley targeted taxonic class variables (diagnoses) in developing the Clinical Scales. With the subsequent abandonment of differential diagnosis as the primary application of the instrument, and ensuing efforts to discover and flesh out the correlates of new classes, use of the MMPI remained focused on typological classification, with the Clinical Scales now serving as the ingredients of code types and cookbooks. On the other hand, further scale construction with the MMPI (e.g., the Welsh A and R scales, the Wiggins Content Scales) and nearly all scale development efforts with the MMPI-2 (e.g., the MMPI-2 Content Scales, the PSY-5 Scales) produced dimensionally focused measures of dimensionally conceived constructs.

Any effort to address the significant structural problems of the Clinical Scales (just noted) would require thoughtful consideration of, and ultimately adopting a position on, the fundamental nature (dimensional or categorical) of the constructs targeted in the revision. Contemplating this possibility, Meehl (1972) noted, "I cannot imagine myself starting to 'build a new MMPI' without having tentatively settled this kind of question for at least the major variables of clinical interest" (p. 179).

CONCLUSIONS

Judged by the frequency with which the MMPI-2 came to be used in practice and research, the revision was clearly successful. This is particularly true in light of the skeptical reaction of some original MMPI enthusiasts who opined that the test had changed too much and mistakenly predicted that, as a result, the MMPI-2 would fail to replace its classic predecessor. This initial tepid reaction suggests that the strategic decision of the Restandardization Committee to update the test norms and forgo any meaningful changes to the Clinical Scales was wise, insofar as the goal of fostering transition to the MMPI-2 was concerned.

The strategic decision to leave the Clinical Scales essentially unchanged did, however, have negative consequences. As discussed earlier, up until the 1960s, the MMPI played a significant role in basic research in personality and psychopathology and in studies of important applied questions in personality assessment. As concerns about the psychometric soundness of the Clinical Scales mounted, basic researchers lost interest in the MMPI, as did many investigators interested in fostering improvements in applied personality assessment. This schism disadvantaged MMPI users, who could no longer rely on direct links to these lines of investigation, and it was also detrimental to investigators in these areas, who lost access to the wealth of clinically rich data available on the hundreds of thousands of individuals tested yearly with the inventory. The continuity achieved by protecting the Clinical Scales had the negative consequence of maintaining the growing gulf between MMPI-2 users and innovative research in personality and psychopathology.

Successful efforts to link the MMPI-2 to contemporary approaches to the measurement and study of psychopathology and personality were nevertheless carried out. The PSY-5 Scales provided a link to a dimensional model of Axis II psychopathology, which could also be associated with the widely studied Five Factor Model of personality. On the applied side, a substantial body of research on the MMPI-2 Content Scales indicated that content-based, largely transparent MMPI-2 measures could perform at least as well as the Clinical Scales in assessing psychopathology and personality constructs. Finally, an extensive literature accumulated on applications of new and old MMPI-2 Validity Scales (in particular, VRIN, TRIN, and F_p), providing test users with a firm foundation for using the instrument to assess a variety of threats to the validity of test protocols.

TOWARD THE MMPI-2-RF

The structural problems with the MMPI-2 Clinical Scales discussed at length by Jackson (1971), Loevinger (1972), Meehl (1972), and Norman (1972), and revisited by Helmes and Reddon (1993), led Auke Tellegen, a member of the Restandardization Committee, to begin exploring ways they might be addressed. This work culminated in the development of the RC Scales (Tellegen et al., 2003), which was the first step toward the construction of the MMPI-2-RF. A detailed discussion of these structural challenges, the methods used to address them, and the outcome of Tellegen's efforts to restructure the Clinical Scales is provided in the next chapter.

CHAPTER 2

Transitioning to the MMPI-2-RF:
The Restructured Clinical (RC) Scales

Soon after the MMPI-2 was published, Auke Tellegen, a member of the MMPI Restandardization Committee, began to explore ways to address long-recognized problems with the Clinical Scales. As discussed in Chapter 1, the MMPI-2 item pool served as a rich source of clinically relevant information for nearly seven decades. However, significant questions had been raised over the years about the psychometric adequacy of the Clinical Scales, which, for the sake of continuity, were left intact in the MMPI-2. Approximately 10 years after Tellegen initiated his project, the resulting set of Restructured Clinical (RC) Scales was added to the inventory. This turned out to be the first phase of a comprehensive effort to modernize the test, which ultimately generated the MMPI-2-RF.

Development of the RC Scales played a critical role in the construction of the MMPI-2-RF. The procedures Tellegen designed for revising the Clinical Scales were later implemented in the development of many of the additional measures included in the MMPI-2-RF. This chapter begins with a detailed discussion of the rationale for the revision of the Clinical Scales, followed by a description of the methods Tellegen used and a detailed delineation of the constructs assessed by the restructured scales. The chapter concludes with a discussion of appraisals of the RC Scales.

WHY RESTRUCTURE THE CLINICAL SCALES?

Although they contain compelling and informative items, it had long been recognized that as aggregate measures, the Clinical Scales were not psychometrically optimal. Two primary problems were the higher than expected intercorrelations between the scales and the substantial heterogeneity within them.

Excessive Intercorrelations of the Scales

Chief among the identified shortcomings of the Clinical Scales were the higher than expected intercorrelations between them. For example, the correlation between Clinical Scale 7, a measure of emotional dysfunction associated with anxiety, and Clinical Scale 8, designed to assess disordered thinking, averages around .90 in clinical samples (Tellegen, Ben-Porath, McNulty, Arbisi, Graham & Kaemmer, 2003). Although anxiety-related problems and disordered thinking certainly co-occur, epidemiological findings (cf. Buckley, Miller, Lehrer & Castle, 2009) are inconsistent with an 80% comorbidity rate implied by these correlations. As a second illustration, the correlation between Clinical Scale 2, a measure of depression, and Clinical Scale 4, intended to assess features of psychopathy, averages approximately .60 in clinical samples (Tellegen et al., 2003). However, depression has generally been found to be either uncorrelated or only modestly associated with measures of psychopathy (Patrick, 2007). In general, correlations between the Clinical Scales often exceed substantially the known rates of co-occurrence of the phenomena they were designed to assess.

One source of these excessive intercorrelations is item overlap. For example, Clinical Scales 7 and 8 share 17 items. An extreme example is that item 31—"I find it difficult to keep my mind on a task or job"—was keyed true on five of the eight original Clinical Scales (2, 3, 4, 7, and 8). This was not an oversight. Hathaway's (1956) rationale for allowing item overlap on the Clinical Scales was that the syndromes they targeted had overlapping clinical features:

> In some cases, as with Pt and Sc, an arbitrary decision had to be made about the proper amount of overlap. These scales correlate and the syndromes as observed in clinical cases also overlap. It would be undesirable to eliminate this correlation in measurement of syndromes. The correlation was deliberately built in by leaving in each scale certain items that had been observed to be valid for the other syndrome. (pp. 104–105)

It is now recognized that allowing the same item response to contribute variance to more than one measure artificially inflates intercorrelations between item-overlapping scales by introducing correlated measurement error. Item overlap on scales that are analyzed comparatively (e.g., scales plotted on the same profile) is inconsistent with current standards of psychological test construction.

Although clearly a problem, item overlap was not the primary source of the excessive intercorrelations between the Clinical Scales. As discussed later, Demoralization, a construct that in the past had been labeled the "MMPI first factor," "General Maladjustment," and "Anxiety," was the primary contributor to this phenomenon. Regardless of their origin, excessive correlations between the Clinical Scales substantially limited their discriminant validities. As correlations between measures of two constructs range higher, it becomes increasingly difficult for those measures to adequately differentiate between the constructs they are intended to assess.

Substantial Heterogeneity of the Scales

A second major source of difficulty with the Clinical Scales was their heterogeneous, overinclusive item content, which significantly attenuated their convergent validities. Like item overlap, heterogeneity was built into the scales intentionally to assess multifaceted syndromes (Hathaway, 1956). However, attempting to assess multifaceted syndromes with heterogeneous, univariate scales is problematic and unlikely to be effective (Nunnally, 1967). Item heterogeneity has the effect of producing ambiguous scale scores. The same score on a heterogeneous scale may reflect very different sets of responses, associated with dissimilar problems, unless the score approaches its maximal value.

The Subtle Items

The subtle items, long the focus of MMPI critics (e.g., Jackson, 1971; Norman, 1972), are an example of the problem caused by overinclusive item content. As discussed in Chapter 1, Meehl (1972), who had previously defended the inclusion of subtle items on the Clinical Scales (Meehl, 1945a), no longer viewed it desirable to include on a scale items whose content could not be understood in the context of the targeted construct.

Doubts about the subtle items can be traced to data presented by Wiener (1948) in initial support of the Wiener–Harmon Subtle and Obvious subscales. These data showed that scores on the obvious subscales were more highly correlated with relevant criteria than were scores on the full Clinical Scales. On the other hand, subtle subscale scores were uncorrelated with the criteria in Wiener's study. Taken together, these findings indicated that the subtle items contributed construct-irrelevant variance (i.e., noise) to the full scales and thus attenuated their validities.

Jackson (1971) speculated that a large number of invalid subtle items were included on the Clinical Scales as a result of sampling error. This is a plausible hypothesis. Hathaway and McKinley had very limited resources when constructing the Clinical Scales. Most of the original criterion samples were quite small (20–50 subjects were available for the development of all but Scale 4), and cross-validation of item selections with independent samples was generally not possible. Moreover, thousands of correlations were calculated by hand in the process of developing the Clinical Scales, creating many opportunities for clerical error.[1]

Weed, Ben-Porath, and Butcher (1990) tested the random variance hypothesis by replacing the subtle items with items selected randomly from the MMPI-2 to create "pseudo-subtle" subscales. Consistent with the hypothesis that the subtle items, for the most part, contribute random variance or psychometric noise to the Clinical Scales, Weed at al. (1990) found that pseudo–Clinical Scale scores, composed of the obvious plus pseudo-subtle subscales, had validities comparable to those found with the actual Clinical Scales.

These findings, indicating that the subtle items were most likely included on the Clinical Scales as a result of random error, coupled with the absence of any consistent evidence of the extratest validity of subtle subscale scores, resulted in the publisher's decision to discontinue their use with the MMPI-2 in 1999. However, the subtle items themselves were not removed from the Clinical Scales and continued to exacerbate the problem of scale heterogeneity.

In sum, excessive intercorrelations, which reduced their discriminant properties, and heterogeneity, which attenuated their convergent validities, were the primary shortcomings that motivated Tellegen to explore a restructuring of the Clinical Scales.

Pre–Restructured Clinical Scale Solutions

It may be instructive to consider how these challenges were met prior to the development of the RC Scales. Two relatively early developments, the shift to code-type interpretation and the introduction of the Harris–Lingoes subscales, provided the primary means for dealing with these problems.

Scale 4 can be used to illustrate the problem and its pre–RC Scale solutions. Following in the tradition of the large-scale cookbook studies of the original MMPI, Graham, Ben-Porath, and McNulty (1996) conducted a comprehensive investigation of the empirical correlates of MMPI-2 scales and code types in a community mental health center. Extratest criterion data, consisting of historical and mental status findings reported by intake workers and ratings provided later by therapists (without access to the MMPI-2 results), served as the criteria. The correlates obtained for Scale 4 included those that would be expected for a measure of so-called psychopathic deviance (e.g., substance abuse, family problems, anger). However, a larger number of correlates, with generally stronger associations with Scale 4, reflected features such as depression, anxiety, insecurity, and pessimism, which would not be expected to correlate with a psychopathy measure.

Examination of the items scored on Scale 4 provides an explanation for these unexpected findings. They include statements such as "I wish I could be as happy as others seem to be" (keyed true [T]), "I have not lived the right kind of life" (T), "I am happy most of the time" (F), and "These days I find it hard not to give up hope of amounting to something" (T).[2]

Given the diversity of features associated with higher scores on Scale 4, how was an interpreter to characterize an individual with a clinically significant elevation on the scale? The code types and subscales provided some necessary guidance. If, along with a Scale 4 elevation, the test taker produced a clinically significant elevation on Scale 9, and scores on the remaining scales were substantially lower than those on Scales 4 and 9 (i.e., the test taker produced a well-defined 49-94 code type), the empirical correlates identified by Graham et al. (1996) for the 49-94 code type included impulsivity, narcissism, and problems with authority figures but not the unexpected emotional correlates of Scale 4. For a different test taker who produced exactly the same score on Scale 4 but, rather than having an elevated Scale 9 score, scored high on Scale 2 (thus forming a well-defined 24-42 code type), the correlates reported by Graham and colleagues included depression, anxiety, and feelings of inferiority, and none of the acting-out descriptors were correlated significantly with this code type. Thus, by considering scores on other scales on the profile, the interpreter was able to distinguish between the two very different types of Scale 4 correlates. However, this method for indirect dismantling of heterogeneous scales can hardly be considered an ideal solution.

Moreover, not all MMPI-2 test takers with elevated scores on Scale 4 produced well-defined code types. In such cases, the Harris–Lingoes subscales could be of assistance. For example, the correlates Graham et al. (1996) reported for the Harris–Lingoes subscale Authority Problems (Pd2) included substance abuse, a criminal history, and being described by their therapist as antisocial, but none of the emotional correlates of Scale 4, whereas the correlates found for Self-Alienation (Pd5) included depression, anxiety, acute psychological turmoil, and feelings of inferiority, but no acting-out descriptors were associated with this subscale.

These armchair-constructed measures had their own shortcomings, including overlapping items within subscale sets, subscales for which the highest T scores did not exceed the cutoffs for clinically significant elevation, and some very low reliabilities. Perhaps because of these difficulties, the Harris–Lingoes subscales were never subjected to systematic empirical investigation.

Conclusion

Although the code types and Harris–Lingoes subscales were, in some cases, helpful in meeting the challenges of excessive intercorrelations and heterogeneity, neither approach provided a psychometrically sound solution. As additional Supplementary Scales were added to the MMPI and MMPI-2, they, too, were enlisted in the increasingly complex task of deciphering Clinical Scale scores. The basic aim of the restructuring process was to revise these scales to provide a more efficient and psychometrically sound solution to the problems just discussed.

DEVELOPING THE RESTRUCTURED CLINICAL SCALES

Tellegen's first task in attempting to revise the Clinical Scales was to devise a method for doing so. As discussed in Chapter 1, critics of the Clinical Scales (e.g., Jackson, 1971; Loevinger, 1972; Meehl, 1972; Norman, 1972) had proposed various strategies for addressing the psychometric challenges just described. This section begins with a discussion of the methods available for revising the Clinical Scales, followed by a description of the approach adopted by Tellegen.

Methodological Considerations

Jackson (1971) articulated a detailed formula for creating new Clinical Scales for the MMPI. The first step would involve a theory-informed designation of the targeted constructs. This would be followed by the writing of items guided by theory and then empirical analyses designed to maximize the internal consistency of the developed scales, enhance their convergent and discriminant properties, and minimize the impact of response styles. Norman (1972) and Meehl (1972) offered similar, more narrowly focused recommendations for addressing specific problems but did not propose an overall strategy.

An alternative scale construction approach, based on exploratory factor-analytic techniques, had previously been devised by Cattell (1966), culminating in the development of the 16PF. Applying this methodology to the Clinical Scales would have involved conducting factor analyses designed to identify the primary sources of variance in the item pool, rotating the resulting factors to simple structure, and retaining items associated uniquely with a single factor.

Tellegen did not share Jackson's optimism that the fields of personality and psychopathology had converged on a consensual set of constructs that could be targeted in a clinical assessment device, let alone a fully delineated theory that could guide item writing or selection. He opted instead to rely on exploratory analyses designed to discover the primary, distinctive sources of Clinical Scale variance and treat the identified dimensions as "open concepts" (Cronbach & Meehl, 1955; MacCorquodale & Meehl, 1948; Meehl, 1978), to be fleshed out conceptually and empirically. Tellegen concluded that Cattell's (1966) dimensional simplification approach to construct identification was inappropriate for the revision of the Clinical Scales because of the very real possibility that factorially pure dimensions might miss important clinical phenomena, that is, those that are rare and/or do not conform to the requirements of simple structure.

Having concluded that the two primary methods used to construct modern self-report inventories (Jackson's and Cattell's) were not appropriate for revising the Clinical Scales, Tellegen had to devise an alternative. He was guided by his experience developing the Multidimensional Personality Questionnaire (MPQ; Tellegen, 1995/2003), a normal personality inventory assembled by "exploratory test construction." Tellegen and Waller (2008) chronicle the development of the MPQ through an iterative process over a 10-year period of theoretically informed item writing, followed by data collection, empirically guided construct refinement, new item writing, new data collection, further construct refinement, and so on.

Applying exactly the same methodology to a revision of the Clinical Scales was neither feasible nor necessary. It was not feasible because it would have entailed repeated collection of new clinical samples and, in the end, would have produced a set of scales that required new norms and lacked a comprehensive foundation for empirically grounded interpretation. This was the very problem that led the MMPI Restandardization Committee to avoid making substantive changes to the Clinical Scales. It was unnecessary because the carefully assembled MMPI-2 item pool was available to Tellegen for a revision that would not necessarily require writing additional items. By the time RC Scale construction was complete (in the late 1990s), abundant MMPI-2 data were available to help delineate the open constructs assessed by the new scales and establish an empirical foundation for their interpretation.

The methodology adopted for revising the Clinical Scales, described in detail by Tellegen et al. (2003), retained the use of exploratory factor analyses to guide the identification of targets for scale development, while adopting a flexible approach to the process of assembling a revised set of scales from the entire MMPI-2 item pool. As detailed next, it was guided conceptually by the results of Tellegen's prior work on the interrelatedness of mood, personality, and psychopathology.

Scale Development

Development of the RC Scales proceeded in four steps, each designed to accomplish a particular goal and predicated on specified assumptions. To achieve reliable results, empirically based decisions were guided by consistent findings using four large samples (composed of male and female psychiatric inpatients and male and female substance abuse treatment patients). The first step addressed the primary source of the excessive correlations between the Clinical Scales: demoralization.

Step 1: Defining and Capturing the Common Factor

The existence of a common factor that contributed substantial variance to the MMPI Clinical Scales and, as a result, markedly increased the intercorrelations between them had been recognized for some time. MMPI critics disagreed about whether this was a substantive source of variance (Norman, 1972) or an artifactual response style (Jackson, 1971; Loevinger, 1972). Meehl (1972) argued that regardless of its origin (about which he remained uncertain), any effort to improve the Clinical Scales—in particular, their discriminant validities—required that the common factor be identified and removed.

Tellegen's view on the nature of this common factor was articulated in a chapter devoted to the assessment of anxiety by self-report (Tellegen, 1985):

> It is generally the case that correlations between measures of adjustment tend to be substantial, giving rise to a large—sometimes very large—general demoralization or subjective discomfort factor in such inventories as the MMPI. . . . One challenge in developing new self-report scales is to find ways of *not* measuring this general factor. (p. 692)

Tellegen's observation that an affect-laden common factor—*demoralization*—was responsible for the excessive intercorrelations between the Clinical Scales (and scales on similar measures) was based on his study of the structure of mood (discussed later). The demoralization construct had similarly been implicated as playing a role in the common (i.e., nonspecific) effects of psychotherapy and in creating a common distress factor in psychiatric screening scales.

In the 1960s and 1970s, Jerome Frank became interested in what was then a much-debated issue in the psychotherapy literature: the nonspecific effects of psychotherapeutic interventions. As alternatives to psychodynamic orientations to psychotherapy emerged in the second half of the 20th century, clinicians began to observe, and research later confirmed, that no form of treatment consistently produced better therapeutic outcomes than others. Moreover, common therapeutic outcomes were found regardless of the specific presenting complaints (cf. Strupp, 1973). Frank (1974) postulated that if disparate therapeutic modalities had common results, this might be because they address a problem that is common across patient types and presenting complaints. He labeled this common variable *demoralization* and commented, "Of course, patients seldom present themselves to therapists with the complaint that they are demoralized; rather they seek relief for an enormous variety of symptoms and behavior disorders" (p. 271). Frank went on to observe that

> only a small proportion of persons with psychopathology come to therapy; apparently something else must be added that interacts with their symptoms. This state of mind, which may be termed "demoralization," results from

persistent failure to cope with internally or externally induced stresses. . . . Its characteristic features, not all of which need to be present in any one person, are feelings of impotence, isolation, and despair. (p. 271)

Thus, according to Frank, demoralization is common across various forms of psychopathology and unique to none. It is what motivates individuals to seek treatment, and its amelioration, regardless of the therapeutic modality employed, is responsible for the common outcomes of different modes of psychotherapy.

To understand the link between Frank's concept of demoralization and Tellegen's conclusion that a similar affectively colored dimension was responsible for the MMPI common factor, it is necessary to revisit how the Clinical Scales were constructed. Recall that the items for each scale were selected by contrasting the responses of a group of patients with a specific disorder (e.g., hypochondriasis) with those of a nonclinical control sample. The same control sample, made up of friends and relatives of hospital patients approached in the hospital hallways about volunteering for a research study and who agreed to do so, was used in developing each of the scales. Individuals receiving medical or mental health services were excluded from the control sample. Items were assigned to a given Clinical Scale if the proportion of patients responding in the keyed direction differed significantly from the proportion of nonpatients responding to that item. As a result, some of the items selected for each scale described unique features of the targeted disorder (e.g., somatic complaints for the patients with hypochondriasis), whereas others reflected attributes and experiences that would generally differentiate a hospitalized inpatient from a nonpatient cohort (e.g., being upset and feeling demoralized).

Recall from the earlier example that Scale 4 included items keyed to reflect unhappiness, living the wrong kind of life, and giving up. Such statements, seemingly incongruent with psychopathy, can be understood if one considers that many of the diagnosed patients in the development sample for Scale 4, having been arrested and charged with various minor crimes, were hospitalized under court order. When asked (in responding to the item pool used to develop the MMPI) to describe their mood, it is not surprising that they endorsed statements akin to Frank's concept of demoralization.

Other self-report measures were similarly found to be influenced by a common demoralization factor. Dohrenwend, Shrout, Egri, and Mendelsohn (1980) linked Frank's concept of demoralization to a common general distress dimension found in many psychiatric screening scales. They observed that

these screening scales measured a dimension of nonspecific psychological distress. . . . The items in these scales are generally associated with affective distress but are not specific to any particular psychiatric disorder. What they measure is analogous in important ways to measures of temperature in physical medicine. . . . Clearly, elevated scores on these scales, like elevated temperature, tell you something is wrong. However, just as in physical medicine, where many diseases are not associated with elevated temperature, a respondent may have serious psychopathology without having an elevated score [on nonspecific distress]. Some of the symptoms described by Frank in his formulation of "demoralization" are very similar to items in these brief screening scales of nonspecific distress. (pp. 1229–1230)

In sum, Tellegen conceptualized the common factor to be a broad, affectively colored construct labeled *demoralization.* Although the method used to develop the Clinical Scales undoubtedly contributed to its prominence in the scales, the identification of demoralization as a source of common variance in other self-report measures indicates that this problem was not caused exclusively by the criterion keying approach or its specific application by Hathaway and McKinley.

Capturing Demoralization

Having identified demoralization as the common factor responsible for excessive correlations between the Clinical Scales, Tellegen next sought to develop a measure of this construct, which would be required for the restructuring process. His approach to capturing demoralization with the MMPI-2 item pool was guided by his and others' work investigating links between mood, personality, and psychopathology.

D. Watson and Tellegen (1985) reviewed the literature and reanalyzed previously published data on the structure of mood. They concluded that two factors, labeled *Positive Affect* (PA) and *Negative Affect* (NA), could account for a substantial amount of variance in self-reported affective states. PA was described as a bipolar dimension marked by adjectives such as *enthusiastic* and *peppy* on its high end and *dull* and *sluggish* on the other. NA was described as a bipolar dimension marked by descriptions such as *fearful* and *nervous* on its high end and *calm* and *relaxed* on the other. D. Watson and Tellegen noted that an alternative two-factor structure, achieved through a 45° rotation of the factors, could yield bipolar factors labeled *Pleasantness/Unpleasantness* (PU) and *Strong Engagement/Disengagement* (SD), which had previously been identified in the mood literature. The two two-factor structures were not competing models but rather alternative ways of organizing the same findings.

The two affect dimensions were later renamed more descriptively *Positive Activation* and *Negative Activation,* respectively (D. Watson, Wiese, Vaidya & Tellegen, 1999; Tellegen, Watson & Clark, 1999a, 1999b), without changing the PA and NA labels. In a subsequent empirical hierarchical elaboration of D. Watson and Tellegen's model, Tellegen et al. (1999a, 1999b) demonstrated that PU, relabeled *Happiness/Unhappiness,* emerged as a broad bipolar dimension, overarching PA and NA. Tellegen's (1985) conception of this mood dimension, marked at its dysfunctional end by a combination of high NA and low PA, and characterized by adjectives such as *sad, discouraged,* and *blameworthy,* as the common demoralization component of self-report measures of personality and psychopathology. A comparison of the adjectives just listed with Frank's (1985) description of demoralization—"the demoralized person suffers from a sense of failure, a loss of self-esteem, feelings of hopelessness or helplessness, of alienation or isolation" (p. 17)—reveals that two very distinct lines of research (on the structure of mood and nonspecific components of psychotherapy) converged on a remarkably congruent (and similarly labeled) construct.

Tellegen (1985) observed that the mood (state) PA and NA variables had dispositional (trait) counterparts he labeled *Positive Emotionality* and *Negative Emotionality* (abbreviated PEM and NEM, respectively). He conceptualized a high NEM level as a risk factor for anxiety-related psychopathology and a low PEM level as increasing vulnerability to depression, and reviewed research findings that supported this perspective on the links between personality and psychopathology. Guided by this conceptualization, Tellegen sought to identify MMPI-2 markers of demoralization through a series of factor analyses of the combined items of Clinical Scales 2 and 7, MMPI-2 markers of depression and anxiety. These analyses yielded a 23-item measure made up of items keyed to denote features such as unhappiness, a poor self-concept, a sense of being overwhelmed, and a desire to give up. The content of these items provided empirical support for Tellegen's supposition that demoralization represented the MMPI common factor.

With the identification of a theoretically grounded, empirically derived measure of the common factor, it was possible to move on to the next step in RC Scale construction.

Step 2: Identifying the Core Components of the Clinical Scales

The second step in developing the RC Scales was to identify a major distinctive core component of each of the Clinical Scales.[3] Tellegen assumed that each scale included items that assess (at least) one major construct distinct from demoralization. Analyses were conducted to designate the subset of items in each of the Clinical Scales that represented this component.

Following an exploratory scale construction approach, Tellegen conducted separate factor analyses of the items of each of the 10 Clinical Scales augmented by the 23 demoralization markers identified in Step 1. Two to four factors were extracted and rotated for each scale. The solution with the smallest number of factors that included a clear demoralization component and an additional factor that reflected a separate substantive attribute was selected and used to identify items that marked the distinctive core component of that scale. Inclusion of the demoralization items allowed Tellegen to identify in each Clinical Scale items that were associated primarily with the common factor and were the primary sources of excessive demoralization variance on that scale. The number of these items ranged from 3 to 32, with a median of 17 Clinical Scale items per scale identified as being primarily markers of demoralization. These exploratory factor analyses resulted in the identification of a set of items that marked a major distinctive component for each of the Clinical Scales.

For Scale 1, a two-factor solution identified a demoralization factor, which included the smallest number of items on any Clinical Scale (three) identified as measures of this construct. The second factor, which loaded on a set of items that described various somatic complaints, was selected as the major distinctive component for this scale.

For Scale 2, a two-factor solution included a demoralization factor and a second factor that loaded on items that, as keyed, identified the absence of positive emotional experiences, or anhedonia, as the major distinctive component of the scale. These findings corroborated Tellegen's (1985) model in which a low level of positive emotions was hypothesized to be a distinctive risk factor for depression.

For Scale 3, a three-factor solution identified a demoralization component, a second component very similar to (and made up of several of the same items as) the somatic complaints factor identified for Scale 1, and a third component marked by items keyed on Scale 3 to denote disavowal of cynical beliefs about others. Although the second component was a stronger contributor to the overall score on Scale 3, because the goal of Step 2 was to identify *distinctive* components of the Clinical Scales, the third component was selected to represent this scale.

For Scale 4, a three-factor solution included a demoralization component, a second factor marked primarily by items that reflect interpersonal suspiciousness, and a third factor that loaded on items that describe various antisocial behaviors. Here, too, although the second factor accounted for more variance in Scale 4, the third factor was selected because the items that best defined the second factor were also markers of the major component of Scale 6.

For Scale 5, a four-factor solution included a demoralization component; a second factor marked by items that describe various aesthetic and literary interests; a third factor that consisted of a mixture of items with aggressive, cynical, and extraverted content; and a fourth that loaded on items that describe various mechanical and physical interests. Because a significant body of literature had indicated that Scale 5 included items that mark two distinct factors (designated often as measures of traditional feminine and masculine gender roles), items associated consistently with the second and fourth factors were selected to represent these two distinctive components of Scale 5.

For Scale 6, a three-factor solution identified a demoralization component, a second factor made up of items that described various persecutory beliefs, and a third factor marked by items that reflected cynical beliefs, many of which were selected to represent the cynicism component of Scale 3. Items associated consistently with the second factor were selected to represent the major distinctive component of Scale 6.

For Scale 7, a two-factor solution designated a demoralization component and a second factor associated with items that describe various dysfunctional negative emotions. This second factor was determined to be the major distinctive component of this scale. These findings corroborated Tellegen's (1985) model in which NEM was hypothesized to be a dispositional risk factor for anxiety-related psychopathology.

For Scale 8, a two-factor solution included a demoralization component and a second factor marked by items that describe various unusual perceptual or thought processes. Items describing these aberrant experiences, on which the second factor loaded consistently, were selected to represent the major distinctive component of this scale.

For Scale 9, a two-factor solution identified a demoralization component and a second factor associated with items that describe overactivation, grandiosity, aggression, and poor impulse control. Items describing these manifestations of hypomanic activation on which the second factor loaded consistently were designated to represent the major distinctive component of this scale.

For Scale 0, a two-factor solution identified a demoralization component, the largest number of items of any Clinical Scale to load on this factor (32). A second factor was marked by items that (as keyed) reflect various manifestations of low sociability. This factor, which included items that describe a lack of interpersonal assertiveness, avoidance of social situations, and discomfort when interacting with others, was designated to represent the major distinctive component of Scale 0.

At the end of Step 2, a subset of the items of each Clinical Scale was selected to represent its major distinctive core component. Eleven distinctive components were identified. As just described, the factor finally identified as representing the distinctive component of a given scale was not always the second major source of variance on that measure. To avoid developing redundant measures and reflecting the flexible scale-construction approach described earlier, Tellegen, when designating a distinctive component for each scale, exercised judgment when the same component, often made up of some of the same items, emerged from analyses of more than one scale.

Step 3: Deriving Seed Scales

The next step in developing the RC Scales was designed to optimize their internal coherence and mutual distinctiveness. In keeping with the idea that a set of completely orthogonal scales was unlikely to accurately represent how psychopathology is manifested (i.e., the reality of comorbidity or co-occurring features), Tellegen made no effort in Step 2 to ensure that items selected to represent the major distinctive component of one scale were *completely* independent of items designated to represent the others. However, he considered it undesirable (insofar as optimizing the discriminant validity of the RC Scales was concerned) for an item selected to represent the distinctive component of a given scale to be too highly correlated with the major component of another. Analyses undertaken in Step 3 were designed to preclude this possibility while enhancing the internal consistency of the item sets that emerged from Step 2.

A series of analyses was conducted to achieve the desired optimization of internal consistency and distinctiveness for the 11 sets of items identified in Step 2. First, only items with sufficient loadings on the factor they were designated to represent were retained. Next, any item that satisfied this criterion for more than one scale was deleted. This yielded 11 nonoverlapping provisional Seed Scales. This was followed by deletion of items that did not correlate sufficiently with their provisional Seed Scale and then deletion of items that did not consistently have higher correlations with their provisional scale than they did with the 10 other provisional measures. A small number of exceptions and the specific statistical criteria used in these analyses are described by Tellegen et al. (2003).

A final analysis conducted in Step 3 produced a 12th Seed Scale representing demoralization. This analysis was designed to accomplish two distinct goals: first, to ensure that undue demoralization variance would not slip back into the RC Scales in the fourth and final step, and second, to facilitate the development of a Restructured

Clinical Scale to assess the demoralization construct. Recall (from Chapter 1) that critics of the Clinical Scales differed as to whether the common factor responsible for the excessive Clinical Scale intercorrelations was substantive (Norman, 1972) or stylistic (Jackson, 1971; Loevinger, 1972), although they agreed that this variable needed to be accounted for in any revision of the scales. Norman (1972) elaborated that if the common factor did indeed represent a substantive construct, it should be measured separately, along with the revised scales. Tellegen's research in the area of mood persuaded him that demoralization is an important, substantive construct worthy of separate measurement. He assembled a Seed Scale to represent this construct by deleting four items from the 23-item set of demoralization markers used in Step 2. The four deleted items were either weakly correlated with a provisional demoralization scale or judged to be redundant in content.

Step 3 yielded 12 Seed Scales made up of relatively small, mutually exclusive subsets of items from the original Clinical Scales. These seeds were used to derive the final RC Scales in Step 4.

Step 4: Deriving the Final Restructured Clinical Scales

The fourth step in deriving the RC Scales was designed to build on the structural changes attained in Steps 1–3 by recruiting items from the entire MMPI-2 item pool for the final set of scales. The goal was to achieve a balance of internal consistency, convergent and discriminant validity, and content representativeness in a set of measures that assesses the major distinctive core components of the Clinical Scales. Four sets of analyses were conducted to accomplish this goal.

Tellegen first calculated correlations between the 567 MMPI-2 items and the 12 Seed Scales in the four samples used throughout this process. An item was added provisionally to an RC Scale if (1) its correlation with the seed for that scale was higher than it was with the other 11 Seed Scales, (2) its correlation with that Seed Scale was high enough, and (3) its correlations with the remaining Seed Scales were low enough. Tellegen et al. (2003) reported the specific correlation values that were used to satisfy these three criteria, which, by necessity, varied across scales.

Examination of the content of the resulting scales indicated that the items assigned to RC7 and RC9 were too heterogeneous for the targeted constructs (Negative Emotionality and Hypomanic Activation). For each of these scales, Tellegen identified a subset of items whose content unequivocally represented the intended constructs and correlated those subsets with the other items assigned provisionally to that scale. Items that did not correlate sufficiently with the unequivocal subset were deleted from the provisional scales.

Next, for each of the provisional RC Scales, analyses were conducted to identify items that lowered or contributed weakly to internal consistency. Only one item was deleted as a result of these analyses.

Finally, correlations between the items in the provisional restructured versions of Scales 1, 2, 4, 6, 7, and 8 and appropriate external criterion measures were examined. No suitable criterion measures were available for similar analyses of the provisional restructured versions of Scales 3 and 9. These analyses led to a small number of final item assignment changes for the restructured versions of Scales 2, 6, and 8 (detailed by Tellegen et al., 2003).

Step 4 yielded nine RC Scales composed of 192 nonoverlapping items. As noted earlier, final RC Scales were not assembled for Clinical Scales 5 and 0, although the three Seed Scales derived from these two measures were used along with the other nine Seed Scales in the first set of analyses conducted in Step 4. Thus, the final RC Scales were designed to be distinctive from the major components of Scales 5 and 0 as well, although final measures of these constructs were not derived until later in the development of the MMPI-2-RF (see Chapter 3).

Initial Psychometric Findings

The data used to develop the RC Scales were collected during the MMPI Restandardization Project and could have been used to devise these scales at the same time. However, no data were available at that point for independent (of these samples) examination of the psychometric properties of the resulting measures. By the time the RC Scales were completed, new data were available to evaluate and characterize their psychometric functioning. With several large clinical samples and a diverse array of criteria, Tellegen et al. (2003) compared the psychometric properties of the RC Scales and original Clinical Scales and found that scores on the considerably shorter restructured scales showed comparable to improved reliability, substantial reduction in saturation with demoralization, reduced intercorrelations, comparable to improved convergent validity, and improved discriminant validity.

On the basis of these findings, Tellegen et al. (2003) recommended that the RC Scales be used to help clarify scores on the Clinical Scales. They anticipated that the ultimate role of the new measures would be determined by further research and noted that an abundance of previously collected data were already available for this purpose because all the items scored on the RC Scales were embedded within the MMPI-2. As anticipated, a substantial body of empirical studies of the RC Scales has accumulated since they were added to the MMPI-2 in 2003. The findings of these investigations, along with a review of the conceptual and empirical literature related to the constructs assessed by the RC Scales, are integrated into the next section on the RC Scale constructs.

DELINEATING THE RESTRUCTURED
CLINICAL SCALE CONSTRUCTS

As discussed earlier, Tellegen's exploratory scale construction approach produced a set of nine RC Scales: one designed to assess the long-recognized MMPI common factor and eight measures of distinctive core components of the original Clinical Scales. This approach to scale development produced measures of open constructs, the delineation of which can be accomplished by considering the theoretical formulations that guided their development, the content of the resulting scales, and empirical findings on their convergent and discriminant associations with other, known constructs. This section provides a detailed description of the RC Scale constructs and scales based on these three recognized indicators of construct validity (Loevinger, 1957).

Demoralization (RCd)

Conceptualizing Demoralization

The demoralization construct was introduced in the previous section. As noted, Tellegen concluded that this affect-laden phenomenon was the source of problematic excessive intercorrelations between the Clinical Scales and conceptualized it as the equivalent of the Pleasant/Unpleasant or Happy/Unhappy dimension of self-reported mood. Frank (1974, 1985) identified amelioration of demoralization as the mechanism underlying the nonspecific effects of psychotherapy. Dohrenwend et al. (1980) linked Frank's demoralization construct to their finding of substantial intercorrelations between scores on psychiatric rating scales and equated its role in the assessment of psychopathology with that of taking a patient's temperature in medicine. Consistent with these views of demoralization, the RCd items reflect the presence of dysphoric affect, distress, self-attributed inefficacy, low self-esteem, and a sense of having given up.

With the exception of Tellegen's work linking mood, personality, and psychopathology, prior to the introduction of the RC Scales, the demoralization construct did not figure prominently in the assessment literature. An exception was the work of Dohrenwend et al. (1980), who observed that there was considerable phenotypic overlap between demoralization and depression. They also noted that there were important differences between the constructs and that demoralization appeared closer to minor depressive disorder, as described by Spitzer, Endicott, and Robins (1978) in the research diagnostic criteria that preceded the *DSM-III* (American Psychiatric Association [APA], 1980).

Following Dohrenwend et al. (1980), other authors have commented on and investigated similarities and differences between demoralization and depression. De Figuiredo (1993), a former student of Frank's who continued to develop the demoralization construct, noted that whereas both conditions may manifest in subjective distress and dysphoric affect, vegetative symptoms of depression such as poor sleep and appetite are less likely to accompany demoralization. De Figuiredo also observed that the dysphoric affect often found in individuals with medical disorders is more likely a product of demoralization than of depression, and Clarke and Kissane (2002) noted that depression is characterized uniquely by anhedonia.

Empirical Findings on Demoralization

In contrast with the paucity of attention paid to demoralization in the personality assessment literature, investigators in the area of behavioral medicine, building on Frank's conceptualization, have studied this construct extensively and concluded that it plays a prominent role in the mental health of medical patients suffering from a variety of chronic and, in particular, life-threatening diseases. Recognition of the role demoralization plays in the psychological problems experienced by individuals with physical illness led to its inclusion as a distinct diagnostic category in the *Diagnostic Criteria for Psychosomatic Research* (*DCPR*; Fava et al., 1995). Using these criteria, researchers have found significant rates of demoralization in breast cancer patients (Grassi, Rossi, Sabato, Cruciani & Zambelli, 2004), patients with coronary artery disease (Rafanelli et al., 2005), and general medical outpatients (Mangelli, Fava, Grandi, Grassi, Ottolini & Porcelli, 2005). Investigators have also found that demoralization plays a significant role in the psychological reactions of individuals exposed to trauma, including military veterans (e.g., Frank & Frank, 1996), Holocaust survivors (Fenig & Levav, 1991), Southeast Asian refugees (Kroll, 2003; Kroll & McDonald, 2003; Ying & Akutsu, 1997), and immigrants (Gutkovich, Rosenthal, Galynker, Muran, Batchelder & Itskhoki, 1999).

Demoralization and Depression

Empirical studies have examined the co-occurrence of depression and demoralization and found, as expected, evidence of considerable comorbidity but also substantial independence of the two phenomena. Relying on *DSM-IV* (APA, 1994) diagnostic criteria for Major Depression and on *DCPR* (Fava et al., 1995) criteria for demoralization, Mangelli et al. (2005) assessed a large sample of medical outpatients and found that roughly 30% met diagnostic criteria for demoralization and 17% met diagnostic criteria for Major Depression. Of the patients diagnosed with Major Depression, 44% did not meet criteria for demoralization. Of those diagnosed with demoralization, 69% did not meet criteria for Major Depression.

Summarizing the literature on depression and demoralization, Strada (2009) concluded that

> while the core feature of depression is anhedonia and loss of pleasure or interest in present or future activities that used to elicit pleasure, the core feature of demoralization is meaninglessness and helplessness. Patients who are demoralized may not exhibit the psychomotor changes typical of depression, such as retardation or agitation. Unlike patients suffering from MDD, patients who are demoralized can exhibit normal behavior or full range of affect and are capable of experiencing pleasures from engaging in pleasurable activities. (p. 54)

Demoralization and Suicidality

Clarke and Kissane (2002) reasoned that in light of the prominent role of helplessness and hopelessness in demoralization, and the established links between these phenomena and suicidality, suicidal ideation is more likely to be associated with demoralization than with Anhedonic Depression. Several studies have indeed documented a demoralization-linked increased risk for suicide in individuals with Schizophrenia (Restifo, Harkavy-Friedman & Shrout, 2009; Tandon & Jibson, 2003), individuals with severe disabilities (Tweed, Shern & Ciarlo, 1988), and elderly Japanese struggling with modernization (Watanabe, Hasegawa & Yoshinaga, 1995).

Empirical Findings with RCd

Several studies have examined the conceptualized link between RCd and positive and negative activation. Tellegen et al. (2003, 2006) found demoralization to be the MMPI-2 equivalent of the Pleasant/Unpleasant (or Happy/Unhappy) mood dimension in D. Watson and Tellegen's (1985) widely studied model of affect. Consistent with this model, RCd is strongly associated with both (low) positive and (high) negative temperament, as measured in three different personality inventories: Tellegen's (1995/2003; Tellegen & Waller, 2008) MPQ (Sellbom & Ben-Porath, 2005, in college students); Costa and McCrae's (1992) revised NEO Personality Inventory (NEO PI-R), a measure of the Five Factor Model of personality (Forbey & Ben-Porath, 2008, in college students; Sellbom, Ben-Porath & Bagby, 2008b, in mental health patients and college students); and L. A. Clark's (1993) Schedule for Nonadaptive and Adaptive Personality (SNAP; Simms, Casillas, Clark, Watson & Doebbeling, 2005, in a clinical sample and community-dwelling veterans).

Consistent with the broadly unhappy content endorsed by individuals scoring high on demoralization, external correlates of RCd include generalized emotional distress and unhappiness, depressed mood, and anxiety (Arbisi, Sellbom & Ben-Porath, 2008, in psychiatric inpatients; Binford & Liljequist, 2008, in mental health outpatients; Burchett & Ben-Porath, 2010, in college students; Forbey & Ben-Porath, 2008, in college students; Forbey, Ben-Porath & Gartland, 2009, in prison inmates; Handel & Archer, 2008, in psychiatric inpatients; McCord & Drerup, 2011, in chronic pain patients; McDevitt-Murphy, Weathers, Flood, Eakin & Benson, 2007, in psychiatric inpatients; Monnot, Quirk, Hoerger & Brewer, 2009, in substance abuse treatment patients; Osberg, Haseley & Kamas, 2008, in college students; Sellbom, Ben-Porath & Bagby, 2008b, in college students and mental health outpatients; Sellbom, Ben-Porath & Graham, 2006, in a college counseling setting; Sellbom, Graham & Schenk, 2006, in an independent mental health practice; Simms et al., 2006, in a clinical sample and community-dwelling veterans; Tellegen et al., 2003, in mental health inpatients and outpatients; Wolf et al., 2008, in veterans assessed for Posttraumatic Stress Disorder [PTSD]; Wygant, Boutacoff et al., 2007, in bariatric surgery candidates). Congruent with these findings, RCd is also associated with symptoms of nonspecific distress such as decreased sleep, decreased appetite, guilt, feelings of worthlessness, decreased energy, and poor concentration (Arbisi et al., 2008, in psychiatric inpatients; Handel & Archer, 2008, in a different sample of psychiatric inpatients).

Consistent with Frank's (1974) conceptualization of demoralization as a condition characterized by helplessness and hopelessness, low self-esteem, and insecurity, RCd correlates include all these features (Arbisi et al., 2008, in psychiatric inpatients; Burchett & Ben-Porath, 2010, in college students; Forbey & Ben-Porath, 2007, in individuals receiving substance abuse treatment; Osberg et al., 2008, in college students; Sellbom, Ben-Porath & Graham, 2006, in a college counseling setting; Tellegen et al., 2003, in psychiatric inpatients). And congruent with research linking demoralization with increased risk for suicidal ideation, findings from various settings and samples indicate an association between scores on RCd and current suicidal ideation and/or recent suicide attempts (Arbisi et al., 2008, in psychiatric inpatients; Binford & Liljequist, 2008, in mental health outpatients; Handel & Archer, 2008, in psychiatric inpatients; Tellegen & Ben-Porath, 2008/2011, in criminal defendants undergoing court-ordered evaluations).

Summary

Empirical findings support the construct validity of RCd as a measure of a general, affectively colored distress factor linked, as conceptualized by Frank (1974), with symptomatic anxiety and depression, helplessness and hopelessness, low self-esteem, and a sense of inefficacy, and, as conceptualized by Tellegen (1985), with low Positive Activation and high Negative Activation. Scores on this scale are associated with an increased risk for current suicidal ideation and recent suicide attempts. Consistent with findings from behavioral medicine research, where demoralization has been identified as a separate (from depression), incrementally informative construct, Sellbom, Ben-Porath, and Bagby (2008a) found that demoralization, as assessed by RCd, represents a distinctive primary marker of distress disorders, including Major Depression, Dysthymia, Generalized Anxiety, and PTSD.

Somatic Complaints (RC1)

Conceptualizing Somatic Complaints

Psychological disorders involving unexplained somatic complaints have been described and diagnosed since at least the civilization of ancient Egypt (Trimble, 2004). Lamberty (2008) recounts that a "wandering uterus" was first implicated as causing unexplained physical symptoms in women in ancient Egypt, a theory later formalized in the label *Hysteria*, coined by Greek physician Hippocrates. During the Renaissance, British physician Thomas Sydenham observed that symptoms of Hysteria could also be found in men and coined the term *Hypochondriasis* to designate Hysteria's male counterpart. Sydenham is also credited with advancing the view that these conditions were a product of the nervous system, a notion reiterated by 19th-century French psychiatrist Paul Briquet (Lamberty, 2008). Two other 19th-century French physicians, Jean-Martin Charcot and Pierre Janet, began their influential work in this area, adhering to Briquet's conceptualization that excessive somatic complaining was a neurologically based disease. However, after collaborating with Freud, they shifted to a view that it was a disorder of the mind that could afflict both women and men (Lamberty, 2008). Freud's notion of *conversion*, a psychological process that transformed traumatic experiences into symbolic physical symptoms, became the dominant viewpoint in the first part of the 20th century and remains embedded in the label *Conversion Disorder*, still used in the *DSM-IV* (APA, 1994).

The *DSM-IV* (APA, 1994) assigns the label *Somatoform Disorders* to conditions characterized by

the presence of physical symptoms that suggest a general medical condition (hence, the term *somatoform*) and are not fully explained by a general medical condition, by the direct effect of a substance, or by any other mental disorder (e.g., Panic Disorder). (p. 485)

This definition recognizes that excessive somatic complaints are not an exclusive symptom of somatoform conditions, though this is the defining feature of this class of disorders. The manual goes on to indicate that grouping various specific disorders under this label was done for clinical utility rather than as a reflection of a presumed common etiology for these conditions (APA, 2004). Among the major disorders included in the somatoform category are the following:

- *Somatization Disorder.* A polysymptomatic disorder characterized by a combination of pain and gastrointestinal, sexual, and pseudoneurological symptoms (historically referred to as hysteria or Briquet's syndrome).
- *Conversion Disorder.* A condition that involves unexplained medical symptoms or deficits affecting voluntary motor or sensory function that suggest a neurological condition but are actually associated with psychological factors.
- *Pain Disorder.* A disorder characterized by pain as the predominant focus of clinical attention, with psychological factors playing an important role in its onset, severity, exacerbation, or maintenance.
- *Hypochondriasis.* Preoccupation with the fear of having, or the idea that one has, a serious disease based on the person's misinterpretation of bodily symptoms or functions.

The (acknowledged) inclusion of etiologically distinct phenomena under one heading, "Somatoform Disorders," has garnered substantial criticism and calls for reform (Lamberty, 2008). Accordingly, Dimsdale and Creed (2009) reported on behalf of the DSM-5 Workgroup on Somatic Symptom Disorder that the overall label for these conditions is likely to be changed to *Somatic Symptom Disorders* and that the Somatization, Hypochondriasis, and Pain Disorder diagnoses would be subsumed under the label *Chronic Somatic Symptom Disorder,* with the defining feature being

> the patient's difficulty in tolerating physical discomfort and in coping adaptively with bodily symptoms. Patients with this diagnosis typically have multiple, current, somatic symptoms that are severe, intense, and bothersome, but some may have a single severe symptom. . . . Such patients often manifest a poorer health-related quality of life than patients with other serious medical disorders. (Dimsdale & Creed, 2009, p. 474)

Diagnosis of a Chronic Somatic Symptom Disorder would also require "misattributions, excessive concern, or preoccupation with symptoms and illness" and/or an "increased pattern of health care utilization" (p. 474). An acute counterpart condition would have similar features but transient severe symptoms of less than six months' duration.

Dimsdale and Creed report that the *DSM-IV* Conversion Disorder would be maintained as a separate disorder in *DSM-5*, rebranded Functional Neurological/

Conversion Disorder, but this disorder is still under discussion. Two other disorders, Factitious Disorder, presently included as a separate class of conditions in *DSM-IV,* and Factitious Disorder by Proxy, presently listed in an appendix as a condition requiring further study, would be added to the list of *DSM-5* Somatic Symptom Disorders. Dimsdale and Creed indicate that the diagnostic criteria for these disorders would require a pattern of falsification of physical or psychological signs or symptoms associated with deception, including presentation to others (or of the other, in the case of disorder by proxy) as ill or impaired, in the absence of external reward.

Implications for RC1

The proposed revamping of the disorders presently labeled *Somatoform* nicely illustrates one of the advantages of delinking the RC Scales from any given nosological system or version. A relabeling of these conditions as *Somatic Symptom Disorders* would bring them closer to the label for RC1: *Somatic Complaints.* More important, it would be consistent with the intended use of RC1: identification of individuals who present with an unrealistically large number and type of somatic symptom complaints. Moreover, the items of RC1 include a combination of gastrointestinal, pain, and neurological symptoms, thus tapping all but the sexual symptoms required for a *DSM-IV* Somatization or proposed *DSM-5* Chronic Symptom Disorder—a testament to the richness of the original MMPI item pool. Specific Problems Scales designed to assess these three types of complaints are included in the MMPI-2-RF and are described in Chapter 3.

Empirical Findings on Somatic Complaints

The *DSM-IV* lists prevalence rates for Somatoform Disorder that range up to 2% of the population for Somatization Disorder, 3% for Conversion Disorder, 15% for Pain Disorder (primarily work-related disability for back pain), and 9% for Hypochondriasis. However, Lamberty (2008) notes that these figures likely underestimate the true prevalence of somatoform conditions because of the stringent requirements for numbers of symptoms in the *DSM* diagnostic criteria for these conditions. Moreover, Somatoform Disorders are rarely the primary diagnoses in mental health treatment settings because individuals who have these conditions are prone to seeking medical explanations for their symptoms and therefore are more likely to present in primary medical care settings or neurology clinics (Lamberty, 2008).

Barsky, Orav, and Bates (2005) reported that 20% of patients seen consecutively at an urban and suburban primary care clinic met diagnostic criteria for a Somatoform Disorder. These patients were found to utilize medical services at twice the rate of others. On the basis of a review of epidemiological studies conducted in neurology clinics, Lamberty (2008) concluded that about 30% of patients referred to these facilities meet diagnostic criteria for a Somatoform Disorder. Moreover, as is the case with primary care settings, individuals with Somatoform Disorders in neurology clinics have a high level of comorbid psychiatric disorders.

The prevalence rates just cited pertain only to somatic complaints associated with

Somatoform Disorders. Somatic complaints feature prominently in the diagnostic criteria for several other *DSM-IV* diagnoses, including Delusional Disorder, Somatic Type, Panic Disorder, Generalized Anxiety Disorder, and Factitious Disorder, and are associated features of many more (APA, 2004). Malingering, as defined by *DSM-IV,* may also involve somatic complaints. Taken together, these data indicate that somatic complaints are ubiquitous in a variety of settings and types of assessments in which the MMPI-2-RF is likely to be administered.

Empirical Findings with RC1

Identified empirical correlates for RC1 include various forms, indexes, and manifestations of somatoform psychopathology. Substantial correlations between RC1 scores and a screener for Somatoform Disorders (Janca et al., 1995) have been reported by Forbey and Ben-Porath (2008) in college students, Forbey, Ben-Porath and Gartland (2009) in prison inmates, and Tellegen and Ben-Porath (2008/2011) in mental health and medical outpatient samples. Burchett and Ben-Porath (2010) reported comparable findings with the Somatization Scale of the Symptom Checklist 90–Revised (Derogatis, 1994) with college students.

Data reported in the *MMPI-2-RF Technical Manual* (Tellegen & Ben-Porath, 2008/2011) indicate that individuals with elevated scores on RC1 are preoccupied with physical health concerns, prone to developing somatic symptoms in response to stress, likely to have a psychological component to their somatic complaints, complain of fatigue, and present with multiple somatic complaints. Arbisi et al. (2008) found scores on RC1 to be associated with sleep disturbance, decreased appetite, decreased energy, and chronic pain in three large samples of psychiatric inpatients. Handel and Archer (2008) similarly reported significant associations of RC1 scores with physical complaints in psychiatric inpatients.

In mental health outpatient samples, Sellbom, Ben-Porath, and Graham (2006) reported significant correlations of RC1 scores with therapist ratings of somatization and excessive somatic concern in individuals receiving treatment at a college counseling clinic. Tellegen et al. (2003) reported similar findings with individuals receiving treatment at an outpatient community mental health center. Sellbom, Graham et al. (2006) reported a sizable correlation for RC1 scores with self-reported somatization symptoms in a sample of individuals seen for outpatient treatment by independent practitioners.

Simms et al. (2005) found significant correlations for RC1 scores with Structured Clinical Interview for DSM Disorders diagnoses of current and lifetime Somatoform Disorders in a sample of community-dwelling veterans. In a different sample of veterans, Wolf et al. (2008) reported particularly high correlations for RC1 with hyperarousal symptoms in a sample of individuals diagnosed with PTSD.

Locke et al. (2010) evaluated the ability of the MMPI-2-RF to differentiate patients diagnosed with epileptic seizures from patients diagnosed with psychogenic nonepileptic seizures in an epilepsy monitoring unit. These authors found RC1 to perform best in this task, with a sensitivity of .76 and specificity of .60. The authors also reported that RC1 was able to account for unique variance in this differential diagnosis, beyond that explained by demographic variables and medical history risk factors. Thomas and Locke (2010) conducted a series of taxometric and Item Response Theory analyses of the RC1 items and scores with the same sample and concluded that the scale accurately assesses the latent structure of somatization for individuals who produce clinically elevated scores.

In studies related to symptom overreporting, Wygant, Sellbom et al. (2007) found that criminal defendants and civil litigants who fail symptom validity or effort tests are likely to produce higher RC1 scores than are their counterparts who show no signs of reduced effort on these measures. Henry, Heilbronner, Mittenberg, Enders, and Stanczal (2008) reported that RC1 scores were less highly correlated with effort test failure than were relevant MMPI-2 overreporting measures. Together, these findings indicate, as expected, that individuals suspected of symptom overreporting produce elevated scores on RC1. However, the scale is not ideally suited to serve as a validity indicator. Tellegen and Ben-Porath (2008/2011) also reported sizable correlations for RC1 with a broad range of somatic complaints in a large sample of disability claimants.

Summary

Medically unexplained somatic complaints have garnered the attention of physicians and mental health professionals for as long as written historical records have been available. Specific types of complaints have varied, depending in part on cultural factors and advances in medical knowledge and technology. As chronicled by Lamberty (2008), unexplained paralyses, a hallmark of these conditions in the late 19th and early 20th centuries, have largely given way to other, more vaguely manifested conditions (e.g., multiple chemical sensitivities). Epidemiological data indicate a relatively high prevalence rate for medically unexplained somatic complaints, with most individuals experiencing these conditions seen (initially) in primary care and neurology clinics rather than by mental health professionals.

Empirical findings just summarized indicate that the MMPI-2-RF Somatic Complaints Scale (RC1) is sensitive to somatoform symptomatology, but it is not specific to one type of condition within this family of disorders. Moreover, because somatic complaints are primary or secondary features of a number of non-somatoform conditions, elevations in RC1 are not specific to that class of disorders and can be found in individuals with somatic delusions, anxiety disorders, and numerous other psychological conditions.

Low Positive Emotions (RC2)

Conceptualizing Low Positive Emotions

As discussed earlier, Tellegen (1985) posited that a lack of positive emotional responsiveness is a core personological risk factor for depression, related to, but distinguishable from, demoralization (see the section "Capturing Demoralization"). Analyses designed to identify the distinctive core of Clinical Scale 2 corroborated this hypothesis when a subset of Scale 2 items with content reflecting low positive emotions emerged as markers of the major distinctive core component of this scale.

Tellegen's conceptualization was consistent with a model proposed by Klein (1974), who distinguished acute dysphoria, an acute depressive reaction to situational factors, from Neurotic Depression, which he characterized as a chronic emotional or personality disorder related to low self-esteem, overly severe disappointment reactions, feelings of helplessness, and "Endogenomorphic Depression," which Klein postulated was associated with "a sharp, unreactive pervasive impairment of the capacity to experience pleasure or to respond affectively to the anticipation of pleasure" (p. 449). Klein went on to posit that only the endogenomorphic group would be characterized by "an inhibited pleasure mechanism leading to a decreased ability to respond affectively to pleasurable sensations" (p. 450), whereas "all [three] groups would show symptomatology associated with . . . two intervening variables . . . demoralization associated with low self esteem and anticipation of decreased pleasure and relatively increased pain" (p. 450). Klein's characterization of Neurotic Depression is clearly consistent with Frank's concept, although he did not refer to his work when using the term *demoralization.*

Klein (1974) went on to identify one important difference between Neurotic and Endogenomorphic Depression: individuals experiencing either condition were likely to present with phenotypic demoralization, which may include the *anticipation* of decreased pleasure; however, only the latter was uniquely associated with an *actual* deficit in the ability to experience positive emotions. He also characterized Endogenomorphic Depression as having a clearer link to biological vulnerabilities and hypothesized that, as a consequence, it should be more amenable to treatment with antidepressant medication.

A lack or loss of positive emotional responsiveness characterizes other medical and mental health conditions and therefore cannot be considered pathognomonic of depression. Kring and Germans (2000) noted that French physician T. H. Ribot coined the term *anhedonia* when describing a patient who experienced loss of pleasure secondary to liver damage, and following Rado (1956), Meehl (1962) characterized anhedonia, which he defined as "a marked, widespread and refractory deficit in pleasure capacity" (p. 829), as "one of the most consistent and dramatic behavioral signs of [Schizophrenia]" (p. 829). Although he initially characterized anhedonia as a "quasi-pathognomonic sign" of Schizophrenia (Meehl, 1962, p. 829), Meehl (2001) later amended his view on this point, noting,

> Manifest impairment of the pleasure propensity (clinical anhedonia), although found in many schizotypes in varying degrees of decompensation, is also found in other mental disorders, especially major depression. Whether it can be used as a strong diagnostic sign of schizotypy is unclear, but it is not pathognomonic. (p. 192)

Meehl (2001) advocated that the term *anhedonia* be replaced with *hypohedonia,* which he thought was preferable because the former suggests a complete absence of pleasure, whereas he conceptualized the construct as "an individual differences variable of hedonic capacity, not requiring anything pathological in the usual sense, analogous to traits like Spearman's g, social introversion, or dominance, that show wide dispersion in the general population" (p. 189). He characterized Hypohedonia as "an impaired disposition to experience pleasure" (p. 189). Although Meehl's alternative term did not take hold, the label of RC2, *Low Positive Emotions*, reintroduces Meehl's descriptively more accurate terminology.

Empirical Findings on Low Positive Emotions

Klein's (1974) model of depression, distinguishing a more chronic "Neurotic" Depression akin to demoralization from an endogenous and more clearly biologically linked depression marked by anhedonia, has received considerable empirical support. Santor and Coyne (2001) studied individuals with and without a clinical diagnosis of depression who reported equal levels of depressed mood (i.e., demoralization) and found that those who met diagnostic criteria for a Depressive Disorder had considerably higher levels of anhedonia than those who did not. They concluded that this finding refutes a view of depression as falling on a single continuum ranging from depressed mood to Major Depression. Brown, Chorpita, and Barlow (1998) similarly found that low positive affect contributed uniquely to Depressive Disorder, whereas a variable they labeled *Negative Affect*, which, as shown by Sellbom, Ben-Porath, and Bagby (2008a), is better represented by demoralization as measured by RCd, was associated with a broad range of disorders, including Generalized Anxiety Disorder, Panic Disorder/Agoraphobia, Obsessive–Compulsive Disorder, Social Phobia, and also depression. Lewinsohn, Pettit, Joiner, and Seeley (2003) examined the concordance of depressed mood and anhedonia in a sample of individuals with a diagnosis of Major Depression and found that 64% of their sample concurrently experienced both symptoms, 28% experienced depressed mood without anhedonia, and 5% had anhedonia but not depressed mood.

Surveying these and similar findings, Joiner, Walker, Pettit, Perez, and Cukrowicz (2005) highlighted the importance of distinguishing between demoralization and anhedonia when assessing for Depressive Disorder. They concluded, "Depression is clearly more than just distress, demoralization, or Depressed mood. . . . Depressed mood, although very common among those experiencing major depression, is not very specific to the syndrome; anhedonia, by contrast, is more unique to major depression" (p. 270). Similar findings continue to accumulate in the literature. For example, in a study of a measure of postnatal depression, Tuohy and McVey (2008) found distinctive factors assessing so-called nonspecific depression (i.e., demoralization), anhedonia, and anxiety.

The findings just cited demonstrate the importance of separate assessment of demoralization and anhedonia for psychodiagnostic purposes. Klein (1974) also identified potential implications for treatment stemming from his supposition that anhedonia-linked depression has a clearer biological origin than does demoralization, making it potentially more amenable to treatment with antidepressant medication. Several studies have provided support for the biological link hypothesis and its treatment implications. Using an animal model research design, Sammut, Bethus, Goodall, and Muscat (2002) demonstrated an ability of antidepressant medication to alleviate signs of chemically induced anhedonia. Stones, Clyburn, Gibson, and Woodbury (2006) found in a sample of older adults that individuals displaying prominent symptoms of anhedonia were more likely to be prescribed antidepressant medication than those who were not anhedonic. Schlaepfer et al. (2008) found that deep brain stimulation to reward circuitry alleviated anhedonia in patients with refractory Major Depression. It is interesting that the study patients did not report feeling differently with the onset of stimulation, but they spontaneously expressed a desire to engage in pleasurable activity (e.g., take up bowling again).

The research just cited established a clear and distinctive link between anhedonia and depressive disorders. However, as noted earlier, low positive emotions are not specific to depression. Meehl's (1962, 1975, 1987, 2001) writings on anhedonia's role in Schizophrenia have stimulated a sizable empirical literature on this topic as well as the development of several measures of this construct. Chapman, Chapman, and Raulin (1976) constructed measures of physical and social anhedonia and found patients with Schizophrenia to score higher than normal on both. Using a revised version of the Social Anhedonia Scale, Blanchard, Horan, and Brown (2001) found that patients with Schizophrenia demonstrated stable, traitlike high levels of social anhedonia, whereas individuals diagnosed with depression showed reduced social anhedonia on recovery from a depressive episode. Horan, Kring, and Blanchard (2006) reviewed the subsequent literature on this topic and concluded that there is good evidence that anhedonia reflects an enduring trait in Schizophrenia and is episodic in depressed patients.

The distinction between physical and social anhedonia has not been associated with differential findings in patients with Schizophrenia. More recently, building on animal studies that have demonstrated distinctions between "wanting" and "liking" reward-seeking behaviors, Gard, Gard, Kring, and John (2006) constructed the Temporal Experience of Pleasure Scale with separate measures of anticipatory and consummatory pleasure. The item "When ordering something off the menu, I imagine how good it will taste" exemplifies the former, and the item "I enjoy taking a deep breath of fresh air when I walk outside" is an example of the latter. Using this measure, Gard, Kring, Gard, Horan, and Green (2007) found that deficits in anticipatory but not consummatory pleasure were associated with impairment in patients with Schizophrenia. In contrast, as just discussed, Klein (1974) hypothesized that individuals with Anhedonic Depression experience deficits in actual (i.e., consummatory) pleasure.

Low positive emotions are also relevant to the assessment and diagnosis of PTSD, in particular, emotional numbing symptoms such as markedly diminished interest or participation in significant activities, detachment or estrangement from others, and a restricted range of affect. Supporting this specific link between anhedonia and PTSD, Kashdan, Elhai, and Frueh (2006) found anhedonia to be associated with emotional numbing but not with the other types of symptoms required for the diagnosis of PTSD.

To summarize, empirical findings have established a clear link for anhedonia with depression, Schizophrenia, and PTSD. Assessing for low positive emotions provides information relevant to diagnostic consideration of each of these disorders, although for each, different additional symptoms also need to be present.

Empirical Findings with RC2

The external correlates of RC2 are consistent with a lack of positive emotional responsiveness and corroborate its construct validity. RC2 is strongly correlated with various measures of (low) positive temperament in broad-spectrum personality inventories—the MPQ (Sellbom & Ben-Porath, 2005, in college students), the NEO PI-R (Sellbom, Ben-Porath & Bagby, 2008b, in a mental health setting; Tellegen & Ben-Porath, 2008/2011, in veterans in treatment for substance abuse), and the SNAP (Simms et al., 2005, in a clinical sample and a sample of community-dwelling veterans). It is the strongest RC marker of the PEM construct on all three measures.

RC2 is correlated with depressive mood symptoms in a broad range of settings and populations (Arbisi et al., 2008, in psychiatric inpatients; Binford & Liljequist, 2008, in mental health outpatients; Forbey & Ben-Porath, 2007, in individuals in substance abuse treatment; Forbey & Ben-Porath, 2008, in college students; Forbey, Ben-Porath & Gartland, 2010, in prison inmates; Handel & Archer, 2008, in psychiatric inpatients; McCord & Drerup, 2009, in chronic pain patients; Monnot et al., 2009, in individuals in treatment for substance abuse; Osberg et al., 2008, in college students; Sellbom, Ben-Porath & Bagby, 2008a, in college students and mental health outpatients; Sellbom, Ben-Porath & Graham, 2006, in a college counseling clinic; Sellbom, Graham et al., 2006, in individuals in treatment at a private practice; Tellegen et al., 2003, in mental health inpatients and outpatients; Tellegen et al., 2006, in college students; Tellegen & Ben-Porath, 2008/2011, in civil and criminal justice forensic samples; Wygant, Boutacoff et al., 2007, in candidates for bariatric surgery). Specific depression markers, such as anhedonia and loss of interest, as well as nonspecific markers, such as decreased appetite, decreased sleep, diminished concentration, low energy, suicide, and feelings of worthlessness or hopelessness (but no specific anxiety markers), are also associated with RC2 (Arbisi et al., 2008, in psychiatric inpatients; Forbey & Ben-Porath, 2007, in college students; Handel & Archer, 2008, in psychiatric inpatients).

Consistent with the broader empirical literature on anhedonia, scores on RC2 are correlated with an increased likelihood of being prescribed antidepressant medication (Arbisi et al., 2008, in inpatients) and with PTSD symptoms, most prominently those associated with emotional numbing (Miller, Wolf, Harrington, Brown, Kaloupek & Keane, 2010; Tellegen & Ben-Porath, 2008/2011, in a sample of disability claimants and personal injury litigants; Wolf et al., 2008, in veterans diagnosed with PTSD). On the other hand, in contrast with the well-established association between anhedonia and Schizophrenia, Tellegen and Ben-Porath (2008/2011) reported negligible to modest negative correlations between RC2 and this diagnosis in psychiatric inpatients. Examination of the RC2 items reveals a possible reason for this finding. As just reviewed, Gard et al. (2007) found that deficits in anticipatory but not consummatory pleasure were associated with impairment in patients with Schizophrenia. Only two of the 17 RC2 items have anticipatory pleasure content, whereas a sizable number of items on this scale have consummatory content.

Summary

A lack of positive emotional experiences has long been recognized as a primary (although neither defining nor exclusive) feature of depression and Schizophrenia and, more recently, PTSD. Research reviewed in this section indicates that an elevation on RC2, particularly if accompanied by a high score on RCd (indicating the presence of both dysphoric mood and anhedonia), is associated with an increased likelihood that the test taker would meet diagnostic criteria for a major depressive episode and may benefit from antidepressant medication. Elevations on RC2 coupled with high scores on other scales may reflect the presence of anhedonia associated with other disorders (e.g., Schizophrenia if RC8 is also elevated; PTSD if the score on RC7 or the Anxiety Specific Problem Scale [AXY] is elevated). As discussed in Chapter 8, a positive finding on the MMPI-2-RF provides direction for further diagnostic consideration rather than the final word on a diagnosis.

Cynicism (RC3)

Conceptualizing Cynicism

Cynicism, as assessed by RC3, reflects the degree to which an individual holds misanthropic, negativistic, and mistrusting views of others. Cynicism is non-self-referential; it entails a generalized negative system of beliefs that humans are bad and not to be trusted rather than a belief that one is being singled out by others for mistreatment. The cynicism construct has been the focus of two distinct bodies of literature in psychology: one, originating in behavioral medicine, focuses on cynicism as a risk factor for cardiovascular disease and other physical health problems; the other, emerging from police psychology, has centered on cynicism as a risk factor for police burnout and misconduct. The MMPI played a major role in the former area of research, with a sizable component of the literature relying on the original and subsequent variations of the Hostility (Ho) Scale developed by Cook and Medley (1954).

Empirical Findings on Cynicism

Cynicism in Behavioral Medicine

In the first part of the 20th century, coronary heart disease (CHD) became the leading cause of death in the United States (Myrtek, 2007), spurring efforts to identify its causes and develop potentially preventive interventions. Findings that diet and activity level alone, though clearly associated with increased risk for CHD, could not account for important individual differences in its occurrence sparked interest in identifying additional, nonphysiological risk factors. In a survey of executives and physicians, Friedman, Rosenman, Carroll, and Tat (1958) found that "70 percent of each group believed that the major cause of clinical coronary disease was a particular and rather specific type of emotional activity, namely that concerned with excessive 'drive,' competition, meeting 'deadlines,' and economic frustration" (p. 853). The authors then studied a sample of accountants for a period of six months and found a clear pattern of covariation between their subjective reports of stress and objective indicators (i.e., tax-filing deadlines) and their levels of serum cholesterol and blood clotting.

On the basis of this research, Friedman and Rosenman (1959) formulated a behavior pattern they labeled *Type A*, characterized by (1) an intense, sustained drive to achieve self-selected but usually poorly defined goals; (2) profound inclination and eagerness to compete; (3) persistent desire for recognition and advancement; (4) continuous involvement in multiple and diverse functions constantly subject to time restrictions (deadlines); (5) habitual propensity to accelerate the rate of executing many physical and mental functions; and (6) extraordinary mental and physical alertness. They studied its association with CHD by comparing a group of men who met this definition with a second group, labeled *Type B*, who manifested the opposite pattern and a third group of blind, unemployed men who also met the Type B definition but were considered to be experiencing chronic stress as a result of their disability. Friedman and Rosenman found that clinical coronary artery disease was seven times more frequent in the Type A group when compared with each of the other groups.

The finding of a behavioral risk factor for CHD led to the launching, in 1960, of the Western Collaborative Group Study (WCGS), a prospective eight-year investigation of the Type A–CHD link (Rosenman et al., 1964). Assessment for Type A Behavior was conducted with a structured interview developed for the study. Based on this interview, over 1,500 men were classified as Type A, and a comparable number were classified as Type B. In their final report of the follow-up analyses, Rosenman, Brand, Jenkins, Friedman, Strauss, and Wurum (1975) concluded that "the Type A Behavior pattern was strongly related to the CHD incidence, and this association could not be explained by association of behavior pattern with any single [nonbehavioral] predictive risk factor or any combination of them" (p. 872).

Subsequent efforts to replicate the WCGS findings were largely unsuccessful, leading some investigators to seek to dismantle the complex Type A construct and attempt to isolate a more narrowly focused component that might better indicate CHD risk. Mathews, Glass, Rosenman, and Bortner (1977) reanalyzed data from the WCGS and concluded that a high potential for hostility was among the strongest of CHD risk factors. This led R. B. Williams, Haney, Lee, Hong-Kong, Blumenthal, and Whalen (1980) to explore whether an MMPI measure, Cook and Medley's (1954) Ho Scale, would be predictive of increased CHD risk. The Ho Scale was developed to assist in identifying teachers likely to have difficulty getting along with students. However, Cook and Medley observed that the scale items, selected empirically on the basis of correlations with the Minnesota Teacher Attitude Inventory, were not specific to that profession and that the scale might therefore "prove useful also in the selection of sales people, officers, and noncommissioned officers in the armed forces, foremen, and other personnel who must be able to establish rapport with others" (p. 414). On the basis of their reading of the items assigned to the final Ho Scale, Cook and Medley concluded that "the hostile person is one who has little confidence in his fellow man. He sees people as dishonest, unsocial, immoral, ugly, and mean" (pp. 417–418), a description that could well characterize the items of RC3.

R. B. Williams et al. (1980) included Cook and Medley's (1954) description of hostility in explaining their selection of the Ho Scale for investigating the hostility–CHD link. Their initial investigation and a host of follow-up studies established a strong, replicable association between hostility and CHD risk. Barefoot, Dahlstrom, and Williams (1983) examined the association between Ho scores and subsequent health status in a 25-year follow-up of 255 medical students who had completed the MMPI between 1954 and 1959. Higher scores on the scale were associated with a significantly increased risk for CHD as well as total mortality.

Like many empirically derived MMPI scales, Ho was subsequently found to be excessively heterogeneous, leading investigators to pursue efforts to discover the structure of the scale and further dismantle the Hostility construct. A factor analysis of the Ho items by Costa, Zonderman, McCrae, and Williams (1986) identified two primary factors, leading to the development of subscales Cynicism and Paranoid Alienation. A subsequent effort to parse the Ho Scale item content (Barefoot, Dodge, Peterson, Dahlstrom & Williams, 1989), based on the judgment of experts, led to the construction of a number of Ho subscales, including one called "Cynicism." Both Cynicism subscales included 9 of the 12 available RC3 items (three RC3 items were added to the inventory in the MMPI-2). Thus, efforts to home in on personological CHD risk factors and identify behaviors that mediate this risk have, for the past 30 years, focused on the misanthropic attitudes assessed by RC3.

Barefoot et al. (1989) examined associations between scores on the Ho subscales and medical outcomes in a sample of 118 lawyers tested 28 years previously with the MMPI. The Cynicism, Hostile Affect, and Aggressive Responding subscales were all associated with survival, while the remaining Ho subscales were not. A sum of scores on these three subsets provided the best prediction of negative health outcomes. Using the Cynicism subscale created by Costa et al. (1986), Almada et al. (1991) studied a sample of 1,871 employed, middle-aged men and found that scores on this scale (but not a measure of neuroticism) were associated with coronary death and total mortality and that this association may be mediated by cigarette smoking and excessive alcohol use. Barefoot, Larsen, von der Leith, and Schroll (1995) examined the association between scores on an abbreviated version of the Cook–Medley Ho Scale (ACM) that included 10 of the 12 available RC3 items in a sample of Danish men and women followed for a period of 27 years after being administered the MMPI. ACM scores were associated with increased risk for myocardial infarction in both men and women after controlling for traditional medical risk factors. This finding led Boyle et al. (2004) to reexamine data from a previous investigation that had failed to find an association between Ho scores and survival in already identified CHD patients. Using the ACM, these investigators found that after controlling for disease severity, the total score was a significant predictor of both CHD mortality and total mortality. Linking back to the original search for behavioral risk factors,

Song, Terao, and Nakamura (2007) investigated the association between Type A Behavior, as measured by a translated version of Rosenman's structured interview, and scores on the full Ho Scale as well as its Cynicism and Paranoid subscales in Japanese college students. Only the Cynicism subscale was found to be associated with an increased prevalence of Type A Behavior.

Several studies have attempted to identify the mechanisms by which cynicism and/or hostility might increase the risk for CHD. As noted earlier, Almada et al. (1991) found that cigarette smoking and excessive alcohol use were potential mediators of this association. A meta-analysis of studies designed to help understand the personality–CHD link found obesity, insulin resistance, damaging health behaviors, and socioeconomic status to be potential contributing factors (Bunde & Suls, 2006). In a large sample of Vietnam veterans, Boyle, Mortensen, Gronbaek, and Barefoot (2008) found that alcohol consumption, particularly the number of drinks per day, was a potential mediator of an association between ACM scores and all-cause mortality. Using the Cynicism subscale (composed of 13 Ho items that included 9 of the 12 available RC3 items) created by Barefoot et al. (1989), Why and Johnston (2008) identified state anger as a potential moderator of the association between cynicism and blood pressure elevation. Using the same subscale, Lepore (1995) found support for a model postulating that cynical attitudes undermine the stress-buffering potential of interpersonal support.

The Ho Scale and its subscales have also been investigated as risk factors for suicidal ideation in individuals diagnosed with depression. Nierenberg et al. (1996) found that the Cynicism subscale, but not the full Ho Scale or other subscales developed by Barefoot et al. (1989), was associated with suicidal ideation in a sample of 42 outpatients diagnosed with Major Depression.

To summarize, the search for psychological/behavioral risk factors for CHD began with the broad Type A Behavior construct and increasingly became focused on hostility as measured by the Cook–Medley Ho Scale and subsequently by a subset of its items scored on a 13-item Cynicism scale that included 9 of the 12 available RC3 items. An increased risk for CHD, CHD-related mortality, and all-purpose mortality in individuals with high levels of cynicism is well established. Smoking, excessive drinking, poor diet, expression of anger, and an impaired ability to rely on social support have been identified as possible mediators of this association.

Cynicism and Police Misconduct

As just noted, Cook and Medley devised the Ho Scale to identify poor candidates for teacher training. They surmised, based on its nonspecific content, that the scale might be useful in identifying problematic candidates for other types of professions and positions. In a review of the job burnout literature, Maslach, Schaufeli, and Leiter (2001) noted that the Maslach Burnout Inventory, developed by Maslach and Jackson (1981), had been used to study burnout in various professions and that this research led to the development of the multidimensional theory of burnout (Maslach & Goldberg, 1998), which identified three primary burnout-related dimensions—exhaustion, depersonalization or cynicism, and inefficiency—all associated with reduced personal accomplishment.

Of these three dimensions, cynicism has been the focus of efforts to identify and understand problematic behavior in law enforcement officers and other public safety employees. Much of this work can be traced back to an influential book on this topic by Niederhoffer (1967), who postulated that cynical beliefs about the public, the legal system, colleagues, and supervisors are endemic to police work at all levels, with heightened cynicism resulting in burnout and misconduct. Using a measure of cynicism related to police work completed by 220 New York City police officers, Niederhoffer (1967) found that police recruits exhibited the lowest level of cynicism, which increased steadily during roughly their first seven years of service and then began to decline but never reached the baseline level found in recruits. Efforts to replicate Niederhoffer's findings met with mixed success, leading to further work designed to refine the police cynicism measure he developed.

Efforts to replicate Niederhoffer's finding of a curvilinear relation between cynicism and length of service have generally failed to find such a pattern. Wilt and Bannon (1976), Rafky, Lawly, and Ingram (1976), and Singer, Singer, and Burns (1984) all reported significant increases in cynicism between the beginning of police training and its completion but found no pattern of change in cynicism thereafter. In contrast, unlike Niederhoffer, R. Regoli (1977) found an association between officer cynicism levels and complaints from members of the public. Poole and Regoli (1979) similarly found an inverse association between officer cynicism and professionalism. Using an alternative (to Niederhoffer's) measure of cynicism, B. Regoli, Crank, and Rivera (1990) found that officers' cynicism about decision makers and rules was associated with a greater likelihood of hostile interactions with the public and job dissatisfaction and that more cynical officers made a larger number of arrests. Using a modified version of Niederhoffer's cynicism measure with a larger sample of police officers, Hickman, Piquero, and Piquero (2004) found higher cynicism to be associated with a greater likelihood of facing departmental charges.

The two lines of research just reviewed converged in a study of Norwegian police officers reported by Richardsen, Burke, and Martinussen (2006). The authors administered a number of measures related to work engagement and health and found that scores on the Cynicism subscale of the Maslach Burnout Inventory were negatively correlated with work engagement and positively associated with a measure of physical health complaints.

Empirical Findings with RC3

Supporting its construct validity, high RC3 scores are associated with hostility, anger, and low trust (Burchett & Ben-Porath, 2010, in a college sample; Sellbom, Ben-Porath & Bagby, 2008b, in a clinical sample; Tellegen & Ben-Porath, 2008/2011, in various settings); negative beliefs about others (Forbey & Ben-Porath, 2007, in a sample of individuals being treated for substance abuse; Forbey & Ben-Porath, 2008, in a nonclinical sample; Handel & Archer, 2008, in psychiatric inpatients); alienation and blame externalization (Sellbom & Ben-Porath, 2005, in a nonclinical sample; Sellbom, Ben-Porath, Baum, Erez & Gregory, 2008, in a sample of male batterers). Ingram, Kelso, and McCord (2011) found RC3 scores to be associated with Machiavellianism and alienation in a college student sample.

As just reviewed, subsets of items scored on the Cook–Medley Ho Scale, which includes 9–10 of the 12 available RC3 items, have established a well-replicated association between MMPI-assessed cynicism and increased risk for CHD, CHD-related mortality, and non-CHD-related mortality. Although this link has yet to be investigated directly with the full RC3 scale, findings reported by Tellegen and Ben-Porath (2008/2011) suggest that this personological risk factor can be assessed with RC3. In several clinical and nonclinical samples, RC3 scores correlated moderately (.25–.40) with scores on RC1 (Somatic Complaints). Moreover, in each of five clinical samples, RC3 had the highest correlation with Ho (.82–.85) of any MMPI-2-RF scale.

Consistent with findings on the link between cynicism and police officer misconduct, in a sample of law enforcement candidates, higher RC3 scores at time of hire predicted a variety of on-the-job problems, including citizen complaints, rude behaviors, abuse of authority, externalizing blame, and uncooperativeness (Sellbom, Fischler & Ben-Porath, 2007).

Summary

Although cynicism typically has not been the focus of assessments conducted in mental health settings, two lines of research, one in behavioral medicine and the other in police psychology, have documented significant health and public safety implications of higher levels of this variable. Data just summarized indicate that RC3 is the best MMPI-2-RF measure of this construct and its correlates. The interpersonal correlates just reported indicate that individuals who produce elevated scores on RC3 are likely to have significantly impaired interpersonal relationships. Such findings are consistent with Lepore's (1995) conclusion that cynicism undermines an individual's ability to benefit from the stress buffering afforded by social support, suggesting a possible mechanism for the health and occupational risks associated with this construct.

Antisocial Behavior (RC4)

Conceptualizing Antisocial Behavior

Antisocial behavior is a core feature of Antisocial Personality Disorder (ASPD) and, depending on which model one follows, is either a core feature or a consequence of psychopathy. Understanding the relation between antisocial behavior and these two disorders can help guide the use of RC4 in diagnosing them and in assessing the propensity toward antisocial conduct more generally.

The items of RC4 cover a broad spectrum of conduct, including adult and/or juvenile criminal behavior, various other manifestations of juvenile misconduct, substance abuse, aggressive behavior, familial conflict, impulsive behavior, and deceit. Although, like all MMPI-2-RF scales, RC4 is not designed or recommended for use as a direct diagnostic indicator, it is noteworthy that of the seven DSM-IV ASPD criteria for "disregard for and violation of the rights of others," the first four (failure to conform to social norms, deceitfulness, impulsivity, and aggressiveness) are clearly represented by the RC4 item pool, and the ASPD diagnostic requirement of evidence of a Juvenile Conduct Disorder is represented as well. However, the last three (reckless disregard for the safety of self or others, consistent irresponsibility, and lack of remorse) are not. On the other hand, the RC4 pool includes several items describing substance abuse and familial discord that are not related directly to any of the ASPD criteria. Thus, although there is substantial overlap between the antisocial behaviors covered by RC4 and ASPD, the two constructs are by no means veridical.

The starting point of most efforts to delineate psychopathy is Cleckley's (1941) list of psychopathic features, including superficial charm and good intelligence; absence of delusions and other signs of irrational thinking; absence of nervousness, unreliability, untruthfulness, or insincerity; lack of remorse or shame; inadequately motivated antisocial behavior; poor judgment and failure to learn from experience; egocentricity; impoverished affective relationships; lack of insight; uninviting behavior (related and unrelated to substance use); low probability of suicide; casual sexual behavior; and failure to follow a life plan. This list encompasses a far more extensive domain than the one represented by the RC4 item pool. Thus, psychopathy, as conceptualized by Cleckley and incorporated into most measures of the construct, is clearly a broader phenomenon than the one represented by the diagnostic criteria for ASPD or the item pool of RC4.

The most widely studied and best-validated measure of the construct—Hare's (1991, 2003) Psychopathy Checklist–Revised (PCL-R)—was designed to follow closely Cleckley's conceptualization and has been the focus of efforts to delineate the relation between psychopathy and antisocial behavior. As summarized in the following section, PCL-R structural modeling studies have been interpreted as providing evidence that antisocial behavior is either a primary aspect of psychopathy or, alternatively, a secondary consequence of a preexisting disorder. Commenting on this topic more broadly, Lykken (1995) observed, "The antisocial personalities who are responsible for most crime, including violent crime, in the United States are not psychopaths but rather *sociopaths*, persons of broadly normal temperament who have failed to acquire the attributes of socialization" (p. vii). Lykken's (1957, 1995, 2006) conceptualization of psychopathy posited a genetically inherited deficit in the ability to experience anxiety as a primary cause of the failure of psychopaths to socialize. By contrast, he viewed the antisocial behavior of sociopaths as resulting from an upbringing that failed to provide the experiences necessary for proper socialization. These etiological distinctions have important implications for the assessment of antisocial behavior, ASPD, and psychopathy as measured by RC4.

Hare and Neumann (2006) describe an asymmetric association between psychopathy and ASPD, noting that in studies of criminal offenders, most who have high scores on the PCL-R, also meet diagnostic criteria for ASPD, whereas most who meet the ASPD criteria do not also score high on the PCL-R. They explain this asymmetry in the context of efforts to identify facets of psychopathy through structural analyses of the PCL-R item pool. Hare (1991) initially introduced a two-factor structure, with Factor 1 representing the affective and interpersonal aspects of psychopathy and Factor 2 linked to antisocial behavior. In the second edition of the PCL-R manual, Hare (2003) introduced a four-factor model, with separate scales assessing interpersonal, affective, lifestyle, and antisocial aspects of psychopathy. In both models, antisocial behavior is viewed as a necessary (but not sufficient) component of the broader psychopathy construct.

Cooke, Michie, and Hart (2006) posit, in contrast, that antisocial behavior is a consequence rather than a core feature of psychopathy. Recognizing that the link between psychopathy and antisocial behavior is formalized in both the *DSM-IV* (APA, 1994) and the ICD-10 (World Health Organization, 1992), these authors assert that the nature of the association between psychopathy and antisocial behavior is not made clear in these diagnostic systems and that empirical findings indicate that the latter is in fact a consequence rather than a symptom of the former.

Seeking to integrate the models just described, Patrick, Fowles, and Krueger (2009) proposed a triarchic conceptualization, positing that

> psychopathy encompasses three distinct phenotypic constructs: *disinhibition*, which reflects a general propensity toward problems of impulse control, *bold-ness:* which is defined as the nexus of social dominance, emotional resiliency, and venturesomeness, and *meanness*, which is defined as aggressive resource seeking without regard for others. (p. 913)

Patrick et al. (2009) indicate that prominent behavioral manifestations of disinhibi-tion include irresponsibility, impulsivity, alienation and distrust, aggressive acting out, untrustworthiness, substance misuse, and engagement in illicit or other norm-violating activities. Boldness is described as entailing a capacity to remain calm in stressful situations, an ability to recover quickly from stressful events, high self-assurance and social efficacy, and a tolerance for unfamiliarity and danger. Meanness is characterized by deficient empathy, disdain for and lack of close relationships, rebelliousness, excitement seeking, exploitiveness, and empowerment through cruelty. Antisocial behavior in this model would be associated with disinhibition.

Empirical Findings on Antisocial Behavior

Hare and Neumann (2006) summarize the empirical literature supporting their con-ceptualization of antisocial behavior as an integral component of psychopathy and observe that "both basic research on normal personality and studies on psychopathy support the position that characteristic adaptations, reflecting undercontrolled or externalizing antisocial tendencies, are important components of the psychopathy construct" (p. 74). As examples of evidence that antisocial behavior is a feature rather than an outcome of psychopathy, they cite findings showing that antisocial behav-ior is heritable and often precedes the development of other facets of psychopathy (Blonigan, Carlson, Krueger & Patrick, 2003; Blonigan, Hicks, Krueger, Patrick & Iacono, 2005; Slutske et al., 2001; Viding, James, Blair, Moffitt & Plomin, 2005).

By contrast, Cooke et al. (2006) note that in structural analyses of the PCL-R, Cooke and Michie (2001) identified a three-factor model that yielded measures labeled

"Impulsive and Irresponsible Behavioral Style," "Deficient Affective Experience," and "Arrogant and Deceitful Interpersonal Style." In a subsequent study, Cooke, Michie, Hart, and Clark (2004) identified two additional PCL-R factors involving seven PCL-R items related to antisocial behavior (Criminal Behavior and Relationship Lability) and evaluated the fit of a structural model that treated the two additional factors as coequal facets of psychopathy. Cooke, Michie, Hart, and Clark (2004) found that the five-factor model provided a poorer fit than the previously delineated three-factor model, and overall, the five-factor model produced an inadequate fit with the data. They subsequently developed and replicated an alternative path model in which the seven PCL-R items that involve antisocial behavior loaded on factors that functioned as products of the three primary psychopathy factors just listed.

Whether antisocial behavior is a facet or outcome of psychopathy is of secondary importance to understanding the construct assessed by RC4. Numerous studies have found that the PCL-R items related to antisocial behavior, whether represented by Factor 2 in the two-factor PCL-R model or Factor 4 in the four-factor model, are the best predictors of future antisocial behavior in a broad range of settings and populations (cf. meta-analyses by Gendreau, Goggin & Smith, 2002; Hemphill, Hare & Wong, 1998; Leistico, Salekin, DeCoster & Rogers, 2008; Walters, 2003, for Factor 2, and studies by Walters & Heilbrun, 2009, and Walters, Knight, Grann & Dahle, 2008, for Factor 4). Thus, a set of PCL-R items that overlap to some extent with the RC4 item pool has been found repeatedly to be predictive of future antisocial conduct.

RC4 includes several items relating to substance misuse, a particular antisocial behavior that is not included in the ASPD diagnostic criteria or in the 20 PCL-R items. However, epidemiological investigations have established a high comorbidity rate for Substance Use Disorders and ASPD. For example, Moran (1999) reported that in a community sample, up to 80% of individuals diagnosed with ASPD met lifetime criteria of at least one Substance Use Disorder, and 70% of individuals who met diagnostic criteria for a Substance Use Disorder were also diagnosed with ASPD. Moreover, behavioral genetic studies have demonstrated a common genetic liability for ASPD and Substance Use Disorders (cf. Waldman & Slutske, 2000), leading Krueger, Markon, Patrick, Benning, and Kramer (2007) to assert that "DSM-defined Substance Use Disorders and Antisocial Behavior Disorders can be understood as elements within a genetically coherent, continuously varying liability spectrum" (p. 647). Krueger and colleagues posited that "disinhibitory personality traits" are an additional element of the broad domain of externalizing psychopathology, noting that "extensive evidence documents significant correlations between personality traits and externalizing forms of psychopathology. In particular, the most specific traits entail aggression and impulsivity" (p. 646).

Empirical Findings with RC4

Scores on RC4 are correlated with a variety of antisocial behaviors. Correlations with a history of juvenile delinquency and adult criminal conduct—recorded by others and self-reported—have been found in a variety of settings (Arbisi et al., 2008, in psychiatric inpatients; Binford & Liljequist, 2008, in mental health outpatients; Burchett & Ben-Porath, 2010, in college students; Handel & Archer, 2008, in psychiatric inpatients; Sellbom et al., 2008, in a sample of men tested at intake to a batterer's intervention program; Sellbom, Ben-Porath & Graham, 2006, in a sample of private practice outpatients; Sellbom, Ben-Porath & Stafford, 2007, in a sample of pretrial criminal defendants; Tellegen & Ben-Porath, 2008/2011, in a broader sample of pretrial criminal defendants; Tellegen et al., 2003, in a sample of community mental health center outpatients). Correlations with alcohol and substance abuse, both current and lifetime, have also been reported in various settings and populations (Arbisi et al., 2008, in psychiatric inpateints; Binford & Liljequist, 2008, in mental health outpatients; Forbey & Ben-Porath, 2008, in a college student sample; Forbey, Ben-Porath & Gartland, 2009, in a correctional setting; Handel & Archer, 2008, in psychiatric inpatients; Sellbom et al., 2008, in a sample of male batterers; Sellbom, Ben-Porath & Graham, 2006, in a college counseling sample; Sellbom, Ben-Porath et al., 2007, in a sample of pretrial criminal defendants; Tellegen & Ben-Porath, 2008/2011, in medical and mental health outpatients, criminal defendants, and disability claimants; Tellegen et al., 2003, in mental health outpatients). Scores on RC4 are also correlated with aggressive and violent behavior (Forbey & Ben-Porath, 2007, in a sample of men receiving substance abuse treatment; Sellbom et al., 2008, in a sample of men enrolled in a batterer's intervention program) and family dysfunction (Tellegen & Ben-Porath, 2008/2011, in mental health outpatients, psychiatric inpatients, medical patients, and criminal defendants; Wygant, Boutacoff et al., 2007, in a sample of bariatric surgery candidates).

In the personality domain, high RC4 scores are associated with low Constraint, particularly with low behavioral control, low Agreeableness and Conscientiousness, Impulsiveness, and Anger (Forbey & Ben-Porath, 2007, in a nonclinical sample; Forbey & Ben-Porath, 2008, in a nonclinical sample; Forbey, Ben-Porath & Gartland, 2009, in a male prison inmate sample; Sellbom & Ben-Porath, 2005, in a nonclinical sample; Sellbom, Ben-Porath & Bagby, 2008b, in a mental health setting; Sellbom et al., 2008, in a sample of male batterers; Simms et al., 2005, in a clinical setting and a sample of community-dwelling veterans; Wygant, Boutacoff et al., 2007, in a sample of bariatric surgery candidates).

Several studies have reported correlations between RC4 scores and measures of psychopathy. Using Lilienfeld and Andrews's (1996) Psychopathic Personality Inventory (PPI), Sellbom, Ben-Porath, Lilienfeld, Patrick, and Graham (2005) reported a correlation of .52 with the total score, .56 with a Social Deviance factor score, and correlations in the .40s with related measures of Machiavellian Egocentricity, Carefree Nonplanfullness, Blame Externalization, and Impulsive Nonconformity. In a sample of pretrial criminal defendants, Sellbom, Ben-Porath et al. (2007) reported a correlation of .50 with the total score on the Screening Version of the PCL-R (PCL-SV; Hart, Cox & Hare, 1995) and correlations of .29 and .62, respectively, with Factors 1 and 2 of the PCL-SV. Sellbom (in press) reported substantial correlations between RC4 scores and psychopathy, as measured by the Levenson Self-Report Psychopathy Scale (Levenson, Kiehl & Fitzpatrick, 1995) in a correctional sample. Sellbom (in press) found similar correlations between RC4 and PPI-assessed psychopathy in the same sample. These findings show, as expected, that scores on RC4 are associated primarily with the antisocial behavior component of the PCL-R, but they are also associated with the affective/interpersonal component assessed by Factor 1. Bolinskey, Trumbetta, Hanson, and Gottesman (2010) found in a prospective study that scores on an abridged version of RC4 (made up of original MMPI items) predicted risk for adult psychopathy 30 years later in a cohort of adolescents tested in the 1950s.

Several studies have reported correlations between scores on RC4 and an ASPD diagnosis (Monnot et al., 2009, in a sample of veterans receiving treatment for substance abuse; Simms et al., 2005, in a sample of community-dwelling veterans; Tellegen & Ben-Porath, 2008/2011, in pretrial criminal defendants; Wolf et al., 2008, in veterans receiving PTSD treatment).

In two prospective studies, scores on RC4 were associated with an increased risk for problematic behavior. In a study of law enforcement candidates tested at the prehire evaluation, Sellbom, Fischler et al. (2007) found scores on RC4 to be associated with future report of being uncooperative toward peers and supervisors, using their position for personal advantage, abuse of sick leave, and conduct unbecoming a police officer. Wygant et al. (2007) found scores on RC4 to be associated with failing to adhere to the aftercare program in a sample of bariatric surgery candidates.

Summary

The RC4 correlates just reviewed provide evidence in support of the construct validity of the scale as a measure of antisocial behavior. Across a wide range of settings, scores on RC4 are associated with rule breaking and irresponsible conduct linked empirically and conceptually to ASPD and psychopathy. With regard to the former, RC4 correlates include behaviors indicative of failure to conform to social norms, deceitfulness, impulsivity, aggressiveness, and consistent irresponsibility as well as a history of juvenile misconduct. Strong associations between RC4 and substance abuse are consistent with the high comorbidity rates for the two conditions and the generally higher base rate of substance abuse compared with criminal conduct. Elevations on RC4 have robust associations with the acting-out or social deviance facets of psychopathy as well as the total psychopathy score on the two leading measures of this construct. As is the case with all MMPI-2-RF scales, these correlates do not allow for the direct diagnosis of either disorder but, rather, indicate that both should be given consideration in differential diagnosis. Moreover, elevations on RC4 indicate a strong likelihood of acting-out behaviors that are likely to occur regardless of whether an individual meets diagnostic criteria for Antisocial Personality Disorder or psychopathy.

Ideas of Persecution (RC6)

Conceptualizing Ideas of Persecution

The RC6 items describe self-referential beliefs that one is being singled out for mistreatment, ranging from being called names to being poisoned. Data reported later in this section show, as expected, that scores on this scale are associated with paranoid delusional thought dysfunction; however, as implied by its label, the scale most directly assesses the extent to which a test taker reports experiencing persecutory thoughts. In a review of the concept of paranoid thinking and its assessment, Manschreck (1979) noted that that the term *paranoia* was coined by the ancient Greeks and that Hippocrates used it to describe delirium associated with high fever. It subsequently fell into disuse until the 19th century, when Karl Kahlbaum (as quoted in Lewis, 1970) classified paranoia as a separate mental illness, "a form of partial insanity, which, throughout the course of the disease, principally affect[s] the sphere of the intellect" (p. 3). Manschreck (1979) also noted that in addition to thought disorder, paranoid features are associated with a wide range of conditions, including neurological, metabolic, and other psychiatric conditions; sex chromosome anomalies; infections; substance misuse; and use of various pharmacologic agents. Most efforts to conceptualize paranoid thinking and identify its origins have, however, focused on the domain of thought dysfunction.

Maher (1974) noted that efforts to study paranoia had, to the point of his review, been either descriptive, yielding systematic descriptions of delusional thought processes, or explanatory, involving an inner state that disrupts the process of logical reasoning. He offered and studied an alternative explanation, whereby "a delusion is a hypothesis designed to explain unusual perceptual phenomena and developed through operation of normal cognitive processes" (p. 103). He postulated that

> the explanations (i.e., the delusions) of the patient are derived by cognitive activity that is essentially indistinguishable from that employed by non-patients, by scientists, by people generally. The structural coherence and internal consistency of the explanation will be a reflection of the intelligence of the individual patient. (p. 103)

More recently, Freeman (2007) postulated that in addition to the factors described by Maher, "there is a large direct affective contribution to the experience [of persecutory delusions]" (p. 425). In particular, he proposed and cited empirical findings to support the notion that anxiety affects the content, distress, and persistence of paranoia, although affect alone is not sufficient to induce paranoid experiences. He proposed a threat anticipation cognitive model of persecutory delusions, which were hypothesized to arise from an interaction of emotional processes, anomalous experiences (à la Maher, 1974), and reasoning biases. Freeman (2007) also noted that owing to their self-referential nature, persecutory delusions were disruptive of the individual's social functioning.

Freeman and Garety (2000) had previously proposed that to be classified as persecutory delusions, the individual's beliefs must include both the anticipation that harm (not necessarily physical) is occurring or going to occur to him or her and that the persecutor has the intent to cause harm. Freeman (2007) elaborated that paranoia is a hierarchical phenomenon, characterized by five levels of perceived threat ranging from (1) social evaluative concerns (fear of rejection and feelings of vulnerability) to (2) ideas of reference (being talked about or watched by others), (3) mild threat (people trying to cause minor distress such as irritation), (4) moderate threat (people going out of their way to get at the individual), and (5) severe threat (people trying to cause significant physical, psychological, or social harm to the individual). Examination of the RC6 items indicates that most range from descriptions of mild to severe threat, with roughly equal numbers of each type.

Empirical Findings on Ideas of Persecution

Investigators following Freeman's (2007) conceptualization of persecutory delusions have sought to elaborate their nature and correlates. C. Green et al. (2006) conducted semistructured interviews with individuals identified as having current persecutory delusions. They found that their beliefs frequently involved multiple human persecutors known to the individual, and for the majority, the perceived threat was severe, ongoing, and coupled with feelings of vulnerability. Specific aspects of these individuals' beliefs were associated with emotional distress (or, in MMPI-2-RF terms, demoralization). For example, those who believed they had more power in the face of persecution were less demoralized.

Freeman et al. (2007) describe the development and validation of a measure of "State Paranoia" that can be used in experimental investigations of the phenomenon. The State Social Paranoia Scale is composed of 10 items designed to assess the two elements of Freeman and Garety's (2000) criteria for paranoia (described earlier): fear of harm and perpetrator intent. Using this scale, along with measures of social anxiety, Freeman et al. (2008) exposed a nonclinical sample to a sophisticated, socially neutral virtual reality situation simulating a train ride on the London Underground. In support of Freeman's (2007) model described earlier, the authors found that social anxiety and persecutory ideation shared many predictive factors but that perceptual anomalies coupled with social anxiety were distinct predictors of paranoia.

Also following Freeman and Garety's (2000) definition, McKay, Langdon, and Coltheart (2006) constructed the 10-item Persecutory Ideation Questionnaire (PIQ), which includes content that very closely resembles that of RC6. The authors found that PIQ scores predicted the severity of persecutory delusions in a sample of individuals already identified as experiencing persecutory delusions.

Noting that an erroneous clinical decision can lead to unnecessary treatment or lack of appropriate treatment, S. A. Brown (2008) reviewed the available literature on the prevalence of actual persecutory experiences to assist in differentiating them from persecutory delusional beliefs. He found events such as race-, gender-, or mental illness–based discrimination; criminal victimization; and stalking to be relatively common, occurring in more than 10% of certain population subgroups, whereas government surveillance and intentional poisoning were very uncommon (less than 0.1%) across all population segments.

Empirical Findings with RC6

The empirical correlates of RC6 show it to be a valid indicator of persecutory ideation and paranoid thinking. They include delusions, particularly of a persecutory nature, and ideas of reference (Arbisi et al., 2008, in a sample of psychiatric inpatients; Handel & Archer, 2008, in a different sample of psychiatric inpatients), paranoia and interpersonal mistrust (Sellbom, Graham et al., 2006, in a sample of outpatients treated in independent practice settings; Simms et al., 2005, in a clinical setting and a sample of community-dwelling veterans), alienation and blame externalization (Handel & Archer, 2008, in psychiatric inpatients; Sellbom & Ben-Porath, 2005, in a nonclinical sample; Sellbom et al., 2008, in a sample of men referred to a batterer's intervention program), and the paranoia and mistrust aspects of Cluster A personality pathology (Simms et al., 2005, in a clinical setting and a sample of community-dwelling veterans).

As would be expected, RC6 is also correlated with a broader range of psychotic symptoms, including hallucinations and nonparanoid delusions in psychiatric inpatients (Arbisi et al., 2008; Handel & Archer, 2008; Tellegen & Ben-Porath, 2008/2011), and with a Schizophrenia diagnosis in a sample of individuals entering substance abuse treatment (Monnot et al., 2009). However, the associations with the more specific criteria listed earlier are generally stronger. Scores on this scale are also correlated with both the Magical Ideation and Perceptual Aberration scales (Chapman, Chapman & Raulin, 1978; Eckblad & Chapman, 1983) but, as expected, more so with Magical Ideation in nonclinical (Forbey & Ben-Porath, 2008), correctional (Forbey, Ben-Porath & Gartland, 2009), mental health outpatient (Tellegen & Ben-Porath, 2008/2011), and medical outpatient (Tellegen & Ben-Porath, 2008/2011) samples.

Studies of three samples in which one would not expect to find thought dysfunction that rises to the level of an Axis I disorder have identified additional, informative correlates of RC6. In a sample of bariatric surgery candidates, Wygant, Boutacoff et al. (2007) found RC6 scores to be associated with a history of weight-related teasing in childhood, offering a possible window onto the development of persecutory thoughts in this population. In a study of risk factors for negative outcomes in law enforcement candidates, Sellbom, Fischler et al. (2007) found moderate deviations from the norm (i.e., T scores in the 55–60 range) to be associated with a number of undesirable outcomes, including involuntary departure, citizen complaints, use of excessive force, rude behavior, having a negative attitude toward the public, being uncooperative with supervisors, being a defendant in civil litigation, deceptiveness, abuse of authority, failing to take responsibility for mistakes, using their position for internal gain, showing biased attitudes toward others, and (negatively) responding to previous constructive feedback. In a college student sample, Tellegen and Ben-Porath (2008/2011) found RC6 scores to be associated most strongly with interpersonal alienation and mistrust.

Summary

Persecutory ideation, in some cases rising to the level of persistent paranoid delusional beliefs, has been recognized as a form of psychological dysfunction for several millennia. Current conceptualizations of persecutory delusional beliefs postulate that they are the product of unusual experiences that are anxiety inducing and misinterpreted as signs of malevolent intent by others. Efforts to develop measures of persecutory beliefs have produced scales that are very similar in content to RC6.

Studies of its empirical correlates support the construct validity of the scale and have identified paranoid delusions, less extreme persecutory beliefs, interpersonal suspiciousness and alienation, and mistrust as the strongest correlates of RC6. The possibility that the test taker is in fact experiencing some persecution needs always to be considered when interpreting scores on this scale.

Dysfunctional Negative Emotions (RC7)

Conceptualizing Dysfunctional Negative Emotions

Tellegen (1985) described Negative Emotionality as a higher-order personality trait characterized by a tendency to worry, be anxious, feel victimized and resentful, and appraise situations generally in ways that foster negative emotions. He linked the construct to two well-known models: Gray's (1970) emotion-based psychobiological model, relating temperament to psychiatric disorder, and Freud's anxiety-signal system. Tellegen (1985) linked Negative Emotionality to Gray's (1970) Behavioral Inhibition System, presumed to regulate extinction and passive avoidance in response to signals of punishment. In Freud's model, Tellegen (1985) associated Negative Emotionality with the two-process anxiety theory that postulates an anxiety-signal system, activated by external and internal drive-related stimuli, which controls avoidance of distress. Tellegen noted that both models included a second system (Behavior Activation in Gray's and a hope-signal system in Freud's) that closely resembled a construct he labeled *Positive Emotionality* (assessed on the MMPI-2-RF with RC2).

Tellegen (1985) linked these two broad personality trait dimensions to two psychological domains: mood and psychopathology. In the mood domain, Tellegen associated NEM and PEM with two broad dimensions labeled *Negative Affect* and *Positive Affect*, which had emerged from a review of the literature on self-reported mood conducted by Watson and Tellegen (1985). Tellegen (1985) conceptualized NEM and PEM as the trait counterparts to these mood states. In the psychopathology domain, in keeping with the models of Gray and Freud, Tellegen postulated that high Negative Emotionality is associated with anxiety-related psychopathology, whereas low Positive Emotionality is related to depression. In support of these conceptually grounded hypotheses about associations between personality traits, mood states, and psychopathology, Tellegen reported findings from analyses of five scales— measures of Negative and Positive Affect, unpleasant mood, anxiety, and depression—showing that whereas scores on the depression and anxiety scales were highly correlated with each other and with unpleasant mood (i.e., demoralization), the measures of Negative and Positive Affect were relatively independent of each other and distinctively correlated with scores on the anxiety and depression scales, respectively. Summarizing these findings and their implications, Tellegen concluded the following:

A more complete description of anxious and depressive mood is possible by taking primary factors as well as higher-order dimensions into consideration.

Anxious mood can then be characterized as heightened Negative Affect . . . with a particularly salient fear component. Depressed mood can be described as lowered Positive Affect . . . often with salient features of sadness and fatigue. (p. 694)

The finding that after controlling for demoralization, NEM and PEM emerge as the major distinctive components of the primary MMPI measures of anxiety and depression (Clinical Scales 7 and 2), described earlier in the section on the development of the RC Scales, provides further corroboration of Tellegen's model.

D. P. Green, Goldman, and Salovey (1993) questioned Watson and Tellegen's (1985) two-factor mood model and suggested instead that mood variance could more parsimoniously be attributed to a single, largely bipolar factor marked by positive and negative affect at its opposing ends. In response, Tellegen et al. (1999a, 1999b) clarified that the single factor emphasized by D. P. Green et al. (1993) corresponded to the *Pleasant/Unpleasant* mood dimension in Watson and Tellegen's (1985) mood model (now relabeled *Happiness/Unhappiness*). They demonstrated that the three mood dimensions conform to a hierarchical structure, with a general Happiness/ Unhappiness dimension and relatively independent positive affect and negative affect dimensions at a lower level. In RC Scale terms, Happiness/Unhappiness corresponds to demoralization and is assessed with RCd, Positive Affect corresponds to (reversed) low positive emotions and is assessed with RC2, and Negative Affect corresponds to dysfunctional negative emotions and is assessed with RC7.

A Terminological Confound

Some authors have used the term *Negative Affectivity* in a manner that is not consistent with the framework just discussed, resulting in conceptual confusion and inconsistent empirical findings. This regrettable mix-up can be traced back to a comprehensive review of personality measures conducted by D. Watson and Clark (1984), who concluded that various scales, labeled alternatively *trait anxiety, neuroticism, ego strength, general maladjustment,* and more, were in fact all measures of a general mood dispositional dimension they labeled Negative Affectivity. Examination of the data reported in D. Watson and Clark's review shows that the single best MMPI marker of this dimension was Welsh's (1956) Anxiety (A) Scale, now recognized as a measure of demoralization (Tellegen et al., 2006). By labeling this factor Negative Affectivity, and associating it with Tellegen's concept of Negative Affect, D. Watson and Clark (1984) confounded two related but distinctive dimensions. This misconstrual was subsequently carried over to L. A. Clark and Watson's (1991) influential tripartite model of anxiety and depression, in which they posited that a general affective dimension labeled Negative Affectivity (but in fact corresponding to demoralization, Pleasant/Unpleasant mood, or Happiness/Unhappiness) was responsible for high rates of comorbidity of these disorders.

This was carried over to subsequent elaborations and revisions of the tripartite model (e.g., Mineka, Watson & Clark, 1998) and remains a source of confusion and ambiguity in the personality, psychopathology, and mood literature. Most recently, Watson (2005) proposed a reconceptualization of the diagnostic categories for mood and anxiety disorders for the *DSM-5*, with Major Depression, Dysthymia, Generalized Anxiety, and PTSD grouped under the heading of "Distress Disorders and Panic," "Agoraphobia," "Social Phobia," and other specific phobic disorders labeled "Fear Disorders." Watson proposed that Negative Affectivity was responsible for variance in, and comorbidity between, the two proposed classes (Distress and Fear Disorders), whereas low Positive Affect was responsible for specific variance in Major Depression and Social Phobia. Sellbom, Ben-Porath, and Bagby (2008a) tested an alternative model in which MMPI-2-RF-measured demoralization was a primary marker of Distress Disorders, dysfunctional negative emotions was a primary marker of Fear Disorders, and low positive emotions was associated with Major Depression and Social Phobia. This elaborated three-factor model produced a better fit than a two-factor (Negative and Low Positive Emotionality only) model with data tested in two studies, indicating that demoralization, rather than Negative Emotionality, corresponds better to the general distress factor D. Watson and Clark (1984) labeled Negative Affectivity.

Empirical Findings on Dysfunctional Negative Emotions

Because, as just described, the term *Negative Affectivity* has been applied to a construct that in the MMPI-2-RF is represented by demoralization, this review of the literature on dysfunctional negative emotions is restricted to studies that have utilized three measures linked directly with Tellegen's (1985) NEM construct. The first is Tellegen's own NEM measure, a higher-order factor score based on the MPQ (Tellegen, 1995/2003). The second is an MMPI-2 scale labeled Negative Emotionality/ Neuroticism (NEGE), developed by Harkness, McNulty, and Ben-Porath (1995) to assess one of the five dimensions incorporated in Harkness and McNulty's (1994) Personality Psychopathology Five (PSY-5) model of Personality Disorder (Axis II) features. Harkness et al. (1995) reported a correlation of .72 between MPQ-NEM and NEGE in a nonclinical sample. They explained that NEGE assesses a more narrowly focused construct in that the anger component associated with the MPQ-NEM is measured by a different PSY-5 Scale: Aggressiveness.[4] In this respect, RC7 more closely resembles Tellegen's MPQ-NEM measure than the PSY-5 NEGE scale. Another important difference between the two MMPI-2-based measures of dysfunctional negative emotions is that RC7 was designed to be distinct from demoralization, which was not considered in the development of NEGE. The third measure reviewed here is D. Watson, Clark, and Tellegen's (1988) NA Scale on the Positive and Negative Affect Schedule (PANAS).

In a study of the similarity of personality in twins reared apart and together, Tellegen et al. (1988) found that genetic heritability accounted for approximately 55% of the variance in NEM. This finding is exemplified by a NEM correlation of .61 in a sample of monozygotic (identical) twins who were separated shortly after birth, contrasted with a correlation of .29 in dizygotic (fraternal) twins who were similarly reared apart. A sizable genetic contribution is consistent with conceptualizations of NEM as a stable, dispositional personality trait. Along the same lines, Blonigen, Carlson, Hicks, Krueger, and Iacono (2008) reported finding substantial rank-order stability in a cohort tested seven years apart (at ages 17 and 24) with an abbreviated MPQ-based NEM measure (Patrick, Curtin & Tellegen, 2002).

A study by Segarra, Ross, Pastor, Montanes, Poy, and Molto (2007) provided empirical support for Tellegen's (1985) conceptualized link between NEM and Gray's (1970) Behavioral Inhibition System (BIS). These authors administered Spanish translations of the MMPI-2 and several measures of Gray's BIS and Behavioral Activation System (BAS) to a sample of Spanish undergraduates and found a correlation of .67 between the PSY-5 NEGE scale and a composite index representing BIS. A substantial literature connects Gray's BIS with anxiety-related psychopathology, thus supporting Tellegen's (1985) conceptualization of dysfunctional negative emotions as a core personological vulnerability to developing anxiety-related psychopathology.

Several studies have explored the role of dysfunctional negative emotions in PTSD. Miller, Greif, and Smith (2003) conducted cluster analyses of the MPQ scores of male combat veterans diagnosed with PTSD and reported finding three primary clusters marked by low psychopathology, externalizing difficulties, and internalizing pathology. Whereas the internalizing subgroup showed evidence of significantly lowered positive emotions and the externalizing group was characterized by low levels of constraint, both subgroups evidenced marked elevations on the MPQ-NEM scale. Miller, Kaloupek, Dillon, and Keane (2004) replicated these findings with the PSY-5 NEGE scale. Souza et al. (2008), using the NA Scale of D. Watson, Clark, and Tellegen's (1988) PANAS, found in a sample of Brazilian peacekeepers deployed to Haiti that predeployment high NA levels prospectively predicted PTSD in peacekeepers exposed to significant stress during deployment. Also using the PANAS, Mendonca-de-Souza et al. (2007) found that high NA levels increased individuals' sensitivity to an acute stressor and were implicated in the stimulation of cortisol release, which has been found to occur in stress-exposed individuals who go on to develop PTSD.

Dysfunctional negative emotions have also been implicated in eating disorders in general and in Bulimia Nervosa in particular. Downey and Chang (2007) found that negative affect (assessed with the PANAS) mediated the observed association between perfectionism and bulimic symptoms. Markey and Vander Wal (2007), also using the PANAS NA measure, found that negative affect and emotion dysregulation contribute independently to the expression of bulimic symptomatology, and Perkins, Klump, Iacono, and McGue (2005) found that dysfunctional negative emotions, as measured by the brief MPQ-NEM measure, likely motivated women with anorexia to seek treatment for their symptoms.

Finally, dysfunctional negative emotions have also been implicated in psychopathy. Hicks, Markon, Patrick, Krueger, and Newman (2004) identified a subset of prison inmates diagnosed with psychopathy based on the PCL-R, which they labeled an aggressive subtype characterized by high NEM scores. Along the same lines, Benning, Patrick, Hicks, Blonigen, and Krueger (2003) found MPQ-measured NEM to be associated positively with the social deviance component of psychopathy and negatively with its affective/interpersonal component.

Empirical Findings with RC7

Empirical findings with RC7 indicate that it is strongly correlated with other, non-MMPI measures of dysfunctional negative emotions (Sellbom & Ben-Porath, 2005, with the NEM score on Tellegen's MPQ in college students; Simms et al., 2005, with the Negative Temperament score on Clark's, 1993, SNAP in a clinical sample and community-dwelling veterans). Consistent with Tellegen's (1985) conceptualization of NEM, scores on RC7 are correlated substantially with a measure of Gray's BIS in mental health and medical outpatients (Tellegen & Ben-Porath, 2008/2011).

RC7 scores are associated with various measures and indicators of anxiety in psychiatric inpatients (Arbisi et al., 2008; Handel & Archer, 2008; Tellegen & Ben-Porath, 2008/2011), individuals in treatment at a community mental health setting (Tellegen & Ben-Porath, 2008/2011), a college counseling setting (Sellbom, Ben-Porath & Graham, 2006), individuals receiving mental health outpatient treatment in an independent practice setting (Sellbom, Graham et al., 2006), a sample of disability claimants (Tellegen & Ben-Porath, 2008/2011), a sample of pretrial criminal defendants, a nonclinical sample (Forbey & Ben-Porath, 2008), and a clinical sample and community-dwelling veterans (Simms et al., 2005). RC7 scores have also been found to be associated with other (than anxiety) dysfunctional negative emotions, including anger in prison inmates (Forbey, Ben-Porath & Gartland, 2009), individuals receiving treatment for substance abuse (Forbey & Ben-Porath, 2007), psychiatric inpatients (Handel & Archer, 2008; Tellegen & Ben-Porath, 2008/2011), mental health outpatients (Tellegen & Ben-Porath, 2008/2011), and a nonclinical sample (Forbey & Ben-Porath, 2008) and fear in mental health and medical outpatients (Tellegen & Ben-Porath, 2008/2011).

Empirical findings with RC7 are also consistent with associations (described earlier) between dysfunctional negative emotions and PTSD. Wolf et al. (2008) reported substantial correlations between RC7 scores and PTSD symptoms and diagnoses in samples of male and female combat veterans. Arbisi et al. (2008) reported significant associations between RC7 scores and flashbacks and sleep difficulties in psychiatric inpatients, and Tellegen and Ben-Porath (2008/2011) reported significant correlations between RC7 scores and a PTSD diagnosis in a sample of male inpatients at a Veterans Administration (VA) medical facility. Miller et al. (2010) found substantial correlations between RC7 and PTSD symptoms related to reexperiencing, avoidance, numbing, and hyperarousal in a Vietnam veterans sample. Forbes, Elhai, Miller, and Creamer (2010) reported higher RC7 scores in a sample of Australian combat veterans diagnosed with PTSD. McDevitt-Murphy et al. (2007) found significant elevations on RC7 in a sample of trauma-exposed college students. Monnot et al. (2009) reported a significant correlation between RC7 scores and a diagnosis of PTSD in a sample of veterans receiving treatment for substance abuse. Tellegen and Ben-Porath (2008/2011) found substantial correlations between various PTSD features and RC7 scores in a forensic sample of disability claimants. In a sample of bariatric surgery candidates, Wygant, Boutacoff et al. (2007) found that RC7 scores were associated with indications that exposure to traumatic events preceded the development of maladaptive eating behaviors.

In a study of associations between RC Scale scores and features of psychopathy, consistent with findings using other measures of dysfunctional negative emotions, Sellbom, Ben-Porath et al. (2005) found RC7 scores to be positively associated with the social deviance facet of psychopathy and negatively correlated with its affective/interpersonal component.

Summary

Tellegen (1985) conceptualized Negative Emotionality as an affectively linked personality trait associated with increased risk for anxiety-related psychopathology. The finding (described earlier) that the major distinctive (from demoralization) component of MMPI Clinical Scale 7 (a measure of anxiety-related psychopathology) is in fact marked by a set of items describing dysfunctional negative emotions corroborated Tellegen's model. Scores on the resulting scale, RC7, are indeed associated with a variety of dysfunctional negative emotions, most notably anxiety and anger, and in expected ways with features of PTSD and psychopathy. They are also associated with measures of Gray's (1970) BIS, consistent with Tellegen's (1985) conceptualization of Negative Emotionality. The findings just summarized thus provide good evidence of the construct validity of RC7.

Some terminological confusion has been introduced by use of the label *Negative Affectivity* to describe a general mood-related disposition associated with a variety of personality variables related to psychological dysfunction (D. Watson & Clark, 1984) and responsible for phenotypic comorbidity reflected in measures of anxiety and depression. Used in this manner, the term *Negative Affectivity* is synonymous with *demoralization* rather than with *Negative Emotionality* or *dysfunctional negative emotions.*

Aberrant Experiences (RC8)

Conceptualizing Aberrant Experiences

RC8 items describe a variety of sensory, perceptual, cognitive, and motor experiences that fall well outside the range of normal experiences. These phenomena have long been associated with thought disturbance, although they are neither unique to this form of psychopathology nor an exhaustive list of its manifestations. Two distinct, discipline-linked lines of clinical research have converged on these experiences as core components of disordered thinking: the medical/psychiatric tradition and the psychometric/psychological approach.

In the medical/psychiatric tradition, thought dysfunction has been linked primarily with Schizophrenia, which, like all psychiatric disorders, has been conceptualized, following Kraepelin and Bleuler, as a categorical phenomenon. In their description of the clinical picture associated with Schizophrenia, Combs and Mueser (2007) identify three classes of characteristic symptoms, including positive symptoms (hallucinations, delusions, and bizarre, disorganized behavior), negative symptoms (blunted or flat affect, poverty of speech, anhedonia, apathy, psychomotor retardation, and physical inertia), and cognitive impairments (difficulties in visual and verbal learning, memory problems, attentional deficits, and impaired capacities for abstract reasoning and executive functions). The aberrant experiences assessed by RC8 fall in the first category. Combs and Mueser note that among the positive symptoms, persecutory delusions are the most common. However, these are assessed by RC6, leaving the domain of RC8 focused on experiences associated with hallucinations and nonpersecutory delusions.

Walker, Bollini, Hochman, Kestler, and Mittal (2007) note that current approaches to the diagnosis of Schizophrenia rely heavily on Schneider's (1959) description of the features of this disorder, involving primarily those he characterized as first-rank symptoms. The first-rank symptoms, all of which would be classified as positive symptoms in the typology just reviewed, include thought broadcasting (a belief that others can hear one's thoughts being broadcast out loud), thought intrusion (a belief that some of one's thoughts are being planted by others), thought withdrawal (a belief that others are removing one's thoughts), somatic hallucinations (unusual, unexplained bodily sensations), passivity experiences (a belief that one's thoughts, feelings, or actions are controlled by others), and delusional perception (a fixed false belief about everyday occurrences). Most of the RC8 items describe one of these Schneiderian first-rank symptoms, with some related to one specific type of symptom and others, worded more broadly, conceivably encompassing more than one type of symptom.

The psychometric/psychological approach is often linked to Meehl's (1962) theory of schizotypy, a personality dimension thought at high levels to place an individual at risk for developing Schizophrenia and at lower levels to manifest in various peculiarities of affect, thinking, and behavior. This theoretical framework led Loren and Jean Chapman and their colleagues to develop measures of five features associated with Meehl's schizotypic personality construct, labeled *Physical Anhedonia, Social Anhedonia, Impulsive Nonconformity, Perceptual Aberration,* and *Magical Ideation.* The first two scales were discussed earlier in the context of RC2. The last two overlap conceptually and in some of their content with RC8. The Perceptual Aberration Scale (PAS) includes items described by Chapman et al. (1978) as designed to tap grossly Schizophrenic-like distortions in the perceptions of one's body as well as other perceptual distortions. The Magical Ideation Scale (MIS) comprises items described by Eckblad and Chapman (1983) as involving beliefs in forms of causation that by conventional standards would be deemed invalid or magical. These scales were conceptualized as measures of psychosis/proneness.

To investigate links between psychosis proneness, as measured by the schizotypy scales, and the development of psychotic symptoms, Chapman and Chapman (1980) also developed an interview-based rating system for identifying psychotic and psychotic-like deviancy. The system yielded ratings of six categories of deviancy, including transmission of one's own thoughts (the individual believes that others can read her or his mind or that thoughts leave her or his head), passivity experiences (such as possession by demonic spirits), auditory experiences (hearing voices), thought withdrawal (the belief that others are able to steal one's thoughts), aberrant beliefs (such as being able to control objects with one's thoughts), and visual experiences (seeing things that others cannot see). A seventh category, olfactory experiences, including olfactory hallucinations, was added later. Nearly all the RC8 items can be linked to one of these rating categories, perceptual aberration, or magical ideation.

Empirical Findings on Aberrant Experiences

The Chapmans' psychosis-proneness scales were administered to approximately 7,800 undergraduate students in the late 1970s and early 1980s. Of these, 534 who either scored substantially higher than average on one or more of the scales or were within normal limits on all were invited to participate in a longitudinal study that included periodic evaluations over the course of 10 years. At the end of the study period, 95% of those enrolled were available for the 10-year follow-up assessment. Of the 153 control subjects who did not produce deviant scores on any of the psychosis-proneness measures, only one went on to develop a psychotic disorder, and another was eventually diagnosed with Major Depression with psychotic features. Of those who produced deviant scores on one or more of the psychosis-proneness scales, only subjects with elevations on the PAS or MIS were significantly more likely to develop a psychotic disorder. By the end of the study period, a total of 10 out of 182 (5.5%) individuals with deviant baseline scores on these scales were diagnosed with a psychotic disorder.

In a more recent study, Horan, Reise, Subotnik, Ventura, and Nuechterlein (2008) sought to examine whether the Chapman psychosis-proneness scales could differentiate individuals recently diagnosed with Schizophrenia from healthy controls. Focusing on the two measures associated with aberrant experiences (PAS and MIS), these authors found elevations on these scales in patients with Schizophrenia during both symptomatic and asymptomatic states, with greater deviations from the norm during symptomatic states. Scores on both scales were also substantially correlated with ratings on a thought disturbance variable derived from the modified Brief Psychiatric Rating Scale (BPRS; Lukoff, Nuechterlein & Ventura, 1986).

Empirical Findings with RC8

In clinical samples, Arbisi, Selbom, and Ben-Porath (2008) found elevations on RC8 in psychiatric inpatients to be associated with various types of hallucinations, nonparanoid delusions, and being prescribed antipsychotic medication on discharge. Also in inpatients, Handel and Archer (2008) reported significant correlations between RC8 and BPRS ratings on conceptual disorganization, hallucinatory behavior, and unusual thought content. Monnot et al. (2009) reported a significant correlation between RC8 scores and a diagnosis of Schizophrenia in a sample of veterans undergoing substance abuse treatment. Sellbom, Graham et al. (2006) found a substantial correlation between RC8 and a measure of bizarre experiences in a sample of individuals receiving outpatient therapy in private practice settings. Finally, Tellegen and Ben-Porath (2008/2011) reported significant correlations between

RC8 scores and dissociative experiences in a sample of individuals undergoing disability evaluations.

At the personality level, Tellegen and Ben-Porath (2008/2011) reported substantial correlations in college students between RC8 scores and the Absorption Scale on Tellegen's (1995/2003) MPQ. Of the two MPQ Absorption subscales, scores on RC8 were most strongly associated with the one measuring proneness to imaginative and altered states. Simms et al. (2005) reported very high correlations between RC8 scores and the Eccentric Perceptions Scale on L. A. Clark's (1993) SNAP in a clinical setting and a sample of community-dwelling veterans. The SNAP also includes personality disorder measures, and with those scales, Simms et al. (2005) found that RC8 scores were associated most strongly with a measure of Schizotypal Personality Disorder.

Reports from several investigations include sizable correlations between RC8 and the PAS and MIS psychosis-proneness measures (Forbey & Ben-Porath, 2008, in a nonclinical setting; Forbey, Ben-Porath & Gartland, 2009, in a sample of prison inmates; Tellegen & Ben-Porath, 2008/2011, in mental health and medical outpatients). RC8 correlations with MIS generally run higher than those with PAS (although both fall primarily in the .50–.70 range) in all settings.

Summary

The aberrant experiences assessed by RC8 have been linked with various psychotic disorders and, more broadly, with characteristics of individuals at increased risk for developing thought disorders. The empirical correlates of the scale include expected associations with personality characteristics related to unusual thinking and perceptual processes, well-established measures of psychosis proneness, and a host of clinical phenomena related to nonpersecutory symptoms of Thought Disorder. It is important to consider, however, that none of the studies just reviewed included measures of psychotic symptoms unrelated to Primary Thought Disorder (e.g., substance-induced psychosis), and there is no reason to assume that the aberrant experiences reported by an individual who scores high on this scale are associated specifically or exclusively with Primary Thought Disorder. Nevertheless, the findings just reported provide evidence of the construct validity of RC8 as a measure of psychosis proneness and nonpersecutory psychotic symptoms.

Hypomanic Activation (RC9)

Conceptualizing Hypomanic Activation

Conceptual and descriptive models of hypomania and mania often trace their origins to Kraepelin's (1921) treatise on Manic-Depressive Insanity and Paranoia. Kraepelin differentiated between

manic states with the essential morbid symptoms of flight of ideas, exalted mood, and pressure of activity, and *melancholia* or *depressive states* with sad or

anxious moodiness and also sluggishness of thought or action. These two opposed phases of the clinical state have given the disease its name. (pp. 3–4)

He went on to note, however, that

besides them we observe also clinical "mixed forms," in which the phenomena of mania and melancholia are combined with each other, so that states
arise, which indeed are composed of the same morbid symptoms as these, but
cannot without coercion be classified either with one or the other. (p. 4)

These descriptions have by and large been retained in the *DSM-IV* criteria for diagnosing various types of Bipolar Disorder.

Kraepelin (1921) differentiated between transient manic states (just described)
and what he called "Fundamental States," which currently might be called *traits*.
With regard to manic states, he singled out one of the three essential features of
mania just cited, noting that "in manic states the morbid picture is dominated by
pressure of activity; here we have to do with general volitional excitement" (p.
26). He associated two fundamental states (i.e., traits) with mania: the manic and
irritable temperaments. Kraepelin described the manic temperament as consisting
of "constitutional excitability" (p. 125), characterized by carelessness, very marked
self-confidence, and a related sense of superiority, restlessness, and irresponsible
conduct. He described the irritable temperament as "a mixture of fundamental
states" (p. 130) and noted,

The patients display from youth up extraordinarily great fluctuations in emotional equilibrium and are greatly moved by all experience, frequently in an
unpleasant way. While on the one hand they appear sensitive and inclined to
sentimentality and exuberance, they display on the other hand great irritability and sensitiveness. They are easily offended and hot tempered; they flare
up, and on the most trivial occasions fall into outbursts of boundless fury. . . .
It then comes to violent scenes with abuse, screaming, and a tendency to
rough behavior. (p. 130)

Kraepelin also noted that the mood of individuals with an irritable temperament

is subject to frequent change. In general the patients are perhaps cheerful,
self-conscious, unrestrained; but periods are interpolated in which they are
irritable and ill-humored, also perhaps sad, spiritless, anxious; they shed tears
without cause, give expression to thoughts of suicide, bring forward hypochondriacal complaints, go to bed. (p. 131)

Kraepelin's (1921) state/temperament distinction has important implications
for the assessment of Mania and Hypomania. Two features associated with manic states, their transient nature and the existence of a mixed state consisting of
seemingly incongruent symptoms create substantial difficulties in the assessment

of acute manic or even less extreme, hypomanic episodes. In contrast, the more stable manic and irritable temperaments are more amenable to reliable assessment. Examination of the items scored on RC9 indicates that the vast majority describe features associated with manic or irritable temperament. A smaller proportion can be linked to Kraepelin's notion of *pressure of activity*, the cardinal feature of a manic or hypomanic state.

Empirical Findings on Hypomanic Activation

Several lines of research have sought to provide empirically based elaborations on Kraepelin's insights regarding manic-depressive illness. One involves efforts to identify salient features of mania and hypomania in patients diagnosed with Bipolar Disorder. Wittenborn (1951) conducted an early factor analysis of symptom ratings of 140 psychiatric patients and linked one of the symptom clusters he identified to Kraepelin's (1921) description of manic patients. The symptom ratings associated with this factor included temper tantrums, loudness, attention-demanding behavior, assaultive behavior, fantastic thinking, exaggerated sense of well-being, feelings of persecution, and abrupt mood changes. More recent factor-analytically based efforts to delineate features of Bipolar Disorder have yielded more distinctive symptom subsets. Cassidy, Forest, Murry, and Carroll (1998) factor analyzed ratings of 237 patients with Bipolar Disorder and reported identifying five factors labeled *dysphoria in mania* (reminiscent of Kraepelin's description of sad, spiritless mood associated with irritable temperament), *psychomotor acceleration, psychosis, increased hedonic function,* and *irritable aggression.* Following up on these findings, Cassidy, Ahearn, and Carroll (2002) examined the interepisodic stability of these five symptom factors in patients with Bipolar Disorder and found that all but psychomotor agitation remained quite stable across manic or hypomanic episodes.

Of the features associated with manic and hypomanic activation, aggression has been singled out for attention because of its potentially destructive (to others and self) consequences. For example, McNeil, Binder, and Greenfield (1988) reported that manic patients who had displayed violent behavior in the community during the two weeks preceding their hospitalization had higher rates of violence during their first three days of inpatient treatment. Binder and McNeil (1988) reported that during the first 24 hours of hospitalization, manic patients had higher rates of violence than those diagnosed with Schizophrenia and other disorders. Barlow, Grenyer, and Ilkiw-Lavalle (2000) found similarly that among hospitalized patients, those diagnosed with Bipolar Disorder were the most likely to act out aggressively. On the basis of a review of the literature in this area, Najt, Perez, Sanches, Peluso, Glahn, and Soares (2007) concluded that poor impulse control was a likely mediator between aggressive impulses and behavior during manic episodes. Michaelis, Goldberg, Davis, Singer, Garno, and Wenze (2004) found that aggression and impulsivity were associated with increased risk for suicide attempts in patients with Bipolar Disorder, and Grunebaum et al. (2006) reported findings indicating that an earlier age of onset of aggression in patients with Bipolar Disorder was associated with later development of comorbid substance abuse.

A second symptom cluster that has emerged repeatedly from studies attempting to identify salient features of Bipolar Disorder involves various manifestations of overactivity. On the basis of a factor analysis of the *DSM-IV* criteria for a Hypomanic episode (from which aggression is notably absent), Benazzi (2004) described three primary symptom clusters involving mental activation (e.g., racing thoughts), elevated mood, and overactivity or behavioral activation, which the author noted had been identified by Kraepelin as the most striking feature of hypomania. Angst et al. (2005) created the Hypomania Checklist (HCL-32) to aid in the assessment of hypomanic symptoms in outpatients and found in a multinational study that two primary factors, labeled "active/elated" and "risk taking/irritable," accounted for most of the variance on this measure.

Empirical Findings with RC9

The external correlates of RC9 in clinical settings include symptoms of manic episodes and Bipolar Disorder. In inpatient settings, Arbisi et al. (2008) found RC9 scores to be correlated with experiencing racing thoughts and increased likelihood of being prescribed mood stabilizers at discharge, and Handel and Archer (2008) identified grandiosity and overexcitement as RC9 correlates. In an outpatient private practice sample, Sellbom, Graham et al. (2006) found that RC9 scores were substantially correlated with a measure of manic symptoms. RC9 scores have also been found to be correlated with behavioral activation in mental health and medical outpatients (Tellegen & Ben-Porath, 2008/2011). Burchett and Ben-Porath (2010) found that RC9 scores correlated with manic symptoms in a college student sample. L. C. Watson, Quilty, and Bagby (2010) compared the MMPI-2-RF scores of individuals diagnosed with Bipolar Disorder or Major Depression and found RC9 to be the best differential diagnostic indicator among the RC Scales.

Construct-relevant correlates have also been reported for RC9, including hostility, aggression, and antisocial features in a college counseling setting (Sellbom, Ben-Porath et al., 2006) and aggression in a sample of individuals in treatment for substance abuse (Forbey & Ben-Porath, 2007), in an outpatient community mental health sample (Tellegen et al., 2003), and in mental health and medical outpatients at a VA medical center (Tellegen & Ben-Porath, 2008/2011). Substantial correlations between RC9 and indexes of aggression have also been reported in a correctional setting (Forbey, Ben-Porath & Gartland, 2009), in a clinical sample and community-dwelling veterans (Simms et al., 2005), and in college student samples (Forbey & Ben-Porath, 2008; Sellbom & Ben-Porath, 2005). In a sample of domestic violence offenders, higher scores on RC9 were associated with lower confidence in offenders' ability to stop acting violently (Sellbom et al., 2008). Other correlates in this population included poorer treatment outcome and increased risk for recidivism (Sellbom et al., 2008). In a sample of law enforcement candidates, scores on RC9 were associated with subsequent use of excessive force (Sellbom, Fischler et al., 2007).

Correlates of RC9 in the personality and personality disorder domain include Narcissism, Manipulativeness, and Dominance/Social Potency (Handel & Archer, 2008, in psychiatric inpatients; Sellbom & Ben-Porath, 2005, in a college student sample; Simms et al., 2005, in a clinical setting and a sample of community-dwelling veterans). Some of the strongest personality correlates of RC9 are a low level on the Five Factor Model Agreeableness domain and low MPQ Harmavoidance (Sellbom & Ben-Porath, 2005). RC9 has also been found to be associated with psychopathy (Sellbom, Ben-Porath et al., 2005). Other personality correlates of RC9 include sensation seeking/behavioral fearlessness (Sellbom, Ben-Porath et al., 2005, in college students; Sellbom, Ben-Porath & Bagby, 2008b, in psychiatric patients; Simms et al., 2005, in a clinical setting and community-dwelling veterans) and disinhibition and impulsivity (Forbey & Ben-Porath, 2007, in individuals receiving treatment for substance abuse; Forbey & Ben-Porath, 2008, in college students; Forbey, Ben-Porath & Gartland, 2009, in prison inmates; Simms et al., 2005, in a clinical setting and a sample of community-dwelling veterans).

Summary

The construct targeted by RC9, hypomanic activation, represents a challenge for assessment devices such as the MMPI-2-RF because of the inherently transient nature of some of its core manifestations. Nevertheless, the correlates just summarized include many of the features of manic and hypomanic states cataloged in Kraepelin's (1921) nosology and captured in subsequent empirical studies as well as the two core temperamental traits identified by Kraepelin: aggression and overexcitation (i.e., activation). RC9 scores are not associated substantially with the expansive mood component of hypomania, which would instead be reflected in low scores on RC2, indicating the need (discussed in Chapter 8) to consider scores on multiple MMPI-2-RF scales in the process of differential diagnosis.

Most individuals with hypomanic personality traits do not go on to develop a full-fledged Bipolar Disorder, although it is associated with an increased risk for this diagnosis (cf. Kwapil, Miller, Zinser, Chapman, Chapman & Eckblad, 2000). Thus, as is the case with all the RC Scales, an elevated score on RC9 indicates a need to consider a *possible* diagnosis of Bipolar Disorder (by referencing the actual diagnostic criteria). However, the behavioral and personological correlates just listed are likely to apply.

General Summary

Following an exploratory test construction approach guided by advances in the fields of personality and psychopathology, and with access to methods and technology unavailable to Hathaway and McKinley, Tellegen identified and developed measures of nine psychological constructs representing the general factor and eight distinctive core components of the eight original Clinical Scales of the MMPI. The literature reviewed in this section shows that each of the constructs assessed by the RC Scales can be linked conceptually and empirically to a broad, contemporary literature. Their empirical correlates provide evidence of the construct validity of RC Scale scores as well as a foundation for generating empirically supported interpretations of MMPI-2-RF results.

This review has focused on the convergent validities of RC Scale scores. Although not delineated here, the literature cited also shows evidence of good discriminant properties for the RC Scales, reflecting the success of Tellegen's effort to address a fundamental shortcoming of the Clinical Scales: inadequate discriminant validity owing to the excessive intercorrelations between the scales (discussed earlier in this chapter).

As features of the constructs assessed by the RC Scales are delineated further, criterion validity–based interpretation of findings with these scales can increasingly be augmented with construct validity–based information in a manner consistent with Cronbach and Meehl's (1955) recommendations. Moreover, consistent with one of the goals for their development, the RC Scales are positioned to provide a link between basic and applied psychopathology and personality research. Because the items scored on the RC Scales are embedded within the full MMPI-2, hundreds of thousands of test protocols are available in a broad range of settings with diverse populations and can be used to study the constructs assessed by these scales as both dependent and independent variables.

APPRAISALS OF THE RESTRUCTURED CLINICAL SCALES

Appraisals of the MMPI and MMPI-2 in Chapter 1 of this volume included consideration of test use and research patterns and scholarly commentary. Because the RC Scales are embedded within the MMPI-2, it is not possible to determine the extent to which clinicians using the test rely on them in its interpretation. As evidenced by the literature reviewed in this chapter, a substantial body of empirical research on the RC Scales accumulated within the first few years following their introduction. Before turning to published appraisals, it might be instructive to consider whether and how the restructuring of the Clinical Scales addressed the criticisms and recommendations offered by reviewers of the original MMPI and its revision (discussed in detail in Chapter 1).

Loevinger (1972) and Jackson (1971), and later, Helmes and Reddon (1993), were very critical of the absence of a theoretical grounding for the selection of constructs and writing of items for the MMPI Clinical Scales. Although they conceded a lack of sufficient theoretical foundation at the time the scales were developed, Loevinger and Jackson both held that advances in the ensuing three decades had remedied this deficiency. They advocated that any effort to revise the scales begin essentially from scratch, targeting theoretically defined constructs for new scale construction. Tellegen's exploratory approach to restructuring the scales was different and more closely matched the recommendations of Norman (1972) and Meehl (1972).

Norman (1972) was very critical of profile interpretation based on heterogeneous (including invalid subtle items), overlapping, and otherwise highly intercorrelated (owing to a strong common factor) scales. The RC Scales address all these concerns. Although not ready to abandon the Kraepelinian nosological system, Meehl (1972) conceded the problems caused by scale heterogeneity (including subtle items) and acknowledged that it is difficult to argue against recommendations to factor analyze the Clinical Scales and identify distinctive components as targets for new scale construction—much the way Tellegen set about identifying the major distinctive core components of the Clinical Scales. The development of a separate measure of the common factor is consistent with the recommendations of Norman (1972) and Meehl (1972), and an emphasis on internal consistency conforms to the recommendations of all four authors.

Tellegen's approach to identifying the common MMPI factor was guided directly by a theoretical model linking personality, mood, and psychopathology—a conceptual framework that remains at the core of contemporary conceptualizations of mood and anxiety disorders. Indeed, all nine RC Scales can be linked conceptually and empirically to current models of personality and psychopathology. Consistent with Loevinger's, Norman's, and Jackson's recommendations, Tellegen made a clear decision to target continuous rather than taxonic constructs, although, as detailed by Meehl (1972), this does not preclude using the resulting scales to assess categorical phenomena.

Jackson's (1971) concerns about the impact of response styles, repeated later by Helmes and Reddon (1993), were discussed earlier in this chapter (and in Chapter 1), where a fundamental problem, the confound of psychopathology and undesirability, was noted, as was the fact that Jackson himself abandoned efforts to develop social desirability–free measures of psychopathology. Moreover, because social desirability measures, particularly the one created by Edwards (1957) and favored by Jackson, are themselves heavily saturated with demoralization (after all, demoralization itself is not desirable), empirical findings reported by Tellegen et al. (2006) show that RC Scale scores, by and large, are substantially less correlated with social desirability measures than are the Clinical Scales. Nonetheless, as discussed in the "Negative Appraisals" section later, adherents of a Jacksonian scale construction approach find fault with the failure to control for social desirability in the steps taken to restructure the Clinical Scales.

Published appraisals of the RC Scales can be divided into two general conclusions: positive and negative. As evident in the following review, authors of positive appraisals have based their conclusions on data analyses that included external criteria, whereas negative views have been based on beliefs about the nature of constructs assessed by the Clinical Scales or internal analyses limited to correlations between subsets of MMPI-2 items.

Positive Appraisals

The section delineating the RC Scales provides the first comprehensive empirically based review of these measures. Authors of specific investigations (limited in the following to those not involved in RC Scale development and initial validation research) have generally concluded that the RC Scales provide psychometrically sound, useful findings in a broad range of assessment types and settings. In mental health settings, Handel and Archer (2008) concluded that their "results generally replicate and support the findings from inpatient samples presented by Tellegen et al. (2003)" (p. 248). In a study of individuals diagnosed with PTSD and various comorbid disorders, Wolf et al. (2008) concluded that

the RCs demonstrated good psychometric properties and patterns of associations with other measures of psychopathology that correspond to current
theory regarding the structure of comorbidity. A notable advantage of the RCs
compared with the MMPI-2 [Clinical Scales] was their enhanced construct
validity and clinical utility in the assessment of comorbid internalizing and
externalizing psychopathology. (p. 340)

Reid and Carpenter (2009) concluded that the RC Scales "appear to capture meaningful characteristics of a substantial portion of hypersexual patients" (p. 184).

In medical settings, based on a comparison of patients with epileptic and pseudo-
nonepileptic seizures, Locke et al. (2010) concluded that "RC1 added significant
incremental validity to a set of demographic and medical history predictors" (p.
6). Using the same sample, Thomas and Locke (2010) conducted a series of sophisticated analyses of the psychometric properties of RC1 and concluded that "overall, the results indicate that the scale has strong psychometric properties. Clinical
researchers and practitioners should feel confident that the RC1 scale accurately
assesses the latent construct of somatization for individuals in the impaired range
of the distribution" (p. 24).

On the basis of a study conducted with a clinical sample and a sample of
community-dwelling veterans, Simms et al. (2005) concluded that "the results of
this study broadly suggest that the RC Scales represent a somewhat successful
attempt to improve on weaknesses often associated with the Clinical Scales while
clarifying the core constructs of each" (p. 355). Discussing their findings in a study
of genetic variation and covariation in the Clinical and RC Scales, Viken and Rose
(2007) commented, "From the standpoint of familial aggregation, little was lost by
using the much shorter RC Scales. . . . Correlations among the basic and Clinical
Scales [suggest] success in the RC goal of deriving more distinct and homogeneous
scales" (p. 846). On the basis of their investigation of the RC Scales with a sample
of young adults, Osberg et al. (2008) concluded that "the RC Scales demonstrated
good convergence with the Clinical Scale counterparts and were more distinctive
than the Clinical Scales" (p. 81). Discussing the results of their study of the RC
Scales with chronic pain patients, McCord and Drerup (2011) remarked that "the RC
Scales have great promise for improving the convergent and discriminant validity
of the MMPI" (p. 6). In a forensic setting, commenting on the results of analyses
of the RC Scales in a sample of individuals with varying levels of traumatic brain
injury (TBI) and effort, Thomas and Youngjohn (2010) concluded that "the MMPI-2
RC Scales can aid in the diagnosis of over-reported TBI symptomatology" (p. 1).

Two studies have compared the predictive validities of the RC Scales in African
Americans and Caucasians. On the basis of analyses conducted with a community
outpatient sample, Castro, Gordon, Brown, Anestis, and Joiner (2008) concluded
that "there is no indication of predictive bias in this sample" (p. 284). Using a sample
of veterans undergoing substance abuse treatment, Monnot et al. (2009) concluded
that "the RC Scales demonstrated strong correlations with diagnoses, however,
like other MMPI-2 scales examined in this study, they displayed a general trend of
predictive bias. . . . However most of these effects were small to modest (accounting

for 3%–5% of variance)" (p. 137). In all but one of the analyses where Monnot and colleagues found evidence of small to modest predictive bias, RC Scale scores underpredicted psychopathology for African Americans.

Negative Appraisals

A special issue of the *Journal of Personality Assessment* included several papers with criticisms of the RC Scales. Rogers, Sewell, Harrison, and Jordan (2006) analyzed an archival data set, and though they were able to replicate many of the scale development steps and findings reported by Tellegen et al. (2003), Rogers et al. (2006) expressed concern that clinically significant elevations on the RC Scales were found in only half the cases in their sample. However, closer examination of the sample made available to Rogers and colleagues for their analyses indicated that contrary to what they had been told, it included a large number of job applicants and child custody litigants who would not be expected to produce elevations on measures of psychopathology (Tellegen et al., 2006). Moreover, Tellegen et al. (2006) reported findings showing in multiple clinical and nonclinical samples that the RC Scales do not produce more profiles within normal limits than do the Clinical Scales. One important actual difference between the two sets of scales is that RC Scale profiles very often have smaller numbers of elevated scales, which is consistent with their improved discriminant properties.

Rogers et al. (2006) were also critical of Tellegen et al.'s (2003) failure to "consider adequately Jackson's (1970) second principle [of scale construction] involving suppression of response variance" (p. 145). Tellegen et al. (2006) discussed the rationale for doing so at length and reported findings showing that although this was not a goal of the restructuring effort, scores on the RC Scales are, in fact, less correlated with measures of social desirability than are Clinical Scale scores.

Nichols (2006) criticized the RC Scales for failing to retain "syndromal fidelity," drifting from the constructs assessed by the original Clinical Scales, and even from the ones targeted by the Seed Scales used in their development, failing to adequately capture the MMPI-2 common factor with the Demoralization Scale, and creating new measures that are largely redundant with existing MMPI-2 scales. Tellegen et al. (2006) provided detailed, empirically based responses to all these criticisms and noted the absence of validity data in Nichols's own analysis, which was based entirely on rational examination of item content and correlations between various subsets of MMPI-2 items.

Briefly, on the topic of syndromal fidelity, Tellegen et al. (2006) acknowledged that the RC Scales were not designed to individually measure complex, multivariate phenomena such as psychiatric diagnoses (a long-recognized major flaw of the Clinical Scales discussed earlier in this chapter) and showed that despite this, the Restructured Scales generally have substantially higher correlations with diagnoses than do the Clinical Scales. Tellegen et al. (2006) also noted that it has long been recognized that psychometric prediction of complex phenomena is best accomplished with multivariate assessment of the different elements of such constructs.

On the topic of construct drift, Tellegen et al. (2006) pointed out that the shift to more narrowly defined constructs was not accidental or haphazard (as implied by the term *drift*) and that the constructs assessed by the RC Scales represent the major distinctive core components of the Clinical Scales (delineated in detail in this chapter). Regarding measurement of the MMPI common factor, Tellegen et al. (2006) reported findings showing the superiority of RCd over the various alternatives Nichols proposed. Finally, regarding redundancy, Tellegen et al. (2006) acknowledged that it was certainly possible that one or more of the RC Scales would be very similar to an already existing MMPI-2 measure and that if this had occurred, those measures could have been adopted, instead of any redundant RC Scales. However, this turned out not to be the case. Moreover, it is a moot point insofar as the MMPI-2-RF is concerned because the scales with which Nichols thought the RC Scales were redundant are not scored on the restructured inventory.

Butcher, Hamilton, Rouse, and Cumella (2006) sought to demonstrate Nichols's point about construct drift by showing that RC3 (Cynicism) does not assess somatic complaints. As would be expected of a scale designed specifically not to measure this construct, Butcher et al. (2006) found that scores on RC3 were not correlated with other MMPI-2 measures of somatic complaints in an eating disorder treatment sample. By most standards, this study would more accurately be viewed as a demonstration of the discriminant validity of RC3 in that the authors found scores on the scale to be unrelated to a construct it was designed explicitly not to measure.

Finally, Caldwell (2006) argued that RC4 represents a good illustration of loss of syndromal fidelity in that it focuses on a considerably narrower construct (antisocial behavior) than its Clinical Scale counterpart, which was designed to measure psychopathy. Caldwell asserted that as a result, Clinical Scale 4 is a better measure of psychopathy, as measured by Hare's (2003) PCL-R or PCL-SV. In contrast with Caldwell's opinion, as discussed earlier in this chapter, Sellbom, Ben-Porath et al. (2007) reported finding that RC4 substantially outperformed Clinical Scale 4 in predicting PCL-SV scores in a sample of criminal defendants.

In several subsequent publications, some of the authors just cited repeated their criticisms of the RC Scales without consideration of the responses just noted.

Summary

Appraisals of the RC Scales based on external validity data have generally been quite positive. Nonetheless, like other psychometric devices, they are fallible measures, and the interpretive recommendations provided in the second part of this book are therefore intentionally conservative. For example, only empirical correlates that have been replicated across settings and samples are listed for the Substantive Scales of the MMPI-2-RF in the *Manual for Administration, Scoring, and Interpretation* (Ben-Porath & Tellegen, 2008/2011). In contrast, authors of negative appraisals of the RC Scales have to this point neglected to incorporate external validity findings into their analyses.

CHAPTER 3

Completing Development of the MMPI-2-RF: The Substantive Scales

The introduction of the RC Scales may stimulate additional MMPI-2 scale development. It may prove worthwhile to search for and measure distinctive core features of important MMPI-2 scales other than the MMPI-2 Clinical Scales, some of which may also be confounded with a strong Demoralization component. Investigations along these lines may lead to additional measures that are incrementally informative beyond the RC Scales. Through such efforts it may be possible eventually to capture the full range of attributes represented by the large body of MMPI-2 constructs with a set of new scales more transparent and effective than those currently available. (Tellegen, Ben-Porath, McNulty, Arbisi, Graham & Kaemmer, 2003, pp. 85–86)

As reflected in this quotation from the monograph that introduced them, the RC Scales were not intended to represent all the information available in the very rich MMPI-2 item pool. Rather, as discussed in Chapter 2, each Restructured Scale was designed to assess a major distinctive core component of an original Clinical Scale. Our[1] goal in completing the MMPI-2-RF was to produce a comprehensive set of measures representing the clinically significant substance of the entire MMPI-2 item pool.

Five additional sets of scales were developed to complete the MMPI-2-RF. Following previous efforts to identify a broad-based dimensional structure of personality and psychopathology, we conducted a series of factor analyses of the RC Scales, which led to the identification of three recognizable broad-band dimensions and the construction of Higher-Order Scales to assess them. We also developed more narrowly focused measures related to Clinical Scale components not captured by the RC Scales, RC Scale facets warranting separate measurement, and constructs assessable with the MMPI-2 items not represented directly in either the Clinical or RC Scales. These analyses produced 23 Specific Problems Scales and two Interest Scales. In addition, we sought to include in the test measures of the Personality Psychopathology Five (PSY-5; Harkness & McNulty, 1994), a dimensional model of personality disorder features that had already been studied extensively and provide a link to other dimensional models of normal and abnormal personality. Harkness and McNulty revised the MMPI-2 versions of these scales using the 338 items of the MMPI-2-RF to construct the five revised PSY-5 Scales. Finally, we sought to build on the solid foundation laid by the MMPI-2 Validity Scales by revising seven of the existing validity measures and adding a new one, yielding a set of eight Validity

Scales for the MMPI-2-RF. In 2011, a ninth Validity Scale was added. The MMPI-2-RF Validity Scales are described in Chapter 4.

As with the RC Scales, the starting point for the development of many of the additional substantive measures was the existing MMPI-2 scales. Like the RC Scales, the 33 measures described in this chapter can be linked to a broad contemporary literature, which, along with empirical findings reported in the *MMPI-2-RF Technical Manual* (Tellegen & Ben-Porath, 2008/2011) and in journal articles and with consideration of item content, made possible the delineation of the constructs assessed by these measures. The following sections describe the processes followed in developing the remaining Substantive Scales of the MMPI-2-RF and the products of these efforts.

HIGHER-ORDER SCALES

Search for a Structure of Personality

Investigators in the fields of personality and psychopathology have long sought to identify meaningful structural models to provide an organizing descriptive framework for psychological assessment and psychodiagnosis. Empirical efforts to discover such structures were greatly facilitated by Francis Galton's (1888) invention of the precursor to the correlation coefficient and the subsequent refinement of the procedure by his student Karl Pearson (Pearson & Filon, 1898). Heymans and Wiersma (1906) were the first to apply the Galton–Pearson correlational technique in an effort to uncover the structure of personality and its association with psychopathology. As detailed by Ben-Porath and Butcher (1991), these investigators constructed a 90-item rating scale and asked some 3,000 physicians to apply it to individuals they knew well. On the basis of correlational analyses of these ratings, the authors identified eight primary character traits they labeled *amorphous, apathetic, nervous, sentimental, sanguine, phlegmatic, choleric,* and *impassioned.* Relying on observations of correlations between the eight primary factors, Heymans and Wiersma (1906) delineated a higher-order structure consisting of constructs labeled *Activity, Emotionality,* and *Primary versus Secondary Function.* These constructs are remarkably similar to broad-band personality dimensions that have been labeled *Extraversion/Positive Emotionality, Neuroticism/Negative Emotionality,* and *Constraint.*

Heymans and Wiersma's (1906) approach as well as some of their items were subsequently revised and incorporated in similar efforts by Hoch and Amsden (1913) and Wells (1914), laying the foundation for Woodworth's (1920) Personal Data Sheet, described by Goldberg (1971) as the forerunner of all self-report personality inventories. Goldberg chronicled additional early developments, including those that entailed factor analyses of primary scales, which also yielded higher-order dimensions reminiscent of those first proposed by Heymans and Wiersma (1906).

Modern efforts to delineate the structure of adult personality and psychopathology have proceeded along two primary lines of research. In one, nonclinical measures were used to study the structure of "normal" personality. The other focused on delineating a higher-order structure of psychopathology measures.[2] Both lines of investigation converged on structures remarkably reminiscent of the ones identified by Heymans and Wiersma (1906).

Wiggins (1968) reviewed efforts to carve out a higher-order structure of normal personality inventories using the major instruments of the time: the Eysenck Personality Inventory (EPI; Eysenck & Eysenck, 1964), the 16PF (Cattell, 1965), the Guilford–Zimmerman Temperament Survey (Guilford, 1959), and the California Psychological Inventory (CPI; Gough, 1957). He observed, "If consensus exists within the realm of temperament structure, it does so with respect to the importance of the large, ubiquitous and almost unavoidable dimensions of extraversion and anxiety (neuroticism)" (Wiggins, 1968, p. 309). Although the authors of these measures used different terms and occasionally disagreed with each others' interpretations of the results of factor analytic studies (e.g., Eysenck, 1977; Guilford, 1977), these dimensions represent two of the three broad domains identified early on by Heymanns and Wiersma (1906): Activity and Emotionality. Their third dimension, Primary versus Secondary Function, was very similar to a third factor in Eysenck's model, Psychoticism (Eysenck & Eysenck, 1975). Eysenck's choice of label for his third factor was misleading. Examination of the content and empirical correlates reveals that this construct represents undercontrolled behavior.

A similar three-factor structure emerged from research on Tellegen's normal personality inventory, the Multidimensional Personality Questionnaire (MPQ; Tellegen, 1995/2003). The three higher-order factors of the MPQ are labeled *Positive Emotionality*,[3] *Negative Emotionality*, and *Constraint*. Tellegen and Waller (2008) reported the results of a joint factor analysis of the MPQ, Gough's CPI, and the Eysenck Personality Questionnaire (EPQ), showing that these three measures yield a highly congruent three-factor higher-order structure.

Efforts to delineate the higher-order structure of the MMPI began shortly after publication of the test. Commenting on a problem that plagued most of these studies from their inception, Wiggins (1968) noted, "The dangers implicit in factoring MMPI scales with overlapping items continues to be announced (Adams & Horn, 1965; Shure & Rogers, 1965) and ignored (Slater & Scarr, 1964)" (p. 314). Other sources of difficulty in this endeavor were reliance on the misleading labels of the Clinical Scales and assignment of alternative labels that also failed to accurately characterize the constructs that emerged from these investigations.

Results of these early studies and his own analyses led Welsh (1956) to identify two primary dimensions in the MMPI that he labeled *Anxiety* (A) and *Repression* (R). Examination of the items that Welsh identified as best markers of these two dimensions and his own descriptions of what they assess indicates that Welsh's chosen psychodynamically colored labels were misleading. He described A as "related to disability of a dysthymic and dysphoric nature in which anxiety is prominent" (p. 280) and a low level of R as accompanying "externalized and 'acting out' behavior" (p. 280). Kassebaum, Couch, and Slater (1959) replicated Welsh's findings with a broader set of MMPI scales. They also linked the higher-order dimensions they recovered to findings with other instruments (e.g., Eysenck, 1953; Guilford, 1939) and concluded that alternative rotations of the MMPI higher-order factors were consistent with findings on other measures.

Factor analytic studies of the Personality Assessment Inventory (PAI; Morey, 1991) have identified similar higher-order dimensions. Using data provided by a large sample of individuals tested in correctional settings, Ruiz and Edens (2008) identified two broad dimensions among the PAI's clinical scales. The authors labeled one dimension, marked by high loading on measures of anxiety, depression, somatization, Schizophrenia, and suicidal ideation, *Internalizing* and a second dimension, marked by high or unique loadings on measures of antisocial behavior, aggression, and drug and alcohol problems, *Externalizing*. Blais (2010) conducted a joint factor analysis of the PAI and the NEO Personality Inventory–Revised (NEO-PI-R; Costa & McCrae, 1992), a measure of normal personality, in a nonclinical sample and reported finding three broad dimensions reminiscent of the higher-order factors identified in the studies of normal personality inventories just described.

The finding and labeling of the higher-order dimensions of Internalizing and Externalizing link the adult psychopathology literature to a structure identified by Achenbach and Edelbrock (1978) as characterizing child and adolescent psychopathology. These authors observed that two broad-band dimensions, labeled alternatively *Overcontrolled/Internalizing Syndromes* and *Undercontrolled/Externalizing Syndromes*, had emerged from several factor analytically based lines of research. The starting point for these investigations was Achenbach's (1966) study of case history data obtained from 600 4- to 15-year-old boys and girls treated at inpatient and outpatient facilities. Behavioral problems reported in these case records were rated and factor analyzed, identifying several more narrowly focused constructs (e.g., aggressive behavior, phobias) as well as the two broad-band dimensions just mentioned. Achenbach and Edelbrock (1978) reviewed the results of 15 subsequent studies, conducted by various investigators with different measures and sources (i.e., case histories, self-report, teacher report, and parent report), and found that all identified a similar pair of higher-order dimensions.

A Common Structure of Normal Personality and Psychopathology

The findings just described point to considerable similarity and overlap in the higher-order dimensions identified with measures of normal personality and psychopathology. On the basis of a review of a broad body of similar research, O'Connor (2002) concluded that "the dimensional universes of normality and abnormality are apparently the same, at least according to data derived from contemporary assessment instruments" (p. 962). Encouraged by such findings, Markon, Krueger, and Watson (2005) sought to delineate the structure of normal and abnormal personality using an integrative hierarchical approach. On the basis of a meta-analysis of previous investigations of measures of normal and abnormal personality and new analyses conducted with a number of instruments, these authors concluded that a hierarchical structure, composed of two higher-order dimensions related to Negative and Positive Emotionality, could account for common variance among these measures. Markon and colleagues also found meaningful subordinate three-, four-, and five-factor structures. Consistent with findings in the normal personality domain, in the three-factor structure, the Negative Emotionality factor bifurcated into one that focuses more specifically on negative emotional experiences and a second dis-inhibition factor analogous to Tellegen's (1995/2003) higher-order Constraint factor.

In the psychopathology domain, investigators have converged on two broad dimensions labeled (following Achenbach & Edelbrock, 1978) *Internalizing* and *Externalizing*. These broad-band dimensions have been identified as likely responsible for high rates of comorbidity within the two domains (Krueger, Chentsova-Dutton, Markon, Goldberg & Ormel, 2003; Krueger, Markon, Patrick & Iacono, 2005) and also as playing an etiological role in the development of internalizing and external-izing disorders (Dick, 2007; Hicks, DiRago, Iacono & McGue, 2009; Krueger, Hicks, Patrick, Carlson, Iacono & McGue, 2002; Krueger & Markon, 2006; Vaidyanathan, Patrick & Cuthbert, 2009). Across the two domains, combinations of internalizing and externalizing dysfunction have been implicated in the development of complex psychiatric disorders such as Posttraumatic Stress Disorder (PTSD; Miller, Fogler, Wolf, Kaloupek & Keane, 2008), Psychopathy (Blonigen, Hicks, Krueger, Patrick & Iacono, 2005), and Borderline Personality Disorder (James & Taylor, 2008), and gender differences on the internalizing and externalizing dimensions have been found to play a role in gender differences in the prevalence of common mental disorders (Kramer, Krueger & Hicks, 2008).

A Missing Construct: Thought Dysfunction

A factor related to disordered thinking is conspicuously absent from the higher-order dimensions discussed thus far. Although understandable in the context of normal personality inventories, consistent failure of factor-analytic studies of the MMPI/MMPI-2 and PAI to identify a distinctive dimension related to thought dysfunction is puzzling, given the inclusion of relevant measures on both inventories.[4]

MMPI users and investigators have long been cognizant of the need to assess for thought dysfunction with the instrument. Meehl (1946), describing an early system for differential diagnosis based on profile patterns (i.e., code types), distinguished three broad domains of psychopathology assessable with the MMPI, labeled *Psychosis*, *Psychoneurosis*, and *Conduct Disorder*. His scheme for differentiating between the first two conditions involved primarily examination of the relative elevations of Clinical Scales 7 and 8. Thirty years later, H. A. Skinner and Jackson (1978) proposed an MMPI-based differential diagnostic model derived from existing code-type sys-tems and concluded that the test is most useful in identifying three broad domains of psychopathology: neurotic, psychotic, and sociopathic. Along similar lines, an effort to develop a shorter version of the MMPI informed by "decades of research and clinical lore" (p. 362) prompted Swanson et al. (1995) to construct three scales: Subjective Distress, Acting-Out, and Psychosis.

Thus, throughout the test's history, clinicians have either explicitly or implicitly used the MMPI to assess three broad types of psychopathology related to emo-tional, thought, and behavioral dysfunction (with the emotional domain at times bifurcating into emotional dysfunction and somatization), yet factor-analytic studies of the instrument consistently failed to identify a distinctive thought dysfunction dimension. Given the generalizability of this finding to other measures of abnormal and normal personality, the inadequacies of the MMPI Clinical Scales alone are insufficient to explain this failure. However, these shortcomings made an already complicated task even more difficult.

As just noted, Meehl's (1946) early approach to differentiating neurosis from psychosis (adopted in one form or another in all code-type schemes) involved examination of the relative elevation of Clinical Scales 7 and 8. Recall from Chapter 2 that in clinical settings, the correlation between these two scales hovers around .90, making it all but impossible for the two measures to define distinctive higher-order dimensions. Furthermore, considered in the context of the restructuring effort, the saturation of Clinical Scales 8 and 6 with demoralization variance rendered infeasible the discernment of a thought dysfunction–related higher-order dimension. This raised the possibility that improvements introduced with the RC Scales might yield a different outcome. Indeed, in two-factor-analytic studies of the RC Scales, the authors found a clearly differentiated thought dysfunction dimension marked by RC6 and RC8 (Hoelzle & Meyer, 2009; Sellbom, Ben-Porath & Bagby, 2008a). Sellbom and colleagues also identified higher-order dimensions of internalizing (marked by RCd, RC2, RC7) and externalizing (marked by RC4 and RC9). Hoelzle and Meyer (2009) identified the same dimensions as well as two more narrowly focused factors marked by single RC Scales (RC1 and RC3, respectively). Our own analyses, reported in detail by Tellegen and Ben-Porath (2008/2011), also indicated that the Restructured Scales conform to a higher-order structure reflective of the long-held code type–based practice of differentiating between emotional, thought, and behavioral dysfunction. Specifically, these analyses pointed to a clear higher-order structure, with the Emotional/Internalizing domain marked by RCd, RC2, and RC7; Thought Dysfunction by RC6 and RC8; and the Behavioral/Externalizing dimension by RC4 and RC9. These domains correspond to the three most commonly occurring Clinical Scale code types: 27-72, 68-86, and 49-94, respectively.

Summary

Converging lines of research have identified two broad domains of psychopathology, internalizing and externalizing, in the child and adolescent psychopathology literature and, more recently, in studies of adult psychopathology. A three-factor structure, dating back to the early work of Heymans and Wiersma (1906), bifurcates the internalizing domain into Negative Emotionality/Neuroticism and Positive Emotionality/Extraversion. With the exception of recent studies of the RC Scales, factor-analytic studies of the MMPI and PAI have failed to isolate a thought dysfunction domain, although code type–based approaches to MMPI/MMPI-2 interpretation have long recognized its importance and, in particular, the need to differentiate emotional dysfunction from thought dysfunction.

Developing the Higher-Order Scales

Rationale and Objectives

An inherent problem with code type–based interpretation is its mutually exclusive nature. By definition, a test taker cannot produce both a 27-72 and a 68-86 code type, yet it is quite possible for an individual to present with significant dysfunction in both these domains. It was our goal to determine whether development of dimensional measures of these higher-order constructs was feasible and would yield scales that conform to expectations for measures of these constructs. To be effective, the resulting measures would need to be only moderately correlated with each other and associated distinctively with a broad range of psychopathology symptoms, personality characteristics, and behavioral proclivities.

Method

The combined items of the RC Scales that had been found to be the primary markers of the three higher-order factors (i.e., RCd, RC2, RC4, RC6, RC7, RC8, and RC9) were factor analyzed in the samples used to derive the RC Scales. From each of these item-level analyses, a rotated three-factor solution and corresponding factor scores were obtained. Next, the three factor scores were correlated with each of the 567 MMPI-2 items in each of the derivation samples. Finally, a set of items was identified for each scale by selecting from the MMPI-2 item pool diverse and distinctive item markers associated statistically and conceptually with one, but not the other, two higher-order factors.

Outcome

The three resulting scales were labeled *Emotional/Internalizing Dysfunction* (EID), a measure of difficulties in the domain of mood and affect; *Thought Dysfunction* (THD), a measure of disordered thinking; and *Behavioral/Externalizing Dysfunction* (BXD), which assesses problems associated with undercontrolled behavior. For EID, most, but not all, of the items selected are scored on one of the three RC Scales that mark this dimension: RCd, RC2, or RC7. For THD, all the selected items are scored on either RC6 or RC8. All but one of the items selected for BXD are scored on RC4 or RC9.

The three nonoverlapping Higher-Order (H-O) Scales provide dimensional measures related to the basic categorical distinctions provided by the classical MMPI 27-72, 68-86, and 49-94 code types, respectively. However, in contrast with the mutually exclusive nature of code-type-based interpretation, a dimensional measurement model allows for the identification of dysfunction in more than one of these broad domains (indicated by clinically elevated scores on more than one of the Higher-Order Scales) and can provide an indication of the relative prominence of problems, as reflected by the relative elevation of the H-O Scales. The scales also provide a link to a rich and expanding literature on internalizing and externalizing psychopathology.

Psychometric Findings with the Higher-Order Scales

In the *MMPI-2-RF Technical Manual*, Tellegen and Ben-Porath (2008/2011) report reliability estimates for the H-O Scales that range from .69 (THD) to .91 (BXD) in the normative sample and from .79 (BXD) to .95 (EID) in several clinical samples. The associated standard errors of measurement (expressed in T-score values) range from three to six across settings, reflecting overall good reliability of H-O Scale scores in clinical and nonclinical samples. Tellegen and Ben-Porath also report intercorrelations between the H-O Scales in the normative and several clinical samples. These range from .18 to .38, with a median of .30, reflecting moderate covariation consistent with the goals and expectations for these scales.

Tellegen and Ben-Porath (2008/2011) report empirical correlate data for the test based on samples of individuals receiving outpatient and inpatient mental health and substance abuse treatment services, medical patients, criminal defendants and civil disability claimants, and college students. Various types of criteria were available for these analyses, including extensive ratings provided by therapists and intake workers at an outpatient community mental center, systematic record reviews conducted at two psychiatric inpatient facilities and a forensic pretrial assessment center, and various commonly used self-report measures for mental health and medical outpatients, individuals receiving substance abuse treatment, disability claimants, and college students. For the latter, scores on Tellegen's (1995/2003) MPQ served as the criteria, providing information about how the H-O Scales map onto a hierarchical normal personality model discussed earlier.

As would be expected, a broad range of clinically relevant correlates was identified for each of the H-O Scales. Following is a summary of the H-O Scale correlates identified in these analyses.

Emotional/Internalizing Dysfunction (EID)

In both men and women assessed at the outpatient community mental health center, higher scores on EID were associated with being described by intake workers as sad and depressed and by their therapists as sad, insecure, depressed, pessimistic, lonely, tearful, experiencing suicidal ideation, self-punishing, feeling inferior, feeling hopeless and helpless, feeling like a failure, self-degrading, self-doubting, being overly sensitive to criticism, not coping well with stress, anxious, experiencing sleep disturbance, overwhelmed, feeling that life is a strain, and complaining of fatigue. Empirical correlates of EID that replicated across gender and settings in the psychiatric inpatients included being described by the admitting psychiatrist as depressed, having sleep difficulties, having low energy, experiencing suicidal ideation, having made a recent suicide attempt, being diagnosed with a depressive disorder on admission, and being prescribed antidepressant medication. In both mental health and medical outpatient men tested at a Veterans Administration (VA) facility, EID scores were correlated substantially with measures of depression, anxiety, anger, behavioral inhibition, and somatization. In the sample of individuals in treatment for substance abuse, higher EID scores were associated with measures of depression, hopelessness, anger, and hostility. In the sample of criminal defendants, scores on EID were correlated in both women and men with dysphoric mood, being diagnosed with a depressive disorder, being prescribed psychotropic medication (antidepressants, in particular), a history of having been physically abused, a history of having attempted suicide, and having been in outpatient mental health treatment. In the disability claimants, higher EID scores were associated with measures of dysphoria, inadequacy, despondence, depression, anxiety, obsessive worry, and emotional features associated with PTSD. On the MPQ, as expected, EID scores were associated positively with Negative Emotionality and stress reactivity and negatively with Positive Emotionality and well-being.

Thought Dysfunction (THD)

Because individuals with thought disorders were referred to a different agency, very few empirical correlates were found for THD at the outpatient community mental health facility, with only one—being viewed by the therapist as low in achievement orientation—replicating across gender. By contrast, in the psychiatric inpatient samples, being admitted for treatment of psychosis, presenting with delusions and hallucinations, being prescribed antipsychotic medication, being diagnosed with Schizophrenia, and being discharged on antipsychotic medication were correlated with THD scores in more than one of the three available samples. In the mental health and medical outpatient VA samples, THD scores were correlated substantially with scores on the Magical Ideation and Perceptual Aberration scales (discussed in Chapter 2 in the context of RC8). In the sample of criminal defendants, higher scores on THD were correlated for both genders with being prescribed antipsychotic medication, a history of suicide attempts, and lower IQ scores and clinician estimates of intellectual functioning. In the disability claimants, THD scores were associated for both genders with measures of psychosis and trauma-related dissociation. On the MPQ, THD scores were correlated in both genders with being alienated and prone to imaginative and altered states.

Behavioral/Externalizing Dysfunction (BXD)

In both the men and women assessed at the outpatient community mental health center, higher BXD scores were associated with being described by intake workers as having been arrested in the past and with having a past suicide attempt and being diagnosed at intake with substance use and Antisocial Personality disorders. BXD scores were correlated in both genders with therapists' ratings on anger, aggression, antisocial behavior, family problems, having difficulty trusting others, being resentful, having stormy interpersonal relationships, being self-indulgent, being power oriented and overbearing in interpersonal relationships, exercising poor judgment, and being excitable and impulsive. In the psychiatric inpatients, higher BXD scores were associated with being intoxicated on admission, and recent drug or alcohol use in more than one sample, and a history of violence and involvement with the criminal justice system in the VA sample. In the mental health and medical outpatient samples, BXD scores were associated with measures of anger and substance abuse. In the substance abuse treatment sample, higher scores on BXD were associated with measures of aggression, anger, and substance abuse. In the sample of criminal defendants, BXD scores were correlated in both genders with a history of school truancy, being arrested and placed on probation as a juvenile, violent behavior, abuse of alcohol and various drugs, having attempted suicide in the past, and diagnoses of substance use and Antisocial Personality disorders. In the disability claimant sample, BXD scores were associated for both genders with trauma exposure and substance abuse. On the MPQ, BXD scores were correlated positively with aggression and negatively with the higher-order constraint factor.

Summary

The empirical correlates just listed illustrate that scores on each of the H-O Scales are associated with a broad range of construct-relevant criteria, as would be expected of broad-band measures of psychopathology and personality. The distinctive nature of these correlates, reflecting very limited cross-scale overlap, illustrates the discriminant validity of the scales. The psychopathology symptoms, personality characteristics, and behavioral proclivities represented by these correlates are consistent with features of the targeted constructs that have been identified in the literature. These findings indicate good construct validity of the H-O Scales, providing a link between the MMPI-2-RF and current perspectives on psychopathology, which include recognition of the association between psychopathology and personality and the hierarchical nature of psychopathology (Markon et al., 2005), with broad dimensional constructs accounting for phenotypic comorbidity and genotypic commonalities.

The EID, THD, and BXD correlates are also quite consistent with those identified previously for the 27-72, 68-86, and 49-94 Clinical Scale code types, respectively, providing a dimensional measurement perspective on these clinically relevant phenomena.

SPECIFIC PROBLEMS AND INTEREST SCALES

Rationale and Objectives

Our goal in developing the Specific Problems and Interest Scales was to augment the RC and H-O Scales with measures needed to derive a comprehensive instrument that assesses the broad range of constructs measurable with the MMPI-2 item pool. Several types of constructs were targeted in developing these scales. First, as described in Chapter 2, in the process of developing the RC Scales, Tellegen constructed Seed Scales for Clinical Scales 5 and 0, although final RC Scales were not derived for these measures because they do not focus on psychopathology. Development of measures of the distinctive constructs associated with these scales would accomplish the goal of canvassing the full range of domains assessed with the MMPI-2.

A second set of constructs targeted for further scale development emerged from Tellegen's factor analyses of the original Clinical Scales (described in Chapter 2, in

Step 2 of deriving the RC Scales). Several of these analyses identified more than one distinctive component. However, only one was deemed the major distinctive component of a scale and was targeted for the restructuring effort. For example, analyses of Clinical Scale 3 identified distinctive demoralization, somatization, and cynicism components (assessed with RCd, RC1, and RC3, respectively) as well as a set of items related to social anxiety, a construct not represented by the RC Scales. These "excess" components of the heterogeneous Clinical Scales were also candidates for further scale development.

A third set of targeted constructs reflected the broader scope of some RC Scales. Although clearly less heterogeneous than the Clinical Scales, some of the RC Scales are multifaceted, suggesting the potential utility of developing more narrowly focused scales targeting subdomains of these measures. For example, RC4 contains items related to juvenile misconduct, substance abuse, and family difficulties, all of which are related conceptually and empirically to the targeted construct of antisocial behavior, but it may also be helpful to assess each of these constructs separately with more focused scales. RC7 assesses a fairly broad range of dysfunctional negative emotions (related to anxiety, anger, and fear) perhaps also worthy of separate assessment. Thus, RC Scale facets that may warrant separate, more narrowly focused assessments were also targeted for further scale development.

A fourth set of constructs considered for further scale development represented clinically significant attributes found in the MMPI-2 item pool but not represented (directly) by either the Clinical or RC Scales. For example, the MMPI-2 item pool includes a number of items that describe suicidal ideation or attempts. These items were added to the MMPI-2 as part of the Restandardization Project and therefore are not scored on any of the Clinical Scales. And although current suicidal ideation and recent suicide attempts are correlated with scores on RCd, these items are not scored on this scale either. Nevertheless, we sought to include them on a possible restructured inventory and explored the development of a scale to do so. To identify similar possibilities, we examined the content of all the scales included in the MMPI-2 manual as well as several prominent research scales. A number of the MMPI-2 Content Component Scales (e.g., Multiple Fears, Suicidal Ideation) were particularly helpful in this context.

Development

Construction of the Specific Problems and Interest Scales followed an iterative process using methods similar to those employed in developing the RC Scales. As was the case with the latter, it was not possible to follow a simple recipe in these analyses. Judgment calls were made throughout the process, with an added final step designed to ensure that the resulting measures successfully assessed the targeted constructs.

First, to minimize the contribution of demoralization variance to scores on the additional measures, a set of items representing each of the targeted constructs was factor analyzed, along with the demoralization items used in constructing the RC Scales (see Chapter 2). Items with excessive demoralization loadings were dropped from further analyses. Exceptions were made for scales that targeted constructs related conceptually or empirically to demoralization (e.g., suicidal ideation).

Next, Seed Scales were developed by further deleting from the item lists identi-fied in Step 1 items that were too highly correlated with any of the other item sets derived in the first step. In a third step, correlations were calculated between the Seed Scales and the 567 items of the MMPI-2 (except those scored on a given scale), and items were added to a scale if they were sufficiently correlated with the seed for that scale, minimally correlated with the other seeds, and related conceptually to the targeted construct. Next, in an effort to maximize the reliabilities of the resulting scales, some of which were quite short (owing to the constraints of the item pool), item analyses were conducted with the scales that emerged from Step 3, and any item that reduced the internal consistency of a scale was dropped.

Finally, empirical correlates were examined with a number of available data sets used later in the validation analyses reported in the *MMPI-2-RF Technical Manual*. Only scales for which we found meaningful empirical correlates were included in the final set of Specific Problems and Interest Scales.

Unlike the H-O and RC Scales, development of the Specific Problems Scales was an iterative process. The first round of additional scale construction yielded 14 measures. Further examination of the MMPI-2 item domain resulted in the addition of three scales. Preliminary examination of external validity data for the 17 scales provided encouraging findings, and this provisional set of scales was presented at the annual MMPI-2 Research Symposium (Tellegen & Ben-Porath, 2005). On the basis of feedback received from symposium attendees and additional analyses, three more scales were added, yielding a preliminary list of 20 scales designed to complement the RC Scales.

The list of 20 scales, including representative items for each, was sent to 14 ex-pert MMPI-2 researchers and users for review. The experts were informed of our goal for the MMPI-2-RF of representing the clinically significant substance of the MMPI-2 item pool with a comprehensive set of psychometrically adequate measures and including in the revised inventory the RC Scales, a revised set of Personality Psychopathology Five (PSY-5) Scales (described later), and possibly the 20 scales described in the materials they received. They were asked whether any of the large number of existing MMPI-2 scales contained clinically significant content that might be lacking adequate representation by the RC, PSY-5, and 20 additional scales. If they answered affirmatively, they were asked to identify the relevant MMPI-2 scales and to describe the item content of the scales in question. Our colleagues Paul Arbisi and Jack Graham also provided very helpful input regarding this preliminary list.

On the basis of feedback provided by the reviewers and others who subsequently examined the scales, we conducted additional analyses that ultimately yielded the set of 25 MMPI-2-RF scales that are the subject of this section.

Outcome

The scales derived by this process are organized according to the areas they assess, with 23 designated as Specific Problems Scales and 2 as Interest Scales. These 25 scales are nonoverlapping and relatively short, and as discussed in the next section, some of the shorter scales yield comparatively low reliability estimates. The extensive empirical correlates for these scales (see Appendix A of the *MMPI-2-RF Technical Manual*) provide evidence of validity for all 25 scales, which, as mentioned, was the determining factor in deciding to include them on the instrument.

Although some of the Specific Problems Scales can be linked conceptually to facets of the RC Scales, they are not subscales analogous to the Harris–Lingoes or Content Component Scales of the MMPI-2. A critical difference is that most of the Specific Problems Scales include items that are not scored on related RC Scales. An important implication of this distinction is that Specific Problems Scale scores can be interpreted regardless of the test taker's scores on related RC Scales. This feature of the Specific Problems Scales is highlighted and illustrated in Chapter 8.

Specific Problems Scales

The 23 Specific Problems Scales are organized into five domains identified through correlational analyses with the H-O and RC Scales.

Somatic/Cognitive Scales

Constructs

The first scale in this set, Malaise (MLS), targets one of the multiple constructs embedded within the item pool of original Clinical Scale 3. The items scored on this scale, all of which were scored on the Harris–Lingoes Lassitude/Malaise (Hy3) scale, describe an overall sense of physical debilitation and poor health. Bigos et al. (1991) reported that in a large sample of employees of the Boeing company, those who scored higher on Scale 3 were more likely to report a back injury at some point later in their careers, and Fordyce, Bigos, Battie, and Fisher (1992) later clarified that the items scored on Hy3 were the strongest predictors of this outcome. Gatchel, Polatin, and Kinney (1995) found higher scores on Scale 3 to be associated with a reduced likelihood of return to work following back injury, a finding replicated later by Vendrig (1999). As with the Boeing study, Vendrig, Derksen, and de May (1999) later clarified that Hy3 was the best predictor of this negative outcome.

Malaise has also been hypothesized and found to play a role in various unexplained medical conditions associated with somatoform psychopathology. For example, Aragona, Tarsitani, De Nitto, and Inghilleri (2008) found that a combination of MMPI-2 items scored on RC1 and MLS on the MMPI-2-RF best differentiated individuals diagnosed with Pain Disorder from individuals experiencing pain with an identified somatic origin. Along the same lines, Fordyce (1998) emphasized the need to distinguish between pain, suffering, and disability in chronic pain patients. Priebe, Fakhoury, and Henningsen (2008) found that perceived functional incapacity (a construct very similar to Malaise as assessed by the MLS scale) was the primary characteristic of Chronic Fatigue Syndrome, another somatic condition that frequently manifests in medically unexplained symptoms.

The next three Somatic/Cognitive Scales, Gastrointestinal Complaints (GIC), Head Pain Complaints (HPC), and Neurological Complaints (NUC), assess specific types of somatic symptom reports. As discussed in Chapter 1, the MMPI was designed to be used in a medical setting with general medical patients as well as individuals with psychiatric disorders. Moreover, two of the original Clinical Scales targeted Somatoform Disorders marked by unexplainable physical symptoms. As a result, the MMPI and MMPI-2 include a relatively large number of items that describe specific somatic symptoms associated with somatoform conditions. It is therefore not surprising that these scales represent three of the four types of somatic complaints (pain, gastrointestinal, and pseudoneurological symptoms) required for a diagnosis of Somatization Disorder in *DSM-IV* (American Psychiatric Association, 1994) and, as discussed in Chapter 2, likely to be required for a Chronic Somatic Symptoms Disorder in *DSM-5* (Dimsdale & Creed, 2009). The fourth type of complaint (sexual) is not represented adequately in the MMPI-2 item pool to yield a separate measure.

A final scale in this set, Cognitive Complaints (COG), was developed by analyzing items scored on two of the Harris–Lingoes subscales for Clinical Scale 8: Lack of Ego Mastery Cognitive and Lack of Ego Mastery Conative. These items (including some scored on both subscales) describe various cognitive complaints related to memory, attention, and concentration. COG was added to the set of Somatic Scales based on correlational analyses revealing considerable covariation with these measures as well as a literature reflecting significant co-occurrence of somatic and cognitive complaints, for example, following mild traumatic brain injury (Stulemeijer, Vos, Bleijenberg & van der Werf, 2007), stroke (Duits, Munnecom, van Heugten & Oostenbrugge, 2008), and seizure (Velissaris, Wilson, Newton, Berkovic & Saling, 2009). Cognitive complaints can also occur without a clear somatic or other origin and without concomitant evidence of impaired cognitive functioning. The ubiquity of this phenomenon, coupled with difficulty diagnosing individuals who present with unexplained cognitive complaints (e.g., often they do not meet diagnostic criteria for Somatoform Disorders), led Delis and Wetter (2007) to propose a new diagnosis, Cogniform Disorder, for these conditions.

Psychometric Findings

Reliability data reported in the *MMPI-2-RF Technical Manual* (Tellegen & Ben-Porath, 2008/2011) indicate that scores on the Somatic/Cognitive Scales are adequately reliable, with test–retest correlations ranging from .54 (NUC) to .82 (MLS) and internal consistency estimates ranging from .52 on NUC in the normative men to .69 (GIC, COG) in the normative women and .71 (GIC) to .83 (COG) in clinical settings. The lower reliability estimates in the normative sample are a function of the restricted range of scores on these scales in nonclinical settings. This is reflected in comparable standard errors of measurement (ranging from four to eight T-score units) in the normative and clinical samples. Intercorrelations within the somatic/cognitive scales range for the most part in the .20s to .30s in the normative sample and from the .40s to .62 in the clinical samples, with the correlation between MLS and COG consistently being highest.

Correlate data reported by Tellegen and Ben-Porath (2008/2011) for men and women at an outpatient community mental health center indicate that MLS scores were associated with preoccupation with being in poor health, presenting with multiple somatic complaints, being described by their therapists as hypochondriacal, and complaining of sleep disturbance and of fatigue and low energy. In psychiatric inpatients, MLS scores were associated with indications of low energy and sleep disturbances in all three samples included in the analyses. In a sample of forensic disability claimants, MLS scores were associated with fatigue, despondency, sexual dysfunction, depression, and pain in both the men and women included in the analyses. In two VA outpatient samples (one consisting of mental health patients, the other of medical patients), scores on MLS were substantially correlated with scores on a screener for Somatoform Disorders (Janca et al., 1995).

GIC scores were correlated with preoccupation with health problems in both men and women in the outpatient community mental health center, reduced appetite in both men and women treated in a tertiary inpatient psychiatric facility, higher scores on a screener for Somatoform Disorders in medical and mental outpatients at a VA facility, and gastric complaints and Somatic Depression in both the men and women in the disability claimant sample. HPC scores were associated with being preoccupied with poor physical health and presenting with multiple somatic complaints for both men and women in the outpatient community mental health center, chronic pain complaints in all three psychiatric inpatient samples and headache complaints in two of the three samples, scores on a screener for Somatoform Disorders in medical and mental health VA outpatients, and head pain–related complaints in the men and women of the disability claimant sample. NUC scores were associated for both men and women in the outpatient community mental health center sample with difficulty concentrating, being preoccupied with health problems, having multiple somatic complaints, and being described by their therapists as hypochondriacal. They were substantially correlated with scores on a screener for Somatoform Disorders in the VA medical and mental health outpatient samples, with complaining of health-related difficulties in a substance abuse treatment sample, and with complaints about neurological and sensory-motor dysfunction in the men and women of the disability claimant sample.

Scores on COG were associated with difficulty concentrating, preoccupation with physical health concerns, and being diagnosed with depression in the men and women of the outpatient community mental health center; memory complaints and being prescribed antidepressant medication in all three psychiatric inpatient samples; scores on a screener for Somatoform Disorders in the VA outpatient mental health and medical patient samples; and memory complaints in the men and women of the disability claimant sample.

In studies published since the release of the MMPI-2-RF, Gervais, Ben-Porath, and Wygant (2009) found that scores on COG were strongly associated with subjective cognitive and emotional complaints, but, as intended, they were not associated with actual cognitive deficits. Forbey, Lee, and Handel (2010) found COG scores to be correlated with scores on the Cognitive Failures Questionnaire (Broadbent, Cooper, Fitzgerald & Parkers, 1982) in a college student sample. Locke et al. (2010) found that scores on RC1 and NUC were best able to differentiate between individuals experiencing epileptic and nonepileptic seizures on an epilepsy monitoring unit.

Internalizing Scales

Constructs

The nine Internalizing Specific Problems Scales can be divided into two subsets, four measures of constructs associated (both conceptually and statistically) with demoralization and five associated similarly with Negative Emotionality. As noted in Chapter 2, of the nine RC Scales, RCd shows the strongest association with current suicidal ideation and recent suicide attempts. It is therefore not surprising that all the demoralization-related Specific Problems Scales are associated with suicide risk factors. The first of these, Suicidal/Death Ideation (SUI), consists of items directly related to suicide and preoccupation with death. Wenzel, Brown, and Beck (2009) offer definitions for various suicide-related terms, and in the nomenclature, they propose two of the SUI items represent suicidal ideation and a third would qualify as a suicidal act. The importance of inquiring about suicide-related thoughts is highlighted by Wingate, Joiner, Walker, Rudd, and Jobes (2004), who, based on a review of the empirical literature, concluded that "patients' own self report of suicidal symptoms deserves considerable attention within the suicide assessment framework. Unless there are clear reasons to the contrary, self report regarding suicide potential should be a major source of data" (p. 663). Glassmire, Stolberg, Greene, and Bongar (2001) found that some individuals willing to endorse suicide-related MMPI-2 items do not acknowledge these experiences in face-to-face interviews, underscoring the importance of incorporating self-report measures when obtaining information about possible suicidal thoughts.

The second demoralization-related Specific Problems Scale, Helplessness/Hopelessness (HLP), includes items keyed to convey pessimism about one's future prospects and the ability to improve them through self-change. The constructs of helplessness and hopelessness have figured prominently in the suicide risk assessment literature. On the basis of a meta-analysis of the literature on the Beck Hopelessness Scale (BHS; Beck, Weissman, Lester & Trexler, 1974), McMillan, Gilbody, Beresford, and Neilly (2007) concluded that the test is useful in identifying individuals at high risk for suicide and nonfatal self-harm. More broadly, hopelessness, specifically negative expectations for the future, has been implicated as a risk factor for depressive and possibly also anxiety disorders (Miranda, Fontes & Morroquin, 2008; C. B. Williams, Galanter, Dermatis & Schwartz, 2008). Consistent with the notion that demoralization-related depression may be less responsive to antidepressant medication than is Anhedonic Depression (discussed in Chapter 2), Papakostas, Crawford, Scalia, and Fava (2007) found that higher levels of hopelessness were associated with nonresponsiveness to fluoxetine in patients diagnosed with a major depressive disorder. Also within the mood disorder domain, hopelessness has been implicated in Bipolar Disorder in general and in different phases of the disorder (Valtonen et al., 2009). Finally, hopelessness and helplessness have also been identified as playing a role in various medical conditions, including hypertension (Stern, Dhanda & Hazuda, 2009), other forms of cardiovascular disease (Pedersen, Denollet, Erdman, Serruys & van Domburg, 2009), and metabolic syndrome (Valtonen et al., 2008).

The next measure of Internalizing dysfunction within the subset of demoralization-linked scales, Self-Doubt (SFD), is made up of items that describe low self-esteem and a sense of being inferior to others. The construct assessed by this scale is closely linked to the one measured by the final scale in this subset, Inefficacy (NFC), which consists of items keyed to convey an inability to make important decisions or achieve one's goals, particularly when facing crises or difficulties. Conceptual and empirical links between the self-doubt and inefficacy constructs have been proposed and demonstrated by Judge, Erez, Bono, and Thoresen (2002), who found that a single trait (analogous to demoralization) could account for variance in both these constructs (as well as locus of control). However, each was also found to predict relevant criteria in a discriminantly valid manner. Lightsey, Burke, Ervin, Henderson, and Lee (2006) similarly found substantial covariation between self-esteem and self-efficacy and concluded that the two constructs are also distinct, though self-efficacy may play a role in the development of self-esteem.

Focusing specifically on self-doubt or low self-esteem, Neiss, Stevenson, Legrand, Iacono, and Sedikides (2009) reported data showing that self-esteem, depression, and Negative Emotionality covary as a function of genetic influences, and Orth, Robins, Trzesniewski, Maes, and Schmitt (2009) reported that strong cross-sectional correlations between low self-esteem and depression reflect a vulnerability to depression associated with premorbid self-doubt. Underscoring the importance of assessing self-doubt as part of a comprehensive psychological evaluation, Bhar, Ghahramanlou-Holloway, Brown, and Beck (2008) found that low self-esteem was a risk factor for suicidal ideation when controlling for depressed mood (i.e., demoralization) and hopelessness. Self-doubt has also been implicated as a risk factor for Borderline and Avoidant Personality disorders (Lynum, Wilberg & Karterud, 2008), eating disorders (Dunkley & Grilo, 2007), and PTSD (Kashdan, Uswatte, Steger & Julian, 2006).

Research in the area of self-efficacy distinguishes between general self-efficacy, defined by Bandura (1994) as "people's beliefs about their capabilities to produce designated levels of performance that exercise influence over events that affect their lives" (p. 71), which, according to Bandura (2001), is the foundation of human agency, and self-efficacy with respect to more narrowly defined areas of functioning. Wu (2009) evaluated the factorial stability of general self-efficacy in 25 countries and found that a single latent factor best accounted for the data in all. The NFC Scale is a measure of general rather than domain-specific efficacy.

The next five Internalizing measures are all linked conceptually and empirically to the Negative Emotionality domain, assessed by RC7. The first, Stress/Worry (STW), includes items that describe experiencing stress and nervousness, time pressure, and being worry prone. Excessive worry (also termed *apprehensive expectation*) is described as the essential feature of Generalized Anxiety Disorder (GAD) in the *DSM-IV*. Investigators have sought to determine whether a related cognitive process, rumination, can be distinguished from worry and whether differentiating between these two phenomena, both of which are marked by repetitive thought, may assist in distinguishing between cognitive aspects of anxiety and depression. Watkins, Moulds, and Mackintosh (2005) found no differences between worry and rumination in terms of the cognitive strategies and appraisals they entail and concluded that the two processes can be distinguished only in terms of content. Worry thoughts were more concerned with the future and less concerned with the past than were ruminative thoughts. Hughes, Alloy, and Cogswell (2008) found that worry and rumination overlap in their associations with depression and anxiety symptoms, and that rumination in particular appears to play a role in the overlap of the two disorders. The rumination measures used by these investigators include items that in the MMPI-2-RF scheme would be viewed as measures of demoralization, suggesting that the construct assessed by STW is associated with both demoralization and Negative Emotionality.

The next Internalizing measure in the Negative Emotionality domain is Anxiety (AXY), a relatively brief scale made up of items that describe pervasive anxiety marked by near-daily experiences of fright and nightmares. Reiss and McNally (1985) differentiated between anxiety expectancy, an associative learning process in which the individual learns that a given stimulus arouses anxiety or fear, and anxiety sensitivity, an individual-differences variable involving the belief that anxiety experiences cause illness, embarrassment, or additional anxiety. The AXY items reflect a combination of both the expectation of frequent experiences of anxiety and anticipation that their impact will be pronounced. Anxiety sensitivity has been implicated in particular in PTSD (cf. Marshall, Miles & Stewart, 2010). Keane, Taylor, and Penk (1997) noted that although PTSD, GAD, and Major Depression manifest substantial phenotypic overlap, clinicians are readily able to differentiate these disorders on the basis of evidence that includes reexperiencing threatening events both while awake and asleep, and heightened arousal, which would be indicated by the report of pervasive anxiety symptoms as reflected in the AXY items.

The following Internalizing measure on the Negative Emotionality cluster, Anger Proneness (ANP), consists of items that describe becoming easily angered, irritable, and impatient when interacting with others and being overwhelmed with anger. Drawing from the work of Spielberger and colleagues (e.g., Spielberger, Jacobs, Russell & Crane, 1983) and Novaco (1994), Eckhardt, Norlander, and Deffenbacher (2004) drew distinctions between hostility, an interpersonal attitude (measured on the MMPI-2-RF by RC3); anger, an affective experience; and aggression, a behavioral construct assessed on the MMPI-2-RF by a similarly named externalizing Specific Problems Scale. Scarpa and Raine (1997) noted that the affective experience of anger does not always lead to aggressive behavior and that aggression and violence do not always occur within the context of angry affect. However, underscoring the importance of assessing anger, Novaco and Taylor (2004) found that patient-reported anger was a significant predictor of postadmission (to an inpatient forensic unit) assaults in a sample of male offenders with various mental and neurological disabilities.

The final two Negative Emotionality–related Internalizing scales are Behavior Restrictive Fears (BRF), made up of items that describe various fears that inhibit and significantly restrict the individual's normal range of behaviors, and Multiple Specific Fears (BRF), which consists of items that describe various specific types of fears and phobias that tend to co-occur. The *DSM-IV* similarly distinguishes between anxiety and fears that result in avoidant behavior that impairs the individual's ability to work or carry out other responsibilities (i.e., agoraphobia) and specific phobias involving persistent fear of circumscribed objects or situations (simple phobia). The latter tend to co-occur and are classified into animal, natural environment, blood-injection-injury, situational, and other subtypes, all of which are represented in the MSF item pool. McLean and Anderson (2009) noted that across age groups, women endorse a greater number and severity of fears than do men, with the exception of social evaluative fears, which are reported with similar frequency by men and women. The *DSM-IV* includes a third fear-related disorder, Social Phobia, which is assessed with the Interpersonal Scale Shyness on the MMPI-2-RF.

Psychometric Findings

Data reported by Tellegen and Ben-Porath (2008/2011) reflect adequate reliability for the Internalizing Specific Problems Scales. Test–retest reliability estimates based on a subset of the normative sample range from .65 (HLP) to .85 (MSF). Internal consistencies range from .34 (SUI, women) to .72 (ANP, men) in the normative sample and from .48 (BRF) to .83 (COG, NFC) in clinical settings. Standard errors of measurement (SEM) expressed in T-score units range from 4 (NFC, MSF) to 6 (SUI, HLP, BRF) based on the normative test–retest reliability estimates and from 5 (SFD, MSF) to 11 (SUI) based on internal consistency estimates in the clinical samples. Tellegen and Ben-Porath note that for scales with larger SEMs, more extreme T scores are needed to justify clinically significant inferences.

Intercorrelations between the Internalizing Scales fall mainly in the .20–.40 range in the normative sample and in the .30–.50 range in the clinical samples. Reflecting their designation as "facets" of RCd and RC7, respectively, correlations of SUI, HLP, SFD, and NFC are generally higher with RCd than with RC7, and correlations of STW, AXY, ANP, BRF, and MSF show generally the opposite pattern.

External correlates reported by Tellegen and Ben-Porath (2008/2011) indicate that in a sample of mental health outpatients, scores on SUI were most highly correlated with a history of suicide attempts (reported by intake workers who initially interviewed these individuals) and current suicidal ideation reported by their therapists. In the psychiatric inpatient samples, SUI scores were correlated with the admitting psychiatrist reporting suicide risk as one of the reasons for admission and describing ongoing suicidal ideation, having a suicide plan, and past suicide attempts in individuals with higher scores on this scale. These patients were also more likely to be described as helpless and hopeless. In a disability claimant sample, SUI scores were highly correlated with a suicidal ideation measure, and in a criminal defendant sample, scores on this scale were correlated with current suicidal ideation and prior suicide attempts.

Scores on HLP were associated with therapist ratings in the mental health outpatient sample reflecting a sense of hopelessness and a belief that one cannot be helped, a pessimistic outlook and being overwhelmed, and believing that life is a strain. Among the psychiatric inpatients, HLP scores were associated with the admitting psychiatrist reporting prominent findings of helplessness and hopelessness on intake to the facility. In a sample of individuals being treated for substance abuse, HLP scores were highly correlated with scores on the Beck Hopelessness Scale and, in particular, with the Feelings of Future and Loss of Motivation subscales. In several of the samples (mental health outpatients, psychiatric inpatients, disability claimants, and criminal defendants) scores on HLP were associated with suicidal ideation and recent suicide attempts, although the correlations were not as high as those found with the SUI Scale.

SFD scores were associated with therapists describing mental health outpatients as insecure, feeling inferior to others, self-doubting, self-degrading, and self-punishing. Among the psychiatric inpatients, SFD scores were correlated with report by the admitting psychiatrist that the individual felt worthless and, consistent with findings on self-esteem described earlier, with various indicators of depression and suicidal ideation. Similar associations were found in the sample of criminal defendants. Among disability claimants, higher scores on SFD were associated with inadequacy, dysphoria, and self-consciousness.

Scores on NFC were correlated negatively with therapists' descriptions of mental health outpatients as being self-reliant and power oriented, and positively with passivity and feeling like a failure. In VA medical and mental health outpatients, NFC scores were substantially correlated with a measure of behavioral inhibition and measures of fear and stress reactivity. In veterans receiving substance abuse treatment, scores on this scale were associated with a sense of vulnerability, and in the criminal defendant sample, NFC scores were negatively correlated with a stable work history. Among the men in that sample, scores on this scale were also negatively correlated with IQ scores.

In a sample of mental health outpatients, scores on STW, as expected, were associated with being described by their therapists as anxious and depressed, prone to worry, being sad, feeling hopeless, and being nervous. In the psychiatric inpatient samples, STW scores were associated with being described by the admitting psychiatrist as depressed and being prescribed antidepressant medication. In the VA medical and mental health outpatient samples, STW scores were correlated with scores on a measure of obsessiveness and compulsiveness and measures of worry, anxiety, and behavioral inhibition. In a substance abuse treatment sample, STW scores were most highly correlated with measures of anxiety and depression, and in a sample of disability claimants, scores on this scale were most highly correlated with a measure of obsessive worry. In a nonclinical sample, STW scores were most highly correlated with a measure of stress reactivity, reflecting that higher scorers on this scale are likely to perceive situations as stressful that others do not find so.

Scores on AXY were correlated with an intake diagnosis of an anxiety disorder in the men of the mental health outpatient sample and with therapists' descriptions of symptoms of anxiety and depression and experiencing nightmares in both genders. Among the psychiatric inpatients, AXY scores were correlated with experiencing intrusive ideation and nightmares, and in the VA subsample, scores on this scale were associated with an indication by the admitting psychiatrist that the individual was experiencing an increase of symptoms associated with PTSD and with diagnoses of anxiety disorder in general and PTSD in particular. In VA medical and mental health outpatients, AXY scores were correlated with fearfulness. In the disability claimant sample, AXY scores were correlated most highly (among the MMPI-2-RF scales) with a number of scales on the Detailed Assessment of Post-Traumatic Stress measure (Briere, 2001), specifically Peritraumatic Distress, Re-experiencing, Avoidance, Hyperarousal, Post-Traumatic Stress, and Post-Traumatic Impairment.

In a paper published after publication of the MMPI-2-RF, studying a sample of National Guard soldiers who had returned from deployment in Iraq, Arbisi, Polusny, Erbes, Thuras, and Reddy (2011) found AXY scores to be substantially correlated with screening positive for PTSD symptoms.

ANP scores in the mental health outpatient sample were correlated with therapists' descriptions of irritability; low tolerance for frustration; holding grudges; having temper tantrums; and being angry, overreactive, excitable, and argumentative. In the medical and mental health outpatient VA samples, ANP scores were correlated with measures of anger, as they were in the sample of individuals undergoing substance abuse treatment. In the disability claimant sample, ANP scores were correlated with hostility, and in the sample of criminal defendants, higher ANP scores were associated with a history of juvenile misconduct.

Finally, consistent with the earlier description of the constructs assessed by these measures, findings on the two fear-related scales indicated that BRF scores were correlated with a measure of Agoraphobia in the VA mental health and medical outpatients and with being phobic in the sample of disability claimants. BRF scores were correlated with the total number of specific fears and with fear of blood and injury in the VA mental health and medical outpatient samples and with harm avoidance in a college student sample.

Externalizing Scales

Constructs

The four Externalizing Specific Problems Scales are divided into two subsets of two scales each, associated respectively with the constructs assessed by RC4 (Antisocial Behavior) and RC9 (Hypomanic Activation). The first of the two RC4-related scales, Juvenile Conduct Problems (JCP), is made up of items that describe a history of juvenile misconduct involving stealing, negative peer group influence, and problematic behavior in school. Diagnostic criteria for adult Antisocial Personality Disorder require a history of juvenile Conduct Disorder, and numerous studies have demonstrated that such a history is predictive of various negative outcomes in adults. Dalsgaard, Mortensen, Frydenberg, and Thomsen (2002) found, for example, that adolescents with conduct problems and Attention-Deficit Hyperactivity Disorder (ADHD), particularly girls, were at increased risk for admission for treatment of psychiatric disorders as adults. Knop et al. (2009) similarly found that juvenile conduct problems comorbid with ADHD were predictive of alcohol dependence in adults. Burke, Loeber, and Lahey (2007) reported finding that Conduct Disorder and teacher-rated interpersonal callousness in adolescence were predictive of psychopathy in young adults. Jaffee, Belsky, Harrington, Caspi, and Moffitt (2006) found that parents who had a history of Conduct Disorder were at elevated risk for socioeconomic disadvantage and relationship violence.

The Substance Abuse (SUB) scale consists of items that describe problematic alcohol use, drug use, and misuse of prescription medication. Historically, efforts to identify individuals at risk for substance abuse with the MMPI avoided using transparent items for this purpose (e.g., MacAndrew, 1965). However, assessment of substance abuse with transparent items has been accomplished successfully with a number of psychometric devices such as the Addiction Severity Index (ASI; McLellan, Luborksy, O'Brien & Woody, 1980), the Michigan Alcoholism Screening Test (MAST; Selzer, 1971), and the Drug Abuse Screening Test (DAST; B. F. Skinner, 1983). On the MMPI-2, the Addiction Acknowledgment Scale (AAS; Weed, Butcher, McKenna & Ben-Porath, 1992) was used successfully in assessing substance abuse, with several studies (e.g., Stein, Graham, Ben-Porath & McNulty, 1999; Weed, Butcher, McKenna & Ben-Porath, 1992) indicating the superiority of AAS over the nontransparent MMPI-2 MacAndrew Alcoholism Scale–Revised in identifying individuals with substance abuse problems. The importance of assessing for potential substance abuse is highlighted by findings indicating an increased risk for interpersonal violence associated with this behavior in a variety of patients and circumstances (e.g., individuals diagnosed with Schizophrenia, Fazel, Langstrom, Hjern, Grann & Lichtenstein, 2009; perpetrators of intimate partner violence, Hirschel, Hutchison & Shaw, 2010; violent offenders, Sacks et al., 2009).

The Aggression (AGG) scale is one of two Externalizing Specific Problems Scales associated with facets of RC9. It includes items that describe engaging in physically violent behavior toward others, acting violently in response to angry affect, and enjoying thoughts about, or actual infliction of, physical aggression toward others. Like SUB, AGG is a transparent measure of a generally undesirable behavior. However, here too, commonly used measures of aggression have relied successfully on transparent items (e.g., the Buss Perry Aggression Questionnaire; Buss & Perry, 1992). The importance of assessing for a propensity toward physically aggressive behavior is highlighted by findings of an increased risk for interpersonal violence in psychiatric outpatients (Posternak & Zimmerman, 2002) and inpatients (Barlow, Grenyer & Ilkiw-Lavalle, 2000). Physical aggression has been linked specifically to Bipolar Disorder (cf. Good, 1978), which is consistent with the finding that AGG represents a facet of hypomanic activation, as assessed by the MMPI-2-RF. Interpersonal aggression, and, in particular, intimate partner violence, has also been the focus of studies of individuals with PTSD (e.g., Taft, Monson, Schumm, Watkins, Panuzio & Resick, 2009).

The second Externalizing Specific Problems Scale associated with RC9, Activation (ACT), is made up of items that reflect racing thoughts, elated mood, a state of overexcitation, and cycling moods. This content resembles many of the items included in Eckblad and Chapman's (1986) Hypomanic Personality Scale (HYP), although the latter covers a somewhat broader domain than does ACT. Studies with the HYP show that higher scores on this scale are associated with an increased likelihood for Bipolar Disorder symptoms. Kwapil, Miller, Zinser, Chapman, Chapman, and Eckblad (2000) found at a 13-year follow-up that former college students who scored high on this scale were more likely than were control participants to have developed Bipolar Disorder, have psychotic-like experiences, manifest symptoms of Borderline Personality Disorder, and have higher rates of substance abuse. Meyer and Hautzinger (2003) found that higher HYP scores were correlated with experiences of manic or hypomanic episodes but not other mood or anxiety disorders. Meyer and Hoffman (2005) reported substantial correlations between HYP scores and the Behavioral Activation Scale (Carver & White, 1994), in particular the Fun Seeking subscale, but not the Behavioral Inhibition Scale.

Psychometric Findings

Data reported by Tellegen and Ben-Porath (2008/2011) indicate that test–retest reliability estimates for the Externalizing Specific Problems Scales in the normative sample range from .77 (ACT) to .87 (SUB). Internal consistencies in the normative sample range from .56 (JCP) to .66 (AGG). In the clinical samples, these coefficients range from .59 (ACT) to .76 (AGG). SEMs expressed in T-score values range from three to six based on the test–retest reliability estimates and from five to nine based on internal consistencies.

Intercorrelations between the Externalizing Specific Problems Scales fall mainly in the .20 to .35 range in the normative sample and from .30 to .45 in the clinical samples (Tellegen & Ben-Porath, 2008/2011). Consistent with their division into two subsets, JCP and SUB are more highly correlated with each other than with AGG and ACT, and vice versa.

External correlates reported by Tellegen and Ben-Porath (2008/2011) indicate that in the mental health outpatient sample, JCP scores are associated with being described by their therapists as engaging in antisocial behavior, acting out, being sociopathic, having problems with authority figures, experiencing difficulties trusting others, and having stormy interpersonal relationships. In the criminal defendant sample, higher JCP scores were correlated with a history of juvenile delinquency, stealing, violence as a juvenile, being committed to a juvenile residential facility, truancy, school suspensions and expulsions, and in adulthood with arrests, violent behavior, and substance abuse, and with a diagnosis of Antisocial Personality Disorder.

Scores on SUB were correlated in the mental health outpatient sample with an intake diagnosis related to substance abuse. In the psychiatric inpatients, scores on this scale were associated with intoxication at admission, identification of substance abuse as precipitating hospitalization, description by the admitting psychiatrist of substance abuse as a significant problem, and a substance abuse–related diagnosis. In the VA mental health and medical outpatient samples, SUB scores were substantially correlated with the Michigan Alcohol Screening Test and Drug Abuse Screening Test. In a sample of individuals undergoing substance abuse treatment, scores on SUB were associated with findings of alcohol and drug use problems on the Addiction Severity Index. In a sample of disability litigants, SUB scores were correlated with findings of substance abuse problems, and in the criminal defendant sample, higher scores on this scale were associated with misuse of alcohol and a broad range of illegal drugs and with a substance abuse–related diagnosis.

AGG scores were correlated with therapists' descriptions of mental health outpatients as being aggressive and physically abusive, with male clients having a history of committing domestic violence. In the psychiatric inpatient samples, higher scores on this scale were associated with homicidal ideation and a history of violent behavior in the VA sample. In a sample of individuals in treatment for substance abuse, higher AGG scores were substantially correlated with the total score on the Buss Perry Aggression Questionnaire and, in particular, the Physical Aggression subscale. In the disability claimant sample, scores on this scale were correlated with hostility, and in the criminal defendant sample, AGG scores were correlated with a history of having been physically abusive and violent toward others. In a sample of college students, AGG scores were substantially correlated with scores on a measure of interpersonal aggression.

Correlations between ACT scores and external criteria were generally lower than those reported for other Specific Problems Scales in the *MMPI-2-RF Technical Manual.* This likely reflects a combination of the relative infrequency of hypomanic activation in these samples and the cyclical nature of the phenomena assessed by these scales. Nevertheless, the patterns of external correlations indicated that relevant criteria were often most highly correlated with scores on this scale. In the mental health outpatient sample, ACT scores were associated with an intake diagnosis of Bipolar Disorder. In the psychiatric inpatient samples, scores on ACT were correlated with presenting with grandiose delusions and pressured speech, and being prescribed mood-stabilizing medication. In the VA medical and mental health outpatient samples, ACT scores were correlated with activation, magical ideation, and perceptual aberrations. For disability claimants, higher scores on this scale were associated with hypomania, and in the criminal defendant sample, ACT scores were correlated with a Bipolar Disorder diagnosis.

In a study published since the MMPI-2-RF was released, L. C. Watson, Quilty, and Bagby (2010) examined the utility of MMPI-2-RF scales in differentiating patients diagnosed with Bipolar Disorder and Major Depression. ACT scores were the best MMPI-2-RF predictors of this differential diagnosis.

Interpersonal Scales

Constructs

Scores on many of the MMPI-2-RF scales already discussed in this chapter and Chapter 2 are associated conceptually and empirically with interpersonal difficulties. What distinguishes the five scales included in this set is an exclusive focus on interpersonal functioning. The first scale, Family Problems (FML), for example, could reasonably have been included among the externalizing facets of RC4. It is made up of items that describe conflictual family relationships and alienation from members of one's family. Because items do not differentiate between current family and family of origin, FML elevations may indicate dysfunction in either set of relationships or both.

The importance of assessing familial dysfunction is underscored by research linking this experience with a broad range of negative outcomes in adults. In a comprehensive longitudinal investigation, Pardis, Reinherz, Giaconia, Beardslee, Ward, and Fitzmaurice (2009) found increased incidences of depression; low self-esteem; antisocial behavior, including substance abuse; unemployment; and physical health problems among individuals exposed to a dysfunctional family environment while growing up. Pilowsky, Wickramartine, Nomura, and Weissman (2006) found family discord to be associated with increased risk for Major Depression and substance abuse in offspring of depressed and nondepressed parents. Klonsky, Oltmanns, Turkheimer, and Fiedler (2000) found familial dysfunction to be associated with increased risk for personality disorder in general but did not identify associations with specific disorders. Kaslow, Thompson, Brooks, and Twomey (2000) reported an association between family problems and risk for suicide attempts in a sample of African American women. Familial dysfunction has also been found to play a detrimental role in psychological interventions. For example, Evans, Cowlishaw, and Hopwood (2009) found that problematic familial relationships can have a negative impact on PTSD treatment efforts. Thus, elevations on FML may be associated with a broad range of psychological dysfunction and have negative implications for treatment efforts, indicating the advisability of addressing these issues in treatment planning.

The second scale in this subset, Interpersonal Passivity (IPP), consists of items that, as keyed, describe submissiveness and unassertiveness in interpersonal functioning. Associations between assertiveness (or lack thereof) and various manifestations of psychological dysfunction have been demonstrated repeatedly. For example, Elliot and Gramling (1990) found that nonassertive individuals relied on different types of social support and were less likely to benefit from it than were those who were more assertive, and Lee and Swanson-Crockett (1994) found that assertiveness training improved the coping skills of a sample of nurses. Interpersonal passivity and submissiveness have also been linked with features of Dependent Personality Disorder. Bornstein (2005) reviewed the theoretical and empirical literature related to this association and concluded that an interaction between passive/submissive tendencies and situational factors best accounts for the long-observed link between this interpersonal style and the development of dependency.

The last three MMPI-2-RF measures of interpersonal functioning, Social Avoidance (SAV), Shyness (SHY), and Disaffiliativeness (DSF), assess various causes and effects of social isolation. The SAV items describe a lack of interest in and efforts to avoid social situations, particularly those in which the individual is likely to be the center of attention. Items scored on SHY describe experiences of anxiety and discomfort associated with interacting with others. DSF is made up of items that reflect a lack of interest in being around others and a preference for being on one's own. The three scales assess features of three *DSM-IV* disorders marked by social withdrawal: Avoidant Personality Disorder (APD), Social Phobia, and Schizoid Personality Disorder, respectively. However, as discussed next, the constructs social avoidance, shyness, and disaffiliativeness are not synonymous with these disorders.

Taylor, Laposa, and Alden (2004) note that socially avoidant behavior is part of a broader pattern of avoidant behavior that includes efforts to avoid emotional experiences and novel situations. Diagnostically, it is a core feature of APD, which is characterized by social isolation resulting from apprehensiveness about being viewed negatively by others rather than a lack of interest in social contact.

Hofmann, Richey, Sawyer, Ansaani, and Rief (2009) characterize shyness as one of the most heritable temperament characteristics and a core component of Social

Anxiety Disorder, also known as Social Phobia. However, Heiser, Turner, Beidel, and Roberson-Nay (2009) found that shyness and Social Phobia are not interchangeable constructs and that it is possible for individuals to be very shy without meeting diagnostic criteria for Social Phobia. Social Phobia is characterized by more symptomatology and impairment and a lower quality of life.

Bernstein, Arntz, and Travaglini (2009) observe that a central distinction between the Avoidant and Schizoid personality disorders is that individuals diagnosed with the latter lack the desire or ability to form social relationships (assessed on the MMPI-2-RF with the DSF scale), whereas those with APD desire interpersonal contact but avoid it out of feelings of inferiority and an intense fear of rejection and humiliation. Millon (1981) was among the first to note this distinction and characterized the difference between the two disorders as one of passive (Schizoid) versus active (Avoidant) detachment.

Psychometric Findings

Tellegen and Ben-Porath (2008/2011) reported normative test–retest coefficients ranging from .60 (DSF) to .88 (SHY) and internal consistency coefficients ranging from .43 (women on DSF) to .78 (men on SAV). Internal consistency coefficients for the Interpersonal Scales in the clinical samples tend to be higher because of larger variances, ranging from .57 (DSF) to .86 (SAV). The reliability estimates for DSF scores are the clearest exceptions and are attributable to the lower variances of this scale. Note, however, that the low variances in turn result in SEM estimates that are only somewhat higher (6–9 T-score points) than those of the remaining Interpersonal Scales (4–7 T-score points).

Intercorrelations between the Interpersonal Scales (reported by Tellegen & Ben-Porath, 2008/2011) range from .10 to .40 in the normative sample and from .20 to .50 in the clinical samples. The correlation between SAV and SHY in both the normative and clinical samples is consistently the highest, followed by that between SAV and DSF. This pattern is consistent with the view (just discussed) that the three scales have a common theme of social isolation but can assist in differentiating the factors leading to and resulting from this experience.

External correlates of FML reported by Tellegen and Ben-Porath (2008/2011) include identification by their therapists of family problems as a significant concern for the mental health outpatients. Therapists also characterized higher scorers on FML as coming from families lacking in love, being resentful of family members, blaming their family members for causing their difficulties, and generally experiencing familial discord. In the VA medical and mental health outpatient samples, FML scores were correlated with scores on a measure of familial dysfunction. In the sample receiving substance abuse treatment, FML scores were correlated with measures of aggression, anger, and hostility. Scores on this scale were also correlated with a measure of hostility in the disability claimant sample and with having had problematic childhood relationships and poor relationships with family members in the sample of pretrial criminal defendants. In a nonclinical college student sample, FML scores were associated with a measure of alienation.

Correlates of IPP for the mental health outpatients include being described by their therapists as passive, submissive, and introverted and not being power oriented or assertive in interpersonal relationships. For VA mental health and medical outpatients, IPP scores were correlated negatively with various manifestations of behavioral activation, and in the sample of individuals in treatment for substance abuse, higher scores on this scale were associated with unassertiveness. In the nonclinical college student sample, IPP scores were negatively correlated with a measure of social potency.

SAV scores were correlated with various therapist indications of introversion in the mental health outpatient sample. In the VA medical and mental outpatient samples, scores on this scale were associated with a measure of social fears and anxiety. Among individuals in substance abuse treatment, SAV scores were negatively correlated with measures of warmth and gregariousness, and in the nonclinical college student sample, scores on this scale were negatively correlated with a measure of social closeness and Positive Emotionality.

In the mental health outpatient sample, higher SHY scores were associated with therapist descriptions of introversion and insecurity. In the VA mental health and medical outpatients, scores on this scale were correlated with general fearfulness, social fears, anxiety, and behavioral inhibition. In the sample of individuals receiving substance abuse treatment, SHY scores were correlated with a relatively broad range of measures related to anxiety and demoralization, and in the nonclinical college student sample, scores on this measure were associated positively with a measure of stress reactivity and negatively with Positive Emotionality and social potency.

Correlates of DSF for the mental health outpatient men included pessimism and depression as well as suicidal ideation. In the psychiatric inpatients, DSF scores were associated with social withdrawal and suicidal ideation in the female sample and a poor course of hospitalization in the men and women evaluated in the community hospitals. In the VA mental health and medical outpatient samples, DSF scores were associated with social fears. In the substance abuse treatment samples, higher DSF scores were correlated negatively with measures of warmth, gregariousness, and trustworthiness, and positively with demoralization indicators. In the sample of criminal defendants, higher DSF scores were correlated with a history of suicide attempts.

Interest Scales

The MMPI-2-RF Interest Scales were derived from analyses of original MMPI Clinical Scale 5, which was included in the development of the RC Scales, but because it is not a measure of psychopathology, it was not used to derive a Restructured Clinical Scale. As described by Tellegen, Ben-Porath, McNulty, Arbisi, Graham, and Kaemmer (2003), in Step 2 of the development of the RC Scales, which involved factor analyses of the items of each Clinical Scale along with a set of demoralization makers, Tellegen found that a four-factor solution for Scale 5 yielded a clear demoralization factor, another factor loading on items with aggressive/cynical content, and two factors marked by items describing aesthetic/literary and mechanical/physical interests, respectively. The latter two were designated as representing two major distinctive components of Scale 5, and Seed Scales representing these domains were developed in Step 3 and used in Step 4 in deriving the final RC Scales (see Chapter 2 for details).

The Scale 5 Seed Scales described by Tellegen et al. (2003) were included in the development of the Specific Problems Scales of the MMPI-2-RF. Correlations with the entire MMPI-2 item pool led to the addition of items that correlated distinctively with the two Seed Scales. Two measures, labeled Aesthetic–Literary Interests (AES) and Mechanical–Physical Interests (MEC), were derived following analyses designed to identify items that attenuated the internal consistency of the resulting scales.

Constructs

Tellegen's finding that the distinctive components of Scale 5 involved "interests" is consistent with Hathaway and McKinley's (1943) original label for the measure, the Interest Scale, which, in the original test manual, they paired with the abbreviation "Mf," an obvious reference to masculinity and femininity. The authors described the scale as measuring "the tendency toward masculinity or femininity of interest pattern" (p. 5) and reported that "the items were originally selected by a comparison of the two sexes. Some were inspired by Terman and Miles, and others are original" (p. 5). Their goal was to develop a measure of homosexuality (at the time considered a psychiatric disorder), and they found that a very small number of men seeking treatment for "sexual inversion" answered the same set of items differently from a sample of male army recruits. Hathaway and McKinley (1943) emphasized that "homosexual abnormality *must not be assumed* on the basis of a high score without confirmatory evidence" (p. 5; emphasis original) and noted that the Mf score is often important in vocational choice.

The items "inspired by Terman and Miles" refers to the work of Terman and Miles (1936), who developed measures designed to facilitate study of the association of gender and personality. Strong (1943), developer of the Strong Vocational Interest Blank (SVIB), which, as discussed in Chapter 1, had inspired Hathaway and McKinley's choice of empirical keying as the method for developing the MMPI Clinical Scales, included a similar measure on his career interest inventory. And Gough (1957) incorporated a similar measure on the California Psychological Inventory (CPI).

In all these early efforts, masculinity and femininity were conceptualized and measured as polar ends of a single construct. Constantinople (1973) took issue with this conceptualization and offered theoretical and empirical arguments supporting the view that these are relatively independent dimensions and that masculinity/femininity scales such as those included in the SVIB, MMPI, and CPI are in fact multidimensional, often including distinguishable "M" and "F" dimensions, among others. Following this line of reasoning, Bem (1974) and Spence, Helmreich, and Strapp (1975) developed separate M and F measures and concluded that they were able to identify meaningful individual differences within samples of men and women. Baucom (1976) adopted a similar conceptualization in developing M and F scales for the CPI by identifying items answered by large proportions of men or women and smaller proportions of members of the other gender. Peterson and Dahlstrom (1992) adopted a very similar approach in developing Gender Role Scales for the MMPI-2, based on endorsement rates of men and women in the normative sample.

Identification of two distinct sources of variance in Clinical Scale 5, reproducible in both genders, guided the development of the MMPI-2-RF Interest Scales. In contrast with Peterson and Dahlstrom's (1992) MMPI-2 Gender Role Scales, gender played no part in the selection of items for AES and MEC. Recognition that these scales measure primarily individual differences in occupational and leisure activities reintroduces Hathaway and McKinley's (1943) original view of the Scale 5 item pool as representing items associated primarily with vocational interests.

Psychometric Findings

Reliability data reported by Tellegen and Ben-Porath (2008/2011) show considerable short-term stability in AES and MEC scores, with some of the highest test–retest correlations (.86 and .92, respectively) among the MMPI-2-RF scales in the normative sample. Internal consistency coefficients were lower, ranging from .49 to .62 in the normative sample and from .60 to .67 in the clinical samples. Because variances on these scales were relatively low in these samples, the corresponding SEMs are comparable to those obtained with the RC Scales, ranging from three to six T-score points.

Consistent with Constantinople's (1973) observations (just discussed), scores on the Interest Scales are relatively independent. Tellegen and Ben-Porath (2008/2011) report negligible correlations between the scales in the normative and most of the male clinical samples and *positive* correlations between AES and MEC, ranging from .22 to .24 in the female clinical samples.

External correlate data reported by Tellegen and Ben-Porath (2008/2011) indicate that in the mental health outpatient sample, AES scores for men were correlated negatively with therapists' ratings of stereotypic masculine interests and behaviors, being physically abusive, and having a low tolerance for frustration and positively with rejecting a traditional gender role and stereotypic feminine behavior. There were no significant correlates for the women in this sample. In the sample of individuals receiving substance abuse treatment, AES scores were correlated with being open to aesthetic experiences and ideas. In a nonclinical sample of college students, scores on this scale were correlated with a measure of openness to sensory experiences and imaginative states.

MEC scores were correlated positively with therapist ratings of stereotypic masculine interests for both men and women in the mental health outpatient sample. They were correlated negatively in men and positively in women with rejection of traditional gender roles. MEC scores were also correlated negatively with difficulty making decisions, self-doubting, and being worry prone and with concerns about homosexuality in the male outpatient sample. In the sample of pretrial criminal defendants, MEC scores were correlated positively with the number of previous arrests for women, and in the nonclinical college students sample, scores on this scale were correlated negatively with a measure of harm avoidance for both genders, indicating a propensity toward risk-taking and sensation-seeking behavior in higher scorers on this scale.

Summary

The measures reviewed in this section are reliable sources of information related to somatic and cognitive complaints, internalizing difficulties, externalizing behavioral proclivities, interpersonal functioning, and interests. The empirical correlates reported for each of the 25 scales are consistent with expectations for measures of the constructs they target, documenting their convergent validities. Although not summarized here, the correlate data reported in Appendix A of the *Technical Manual* also reflect clearly distinctive correlational findings, reflecting the discriminant validities of these measures. Together, these findings provide evidence supporting the construct validity of the Specific Problems and Interest Scales.

PERSONALITY PSYCHOPATHOLOGY FIVE SCALES

The Original PSY-5 Model and Scales

Rationale, Objectives, and Development

Attempts to develop dimensional models of normal personality and psychopathology were reviewed earlier in this chapter. In the psychopathology domain, this review concentrated on Axis I. Efforts to carve out dimensional structures of Axis II disorders have also been undertaken, and one such program of research led to the development of the PSY-5 model (Harkness & McNulty, 1994). Harkness (1992) described his initial work in this area, intended to develop a dimensional measurement model of Axis II disorders. In assembling the item pool he used for this purpose, Harkness augmented a list of *DSM-III-R* Axis II criteria with items reflecting psychopathy and normal personality constructs. Thus, in contrast with other five-factor models, which have been explored ex post facto as dimensional models of personality disorders (e.g., Widiger & Costa, 2002), the PSY-5 constructs originated directly from the clinical criteria for diagnosing these conditions. Abandoning the categorical measurement model embodied in the *DSM-III-R* in favor of a dimensional model of Axis II disorders was quite novel at the time Harkness began work on this project in the 1980s. Such an approach is now being given serious consideration for *DSM-5*.

Harkness (1992) administered to a number of samples a set of items written to canvass the *DSM-III-R* criteria, Cleckley's (1941) psychopathy descriptions, and Tellegen's (1982) primary normal personality factors. Through application of a series of data-reduction techniques, Harkness and McNulty (1994) converged on a model composed of five underlying factors. They described the first dimension, *Aggressiveness*, as entailing a general disposition to engage in offensive, goal-directed behavior or instrumental aggression. The second dimension, *Psychoticism*, was described as representing the verisimilitude or accuracy of the individual's inner perceptions of her or his outer social and object world. The third dimension, *Constraint*, was linked to Tellegen's (1982) similarly labeled higher-order dimension, combining facets of control versus impulsiveness, harm avoidance, and traditionalism. The fourth dimension, *Negative Emotionality/Neuroticism*, related to Tellegen's Negative Emotionality construct and Eysenck's construct Neuroticism (both discussed in Chapter 2), was characterized as a broad affective disposition to experience negative emotions focusing on anxiety and nervousness. Harkness and McNulty (1994) characterized the fifth dimension, *Positive Emotionality/Extraversion*, as representing a broad disposition to experience positive affect and to seek out and enjoy social experiences, assessed with Tellegen's (1982) Positive Emotionality higher-order dimension.

Recognizing that MMPI-2 measures of the PSY-5 constructs could help provide a conceptually grounded assessment of Axis II disorders, Harkness, McNulty, and Ben-Porath (1995) developed the original set of PSY-5 Scales using a method they termed replicated rational selection. Harkness and colleagues reasoned that because proper functioning of the scales was predicated on test takers' accurate comprehension of their content and its relation to the underlying construct, having laypersons participate in item selection would yield items that were most likely to be properly understood. Lay judges were provided detailed descriptions of the five constructs and were asked to select MMPI-2 items they deemed pertinent to each of the five dimensions. Items selected by the majority of the lay judges were assigned to provisional PSY-5 Scales. Harkness and McNulty then deleted some items that, based on their expert review, did not conform to the meaning of the PSY-5 construct for which they had been nominated by the majority of the lay judges. In a final step designed to enhance the discriminant validity of the resulting scales, item analyses were conducted, and items that were more highly correlated with a scale other than the one to which they had been assigned provisionally were dropped. Thus, the original PSY-5 Scales were composed entirely of items selected by lay reviewers. Although some additional items were dropped based on expert review or psychometric analyses, none were added to the lists generated by the reviewers. In the process of developing the PSY-5 Scales, two constructs, constraint and low Positive Emotionality/extraversion, were reflected so that higher scores on all the scales would indicate likely dysfunction. The resulting scales and constructs were labeled Disconstraint (DISC) and Introversion/Low Positive Emotionality (INTR).

Empirical Findings

Bagby, Ryder, Ben Dat, Bacchiochi, and Parker (2002) validated the dimensional structure of the PSY-5 Scales with confirmatory factor analyses conducted with both a clinical and a nonclinical sample. Rouse, Finger, and Butcher (1999) conducted an Item Response Theory (IRT) analysis of the scales and concluded that they assess unidimensional constructs that conform to IRT assumptions. Rouse (2007) examined the reliability generalization of the PSY-5 Scales with a broad range of clinical and nonclinical samples and found, overall, evidence of adequate reliability of PSY-5 Scale scores across settings.

Turning to associations with other self-report measures, Harkness et al. (1995) reported correlations between scores on the PSY-5 Scales and Tellegen's (1995/2003) MPQ in a college student sample. The findings provided evidence of a convergent and discriminant validity of scores on the PSY-5 when evaluated in the context of a measure of normal personality traits. Harkness, McNulty, Ben-Porath, and Graham (2002) similarly found evidence of the convergent and discriminant validity of the PSY-5 Scale scores using a different normal personality measure: Cattell's 16PF (Cattell, Eber & Tatsuoka, 1970), completed by a sample of community-dwelling veterans. Segarra, Ross, Pastor, Montanes, Poy, and Molto (2007) examined associations between PSY-5 Scale scores and Carver and White's (1994) Behavioral Inhibition and Activation Scales (BIS-BAS), measures of Gray's BIS and BAS constructs and model (described in Chapter 2). They reported findings that, overall, supported the construct validity of the PSY-5 model and scales.

In light of the similarities between the PSY-5 model and the Five Factor Model (FFM) of personality, several investigators have examined correlations between scores on the PSY-5 Scales and FFM measures. Trull, Useda, Costa, and McCrae (1995) found expected patterns of correlations between truncated PSY-5 Scales (based on the original MMPI item pool) and the NEO Personality Inventory (NEO-PI; Costa & McCrae, 1985) in a community sample and between the full PSY-5 Scales and the NEO Personality Inventory–Revised (NEO-PI-R; Costa & McCrae, 1992) in a clinical sample. Egger, De Mey, Derksen, and van der Staak (2003) replicated these findings in a sample of Dutch psychiatric inpatients.

A substantial number of studies have focused on correlations between PSY-5 Scale scores and personality disorder–related criteria. Sharpe and Desai (2001), Trull et al. (1995), and Bagby, Sellbom, Costa, and Widiger (2008) compared the predictive power of the PSY-5 and NEO-PI-R scales in a variety of clinical samples and concluded that although there is substantial overlap between the two sets of scales, each provides incrementally valid information in predicting personality disorder–related extratest criteria. Wygant, Sellbom, Graham, and Schenk (2006) found expected patterns of correlations between the PSY-5 Scales and self-reported personality disorder symptoms in a mental health outpatient sample.

Miller, Kaloupek, Dillon, and Keane (2004) used the PSY-5 Scales to replicate and extend prior findings of internalizing and externalizing subtypes of posttraumatic response. These authors conducted cluster analyses of PSY-5 Scale scores with a large sample of combat veterans diagnosed with PTSD and classified these individuals into low-pathology, externalizing, and internalizing subgroups, finding expected correlations between group membership and extratest criteria. Miller, Vogt, Mozley, Kaloupek, and Keane (2006) reported that scores on the PSY-5 DISC scale mediated between PTSD diagnoses and substance abuse. Ferrier-Auerbach, Kehle, Erbes, Arbisi, Thuras, and Polusny (2009) found scores on truncated measures of DISC and NEGE to be associated with alcohol use predeployment in a sample of National Guard solders. Sellbom, Ben-Porath, and Stafford (2007) reported correlations between DISC scores and a psychopathy measure in a sample of criminal defendants. Egger, Delsing, and De Mey (2003) found scores on this scale to differentiate between patients diagnosed with psychotic versus bipolar disorders. Petroskey, Ben-Porath, and Stafford (2003) reported correlations between PSY-5 Scale scores and a wide range of extratest criteria in a forensic sample and concluded that the empirical correlates they found for the scales were consistent with those reported previously for general mental health settings. Vendrig, Derksen, and De Mey (2000) presented evidence that the PSY-5 Scales predict treatment outcome for chronic pain patients.

Finally, consistent with expectations for measures of relatively enduring personality pathology, Harkness et al. (2002) reported five-year stability coefficients ranging from .69 for Psychoticism (PSYC) to .82 for Negative Emotionality/Neuroticism (NEGE) in a large, nonclinical sample of men.

Revising the PSY-5 Scales for the MMPI-2-RF

The literature just reviewed established the PSY-5 Scales as empirically validated measures linked to a conceptually rich model of personality pathology. Seeking to retain this model in the MMPI-2-RF, Harkness and McNulty were invited to revise the PSY-5 Scales using the reduced, 338-item booklet, and they graciously agreed to do so. Harkness and McNulty (2007) described the revision of the scales as an iterative process involving internal (item scale) and external (item criterion) analyses.

They began by identifying the "surviving" 96 of the 139 PSY-5 items and went through a series of steps designed to yield revised scales that would provide comparable and possibly improved measures of the PSY-5 constructs. On the basis of these analyses, 22 of the 96 surviving items were dropped from the revised scales, and 30 items not included on the original measures were added, yielding five nonoverlapping scales composed of 104 items. Harkness and McNulty (2007) compared the original and revised scales and concluded that the new measures showed several improvements, including lower intercorrelations for some and evidence of comparable to improved external validity.

Psychometric Findings with the MMPI-2-RF PSY-5 Scales

Data reported in the *MMPI-2-RF Technical Manual* (Tellegen & Ben-Porath, 2008/2011) indicate that scores on the revised PSY-5 Scales are reliable, with test–retest reliability estimates ranging from .76 for PSYC-r[5] to .93 for DISC-r. Internal consistency estimates in the normative sample range from .69 for men and women on PSYC-r to .78 for men on NEGE-r. In the clinical samples, alpha coefficients range from .72 on Aggressiveness (AGGR-r) for outpatient women to .88 for the male psychiatric inpatients on PSYC-r. SEMs estimated based on these reliability data range from three to six T-score points and are consistent with those found with the H-O and RC Scales.

Intercorrelations between the PSY-5 Scales reported in the *Technical Manual* range from .10 to .40 in the normative sample and from 0 to .54 in the clinical samples. The patterns are consistent with intercorrelations among the MMPI-2 versions of the PSY-5 Scales reported by Harkness et al. (2002). However, the magnitudes of these correlations are generally lower for the MMPI-2-RF PSY-5 Scales. For example, although in both sets the highest correlations are between PSYC and NEGE and PSYC-r and NEGE-r, respectively, the correlations between these scales in the normative sample are .53 (MMPI-2) versus .40 (MMPI-2-RF) for men and .50 versus .38 for women.

Correlates reported in Appendix A of the *Technical Manual* indicate in a sample of mental health outpatients that higher AGGR-r scores are associated with being characterized by therapists as engaging in interpersonally aggressive and antisocial behavior, being grandiose and power oriented, and being less likely to be passive–submissive in interpersonal relationships. In a VA sample of mental health outpatients, higher AGGR-r scores were associated with anger and behavioral activation, and in a VA sample of individuals enrolled in substance abuse treatment, scores on this scale were correlated with verbal and physical aggression and noncompliant behavior. In a nonclinical sample, AGGR-r scores were correlated with a measure of social potency and aggression.

Scores on PSYC-r were correlated with low achievement orientation in the mental health outpatient sample and with admission problems associated with psychotic symptomatology and findings of psychotic symptoms in mental status examinations in psychiatric inpatients. In VA medical and mental health outpatient samples, PSYC-r scores were associated with measures of magical ideation and perceptual aberration, and in a sample of individuals undergoing substance abuse treatment, higher scores on this scale were related to depression and hostility. In a nonclinical sample, PSYC-r scores were correlated with measures of alienation and unusual perceptual processes.

Higher DISC-r scores were associated with a broad range of externalizing-related criteria. In mental health outpatients, scores on this scale were correlated with a history of arrests and having been diagnosed with substance abuse and being rated by their therapists as engaging in antisocial behavior, having family problems, having difficulties with authority figures, being narcissistic, and, most prominently, having poor impulse control. In the psychiatric inpatient samples, DISC-r scores were correlated with a history of substance misuse and being diagnosed with substance abuse. In VA mental health and medical outpatients, scores on this scale were correlated with measures of drug and alcohol misuse, and in a sample of individuals receiving substance abuse treatment, DISC-r scores were correlated with excitement-seeking behavior. Correlates in a forensic sample included a history of juvenile delinquency and current findings of drug and alcohol abuse and dependence. In a nonclinical sample, DISC-r scores were negatively correlated with a measure of constrained behavior.

In the mental health outpatient sample, scores on NEGE-r were correlated with presenting at intake with sad, depressed, and anxious affect and being rated by their therapists as being anxious and worry prone, responding poorly to stress, being depressed, feeling hopeless, and experiencing suicidal ideation. Correlates for this scale in psychiatric inpatients included being admitted with complaints of sleep difficulty and depression and experiencing suicidal ideation. In VA outpatient mental health and medical samples, NEGE-r scores were associated with measures of anxiety, anger, fearfulness, and depression. In a sample of individuals undergoing substance abuse treatment, scores on this scale were correlated with anxiety, hostility, anger, aggression, and depression, and in a nonclinical sample, higher scores were associated with being stress reactive.

INTR-r scores in the mental health outpatient sample were correlated with presenting with sad mood and being diagnosed with depression at intake. Therapists described those who scored higher on this scale as being depressed and introverted and more likely to experience suicidal ideation. In the psychiatric inpatient sample, higher scores on INTR-r were correlated with being admitted for depression and prescribed antidepressant medication on admission, experiencing suicidal ideation, and having a low energy level. In the sample of individuals receiving substance abuse treatment, higher INTR-r scores were associated with measures of depression and hopelessness. In a forensic sample of pretrial criminal defendants, scores on this scale were correlated with being diagnosed with depression, receiving antidepressant medication, and currently experiencing suicidal ideation.

CONCLUSION

The 33 scales discussed in this chapter, along with the nine RC Scales described in Chapter 2, constitute the Substantive Scales of the MMPI-2-RF. Each of these measures can be linked to familiar psychological constructs, and all have been empirically validated. The empirically grounded interpretive recommendations for these scales provided in Chapter 7 are founded on the empirical correlates listed in Chapters 2 and 3. We turn next to the MMPI-2-RF Validity Scales, which must be considered prior to any substantive interpretation of the test results.

CHAPTER 4

Completing Development of the MMPI-2-RF:
The Validity Scales

Validity scales, initially labeled *validating scores,* have been an integral component of the MMPI since its initial publication as the Minnesota Multiphasic Personality Schedule (Hathaway & McKinley, 1942). As implied by their label, these scales were designed to assist the MMPI interpreter in identifying invalid test results. Validity scales have also served a second purpose: informing the interpreter about a test taker's possible feigning or denial of problems. This chapter covers both functions of the MMPI-2-RF Validity Scales. It begins with a conceptual framework for understanding and using Validity Scales as measures of protocol validity, followed by a historical review of the development and use of Validity Scales for the MMPI and MMPI-2. Development and psychometric functioning of the MMPI-2-RF Validity Scales are described next, followed by a discussion of the dual functions of these scales as measures of protocol validity and indicators of possible malingering or efforts to conceal problems.

THREATS TO PROTOCOL VALIDITY

To provide useful information in response to the statements that make up a self-report measure of personality and psychopathology, a test taker must read, comprehend, and respond accurately to the test statements. Failure to do so, intentionally or unintentionally, can compromise the utility of the resulting test scores, in extreme cases rendering them uninterpretable. Therefore, prior to drawing any substantive inferences from self-report inventory test scores, careful consideration must be given to the quality of the information provided by the test taker, that is, to the validity of the individual test protocol.

Ben-Porath (2003) described a conceptual framework for understanding and using Validity Scales as measures of protocol validity. The premise underlying this approach is that even if a hypothetically 100% valid self-report measure were available, any given administration of the instrument could nonetheless yield invalid results. Threats to protocol validity fall broadly into two categories that reflect the role of item content in invalid responding: non-content-based and content-based. Important distinctions can be made within each of these categories as well.

Non-Content-Based Invalid Responding

Non-content-based invalid responding occurs when the test taker's responses are not based on an accurate reading and comprehension of the test items. Its deleterious effects on protocol validity are obvious: to the extent that a test taker's responses do not reflect his or her reactions to the actual items, the responses cannot gauge the individual's standing on the constructs of interest. This invalidating test-taking approach can be divided further into three subtypes: nonresponding, random responding, and fixed responding.

Nonresponding

Nonresponding occurs when the test taker fails to provide a scorable response to an item. Typically, this is the absence of a response, but if the test taker answers both *true* and *false* to a given item, this is also a nonresponse. Nonresponding may occur for a variety of reasons. Test takers who are uncooperative or defensive may fail to respond to a large number of items, or the test taker may be unable to read or understand items, cognitive functioning deficits may result in confusion or obsessing over responses, or the test taker may have limited introspection and insight.

The effect of nonresponding on protocol validity depends, in part, on the response format of the instrument. In tests that use a true–false response format, a nonresponse is typically considered a response in the nonkeyed direction because raw scores are derived by counting the number of responses given in the keyed direction. In measures with a Likert scale response format, a nonresponse typically receives the value 0. These de facto responses cannot be assumed to approximate how the test taker would have actually responded. Therefore, to the extent that nonresponding occurs in a given protocol, this will distort the resulting test scores by lowering them artificially. If not identified and considered, nonresponding may lead to underestimation of the individual's standing on the constructs measured by the affected scales.

Random Responding

Random responding (more accurately described as quasi-random) is characterized by an unsystematic response pattern that is not based on an accurate reading and comprehension of test items. It is not a dichotomous phenomenon, meaning that random responding may be present to varying degrees in a given test protocol. Two types of random responding can be distinguished. Intentional random responding occurs when the individual has the capacity to respond relevantly to test items but chooses to respond irrelevantly in an unsystematic manner. An uncooperative test taker may engage in intentional random responding instead of becoming involved in a confrontation with the examiner over his or her refusal to participate. In this example, the test taker provides answers to items without reading or considering the content. He or she may do this throughout the test protocol or at various points along the way.

Unintentional random responding occurs when the individual cannot respond relevantly to test items but responds without understanding their content. Test takers who respond this way are often not aware that they are doing so.

Several factors may contribute to unintentional random responding. Reading difficulties may compromise the test taker's ability to respond relevantly. Most current self-report measures require from a fourth- to a sixth-grade reading level for the test taker to be able to read, comprehend, and respond relevantly to the items.[1] This is not synonymous with having completed four to six years of education. Comprehension deficits can also lead to random responding. The individual may be able to read the test items but does not have the necessary language comprehension skills to process and understand them. This could be a product of low verbal ability or, for nonnative speakers, a lack of facility with the English language. Reading and comprehension difficulties tend to be relatively stable test taker characteristics that will likely compromise protocol validity regardless of when a test is administered. Other factors, such as confusion and thought disorganization, may be transitory. Finally, unintentional random responding may result from response recording errors. If the test taker mismarks responses on the answer sheet, he or she is essentially providing random responses. This could result from the individual missing just one item on the answer sheet or from a generally careless approach to response recording.

Fixed Responding

Fixed responding is an invalidating test-taking approach characterized by a systematic response pattern that is not based on an accurate reading and comprehension of test items. In contrast to random responding, the test taker provides the same non-content-based responses (e.g., true) to various items without considering their content. If the test taker provides both true and false responses indiscriminately, then he or she is engaging in random responding. In fixed responding, the indiscriminant responses are stereotypic, either true or false, or in the case of a Likert scale response format, the test taker marks items indiscriminately at the same level without considering content.

Like nonresponding and random responding, fixed responding is a matter of degree rather than a dichotomous all-or-none phenomenon. Unlike nonresponding and random responding, fixed responding has received a great deal of attention in the assessment literature. Jackson and Messick (1962) sparked this discussion when they proposed that much (if not all) of the variance in MMPI scale scores was attributable to two response styles, termed *acquiescence* and *social desirability*. Acquiescence was defined as a tendency to respond true to MMPI items without consideration of their content (i.e., fixed responding). (See Chapter 2 for a discussion of Jackson and Messick's arguments.) Essentially, these authors factor analyzed MMPI scale scores in a broad range of samples and found recurrently that two factors accounted for much of the variance in the scores. They attributed variance on these factors to two response styles, acquiescence and social desirability, and cautioned that MMPI scale scores appeared primarily to reflect individual differences on these nonsubstantive dimensions. Furthermore, they suggested that MMPI scales were particularly vulnerable to the effects of acquiescence and its counterpart, counteracquiescence (a tendency to respond false to self-report items without consideration of their content), because the scoring keys were unbalanced; that is, for some MMPI scales, many, if not most, of the items were keyed true, whereas on other scales, most of the items were keyed false. In contrast with Jackson and Messick's findings, Block (1965), in an extensive and sophisticated series of analyses, demonstrated that the two primary MMPI factors reflected substantive personality dimensions rather than stylistic response tendencies.

Although fixed responding does not pose as broad a threat to protocol validity as Jackson and Messick argued, in the relatively infrequent cases when a test taker uses this response style excessively, the resulting scale scores will be invalid and uninterpretable. Contrary to Jackson and Messick's assertion, constructing scales with balanced keys or Likert scale response formats does not make self-report measures less susceptible to this threat to protocol validity (see Chapter 1). An indiscriminant set of true responses is invalid regardless of whether the scoring key is balanced, and Likert scales provide even more possibilities for stereotypic responses.

Content-Based Invalid Responding

Content-based invalid responding occurs when the test taker skews his or her responses to items and, as a result, creates a misleading impression. This test-taking approach falls broadly into two classes discussed under various labels in the literature. The first has been termed *overreporting, feigning, faking bad, negative response bias,* and *malingering;* the second has been labeled *underreporting, faking good, positive response bias, denial,* and *positive malingering.* Because both types of content-based invalid responding can be generated intentionally and unintentionally, the more neutral descriptive terms *overreporting* and *underreporting* are preferred.

Overreporting

Overreporting occurs when a test taker reports problems he or she does not actually have or exaggerates the significance of difficulties he or she does have. In a hypothetical situation, if a completely objective assessment of the individual's functioning were available, the overreporter's subjective self-report would indicate greater dysfunction than the objective assessment.

Intentional overreporting occurs when the individual knowingly slants his or her self-report to appear dysfunctional. Such a test taker may be motivated by some external gain and thus fit the *DSM-IV* definition of malingering (American Psychiatric Association [APA], 1994). However, intentional overreporting is not synonymous with malingering because, for example, in the absence of an external incentive, it may correspond to the *DSM-IV* definition of Factitious Disorder. Moreover, intentional overreporting is not in itself an indication that psychopathology is absent. An individual with genuine psychological difficulties may amplify their extent or significance or may fabricate others but nonetheless be experiencing significant dysfunction.

Unintentional overreporting occurs when a test taker is unaware that she or he is describing herself or himself in an unrealistically negative manner. It is the test taker's self-concept rather than the self-report that is skewed. Individuals who engage in this test-taking approach mistakenly believe that their responses are accurate when in fact they are overreporting. Individuals with Somatoform Disorders, for example, report significant somatic symptoms that cannot be explained by objective medical findings (Lamberty, 2008). By definition, they believe their symptoms to be the result of some heretofore undiagnosed condition. Test takers who tend to catastrophize, seeing things as worse than they actually are, may also unintentionally overreport in response to self-report measures.

Underreporting

Underreporting occurs when a test taker describes himself or herself as having less serious or a smaller number of difficulties (or both) than he or she actually has. Referring back to the hypothetical objective benchmark just mentioned, an underreporting test taker would paint a picture of better functioning than would be indicated by an objective assessment. Here, too, a distinction may be drawn between intentional and unintentional underreporting.

In intentional underreporting, the individual knowingly denies or minimizes the extent of his or her psychological difficulties or negative characteristics. As a result, the test scores underestimate his or her level of dysfunction. Differentiating denial from minimization is important but complex. In the former, an individual blatantly denies problems that she or he knows exist; in the latter, the test taker may acknowledge some difficulties or negative characteristics but minimize their extent or impact. Unintentional underreporting occurs when the individual unknowingly denies or minimizes difficulties or negative characteristics. Here, too, objective and subjective indicators of psychological functioning would be at odds; however, in unintentional underreporting, this discrepancy results from the individual's distorted self-concept rather than from an intentional effort to produce misleading test results.

ASSESSING THREATS TO PROTOCOL VALIDITY WITH THE ORIGINAL MMPI

Regardless of intentionality, content nonresponsiveness, overreporting, and underreporting can produce scale scores that distort the appraisal of a test taker's functioning. Recognizing this inherent limitation of self-report inventories, Hathaway and McKinley (1943) incorporated measures termed *validating scores* (later relabeled *Validity Scales*) in the first MMPI manual, noting that "the evaluation of a profile begins with the problem of whether or not the responses of the subject will yield a valid set of scores" (p. 8). Commenting on the relative paucity of efforts by self-report inventory developers to address threats to protocol validity, Meehl and Hathaway (1946) observed,

> It is almost as though we inventory-makers were afraid to say too much about the problem because we had no effective solution for it, but it was too obvious a fact to be ignored so it was met by a polite nod. (p. 526)

Acting on this concern, Hathaway and McKinley (1943) incorporated three Validity Scales, Cannot Say (then known as the Question Score and abbreviated "?"), L, and F, into the original test. The MMPI was not the first self-report measure to make Validity Scales available to its users. Cady (1923) modified the Woodworth Psychoneurotic Inventory, derived from Woodworth's (1920) original Personal Data Sheet, to assess juvenile incorrigibility and incorporated negatively worded repeated items in the revised inventory to examine respondents' "reliability." Maller (1932) included items that were designed to assess respondents' "readiness to confide" in his Character Sketches measure. Humm and Wadsworth (1935), developers of the Humm–Wadsworth Temperament Scales, incorporated scales designed to identify defensive responding to their measure. Ruch (1942) developed an "honesty key" for the Bernreuter Personality inventory (BPI; Bernreuter, 1933), the most widely used self-report inventory prior to the MMPI.

Hathaway and McKinley's (1943) inclusion of Validity Scales on the original MMPI was thus consistent with a growing recognition among test developers of the need to incorporate formal means for assessing and considering threats to protocol validity. As noted, Hathaway and McKinley commented on the need to assess protocol validity in the initial test manual, which included instructions on how to score and interpret the three original Validity Scales. A fourth validity indicator, K, was added to the test in 1946, rounding out the list of original MMPI Validity Scales. Because revised versions of the four original scales remain part of the MMPI-2-RF, their conceptual origins and initial interpretive recommendations are discussed in detail.

Cannot Say (CNS)

Hathaway and McKinley (1943) described the Question Score (?) as "a validating score consisting simply of the total number of items put in the *Cannot Say* category" (p. 4). This definition pertains to the format used for administering the original MMPI, the "Card Form," in which each item was printed on a separate index card. Test takers were instructed to sort the cards into three categories, reflecting their response to each item: true, false, or "cannot say." Hathaway and McKinley reported that the median value of CNS[2] was approximately 30. T-score values were "arbitrarily assigned on the basis of experience and percentile tables rather than on the usual statistical basis" (p. 8). Consistent with the problem of score deflation discussed earlier in connection with nonresponding, Hathaway and McKinley noted that higher scores on this scale were associated with lower scores on the remaining MMPI scales. Foreseeing contemporaneous approaches to confronting the threat of nonresponding, the authors pointed out that "since the items most often questioned [i.e., answered "cannot say"] make up varying percentages of the total items in each scale, the effect of these items on the scores for the different scales will of course vary from one to another" (p. 8).

Hathaway and McKinley (1943) recommended that a T score of 70 "be taken as a sign of invalidity" (p. 8) and that "some allowance should be made in the range of 60–70" (p. 8). Examination of the T-score lookup table included in the test manual indicates that a T score of 69 was set arbitrarily to correspond to a CNS raw score of 100 and that a T score of 61 was assigned to a raw score of 70. Consistent with the authors' observation that the median value on this scale was approximately 30, a T score of 50 was set to correspond to this value. These frequencies of unscorable items seem quite high by contemporary standards. They reflect the original instructions for administering the MMPI, which did not discourage the "cannot say" response option: "If the statement does not apply to you, or if it is something that you don't know about, put it behind the card that says CANNOT SAY." The only instruction provided in the original test manual was the following: "If more than about one tenth of the cards have been put in the *Cannot say* category, the subject should be encouraged to place more in the other categories" (Hathaway & McKinley, 1943, p. 7).

Dahlstrom and Welsh (1960) noted that at an unspecified time after the initial release of the test, the instructions for administering the MMPI were altered to discourage nonresponding. Test takers were instructed to assign fewer than 10 items to this category. The introduction of booklet and answer sheet administration and response formats in 1946 also influenced a trend toward smaller numbers of "cannot say" responses, and the accompanying instructions were refined further to discourage nonresponding. Dahlstrom and Welsh cite Meehl (1946) as recommending that MMPI protocols with more than 30 unscorable items be excluded from research samples.[3] Although these authors admonished clinicians not to "make rigid and categorical use of cutting scores on Validity Scales" (Dahlstrom & Welsh, 1960, p. 118), in the second edition of their *MMPI Handbook,* Dahlstrom, Welsh, and Dahlstrom (1972) indicated that CNS scores below 30 are generally acceptable for interpretation. This recommendation was adopted by Graham (1977) and Greene (1980) in the first editions of their MMPI textbooks. Both authors recommended considering protocols with more than 30 unscorable responses as invalid.

Lie (L)

Hathaway and McKinley (1943) introduced the Lie score as "a validating score that affords a measure of the degree to which the subject may be attempting to falsify his scores by always choosing the response that places him in the most acceptable light socially" (p. 4). They indicated that construction of this scale was inspired by the work of Hartshorne, May, and Shuttleworth (1930), whose research on honesty in children involved concocting situations in which the subjects of their investigations were led to believe that they could get away with dishonest behavior, when in fact experimenters would be able to record and quantify this conduct. The 15 items selected for the L Scale were designed similarly "to detect the person who is lying in the sense of trying to place himself in a highly conventional and socially acceptable light" (Hathaway & McKinley, 1943, p. 8). Responses in the keyed direction reflected uncommon claims of virtue.

As they did for the CNS score, Hathaway and McKinley (1943) devised arbitrary T- score values for L ("based on experience and percentiles" [p. 9]) because the use of uncommonly answered items produced "extremely skewed distribution of raw scores" (pp. 8–9). They went on to point out that a T score above 70 does not necessarily invalidate the protocol: "The fact that a high L score is likely to accompany a high Hy score does not invalidate the high Hy finding because the hysterical subject frequently seems to believe himself to be more immune to psychological frailties than does the average person" (p. 9). However, Hathaway and McKinley did recommend that a high L score should engender a cautious interpretation, although they did not provide any specific recommendations on how such caution was to be exercised.

Hathaway and McKinley's (1943) interpretive recommendations for L reflect two important, related features of the scale: first, they saw the potential that elevated scores could reflect both intentional and (as in their example of a high score on Hy) unintentional underreporting; second, they advised that elevated scores on Substantive Scales should not be ignored (i.e., deemed invalid) even when test takers produced markedly elevated L scores. Dahlstrom, Welsh, and Dahlstrom (1972) maintained this approach, observing that even markedly elevated L scores were likely to be found in "subjects who are honestly describing themselves as they see themselves" (p. 158) rather than in a "subject that has deliberately slanted his answers to create a special impression of freedom from any psychological problems or characterological fault" (p. 158). These authors also noted that individuals who hold strong religious beliefs and who describe themselves accurately tend to produce elevated scores on L.

Infrequency (F)

Hathaway and McKinley (1943) labeled this scale the *Validity Score* and indicated that it

> serves as a check on the validity of the whole record. If the F score is high, the other scales are likely to be invalid either because the subject was careless or unable to comprehend the items, or because someone made extensive errors in entering items on the record sheet. (p. 4)

The latter interpretation relates to the considerable potential for error in transcribing the three piles of sorted cards (corresponding to true, false, and "cannot say" responses) onto a record sheet that was then used to score the MMPI scales. Hathaway and McKinley explained that the

> F score is derived from a group of 64 items that have been very infrequently answered in the scored direction by normal persons. All the items are answered in the infrequent direction less than ten percent of the time by normals, and the percentage is but little higher for miscellaneous abnormal subjects. (p. 8)

As they did for the other original validity indicators, Hathaway and McKinley (1943) devised arbitrary T scores for F, setting the value 70 to correspond to a raw score of 12. They indicated that "scores above 70 indicate the whole record to be invalid" (p. 8) but noted that exceptions should be made for "persons who are highly individual and independent [who] may honestly make infrequent responses to items making up the F score" (p. 8) and "badly neurotic or psychotic subjects" (p. 8), who would be expected to score above 70 on F but still produce valid scores on the test.

It is noteworthy that assessment of overreporting is not mentioned in Hathaway and McKinley's (1943) discussion of F. The scale was devised to detect content nonresponsiveness or clerical scoring errors. However, soon after its publication, important alternative interpretations were identified. Meehl and Hathaway (1946) observed,

> From the first it was recognized that F represented several things . . . any error in recording, such as mistaking true items for false items and the like, would raise the F score appreciably. Similarly, if a subject could not understand what he was reading adequately enough to make conventional answers to these items, the F score would obviously be higher. It was felt to be axiomatic that this method would eliminate as invalid records of subjects who could not read and comprehend or who refused to cooperate sufficiently to make expected placements. In addition, however, it was early discovered that schizoid subjects *and subjects who apparently wished to put themselves in a bad light* also obtained high scores. (p. 536; emphasis added)

Commenting on the first alternative, Meehl and Hathaway (1946) noted that

> the schizoid group obtained high scores because, due to delusional or other aberrant mental states, they said very unusual things in responding to the items. . . . This is referred to as distortion since we feel that an impartial study would not justify the patient's placements. (p. 536)

Thus, Meehl and Hathaway identified unintentional overreporting as a potential source of elevated scores on F.

With respect to intentional overreporting, Meehl and Hathaway (1946) stated:

> With the problems of measurement that developed in the armed forces where a subject might be expected frequently to attempt to put himself in a bad light in answering the MMPI, the F score became especially interesting. It was, of course, immediately possible to consider the F score as evidence of this attempt to malinger and obtain fallaciously bad scores on other scales. (p. 537)

They went on to describe the first MMPI "malingering" study, in which a group of men enrolled in the Army Specialized Training Program "who had completed a considerable portion of their training in psychology" (p. 537) were asked to take the MMPI twice (in a counterbalanced design), once under standard instructions and another time with instructions "to assume that they wished to avoid being accepted in the draft and in order to be rejected they were to obtain adverse scores without giving themselves away" (p. 537). Meehl and Hathaway reported finding that "96 percent of the 'fake bad' records had a raw score F of 15 or more (T > 78), indicating that even these men who were somewhat cognizant of psychological measurement betrayed themselves when they attempted to fake a bad record" (p. 537). The authors concluded:

> From this experiment it appeared that F was a very good device for identifying the intentional faking that could be set up in an experimental situation. It still seemed desirable, however, to attempt to separate among the individuals obtaining relatively high F scores who were of the above-described schizoid type or who were simply over pessimistic in their view of themselves, from those who for one reason or another faked a bad score or did not understand the items. (p. 537)

In summary, Meehl and Hathaway (1946) identified three possible threats to protocol validity associated with elevated scores on F: content nonresponsiveness in the form of unintentional random responding, unintentional overreporting, and intentional overreporting.

In the first revision of the MMPI manual, Hathaway and McKinley (1951) noted that their initial recommendation that T scores above 70 on F identify invalid protocols was too strong. Instead, they recommended using a cutoff of 80T on F and recognized that even scores at that level did not necessarily imply a priori invalidity. Dahlstrom et al. (1972) also recommended 80T on F as a cut score for identifying very unusual protocols but noted that it is possible to obtain valid information from such protocols produced by test takers with severe psychopathology.

Correction (K)

The K Scale[4] was not included or mentioned in the original MMPI manual. It was formally incorporated in the test material in 1946, with the publication of a supplementary manual. Also introduced was the K correction. Although concerns were expressed about it from its inception, the procedure was applied routinely in MMPI interpretation and was carried over to the MMPI-2 when it was published in 1989. The K correction was not included in the MMPI-2-RF—a substantial change that, although consistent with subsequent developments with the MMPI-2, requires a somewhat detailed examination.

The K Correction

McKinley, Hathaway, and Meehl (1948) indicated that the K Scale was developed in an attempt to "correct the scores obtained on the personality variables proper for the influence of attitudes toward the test situation" (p. 20). Nonrelevant sources of variance in the MMPI Clinical Scales were to be removed to improve prediction. The basic idea was that the correction would increase scores on the Clinical Scales in cases of underreporting, producing higher scores that more accurately reflected the individual's psychopathology, and reduce scores on the Clinical Scales in cases of overreporting.

A more detailed account of the rationale for constructing the K Scale was articulated by Meehl and Hathaway (1946), who described its development as a "suppressor variable" designed to correct scores on the Clinical Scales for the effects of invalid responding. Following Horst's (1941) development of the subject, Meehl (1945b) had previously described the function of a potential suppressor variable in psychological testing as one designed "to 'suppress' these components of the independent variable which are not correlates of the criterion" (p. 550). He went on to explain that a useful suppressor variable would be correlated with a predictor (e.g., an MMPI Clinical Scale) but not the criterion it is designed to predict. Removal from the predictor of variance associated with the suppressor (i.e., variance that does not contribute to the prediction task) would leave a residual score (predictor minus suppressor) that is better able to account for variance in the criterion.

Meehl and Hathaway (1946) indicated that initial consideration was given to using the L Scale in this manner. However,

> while the positive presence of the rise in the L score seemed quite valid as an indicator that the individual taking the test was being dishonest and might be somewhat unreliable, if no rise in L was observed, the finding could not be so positively and clearly interpreted. The L score was a trap for the naïve subject but easily avoided by more sophisticated subjects. (p. 538)

To support this assertion, Meehl and Hathaway (1946) reported the results of the first MMPI "fake good" study, which, like the first "malingering" investigation just discussed with regard to F, involved a sample of Army Special Training Program psychology students. These 53 individuals completed the test twice (counterbalanced), once under standard instructions and then under instructions to "make certain in taking the test that they would be acceptable to army induction" (p. 538). Meehl and Hathaway reported that

> these records showed no appreciable rise in L. It is also true, however, that the majority of profiles were only slightly better, if any, than the corresponding non-fake profiles. . . . At least, one may conclude that the intent to deceive is not often detectable by L when the subjects are relatively normal and sophisticated. (p. 538)

Meehl and Hathaway (1946) went on to describe two general strategies that were pursued in an attempt to develop a more sensitive measure of underreporting. The first, which, using contemporary terminology, can be characterized as utilizing a simulation design, asked subjects to "deliberately assume a generally defined attitude" (p. 539), instructing them to "fake good" or "fake bad." These responses were then compared to those they provided when they took the MMPI under standard instructions. Items answered differently as a result of the manipulation would be candidates for scales assessing misleading responding. Meehl and Hathaway reported finding that the two sets of instructions did not identify the same items and that scales based on both sets of items were equally effective in detecting underreported and overreported protocols. They also concluded that none of the scales devised in this manner improved on F in identifying overreporting, and like L, they were not effective in detecting "sophisticated persons who deliberately attempted to obtain better scores" (p. 539).

The second approach described by Meehl and Hathaway (1946), which today would be labeled a *known groups* design, identified

> among presumably functional and normal [cases] those [protocols] which are so abnormal as to indicate that the individual should have been in a hospital and attempt to discover the items among these records that will differentiate them from the records of actually abnormal persons (pp. 539–540)

and a counterpart where "one chooses cases who were in the hospital but whose records show a normal profile" (p. 540) and contrasted their item responses with those of "hospital patients with suitably abnormal profiles" (p. 540). Meehl and Hathaway reported that they developed several scales following these procedures, and "whichever of these methods was used . . . the resultant scales were about equally effective and about equally unsatisfactory regardless of the approach and the particular item content" (p. 540). They went on to report that "after some two years of this experimentation all of the scales that had showed any promise were reconsidered by applying them to various available groups that had not been used in their derivation and from among them all a single scale which was originally called L_6 was chosen as the best" (p. 540).

Meehl and Hathaway (1946) reported that L_6, the precursor to K, was derived by comparing the responses of two samples. A group of 25 men and 25 women receiving treatment at a "psychopathic hospital" who scored 60T or higher on L and had diagnoses indicating that they should have produced abnormal MMPI profiles, but actually generated normal-range scores on the Clinical Scales, constituted the target group. Their responses were compared with those of men and women in the general group (i.e., the original Minnesota normals used to develop the Clinical Scales described in Chapter 1). In this manner, 22 items were assigned to L_6. The authors reported that "all of these items showed a percent difference of 30 or more between the criterion cases and the control group, males and females being considered separately" (p. 541), and they observed that "the content of these items would seem to suggest an attitude of denying worries, inferiority feelings and psychiatrically unhealthy symptoms, together with a disposition to see only good in others as well as oneself" (p. 541).

Meehl and Hathaway (1946) indicated that after selecting the 22 L_6 items, they examined a large number of archival records of cases not used in the development of the measure and found that although it was effective as a measure of underreporting and overreporting, the scale "left much to be desired" (p. 542). Specifically, they were concerned that scores on L_6 "tended to be low in severe depressive or Schizophrenic patient records and thus lead to an under-interpretation in spite of the fact that the patients were very grossly abnormal" (p. 543). Because when applied as a correction factor, low scores on L_6 had the effect of inappropriately lowering scores on the Clinical Scales in cases where test takers were actually disordered, Meehl and Hathaway sought to apply a correction to the correction. They did so by identifying eight items found to be insensitive to underreporting or overreporting (reflected in comparable responses in the Army Special Training Program "fake good," "fake bad," and standard instruction samples just described) that differentiated patients diagnosed with depressive disorders or Schizophrenia from the general contrast group. The eight correction items were keyed in the direction of the patients' responses and were added to the 22 L_6 items to form the K Scale.

Meehl and Hathaway (1946) explored the potential utility of K as a suppressor variable by examining whether it differentiated normals from abnormals who produced borderline profiles, defined as having at least one Clinical Scale score at 65T or above but no score above 80T. They found that a cutoff on K that produced a selection ratio comparable to the base rate of abnormal cases in the sample accurately identified 72% of the abnormal men and 61% of the normal men, and 66% of the abnormal women and 59% of the normal women. Further analyses indicated that some Clinical Scales better differentiated normal from abnormal cases when K was considered than did others. In limiting their analyses to borderline cases, Meehl and Hathaway admonished that

> there are upper and lower limits beyond which deviations on K cannot effectively operate. Profiles showing scores [on the Clinical Scales] above 80 are to be interpreted as abnormal no matter how low the score on K falls; while if a profile shows no scores above 65 [on the Clinical Scales] we cannot tell whether a high K means the profile should be adjusted toward more severe scores or is merely that of an actually normal person who for some reason or other took a defensive attitude when being tested. (p. 544)

The final development of the K-correction was described by McKinley et al. (1948), who reported on the derivation of the correction weights used in this procedure. The authors explained, "Since high K scores represent the defensive or 'fake good' end of the test attitude continuum, the most obvious approach to the problem is to add K (or some function of K) to the raw score on each personality variable, i.e., increase the score in the direction of abnormality" (p. 21). Identifying the proportion of the K raw score to be added involved trial-and-error testing of alternative weights and selection of those that optimized separation between normals and individuals diagnosed with the disorder corresponding to each of eight of the original Clinical Scales. For three of the scales (2, 3, and 6), the authors concluded that adding a K correction did not improve prediction. For the remaining five scales, weights ranging from 20% to 100% of the K raw score were selected. Commenting on the weights they derived in this manner, McKinley and colleagues noted that "it must be emphasized that these weights are optimal, within our sample, for the differentiation of largely inpatient psychiatric cases of full-blown psychoneurosis and psychosis from a general Minnesota 'normal' group. For other clinical purposes it is possible that other [weights] would be more appropriate" (p. 24).

Two important caveats were thus proffered by the developers of the K correction. Meehl and Hathaway (1946) recommended that the correction be applied only to scales with noncorrected T scores ranging from 65 to 80. And McKinley et al. (1948) reiterated throughout their article introducing the procedure that the identified weights were best viewed as provisional, subject to refinement with more rigorous methodology and cross-validation with other samples and populations. Nonetheless, McKinley and colleagues concluded their introductory article with the following recommendation: "It is suggested that the K-correction should be made routinely by users of the MMPI and that old records should be scored and redrawn if any research or validation study is to be carried on" (p. 31).

McKinley et al.'s (1948) surprisingly sweeping recommendation was largely followed, and application of the correction soon became routine in clinical practice. Summarizing the results of subsequent efforts to validate the procedure, Dahlstrom and Welsh (1960) observed that "the few studies available that provide cross-validational evidence on the K correction have . . . [indicated that] the K scale corrections do not seem to be beneficial, and may actually reduce the effective separations obtained without K corrections" (p. 154). This included a study cited in the 1946 *Supplementary Manual for the MMPI* (Hathaway & McKinley, 1946). In an updated review of the literature, Dahlstrom et al. (1972) noted that subsequent studies of the K correction also failed to support its use. Nonetheless, they concluded that it was necessary to continue to interpret K-corrected scores because most of the empirical correlates of the Clinical Scales, in particular the code types, were identified using K-corrected profiles.

Recent empirical studies have shed additional light on the K correction. Barthlow, Graham, Ben-Porath, Tellegen, and McNulty (2002) examined the contribution of the correction to the predictive validity of the Clinical Scales in two outpatient samples and also explored whether alternative weights could improve on those that were applied to the scales. They concluded that neither the routine nor any other correction weights improved the validity of the Clinical Scales. On the other hand, noncorrected scores were no more valid than corrected ones. By contrast, Detrick, Chibnall, and Rosso (2001) explored correlations between scores on the MMPI-2 Clinical Scales and the Inwald Personality Inventory (IPI; Inwald, 1992), a measure often used in screening candidates for law enforcement positions. Their results indicated a very substantial attenuation of correlations between MMPI-2 scales and relevant IPI scales when the K correction was applied. This effect was most pronounced—essentially removing the predictive validity of the scales—for Clinical Scales 7 and 8, which received the highest weighted K correction, and least prominent for Scale 9, which received the lowest weighted correction.

On the basis of this body of research, modern MMPI textbook authors have concluded that the K correction does not work. For example, Greene (2011) commented that "there appears to be little empirical data that justifies the use of the K-correction process" (p. 82). Graham (2006) reached the same conclusion. However, both authors agreed with Dahlstrom et al. (1972) that the K correction cannot be abandoned altogether in MMPI-2 interpretation because the preponderance of research establishing the correlates of the Clinical Scales and code types was conducted with K-corrected scores. Because this constraint does not apply to the MMPI-2-RF, no correction weights are applied to the Substantive Scales of the test.

K as a Measure of Underreporting

Although intended originally to function only as a correction factor, evidence that the K Scale contributed incrementally (beyond L) in identifying underreporting led early on to its addition as the fourth and final Validity Scale of the original MMPI. In the 1951 revised MMPI manual, Hathaway and McKinley noted that in contrast to L, K "is somewhat more subtle and taps a slightly different set of distorting factors. A high K score represents defensiveness against psychological weakness, and may indicate a defensiveness that verges upon deliberate distortion in the direction of making a more 'normal' appearance" (p. 18). Dahlstrom and Welsh (1960) recommended that T scores of 75 or above on K be interpreted as reflecting "extreme facades of adequacy and freedom from personal defects" (p. 150).

Heilbrun (1961) identified an important caveat for interpreting K scores in nonclinical settings. Following up on concerns raised by McKinley et al. (1948), who observed that individuals with higher educational levels tested in these settings scored above average on K, Heilbrun (1961) found that in nonclinical settings, higher scores on K were associated with better than average levels of adjustment rather than with defensiveness. Smith (1959) had previously reported similar findings.

Summary

Recognizing the inherent susceptibility of self-report measures to misleading responding and scoring errors, Hathaway, McKinley, and Meehl endeavored to develop a set of validity indicators for the MMPI to alert users to potential threats to the validity of individual test protocols. Nonresponding was assessed with the CNS score, although Hathaway and McKinley (1943) recognized that this was a crude measure because the threat to the validity of a given scale was dependent on the percentage of unscorable items on it. The F Scale, developed to detect random responding and clerical scoring errors, was found to be an effective overreporting measure as well. However, the authors recognized that in addition to being sensitive to intentional overreporting, elevated scores on F in clinical settings for some individuals reflected genuine symptoms of psychopathology, and for others, they represented the effects of unintentional overreporting. L was developed to detect underreporting. From their initial discussions of the scale, it is clear that Hathaway and McKinley perceived the measure to be sensitive to both intentional and unintentional underreporting. Dahlstrom et al. (1972) reiterated this point and also observed that certain cultural factors (e.g., being raised in a religious home) were associated with above average scores on L.

When Meehl began his quest to develop a scale that could be used to correct Clinical Scale scores for the effects of over- and underreporting, he found L and F to be inadequate for this purpose. Two years of experimentation resulted in the identification of a set of items he labeled the K Scale, which was used for this purpose.

It was subsequently adopted as a complementary measure of this construct and considered a more subtle measure of underreporting than L. However, as with L, Hathaway and Meehl characterized scores on K as reflecting both intentional and unintentional underreporting. Subsequent investigations indicated that in nonclinical settings, higher scores on K were actually associated with better than average psychological adjustment.

THE MMPI-2 VALIDITY SCALES

The Restandardization Project that produced the MMPI-2 was described in detail in Chapter 1. With regard to the Validity Scales, the committee retained the four MMPI validity indicators just reviewed and added three new measures: Back F (F_B), Variable Response Inconsistency (VRIN), and True Response Inconsistency (TRIN), described initially as *Additional Validity Indicators* (Butcher, Dahlstrom, Graham, Tellegen & Kaemmer, 1989). Two more scales, Infrequency Psychopathology (F_p), developed by Arbisi and Ben-Porath (1995), and Superlative Self-Presentation (S), developed by Butcher and Han (1995), were added to the test material and incorporated in the 2001 update of the MMPI-2 manual (Butcher, Graham, Ben-Porath, Tellegen, Dahlstrom & Kaemmer, 2001). This update also introduced a reorganized Validity Scale profile. A final measure, the Symptom Validity Scale (FBS), developed by Lees-Haley, English, and Glenn (1991) and originally labeled the *Fake Bad Scale*, was added to the MMPI-2 Validity Scale profile in 2007 and documented in a 2009 research monograph (Ben-Porath, Graham & Tellegen, 2009).

MMPI Validity Indicators Carried Over to the MMPI-2

The standard validity indicators, CNS, L, F, and K were carried over to the MMPI-2 in nearly identical form. As discussed, original MMPI "norms" for these measures were devised arbitrarily by Hathaway and McKinley (1943) for all but the K Scale. Although the authors subsequently concluded that these norms "were not appropriately chosen" (Hathaway & McKinley, 1951, p. 12), no changes were made to the MMPI T scores for these scales. The Restandardization Committee decided to use the new normative sample to set the norms for the MMPI-2 versions of these measures, which resulted in several substantial changes. Some interpretive recommendations made in the 1989 MMPI-2 manual (e.g., for K) reflected these changes, whereas others (e.g., for L and F) did not.

Cannot Say (CNS)

As with the MMPI, the CNS score on the MMPI-2 is the number of unanswered or double-answered items in a protocol. Hathaway and McKinley (1943) had set the mean T-score level for this scale at 30, the modal number of items sorted in the "cannot say" category by the original normative sample. However, as discussed earlier, with the change from instructions that gave the CNS response equal standing with true and false responses to instructions that strongly discouraged this response, revised MMPI interpretive recommendations were based on raw CNS scores. This practice was carried over to the MMPI-2, and no T scores were developed for CNS. Because the two versions of the test included roughly the same number of items, similar cutoffs were adopted for the MMPI-2. Raw scores of 30 and higher on this scale were identified as indicating that "the test records must be considered highly suspect, if not completely invalid" (Butcher et al., 1989, p. 22).

Lie (L)

The L Scale was carried over to the MMPI-2 in its entirety. Consistent with Hathaway and McKinley's concerns about the skewness of L-score distributions, and contrary to the pattern for all other MMPI scales but F, T scores on the MMPI-2 version of L were notably higher than those assigned by Hathaway and McKinley for the MMPI. For example, whereas a raw score of 10 corresponded to a T score of 70 on the original MMPI, the corresponding MMPI-2 T scores for men and women were 78 and 81, respectively. Interpretive recommendations indicated that T scores at or above this level "very likely reflect a pervasive test-taking orientation that adversely affects the meaning of scores on all the clinical scales" (Butcher et al., 1989, p. 23). Such protocols were characterized as "probably invalid." This interpretation contradicted Hathaway and McKinley's (1943) observation (cited earlier) that Substantive Scale findings should not be deemed invalid based only on an elevated L score.

Infrequency (F)

The F Scale lost four "objectionable" items (see Chapter 1) in the restandardization, resulting in a 60-item MMPI-2 scale. Like L scores, MMPI-2 T scores on F were considerably higher than those the authors set arbitrarily for this scale on the MMPI. For example, whereas a raw score of 21 corresponded to 90T on the MMPI, the same raw score yielded MMPI-2 F Scale T scores of 101 and 109 for men and women, respectively. Interpretive recommendations for the scale focused on random responding and overreporting, with T scores of 91 or above indicating a protocol that is probably invalid owing to problems such as random responding, reading problems, or "faking bad."

Correction (K)

The MMPI-2 K Scale was identical in composition to the original version of this measure. However, because T scores on the MMPI K Scale were based on the actual responses of the original MMPI normative sample, unlike L and F, corresponding MMPI-2 K Scale T scores were lower. For example, whereas a T score of 70 corresponded to a raw score of 23 on the MMPI, the same raw score produced MMPI-2 T scores of 66 for men and 67 for women. The authors recommended that T scores of 71 and higher indicate marked defensiveness or "faking good" but noted that lesser deviations from the mean could be found in normal, well-adjusted individuals.

Validity Scales Introduced in the Initial (1989) MMPI-2 Manual

Three new Validity Scales were included in the 1989 MMPI-2 manual. They were described as complementing the original validity indicators but were afforded secondary status. They were not included on the Validity Scale profile, and no specific T-score-based interpretive cutoffs were provided in the manual. For example, regarding the inconsistent responding indicators, the authors stated that "the use of VRIN and TRIN is experimental at this stage and requires caution until more empirical evidence has been accumulated" (Butcher et al., 1989, p. 28).

Back F (F_B)

All the items needed to score the "basic" MMPI-2 profile (consisting of L, F, K, and the 10 Clinical Scales) were placed in the first 370 items of the test booklet. This was done to facilitate an abbreviated administration of the test for individuals thought to be incapable of completing the full inventory. As a result, no F item appeared in the MMPI-2 booklet after number 361, resulting in no F Scale assessment of infrequent responding past that point in the booklet. Consisting of 40 items, the F_B Scale was developed to facilitate continued measurement of infrequent responding in the latter part of the test booklet. The 1989 manual indicated that these items were answered in the keyed direction by less than 10% of the normative sample (the criterion used to develop F for the MMPI). The actual cutoff used to select items for F_B was 20% or less of the men and women of the MMPI-2 normative sample. Although no specific interpretive guidelines were provided for the scale, the authors indicated that it could be used "to identify records in which the individual has stopped paying attention to the test items, and has shifted to an essentially random pattern of responding" (Butcher et al., 1989, p. 27). They noted that this would be particularly salient when considering the validity of scores on the Supplementary and Content Scales, presumably because items that appeared in the latter part of the MMPI-2 booklet were scored primarily on those scales.

Variable Response Inconsistency (VRIN) and
True Response Inconsistency (TRIN)

Although the F Scale was developed to identify invalid protocols resulting from content nonresponsiveness (or clerical error), as detailed earlier, use of the scale evolved rapidly to focus on overreporting. Measures of inconsistent responding were developed subsequently to focus specifically on content nonresponsiveness. However, they did not become part of the standard battery of validity indicators on the original MMPI.

Buechley and Ball (1952) were the first to develop an inconsistent responding measure for the MMPI. Using the 16 repeated items in the Group Form of the inventory (added to the answer sheet to facilitate machine scoring), they developed the Test–Retest (TR) Scale, which consisted of a count of the number of inconsistent responses to the 16 repeated items. The authors proposed that TR be used as a supplementary validity indicator that could "detect those persons making random responses" (Buechley & Ball, 1952, p. 299). Recognizing that elevations on F could reflect two types of validity problems (random responding or overreporting) and severe psychopathology, Buechley and Ball proposed that protocols with high F scores coupled with a deviant finding on TR be interpreted as invalid owing to random responding.

Commenting on the utility of the TR index, Dahlstrom et al. (1972) noted the work of Haertzen and Hill (1963), who had developed a scale labeled Carelessness (Ca) for the Addiction Research Center Inventory. Haertzen and Hill included 15 repeated items as well as eight pairs of items with opposite content on the Ca scale and concluded that a subscale made up of the eight opposite-keyed items was more sensitive to random responding than one based on the repeated subset of items. Dahlstrom et al. (1972) consequently recommended that a similar measure be developed for the MMPI. Greene (1978) pursued this recommendation and developed a Carelessness (CS) Scale by selecting 12 pairs of highly correlated MMPI items judged to be either very similar or opposite in content. Seven negatively correlated pairs of items with very similar content and five positively correlated pairs of items with opposite content constituted the CS Scale. Greene recommended that the scale be used as an adjunct to F and TR to determine "whether the client or patient is willing or able to complete the MMPI in an appropriate manner" (pp. 409–410).

The MMPI-2 inconsistent response indicators, VRIN and TRIN, were developed by Tellegen, who had earlier constructed similarly labeled measures for the Multidimensional Personality Questionnaire (MPQ; Tellegen, 1995/2003). Tellegen (1988) conceptualized Consistency Scales such as TR and CS as analogous to measures of aberrant responding used in ability testing to detect "faulty" response patterns (i.e., answering difficult items correctly more often than easier ones). He distinguished between two types of inconsistent responding—same (i.e., items answered true in an inconsistent manner or items answered false inconsistently) and opposite (i.e., items answered true and false inconsistently)—and noted that a scale such as TR was not sensitive to "same" inconsistent responding because only opposite responses to its item pairs were inconsistent. In an extreme case, if a test taker were to respond true to every MMPI item, the raw score on TR would be 0.

Tellegen (1988) described the MPQ VRIN scale as being made up of pairs of items, the content of which "varies greatly from pair to pair but is quite homogeneous within each pair" (p. 631). MPQ TRIN was also made up of item pairs covering different content domains, but the items making up these pairs were very dissimilar in content so that the same response (both true or both false) would be inconsistent. Tellegen reported findings showing that MPQ TRIN was sensitive to both simulated acquiescent (i.e., inconsistent true) and nonacquiescent (i.e., inconsistent false) responding, and VRIN was effective at detecting simulated variable (i.e., randomly inserted true or false) responding. Neither scale was effective at detecting the type of inconsistent responding detected by the other, demonstrating the need for both types of scales for detecting fixed (TRIN) and random (VRIN) responding.

The MMPI-2 versions of VRIN and TRIN were designed to serve the same function as Tellegen's MPQ scales, with three noteworthy variations. As just mentioned,

Tellegen sought to ensure content heterogeneity across item pairs to keep scores on the MPQ Inconsistency Scales as free as possible from the effects of individual differences in actual personality traits. For the MMPI, it was thought particularly important that scores on the Inconsistency Scales not be affected by psychopathology. To accomplish this goal, we[5] selected for the MMPI-2 VRIN and TRIN Scales only item pairs that, as scored, were correlated below a maximal level with scores on the Clinical Scales. For example, if a TRIN item pair was keyed so that a true response to both items was inconsistent, that combination of responses, treated like a mini two-item scale, would be selected only if it were minimally correlated with any of the Clinical Scales.

A second variation involved expanding the MMPI-2 version of VRIN to include item pairs that would also qualify for TRIN. Whereas, like the original MMPI TR scale, the MPQ version of VRIN included only pairs of items with very similar content, keyed so that opposite responses would be inconsistent, the MMPI-2 VRIN scale also included items with opposite content, keyed so that the same response to the items would be inconsistent. This change was designed to expand the VRIN scale to include a broader range of variable inconsistent responses. It also introduced considerable overlap between the scales, with 10 of the 23 TRIN item pairs also scored on VRIN.

A final modification was designed to accommodate the fact that inconsistency can be asymmetrical. Consider the following hypothetical pair of items:

1. My life is full of stress.
2. I lead a stress-free life.

Responding true to both items would undoubtedly be inconsistent. However, a false response to both is plausible. An individual may experience sufficient stress from time to time to respond false to item 2 but not frequently enough to respond true to item 1. Thus, whereas a true–true response combination would be inconsistent, a false–false response would not.

Item pairs for the MMPI-2 VRIN and TRIN scales were selected after examination of correlations between responses to all possible pairs of items in two large clinical samples. Item pairs with high negative correlations (indicating empirically that the same response to both was uncommon) were candidates for inclusion on both VRIN and TRIN. Item pairs with high positive correlations (indicating empirically that an opposite response to both was uncommon) were candidates for VRIN. To be assigned to these scales, a candidate pair had to be made up of items that were sufficiently highly correlated with each other and minimally correlated (when scored as a mini-scale) with the Clinical Scales across samples. To detect pairs that should be scored asymmetrically, the observed to expected (based on chance) frequency of each pair of responses was compared. This identified response combinations that were unexpected statistically and would therefore likely be inconsistent. As a final hurdle, any pair of responses that satisfied these statistical criteria had to be judged by both Tellegen and me to be semantically inconsistent as keyed.

This process yielded a VRIN scale made of 67 possible pairs of inconsistent responses and a TRIN scale comprising 23 possible response pairs. In light of their novelty as MMPI validity indicators, interpretive recommendations for VRIN and TRIN in the 1989 manual were relatively vague. The scales were described as "expected to complement L, F, and K in unique and useful ways" (Butcher et al., 1989, p. 28) by identifying possible origins of elevated scores on the original Validity Scales. "For example, a high F score combined with a high VRIN score is more likely to indicate a profile that is uninterpretable owing to carelessness, confusion, etc., than if VRIN is not elevated" (p. 28). Raw score cutoffs corresponding to a T score of 80 were recommended for identifying significant inconsistent responding. T scores on TRIN were set up to always be equal to or greater than 50, with a designation of "T" or "F" indicating the direction of inconsistent responding if the T score exceeded 50. Studies by Berry et al. (1991) and Handel, Arnau, Archer, and Dandy (2006) supported these cutoffs.

Validity Scales Incorporated in the Revised (2001) MMPI-2 Manual

As has been the case throughout the MMPI's history, efforts to improve the test, including development of additional Validity Scales, continued following the introduction of the MMPI-2. During the decade after publication of the revised inventory, empirical data on the Validity Scales introduced in the MMPI-2 manual accumulated, and new scales (including new validity indicators) were constructed and tested, leading the University of Minnesota Press to initiate publication of an updated test manual to reflect these advances with the test. In the revised edition of the MMPI-2 manual (Butcher et al., 2001), two validity indicators, Infrequency Psychopathology (F_p) and Superlative Self-Presentation (S), were added to the standard set of validity indicators. These measures plus the scales first introduced in 1989 (F_B, VRIN, and TRIN) were incorporated into a reorganized Validity Scale profile corresponding to the conceptual framework outlined at the beginning of this chapter.

Infrequent Psychopathology (F_p)

Arbisi and Ben-Porath (1995) developed the F_p Scale to address a significant challenge in interpreting scores on the multifaceted F Scale. As reviewed earlier, Hathaway and McKinley (1943) developed F to identify protocols compromised by random responding or scoring errors. In their initial publication on the scale, the authors stated, "If the F score is high, the scales are likely to be invalid either because the subject was careless or unable to comprehend the items, or because of extensive errors in entering the items on the record sheet. A high F score has no other known interpretation" (p. 9). The authors soon discovered another possible reason why test takers might produce deviant scores on F and noted that "F scores will validly be somewhat high for certain persons. These are most often of two types: First, some persons who are highly individual and independent . . . second, a number of rather badly neurotic or psychotic subjects obtain high F scores validly" (p. 8). As discussed earlier, a third reason why test takers may produce elevated F scores—overreporting—was discovered in the context of military applications of the MMPI (Meehl & Hathaway, 1946). Thus, three non–mutually exclusive factors could contribute to elevated F Scale scores: overreporting, random responding, and genuine psychopathology. MMPI users were challenged to distinguish these very different factors in their interpretations.

This challenge became even greater with publication of the MMPI-2, when, as discussed earlier, deriving standard scores for the scale resulted in T scores that were substantially higher than on the original version of the test. This proved to be particularly problematic in settings in which individuals with severe psychopathology were likely to be assessed (e.g., psychiatric inpatient units and facilities). These individuals were now much more likely to produce F scores in ranges that would raise questions about the validity of the protocol and possible symptom overreporting. With the addition of VRIN, MMPI-2 users were able to effectively consider the possible contribution of random responding (both intentional and unintentional) to high F scores, but this still left in place the very substantial confound of genuine psychopathology and overreporting. Arbisi and Ben-Porath (1995) developed the F_p scale to address this challenge.[6]

Using a data set collected at a Veterans Administration (VA) inpatient unit, Arbisi and Ben-Porath (1995) first sought to document the problem and its origin. They applied the cutoff of 91T or higher recommended in the manual for detecting likely invalid protocols (after removing invalid protocols detected by VRIN and TRIN) and found that approximately 30% of the sample produced invalid test results based on F. Applying the same cutoff to the recently introduced F_B Scale, nearly 44% of the sample reached or exceeded 91T. Examination of F and F_B scale item response frequencies pointed to the reason why so many protocols appeared to be invalid. A sizable proportion of the items scored on these scales were quite commonly answered in the "infrequent" direction. In fact, more than half of the inpatients responded to some items in the scored direction. High F_B findings were more prevalent because all the items on the scale were answered infrequently by the current normative sample, which had been used to select the items, whereas some of the F Scale items, which had been selected on the basis of response patterns of the original normative sample, were not answered infrequently in the keyed direction by the MMPI-2 normative sample. For example, an original F item related to excessive use of alcohol was answered in the keyed direction by 44% of the MMPI-2 normative sample.

On the basis of these findings, we concluded that a scale composed of items answered infrequently by psychiatric inpatients would be less confounded than F with genuine psychopathology and consequently more effective at detecting overreporting in settings with high base rates of significant psychopathology. Using the same inpatient sample, we identified a set of MMPI-2 items answered true or false by 20% or less of subjects in this sample. Using an archival sample of (non-VA) psychiatric inpatients, we found 27 items from the original list that were also answered by 20% or less of the men and women in the second sample. After confirming that all these items were also answered more infrequently by the men and women in the normative sample, we designated these 27 items for the Infrequent Psychopathology F_p Scale.

We next sought to test the new scale empirically, reasoning that to be more effective than F because it is less confounded with actual psychopathology, (1) F_p scores should be lower than F scores in clinical samples and, relatedly, use of comparable cutoffs should result in fewer cases identified as invalid in such samples; (2) scores on F_p should be less correlated with substantive measures of psychopathology than F; (3) greater differences between clinical and nonclinical samples would be found on F than on F_p; (4) F_p should better distinguish psychiatric patients from individuals simulating a "fake bad" approach to the test than F does; and (5) F_p should add incrementally to F in discriminating psychiatric patients from individuals instructed to overreport in responding to the MMPI-2. We presented data supporting all these hypotheses (Arbisi & Ben-Porath, 1995).

Following the introduction of F_p, a considerable body of research replicated and expanded on these findings. On the basis of a meta-analysis of studies of MMPI-2 overreporting indicators, Rogers, Sewell, Martin, and Vitacco (2003) concluded that

> the most important clinical finding from the current meta-analysis involves the usefulness of the F_p across settings and diagnoses. The F_p yielded strong effect sizes and comparatively consistent cut scores that appear useful across settings and diagnostic groups. Despite time honored traditions, we recommend the F_p as the primary MMPI-2 scale for the assessment of feigning. (p. 173)

Although encouraging, this appraisal overstated somewhat the potential for using F_p. In some studies, the F Scale (e.g., Barber-Rioja, Zottoli, Kucharski & Duncan, 2009) or F_B (e.g., Bagby, Marshall & Bacchiochi, 2005) were more effective than F_p in detecting overreporting, indicating the advantage of having multiple infrequent response indicators on the MMPI-2.

Superlative Self-Presentation (S)

Noting that L was developed rationally and that K was developed in reference to psychiatric patients, Butcher and Han (1995) designed the S Scale "to explore a different approach to assessing some individuals' tendency to proclaim possession of extreme virtue and absence of psychopathology on the MMPI-2 item pool" (p. 28). The authors used a known-groups design to identify items answered differently by college-educated candidates for airline pilot positions when their responses to the test items were contrasted with those of the MMPI-2 normative sample. Airline pilot candidates were chosen because "they present themselves in a superlative manner, claiming to be superior in terms of their mental health and morality than people in general" (Butcher & Han, 1995, p. 28).

Butcher and Han (1995) contrasted the responses of 274 male airline pilot applicants with those of the 1,138 men of the MMPI-2 normative sample and initially identified 52 items with a 25% or greater response frequency difference across the two groups. Two items that lowered the internal consistency estimates for the scale were dropped, resulting in the 50-item S Scale. The authors reported that scores on

S were quite highly correlated (approximately .80) with K and that the two scales shared nine items. Removal of the nine overlapping items lowered the correlation between the truncated S Scale and K to approximately .75. Correlations with L were considerably lower. Butcher and Han also reported that higher scores on S were correlated with positive descriptions of test takers by their spouses. Finally, based on factor analyses of the S Scale item pool, Butcher and Han constructed five subscales for S.

Although its authors did not provide data on the utility of S as an underreporting measure, subsequent studies did demonstrate the effectiveness of the scale in this task (Archer, Handel & Couvadelli, 2004; Baer, Wetter, Nichols, Greene & Berry, 1995; Bagby, Nicholson, Buis, Radvanovic & Fidler, 1999; Bagby, Rogers, Nicholson, Buis, Seeman & Rector, 1997; Lim & Butcher, 1996). Archer et al. (2004) focused specifically on the incremental validity of S (in reference to L and K) and concluded that the scale "added incrementally to the prediction levels achieved by the optimal combination of L and K scores" (p. 102).

Revised Validity Scale Profile

To reflect the increased role of the validity indicators introduced in the 1989 manual and accommodate the newly included F_p and S scales, the MMPI-2 Validity Scale profile was expanded and reorganized in the 2001 manual. The framework for identifying threats to protocol validity outlined in the first part of this chapter guided this reorganization.

Because content nonresponsiveness can affect scores on the Substantive Scales as well as on Validity Scales designed to detect content-based invalid responding, the VRIN and TRIN scales were placed first on the profile. The interpretive recommendation emphasized the need to first examine the CNS score for evidence of excessive nonresponding prior to moving on to VRIN and TRIN. The remaining Validity Scales could be interpreted only if significant content nonresponsiveness was ruled out. Interpretive recommendations for VRIN related to the possibility that both intentional and unintentional random responding could contribute to elevated scores on this scale.

The three overreporting indicators F, F_B, and F_p were placed next, with interpretive recommendations emphasizing the need to consider the score on F_p when interpreting elevated scores on F. In addition, interpretive guidelines for F and F_B emphasized the need to consider the setting in which the test was administered. This served as a proxy for incorporating extratest indications of the likely presence of severe psychopathology when interpreting scores on F and F_B in light of their significant confound with psychopathology. Cutoffs for identifying overreporting in clinical settings were set higher than they had been in the 1989 manual based on findings (discussed earlier) indicating the substantial contribution of psychopathology to elevated scores on these scales. Consistent with Meehl and Hathaway's (1946) caveat that unintentional overreporting stemming from a distorted self-view may also affect scores on F, interpretive recommendations for F and F_B included psychopathology among the possible reasons for elevation, even at the highest cutoff levels.

The three underreporting indicators L, K, and S were placed next. For these scales as well, different cutoffs were recommended for clinical and nonclinical settings. These differences were designed to reflect the possibility that alternative (to underreporting) interpretations (e.g., better than average psychological adjustment in the case of K and S) were more likely to be appropriate in nonclinical settings. The S subscales were also listed in the manual, but no scoring keys, T-score conversion tables, or interpretive recommendations were provided for these measures.

Symptom Validity Scale (FBS)

The final component of the MMPI-2 Validity Scale profile was put in place in 2007 with the addition of the Symptom Validity Scale (FBS).[7] The scale was developed to address concerns articulated by Lees-Haley (1989), who observed that although the traditional MMPI overreporting indicator F had proven effective at identifying misrepresentation of severe psychiatric symptoms (e.g., in individuals undergoing insanity evaluations), it seemed implausible to assume that this measure would operate the same, or as effectively, in detecting noncredible responding to the MMPI items by personal injury litigants or other disability claimants. Lees-Haley concluded that simply adjusting the cutoffs on F was insufficient because the types of responses likely to be given by individuals who present with noncredible symptoms in personal injury litigation (e.g., somatic and cognitive complaints) were qualitatively different from overreporting severe psychopathology.

Lees-Haley et al. (1991) developed FBS to address this concern, taking item content into consideration and comparing the responses of personal injury litigants judged (independently of the MMPI-2) to be malingering with those judged not to be malingering. Content-based item selection was guided by the assumption that overreporting in the context of personal injury litigation involves, on one hand, an effort to appear honest and psychologically normal, except for the influence of the alleged cause of injury, while, on the other, avoiding admission of or minimizing preexisting psychopathology or preinjury antisocial behavior. The authors compared raw scores on the FBS generated by various samples, including a group of personal injury claimants judged to be credible, another group of claimants judged to be malingering emotional distress, and several groups of medical patients instructed to simulate various conditions. They concluded that a raw score of 20 optimally separated the credible personal injury litigants from the other groups. Lees-Haley (1992) subsequently compared FBS scores of a sample of personal injury claimants judged to be malingering symptoms of PTSD—if, for example, the triggering traumatic event was insufficient to account for the claimed symptoms—with those of litigants who did not present with malingered symptoms. He concluded that higher raw score cutoffs (24 for men and 26 for women) were needed to optimally differentiate the two groups.

The FBS was the subject of extensive validation research following its introduction. Consistent with the target population for the scale, the majority of participants in these investigations were personal injury litigants claiming damages resulting from an injury they had sustained. These individuals typically completed the MMPI-2 as part of neuropsychological evaluations, and the criteria used to validate the scale often included the results of symptom validity tests, which are used routinely to identify individuals who do not exert adequate effort on cognitive tests in these evaluations. These "known-groups" design studies, which contrast the MMPI-2 scores of individuals who "pass" versus those who score below the threshold of adequate performance on symptom validity tests, established that among the MMPI-2 overreporting indicators, FBS performed best in predicting noncredible cognitive symptom presentation (Greve, Bianchini, Love, Brennan & Heinly, 2006; Nelson, Hoelzle, Sweet, Arbisi & Demakis, 2010; Nelson, Sweet & Demakis, 2006). Although the vast majority of studies that established the effectiveness of the scale in predicting noncredible cognitive symptom presentation were conducted with personal injury litigants or disability claimants, this finding was extended to criminal forensic settings as well (e.g., Wygant, Sellbom et al., 2007).

The Question of False Positives

Concerns about false positives on the FBS led Butcher, Arbisi, Atlis, and McNulty (2003) to recommend against using the scale in MMPI-2 interpretation. Butcher and colleagues' methodology and conclusions were challenged by several authors (Greiffenstein, Baker, Axelrod, Peck & Gervais, 2004; Greiffenstein, Fox & Lees-Haley, 2007; Greve & Bianchini, 2004; Larrabee, 2007; Lees-Haley & Fox, 2004). Butcher et al.'s (2003) admonition against use of the scale went unheeded (although it did call attention to the need to use higher cutoffs than the ones proposed initially for use with the scale), as evidenced by a survey of neuropsychologists reported by Sharland and Gfeller (2007) showing that the FBS was among the most widely used measures among all the psychological tests they relied on to detect problematic performance in neuropsychological evaluations. Butcher, Gass, Cumella, Kally, and Williams (2008) repeated Butcher et al.'s (2003) concerns about false positive findings in general and in women, in particular, and cited court rulings that had relied on this information in excluding FBS testimony in three Florida cases. Ben-Porath, Greve, Bianchini, and Kaufmann (2009) cited empirical findings that contradicted Butcher et al.'s (2008) assertions and reported new results showing that a very small proportion of individuals with genuine medical problems, even severe ones, score above 28 on FBS. Scores in the 23–28 range less clearly differentiated between individuals presenting with credible versus noncredible symptoms. Ben-Porath, Greve et al. (2009) also presented data showing that there is no correlation between gender and false positive findings on FBS and outlined a number of problems with Butcher et al.'s (2008) analysis of legal findings about the scale.

Addition to the MMPI-2

The substantial empirical literature documenting the effectiveness of FBS in detecting noncredible somatic and cognitive symptom reporting led the University of

Minnesota Press to conduct a review of the scale for possible inclusion on the test. On the basis of the largely positive results of this review, the scale was added to the standard MMPI-2 materials. Ben-Porath, Graham et al. (2009) summarized the psychometric literature supporting and guiding use of the FBS in MMPI-2 interpretation and provided interpretive guidelines for the scale. Like the ones included for the other overreporting indicators in the 2001 MMPI-2 manual, the guidelines recommended by Ben-Porath, Graham, and colleagues emphasized the need to consider alternative (to intentional overreporting) interpretations of FBS at more moderate levels of deviation from the test norms.

Summary

The 10 MMPI-2 validity indicators (CNS and the nine Validity Scales) expanded considerably measurement of various threats to the validity of a test protocol. Referring to the conceptual framework described in the first part of this chapter, CNS, VRIN, and TRIN were designed to assist in detecting nonresponding, random responding (intentional and unintentional) and fixed responding, respectively.

F, F_B, F_p, and FBS assessed overreporting, and L, K, and S identified threats related to underreporting. As summarized earlier in the review of the MMPI validity indicators, the original test authors noted that scores on L, F, and K could reflect either intentional or unintentional over- or underreporting. These possibilities were incorporated into the 2001 interpretive recommendations for the original and newer validity measures. In addition, interpretive recommendations focused increasingly on simultaneous consideration of Validity Scale scores. For example, interpretation of F required consideration of scores on VRIN, TRIN, and F_p. Updated recommendations also called for consideration of collateral information in interpreting MMPI-2 Validity Scale scores. For example, scores on F, F_B, and FBS needed to be considered in light of extratest indicators of psychopathology or medical illness, and interpretation of scores on L required consideration of cultural factors. A substantial body of empirical research was available to support the interpretive recommendations developed for the MMPI-2 validity indicators.

THE MMPI-2-RF VALIDITY SCALES

Protocol validity measures were the last set of scales developed for the MMPI-2-RF. We[8] approached this process from the perspective that the conceptually and empirically grounded MMPI-2 validity indicators provided a solid framework on which we could build to achieve three goals. First, we sought to eliminate item overlap within subsets of scales. Second, we wished to address deficiencies, noted earlier, in some of the MMPI-2 Validity Scales. Finally, we sought to canvass the array of threats to protocol validity, delineated in the first part of this chapter, as comprehensively as possible.

Development

Non-Content-Based Invalid Responding Measures

CNS

The impact of nonresponding is assessed with the CNS score, which reflects the number of unscorable responses to the 338 test items. As noted earlier, Hathaway and McKinley (1943) observed that the impact of nonresponding could vary dramatically as a function of the proportion of unscorable responses per scale. Computer scoring enables consideration of the scale-specific impact of nonresponding by providing the Response % statistic, which indicates the percentage of scorable responses to the items of each scale.

VRIN-r and TRIN-r

The two other types of non-content-based threats, random and fixed responding, are assessed with revised versions of the MMPI-2 VRIN and TRIN scales. Tellegen and Ben-Porath (2008/2011) provide a detailed description of the method used to revise these scales. Two primary considerations guided the revision. First, we sought to eliminate the considerable overlap between the MMPI-2 versions of these scales. (Recall that 10 of the 23 TRIN item response pairs were also scored on VRIN.) To accomplish this goal, VRIN-r item pairs were restricted to positively correlated items, whereas TRIN-r item pairs consist only of negatively correlated items. Second, because we were working with a smaller item pool (338 vs. 567 items), we used a different approach to reducing the impact of substantive content variance on scores on these scales. The alternative approach used in constructing VRIN-r and TRIN-r generated a broader selection of item pairs to be considered for inclusion in the revised scales.

Item pairs were selected on the basis of statistical and semantic analyses of possible response combinations. A test taker may respond to a pair of items in one of four possible combinations:[9] both true (TT), both false (FF), the first true and the second false (TF), or the first false and the second true (FT). The items of VRIN-r and TRIN-r are actually composites made up of a specific combination of responses (e.g., TT) to a pair of MMPI-2-RF items. For example, for a TT composite, a true response to both items in a pair adds a point to the raw score of the scale on which that composite is scored. Each composite chosen for VRIN-r and TRIN-r had to meet five criteria:

1. The items in a composite had to be sufficiently correlated with each other (positively for VRIN-r, negatively for TRIN-r) in two clinical samples. Rather than require a specific minimal correlation, we sought item pairs that were correlated reliably in both samples and met the remaining four criteria. This allowed us to examine a broader range of items than those considered when we constructed the VRIN and TRIN scales of the MMPI-2.
2. The observed frequency of a composite had to be low when compared with the frequency expected by chance if the two responses making up

that composite were independent. For example, if a TT composite occurs in 5% of the cases in a sample, and the expected (by chance) frequency of responding true to both items is 25%, the observed to expected ratio would be .20, indicating that this combination of responses is unlikely and therefore indicative of inconsistency. This was also the method used to determine which combination of responses was statistically inconsistent for the MMPI-2 Inconsistency Scales.

3. The combination of responses in a composite had to be judged by the authors to be content inconsistent.

4. The correlation between a composite and a mini-scale made up of the two items keyed in the direction they are scored in the composite was low. This criterion replaced the requirement that composites be minimally correlated with scores on the Clinical Scales. Instead, we required that they be minimally correlated with measures (the mini-scales) that were specific to the content of the items in a pair.

5. Neither item in a composite could belong to another composite of the same type. For example, if a given composite consisting of items A and B was scored TT, then neither item A nor item B could be scored TT in a composite with a different item. This criterion was adopted to ensure that an inconsistent true response or false response to a given item could contribute only once to the score on VRIN-r or TRIN-r.

Application of these criteria is illustrated in the *MMPI-2-RF Technical Manual* with a composite consisting of items 269 ("When things get really bad, I know I can count on my family for help") and 314 ("I hate my whole family") selected for TRIN-r. As reported in Table 2-1 of the *Technical Manual,* the correlation between responses to these two items in the sample used for the illustration was −.23, indicating that test takers tended to answer them in the opposite direction, meaning that this was a candidate for the TRIN-r scale.

The observed/expected ratio was .27 for the TT composite and .93 for the FF composite, indicating that the first combination was statistically unlikely, whereas the second was not. Therefore, only the TT composite is scored for this item pair. Considering the content of the two items, this makes sense. Responding *true* to both items (i.e., saying "I know I can count on my family" and "I hate my family") seems very inconsistent; however, responding *false* to both is not. This example illustrates how the TT composite satisfied the third criterion, that it be content inconsistent.

The fourth criterion involved scoring the two items as a mini-scale (in this case, reflecting family problems) and then calculating a correlation between each composite and this mini-scale. The correlation for the TT composite was −.10, demonstrating a minimal association between that combination of responses and actually having family problems. The correlation for the FF composite was −.70, indicating a substantial negative correlation between responding false to both items and having family problems. This finding also disqualifies the FF composite, ensuring that TRIN-r variance will remain relatively content free. Finally, assignment of the TT composite for this item pair meant that neither item (269 or 314) could be scored in another TT composite.

Application of these criteria resulted in the selection of 53 composites for VRIN-r and 26 composites for TRIN-r. Because of the substantially reduced length of the inventory, the revised scales sample a larger proportion of the item pool for indications of random or fixed responding.

Content-Based Invalid Responding Measures

Overreporting Indicators

Four overreporting indicators (revised versions of F, F_p, and FBS) and new scale Fs (Infrequent Somatic Complaints) were included in the initial release of the MMPI-2-RF. A fifth measure, Response Bias Scale (RBS; Gervais, Ben-Porath, Wygant & Green, 2007), was added in 2011.

Infrequent Responses (F-r)

Two factors led to the restructuring of the MMPI-2 F scale. As noted earlier, Arbisi and Ben-Porath (1995) reported that a number of the original F Scale items, selected because they were answered in the keyed direction by 10% or less of the original normative sample, no longer met this criterion in the MMPI-2 normative sample. In addition, the F_B scale, made up entirely of items answered infrequently by the MMPI-2 normative sample, outperformed both F and F_p in detecting overreporting in some studies (e.g., Bagby et al., 2005). Taken together, these findings suggested that a revised F Scale, made up of MMPI-2-RF items answered infrequently by the current normative sample, could contribute incrementally to the detection of symptom overreporting.

Two criteria were used in selecting items for F-r. First, we reverted to Hathaway and McKinley's (1943) original criterion for infrequent responding and required that candidate items be answered in the keyed direction by 10% or less of both the men and women in the current normative sample. Second, we did not include any item assigned to the revised F_p, FBS, L, and K scales or to the new Fs scale, which had already been developed. Thus, all 32 F-r items are answered infrequently by the current normative sample and are not scored on the other infrequency scales or the revised underreporting indicators. Four F-r items are scored on RBS.

Infrequent Psychopathology Responses (Fp-r)

Our primary goal in revising F_p was to eliminate overlap with other validity indicators. Arbisi and Ben-Porath (1995) did not require that the items selected for F_p be nonoverlapping with existing MMPI-2 Validity Scales. As a result, 14 of the 27 F_p items overlapped with F, and four F_p items overlapped with L. Gass and Luis (2001) suggested that the inclusion of four L items on F_p might compromise the validity of the scale. However, Arbisi, Ben-Porath, and McNulty (2003) demonstrated that overall, the F_p scale functioned more effectively when the four L items were included. Nevertheless, in light of our goal of eliminating overlap among the MMPI-2-RF content-based invalidity indicators, we dropped the four L items as well as three items assigned to Fs. Correlational analyses indicated that two other Fp items did not function as effectively as the remaining items, while the addition of three items not scored on F_p was found to improve the scale. The resulting 21-item Fp-r scale does not overlap with any of the content-based invalid responding indicators, although it does share two items with the subsequently added RBS.

Infrequent Somatic Responses (Fs)

Wygant, Ben-Porath, and Arbisi (2004) developed the Fs scale to identify individuals overreporting somatic symptoms. As with F-r and Fp-r, construction of Fs was predicated on the assumption that individuals who report a relatively large number of uncommon symptoms are likely overreporting.

Applying to the somatic symptom domain Arbisi and Ben-Porath's (1995) methodology of using psychiatric inpatients to identify uncommon psychopathology responses, Wygant et al. (2004) examined item response frequencies in three large medical samples. The first scale development sample was from an original MMPI study of some 50,000 medical patients tested at the Mayo Clinic in the 1960s, for which item response frequencies had been published (Swenson, Pearson & Osborne, 1973). The other samples were from two large archival MMPI-2 data sets collected by the test distributor between 1989 and 1998. The first was a general medical sample made up of 2,568 patients, the second of 4,590 chronic pain patients.

Item response frequencies were examined in the three samples, and 166 items answered (true or false) by less than 25% of subjects in all three samples (and less than 20% in the MMPI-2 normative sample) were identified as candidates for the Fs scale. Next, the first two authors examined the content of the 166 items independently and selected items they judged to contain somatic content. Both judges selected the same set of 16 items, and these items make up the Fs scale. The 16 Fs items were excluded from consideration for the other MMPI-2-RF infrequent response indicators, and therefore this scale does not overlap with F-r and Fp-r. Three Fs items appear on FBS-r, and two are scored on RBS.

Symptom Validity (FBS-r)

Of the 43 items included on the original FBS scale, 30 were retained in the 338-item MMPI-2-RF pool. A series of analyses, described later under psychometric findings, indicated that scores on the truncated measure were highly correlated with the original and as effective (if not more so) in identifying protocols of individuals presenting with noncredible cognitive and somatic symptoms. Thus, no further analyses were conducted, and the 30 remaining items make up FBS-r. One FBS-r item is scored on Fp-r, three are on Fs, and four appear on RBS.

Response Bias Scale (RBS)

Gervais et al. (2007) developed RBS "to detect negative response bias in forensic neuropsychological or disability assessment settings" (p. 196). The scale consists of 28 MMPI-2-RF items that discriminate between persons who passed or failed the Word Memory Test (WMT; P. Green, Allen & Astner, 1996), the Computerized Assessment of Response Bias (CARB; Allen, Conder, Green & Cox, 1997), and/or the Test of Memory Malingering (TOMM; Tombaugh, 1997) in a sample of 1,151 non-head-injured disability claimants.

The development sample was split into random halves for the purpose of item selection and scale validation. The 28 RBS items were identified through a series of multiple regression analyses. Dichotomous variables representing passing or failing the three criterion measures (based on standard criteria) were regressed on the MMPI-2 item pool. The 28 items selected for the RBS were those that appeared commonly as significant predictors in the regression analyses. A small number of RBS items are on each of the other overreporting indicators: four on F-r, two on Fp-r, two on Fs, and four on FBS-r.

Underreporting Indicators

MMPI investigators and users have long recognized that detecting underreporting is more difficult than identifying protocols marked by overreporting (Meehl & Hathaway, 1946). The K Scale was developed for use as a correction for underreporting after Meehl and Hathaway (1946) concluded that L, the original MMPI underreporting indicator, was inadequate for this task. The S Scale (Butcher & Han, 1995) was added to the MMPI-2 on the basis of evidence (reviewed earlier) that it added to L and K in detecting underreporting. In a meta-analysis of the detection of underreporting with the MMPI-2, Baer and Miller (2002) found that two older MMPI underreporting indicators, the Positive Malingering Scale (Mp; Cofer, Chance & Judson, 1949) and the Wiggins (1959) Social Desirability (Sd) Scale, outperformed L, K, and S in this task. Given these findings, we decided to examine the unique (i.e., nonoverlapping) items of these five scales as candidates for developing underreporting indicators for the MMPI-2-RF.

We conducted factor analyses of this item pool in several samples that included individuals tested in the context of personnel selection, underreporting simulation, and clinical settings. Replicating results of a similar study conducted at the scale level by Bagby and Marshall (2004), we consistently found two primary factors in these analyses.[10] We constructed two nonoverlapping scales by selecting items that loaded substantially and consistently on one factor without substantial cross-loadings on the other. Labels were assigned to the two scales based on item content, and abbreviations were used to link each MMPI-2-RF underreporting indicator to the MMPI-2 scale with which it shared the most items.

Uncommon Virtues (L-r)

L-r consists of 14 items, 11 of which were on the original L Scale. Two new items come from Sd, and one comes from Mp. In contrast with the MMPI-2 L Scale, for which all 15 items are keyed false, all three new L-r items are keyed true, reducing the likelihood that an extreme score on this scale is an artifact of fixed responding. The label "Uncommon Virtues" describes the content of the items scored on this scale, which, as keyed, describes virtuous behavior in which most individuals are unlikely to engage on a regular basis. Indeed, most of the items are rarely answered in the keyed direction by the MMPI-2-RF normative sample.

Adjustment Validity (K-r)

K-r consists of 14 items, all of which appear on the original K Scale. Five of these items were also scored on S. One of the K-r items was actually scored in the opposite direction as one of the control items (discussed earlier) on K. The label assigned to K-r describes its item content, which, as keyed, comprises assertions of good psychological adjustment. As discussed earlier, it has indeed long been recognized that individuals who are better adjusted than average score above average on K (Meehl & Hathaway, 1946), leading some authors to suggest that the scale should not be interpreted for "normals" (e.g., Heilbrun, 1961). However, as was the case with L, empirical findings (cited in the next section) show that at higher levels, K-r scores are associated with underreporting.

Psychometric Findings with the MMPI-2-RF Validity Scales

Reliability

Reliability estimates for the MMPI-2-RF Validity Scales are reported in Table 3-2 of the *Technical Manual*. Test–retest reliability estimates range from .40 for TRIN-r to .84 for K-r. Internal consistency coefficients in the normative sample range from .20 for women on VRIN-r to .71 for men on F-r. Internal consistency findings in the clinical samples are generally higher, ranging from .16 on VRIN-r for a sample of female psychiatric inpatients to .88 on F-r for the male psychiatric inpatient sample. Standard errors of measurement (SEM; expressed in T-score values) based on the normative test–retest data range from four on several scales to as high as eight on TRIN-r. SEMs based on the internal consistency coefficients in the normative sample range from five for women on F-r to nine for men on VRIN-r and TRIN-r. For the clinical samples, SEMs range from 6 on K-r to 12 on Fs.

These reliability findings need to be considered in light of the composition of the samples used in the analyses, which consisted largely of cooperative and test-competent individuals for whom one would not expect to encounter large, reliable variations in invalid responding. Relatively low reliability estimates stand out, in particular, for the inconsistent responding indicators VRIN-r and TRIN-r. These results are not surprising because the Inconsistency Scales were designed to be content-free indicators and have an even greater restriction of range than do the other validity indicators. Thus, range restriction owing to sample characteristics and the nature of the Validity Scales attenuates the reliability estimates to some extent. This is borne out by the SEM findings, which incorporate variability in the analyses and generally reflect only marginally greater measurement error in the validity indicators than that found with the Substantive Scales.

Higher SEM values indicate a need to use higher cutoffs to identify significant deviations from the norm. Interpretive recommendations for most of the MMPI-2-RF Validity Scales do in fact require more substantial deviation from the norm (than that required for the Substantive Scales) to raise substantial concerns about the validity of a test protocol. Exceptions to the requirement for greater deviations from the mean are L-r and K-r, for which SEM findings are comparable to those reported for the Substantive Scales.

Validity

Validation data reported in the *Technical Manual* were limited to internal correlates. Correlations between the new validity indicators and the MMPI-2 Validity Scales were reported for a number of samples used in prior MMPI-2 Validity Scale studies. Extratest findings with the MMPI-2-RF Validity Scales have been reported in journal articles published after the test was released.

Internal Correlates

Data sets generated by Handel, Ben-Porath, Tellegen, and Archer (2007), who manipulated the responses of normative sample participants, were used to examine associations between the revised and original versions of the Inconsistency Scales. To examine VRIN-r, Handel and colleagues replaced half the responses generated by members of the normative sample with randomly generated responses. For the TRIN-r analyses, 70% of the normative sample responses were replaced twice, once with all true responses and a second time with all false responses. As seen in *Technical Manual* Tables 3-7–3-9, the correlation between VRIN-r and VRIN was .84. Correlations between TRIN-r and TRIN were .95 and .91 with false and true response insertion, respectively. The lower correlation between the two versions of VRIN was expected because of the changes made to this scale, as discussed earlier.

Four samples were used to study the internal correlates of the overreporting indicators. In two clinical samples, test takers were instructed to simulate overreporting of psychiatric and medical symptoms, respectively. The other two samples included MMPI-2 data generated in forensic evaluations in which test takers had incentives for symptom overreporting. These data are presented in Tables 3-10–3-13 of the *Technical Manual*. Correlations between F-r and F ranged from .86 to .96 and were highest (.95 and .96) in the two simulation samples. Correlations between Fp-r and F_p ranged from .73 to .99, with the two highest correlations (.98 and .99) again found in the two simulation samples. Correlations between FBS-r and FBS ranged from .96 to .97 in all four samples.

Although Fs and RBS do not have MMPI-2 counterparts, it is instructive to identify the most highly correlated MMPI-2 validity indicators for these scales. Scores on Fs were most highly correlated with F in all four samples, with correlations ranging from .65 to .95. RBS scores were most highly correlated with F in two samples, F_B in another, and FBS in the fourth sample, with correlations ranging from .74 to .87.

Two samples, both including the responses of individuals instructed to simulate underreporting, were used to examine correlations between the MMPI-2-RF and MMPI-2 underreporting indicators. Correlations between L-r and L were .91 and .93 in the two samples, respectively. Correlations between K-r and K were .88 in both samples. The lower correlation for K-r reflects the removal of seven of the eight control items and scoring reversal of the eighth.

Overall, the internal validation results provided expected patterns of correlation between the MMPI-2-RF validity indicators and the MMPI-2 scales they were designed to replace or expand.

Extratest Findings

A substantial body of empirical studies of the MMPI-2-RF Validity Scales accumulated following publication of the test. The research designs employed in these investigations include simulations of invalid responding and differential prevalence or known-groups comparisons.

Non-Content-Based Invalid Responding

Dragon, Ben-Porath, and Handel (2011) examined in two clinical samples the impact of unscorable item responses on the validity and interpretability of scores on the MMPI-2-RF Restructured Clinical (RC) Scales. Unscorable responses were inserted randomly in place of the subjects' actual responses to the items of each of the RC Scales. Unscorable response insertion was increased in 10% increments ranging from 10% to 90% of the items of each scale. With only a 10% insertion of unscorable responses, a sizable proportion of individuals who scored at or above 65T on each RC Scale no longer produced a clinically elevated score on that scale. Scores that remained elevated when 10% unscorable responses were inserted declined considerably. In contrast, examination of correlations between RC Scale scores and extratest criteria indicated that the validity coefficients were remarkably robust when substantial levels of unscorable responses were inserted. Nevertheless, in light of the significant reduction in the proportion of elevated scores resulting from unscorable responses, and the substantial lowering of scores that remained elevated, the authors recommended that scores on scales with 10% or more unscorable responses be interpreted with caution. Specifically, nonelevated scores should not be interpreted as indicating the absence of problems measured by the scale, and elevated scores should be interpreted noting the possibility that the resulting scale score may underestimate the problems assessed by that measure.

Handel, Ben-Porath, Tellegen, and Archer (2010) evaluated the effects of increasing degrees of simulated random and fixed responding on VRIN-r and TRIN-r scores and compared the performance of these scales with their MMPI-2 counterparts. Overall, the authors concluded that their findings supported the interpretive recommendations for VRIN-r and TRIN-r in the *Manual for Administration, Scoring, and Interpretation* (Ben-Porath & Tellegen, 2008/2011). These guidelines recommend that T scores at or above 80 on the Inconsistency Scales be interpreted as indicating that the protocol is invalid and uninterpretable owing to excessive variable or fixed responding. The authors noted that at lower T-score levels (70–79 on VRIN-r or TRIN-r in the true direction), caution should be exercised when interpreting scores on RC6 and RC8. TRIN-r T scores in the 70–79 range in the false direction indicate that caution should be exercised in interpreting scores on RC1 and RC2.

Overreporting

The following review summarizes the results of 19 empirical studies of the MMPI-2-RF overreporting indicators. Because RBS was not included on the MMPI-2-RF when the test was released in 2008, a number of the studies reviewed focus only on F-r, Fp-r, Fs, and FBS-r. Similarly, because RBS was first published in the MMPI-2 literature in 2007, several of the studies reviewed here did not include the other MMPI-2-RF overreporting measures.

Two research designs have been applied in studies of the MMPI-2-RF overreporting indicators. In simulation research, participants are instructed to respond to the test items as though they have problems they do not actually have or to exaggerate problems they do have. Validity scale scores of individuals in the simulated overreporting groups are compared with those of nonclinical and, in some cases, clinical samples tested under standard instructions. In known-groups investigations, individuals are classified into overreporting and non-overreporting groups on the basis of other response bias measures, and Validity Scale scores are then compared for the resulting samples.

In a simulation study with college students as participants, Burchett and Ben-Porath (2010) found that scores on F-r, Fp-r, Fs, and FBS-r all differentiated participants overreporting psychopathology symptoms or somatic complaints from others tested under standard instructions. The highest effect sizes for detecting overreported psychopathology were found for F-r and Fp-r. Fs performed best at detecting overreported somatic symptoms.

Sellbom and Bagby (2010) compared overreporting scale scores produced by a sample of psychiatric inpatients with those of undergraduates instructed to feign psychopathology. Some of the undergraduates were assigned to a coaching condition in which they were informed about the existence of the Validity Scales. F-r, Fp-r, and Fs differentiated patients from overreporters in both the coached and uncoached conditions. FBS-r scores differentiated only the uncoached feigners from the patients. Consistent with findings in MMPI-2 studies, Fp-r performed best in differentiating both groups of overreporters from psychiatric inpatients.

Marion, Sellbom, and Bagby (2011) examined whether the MMPI-2-RF overreporting indicators differentiated college students simulating Major Depression, Schizophrenia, or PTSD from patients diagnosed with these disorders. F-r, Fp-r, Fs, and FBS-r differentiated all three simulation groups from their patient counterparts. In this study, also, the strongest effect sizes were found for Fp-r.

Wygant, Ben-Porath, Arbisi, Berry, Freeman, and Heilbronner (2009) examined the performance of the MMPI-2-RF overreporting indicators in simulation studies of somatic symptom overreporting. A sample of individuals with a history of head injuries was divided into random halves, with one group tested under standard instructions and the other group instructed to feign head injury symptoms. The two groups differed significantly on F-r, Fp-r, and Fs, with Fs showing the strongest effect size. A second sample consisted of medical patients in treatment at a VA medical facility. A subset was tested under standard instructions, and the other participants were instructed to exaggerate the extent of the medical problems for which they were being treated and any resulting emotional difficulties. F-r, Fp-r, Fs, and FBS-r all differentiated significantly between the two groups, with FBS-r, followed by F-r, having the strongest effect sizes.

Harp, Jasinski, Shandera-Ochsner, Mason, and Berry (2011) investigated the detection of malingered symptoms of Attention-Deficit Hyperactivity Disorder (ADHD) by comparing the MMPI-2-RF Validity Scale scores of college students simulating the condition with scores of a sample of students actually diagnosed with ADHD. They found Fp-r scores to best differentiate the two groups.

Youngjohn, Wershba, Stevenson, Sturgeon, and Thomas (2011) studied the MMPI-2-RF overreporting indicators in a sample of traumatic brain injury (TBI) litigants. The authors found that FBS-r differentiated TBI litigants who passed from those who failed symptom validity tests administered as part of a forensic neuropsychological evaluation. F-r and Fs showed nonsignificant trends in the same direction.

Using a known-groups design, Sellbom, Toomey, Wygant, Kucharski, and Duncan (2010) investigated whether the MMPI-2-RF overreporting measures could identify criminal defendants classified as malingering using the Structured Interview of Reported Symptoms (SIRS; Rogers, Bagby & Dickens, 1992). Scores on F-r, Fp-r, Fs, and FBS-r were all significantly higher in the malingering group. The strongest effect sizes were found with F-r and Fp-r.

Wygant et al. (2010) examined associations between the MMPI-2-RF overreporting indicators and evidence of noncredible responding in a different sample of criminal defendants. However, in their investigation, groups were defined using the test takers' performance on symptom validity tests (SVTs), including the RBS. All five MMPI-2-RF overreporting measures differentiated significantly defendants who passed versus those who failed the criterion measures. RBS, F-r, and Fp-r had the strongest effect sizes. Wygant and colleagues also examined associations between SVT failure and MMPI-2-RF overreporting scale scores in a civil forensic sample made up of personal injury litigants and disability claimants. Here, too, all five MMPI-2-RF measures differentiated significantly groups of individuals who passed versus those who failed SVTs. In these analyses, RBS, F-r, Fs, and FBS-r had the strongest effect sizes. Consistent with MMPI-2 findings with civil forensic samples, Fp-r produced markedly weaker effect sizes than did the other measures.

Gervais, Ben-Porath, Wygant, and Sellbom (2010) investigated whether the MMPI-2-RF overreporting scales detected overreported memory complaints as assessed by the Memory Complaints Inventory (MCI; P. Green, 2004). Scores on all five measures were associated with noncredible memory complaints, with RBS showing the strongest effect size, followed by F-r. In a series of hierarchical regression analyses, RBS was found to add incrementally to each of the other four overreporting indicators in predicting MCI overreporting scores. Gervais et al. (2010) also compared the ability of F-r, Fp-r, and FBS-r and their MMPI-2 counterparts to predict MCI findings of overreported memory complaints and found that the MMPI-2-RF versions of all three added incrementally to the prediction. In reverse-order analyses, none of the MMPI-2 scales added significantly to the prediction equations beyond their MMPI-2-RF counterparts.

Rogers, Gillard, Berry, and Granacher (2011) found scores on F-r and Fp-r to detect individuals assessed for chronic pain who were deemed to be feigning psychopathology and scores on FBS-r and RBS to best detect those in the sample who scored below chance on cognitive effort measures. Using a sample assessed for chronic pain–related disability claims at the same practice, Wygant, Anderson, Sellbom, Rapier, Algeier, and Granacher (2011) found scores on F-r, Fs, FBS-r, and RBS to be sensitive to malingering symptoms of neurocognitive dysfunction based on the Slick, Sherman, and Iverson (1999) criteria and to malingering of pain symptoms based on the criteria developed by Bianchini, Greve, and Glynn (2005).

Several investigations have focused on RBS as an MMPI-2 measure. These findings apply to its use on the MMPI-2-RF because the scale is made up of the same 28 items on both versions of the inventory. In the initial study introducing the scale, Gervais et al. (2007), using a disability claimant sample, found RBS scores to be associated with failure on the Word Memory Test (P. Green et al., 1996) and/ or the Medical Symptom Validity Test (P. Green, 2004). Employing a classification tree analysis with a known-groups design, Smart et al. (2008) found RBS to be the best predictor of failed symptom validity testing. Whitney, Davis, Shephard, and Herman (2008) found RBS scores to be associated with failure on the TOMM in a sample of VA outpatients referred for neuropsychological evaluations. In another sample of individuals referred for outpatient neuropsychological evaluations, Dionysus, Denney, and Halfaker (2011) found RBS scores to be associated with probable negative response bias as defined by the criteria established by Slick et al. (1999).

Using a differential prevalence design, a variant of the known-groups procedure that involves comparing samples of individuals assumed to differ on a variable of interest, Nelson, Sweet, and Heilbronner (2007) found increased scores on a preliminary version of RBS when comparing samples of individuals who had undergone neuropsychological evaluations with and without potential for secondary gain. Applying a mixed-group validation approach, another differential prevalence research design, Tolin, Steenkamp, Marx, and Litz (2010) found RBS scores to be associated with symptom exaggeration in the context of VA compensation and pension evaluations. Lange, Sullivan, and Scott (2010) conducted a simulation study comparing detection by the MMPI-2 and Personality Assessment Inventory (PAI) validity indicators of feigned depression and PTSD symptoms. Undergraduate students were administered the two tests under standard instructions or instructions to feign symptoms of one of these disorders, accompanied by information readily available on the Internet about the symptoms associated with the conditions they were instructed to simulate. RBS outperformed all of the MMPI-2 and PAI Validity Scales in differentiating simulators from participants tested under standard instructions.

In summary, studies employing simulation and known-groups methodologies have established that the MMPI-2-RF overreporting indicators can effectively detect noncredible reporting of psychological, somatic, and cognitive symptoms. F-r is sensitive to the broadest range of overreported symptoms and performed well, but not always best, in all of the studies just reviewed. Fp-r is most sensitive to overreported psychological symptoms and less effective than the other measures in detecting overreported somatic and cognitive complaints. It is particularly effective in differentiating genuine, severe psychopathology from overreported psychological symptoms. Fs and FBS-r are the best MMPI-2-RF predictors of overreported somatic symptoms, and FBS-r and RBS are the best measures of noncredible cognitive complaints. RBS is most specifically associated with overreported memory complaints. Most of the studies just reviewed also included classification accuracy findings that support the interpretive cutoffs recommended in the *Manual for Administration, Scoring, and Interpretation.*

Underreporting

As was the case with the MMPI-2, a smaller number of studies have examined the utility of the MMPI-2-RF underreporting indicators. Sellbom and Bagby (2008) reported the results of two studies designed to examine the validity of L-r and K-r. In their first investigation, both scales differentiated significantly a sample of patients diagnosed with Schizophrenia who took the test under standard instructions from a randomly selected patient cohort instructed to "answer the questions as if you were applying for employment and wanted to keep your history of psychiatric problems or symptoms private" (Sellbom & Bagby, 2008, p. 372). The patients who took the test under the simulation instructions scored lower than did their counterparts tested under standard instructions on all the RC Scales, except RC3 and RC9. The simulators scored higher than the control group on both L-r and K-r. Hierarchical regression analyses showed that each scale added incrementally to the detection of underreporting beyond the other. Sellbom and Bagby replicated these findings with a sample of undergraduate students, with the exception that the underreporting students scored lower than did their counterparts tested under standard instructions on RC6 and RC9, and L-r did not add incrementally beyond K-r in differentiating the two subsamples from each other.

In their second study, Sellbom and Bagby (2008) sought to replicate and extend their findings across research designs and settings. This study included a sample of undergraduates tested with standard instructions or with instructions to "fake good" in scenarios that included gaining custody of or access to a child. A second sample used in this study consisted of 86 individuals tested in child custody evaluations, in which it is assumed that individuals are motivated to present themselves in a favorable manner. The first sample was used to replicate the simulation findings from study 1, and the second sample was used to examine whether these results would extend to a differential prevalence design.

Scores on the RC, L-r, and K-r Scales of the students simulating a custody evaluation and of the custody litigants were compared with those of the students tested under standard instructions. The simulating students scored lower than did their counterparts on all the RC Scales, except for RC6. The custody litigants scored lower than did the nonsimulating students on all but RC1, RC2, and RC6. Significant differences were found for both groups on L-r and K-r, with the custody litigants and custody litigation simulators scoring higher than the control group on both measures. In hierarchical regression analyses, each scale added incrementally to the other in predicting underreporting.

Sellbom and Bagby (2008) concluded that their results support the utility of the MMPI-2-RF underreporting indicators and noted that the effect sizes they obtained were similar to the ones reported in Baer and Miller's (2002) meta-analysis of the MMPI-2 measures of underreporting.

Summary

Findings reported in this section show that the MMPI-2-RF Validity Scales have sound psychometric properties. Reliability estimates, with the exception of the underreporting measures, indicate that observed scores on the Validity Scales are moderately more susceptible to measurement error than are most Substantive Scale scores. This is accommodated by requiring greater deviations from the norm to raise concerns about protocol validity. Substantial effect sizes found consistently in validation studies indicate that the MMPI-2-RF Validity Scales function effectively as protocol validity indicators.

Two Functions of the Scales

This chapter began with an overview of threats to the validity of individual test protocols. Two general classes of threats—non-content-based and content-based—were described, and subsets of potential validity problems were identified within each. The non-content-based threats include nonresponding, random responding, and fixed responding. The content-based threats include overreporting and under-reporting. With regard to three of these threats—random responding, overreporting, and underreporting—a distinction was made between intentional and unintentional responses by test takers to self-report measures.

The MMPI-2-RF Validity Scales canvass the full range of threats to protocol validity. Like their predecessors, they serve a second function by providing information relevant to the assessment of malingering and its counterpart: intentional concealment of problems.

Assessing Threats to Protocol Validity

Validity problems associated with nonresponding are assessed with CNS and the Response % statistic reported for each scale in the computerized reports. Random (or quasi-random) responding is assessed with VRIN-r, which is equally sensitive to intentional and unintentional random responding but does not distinguish between the two. Regardless of intentionality, excessive levels of random responding invalidate the test protocol. Fixed responding in either the true or false direction is assessed with TRIN-r, and excessive levels of either type of fixed responding also invalidate the resulting test protocol.

The MMPI-2-RF overreporting indicators identify noncredible reports of psychopathology, somatic symptoms, and cognitive difficulties, which can distort scores on various Substantive Scales. Because the primary focus of the MMPI-2-RF Substantive Scales is psychopathology, very substantial deviations from the general population mean on F-r or Fp-r indicate that a test protocol is invalid and uninterpretable owing to excessive overreporting. Scores on all five MMPI-2-RF overreporting indicators are affected by both intentional and unintentional overreporting. For example, individuals with Somatoform Disorder or a psychotic disorder that includes somatic delusions may produce very high scores on Fs by reporting problems they genuinely but mistakenly believe they are experiencing. Extremely demoralized individuals may perceive and present themselves as having more problems than they actually have.

L-r and K-r alert the interpreter to the possible impact of underreporting on Substantive Scale scores. Elevated L-r scores indicate that a test taker presents an unlikely picture of moral virtues associated with underreporting. High K-r scores reflect an unlikely presentation of good psychological adjustment.

A distinction between intentional and unintentional underreporting is often associated with Paulhus's (1984) conceptualization of the roles of self-deception and impression management in self-report. Paulhus cited Meehl and Hathaway's distinction between "conscious falsehood" and self-deception in this regard. However, identification of L or L-r as reflecting primarily impression management and K or K-r as a measure of self-deception is inconsistent both with how the developers conceptualized these scales and with subsequent empirical findings. Hathaway, McKinley, and Meehl viewed both scales as measures of intentional and unintentional underreporting. Simulation studies conducted with the original and revised versions of these scales indicate that scores on both L-r and K-r change significantly when subjects are instructed to appear better adjusted than they actually are. Thus, both scales are sensitive to impression management. Both may also be affected by (and reflect) distorted self-perceptions.

Detecting Malingering and Concealment of Psychopathology

Although they were not developed for this purpose, a second function of MMPI validity indicators was identified shortly after the test was introduced. As has often been the case with psychological testing, this development occurred in the context of efforts to use the MMPI in screening military personnel. Recall that Meehl and Hathaway (1946) described what was likely the first MMPI "faking" study, in which military personnel simulated faking bad to "avoid being accepted into the draft" (p. 537) and faking good "to make certain that they would be acceptable to army induction" (p. 538). Follow-up studies explored the utility of the MMPI validity indicators in detecting externally motivated, intentional overreporting and underreporting (Cofer et al., 1949; Gough, 1947; Hunt, 1948).

Following the conclusion of World War II, there was a lull in efforts to investigate the utility of the MMPI in detecting malingering. Dahlstrom and Welsh (1960) allocated just two pages to the topic in the first edition of their *MMPI Handbook* and even less space in the second edition (Dahlstrom et al., 1972). Graham (1977) devoted approximately two pages of text to the topic in the first edition of his MMPI textbook, and the term does not appear in the index of Greene's (1980) first MMPI interpretive manual.

Interest in using the MMPI to detect malingering was revived as psychologists became increasingly involved with the legal system in the 1980s. Discussions and investigations of use of the test to detect malingering focused on disability claimants and personal injury litigants (e.g., Butcher, 1985; Fairbank, McCaffrey & Keane, 1985; Lees-Haley, 1984; Pollack & Grainey, 1984; Snibe, Peterson & Sosner, 1980), criminal defendants (e.g., Hawk & Cornell, 1989; Parwatiker, Holcomb & Menninger, 1985; Wasyliw, Grossman, Haywood & Cavanaugh, 1988), and prison inmates (Schretlen & Arkowitz, 1990; Walters, White & Greene, 1988). With the transition to the MMPI-2, and even greater involvement of psychologists in the civil and criminal justice systems during the 1990s, the pace of research on using the Validity Scales to detect malingering grew exponentially. This pattern has carried over to the MMPI-2-RF. In fact, the overwhelming majority of empirical studies of the MMPI, MMPI-2, and MMPI-2-RF validity indicators have focused on their use in the detection of malingering and, to a lesser extent, on concealment of psychopathology.

CONCLUSION

Although they were developed to assess threats to protocol validity, most of the published research on the MMPI validity indicators has focused on their second function, detecting malingering or underreporting of problems. A substantial body of empirical findings demonstrates the utility of the MMPI-2-RF Validity Scales in serving both functions. This chapter has focused on the conceptual and empirical foundations for using these measures to assess protocol validity. Interpretive guidelines for this use of the validity indicators are provided in Chapter 6. Detection of malingering and concealment of psychopathology have been studied primarily in forensic settings. Interpretive guidelines for this application of the MMPI-2-RF validity indicators, emphasizing the need to consider extratest data, are provided in Chapter 8.

CHAPTER 5

Administering and Scoring the MMPI-2-RF

This chapter describes and illustrates standard administration and scoring procedures for the MMPI-2-RF. Standard procedures enhance the reliability of psychological test scores and facilitate comparison of a test taker's results with relevant reference groups, including the MMPI-2-RF normative sample. Adherence to the procedures presented in this chapter increases the likelihood that MMPI-2-RF findings will reflect characteristics of the test taker rather than idiosyncrasies introduced in the administration or scoring of the test. Deviations from standard procedures should be mentioned, and their impact considered, when reporting MMPI-2-RF results.

The chapter begins with a delineation of standard administration procedures for the MMPI-2-RF. Standard scoring procedures are reviewed next, including a description of the normative sample and methods used to derive standard scores for the test. Software-based reports available for the MMPI-2-RF are described in detail in the third and final part of the chapter.

ADMINISTERING THE MMPI-2-RF

The MMPI-2-RF can be administered by a qualified test user (see Chapter 2 of the *Manual for Administration, Scoring, and Interpretation*) or a trained assistant working under a qualified user's supervision. Proper administration of the test requires consideration of whether the potential test taker is an appropriate candidate for assessment with the inventory, use of standard administration and response-recording modalities, and adherence to standard administration procedures.

Before Testing

Consider the Test Taker's Age

The MMPI-2-RF is normed for use with individuals 18 years of age and older. The top of the age range for the adolescent version of the inventory is also 18, creating a one-year overlap in the test norms. Shaevel and Archer (1996) noted that the two sets of norms produce substantially different T scores for 18-year-olds, with MMPI-2 norms generally producing lower Validity Scale scores and higher Clinical Scale values than do the MMPI-A norms. Therefore, the choice of norms for this age group is consequential. The authors of the MMPI-A manual (Butcher et al., 1992) recommended that 18-year-olds who are still living at home and attending high school be administered the MMPI-A and that the MMPI-2 be used with those who are in college, working, or otherwise living on their own. Osberg and Polland (2002) found that 18-year-old college students were overpathologized by the MMPI-2 norms and underpathologized by the MMPI-A norms. Similar studies are needed to explore the potential for overpathologizing independently living 18-year-olds (e.g., military personnel) before any firm conclusions can be drawn. In the interim, the rule of thumb recommended by the MMPI-A manual authors seems reasonable. However, the potential for overpathologizing should be considered when interpreting MMPI-2-RF results of 18-year-old test takers.

Inquire about Prior Testing

Individuals involved previously with mental health or behavioral medicine systems, or those who have already been evaluated in a forensic or preemployment screening context, may have had prior experience with the MMPI. Inquiring about prior testing and, if the individual has previously completed the test, about her or his experiences, impressions, and expectations for the current evaluation can help identify and correct misconceptions. However, to avoid undue influence on current test results, asking about previous experiences is best conducted in the early stages of an assessment rather than immediately before the MMPI-2-RF is administered.

Assess the Testability of the Test Taker

The MMPI-2-RF is typically administered via a visual medium: a test booklet or a computer screen. For a test taker to provide meaningful results, he or she must be able to see, read, and comprehend the test items. The individual administering the test should conduct a preliminary assessment of the testability of the test taker by determining whether he or she has any limitations or conditions that might impair his or her ability to respond meaningfully to the test items and, if so, whether corrective steps can properly be taken. Individuals experiencing acute psychotic episodes or delirium and some potential test takers with severe cognitive impairments may be unable to complete a valid and interpretable MMPI-2-RF.

Physical disabilities may require that accommodations be made to ensure valid testing. The test taker should be asked whether he or she has any visual impairment. If he or she requires reading glasses, these should be available. If the test taker's visual impairment is not correctable with reading glasses, a standard audio administration of the MMPI-2-RF should be done (see description below) and arrangements made for the test taker to record his or her responses privately. It is strongly recommended that the test taker not be asked to respond to the test items orally and that the items not be read to the test taker. Private recording of the test taker's responses can be implemented by providing an appropriate means for recording the responses (e.g., a notepad or a computer), which can later be transcribed onto an answer sheet or entered into the computerized scoring software. An alternative is standard computerized administration of the MMPI-2-RF with Pearson software (described later in this chapter and in greater detail in the *MMPI-2-RF User's Guide for Reports*; Ben-Porath & Tellegen, 2011), which includes audio as well as visual administration of the test items and ensures privacy.

Reading Level

After confirming that the test taker can see the test items or providing accommodations that make this possible, his or her reading ability should be considered. The reading level required for test takers to respond meaningfully to the MMPI-2 has been the subject of some discussion and confusion. In the last edition of the original MMPI manual, Hathaway and McKinley (1967) indicated that an individual "with at least six years of successful schooling can be expected to complete the MMPI without difficulty" (p. 9). By contrast, the authors of the initial edition of the MMPI-2 manual indicated that "based on contemporary proficiency levels, the test would now require an eighth grade reading level to comprehend the content of all the test items and to respond to them appropriately" (Butcher, Dahlstrom, Graham, Tellegen & Kaemmer, 1989, p. 14). The apparent increase in reading level required to complete the MMPI-2 was unexpected in light of the historical trend for generational improvement in reading proficiencies, simplification of wording for some of the original MMPI items in the MMPI-2 booklet, and attention paid to wording of the items that were added to the MMPI-2.

Prompted by these unexpected findings, Dahlstrom, Archer, Hopkins, Jackson, and Dahlstrom (1994) conducted a comprehensive analysis of the readability of the MMPI, MMPI-2, and MMPI-A item pools and concluded that the *average* reading difficulty of all three MMPI instruments was about the sixth-grade level. Schinka and Borum (1993) had previously conducted an item-by-item examination of standard reading difficulty indicators and concluded that the majority of MMPI-2 items were written at a fourth- or fifth-grade level, although some required a greater reading ability. These findings indicate that establishing a reading level requirement does not guarantee that a test taker will be able to read every item of an instrument, unless the level is set considerably higher than what is required to read most of the test items. Because the data reported by Dahlstrom et al. (1994) indicated that most of the MMPI-2 items require less than a seventh-grade reading ability, the recommended reading level for the MMPI-2 was changed from eighth to sixth grade in the revised edition of the test manual (Butcher, Graham, Ben-Porath, Tellegen, Dahlstrom & Kaemmer, 2001).

A second source of confusion regarding the reading difficulty of MMPI-2 items stems from comparisons with other tests. Morey (2007) reported that the Personality Assessment Inventory (PAI) requires the ability to read at the fourth-grade level. Some authors have inferred that this makes the PAI a more appropriate instrument in settings where test takers may have lower reading levels. For example, Morey, Warner, and Hopwood (2007) commented that the lower reading level required for the PAI is "an important issue in forensic settings where reading ability is commonly lower than average" (p. 108). However, comparisons of the MMPI-2 and PAI reading levels, estimated at the sixth- and fourth-grade levels, respectively, are incomplete because the two estimates were derived with different methodologies. Butcher et al. (2001) relied on analyses using Lexile values (Stenner, Horabin, Smith & Smith, 1988), whereas Morey (2007) derived the PAI estimate based on analysis of the test's entire item pool using the Flesch–Kincaid reading level index available in the Microsoft Word spell-checker, which yields a score of 4.0. Applying the same procedure to the MMPI-2-RF item pool produces a Flesch–Kincaid index of 4.5, consistent with the results reported by Dahlstrom et al. (1994) and Schinka and Borum (1993).

Establishing and comparing reading levels for self-report inventories is complicated further when different response formats are used. The true–false response format of the MMPI-2-RF is less complex than Likert-scale response formats and, all things being equal, should be less challenging for test takers with limited cognitive abilities. This is particularly true of items that include quantifiers (e.g., "I sometimes . . ." or "I frequently . . .") or are worded negatively (e.g., "I don't . . ." or "I rarely . . ."), which gives rise to ambiguities when used with a Likert response format that also includes quantifiers (such as "somewhat true"). Therefore, evaluations of the difficulties involved in administering tests based solely on item content and ignoring response format differences do not offer a complete comparison of the cognitive resources needed to meaningfully respond to self-report measures such as the MMPI-2-RF.

If a test taker's ability to read the MMPI-2-RF items is in doubt (e.g., because of possible reading limitations or because the test taker is not a native English speaker), administration of a standard test of reading ability is recommended. If the test taker's reading level is less than sixth grade, or if it is not feasible to administer a reading test when reading comprehension is in doubt, audio administration of the MMPI-2-RF using the standard compact disc or computer software (described later) is recommended.

Reading the items to the test taker represents a deviation from standard administration procedures and introduces an uncontrolled interpersonal element into the testing. Because this compromises being able to rely on the test norms and comparison group data for interpreting MMPI-2-RF results, it should be avoided.

Test takers who have the visual ability to respond to a conventional administration of the MMPI-2-RF and the requisite reading skills (or who receive an audio administration of the test) may still be unable to respond meaningfully to the test items because of a lack of comprehension. This may occur with nonnative English speakers as well as test takers whose cognitive functioning is compromised by dementia, delirium, intoxication, or acute primary psychopathology. The test taker's English-language proficiency and mental status should be examined prior to administration of the MMPI-2-RF.

If an individual lacking the requisite reading ability or language facility is administered the MMPI-2-RF without the aid of an audio presentation of the items, the Validity Scales, particularly Variable Response Inconsistency (VRIN-r), will probably detect it (following the interpretive recommendations described in Chapter 6). A T score of 60 or below on VRIN-r is very unlikely when the test taker lacks the ability to read and respond meaningfully to the items.

To summarize, setting a specific reading level for a self-report instrument can be misleading because individual items vary in difficulty. However, for comparison purposes, if the standards used to set the recommended reading level for the MMPI-2 are applied to the MMPI-2-RF item pool, this results in a recommended sixth-grade reading level for the test. Estimating MMPI-2-RF reading difficulty by calculating the Flesch–Kincaid index produces a recommended reading level of 4.5 grades. For individuals with limited cognitive abilities, the true–false response format may be less challenging than responding on a Likert scale. Audio administration can facilitate testing if the individual lacks the requisite reading ability to complete the MMPI-2-RF; however, this does not address language comprehension deficits.

Standard Administration and Response-Recording Modalities

Standard MMPI-2-RF administration modalities[1] include a test booklet, computer administration using Pearson software, and audio recordings of the test items. Audio administration can be accomplished with a standard compact disc or as an optional accompaniment to computerized test administration. As discussed earlier, reading the test items aloud to the test taker is not recommended because it deviates from standard administration procedures and introduces an interpersonal element to the assessment. When the booklet or audio recording is used to administer the test, an answer sheet is the recording modality.

To avoid content clustering, items composing the MMPI-2-RF scales are distributed throughout the test booklet. The items are presented in the computerized administration of the test in the same order as they appear in the test booklet. The test taker is presented the standard instructions and then the 338 test items. The examinee inputs her or his response to each item with a keyboard or mouse, and the computer software records the test taker's responses, creating a record that can then be scored with the same software.

Booklet or Computer Administration

Several studies have established that booklet and computer administrations of the MMPI yield comparable results (cf. Forbey, Ben-Porath & Gartland, 2009). On-screen administration offers two primary advantages. First, it is appreciably faster than using a booklet and answer sheet. Test takers with normal-range cognitive functioning and reading skills can typically complete a computer administration of the MMPI-2-RF in 25–35 minutes. Booklet and answer sheet administration typically requires 35–50 minutes. Computerized administration is faster because the test taker does not need to go back and forth between the booklet and answer sheet and fill in 338 bubbles. In addition, in an on-screen administration, the test taker inputs his or her responses directly into the computer, allowing for an immediate scoring of the test, saving the time needed to input the responses and avoiding potential error associated with manual entry (discussed later). The primary disadvantage of on-screen administration is that in its present form, it requires that a test taker have access to a computer, which is not feasible or practical in some settings. However, on-screen administration is becoming increasingly feasible as computer technology proliferates. It will be greatly facilitated when it becomes possible to administer the MMPI-2-RF with hand-held devices.

Standard Administration Procedures

Use Standard Administration Instructions

Each of the administration modalities provides standard instructions for completing the inventory, which are the same as those that were used in collecting the test norms. The instructions are as follows:

> This inventory consists of numbered statements. Read each statement and decide whether it is *true as applied to you or false as applied to you.*
>
> You are to mark your answers on the answer sheet you have. Look at the example of the answer sheet shown at the right. If a statement is **true** or **mostly true** as applied to you, blacken the circle marked **T.** If a statement is **false** or **not usually true** as applied to you, blacken the circle marked **F.** If a statement does not apply to you or if it is something that you don't know about, make no mark on the answer sheet. But try to give a response to every statement.
>
> Remember to give **your own** opinion of yourself.

Instructions for using the mouse or keyboard to enter responses to the items replace the directions for recording responses on the answer sheet in an on-screen computerized administration.

Deviations from these instructions may compromise the interpretability of the resulting test scores. If a test taker asks procedural questions about the administration process, they are best answered using language that approximates the standard instructions. Questions about the meaning of test items are best answered with a polite indication that the procedures for using this test do not allow the administrator to explain the statements.

It is tempting, particularly in clinical settings, to deviate from the standard procedures and attempt to assist the test taker, who, after all, in these settings is typically being evaluated for treatment planning or monitoring purposes. However, any advantages in doing so should be weighed against the potential cost of compromising the interpretability of the results. In other settings, in which test takers have a particularly significant stake in the outcome of the assessment (e.g., insanity pleas, personal injury litigation, preemployment evaluations, presurgical assessments), to avoid obtaining invalid or otherwise problematic results, it might be tempting to encourage "honesty." However, it is not appropriate to provide this direction in conjunction with the standard test instructions. The best time to provide general encouragement to respond candidly is during an initial orientation to the assessment process. It is never appropriate to caution test takers about the validity indicators because research has shown that this compromises their utility (cf. Bagby, Nicholson, Bacchiochi, Ryder & Bury, 2002).

Supervise Testing

The Standards for Educational and Psychological Testing (standard 5.6) require that test users make reasonable efforts to protect the integrity of test scores by eliminating opportunities for test takers to obtain scores fraudulently. Although the

MMPI-2-RF is a self-administered test, completion of the inventory should be supervised by a qualified user or a technician working under the supervision of a qualified user. Adequate supervision ensures that the test taker completes the inventory on his or her own, that any unusual events that occur during testing are recorded and can be considered in the interpretation of the test results, and that conditions conducive to obtaining optimally valid information are maintained. Supervision does not require that the individual administering the test be in the same room as the test taker throughout the session, although it is desirable that the test taker be within the supervisor's line of sight. MMPI-2-RF materials should not be sent home with test takers, nor, in institutional settings, should test takers be allowed to complete the instrument in their rooms or anywhere else where supervision is not possible.

Maintain a Quiet, Comfortable Environment

MMPI-2-RF administration should occur in a quiet, comfortable environment in which the test taker is free of distraction. Testing can be conducted individually or in groups, but when more than one individual is tested, it is essential that the supervisor remain in the room to ensure that test takers do not bother or distract each other.

SCORING THE MMPI-2-RF

Scoring the MMPI-2-RF involves calculating a raw score for each of the 51 scales that in turn is converted to a standard T score based on the MMPI-2-RF norms.

The Normative Sample

The MMPI-2-RF normative sample is essentially the same one used in standardizing the MMPI-2, with one modification. Since the original MMPI was developed, most MMPI standard scores have been gender specific. Apparently, Hathaway and McKinley (1943) used gendered norms because they observed differences in the raw scores of women and men in the original MMPI normative sample. They did not address this issue in the test manual. However, later, when normative data for several new MMPI scales were reported, Hathaway and Briggs (1957) indicated that nongendered norms might be used if gendered norms yielded "nearly identical T-scores for the same raw score at about + 2 S.D." (p. 366).

Use of group-specific norms (such as the gendered norms) is predicated on the assumption that group differences in raw scores are irrelevant with respect to the attributes being assessed and must therefore be eliminated when transforming raw scores to standard scores. This would be the case, for example, if members of a group were more willing to report certain characteristics about themselves than were nonmembers of that group, resulting in scale score differences that are a product of response style rather than true differences in the attribute being measured. Although they did not state this explicitly, Hathaway and McKinley apparently assumed that the gender differences they observed reflected a differential willingness of men and women to report certain personality characteristics rather than reflecting relevant group differences.

The practice of reporting and interpreting gendered norms for MMPI scales became standard and was maintained with the MMPI-2 (Butcher et al., 1989). Gendered norms were also reported for all the scales included in the revised edition of the MMPI-2 manual (Butcher et al., 2001). However, testing in certain areas, particularly in personnel screening, is governed by laws that prohibit the use of group-specific norms. The federal Civil Rights Act of 1991 explicitly prohibits consideration of race, color, religion, sex, or national origin in employment practices and has been interpreted as prohibiting use of gendered norms in personnel screening.

Soon after this act was passed, Tellegen, Butcher, and Hoeglund (1993) explored the possibility of developing nongendered norms for the MMPI-2 and concluded that they seemed to operate in a manner similar to that of traditional gender-specific norms. They further observed that nongendered norms did not appear to "disadvantage" either gender. Tellegen and colleagues' analyses did not incorporate all the MMPI-2 scales then being used. Subsequently, a set of nongendered norms for all MMPI-2 scales included in the test manual was developed by Ben-Porath and Forbey (2003), and this normative data set was used to derive standard scores for the MMPI-2-RF.

The nongendered MMPI-2-RF normative sample was created by combining data for the 1,138 men of the MMPI-2 normative sample with those of 1,138 women selected randomly from the 1,462 normative women. Demographic information for the 2,276 individuals who make up the MMPI-2-RF normative sample and a comparison with the 1990 census, which was conducted around the same time that the normative data were collected, are provided in the *MMPI-2-RF Manual for Administration, Scoring, and Interpretation* (Ben-Porath & Tellegen, 2008/2011). The ethnic origin data reported in the manual indicate that the MMPI-2-RF normative sample slightly overrepresents Caucasians and underrepresents Asians and Hispanics. Given the increased rate of growth of the Hispanic population in the United States, the underrepresentation of that group in the normative sample is now even greater. This stems in part from the fact that many Hispanics (and Asians) are immigrants who are not native English speakers and may not have the requisite language skills to complete the MMPI-2 instruments. Standard, approved translations of the MMPI-2-RF are in development and will be added to the materials for the instrument.[2]

Ben-Porath and Forbey (2003) conducted analyses to explore the impact of using nongendered versus gendered MMPI-2 norms on each of the 118 MMPI-2 scales and subscales (except for Clinical Scale 5 and the Gender Role–Masculine [GM] and Gender Role–Feminine [GF] Supplementary Scales) included in the MMPI-2 manual. The nongendered T score was subtracted from the corresponding gendered T score for each raw-score level for every MMPI-2 scale. There was a remarkable dearth of meaningful differences between gendered and nongendered norms. Among the 118 comparisons conducted for each gender, nearly all of the mean differences were below three T-score points. Overall, these analyses indicated considerable similarity in T scores based on gendered versus nongendered norms. Moreover, it was reasonable to conclude that the few instances of clinically significant differences were substantive (which would be masked by gendered norms) rather than nonsubstantive (e.g., stylistic).

Only nongendered norms were derived for the MMPI-2-RF. Note that rather than gendered norms, the common metric of nongendered norms is a prerequisite for recognizing gender differences, just as it is for other group- and setting-specific characteristics. Accordingly, as described later, Appendix D of the *MMPI-2-RF Technical Manual* provides descriptive statistics (T-score means and standard deviations) by gender for a wide range of settings, including the current normative sample. This information, which can also be obtained with the scoring software, makes it possible to compare the scores produced by a given test taker with those of other members of his or her gender tested in a similar setting.

Figures 5-1–5-5 provide the mean T scores and associated standard deviations for the 51 MMPI-2-RF scales for the men and women in the MMPI-2-RF normative sample. Figure 5-1 shows scores on the MMPI-2-RF Validity Scales. As would be expected, mean T scores for both men and women are at or about 50, with associated standard deviations of 10. None of the gender differences reaches or exceeds five T-score points, which, by convention, is the minimal mean difference of clinical significance. For all but two of the validity indicators, the means are within one T-score point across genders. A similar pattern occurs for the Substantive Scales in Figures 5-2–5-5. Noteworthy exceptions occur for Behavioral/Externalizing Dysfunction (BXD) and Disconstraint–Revised (DISC-r), on which men score higher than women, and Multiple Specific Fears (MSF), on which women score higher than men. These differences are consistent with MMPI-2 findings reported by Ben-Porath and Forbey (2003).

Derivation of Standard Scores

Standard T scores for the original MMPI Clinical Scales were derived through a linear transformation of raw scores to standard scores with a mean of 50 and a standard deviation of 10 based on the responses of members of the original normative sample (Hathaway & McKinley, 1943). Because the distribution of raw scores varied across scales, the linear transformation procedure yielded differential amounts of skew in the T-score distributions, resulting in the potential for the same T-score value (e.g., 70) to reflect different degrees of deviation from the norm in percentile terms. This, coupled with concerns about the interpretability of T-score values forming a skewed distribution, led some researchers (e.g., Colligan, Osborne, Swenson & Offord, 1983; Finney, 1968) to propose that normalized T-score values be adopted instead.

Examination of the raw-score distributions of the MMPI-2 Clinical Scales revealed that the positive skew characterized the normative distributions of most of the scales in the 1940s and also in the 1989 normative data. The positive skew is to be expected for measures of psychopathology and can be viewed as typical for such measures and also as more appropriate than, for example, a normal distribution (Tellegen & Ben-Porath, 1992). However, for both sets of norms, the degree of skewness of the raw-score distributions and of the corresponding linear T-score distributions varied from scale to scale. Consequently, the same linear T-score value (e.g., a T score of 70) could have different percentile values for different scales.

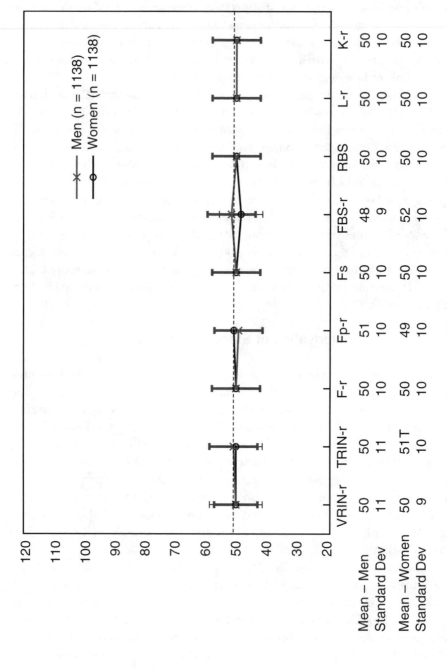

	VRIN-r	TRIN-r	F-r	Fp-r	Fs	FBS-r	RBS	L-r	K-r
Mean – Men	50	50	50	51	50	48	50	50	50
Standard Dev	11	11	10	10	10	9	10	10	10
Mean – Women	50	51T	50	49	50	52	50	50	50
Standard Dev	9	10	10	10	10	10	10	10	10

Figure 5-1. MMPI-2-RF Validity Scales: Normative sample mean T scores and associated standard deviations.

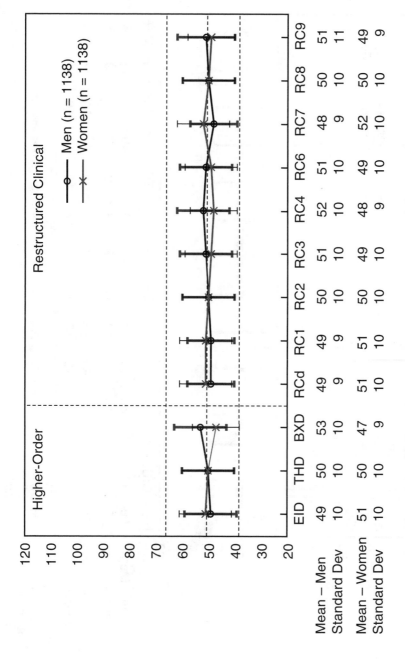

Figure 5-2. MMPI-2-RF Higher-Order (HOD) and Restructured Clinical (RC) Scales: Normative sample mean T scores and associated standard deviations.

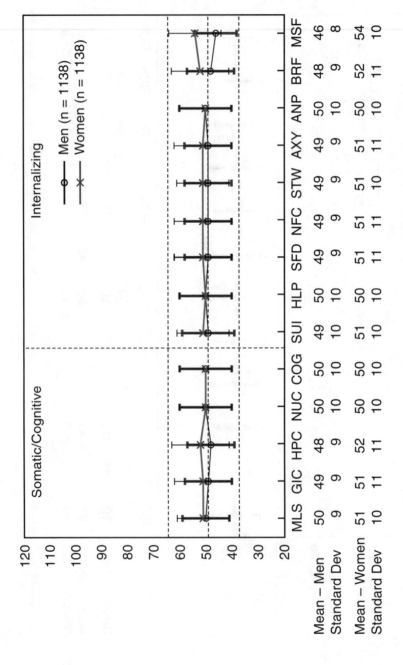

Figure 5-3. MMPI-2-RF Somatic/Cognitive and Internalizing Scales: Normative sample mean T scores and associated standard deviations.

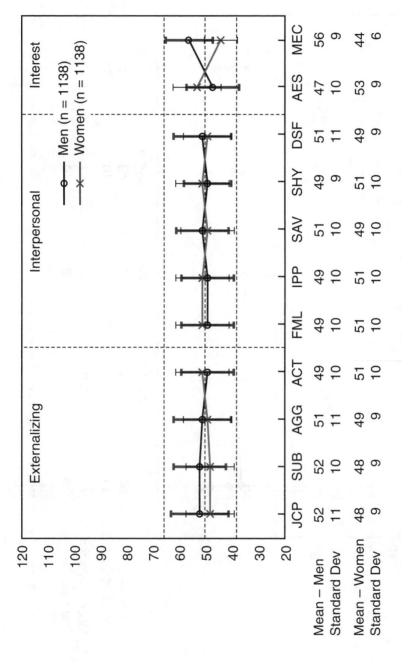

Figure 5-4. MMPI-2-RF Externalizing, Interpersonal, and Interest Scales: Normative sample mean T scores and associated standard deviations.

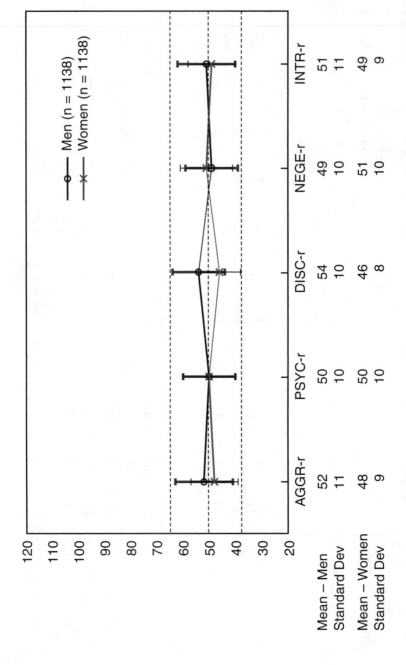

Figure 5-5. MMPI-2-RF Personality Psychopathology Five (PSY-5) Scales: Normative sample mean T scores and associated standard deviations.

For the MMPI-2, this undesirable feature of linear T scores was corrected with a minimum of change in the original linear T-score distributions, preserving the typical positive skewness of the MMPI Clinical Scales. This was accomplished by deriving Uniform T scores (Tellegen & Ben-Porath, 1992), which were designed to have distributions approximating the "prototypical" linear T-score distribution of the MMPI-2 Clinical Scales. Such a distribution was derived empirically for that purpose and was adopted as a standard. This prototypical distribution is essentially a composite of 16 individual distributions, namely, the non-K-corrected linear T-score distributions of the eight original MMPI Clinical Scales in the normative samples for both men and women (omitting Scales 5 and 0 because of their distinctive distributions and methods of derivation).

To arrive at this composite target distribution, linear T scores were first derived for each of the 16 raw-score distributions using the formula $T = 50 + [10(X - M)]/SD$, where X is the raw score and M and SD are the mean and standard deviation of the raw score, respectively. Next, a series of linear T-score values was derived through interpolation, namely, the T-score values corresponding to percentiles 0.5, 1, 2, . . . 98, 99, 99.5 in each of the 16 distributions. In other words, for each percentile value, 16 linear T-score values were derived and then averaged. The resulting series of average or composite T-score values (one average T-score value for each percentile) was adopted as the composite target distribution. As expected, this distribution is positively skewed, as illustrated in Figure 5-6. The composite standard is numerically illustrated in Table 5-1, which provides the percentile values for a subset of representative composite T-score values. Reflecting the same positive skew as Figure 5-6, Table 5-1 shows, for example, that a high composite T score of 70 (two standard deviations above 50) has a percentile value of 96, whereas the correspondingly low composite T score of 30 (two standard deviations below 50) has a more extreme percentile value of less than 1. Regression methods were then developed to transform the raw scores of each scale directly into Uniform T scores that would conform as closely as possible to the composite standard. The Uniform T-score transformation largely eliminated the original linear T-score distributional differences between the Clinical Scales because the obtained Uniform T-score distributions do conform well to the adopted standard and are consequently quite similar (Tellegen & Ben-Porath, 1992). Uniform T scores were developed for the (eight original) MMPI-2 Clinical Scales as well as for the Content Scales (Butcher, Graham, Williams & Ben-Porath, 1990), the Personality Psychopathology Five (PSY-5) Scales (Harkness, McNulty & Ben-Porath, 1995), the Restructured Clinical (RC) Scales (Tellegen, Ben-Porath, McNulty, Arbisi, Graham & Kaemmer, 2003), and other selected Supplementary Scales. Uniform T scores have also been adopted for the MMPI-2-RF, with the exception of the Validity and Interest Scales (for which linear T scores were adopted because these scales have distinctive distributions dissimilar to the composite uniform distribution). The composite distribution that was targeted to derive Uniform T scores for the MMPI-2 was also used in calculating Uniform T scores for the MMPI-2-RF so that the standard scores are directly comparable across the two versions of the instrument. Raw-score to T-score conversions for all the MMPI-2-RF scales are

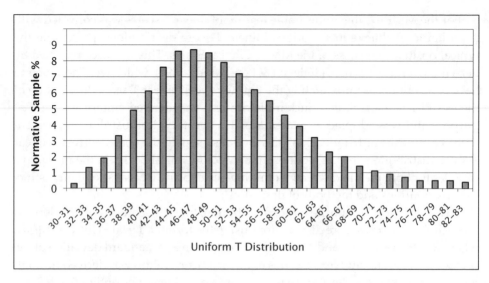

Figure 5-6. Prototype distribution used as a target for deriving the Uniform T scores.

reported in Appendix A of the *MMPI-2-RF Manual for Administration, Scoring, and Interpretation* (Ben-Porath & Tellegen, 2008/2011).

Hand Scoring or Computer Scoring?

MMPI-2-RF protocols can be scored by computer or by hand. Computerized scoring offers a number of advantages (discussed in detail later). It can also be cost-effective if the clerical costs of hand scoring are considered. The most efficient way to implement computerized scoring is to administer the MMPI-2-RF using Pearson software. As noted, this eliminates the need to enter the test taker's responses into the system and shortens administration time considerably. If the MMPI-2-RF is administered by booklet and answer sheet, a scanner can be used to enter the item responses into the Pearson scoring software, or the software can be used to enter the test taker's responses by keyboard. If keyboard entry is used, the software provides the option of reentering a protocol (double entry), which is recommended to reduce the likelihood of entry error. Users can also mail answer sheets to Pearson for computerized scoring.

Hand scoring requires the use of answer keys (plastic templates) available from Pearson. Given the number of scales on the MMPI-2-RF (51) and the complexity of scoring some of these scales (in particular, VRIN-r and TRIN-r), hand scorers may be tempted not to score all of the scales. This is not recommended because scores on all the MMPI-2-RF scales need to be considered to develop a comprehensive and complete interpretation of a protocol. Even the most time-consuming mode of response entry for computer scoring (double-entry by keyboard) requires considerably less time than does hand scoring the 51 scales of the MMPI-2-RF. An experienced user or clerical assistant can typically double-enter an MMPI-2-RF protocol in 10–12 minutes. Hand scoring by an experienced user or assistant typically requires 25–30

Table 5-1. Percentile Equivalents of Uniform T Scores

Uniform T Score	Equivalent Percentile
30	< 1
35	4
40	15
45	34
50	55
55	73
60	85
65	92
70	96
75	98
80	> 99

minutes. Moreover, research has shown that hand scoring is error prone (Allard & Faust, 2000; Simon, Goddard & Patton, 2002). By contrast, as just noted, the only error possible when using automated scoring is inaccurate keyboard entry of item responses, which can be greatly reduced by using the double-entry option.

The accuracy advantage afforded by automated scoring is, of course, contingent on the accuracy of the scoring software. Allard and Faust (2000) found substantial scoring errors in several nonstandard software systems used in the clinical settings in which they collected their data. Furthermore, the creation and use of unauthorized computer scoring programs is illegal. The MMPI-2-RF scoring algorithm included in Pearson software is rigorously checked for errors, and it is the only authorized, commercially available system for computer scoring the MMPI-2-RF.

A final and noteworthy advantage of computer scoring involves the additional information provided in the MMPI-2-RF Score Report and Interpretive Report.

COMPUTER-GENERATED REPORTS

Two reports can presently be generated with Pearson software. The MMPI-2-RF Score Report provides a test taker's scores on the 51 scales of the inventory along with information about the individual's responses to the test items. The MMPI-2-RF Interpretive Report includes all of the elements of the Score Report and a computer-generated interpretation of the results.[3] The Pearson software used to produce these reports provides opportunities to customize by including a variety of optional data, described next. Additional information about the reports and how to interface with the software to generate them is provided in the *MMPI-2-RF User's Guide for Reports* (Ben-Porath & Tellegen, 2011).

MMPI-2-RF Score Report

A sample MMPI-2-RF score report is reproduced in Figures 5-7–5-15. The scores are those of a 36-year-old man, "Mr. I," tested at intake to an inpatient psychiatric facility. The cover page for the report (Figure 5-7) provides identifying information as recorded on the MMPI-2-RF answer sheet or during on-screen administration. Scores on the 51 scales of the MMPI-2-RF are reported on five profiles that appear on pages 2–6 of the score report (Figures 5-8–5-12). They are followed by a summary of the scale scores under the heading "MMPI-2-RF T Scores (By Domain)" (Figure 5-13). Item-level information is provided in the remaining pages of the report (Figures 5-14 and 5-15).

Profiles

The second page of the report (Figure 5-8) provides a profile of the scores on the Validity Scales. Standard linear T scores are plotted in four groups: (1) inconsistent responding (VRIN-r and TRIN-r); (2) overreporting psychopathology (Infrequent Responses [F-r] and Infrequent Psychopathology Responses [Fp-r]); (3) overreporting somatic and cognitive complaints (Infrequent Somatic Responses [Fs], Symptom Validity [FBS-r], and Response Bias Scale [RBS]); and (4) underreporting (Uncommon Virtues [L-r] and Adjustment Validity [K-r]). The Validity Scales profile has a horizontal line drawn at T score 50, representing the mean score for the MMPI-2-RF normative sample. Unlike the remaining profiles, this is the only demarcation line on the Validity Scales profile because different cutoffs are used in the interpretation of scores on these scales (see Chapter 6 for details). Three hyphens denote the highest and lowest possible T scores on each scale.

The first three rows of numbers below the profile show the raw score, T score, and percentage of scorable responses to the items on each of the nine scales. Responses are unscorable when the test taker fails to mark an answer or responds both true and false to an item. The fourth row of numbers provides a count of the number of unscorable responses ("cannot say") and the percentage of true scorable item responses in the protocol.

As described in Chapters 6 and 8, consideration of scores on the MMPI-2-RF begins with an examination of the Cannot Say score, the count of unscorable responses in the protocol. The interpretive guidelines indicate that for scales on which less than 90% of the item responses are scorable, the absence of elevation is uninterpretable. Moreover, elevated scores on such scales may underestimate the significance or severity of associated problems. To facilitate identification of scales potentially compromised by an excessive number of unscorable responses, if the percentage of scorable items on a scale falls below 90, it is highlighted in bold in the third row of numbers under the profile. In Mr. I's case, less than 90% of the items on FBS-r and K-r are scorable. A list of the 17 unscorable items is provided later in the report (Figure 5-14).

The third page of the report (Figure 5-9) provides scores on the three Higher-Order (H-O) Scales and the nine RC Scales. In addition to the features just described for the Validity Scales, the profiles for these and the remaining Substantive Scales include two more lines of demarcation, drawn at T scores of 65 and 38. The higher line, drawn at the 92nd percentile for Uniform T scores, indicates the minimal level of elevation required for most of the interpretive recommendations made for the

Minnesota Multiphasic
Personality Inventory-2
Restructured Form®

Score Report

MMPI-2-RF®

Minnesota Multiphasic Personality Inventory-2-Restructured Form®

Yossef S. Ben-Porath, PhD, & Auke Tellegen, PhD

ID Number:	Mr. I
Age:	36
Gender:	Male
Marital Status:	Married
Years of Education:	Not reported
Date Assessed:	04/22/2011

PEARSON

🕲 *PsychCorp*

Figure 5-7. Mr. I's MMPI-2-RF Score Report, page 1.

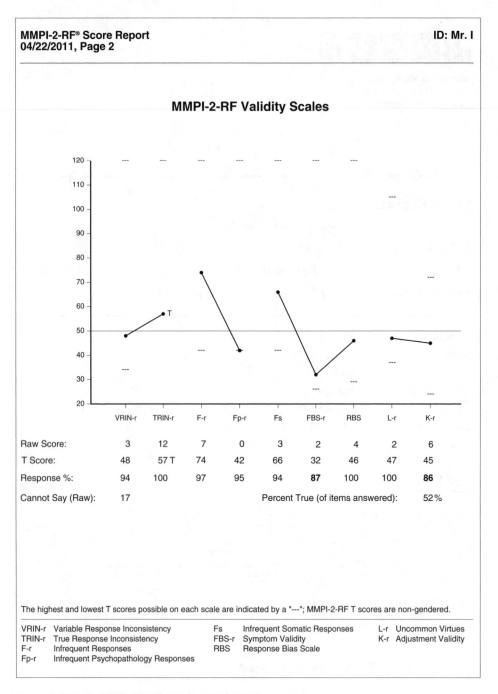

Figure 5-8. Mr. I's MMPI-2-RF Score Report, page 2.

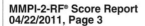

MMPI-2-RF® Score Report
04/22/2011, Page 3

ID: Mr. I

MMPI-2-RF Higher-Order (H-O) and Restructured Clinical (RC) Scales

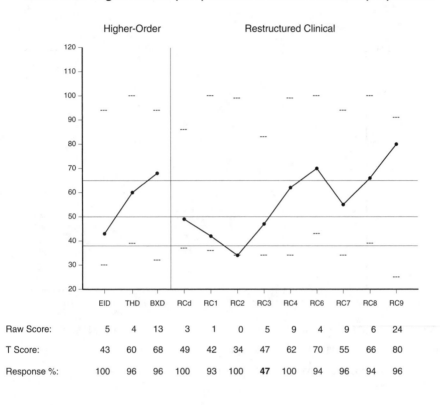

	EID	THD	BXD	RCd	RC1	RC2	RC3	RC4	RC6	RC7	RC8	RC9
Raw Score:	5	4	13	3	1	0	5	9	4	9	6	24
T Score:	43	60	68	49	42	34	47	62	70	55	66	80
Response %:	100	96	96	100	93	100	**47**	100	94	96	94	96

The highest and lowest T scores possible on each scale are indicated by a "---"; MMPI-2-RF T scores are non-gendered.

EID Emotional/Internalizing Dysfunction	RCd Demoralization	RC6 Ideas of Persecution
THD Thought Dysfunction	RC1 Somatic Complaints	RC7 Dysfunctional Negative Emotions
BXD Behavioral/Externalizing Dysfunction	RC2 Low Positive Emotions	RC8 Aberrant Experiences
	RC3 Cynicism	RC9 Hypomanic Activation
	RC4 Antisocial Behavior	

Figure 5-9. Mr. I's MMPI-2-RF Score Report, page 3.

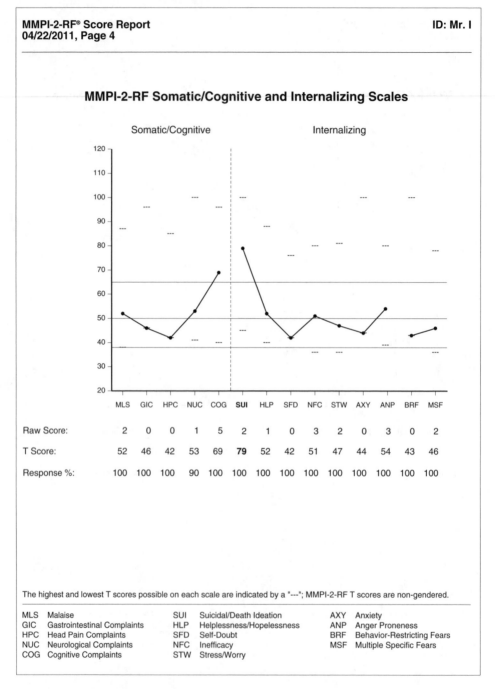

MMPI-2-RF Somatic/Cognitive and Internalizing Scales

Somatic/Cognitive   Internalizing

	MLS	GIC	HPC	NUC	COG	SUI	HLP	SFD	NFC	STW	AXY	ANP	BRF	MSF
Raw Score:	2	0	0	1	5	2	1	0	3	2	0	3	0	2
T Score:	52	46	42	53	69	79	52	42	51	47	44	54	43	46
Response %:	100	100	100	90	100	100	100	100	100	100	100	100	100	100

The highest and lowest T scores possible on each scale are indicated by a "---"; MMPI-2-RF T scores are non-gendered.

MLS	Malaise	SUI	Suicidal/Death Ideation	AXY	Anxiety
GIC	Gastrointestinal Complaints	HLP	Helplessness/Hopelessness	ANP	Anger Proneness
HPC	Head Pain Complaints	SFD	Self-Doubt	BRF	Behavior-Restricting Fears
NUC	Neurological Complaints	NFC	Inefficacy	MSF	Multiple Specific Fears
COG	Cognitive Complaints	STW	Stress/Worry		

Figure 5-10. Mr. I's MMPI-2-RF Score Report, page 4.

MMPI-2-RF® Score Report   **ID: Mr. I**
04/22/2011, Page 5

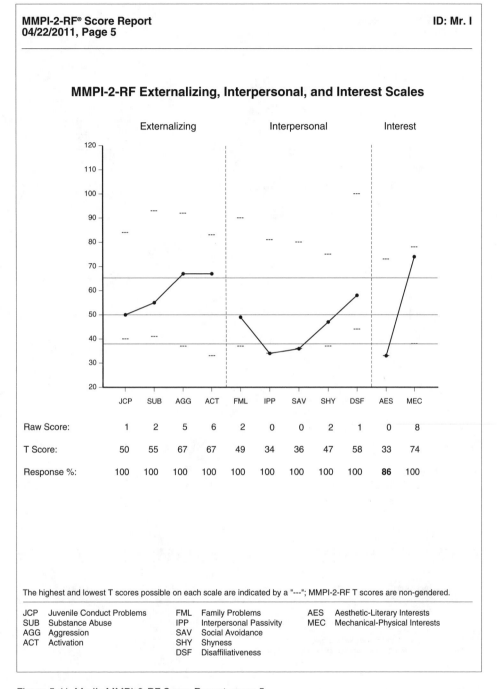

Figure 5-11. Mr. I's MMPI-2-RF Score Report, page 5.

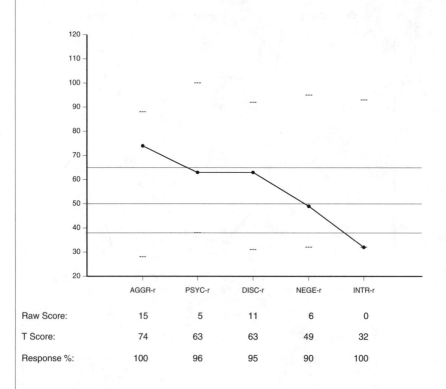

MMPI-2-RF PSY-5 Scales

	AGGR-r	PSYC-r	DISC-r	NEGE-r	INTR-r
Raw Score:	15	5	11	6	0
T Score:	74	63	63	49	32
Response %:	100	96	95	90	100

The highest and lowest T scores possible on each scale are indicated by a "---"; MMPI-2-RF T scores are non-gendered.

AGGR-r	Aggressiveness-Revised
PSYC-r	Psychoticism-Revised
DISC-r	Disconstraint-Revised
NEGE-r	Negative Emotionality/Neuroticism-Revised
INTR-r	Introversion/Low Positive Emotionality-Revised

Figure 5-12. Mr. I's MMPI-2-RF Score Report, page 6.

MMPI-2-RF® Score Report
04/22/2011, Page 7

ID: Mr. I

MMPI-2-RF T SCORES (BY DOMAIN)

PROTOCOL VALIDITY

Content Non-Responsiveness		17	48	57 T				
		CNS	VRIN-r	TRIN-r				

Over-Reporting		74	42		66	32*	46
		F-r	Fp-r		Fs	FBS-r	RBS

Under-Reporting		47	45*
		L-r	K-r

SUBSTANTIVE SCALES

Somatic/Cognitive Dysfunction		42	52	46	42	53	69
		RC1	MLS	GIC	HPC	NUC	COG

Emotional Dysfunction	43	49	**79**	52	42	51		
	EID	RCd	**SUI**	HLP	SFD	NFC		
		34	32					
		RC2	INTR-r					
		55	47	44	54	43	46	49
		RC7	STW	AXY	ANP	BRF	MSF	NEGE-r

Thought Dysfunction	60	70
	THD	RC6
		66
		RC8
		63
		PSYC-r

Behavioral Dysfunction	68	62	50	55		
	BXD	RC4	JCP	SUB		
		80	67	67	74	63
		RC9	AGG	ACT	AGGR-r	DISC-r

Interpersonal Functioning		49	47*	34	36	47	58
		FML	RC3	IPP	SAV	SHY	DSF

Interests		33*	74
		AES	MEC

*The test taker provided scorable responses to less than 90% of the items scored on this scale. See the relevant profile page for the specific percentage.

Note. This information is provided to facilitate interpretation following the recommended structure for MMPI-2-RF interpretation in Chapter 5 of the *MMPI-2-RF Manual for Administration, Scoring, and Interpretation*, which provides details in the text and an outline in Table 5-1.

Figure 5-13. Mr. I's MMPI-2-RF Score Report, page 7.

ITEM-LEVEL INFORMATION

Unscorable Responses

Following is a list of items to which the test taker did not provide scorable responses. Unanswered or double answered (both True and False) items are unscorable. The scales on which the items appear are in parentheses following the item content.

    9. Item content removed. (RC7, NEGE-r)
  15. Item content removed. (Fs, FBS-r, RC1)
  36. Item content removed. (FBS-r, K-r, RC3)
  55. Item content removed. (VRIN-r, FBS-r, RC3)
  99. Item content removed. (VRIN-r, FBS-r, K-r, RC3)
107. Item content removed. (BXD, RC9, DISC-r)
121. Item content removed. (RC3)
185. Item content removed. (RC3)
191. Item content removed. (Fp-r)
194. Item content removed. (VRIN-r, RC6)
203. Item content removed. (F-r, THD, RC8, PSYC-r)
209. Item content removed. (NEGE-r)
238. Item content removed. (RC3)
296. Item content removed. (AES)
304. Item content removed. (RC3)
313. Item content removed. (RC1, NUC)
326. Item content removed. (RC3)

Critical Responses

Seven MMPI-2-RF scales--Suicidal/Death Ideation (SUI), Helplessness/Hopelessness (HLP), Anxiety (AXY), Ideas of Persecution (RC6), Aberrant Experiences (RC8), Substance Abuse (SUB), and Aggression (AGG)--have been designated by the test authors as having critical item content that may require immediate attention and follow-up. Items answered by the individual in the keyed direction (True or False) on a critical scale are listed below if his T score on that scale is 65 or higher. The percentage of the MMPI-2-RF normative sample that answered each item in the keyed direction is provided in parentheses following the item content.

Suicidal/Death Ideation (SUI, T Score = 79)
   251. Item content removed. (True, 3.0%)
   334. Item content removed. (True, 13.5%)

Ideas of Persecution (RC6, T Score = 70)
   14. Item content removed. (True, 2.9%)
   34. Item content removed. (True, 10.6%)
   71. Item content removed. (True, 2.0%)
110. Item content removed. (True, 9.9%)

Figure 5-14. Mr. I's MMPI-2-RF Score Report, page 8.

MMPI-2-RF® Score Report
04/22/2011, Page 9

Aberrant Experiences (RC8, T Score = 66)

    32. Item content removed. (True, 21.1%)
    85. Item content removed. (False, 17.1%)
  106. Item content removed. (True, 8.7%)
  159. Item content removed. (True, 6.0%)
  240. Item content removed. (True, 8.8%)
  257. Item content removed. (True, 12.4%)

Aggression (AGG, T Score = 67)

    23. Item content removed. (True, 39.0%)
  312. Item content removed. (True, 5.5%)
  316. Item content removed. (True, 45.1%)
  329. Item content removed. (True, 12.7%)
  337. Item content removed. (True, 50.2%)

User-Designated Item-Level Information

The following item-level information is based on the report user's selection of additional scales, and/or of lower cutoffs for the critical scales from the previous section. Items answered by the test taker in the keyed direction (True or False) on a selected scale are listed below if his T score on that scale is at the user-designated cutoff score or higher. The percentage of the MMPI-2-RF normative sample that answered each item in the keyed direction is provided in parentheses following the item content.

Hypomanic Activation (RC9, T Score = 80)

    13. Item content removed. (True, 40.9%)
    39. Item content removed. (True, 51.0%)
    47. Item content removed. (True, 42.7%)
    61. Item content removed. (False, 61.6%)
    72. Item content removed. (True, 81.5%)
    97. Item content removed. (True, 50.5%)
  118. Item content removed. (True, 57.4%)
  131. Item content removed. (True, 43.3%)
  143. Item content removed. (True, 27.5%)
  155. Item content removed. (True, 41.6%)
  166. Item content removed. (True, 38.9%)
  181. Item content removed. (True, 35.3%)
  193. Item content removed. (True, 32.8%)
  207. Item content removed. (True, 66.9%)
  219. Item content removed. (True, 51.5%)
  244. Item content removed. (True, 56.9%)
  248. Item content removed. (True, 16.1%)
  256. Item content removed. (True, 65.7%)
  267. Item content removed. (True, 12.9%)
  292. Item content removed. (True, 26.1%)
  305. Item content removed. (True, 37.6%)
  316. Item content removed. (True, 45.1%)

Figure 5-15. Mr. I's MMPI-2-RF Score Report, pages 9–10.

MMPI-2-RF® Score Report   ID: Mr. I
04/22/2011, Page 10

---

327. Item content removed. (True, 41.7%)
337. Item content removed. (True, 50.2%)

Activation (ACT, T Score = 67)
72. Item content removed. (True, 81.5%)
166. Item content removed. (True, 38.9%)
181. Item content removed. (True, 35.3%)
207. Item content removed. (True, 66.9%)
219. Item content removed. (True, 51.5%)
267. Item content removed. (True, 12.9%)

End of Report

This and previous pages of this report contain trade secrets and are not to be released in response to requests under HIPAA (or any other data disclosure law that exempts trade secret information from release). Further, release in response to litigation discovery demands should be made only in accordance with your profession's ethical guidelines and under an appropriate protective order.

Figure 5-15. Mr I's MMPI-2-RF Score Report, pages 9–10, continued.

Substantive Scales. The lower line, indicating the eighth percentile for Uniform T scores, is designed to assist in identifying interpretable low scores.

The fourth page of the report (Figure 5-10) provides scores on two sets of MMPI-2-RF measures, the Somatic/Cognitive and Internalizing Scales. Scores for the Internalizing Scales are plotted in two groups, with scores on the two fear-related scales, Behavior-Restricting Fears (BRF) and Multiple Specific Fears (MSF), separated from the rest. This separation reflects the results of factor analyses indicating that although they are clearly related to the higher-order internalizing dimension, scores on the fear-related measures load on a separate factor. Another unique feature on this page of the report appears in cases (such as Mr. I) when the score on the Suicidal/Death Ideation (SUI) Scale is elevated. The abbreviated scale name and the T score appear in boldface below the profile to draw the user's attention to that score. The fifth page of the report (Figure 5-11) provides scores for the Externalizing, Interpersonal, and Interest Scales. Scores for the PSY-5 Scales are provided on page 6 of the report (Figure 5-12).

MMPI-2-RF T Scores (By Domain)

The seventh page of the report (Figure 5-13) provides a summary of scores on the 51 MMPI-2-RF scales organized by domain. This summary page is intended to facilitate the interpretation process by arranging the individual's scores according to the recommended structure for MMPI-2-RF interpretation detailed in Chapter 8. This interpretive approach indicates, for example, that interpretation of Substantive Scale scores begins with the highest elevated H-O Scale, followed by the RC Scales associated with it in order of elevation. RC Scale interpretation incorporates the affiliated Specific Problems Scales. In Figure 5-13, Mr. I has an elevated score on BXD, which would be interpreted first, followed by Hypomanic Activation (RC9), Aggression (AGG), Activation (ACT), and Aggressiveness–Revised (AGGR-r). An asterisk identifies scales for which Mr. I provided less than 90% scorable item responses, which limits their interpretability as noted. A complete interpretation of Mr. I's MMPI-2-RF results is provided in Chapter 8.

Item-Level Information

Easily accessible item-level information is another important advantage of automated scoring over hand scoring of the MMPI-2-RF. Although this information can be obtained by detailed examination of the answer sheet, doing so would add considerably to the already time-consuming process of hand scoring the protocol. In the following sections, the three types of item-level information available in the score report are described. To maintain test item security, the content of the items, which appears in the actual report printout, is removed from the sample reports reproduced in this book. Item numbers are reported so that interested readers can consult an MMPI-2-RF booklet to find the content of the items.

Unscorable Responses

A list of items to which the test taker did not provide scorable answers appears under the heading "Unscorable Responses" (see Figure 5-14). As defined earlier, unscorable responses occur when the test taker either fails to mark an answer or responds both *true* and *false* to an item. Unscorable items are listed in the order in which they appear in the MMPI-2-RF protocol. The scale or scales on which each item is scored appear in parentheses following the item number and its content. This makes it possible to examine the content of the unscorable items to detect possible themes. If the test taker is available for a follow-up interview, he or she could be asked why no response or a double response was given to these items.

In the example provided in Figure 5-14, 8 of the 17 unscorable items appear on the Cynicism (RC3) Scale. Examination of Figure 5-4, containing scores on the RC Scales, indicates that Mr. I provided scorable responses to only 47% of the RC3 items. This finding should not be interpreted as an indication that he holds cynical views of others, but it does indicate that he avoided responding to test items relating to such attitudes. This could be an area for follow-up as part of the assessment, which could include a discussion about why Mr. I did not respond to these specific items.

Critical Responses

A second type of item-level information appears under the heading "Critical Responses." The critical responses approach relies on scale-level data to identify a test taker who is probably experiencing critical difficulties that warrant immediate attention. If he or she generates an elevated score on one or more of the scales designated as having critical content, then item-level data can be used to identify the specific difficulties being reported by the test taker. We[4] designated seven MMPI-2-RF Substantive Scales as having critical item content that might require immediate attention and follow-up: Suicidal/Death Ideation (SUI), Helplessness/Hopelessness (HLP), Anxiety (AXY), Ideas of Persecution (RC6), Aberrant Experiences (RC8), Substance Abuse (SUB), and Aggression (AGG). Items answered by the individual in the keyed direction on a critical scale are listed if the test taker's T score on that scale is 65 or higher. The percentage of the MMPI-2-RF normative sample who answered each item listed in the keyed direction is provided in parentheses following the item content.

Because the items scored on the SUI Scale were very rarely endorsed by members of the normative sample, a raw score of 1 is sufficient to generate a T score above 65 on this scale. Therefore, if a test taker answers *any* of the SUI items in the keyed direction, they will be listed in this section. Because of the particularly serious nature of this information, if the test taker has an elevated score on SUI, all the information regarding this scale is presented in boldface in this section of the report.

The critical responses list informs the interpreter of the specific responses a test taker gave to obtain an elevated score on the seven scales identified as having critical item content. This information can be used to guide a follow-up interview that might include asking the test taker to elaborate on certain responses that he or she gave. Test takers sometimes attribute their responses to misunderstanding the item content or incorrectly recording their answers. However, if a test taker cites multiple such misunderstandings or mistakes in an effort to explain away a pattern of unusual or otherwise worrisome responses, this may raise questions about the credibility of her or his explanations.

In the example provided in Figure 5-14, Mr. I has elevated scores on four of the seven scales: SUI, RC6, RC8, and AGG. The SUI item-level responses show that he reported an attempt to kill himself that is unknown to anyone else and a preoccupation with death. This information should trigger an immediate assessment of suicide risk. Responses to critical items on RC6 and RC8 provide insight into the types of persecutory thoughts and unusual sensory-perceptual experiences reported by Mr. I. His responses to the AGG items illustrate the kind of aggressive behaviors he reported.

User-Designated Item-Level Information

The Pearson software provides an option for the user to designate additional scales and/or alternative cutoff levels for generating a third type of item-level information. Users can select any MMPI-2-RF scale for inclusion in this part of the report. By default, if a scale is selected, item-level information will be printed if a test taker's score reaches a level for which interpretive recommendations are provided for that scale in Chapters 6 and 7 (excluding low-score interpretive recommendations). For the Substantive Scales, the default T-score cutoff is 65. The default values for the validity indicators vary depending upon the interpretive recommendations listed in Chapter 6.

The ability to customize cutoffs can be particularly helpful in settings in which interpretable deviations from reference group means occur at lower levels. For example, as discussed and illustrated in Chapter 9, cutoffs of 60 and 55 can be used to identify potentially problematic characteristics in law enforcement candidates. In such cases, users may wish to select alternative cutoffs for generating supplementary item-level information.

The option to select additional scales can be helpful when an initial review of the results identifies areas requiring further attention in addition to those incorporated in the "Critical Responses" section. For example, an elevated score on RC9 is a central finding in Mr. I's case. Although RC9 and ACT are not among the scales in the "Critical Responses" section, selecting them for inclusion in the "User-Designated Item-Level Information" section in this case provides additional information about a possible mood disorder (see Figure 5-15). Most but not all of the ACT items are also scored on the higher-level RC9 scale. By examining the items listed in this section, the interpreter can get a sense of the relatively broad content of the items Mr. I answered in the keyed direction on RC9 and the more narrowly focused statements on ACT, which identify racing thoughts, elevated mood, and overexcitation as specific indications of overactivation in Mr. I's test results.

An MMPI-2-RF score report can be reprinted with different options selected (e.g., adding scales to the user-designated item-level information list) without incurring additional cost. One approach to using this option is to begin with a preliminary examination of the report with no scales selected for this section. If the user then identifies additional scales or alternative cutoffs that might provide useful information, these options can be selected and the report reprinted. A detailed illustration of how to use the Pearson software to select additional scales and alternative cutoffs for inclusion in this section can be found in the *MMPI-2-RF User's Guide for Reports* (Ben-Porath & Tellegen, 2011).

Comparison Groups

The Pearson software used to generate the score report and interpretive report provides an option to plot the test taker's standard scores along with descriptive data for various comparison groups. The descriptive data include means and standard deviations on all 51 scales, the percentage of individuals in the comparison group who score at or below the test taker on each scale, and the percentage of individuals in the comparison group who responded the same as the test taker to the items listed under "Critical Responses" and "User-Designated Item-Level Information." These data make it possible to compare a test taker's scores and item-level responses with those of individuals tested in a similar setting, usually under similar circumstances. This additional, setting-specific information complements what can be learned from the standard T scores and item-level information included in the reports, which characterize the test taker's scores and responses in reference to the general population norms. Two options are available for selecting comparison groups.

Standard Comparison Groups

A set of standard comparison groups, representing the range of settings in which the MMPI-2-RF is used, is available for selection with the Pearson software. As of this writing, the set includes 31 samples representing 18 settings or types of evaluation.[5] A list of the currently available standard comparison groups and the demographic characteristics of their subjects is provided in Table 5-2. The means and standard deviations of these samples are reported in Appendix D of the *MMPI-2-RF Technical Manual*.

Composition of the normative sample was described earlier in this chapter. The remaining comparison groups represent various settings in which the MMPI-2-RF is used. For most groups, sufficient numbers of men and women were available, and the comparison group data are gender specific. An exception was made for the three comparison groups of individuals tested as part of a personnel screening assessment (law enforcement officer, corrections officer, and clergy candidates). In the *Technical Manual*, we report descriptive data for men, women, and a combined-gender sample for these settings. In the MMPI-2-RF reports, only the combined-gender data can be selected because of the previously noted legal prohibition against using gender-based norms in employment-related assessments.

The list of comparison groups in Table 5-2 is current for the 2.7 release of Pearson's Q Local software. Comparison groups subsequently added to the software will be listed in periodic updates of the *MMPI-2-RF User's Guide for Reports*.

Table 5-2. Demographic Characteristics of the Standard Comparison Groups

Comparison Group	n	Age M (SD)	Ethnicity (%) Caucasian	African American	Other
MMPI-2-RF Normative					
Men	1,138	41.7 (15.3)	82.0	11.1	5.9
Women	1,138	40.4 (15.2)	81.5	12.0	6.5
Outpatient, Community Mental Health Center					
Men	370	33.8 (10.8)	82.0	16.4	1.6
Women	582	32.8 (9.8)	80.8	18.2	1.0
Outpatient, Independent Practice					
Men	246	37.2 (10.5)	80.3	11.5	8.2
Women	432	37.0 (11.0)	90.1	4.7	5.2
Psychiatric Inpatient, Community Hospital					
Men	659	34.0 (10.6)	77.9	16.4	5.7
Women	498	34.1 (11.3)	75.8	17.8	6.4
Psychiatric Inpatient, VA Hospital					
Men	1,059	47.8 (13.7)	90.4	6.6	3.0
Substance Abuse Treatment, VA Hospital					
Men	1,151	44.7 (8.6)	39.1	59.8	1.1
Bariatric Surgery Candidate					
Men	228	45.4 (10.4)	84.0	8.0	8.0
Women	435	36.8 (9.8)	85.9	10.2	3.9
Spine Surgery/Spinal Cord Stimulator Candidate					
Men	263	47.9 (12.2)	85.9	3.9	10.2
Women	265	48.4 (13.4)	87.1	9.7	3.2
College Counseling Clinic					
Men	367	26.3 (8.5)	89.1	5.5	5.4
Women	894	23.8 (6.7)	90.3	4.3	5.4
College Student					
Men	1,227	19.6 (2.5)	91.2	5.9	2.9
Women	1,989	19.4 (3.6)	87.4	9.5	3.1
Forensic, Child Custody Litigant					
Men	244	40.3 (7.8)	NA	NA	NA
Women	238	36.9 (7.2)	NA	NA	NA
Forensic, Disability Claimant					
Men	523	41.0 (10.7)	92.0	2.6	5.4
Women	480	40.1 (11.0)	90.4	4.3	5.3

Continued, next page

Table 5-2, continued

Comparison Group	n	Age M (SD)	Ethnicity (%) Caucasian	African American	Other
Forensic, Neuropsychological Examination Litigant/Claimant					
Men	463	38.7 (11.8)	NA	NA	NA
Women	578	39.2 (11.9)	NA	NA	NA
Forensic, Pre-Trial Criminal					
Men	551	35.8 (18.3)	77.6	21.2	1.2
Women	223	36.3 (11.9)	82.8	15.8	1.4
Prison Inmate					
Men	34,933	29.1 (8.9)	49.6	49.5	0.9
Women	7,353	31.6 (8.4)	43.3	56.5	0.2
Personnel Screening, Law Enforcement Officer					
Men and Women (Combined Gender)	674	27.3 (5.4)	NA	NA	NA
Personnel Screening, Corrections Officer					
Men and Women (Combined Gender)	3,036	31.6 (8.9)	NA	NA	NA
Personnel Screening, Clergy					
Men and Women (Combined Gender)	1,738	43.9 (14.0)	NA	NA	NA

Note. NA = not available.

   Combined-gender groups are made up of equal numbers of men and women.

Case Illustration

   The comparison group data option is illustrated in Figures 5-16–5-20 for the same case used earlier to illustrate the score report. As a reminder, the scores are those of Mr. I, a 36-year-old man tested at intake to an inpatient psychiatric unit of a community hospital. Therefore, the Psychiatric Inpatient, Community Hospital sample of men was selected as the comparison group for this protocol. All the standard information included in the MMPI-2-RF reports (i.e., raw scores, T scores, percentage of items answered on each scale, and item-level information) is printed when the comparison group option is chosen. As shown in Figures 5-16–5-20, the comparison group data are plotted with dashed lines connecting the sample's mean scores (marked by open diamonds) and bars reflecting the associated standard deviation for each mean. (By contrast, the test taker's scores are connected by a solid line.) These descriptive data are also reported numerically under the test taker's scores below the profile. A third row below the comparison group means and standard deviations reports for each scale the percentage of comparison group members who score at or below the test taker's score for that scale.

MMPI-2-RF® Score Report   ID: Mr. I
04/22/2011, Page 2

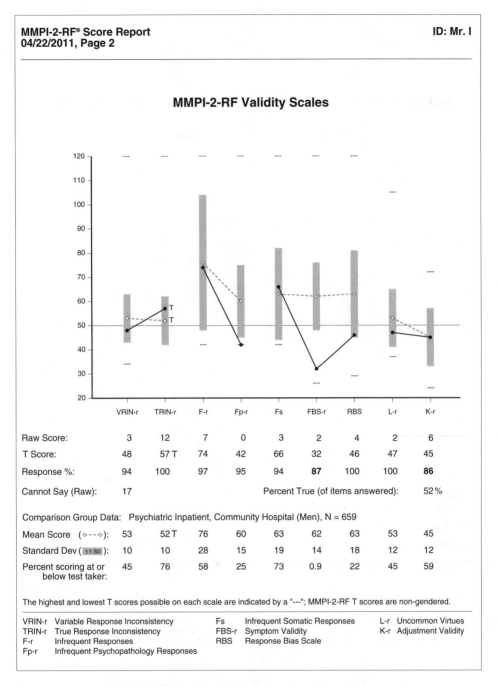

MMPI-2-RF Validity Scales

	VRIN-r	TRIN-r	F-r	Fp-r	Fs	FBS-r	RBS	L-r	K-r
Raw Score:	3	12	7	0	3	2	4	2	6
T Score:	48	57 T	74	42	66	32	46	47	45
Response %:	94	100	97	95	94	**87**	100	100	**86**

Cannot Say (Raw):   17   Percent True (of items answered):   52%

Comparison Group Data: Psychiatric Inpatient, Community Hospital (Men), N = 659

	VRIN-r	TRIN-r	F-r	Fp-r	Fs	FBS-r	RBS	L-r	K-r
Mean Score (◇--◇):	53	52 T	76	60	63	62	63	53	45
Standard Dev (±1 SD):	10	10	28	15	19	14	18	12	12
Percent scoring at or below test taker:	45	76	58	25	73	0.9	22	45	59

The highest and lowest T scores possible on each scale are indicated by a "---"; MMPI-2-RF T scores are non-gendered.

VRIN-r	Variable Response Inconsistency	Fs	Infrequent Somatic Responses	L-r	Uncommon Virtues
TRIN-r	True Response Inconsistency	FBS-r	Symptom Validity	K-r	Adjustment Validity
F-r	Infrequent Responses	RBS	Response Bias Scale		
Fp-r	Infrequent Psychopathology Responses				

Figure 5-16. Mr. I's MMPI-2-RF Score Report with Comparison Group data, page 2.

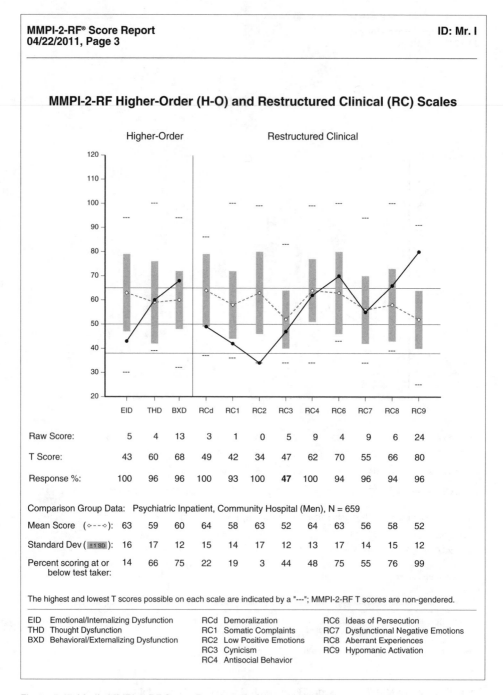

MMPI-2-RF Higher-Order (H-O) and Restructured Clinical (RC) Scales

Higher-Order   Restructured Clinical

	EID	THD	BXD	RCd	RC1	RC2	RC3	RC4	RC6	RC7	RC8	RC9
Raw Score:	5	4	13	3	1	0	5	9	4	9	6	24
T Score:	43	60	68	49	42	34	47	62	70	55	66	80
Response %:	100	96	96	100	93	100	47	100	94	96	94	96

Comparison Group Data: Psychiatric Inpatient, Community Hospital (Men), N = 659

Mean Score (◇--◇):	63	59	60	64	58	63	52	64	63	56	58	52
Standard Dev (±1 SD):	16	17	12	15	14	17	12	13	17	14	15	12
Percent scoring at or below test taker:	14	66	75	22	19	3	44	48	75	55	76	99

The highest and lowest T scores possible on each scale are indicated by a "---"; MMPI-2-RF T scores are non-gendered.

EID	Emotional/Internalizing Dysfunction	RCd	Demoralization	RC6	Ideas of Persecution
THD	Thought Dysfunction	RC1	Somatic Complaints	RC7	Dysfunctional Negative Emotions
BXD	Behavioral/Externalizing Dysfunction	RC2	Low Positive Emotions	RC8	Aberrant Experiences
		RC3	Cynicism	RC9	Hypomanic Activation
		RC4	Antisocial Behavior		

Figure 5-17. Mr. I's MMPI-2-RF Score Report with Comparison Group data, page 3.

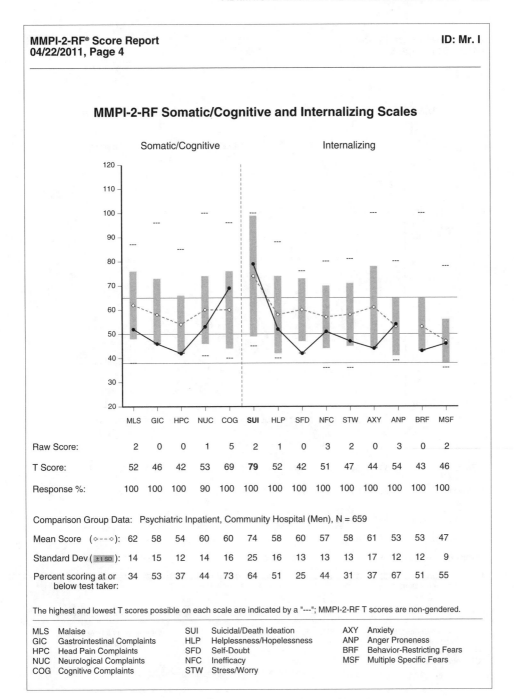

MMPI-2-RF Somatic/Cognitive and Internalizing Scales

Somatic/Cognitive   Internalizing

	MLS	GIC	HPC	NUC	COG	SUI	HLP	SFD	NFC	STW	AXY	ANP	BRF	MSF
Raw Score:	2	0	0	1	5	2	1	0	3	2	0	3	0	2
T Score:	52	46	42	53	69	**79**	52	42	51	47	44	54	43	46
Response %:	100	100	100	90	100	100	100	100	100	100	100	100	100	100

Comparison Group Data: Psychiatric Inpatient, Community Hospital (Men), N = 659

	MLS	GIC	HPC	NUC	COG	SUI	HLP	SFD	NFC	STW	AXY	ANP	BRF	MSF
Mean Score (◇--◇):	62	58	54	60	60	74	58	60	57	58	61	53	53	47
Standard Dev (±1 SD):	14	15	12	14	16	25	16	13	13	13	17	12	12	9
Percent scoring at or below test taker:	34	53	37	44	73	64	51	25	44	31	37	67	51	55

The highest and lowest T scores possible on each scale are indicated by a "---"; MMPI-2-RF T scores are non-gendered.

MLS	Malaise	SUI	Suicidal/Death Ideation	AXY	Anxiety
GIC	Gastrointestinal Complaints	HLP	Helplessness/Hopelessness	ANP	Anger Proneness
HPC	Head Pain Complaints	SFD	Self-Doubt	BRF	Behavior-Restricting Fears
NUC	Neurological Complaints	NFC	Inefficacy	MSF	Multiple Specific Fears
COG	Cognitive Complaints	STW	Stress/Worry		

Figure 5-18. Mr. I's MMPI-2-RF Score Report with Comparison Group data, page 4.

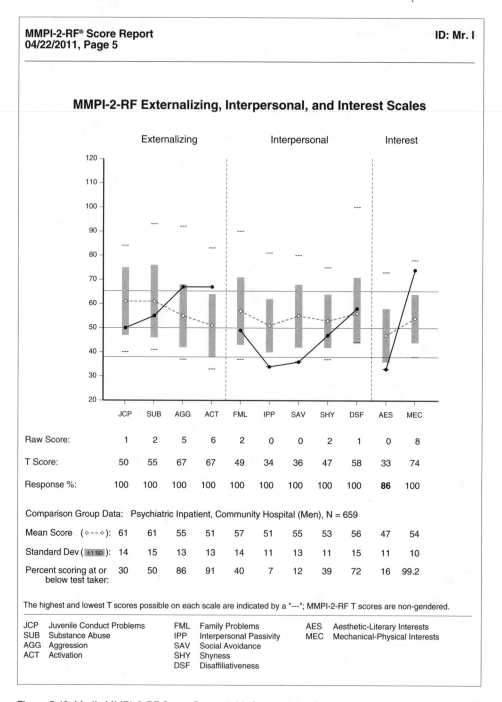

MMPI-2-RF Externalizing, Interpersonal, and Interest Scales

	JCP	SUB	AGG	ACT	FML	IPP	SAV	SHY	DSF	AES	MEC
Raw Score:	1	2	5	6	2	0	0	2	1	0	8
T Score:	50	55	67	67	49	34	36	47	58	33	74
Response %:	100	100	100	100	100	100	100	100	100	**86**	100

Comparison Group Data: Psychiatric Inpatient, Community Hospital (Men), N = 659

	JCP	SUB	AGG	ACT	FML	IPP	SAV	SHY	DSF	AES	MEC
Mean Score (◇--◇):	61	61	55	51	57	51	55	53	56	47	54
Standard Dev (±1 SD):	14	15	13	13	14	11	13	11	15	11	10
Percent scoring at or below test taker:	30	50	86	91	40	7	12	39	72	16	99.2

The highest and lowest T scores possible on each scale are indicated by a "---"; MMPI-2-RF T scores are non-gendered.

JCP	Juvenile Conduct Problems	FML	Family Problems	AES	Aesthetic-Literary Interests
SUB	Substance Abuse	IPP	Interpersonal Passivity	MEC	Mechanical-Physical Interests
AGG	Aggression	SAV	Social Avoidance		
ACT	Activation	SHY	Shyness		
		DSF	Disaffiliativeness		

Figure 5-19. Mr. I's MMPI-2-RF Score Report with Comparison Group data, page 5.

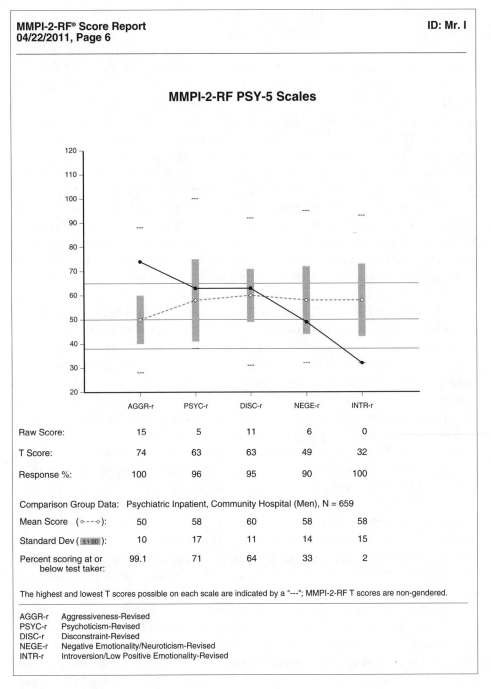

MMPI-2-RF® Score Report
04/22/2011, Page 6

ID: Mr. I

MMPI-2-RF PSY-5 Scales

	AGGR-r	PSYC-r	DISC-r	NEGE-r	INTR-r
Raw Score:	15	5	11	6	0
T Score:	74	63	63	49	32
Response %:	100	96	95	90	100

Comparison Group Data: Psychiatric Inpatient, Community Hospital (Men), N = 659

	AGGR-r	PSYC-r	DISC-r	NEGE-r	INTR-r
Mean Score (◇--◇):	50	58	60	58	58
Standard Dev (±1 SD):	10	17	11	14	15
Percent scoring at or below test taker:	99.1	71	64	33	2

The highest and lowest T scores possible on each scale are indicated by a "---"; MMPI-2-RF T scores are non-gendered.

AGGR-r	Aggressiveness-Revised
PSYC-r	Psychoticism-Revised
DISC-r	Disconstraint-Revised
NEGE-r	Negative Emotionality/Neuroticism-Revised
INTR-r	Introversion/Low Positive Emotionality-Revised

Figure 5-20. Mr. I's MMPI-2-RF Score Report with Comparison Group data, page 6.

Figure 5-16 shows that the mean T score on VRIN-r for the 659 men in the comparison group of psychiatric inpatients is 53, with a standard deviation of 10. The bar for VRIN-r on the profile represents a range of one standard deviation above and below the group's mean score on this scale (i.e., 43–63). Mr. I's score (48) is five points lower than the comparison group mean. The final row of data below the VRIN-r score shows that 45% of the individuals in the comparison group scored at or below Mr. I's T score of 48. His scores fall within one standard deviation of the mean on TRIN-r, F-r,[6] Fs, RBS, L-r, and K-r. On Fp-r, Mr. I's score (42) is three points lower than one standard deviation below the comparison group's mean, and on FBS-r, his score (32) is more than two standard deviations below the comparison group's mean. Because low scores on the Validity Scales are generally not interpretable, these findings would probably not alter the interpretation. Moreover, in the case of FBS-r, even if a low score were interpretable, it would not be appropriate to interpret it here because less than 90% of the item responses on this scale (87%) are scorable. As indicated in Chapter 6, low scores are not interpretable when this occurs.

Figure 5-17 shows Mr. I's scores and the comparison group findings on the H-O and RC Scales. One of two noteworthy findings on this profile is the low score on Low Positive Emotions (RC2), which is more than one standard deviation and a half below the comparison group mean. Only 14% of the comparison group members score this low. The second noteworthy finding is the high score on RC9, which is more than two standard deviations above the mean for this group. Mr. I's 80 T score on RC9 is as high as that of 99% of the members of the comparison group. Interpretation of Mr. I's scores on these scales can include the observation that his co-occurring psychological activation and heightened sense of well-being are substantially greater than those of most psychiatric inpatients.

Figure 5-18 illustrates an important caveat regarding interpretation of comparison group data. Although Mr. I's score on the SUI Scale falls very near the mean for male psychiatric inpatients, this in no way mitigates the significance of the finding that Mr. I produced a substantially elevated score on this scale, indicating that he is preoccupied with suicide and death and at risk for a suicide attempt, which is exacerbated by poor impulse control (indicated by his high score on RC9). Significant deviations from the comparison group mean on a scale may provide additional information about the test taker, but any scores reaching the cutoffs for interpretation recommended in Chapter 6 remain interpretable. Figures 5-19 and 5-20 indicate that Mr. I's scores on Interpersonal Passivity (IPP), Social Avoidance (SAV), and Introversion/Low Positive Emotionality–Revised (INTR-r) fall substantially below the comparison group mean (as does his score on Aesthetic–Literary Interests [AES], but this is not an interpretable finding because Mr. I provided scorable responses to less than 90% of the items scored on this scale), and his score on AGGR-r falls considerably above the comparison group mean.

Comparison group data are also provided for item-level information (Figure 5-21). Specifically, if the test taker produces an elevated score on one or more of the seven scales identified as having critical item content or on a scale selected for the user-designated item-level information section, the percentage of the normative sample (NS) and the comparison group (CG) who answered the items on these

ITEM-LEVEL INFORMATION

Unscorable Responses

Following is a list of items to which the test taker did not provide scorable responses. Unanswered or double answered (both True and False) items are unscorable. The scales on which the items appear are in parentheses following the item content.

    9. Item content removed. (RC7, NEGE-r)
   15. Item content removed. (Fs, FBS-r, RC1)
   36. Item content removed. (FBS-r, K-r, RC3)
   55. Item content removed. (VRIN-r, FBS-r, RC3)
   99. Item content removed. (VRIN-r, FBS-r, K-r, RC3)
  107. Item content removed. (BXD, RC9, DISC-r)
  121. Item content removed. (RC3)
  185. Item content removed. (RC3)
  191. Item content removed. (Fp-r)
  194. Item content removed. (VRIN-r, RC6)
  203. Item content removed. (F-r, THD, RC8, PSYC-r)
  209. Item content removed. (NEGE-r)
  238. Item content removed. (RC3)
  296. Item content removed. (AES)
  304. Item content removed. (RC3)
  313. Item content removed. (RC1, NUC)
  326. Item content removed. (RC3)

Critical Responses

Seven MMPI-2-RF scales--Suicidal/Death Ideation (SUI), Helplessness/Hopelessness (HLP), Anxiety (AXY), Ideas of Persecution (RC6), Aberrant Experiences (RC8), Substance Abuse (SUB), and Aggression (AGG)--have been designated by the test authors as having critical item content that may require immediate attention and follow-up. Items answered by the individual in the keyed direction (True or False) on a critical scale are listed below if his T score on that scale is 65 or higher. The percentage of the MMPI-2-RF normative sample (NS) and of the Psychiatric Inpatient, Community Hospital (Men) comparison group (CG) that answered each item in the keyed direction are provided in parentheses following the item content.

Suicidal/Death Ideation (SUI, T Score = 79)
  251. Item content removed. (True; NS 3.0%, CG 20.8%)
  334. Item content removed. (True; NS 13.5%, CG 35.5%)

Ideas of Persecution (RC6, T Score = 70)
   14. Item content removed. (True; NS 2.9%, CG 8.5%)
   34. Item content removed. (True; NS 10.6%, CG 27.3%)
   71. Item content removed. (True; NS 2.0%, CG 17.3%)
  110. Item content removed. (True; NS 9.9%, CG 32.5%)

Figure 5-21. Mr. I's MMPI-2-RF Score Report with item-level information, pages 8–10

Aberrant Experiences (RC8, T Score = 66)

   32. Item content removed. (True; NS 21.1%, CG 51.0%)
   85. Item content removed. (False; NS 17.1%, CG 35.2%)
 106. Item content removed. (True; NS 8.7%, CG 31.7%)
 159. Item content removed. (True; NS 6.0%, CG 27.0%)
 240. Item content removed. (True; NS 8.8%, CG 23.2%)
 257. Item content removed. (True; NS 12.4%, CG 37.0%)

Aggression (AGG, T Score = 67)

   23. Item content removed. (True; NS 39.0%, CG 46.3%)
 312. Item content removed. (True; NS 5.5%, CG 25.8%)
 316. Item content removed. (True; NS 45.1%, CG 50.5%)
 329. Item content removed. (True; NS 12.7%, CG 29.3%)
 337. Item content removed. (True; NS 50.2%, CG 52.2%)

User-Designated Item-Level Information

The following item-level information is based on the report user's selection of additional scales, and/or of lower cutoffs for the critical scales from the previous section. Items answered by the test taker in the keyed direction (True or False) on a selected scale are listed below if his T score on that scale is at the user-designated cutoff score or higher. The percentage of the MMPI-2-RF normative sample (NS) and of the Psychiatric Inpatient, Community Hospital (Men) comparison group (CG) that answered each item in the keyed direction are provided in parentheses following the item content.

Hypomanic Activation (RC9, T Score = 80)

   13. Item content removed. (True; NS 40.9%, CG 43.4%)
   39. Item content removed. (True; NS 51.0%, CG 53.3%)
   47. Item content removed. (True; NS 42.7%, CG 45.7%)
   61. Item content removed. (False; NS 61.6%, CG 73.4%)
   72. Item content removed. (True; NS 81.5%, CG 69.3%)
   97. Item content removed. (True; NS 50.5%, CG 45.2%)
 118. Item content removed. (True; NS 57.4%, CG 61.3%)
 131. Item content removed. (True; NS 43.3%, CG 47.0%)
 143. Item content removed. (True; NS 27.5%, CG 32.3%)
 155. Item content removed. (True; NS 41.6%, CG 37.9%)
 166. Item content removed. (True; NS 38.9%, CG 31.7%)
 181. Item content removed. (True; NS 35.3%, CG 36.7%)
 193. Item content removed. (True; NS 32.8%, CG 38.2%)
 207. Item content removed. (True; NS 66.9%, CG 47.3%)
 219. Item content removed. (True; NS 51.5%, CG 54.9%)
 244. Item content removed. (True; NS 56.9%, CG 64.5%)
 248. Item content removed. (True; NS 16.1%, CG 25.6%)
 256. Item content removed. (True; NS 65.7%, CG 58.1%)
 267. Item content removed. (True; NS 12.9%, CG 32.0%)
 292. Item content removed. (True; NS 26.1%, CG 30.3%)

Figure 5-21. Mr. I's MMPI-2-RF Score Report with item-level information, pages 8–10, continued.

MMPI-2-RF® Score Report   ID: Mr. I
04/22/2011, Page 10

---

 305. Item content removed. (True; NS 37.6%, CG 47.2%)
 316. Item content removed. (True; NS 45.1%, CG 50.5%)
 327. Item content removed. (True; NS 41.7%, CG 46.4%)
 337. Item content removed. (True; NS 50.2%, CG 52.2%)

Activation (ACT, T Score = 67)

  72. Item content removed. (True; NS 81.5%, CG 69.3%)
 166. Item content removed. (True; NS 38.9%, CG 31.7%)
 181. Item content removed. (True; NS 35.3%, CG 36.7%)
 207. Item content removed. (True; NS 66.9%, CG 47.3%)
 219. Item content removed. (True; NS 51.5%, CG 54.9%)
 267. Item content removed. (True; NS 12.9%, CG 32.0%)

End of Report

This and previous pages of this report contain trade secrets and are not to be released in response to requests under HIPAA (or any other data disclosure law that exempts trade secret information from release). Further, release in response to litigation discovery demands should be made only in accordance with your profession's ethical guidelines and under an appropriate protective order.

Figure 5-21. Mr. I's MMPI-2-RF Score Report with item-level information, pages 8–10, continued.

scales in the keyed direction is presented. In Figure 5-21, we see that 3.0% of the normative sample responded *true* to item 251, which reflects a recent suicide attempt, compared to 20.8% of the men in the psychiatric inpatient sample.

Custom Comparison Groups

The Pearson software for scoring the MMPI-2-RF includes a module for generating custom comparison groups from cases scored and stored on a user's system. The procedures for doing so are described in detail in the *MMPI-2-RF User's Guide for Reports* (Ben-Porath & Tellegen, 2011). Following is a brief description of the process. After activating this module, the user is prompted to name the custom comparison group and identify cases to be included. A minimum of 200 valid cases is required to form a comparison group. The same exclusionary criteria used when forming the standard comparison groups are employed with user-designated groups. Protocols with excessive item omissions (Cannot Say ≥ 18), inconsistent responding (VRIN-r or TRIN-r ≥ 80), or infrequent responding (F-r = 120 or Fp-r ≥ 100) are considered invalid for this purpose. After a sample of 200 valid cases is selected, the software calculates raw score means and standard deviations for the 51 MMPI-2-RF scales and converts them to T-score values using the tables in Appendix B of the *MMPI-2-RF Technical Manual*. The custom comparison group is then added to a drop-down menu under the user-supplied name for this group.

An MMPI-2-RF protocol can be printed, along with the means and standard deviations for any of the standard or custom comparison groups. It is possible to reprint the report with different comparison groups at no additional cost. However, it is not possible to include more than one comparison group at a time.

MMPI-2-RF Interpretive Report

Computer-generated interpretive reports have been available for the MMPI since the 1960s, when the first such system was developed at the Mayo Clinic (Rome et al., 1962). Many interpretive systems were developed for the MMPI-2 (for a review, see J. E. Williams & Weed, 2004). Two features of the MMPI-2-RF Interpretive Report set it apart from its predecessors. First, the statements in the report are based entirely on the interpretive guidelines provided in the test manual. In essence, the report applies the interpretive recommendations presented in the *MMPI-2-RF Manual for Administration, Scoring, and Interpretation* to a specific set of scores. Examining the interpretive report is tantamount to looking up the interpretive recommendations for the test taker's scores. The report organizes this information within the structure for MMPI-2-RF interpretation described in the test manual and Chapter 8 of this book.

A second unique aspect of the interpretive report is its transparency. The annotated version of the report, which is provided unless the test user opts to suppress it, identifies the source (i.e., scale scores) for each statement and indicates whether it is based on test responses (i.e., reflects the content of the test taker's responses to the test items) or empirical correlates or is an inference of the report authors. For statements identified as being based on empirical correlates, the report provides references to the literature where the correlational data supporting these statements can be found. As noted, it is possible to suppress the annotation if the user prefers not to have it included in the report.

The MMPI-2-RF Interpretive Report consists of all the information provided in the MMPI-2-RF Score Report, including the optional comparison group data, plus an automated interpretation of the test results. The first part of the report is identical to the score report (see Figures 5-7–5-13) and therefore is not reproduced here. Figure 5-22 provides the computer-generated interpretation of the results for Mr. I, whose MMPI-2-RF protocol is used to illustrate the score report as well.

The opening paragraph of every interpretive report states the following:

> This interpretive report is intended for use by a professional qualified to interpret the MMPI-2-RF. The information it contains should be considered in the context of the test taker's background, the circumstances of the assessment, and other available information.

This statement reflects an important caveat regarding computer-generated interpretive reports. None of the unique circumstances of the individual or the evaluation are considered in the computer-generated interpretation. Because such information is essential for an accurate interpretation of psychological test data, this report does not take the place of a qualified test user who considers extratest factors and integrates them into her or his interpretation of the results. The interpretive report provides a first step in this process. The automated interpretation appears under six major headings, as follows.

Synopsis

This section provides a brief overview of the major findings pertaining to the interpretability of the results and the major conclusions indicated by the test taker's scores on the Substantive Scales. As seen on page 8 of the report (the first page of Figure 5-22), if the findings include possible suicidal ideation, this information is printed in bold.

Protocol Validity

The Protocol Validity section provides information about the three types of threats to the validity of the test results: content nonresponsiveness (i.e., unscorable and/or inconsistent responses), overreporting, and underreporting. A detailed discussion of these issues appears in Chapters 4 and 6. When no protocol validity concerns are indicated by scores on the Validity Scales, a brief statement to that effect will appear in this section. If one or more possible concerns about protocol validity are indicated, the three types of threats (content nonresponsiveness, overreporting, and underreporting) are addressed (see Figure 5-22). If the test taker answered less than 90% of the items on one or more scales, the affected scale(s) (and the percentage of scorable items on each) are listed in this section. A complete list of the test taker's

---

MMPI-2-RF® Interpretive Report: Clinical Settings   **ID: Mr. I**
04/22/2011, Page 8

This interpretive report is intended for use by a professional qualified to interpret the MMPI-2-RF.
The information it contains should be considered in the context of the test taker's background, the
circumstances of the assessment, and other available information.

SYNOPSIS

Scores on the MMPI-2-RF validity scales raise concerns about the possible impact of unscorable
responses on the validity of this protocol. With that caution noted, scores on the substantive scales
indicate cognitive complaints and emotional, thought, behavioral, and interpersonal dysfunction.
Cognitive complaints include difficulties in memory and concentration. Emotional-internalizing findings
relate to **suicidal ideation**. Dysfunctional thinking includes ideas of persecution and aberrant
perceptions and thoughts. Behavioral-externalizing problems include aggression and excessive
activation. Interpersonal difficulties relate to over-assertiveness.

PROTOCOL VALIDITY

Content Non-Responsiveness

Unscorable Responses

The test taker answered less than 90% of the items on the following scales. The resulting scores may
therefore be artificially lowered. In particular, the absence of elevation on these scales is not
interpretable. A list of all items for which the test taker provided unscorable responses appears under the
heading "Item-Level Information."

    Symptom Validity (FBS-r): 87%
    Adjustment Validity (K-r): 86%
    Cynicism (RC3): 47%
    Aesthetic-Literary Interests (AES): 86%

Inconsistent Responding

The test taker responded to the items in a consistent manner, indicating that he responded relevantly.

Over-Reporting

There are no indications of over-reporting in this protocol.

Under-Reporting

There are no indications of under-reporting in this protocol.

Figure 5-22. Mr. I's MMPI-2-RF Interpretive Report, pages 8–17.

MMPI-2-RF® Interpretive Report: Clinical Settings   **ID: Mr. I**
04/22/2011, Page 9

SUBSTANTIVE SCALE INTERPRETATION

Clinical symptoms, personality characteristics, and behavioral tendencies of the test taker are described in this section and organized according to an empirically guided framework. Statements containing the word "reports" are based on the item content of MMPI-2-RF scales, whereas statements that include the word "likely" are based on empirical correlates of scale scores. Specific sources for each statement can be viewed with the annotation features of this report.

The following interpretation needs to be considered in light of cautions noted about the possible impact of unscorable responses on the validity of this protocol.

Somatic/Cognitive Dysfunction

The test taker reports a diffuse pattern of cognitive difficulties[1]. He is likely to complain about memory problems[2], to have low tolerance for frustration[3], not to cope well with stress[3], and to experience difficulties in concentration[4].

Emotional Dysfunction

The test taker reports a history of suicidal ideation and/or attempts[5]. He is likely to be preoccupied with suicide and death[6] and to be at risk for current suicidal ideation and attempts[6]. This risk is exacerbated by poor impulse control[7].

Thought Dysfunction

The test taker reports significant persecutory ideation such as believing that others seek to harm him[8]. He is likely to be suspicious of and alienated from others[9], to experience interpersonal difficulties as a result of suspiciousness[10], and to lack insight[10].

He reports unusual thought processes[11]. He is likely to experience thought disorganization[12], to engage in unrealistic thinking[13], and to believe he has unusual sensory-perceptual abilities[14].

Behavioral Dysfunction

The test taker's responses indicate significant externalizing, acting-out behavior, which is likely to have gotten him into difficulties[15]. More specifically, he is very likely to be restless and become bored[16] and to be acutely over-activated as manifested in aggression[17], mood instability[18], euphoria[16], excitability[19], and sensation-seeking, risk-taking, or other forms of under-controlled, irresponsible behavior[20]. He reports episodes of heightened excitation and energy level[21] and may have a history of symptoms associated with manic or hypomanic episodes[22]. He also reports engaging in physically aggressive, violent behavior and losing control[23], and is indeed likely to have a history of violent behavior toward others[24].

Interpersonal Functioning Scales

The test taker describes himself as having strong opinions, as standing up for himself, as assertive and direct, and able to lead others[25]. He is likely to believe he has leadership capabilities, but to be viewed by others as domineering, self-centered, and possibly grandiose[26]. He also reports enjoying social situations and events[27], and is likely to be perceived as outgoing and gregarious[28].

Figure 5-22. Mr. I's MMPI-2-RF Interpretive Report, continued.

Interest Scales

The test taker reports an above average number of interests in activities or occupations of a mechanical or physical nature (e.g., fixing and building things, the outdoors, sports)[29]. Individuals who respond in this manner are likely to be adventure- and sensation-seeking[30]. The extent to which he lacks aesthetic or literary interests cannot be accurately gauged because of unscorable responses. There is possible evidence that he indicates little or no interest in activities or occupations of an aesthetic or literary nature (e.g., writing, music, the theater)[31].

DIAGNOSTIC CONSIDERATIONS

This section provides recommendations for psychodiagnostic assessment based on the test taker's MMPI-2-RF results. It is recommended that he be evaluated for the following:

Emotional-Internalizing Disorders

- Cycling mood disorder[32]

Thought Disorders

- Disorders involving persecutory ideation[10]
- Disorders manifesting psychotic symptoms[33]
- Personality disorders manifesting unusual thoughts and perceptions[34]
- Schizoaffective disorder[35]

Behavioral-Externalizing Disorders

- Manic or hypomanic episode or other conditions associated with excessive energy and activation[32]
- Disorders associated with interpersonally aggressive behavior such as intermittent explosive disorder[36]

TREATMENT CONSIDERATIONS

This section provides inferential treatment-related recommendations based on the test taker's MMPI-2-RF scores.

Areas for Further Evaluation

- <u>Risk for suicide</u> **should be assessed immediately**[37].
- May require inpatient treatment due to hypomania [38].
- Need for mood-stabilizing medication[39].
- Origin of cognitive complaints[40]. May require a neuropsychological evaluation.

Psychotherapy Process Issues

- Persecutory ideation may interfere with forming a therapeutic relationship and treatment compliance[41].
- Impaired thinking may disrupt treatment[34].

Figure 5-22. Mr. I's MMPI-2-RF Interpretive Report, continued.

MMPI-2-RF® Interpretive Report: Clinical Settings   **ID: Mr. I**
04/22/2011, Page 11

- Unlikely to be internally motivated for treatment[42].
- At significant risk for treatment non-compliance[42].
- Excessive behavioral activation may interfere with treatment[39].

Possible Targets for Treatment

- Mood stabilization in initial stages of treatment[38]
- Persecutory ideation[41]
- Inadequate self-control[42]
- Reduction in interpersonally aggressive behavior[36]

ITEM-LEVEL INFORMATION

Unscorable Responses

Following is a list of items to which the test taker did not provide scorable responses. Unanswered or double answered (both True and False) items are unscorable. The scales on which the items appear are in parentheses following the item content.

     9. Item content removed. (RC7, NEGE-r)
    15. Item content removed. (Fs, FBS-r, RC1)
    36. Item content removed. (FBS-r, K-r, RC3)
    55. Item content removed. (VRIN-r, FBS-r, RC3)
    99. Item content removed. (VRIN-r, FBS-r, K-r, RC3)
   107. Item content removed. (BXD, RC9, DISC-r)
   121. Item content removed. (RC3)
   185. Item content removed. (RC3)
   191. Item content removed. (Fp-r)
   194. Item content removed. (VRIN-r, RC6)
   203. Item content removed. (F-r, THD, RC8, PSYC-r)
   209. Item content removed. (NEGE-r)
   238. Item content removed. (RC3)
   296. Item content removed. (AES)
   304. Item content removed. (RC3)
   313. Item content removed. (RC1, NUC)
   326. Item content removed. (RC3)

Critical Responses

Seven MMPI-2-RF scales--Suicidal/Death Ideation (SUI), Helplessness/Hopelessness (HLP), Anxiety (AXY), Ideas of Persecution (RC6), Aberrant Experiences (RC8), Substance Abuse (SUB), and Aggression (AGG)--have been designated by the test authors as having critical item content that may require immediate attention and follow-up. Items answered by the individual in the keyed direction (True or False) on a critical scale are listed below if his T score on that scale is 65 or higher. The percentage of the MMPI-2-RF normative sample that answered each item in the keyed direction is provided in parentheses following the item content.

Figure 5-22. Mr. I's MMPI-2-RF Interpretive Report, continued.

Suicidal/Death Ideation (SUI, T Score = 79)

    251. Item content removed. (True, 3.0%)
    334. Item content removed. (True, 13.5%)

Ideas of Persecution (RC6, T Score = 70)

    14. Item content removed. (True, 2.9%)
    34. Item content removed. (True, 10.6%)
    71. Item content removed. (True, 2.0%)
    110. Item content removed. (True, 9.9%)

Aberrant Experiences (RC8, T Score = 66)

    32. Item content removed. (True, 21.1%)
    85. Item content removed. (False, 17.1%)
    106. Item content removed. (True, 8.7%)
    159. Item content removed. (True, 6.0%)
    240. Item content removed. (True, 8.8%)
    257. Item content removed. (True, 12.4%)

Aggression (AGG, T Score = 67)

    23. Item content removed. (True, 39.0%)
    312. Item content removed. (True, 5.5%)
    316. Item content removed. (True, 45.1%)
    329. Item content removed. (True, 12.7%)
    337. Item content removed. (True, 50.2%)

User-Designated Item-Level Information

The following item-level information is based on the report user's selection of additional scales, and/or of lower cutoffs for the critical scales from the previous section. Items answered by the test taker in the keyed direction (True or False) on a selected scale are listed below if his T score on that scale is at the user-designated cutoff score or higher. The percentage of the MMPI-2-RF normative sample that answered each item in the keyed direction is provided in parentheses following the item content.

Hypomanic Activation (RC9, T Score = 80)

    13. Item content removed. (True, 40.9%)
    39. Item content removed. (True, 51.0%)
    47. Item content removed. (True, 42.7%)
    61. Item content removed. (False, 61.6%)
    72. Item content removed. (True, 81.5%)
    97. Item content removed. (True, 50.5%)
    118. Item content removed. (True, 57.4%)
    131. Item content removed. (True, 43.3%)
    143. Item content removed. (True, 27.5%)
    155. Item content removed. (True, 41.6%)
    166. Item content removed. (True, 38.9%)

Figure 5-22. Mr. I's MMPI-2-RF Interpretive Report, continued.

MMPI-2-RF® Interpretive Report: Clinical Settings   **ID: Mr. I**
04/22/2011, Page 13

---

   181. Item content removed. (True, 35.3%)
   193. Item content removed. (True, 32.8%)
   207. Item content removed. (True, 66.9%)
   219. Item content removed. (True, 51.5%)
   244. Item content removed. (True, 56.9%)
   248. Item content removed. (True, 16.1%)
   256. Item content removed. (True, 65.7%)
   267. Item content removed. (True, 12.9%)
   292. Item content removed. (True, 26.1%)
   305. Item content removed. (True, 37.6%)
   316. Item content removed. (True, 45.1%)
   327. Item content removed. (True, 41.7%)
   337. Item content removed. (True, 50.2%)

Activation (ACT, T Score = 67)

    72. Item content removed. (True, 81.5%)
   166. Item content removed. (True, 38.9%)
   181. Item content removed. (True, 35.3%)
   207. Item content removed. (True, 66.9%)
   219. Item content removed. (True, 51.5%)
   267. Item content removed. (True, 12.9%)

Figure 5-22. Mr. I's MMPI-2-RF Interpretive Report, continued.

ENDNOTES

This section lists for each statement in the report the MMPI-2-RF score(s) that triggered it. In addition, each statement is identified as a <u>Test Response</u>, if based on item content, a <u>Correlate</u>, if based on empirical correlates, or an <u>Inference</u>, if based on the report authors' judgment. (This information can also be accessed on-screen by placing the cursor on a given statement.) For correlate-based statements, research references (Ref. No.) are provided, keyed to the consecutively numbered reference list following the endnotes.

[1] Test Response: COG=69
[2] Correlate: COG=69, Ref. 2, 6, 14
[3] Correlate: COG=69, Ref. 14
[4] Correlate: COG=69, Ref. 2, 14
[5] Test Response: SUI=79
[6] Correlate: SUI=79, Ref. 14
[7] Inference: BXD=68; RC9=80
[8] Test Response: RC6=70
[9] Correlate: RC6=70, Ref. 1, 2, 7, 8, 12, 14
[10] Correlate: RC6=70, Ref. 14
[11] Test Response: RC8=66
[12] Correlate: RC8=66, Ref. 7, 14
[13] Correlate: RC8=66, Ref. 2, 3, 5, 14
[14] Correlate: RC8=66, Ref. 3, 5, 13, 14
[15] Correlate: BXD=68, Ref. 14
[16] Correlate: RC9=80, Ref. 14
[17] Correlate: RC9=80, Ref. 4, 8, 10, 11, 13, 14
[18] Correlate: RC9=80, Ref. 2, 12, 14
[19] Correlate: RC9=80, Ref. 2, 7, 9, 14
[20] Correlate: RC9=80, Ref. 9, 14
[21] Test Response: ACT=67
[22] Correlate: RC9=80, Ref. 12, 14; ACT=67, Ref. 14, 15
[23] Test Response: AGG=67
[24] Correlate: RC9=80, Ref. 4, 8, 10, 11, 13, 14; AGG=67, Ref. 14
[25] Test Response: IPP=34
[26] Correlate: IPP=34, Ref. 14; AGGR-r=74, Ref. 14
[27] Test Response: SAV=36
[28] Correlate: SAV=36, Ref. 14; INTR-r=32, Ref. 14
[29] Test Response: MEC=74
[30] Correlate: MEC=74, Ref. 14
[31] Test Response: AES=33
[32] Correlate: ACT=67, Ref. 15
[33] Correlate: RC8=66, Ref. 14
[34] Inference: RC8=66
[35] Inference: RC6=70; RC9=80
[36] Inference: AGG=67
[37] Inference: SUI=79
[38] Inference: RC9=80
[39] Inference: RC9=80; ACT=67
[40] Inference: COG=69
[41] Inference: RC6=70
[42] Inference: BXD=68

Figure 5-22. Mr. I's MMPI-2-RF Interpretive Report, continued. Note: Pages 14 and 15 of the report have been consolidated.

RESEARCH REFERENCE LIST

1. Arbisi, P. A., Sellbom, M., & Ben-Porath, Y. S. (2008). Empirical correlates of the MMPI-2 Restructured Clinical (RC) Scales in psychiatric inpatients. *Journal of Personality Assessment, 90,* 122-128.

2. Burchett, D. L., & Ben-Porath, Y. S. (2010). The impact of over-reporting on MMPI-2-RF substantive scale score validity. *Assessment, 17,* 497-516.

3. Forbey, J. D., & Ben-Porath, Y. S. (2007). A comparison of the MMPI-2 Restructured Clinical (RC) and Clinical Scales in a substance abuse treatment sample. *Psychological Services, 4,* 46-58.

4. Forbey, J. D., & Ben-Porath, Y. S. (2008). Empirical correlates of the MMPI-2 Restructured Clinical (RC) Scales in a non-clinical setting. *Journal of Personality Assessment, 90,* 136-141.

5. Forbey, J. D., Ben-Porath, Y. S., & Gartland, D. (2009). Validation of the MMPI-2 Computerized Adaptive Version (MMPI-2-CA) in a correctional intake facility. *Psychological Services, 6,* 279-292.

6. Gervais, R. O., Ben-Porath, Y. S., & Wygant, D. B. (2009). Empirical correlates and interpretation of the MMPI-2-RF Cognitive Complaints scale. *The Clinical Neuropsychologist, 23,* 996-1015.

7. Handel, R. W., & Archer, R. P. (2008). An investigation of the psychometric properties of the MMPI-2 Restructured Clinical (RC) Scales with mental health inpatients. *Journal of Personality Assessment, 90,* 239-249.

8. Sellbom, M., & Ben-Porath, Y. S. (2005). Mapping the MMPI-2 Restructured Clinical (RC) Scales onto normal personality traits: Evidence of construct validity. *Journal of Personality Assessment, 85,* 179-187.

9. Sellbom, M., Ben-Porath, Y. S., & Bagby, R. M. (2008). Personality and psychopathology: Mapping the MMPI-2 Restructured Clinical (RC) Scales onto the five factor model of personality. *Journal of Personality Disorders, 22,* 291-312.

10. Sellbom, M., Ben-Porath, Y. S., Baum, L. J., Erez, E., & Gregory, C. (2008). Predictive validity of the MMPI-2 Restructured Clinical (RC) Scales in a batterers' intervention program. *Journal of Personality Assessment, 90,* 129-135.

11. Sellbom, M., Ben-Porath, Y. S., & Graham, J. R. (2006). Correlates of the MMPI-2 Restructured Clinical (RC) Scales in a college counseling setting. *Journal of Personality Assessment, 86,* 89-99.

12. Sellbom, M., Graham, J. R., & Schenk, P. (2006). Incremental validity of the MMPI-2 Restructured Clinical (RC) Scales in a private practice sample. *Journal of Personality Assessment, 86,* 196-205.

Figure 5-22. Mr. I's MMPI-2-RF Interpretive Report, continued.

13. Simms, L. J., Casillas, A., Clark, L. A., Watson, D., & Doebbeling, B. I. (2005). Psychometric evaluation of the Restructured Clinical Scales of the MMPI-2. *Psychological Assessment, 17,* 345-358.

14. Tellegen, A., & Ben-Porath, Y. S. (2008). *The Minnesota Multiphasic Personality Inventory-2-Restructured Form (MMPI-2-RF): Technical manual.* Minneapolis: University of Minnesota Press.

15. Watson, C., Quilty, L. C., & Bagby, R. M. (2010, November 30). Differentiating bipolar disorder from major depressive disorder using the MMPI-2-RF: A receiver operating characteristics (ROC) analysis. *Journal of Psychopathology and Behavioral Assessment.* Advance online publication. doi:10.1007/s10862-010-9212-7

End of Report

Figure 5-22. Mr. I's MMPI-2-RF Interpretive Report, continued.

unscorable responses appears later, in the "Item-Level Information" section of the report (see page 11 of the report in Figure 5-22).

Substantive Scale Interpretation

The "Substantive Scale Interpretation" section begins on page 9 (Figure 5-22) and concludes at the top of page 10 of the sample output. The standard introductory paragraph reads as follows:

> Clinical symptoms, personality characteristics, and behavioral tendencies of the test taker are described in this section and organized according to an empirically guided framework. Statements containing the word "reports" are based on the item content of MMPI-2-RF scales, whereas statements that include the word "likely" are based on empirical correlates of scale scores. Specific sources for each statement can be viewed with the annotation features of this report.

As indicated, nearly all statements that appear in this section of the report are based either on scale item content, in which case they contain the word *reports*, or on empirical correlates of the scales, in which case they include the word *likely*. The annotation feature mentioned in the introductory paragraph is described later.

If scores on the Validity Scales indicate the need for caution in interpreting the results of the Substantive Scales, a cautionary statement is printed in boldface immediately following the introductory paragraph. In the case of Mr. I, cautions related to unscorable responses are reiterated in bold near the top of page 9 (Figure 5-22).

Following a structure outlined in Chapter 8, the "Substantive Scale Interpretation" section of the report is divided into six subsections: Somatic/Cognitive Dysfunction, Emotional Dysfunction, Thought Dysfunction, Behavioral Dysfunction, Interpersonal Functioning Scales, and Interest Scales. If certain scale score cutoffs are reached, findings on the 42 Substantive Scales are interpreted. Table 5-3 lists the scales considered in generating interpretive statements for each subsection.

Diagnostic Considerations

The "Diagnostic Considerations" section appears on page 10 of Mr. I's report. If no diagnostic possibilities are indicated by a test taker's scores, this statement appears: "No specific psychodiagnostic recommendations are indicated by this MMPI-2-RF protocol." If diagnostic possibilities are indicated by scores on the Substantive Scales, the section begins with this standard introduction:

> This section provides recommendations for psychodiagnostic assessment based on the test taker's MMPI-2-RF results. It is recommended that he/she be evaluated for the following.

Table 5-3. Scales Considered in the Substantive Scale Interpretation Section

Subsection	Scale
Somatic/Cognitive Dysfunction	RC1, MLS, GIC, HPC, NUC, COG
Emotional Dysfunction	EID, RCd, SUI, HLP, SFD, NFC RC2, RC7, STW, AXY, ANP, BRF, MSF NEGE-r, INTR-r
Thought Dysfunction	THD, RC6, RC8, PSYC-r
Behavioral Dysfunction	BXD, RC4, JCP, SUB, RC9, AGG, ACT DISC-r, AGGR-r
Interpersonal Functioning	FML, RC3, IPP, SAV, SHY, DSF
Interest	AES, MEC

If scores on the Validity Scales raise concerns about possible overreporting, the introduction will include a caution to that effect. No such concerns were indicated in the case of Mr. I.

Diagnostic possibilities are listed under four possible subheadings: Emotional/Internalizing Disorders, Thought Disorders, Behavioral/Externalizing Disorders, and Interpersonal Disorders. Table 5-4 lists the types of possible diagnostic considerations but does not necessarily provide the complete statement as it appears in the report. If none of the possibilities listed under one of these subheadings is indicated by the test scores, that subheading is not printed in the report. For example, in Mr. I's case, none of the possibilities listed in Table 5-4 under "Interpersonal Disorders" is indicated by his test results. Therefore, this subheading does not appear in his interpretive report. The list in Table 5-4 includes all the diagnostic considerations incorporated into the report at the time the MMPI-2-RF was released. It will expand as additional research is conducted.

Treatment Considerations

The "Treatment Considerations" section appears on pages 10–11 of Mr. I's report (Figure 5-22). If none of the possible treatment-related recommendations is indicated by the test results, then the statement "No specific recommendations for treatment are indicated by this MMPI-2-RF protocol" appears. If any of the possible treatment considerations are indicated, the first sentence under this heading will state the following:

This section provides inferential treatment-related recommendations based on the test taker's MMPI-2-RF scores.

The recommendations are characterized as *inferential* because they are based on the report authors' judgments of the treatment implications of certain test results. Our judgments were guided by the construct validity (i.e., empirical correlates and content and the resulting links to theoretical constructs) of the Substantive Scales of the test.

Three types of treatment-related recommendations may appear under separate

Table 5-4. Possible Diagnostic Considerations

Emotional/Internalizing Disorders

Internalizing disorders
Somatoform disorder
Depression-related disorder
Anxiety-related disorders
Posttraumatic stress disorder
Agoraphobia
Specific phobias
Anger-related disorders
Cycling mood disorder

Thought Disorders

Disorders associated with thought dysfunction
Disorders involving persecutory ideation
Disorders involving paranoid delusional thinking
Disorders manifesting psychotic symptoms
Personality disorders manifesting unusual thoughts and perceptions

Behavioral/Externalizing Disorders

Externalizing disorders
Antisocial personality disorder
Substance-related disorders
Schizoaffective disorder
Manic or hypomanic episode
Intermittent explosive disorder

Interpersonal Disorders

Personality disorders involving mistrust of and hostility toward others
Dependent personality disorder
Avoidant personality disorder
Social phobia

subheadings in this section of the report: "Areas for Further Evaluation," "Psychotherapy Process Issues," and "Possible Targets for Treatment." If no recommendations are indicated for one of these areas by the test taker's scores, the corresponding subheading is not printed in the report.

Areas for further evaluation may include assessment of risk for suicide (which, if indicated, will be listed first and printed in bold, as on page 10 in Figure 5-22), evaluation of need for medication and/or hospitalization, and evaluation of the origin of various somatic and cognitive complaints. Psychotherapy process issues that may be identified include readiness and motivation for treatment, possible hindrances to the formation of a therapeutic relationship, and factors that may increase the risk for treatment noncompliance. Possible targets for treatment include a broad range of somatic, cognitive, emotional, thought, behavioral, and interpersonal difficulties assessed by the Substantive Scales.

Item-Level Information

The "Item-Level Information" section, including "User-Designated Item-Level Information" for RC9 and ACT (discussed earlier), appears on pages 11–14 of Mr. I's interpretive report (Figure 5-22). The content of this section is identical to Figures 5-14 and 5-15 of the score report.

Annotation

Standard 6.12 of the Standards for Educational and Psychological Testing (AERA, APA & NCME, 1999) states, "Publishers and scoring services that offer computer-generated interpretations of test scores should provide a summary of the evidence supporting the interpretations given." To meet this standard, the annotation feature of the interpretive report identifies the origin of the interpretive statements (i.e., attributes the statements to the individual's score[s] on a specific scale or scales); indicates whether the statements are based on the test taker's responses, direct empirical correlates, or construct-based inferences; and provides citations to empirical studies that support the correlate-based statements.

Figure 5-22 shows the annotation feature as it appears in a report. Each statement is followed by a superscripted number linked to Endnotes that appear on pages 14–15 of the report. The Endnotes are explained in a standard opening paragraph (page 14) that reads as follows:

> This section lists for each statement in the report the MMPI-2-RF score(s) that triggered it. In addition, each statement is identified as a *Test Response*, if based on item content, a *Correlate*, if based on empirical correlates, or an *Inference*, if based on the report authors' judgment. (This information can also be accessed on-screen by placing the cursor on a given statement.) For correlate-based statements, research references (Ref. No.) are provided, keyed to the consecutively numbered reference list following the endnotes.

For example, the first statement in the "Somatic/Cognitive Dysfunction" section (page 9 of the report in Figure 5-22) reads, "The test taker reports a diffuse pattern of cognitive difficulties." In the Endnotes section of the report (page 14), Endnote 1 identifies this statement as being test response based, meaning that it is an item content–based statement reflecting a content theme of the scale and indicates that the source for the statement is a T score of 69 on the Cognitive Complaints (COG) Scale. The next statement—"He is likely to complain about memory problems"—is linked to the same scale score. However, the second Endnote on page 14 indicates that it is identified as a correlate, meaning that it is based on the empirical correlates of the COG Scale. The last entry for this Endnote, "Ref. 2, 6, 14," indicates that the empirical findings that support this statement are reported in references 2, 6, and 14 in the "Research Reference List" that appears on pages 16–17 of the report (Figure 5-22). The list of references supporting empirical correlate-based statements in the report is updated regularly.

As indicated in the standard opening paragraph for the Endnotes section of the report, users who choose to read the interpretive report on-screen while interfacing with the Pearson software can find information on the sources for interpretive statements by pointing the cursor at a statement. This will produce *hover text* that identifies the score(s) on the scale or scales that triggered the statement and whether the scores are based on test responses, correlates, or inferences made by the report authors.

Optional Features of the Interpretive Report

Figure 5-22 includes the standard output for an MMPI-2-RF interpretive report augmented by user-designated item-level information for RC9 and ACT. The "User-Designated Item-Level Information" feature is generated in the same manner as described earlier for the score report. Comparison Group data can also be incorporated into the interpretive report, as described earlier. It is important to note that selecting a comparison group for inclusion in an interpretive report will not alter the content of the interpretation. As noted, Comparison Group data are presented on the profile pages and in the item-level information sections of the report. A final option available for the interpretive report is to suppress the annotation of the report, which can be done by unmarking the annotation box prior to printing the report.

Invalid Protocols

The full text of the interpretive report will not be generated if scores on the Validity Scales raise significant concerns about interpretability of the test results. In such cases, the profiles will be plotted but will be marked by a statement indicating that the protocol is invalid (see Figure 5-23). The automated interpretation in these cases will be limited to addressing concerns about the validity of the protocol (see Figure 5-24).

As noted, three types of validity problems invalidate the protocol: an excessive number of unscorable responses to items on the Validity Scales, excessive inconsistent responding, and indications of excessive infrequent responding that raise serious concerns about overreporting.

Unscorable Responses

If a test taker does not provide scorable responses to at least 70% of the items on all the Validity Scales, the protocol will be identified as invalid. An excessive number of unscorable responses to the items limits the user's ability to rely on the Validity Scales to provide an accurate assessment of the interpretability of the test taker's results. If this occurs, the report provides all the standard information about unscorable responses (i.e., which scales are affected by unscorable items and which items were not answered) and any Validity Scale interpretations that are not compromised by unscorable responses. Scores on the over- and underreporting Validity Scales that have less than 70% scorable responses are not interpreted, nor are any scores on the Substantive Scales. Item-level information (including both unscorable and critical responses) is provided.

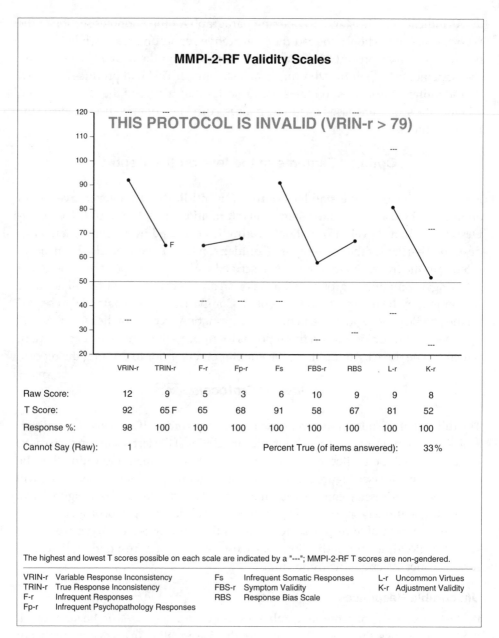

Figure 5-23. An invalid MMPI-2-RF.

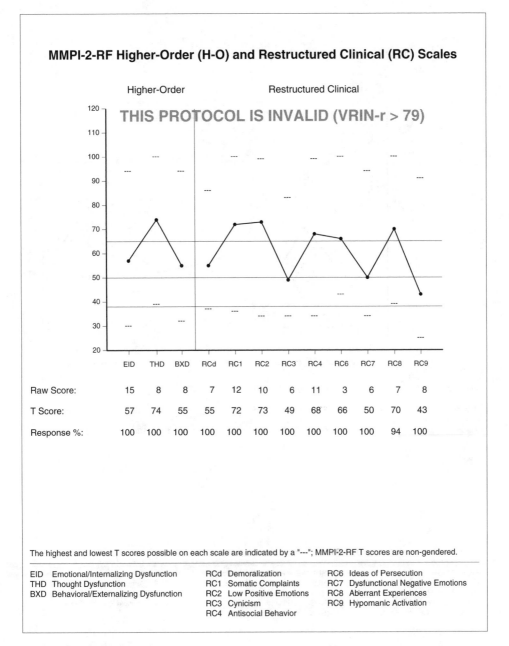

Figure 5-23. An invalid MMPI-2-RF, continued.

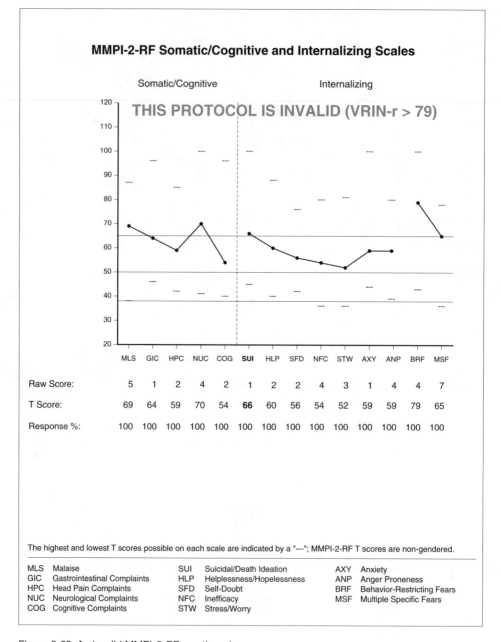

The highest and lowest T scores possible on each scale are indicated by a "---"; MMPI-2-RF T scores are non-gendered.

MLS	Malaise	SUI	Suicidal/Death Ideation	AXY Anxiety
GIC	Gastrointestinal Complaints	HLP	Helplessness/Hopelessness	ANP Anger Proneness
HPC	Head Pain Complaints	SFD	Self-Doubt	BRF Behavior-Restricting Fears
NUC	Neurological Complaints	NFC	Inefficacy	MSF Multiple Specific Fears
COG	Cognitive Complaints	STW	Stress/Worry	

Figure 5-23. An invalid MMPI-2-RF, continued.

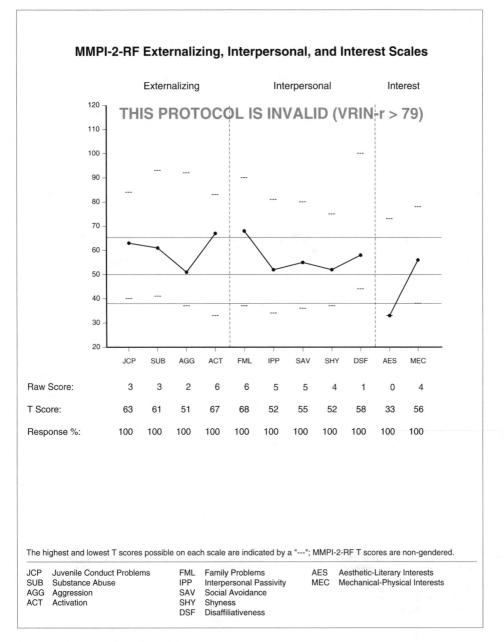

Figure 5-23. An invalid MMPI-2-RF, continued.

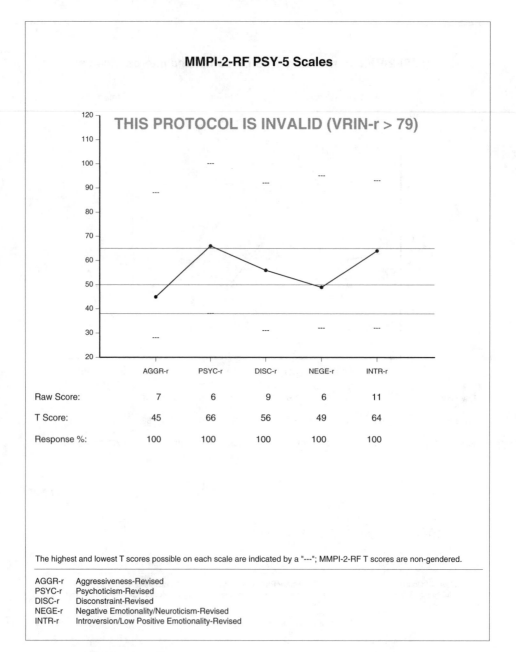

Figure 5-23. An invalid MMPI-2-RF, continued.

This interpretive report is intended for use by a professional qualified to interpret the MMPI-2-RF. The information it contains should be considered in the context of the test taker's background, the circumstances of the assessment, and other available information.

PROTOCOL VALIDITY

This MMPI-2-RF protocol is invalid and uninterpretable due to inconsistent responding. Details are provided below.

Content Non-Responsiveness

Unscorable Responses

The test taker answered at least 90% of the items on each of the MMPI-2-RF scales.

Inconsistent Responding

There is evidence of excessive inconsistency because of variable responding to the MMPI-2-RF items. Therefore, this protocol is invalid and uninterpretable. This may result from reading or language comprehension problems, cognitive impairment, or a non-cooperative test-taking approach. Erroneously recorded item responses can also produce this level of inconsistency.

ITEM-LEVEL INFORMATION

Unscorable Responses

Following is a list of items to which the test taker did not provide scorable responses. Unanswered or double answered (both True and False) items are unscorable. The scales on which the items appear are in parentheses following the item content.

    32. Item content removed. (VRIN-r, RC8)

End of Report

Figure 5-24. An invalid MMPI-2-RF Interpretive Report, page 8.

If a test taker does not provide scorable responses to at least 90% of the items on VRIN-r, TRIN-r, F-r, and Fp-r, and had he or she answered all the unscorable items in the keyed direction so that the score on one, two, or all three of these scales would have reached the thresholds listed below for invalidating the protocol, the results are identified as invalid, and the output is the same as the one we describe next for protocols that are invalid owing to inconsistent responding or overreporting. For example, if a test taker answers only 85% of the items on F-r, and the T score on F-r is below 120, and if his or her score would have reached 120 had he or she answered the unscorable items on F-r in the keyed direction, then the protocol is considered invalid, as described subsequently.

Inconsistent Responding

If a test taker has a T score of 80 or higher on VRIN-r or TRIN-r, the protocol is identified as invalid. In such cases, the report provides the standard information about unscorable responses and an interpretation of scores on VRIN-r and TRIN-r. However, scores on the over- and underreporting indicators and the Substantive Scales are not interpreted because evidence of excessive inconsistent responding indicates that the test taker probably did not respond to the content of the test items. Item-level information is provided about unscorable responses but not about critical responses or user-designated item-level information. Figure 5-24 illustrates the output in a case in which the T score on VRIN-r exceeds the cutoff for invalidity.

Overreporting

If a test taker's T score is 120 on F-r or 100 or higher on Fp-r, the protocol is identified as invalid. In such cases, the report provides a full interpretation of the results of all the Validity Scales but no interpretation of the Substantive Scale scores. Item-level information is provided about unscorable responses, as are critical responses and user-designated item-level information. However, the "Critical Responses" and optional "User-Designated Item-Level Information" sections include the following cautionary statement: "These responses need to be considered with caution in light of the finding, discussed earlier, that this protocol is invalid because of over-reporting."

CONCLUSION

Standard procedures for administration and scoring of the MMPI-2-RF were reviewed in the first part of this chapter. Available Pearson software can substantially facilitate both processes. On-screen administration reduces administration time and allows test takers to input their responses directly into the scoring software. The MMPI-2-RF Score Report and Interpretive Report provide a range of standard and customized information in addition to the test taker's test scores. Guidelines for using this information to interpret an MMPI-2-RF protocol are provided in Chapters 6–8.

CHAPTER 6

Interpreting the MMPI-2-RF Validity Scales

MMPI-2-RF interpretation begins with an inspection of the Validity Scales to de-termine whether the substantive test results are interpretable and, if so, whether any interpretive caveats are called for. This chapter provides detailed interpretive recommendations for the MMPI-2-RF Validity Scales. It begins with interpretive guidelines for the Cannot Say (CNS) score and each of the nine MMPI-2-RF Valid-ity Scales, which are reproduced from the *MMPI-2-RF Manual for Administration, Scoring, and Interpretation.* As detailed in these guidelines, interpretation of specific MMPI-2-RF Validity Scale scores often requires integration of collateral information and findings on other validity indicators. A conceptual framework for doing so, described in Chapter 4, is illustrated with case examples in the second part of this chapter. Empirical findings supporting the guidelines discussed and illustrated in this chapter are also reviewed in Chapter 4.

GUIDELINES FOR INTERPRETING THE
MMPI-2-RF VALIDITY SCALES

Tables 6-1–6-10 identify for different score levels on each Validity Scale con-cerns about protocol validity, possible reasons why a test taker may score in that range, and the interpretive implications of scores falling in the designated ranges.

Cannot Say (CNS)

The CNS score is the count of the number of unscorable responses to the 338 MMPI-2-RF items. The most common type of unscorable response is no response. However, if the test taker marks both *true* and *false* for an item, that response is also unscorable. Table 6-1 provides specific interpretive recommendations for the CNS score. A score of 15 or greater raises concerns about the possibility of compromised validity owing to unscorable responses. As indicated, an excessive number of unscorable responses may reflect lack of cooperation on the part of the test taker, but it may also occur if he or she lacks adequate reading skills (see Chapter 5), is seriously disturbed, is very obsessive, or lacks the necessary insight or self-awareness to respond to some of the test items. The interpreter will need to consider which of these factors may be involved in a given case on the basis of extratest information (e.g., background, interview, results of other testing).

Table 6-1. CNS (Cannot Say) Interpretation

Raw Score	Protocol Validity Concerns	Possible Reasons for Score	Interpretive Implications
≥ 15	Scores on some scales may be invalid.	Reading or language limitations Severe psychopathology Obsessiveness Lack of insight Lack of cooperation	Examine the content of unscorable items to detect possible themes. The impact is scale-dependent. For scales on which less than 90% of the items were scorable, the absence of elevation is uninterpretable. Elevated scores on such scales may underestimate the significance or severity of associated problems.
1–14	Scores on some of the shorter scales may be invalid.	Selective nonresponsiveness	Examine the content of unscorable items to detect possible themes. The impact is scale-dependent. For scales on which less than 90% of the items were scorable, the absence of elevation is uninterpretable. Elevated scores on such scales may underestimate the significance or severity of associated problems.
0	None	The test taker provided scorable responses to all 338 items.	The test taker was cooperative insofar as her or his willingness to respond to the test items is concerned.

Variable Response Inconsistency (VRIN-r)

The Variable Response Inconsistency (VRIN-r) score is based on the test taker's responses to 53 pairs of items similar in content. The raw VRIN-r score is the number of pairs answered inconsistently (i.e., true–false or false–true). The T score derived from it is used to identify protocols marked by excessive quasi-random responding, defined broadly as reflecting both intentional problems (a noncooperative test taker who provides responses without bothering to read the items) and unintentional ones (a test taker lacking the language skills or cognitive faculties needed to respond to the MMPI-2-RF items or who mismarked his or her responses). Excessive variable inconsistency compromises the interpretability of scores on the other Validity Scales and on the Substantive Scales.

Table 6-2 provides interpretive recommendations for VRIN-r. A T score of 80 or higher indicates that the protocol is invalid because of excessive variable response inconsistency. As noted, this score does not necessarily mean that the test taker was intentionally uncooperative. Other possible reasons for a high VRIN-r score need to be considered on the basis of extratest information. However, it does indicate that scores on the remaining Validity Scales and the Substantive Scales cannot be interpreted.

Table 6-2. VRIN-r (Variable Response Inconsistency) Interpretation

T Score	Protocol Validity Concerns	Possible Reasons for Score	Interpretive Implications
≥ 80	The protocol is invalid because of excessive variable response inconsistency.	Reading or language limitations Cognitive impairment Errors in recording responses Intentional random responding An uncooperative test-taking approach	The protocol is uninterpretable.
70–79	There is some evidence of variable response inconsistency.	Reading or language limitations Cognitive impairment Errors in recording responses Carelessness	Scores on the Validity and Substantive Scales should be interpreted with some caution.
39–69	There is evidence of consistent responding.	The test taker was able to comprehend and respond relevantly to the test items.	The protocol is interpretable.
30–38	There is evidence of remarkably consistent responding.	The test taker was deliberate in his or her approach to the assessment.	The protocol is interpretable.

As indicated in Table 6-2, a low score (a T score of 38 or below) on VRIN-r indicates that the individual responded to the MMPI-2-RF items in a remarkably consistent manner. This can occur in individuals who overreport, who underreport, or who respond in an unremarkable manner. Regardless of why a test taker produces a low VRIN-r score, such a finding indicates that the test taker was likely deliberate in her or his approach to the assessment and made a concerted effort to attend and respond consistently to the test items.

True Response Inconsistency (TRIN-r)

The True Response Inconsistency (TRIN-r) score is based on the test taker's responses to 26 pairs of items selected so that the members of each pair are quasi-reversals in content and keyed so that the raw TRIN-r score equals the number of pairs (inconsistently) answered true–true minus the number of pairs (inconsistently) answered false–false. Thus, higher raw TRIN-r scores indicate fixed (semantically inconsistent, indiscriminate) true responding, whereas lower scores indicate fixed false responding. The TRIN-r T scores were derived by first transforming the raw scores into linear T scores and then reflecting all T-score values below 50 (i.e., those deviating from the mean in the nonacquiescent direction). For example, an initial T score of 80, indicative of acquiescence, is left unchanged, but a nonreflected T score of 20, indicating an equally large deviation in the nonacquiescent direction, is reflected and consequently also becomes 80. This was done to ensure that like all the other validity indicators, only high TRIN-r T scores indicate possible invalid responding.

Table 6-3. TRIN-r (True Response Inconsistency) Interpretation

T Score	Protocol Validity Concerns	Possible Reasons for Score	Interpretive Implications
≥ 80T	The protocol is invalid because of excessive fixed, content-inconsistent True responding.	A noncooperative test-taking approach	The protocol is uninterpretable.
70T–79T	There is some evidence of fixed, content-inconsistent True responding.	A noncooperative test-taking approach	Scores on the Validity and Substantive Scales should be interpreted with some caution.
50–69	There is no evidence of fixed, content-inconsistent responding.		The protocol is interpretable.
70F–79F	There is some evidence of fixed, content-inconsistent False responding.	A noncooperative test-taking approach	Scores on the Validity and Substantive Scales should be interpreted with some caution.
≥ 80F	The protocol is invalid because of excessive fixed, content-inconsistent False responding.	A noncooperative test-taking approach	The protocol is uninterpretable.

To distinguish acquiescent from nonacquiescent scores, the former are displayed with the letter *T* (e.g., "80T") and the latter with the letter *F* ("80F").

Table 6-3 provides interpretive recommendations for TRIN-r. A T score of 80 or higher (in either a true or false direction) indicates that the protocol is invalid because of excessive inconsistent fixed responding and that scores on the remaining Validity Scales and on the Substantive Scales cannot be interpreted.

Infrequent Responses (F-r)

Infrequent Responses (F-r) consists of 32 items rarely answered in the keyed direction by members of the MMPI-2-RF normative sample. As discussed in Chapter 4, Hathaway and McKinley's original criterion for selecting F Scale items, that they be answered in the keyed direction by 10% of the normative sample, was applied to the MMPI-2-RF item pool using the current normative sample. Studies reviewed in Chapter 4 show that elevated scores on F-r are associated with overreporting of a broad range of psychological, cognitive, and somatic symptoms.

Table 6-4 provides interpretive recommendations for F-r. As outlined, T scores in the 79–89 range raise concerns about possible overreporting of psychological dysfunction that need to be considered in the context of evidence of a history of or current extratest findings of dysfunction. Significant psychopathology and/or pronounced emotional distress can also result in deviant scores on this scale. As the score on F-r rises, evidence of a greater degree of genuine dysfunction is needed to rule out overreporting. A T score of 120 on F-r is very uncommon even in individuals with genuine, severe dysfunction, indicating that the protocol is invalid and

Table 6-4. F-r (Infrequent Responses) Interpretation

T Score	Protocol Validity Concerns	Possible Reasons for Score	Interpretive Implications
120	The protocol is invalid. Over-reporting is reflected in an excessive number of infrequent responses.	Inconsistent responding Overreporting	Inconsistent responding should be considered by examining the VRIN-r and TRIN-r scores. If it is ruled out, note that this level of infrequent responding is uncommon even in individuals with genuine, severe psychological difficulties who report credible symptoms. Scores on the Substantive Scales should not be interpreted.
100–119	The protocol may be invalid. Overreporting of psychological dysfunction is indicated by a considerably larger than average number of infrequent responses.	Inconsistent responding Severe psychopathology Severe emotional distress Overreporting	Inconsistent responding should be considered by examining the VRIN-r and TRIN-r scores. If it is ruled out, note that this level of infrequent responding may occur in individuals with genuine, severe psychological difficulties who report credible symptoms. However, for individuals with no history or current corroborating evidence of dysfunction, it most likely indicates overreporting.
90–99	Possible over-reporting of psychological dysfunction is indicated by a much larger than average number of infrequent responses.	Inconsistent responding Significant psychopathology Significant emotional distress Overreporting	Inconsistent responding should be considered by examining the VRIN-r and TRIN-r scores. If it is ruled out, note that this level of infrequent responding may occur in individuals with genuine, substantial psychological difficulties who report credible symptoms. However, for individuals with no history or current corroborating evidence of dysfunction, it very likely indicates overreporting.
79–89	Possible over-reporting of psychological dysfunction is indicated by a larger than average number of infrequent responses.	Inconsistent responding Significant psychopathology Significant emotional distress Overreporting	Inconsistent responding should be considered by examining the VRIN-r and TRIN-r scores. If it is ruled out, note that this level of infrequent responding may occur in individuals with genuine psychological difficulties who report credible symptoms. However, for individuals with no history or current corroborating evidence of dysfunction, it probably indicates overreporting.
< 79	There is no evidence of overreporting.		The protocol is interpretable.

uninterpretable. Interpretation of F-r scores in the 100–119 range should include consideration of scores on Infrequent Psychopathology Responses (Fp-r) to assist in differentiating between genuine psychopathology and symptom overreporting, as discussed next.

Infrequent Psychopathology Responses (Fp-r)

The Fp-r Scale consists of 21 items rarely answered in the keyed direction by individuals with genuine, severe psychopathology. As a result, in contrast with F-r, scores on Fp-r are less likely to be confounded with severe disorder or distress. The scale is therefore particularly helpful in assessing overreporting in settings and populations characterized by high base rates of significant psychological disorders, most notably those marked by psychotic symptoms.

Table 6-5 provides interpretive recommendations for Fp-r. As indicated, T scores in the 80–99 range raise significant concerns about the possibility of symptom exaggeration, even for test takers with a significant mental health history. T scores that reach or exceed 100 indicate that the protocol is invalid owing to the strong likelihood of substantial overreporting.

Scores on Fp-r can be particularly helpful when a test taker produces a substantially elevated score on F-r and the interpreter needs to determine whether this indicates overreporting or genuine dysfunction. The lower the score on Fp-r, the less likely it is that an elevation on F-r reflects overreporting, and the more likely it is that it reflects accurate reporting of experiences that are uncommon in the general population but not in individuals with significant psychological difficulties. This is particularly true if the individual presents with symptoms of thought dysfunction. Test takers who overreport problems associated with emotional rather than thought dysfunction may produce substantially higher scores on F-r than on Fp-r. Higher F-r than Fp-r scores may also result when test takers report noncredible somatic or cognitive symptoms. These test takers would also be expected to generate elevated scores on Infrequent Somatic Responses (Fs), Symptom Validity (FBS-r), and the Response Bias Scale (RBS).

Infrequent Somatic Responses (Fs)

The Fs Scale consists of 16 items with somatic content that are uncommonly endorsed by medical patients receiving treatment for various physical diseases. Based on the same rare-symptoms rationale as the other two MMPI-2-RF infrequent response indicators (F-r and Fp-r), Fs is designed to identify test takers who overreport somatic symptoms by endorsing a large number of somatic complaints rarely reported by medical patients. Studies reviewed in Chapter 4 indicate that the scale is indeed particularly sensitive to overreported somatic complaints.

Table 6-6 provides interpretive recommendations for scores on Fs. T scores in the 80–99 range raise concerns about possible overreporting of somatic symptoms. T scores of 100 or higher indicate that overreporting of somatic complaints has

Table 6-5. Fp-r (Infrequent Psychopathology Responses) Interpretation

T Score	Protocol Validity Concerns	Possible Reasons for Score	Interpretive Implications
≥ 100	The protocol is invalid. Overreporting is indicated by assertion of a considerably larger than average number of symptoms rarely described by individuals with genuine, severe psychopathology.	Inconsistent responding Overreporting	Inconsistent responding should be considered by examining the VRIN-r and TRIN-r scores. If it is ruled out, note that this level of infrequent responding is very uncommon even in individuals with genuine, severe psychopathology who report credible symptoms. Scores on the Substantive Scales should not be interpreted.
80–99	Possible overreporting is indicated by assertion of a much larger than average number of symptoms rarely described by individuals with genuine, severe psychopathology.	Inconsistent responding Severe psychopathology Overreporting	Inconsistent responding should be considered by examining the VRIN-r and TRIN-r scores. If it is ruled out, note that this level of infrequent responding may occur in individuals with genuine, severe psychopathology who report credible symptoms, but it could also reflect exaggeration. For individuals with no history or current corroborating evidence of psychopathology it very likely indicates overreporting.
70–79	Possible overreporting is indicated by assertion of a larger than average number of symptoms rarely described by individuals with genuine, severe psychopathology.	Inconsistent responding Severe psychopathology Overreporting	Inconsistent responding should be considered by examining the VRIN-r and TRIN-r scores. If it is ruled out, note that this level of infrequent responding may occur in individuals with genuine, severe psychopathology who report credible symptoms. However, for individuals with no history or current corroborating evidence of psychopathology, it likely indicates overreporting.
< 70	There is no evidence of overreporting.		The protocol is interpretable.

likely occurred, limiting the interpretability of scores on the Somatic Scales of the MMPI-2-RF, including Somatic Complaints (RC1), Malaise (MLS), Gastrointestinal Complaints (GIC), Head Pain Complaints (HPC), and Neurological Complaints (NUC). In such cases, elevated scores on these scales may reflect the particular types of complaints the individual is overreporting.

Test takers may present with noncredible somatic complaints for a variety of reasons, including an external incentive as well as the internal psychological factors underlying a Somatoform Disorder or somatic delusions. Extratest data (in this case, a detailed medical and psychological history) are needed to make these distinctions.

Table 6-6. Fs (Infrequent Somatic Responses) Interpretation

T Score	Protocol Validity Concerns	Possible Reasons for Score	Interpretive Implications
≥ 100	Scores on the Somatic Scales may be invalid. Overreporting of somatic symptoms is reflected in the assertion of a considerably larger than average number of somatic symptoms rarely described by individuals with genuine medical problems.	Inconsistent responding Overreporting of somatic complaints	Inconsistent responding should be considered by examining the VRIN-r and TRIN-r scores. If it is ruled out, note that this level of infrequent responding is very uncommon even in individuals with substantial medical problems who report credible symptoms. Scores on the Somatic Scales should be interpreted in light of this caution.
80–99	Possible overreporting of somatic symptoms is reflected in the assertion of a much larger than average number of somatic symptoms rarely described by individuals with genuine medical problems.	Inconsistent responding Significant and/or multiple medical conditions Overreporting of somatic complaints	Inconsistent responding should be considered by examining the VRIN-r and TRIN-r scores. If it is ruled out, note that this level and type of infrequent responding may occur in individuals with substantial medical conditions who report credible symptoms, but it could also reflect exaggeration. In individuals with no history or corroborating evidence of physical health problems, this probably indicates noncredible reporting of somatic symptoms. Scores on the Somatic Scales should be interpreted in light of this caution.
< 80	There is no evidence of overreporting.		The protocol is interpretable.

Symptom Validity (FBS-r)

The FBS-r Scale consists of 30 items that are a subset of the 43 items that comprised the MMPI-2 version of this measure. As discussed in Chapter 4, the scale was originally developed to complement the MMPI-2 F Scale by identifying individuals presenting with noncredible symptoms in the context of civil litigation. It has been widely studied and is commonly used by neuropsychologists.

Table 6-7 provides interpretive recommendations for FBS-r. As indicated, T scores in the 80–99 range identify possible overreporting, as reflected in an unusual combination of responses that is associated with noncredible presentation of somatic and/or cognitive symptoms. T scores of 100 or higher indicate likely overreporting of such symptoms, limiting the interpretability of the Somatic Scales (RC1, MLS, GIC, HPC, and NUC) and the Cognitive Complaints (COG) Scale to indicating what type of complaints the test taker is likely overreporting. The extratest data needed to make inferences about possible motives for noncredible symptom reporting just described for Fs should also be considered in the interpretation of scores on

Table 6-7. FBS-r (Symptom Validity) Interpretation

T Score	Protocol Validity Concerns	Possible Reasons for Score	Interpretive Implications
≥ 100	Scores on the Somatic and Cognitive Scales may be invalid. Over-reporting is indicated by a very unusual combination of responses that is associated with noncredible reporting of somatic and/or cognitive symptoms.	Inconsistent responding Overreporting of somatic and/or cognitive symptoms	Inconsistent responding should be considered by examining the VRIN-r and TRIN-r scores. If it is ruled out, note that this combination of responses is very uncommon even in individuals with substantial medical problems who report credible symptoms. Scores on the Somatic and Cognitive Scales should be interpreted in light of this caution.
80–99	Possible overreporting is indicated by an unusual combination of responses that is associated with noncredible reporting of somatic and/or cognitive symptoms.	Inconsistent responding Significant and/or multiple medical conditions Overreporting of somatic and/or cognitive complaints	Inconsistent responding should be considered by examining the VRIN-r and TRIN-r scores. If it is ruled out, note that this combination of responses may occur in individuals with substantial medical problems who report credible symptoms, but it could also reflect exaggeration. Scores on the Somatic and Cognitive Scales should be interpreted in light of this caution.
< 80	There is no evidence of overreporting.		The protocol is interpretable.

FBS-r. Scores on both scales need to be considered with due attention to the setting.

As reflected in the respective interpretive recommendations, both Fs and FBS-r provide information about possible noncredible somatic symptom reporting. The two scales are only moderately correlated (.54–.66 in the clinical samples reported by Tellegen and Ben-Porath, 2008/2011), indicating relatedness but by no means redundancy.

Response Bias Scale (RBS)

The RBS is made up of 28 items designed to detect negative response bias in forensic evaluations. The RBS items were selected on the basis of correlations with performance on symptom validity measures in a sample of disability claimants and personal injury litigants. Research reviewed in Chapter 4 indicates that the scale is particularly sensitive to noncredible memory complaints.

Table 6-8 provides interpretive recommendations for RBS. As noted, T scores in the 80–99 range indicate possible overreporting manifested as an unusual combination of responses associated with noncredible memory complaints. However, scores in this range may also be found in individuals experiencing substantial emotional dysfunction. T scores of 100 or higher indicate likely overreporting

Table 6-8. RBS (Response Bias) Interpretation

T Score	Protocol Validity Concerns	Possible Reasons for Score	Interpretive Implications
> 100	Scores on the Cognitive Complaints Scale may be invalid. Overreporting is indicated by a very unusual combination of responses that is strongly associated with noncredible memory complaints.	Inconsistent responding Overreporting of memory complaints	Inconsistent responding should be considered by examining the VRIN-r and TRIN-r scores. If it is ruled out, note that this combination of responses is very unusual even in individuals with substantial emotional dysfunction who report credible symptoms. Scores on the Cognitive Complaints Scale should be interpreted in light of this caution.
80–99	Possible overreporting is indicated by an unusual combination of responses that is associated with noncredible memory complaints.	Inconsistent responding Significant emotional dysfunction Overreporting of memory complaints	Inconsistent responding should be considered by examining the VRIN-r and TRIN-r scores. If it is ruled out, note that this combination of responses may occur in individuals with substantial emotional dysfunction who report credible symptoms, but it could also reflect exaggeration. Scores on the Cognitive Complaints Scale should be interpreted in light of this caution.
< 80	There is no evidence of overreporting		The protocol is interpretable.

of memory problems, limiting the interpretability of scores on the COG Scale.

Although symptom validity (or effort) tests were used in the development of RBS, it was not designed, nor is it recommended, for use as a measure of effort on cognitive tests. However, an elevated RBS score could indicate the advisability of administering effort tests and considering scores on embedded effort measures.

Uncommon Virtues (L-r)

The Uncommon Virtues (L-r) Scale consists of 14 items. Elevated L-r scores indicate that the test taker presented himself or herself in a favorable light by denying minor faults and shortcomings that most individuals acknowledge. Table 6-9 provides interpretive recommendations for L-r. Scores in the 65–69 and 70–79 ranges reflect possible underreporting, with higher scores indicating an increased likelihood of this being the case. T scores of 80 or higher indicate that substantial underreporting very likely occurred and raise the possibility that the protocol is consequently invalid. When L-r scores reach this level, the absence of elevation on the Substantive Scales is uninterpretable. However, elevated Substantive Scale scores can be interpreted with the understanding that they may underestimate the magnitude or severity of the problems they assess.

Table 6-9. L-r (Uncommon Virtues) Interpretation

T Score	Protocol Validity Concerns	Possible Reasons for Score	Interpretive Implications
≥ 80	The protocol may be invalid. Under-reporting is indicated by the test taker pre-senting himself or her-self in an extremely positive light by denying many minor faults and shortcom-ings that most people acknowledge.	Inconsistent responding Underreporting	Inconsistent responding should be considered by examining the VRIN-r and TRIN-r scores. If it is ruled out, note that this level of virtuous self-presentation is very uncommon even in individuals with a background stressing traditional values. Any absence of elevation on the Substantive Scales is unin-terpretable. Elevated scores on the Substantive Scales may underes-timate the problems assessed by those scales.
70–79	Possible under-reporting is indicated by the test taker presenting himself or herself in a very posi-tive light by denying several minor faults and shortcomings that most people acknowledge.	Inconsistent responding Traditional upbringing Underreporting	Inconsistent responding should be considered by examining the VRIN-r and TRIN-r scores. If it is ruled out, note that this level of vir-tuous self-presentation is uncom-mon, but may, to some extent, reflect a background stressing traditional values. Any absence of elevation on the Substantive Scales should be interpreted with caution. Elevated scores on the Substan-tive Scales may underestimate the problems assessed by those scales.
65–69	Possible under-reporting is indicated by in the test taker presenting himself or herself in a posi-tive light by denying some minor faults and shortcomings that most people acknowledge.	Inconsistent responding Traditional upbringing Underreporting	Inconsistent responding should be considered by examining the VRIN-r and TRIN-r scores. If it is ruled out, note that this level of vir-tuous self-presentation may reflect a background stressing traditional values. Any absence of elevation on the Substantive Scales should be interpreted with caution. Elevated scores on the Substantive Scales may underestimate the problems assessed by those scales.
< 65	There is no evidence of underreporting		The protocol is interpretable.

An important consideration in understanding the significance of an elevated L-r score is whether the test taker was raised in an environment in which traditional values were stressed. A number of the L-r items are keyed to reflect uncommon moral virtues to which individuals raised in such environments are expected to aspire. Consequently, inferences about underreporting need to be tempered at moderate levels of elevation on this scale for individuals known to have been raised in environments stressing traditional values.

Adjustment Validity (K-r)

Adjustment Validity (K-r) consists of 14 of the original MMPI K Scale items. Elevated K-r scores indicate that the test taker presented himself or herself as well adjusted, with higher scores representing a higher level of adjustment. This type of self-presentation is associated with underreporting. However, the possibility that the test taker is in fact better adjusted than average also needs to be considered in interpreting an elevated K-r score. Extratest indications that the individual is not well adjusted would support the conclusion that an elevated K-r score indicates underreporting, whereas evidence that he or she is well adjusted would temper this interpretation.

Table 6-10 provides interpretive recommendations for K-r. T scores in the 60–65 and 66–69 ranges indicate possible underreporting, with higher scores suggesting a greater likelihood of underreporting and requiring evidence of better adjustment to rule out this interpretation. The highest possible T-score value on K-r, 72, indicates that the test taker presented himself or herself as remarkably well adjusted. Absent extratest indications that this is in fact the case, this level of elevation on K-r indicates in most settings that nonelevated scores on the Substantive Scales represent favorable self-portrayals, reflecting an underreporting tendency.

As with L-r, the primary interpretive implication of an elevated K-r score that denotes underreporting is that nonelevated scores on the Substantive Scales cannot be interpreted as indicating an absence of the problems they are designed to assess, and elevated scores may be an underestimate of the magnitude or severity of such problems. Low scores on Substantive Scales cannot be interpreted if scores on K-r (or L-r) indicate likely underreporting.

INTEGRATING MMPI-2-RF VALIDITY SCALE FINDINGS

A conceptual framework for assessing threats to the validity of an MMPI-2-RF protocol was discussed in detail in Chapter 4, which also provides descriptions of the development of the test's validity indicators and reviews the literature supporting their use. As a reminder, non-content-based threats to protocol validity include nonresponding, random responding, and fixed responding. *Nonresponding* occurs when a test taker provides unscorable responses to MMPI-2-RF items. This is most likely to occur if no response is provided, but responding both *true* and *false* to an item is also unscorable. *Random responding* occurs when a test taker provides variable responses (some true and others false) to test items without actually reading and considering their content. It can be intentional, if, for example, a test taker does not bother to read some of the test items before marking the answer sheet, or unintentional, if a test taker lacks the requisite reading or language skills or cognitive faculties needed to understand and respond relevantly to the test items and nonetheless attempts to respond without a clear understanding of their content. *Fixed responding* occurs if a test taker provides indiscriminate true or indiscriminate false responses to the test items (but not both).

Content-based threats to protocol validity involve overreporting and underreporting. *Overreporting* occurs when a test taker portrays herself or himself as

Table 6-10. K-r (Adjustment Validity) Interpretation

T Score	Protocol Validity Concerns	Possible Reasons for Score	Interpretive Implications
≥ 70	Underreporting is indicated by the test taker presenting herself or himself as remarkably well adjusted.	Inconsistent responding Underreporting	Inconsistent responding should be considered by examining the VRIN-r and TRIN-r scores. If it is ruled out, note that this level of psychological adjustment is rare in the general population. Any absence of elevation on the Substantive Scales should be interpreted with caution. Elevated scores on the Substantive Scales may underestimate the problems assessed by those scales.
66–69	Possible underreporting is reflected in the test taker presenting himself or herself as very well adjusted.	Inconsistent responding Very good psychological adjustment Underreporting	Inconsistent responding should be considered by examining the VRIN-r and TRIN-r scores. If it is ruled out, note that this level of psychological adjustment is relatively rare in the general population. For individuals who are not especially well adjusted, any absence of elevation on the Substantive Scales should be interpreted with caution. Elevated scores on the Substantive Scales may underestimate the problems assessed by those scales.
60–65	Possible underreporting is reflected in the test taker presenting himself or herself as well adjusted.	Inconsistent responding Good psychological adjustment Underreporting	Inconsistent responding should be considered by examination of scores on VRIN-r and TRIN-r. In individuals who are not well adjusted, any absence of elevation on the Substantive Scales should be interpreted with caution. Elevated scores on the Substantive Scales may underestimate the problems assessed by those scales.
< 60	There is no evidence of underreporting		The protocol is interpretable.

functioning worse than an objective appraisal would indicate. It can be intentional if the test taker knowingly exaggerates or fabricates difficulties or unintentional if the test taker does so unknowingly, believing that he or she is functioning worse than an objective evaluation would indicate. *Underreporting* occurs when a test taker presents as functioning better than an objective evaluation would indicate. It, too, can be intentional if the test taker knowingly denies or minimizes problems or unintentional if she or he does so without awareness.

Table 6-11 lists the possible threats to protocol validity assessed by the MMPI-2-RF Validity Scales as well as other potential influences that, if not considered, can confound Validity Scale interpretation. An "×" in the grid identifies the primary MMPI-2-RF source(s) for assessing each threat. Interpretation of scores on these primary indicators can be confounded by invalid responding other than the type assessed by a scale as well as by extratest factors listed in Table 6-11. For example, nonresponding can confound interpretation of scores on all the MMPI-2-RF validity indicators, except CNS. Psychopathology is a potential extratest confound that can affect scores on all the overreporting indicators.

A plus sign (+) in the grid indicates a potential confound that can artifactually elevate scores on a validity indicator; a minus sign (−) denotes confounds that can artifactually lower scores. Confounds listed in the shaded cells can reach levels that invalidate scores on a validity indicator, rendering them uninterpretable. For example, under VRIN-r, nonresponding is identified as a confound that can artifactually lower scores on this scale. In an extreme example, if a test taker does not provide scorable responses to any of the VRIN-r items, the resulting raw score of zero is uninterpretable insofar as assessment of random responding is concerned. Although extratest confounds do not render Validity Scale scores uninterpretable, they must be considered carefully in the interpretation.

The interpretive guidelines listed in Tables 6-1–6-10 incorporate consideration of the confounds listed in Table 6-11. Applying these statements and weighing potential confounds in an assessment of protocol validity are discussed and illustrated next.

Content Nonresponsiveness

Of the threats to protocol validity, content nonresponsiveness must always be considered first because, as shown in the shaded areas of Table 6-11, it can confound and invalidate scores on all the MMPI-2-RF Validity Scales.

Nonresponding

As discussed in Chapter 4, unscorable responses, which, by and large, occur when a test taker provides no response to an item, artifactually lower scores on MMPI-2-RF scales. This occurs because the method used to score MMPI-2-RF scales (counting the number of scale items the test taker answered in the keyed direction) treats unscorable responses the same as responses in the nonkeyed direction. Scores on scales for which at least 90% of the items were answered are not likely to be affected by unscorable responses to a degree that would compromise interpretability. However, as the proportion of unscorable item responses on a given scale increases beyond 10%, the absence of elevation (including a low score) on that scale becomes increasingly uninterpretable. Elevated scores on a scale are still interpretable as such when the test taker has responded to less than 90% of the items, but they may underestimate the problems assessed by that scale.

Determining which of the MMPI-2-RF scales are affected by nonresponding is facilitated by computerized scoring (see Chapter 5). As shown in Figure 6-1, in the third row of numbers under each scale, the computer-generated MMPI-2-RF reports provide the Response % statistic, which indicates the percentage of scorable

Table 6-11. MMPI-2-RF Validity Scales: Threats to Protocol Validity and Confounds

Threat	CNS	VRIN-r	TRIN-r	F-r	Fp-r	Fs	FBS-r	RBS	L-r	K-r
				Scale						
Non-Content Based										
Nonresponding	×	−	−	−	−	−	−	−	−	−
Random responding		×		+	+	+	+	+	+	+
Fixed "true" responding			×	+	+	+	+	+	−	−
Fixed "false" responding			×	+	+	+	+	+	+	+
Content-Based										
Overreporting				×	×	×	×	×		
Underreporting									×	×
Extratest Confounds										
Psychopathology				+	+	+	+	+		
Medical conditions						+	+			
Traditional upbringing									+	
Good adjustment										+

Note. × = Scale designed to assess this threat; + = Confound artifactually increases score;
− = Confound artifactually lowers score. Shaded area identifies confounds that can invalidate
scores on the corresponding Validity Scales.

responses to the items of that scale. If the percentage of scorable responses falls below 90%, it is printed in bold to draw the interpreter's attention. In this case, the test taker provided unscorable responses to 34 items (reflected in the CNS score) and more than 10% of the items on all the Validity Scales but Fs and RBS.

Because of the critical role of the Validity Scales in informing the interpreter about threats to the validity of an MMPI-2-RF protocol, special consideration needs to be given when more than 10% of responses to a Validity Scale are unscorable. As mentioned earlier, scores on VRIN-r, TRIN-r, F-r, and Fp-r can reach levels indicating that a protocol is invalid and uninterpretable. If the percentage of scorable items on these scales falls below 90% and responses in the keyed direction to those items would have raised the score to or beyond the cutoff indicating an invalid protocol, the test results should be considered potentially invalid.

Such a scenario is shown in Figure 6-1. The test taker in this case provided unscorable responses to 22% of the 53 VRIN-r items,[1] meaning that 12 item pairs could not be scored. If all 12 pairs had been answered in the keyed direction, the VRIN-r raw score would have increased from 1 to 13, and the T score would have increased from 39 to 97, indicating a clearly invalid protocol owing to random responding. The test taker also provided unscorable responses to 22% of the 32 F-r items, meaning that responses to seven items could not scored. If just three of these seven items were answered in the keyed direction, the F-r raw score would have increased from 14 to 17, and the T score would have increased from 106 to 120, indicating an invalid protocol owing to excessive overreporting. However, the potentially extreme F-r T score of 120 could also be an artifact of random responding,

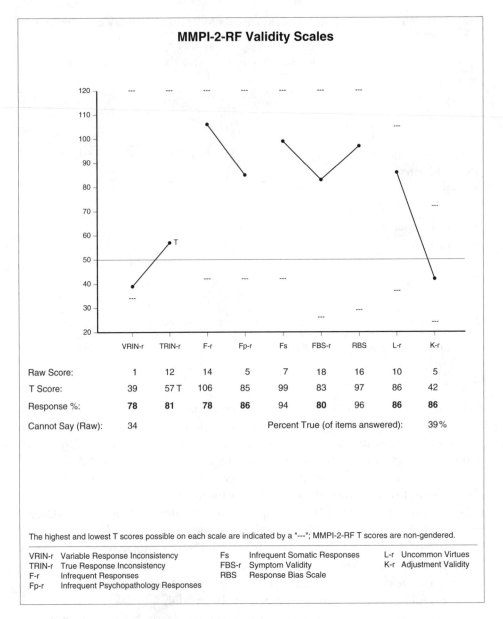

Figure 6-1. MMPI-2-RF Score Report Validity Scales profile showing nonresponding.

which, as just illustrated, also cannot be ruled out in this case. This protocol should be interpreted very cautiously (if at all), with caveats regarding possible random responding or overreporting emphasized throughout the report.

A CNS score as low as 1 indicates that scores on some of the shorter MMPI-2-RF scales may be invalid. For example, the Suicidal/Death Ideation (SUI) Scale is composed of five items. If just one is unanswered, the percentage of scorable responses to the SUI items falls to 80%, rendering a nonelevated score, in this case, uninterpretable. Therefore, for any case when CNS is greater than 0, the Response % statistic should be examined for all MMPI-2-RF scales. In such cases, the computer-generated reports will also include a list of the unscorable items with an indication of which scale(s) they are scored on. This list can provide the interpreter a sense of the content of items to which the test taker did not respond and facilitate identification of topics for follow-up with the examinee. For example, if a test taker does not provide scorable responses to a large number of items describing family conflict, this does not necessarily indicate that he or she experiences difficulties in this area, but it does identify an area for follow-up to determine why the examinee chose not to respond to those items.

Hand scorers do not have ready access to scale-by-scale Response % information. To implement the steps just outlined when hand scoring, any time the CNS score is greater than 0, the scale(s) on which unscorable items appear should be determined with the aid of Appendix C of the *Manual for Administration, Scoring, and Interpretation.* For each scale identified as having unscorable responses, the percentage will need to be calculated and considered as just described.

Random Responding

Random responding (more accurately characterized as quasi-random) occurs when a test taker provides variable true and false answers that are not based on reading, comprehension, and response to the content of MMPI-2-RF items. It is detected with VRIN-r, which can identify protocols marked by excessive variable-inconsistent responses. As indicated in Table 6-2, VRIN-r T scores in the 70–79 range raise concerns about the test taker's motivation or ability to respond meaningfully to the test items. T scores of 80 and above indicate that the protocol is invalid and uninterpretable.

When a VRIN-r score indicates that a protocol is invalid, the interpreter will typically want to determine why a test taker produced this result. VRIN-r scores can reflect both intentional and unintentional random responding. The former would indicate an uncooperative test taker, whereas the latter can reflect permanent or transitory impediments to meaningful assessment with the MMPI-2-RF. Test data alone cannot resolve the important distinction between intentional and unintentional random responding. This requires consideration of the test taker's reading ability and language skills (as reflected in educational records, achievement testing, employment status, or other collateral sources) and cognitive status (as reflected in interview or cognitive testing). Possible errors in recording responses (e.g., if a test taker inadvertently skips an item while marking the answer sheet) can also result in random responding. If either transitory impediments or errors in recording responses are determined to have caused a test taker to produce an invalid protocol, retesting may be considered.

Regardless of whether a VRIN-r score reflects intentional or unintentional random responding, a T score of 80 or greater on this scale indicates that the entire MMPI-2-RF protocol is invalid and uninterpretable. This includes scores on the remaining validity indicators. As shown in Table 6-11, random responding can

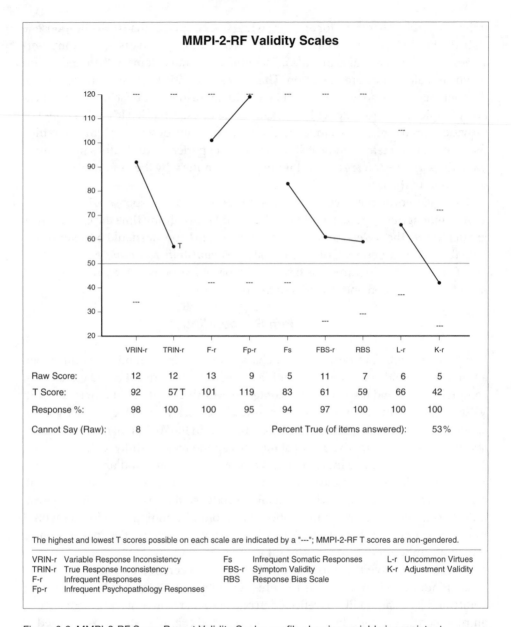

Figure 6-2. MMPI-2-RF Score Report Validity Scales profile showing variable inconsistent responding.

artifactually inflate scores on all the overreporting and underreporting indicators, rendering them uninterpretable. Such a case is illustrated in Figure 6-2, where a test taker scored 92 on VRIN-r. In addition to indicating that scores on the Substantive Scales are uninterpretable, this finding also means that the test taker's 119 T score on Fp-r cannot be interpreted as indicating a pattern of overreporting. The Fp-r score is uninterpretable in this case because excessive random responding can result in non-content-based infrequent responding.

Fixed Responding

Fixed responding occurs when a test taker provides fixed true or false responses that are not based on reading, comprehension, and response to the content of MMPI-2-RF items. As detailed in Chapter 4, the former is sometimes termed *acquiescence* and the latter *nonacquiescence*. Invalid fixed responding is detected with TRIN-r, which can identify protocols marked by excessive acquiescence or nonacquiescence. As detailed in Table 6-3, TRIN-r T scores in the 70–79 range raise concerns about the possible impact of fixed responding to the test items. T scores of 80 and above indicate that the protocol is invalid and uninterpretable. As discussed earlier, T scores on TRIN-r are set to always equal 50 or higher. A 50 T score on TRIN-r indicates the absence of a predominant pattern of fixed responding. T scores above 50 are followed by the letter *T* or *F* to distinguish acquiescent from nonacquiescent responding, respectively.

Unlike random responding, which may be unintentional, excessive fixed responding most often indicates an uncooperative test-taking approach. A possible exception involves items with double negatives. Individuals who struggle with double negatives—for example, nonnative English speakers tested in English or individuals with particularly low verbal abilities—may provide a sufficient number of fixed inconsistent responses to elevate TRIN-r to an interpretable level. For native English speakers and individuals with adequate verbal skills, an elevated score on TRIN-r most likely reflects an uncooperative test-taking approach.

Regardless of why a test taker produces an elevated TRIN-r score, excessive fixed responding, as shown in Table 6-11, can invalidate scores on the overreporting and underreporting indicators. Fixed false responding can artifactually inflate scores on all these measures. Scores on L-r and K-r are particularly susceptible to this effect because most of the items scored on these scales are keyed false. For example, in Figure 6-3, the TRIN-r T score of 95F indicates that the protocol is invalid and uninterpretable. The T score of 71 on L-r in this case is invalid and cannot be relied on to assess possible underreporting. Fixed true responding can also artifactually inflate scores on the overreporting indicators. Because of the large proportion of false-keyed items just mentioned, it can deflate scores on the underreporting measures. Such a scenario is illustrated in Figure 6-4, in which a TRIN-r T score of 110T indicates that the protocol is invalid and uninterpretable. In this case, both the high T score on F-r (101) and the low score on K-r (35) may be artifacts of fixed true responding and are therefore uninterpretable.

It is possible, but rare, for both VRIN-r and TRIN-r to be elevated in the same protocol. Such a finding, illustrated in Figure 6-5, indicates that the test taker alternated his or her content nonresponsive test-taking approach by responding variably to some items and in a stereotypic, fixed manner to others. In this particular case, excessive levels of random and fixed responding render highly elevated scores on F-r, Fp-r, Fs, and RBS uninterpretable.

For cases in which T scores on both VRIN-r and TRIN-r fall below 70, inconsistent responding can be ruled out, and the interpretation of scores on the remaining Validity Scales can proceed to consideration of possible over- or underreporting.

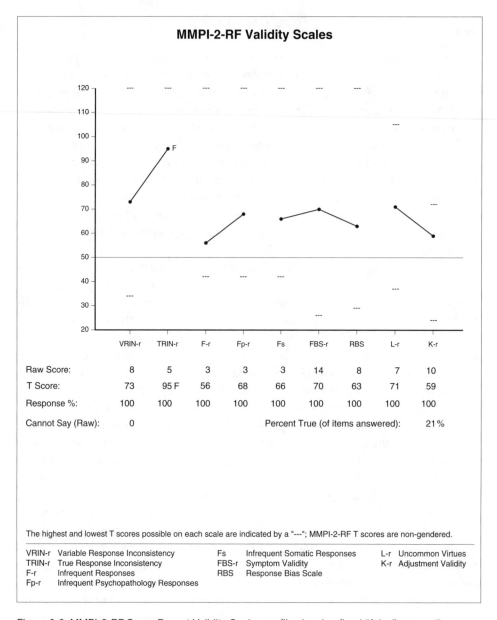

MMPI-2-RF Validity Scales

	VRIN-r	TRIN-r	F-r	Fp-r	Fs	FBS-r	RBS	L-r	K-r
Raw Score:	8	5	3	3	3	14	8	7	10
T Score:	73	95 F	56	68	66	70	63	71	59
Response %:	100	100	100	100	100	100	100	100	100

Cannot Say (Raw):   0   Percent True (of items answered):   21%

The highest and lowest T scores possible on each scale are indicated by a "---"; MMPI-2-RF T scores are non-gendered.

VRIN-r	Variable Response Inconsistency	Fs	Infrequent Somatic Responses	L-r	Uncommon Virtues
TRIN-r	True Response Inconsistency	FBS-r	Symptom Validity	K-r	Adjustment Validity
F-r	Infrequent Responses	RBS	Response Bias Scale		
Fp-r	Infrequent Psychopathology Responses				

Figure 6-3. MMPI-2-RF Score Report Validity Scales profile showing fixed "false" responding.

Overreporting

Overreporting is defined as occurring when the test taker's self-presentation indicates a degree of dysfunction that is noncredible (i.e., more extreme than would be indicated by a hypothetical objective assessment of the individual). The term *over-reporting* is preferred over alternatives such as *faking bad,* which make an inference of intentionality that typically requires consideration of extratest data.

Particularly with regard to intentionality, it is necessary to consider the possible

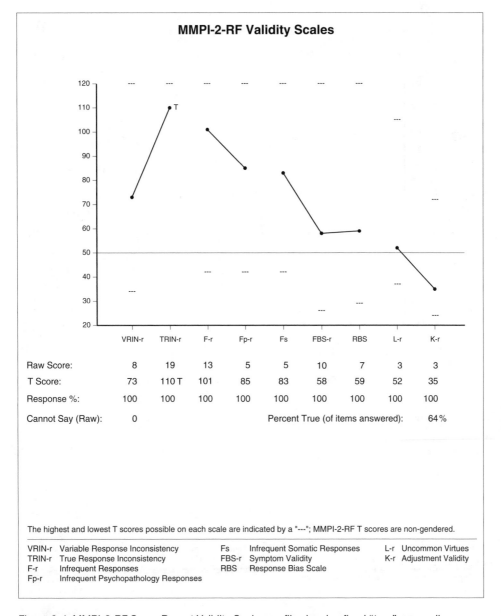

Figure 6-4. MMPI-2-RF Score Report Validity Scales profile showing fixed "true" responding.

impact of various mental disorders characterized by unintentional overreporting of symptoms (e.g., Somatoform Disorder) or misperception of reality (e.g., thought disorders). In both instances, the test taker's reported symptoms are inconsistent with indicators of objective findings. However, she or he believes genuinely in their existence. Moreover, even when there is extratest evidence of intentionality, the current diagnostic system requires for a diagnosis of malingering an external motive (e.g., avoidance of legal responsibility). By contrast, Factitious Disorder is indicated if there is evidence of an internal motive (i.e., a psychogenic need to assume the sick role).

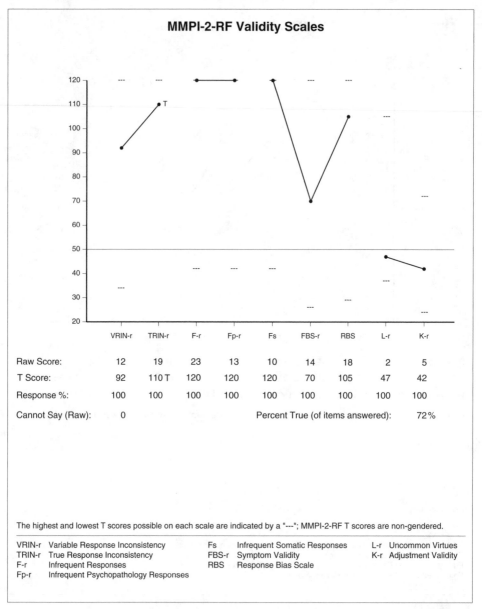

MMPI-2-RF Validity Scales

	VRIN-r	TRIN-r	F-r	Fp-r	Fs	FBS-r	RBS	L-r	K-r
Raw Score:	12	19	23	13	10	14	18	2	5
T Score:	92	110 T	120	120	120	70	105	47	42
Response %:	100	100	100	100	100	100	100	100	100

Cannot Say (Raw):   0   Percent True (of items answered):   72%

The highest and lowest T scores possible on each scale are indicated by a "---"; MMPI-2-RF T scores are non-gendered.

VRIN-r	Variable Response Inconsistency	Fs	Infrequent Somatic Responses
TRIN-r	True Response Inconsistency	FBS-r	Symptom Validity
F-r	Infrequent Responses	RBS	Response Bias Scale
Fp-r	Infrequent Psychopathology Responses		

L-r Uncommon Virtues
K-r Adjustment Validity

Figure 6-5. MMPI-2-RF Score Report Validity Scales profile showing variable and fixed responding.

Scores on the MMPI-2-RF Validity Scales do not provide specific indications of intentionality or motivation when there is evidence of overreporting. However, test results indicative of overreporting (or lack thereof) can be used to support (or refute) inferences about feigning or malingering, just as scores on the Substantive Scales can suggest diagnostic possibilities to be considered and evaluated with the aid of extratest data (e.g., interview, other test results, historical records). It is worth noting in this regard that all the validation studies of the MMPI-2-RF overreporting indicators reviewed in Chapter 4 involve simulation or detection of intentional overreporting.

Broadly speaking, test takers may overreport psychological symptoms (e.g., depression, psychosis), cognitive symptoms (e.g., attention difficulties, memory impairment), or somatic/cognitive symptoms (e.g., pain, poor health, memory deficits). The MMPI-2-RF Validity Scales are differentially associated with these types of overreporting. F-r is sensitive to the broadest range of overreported symptoms. Fp-r is most sensitive to overreported psychological symptoms and is less effective than the other measures in detecting overreported somatic and cognitive complaints. Scores on this scale are particularly effective in differentiating genuine, severe psychopathology from overreported psychological symptoms. Fs and FBS-r are the best MMPI-2-RF predictors of overreported somatic symptoms, and FBS-r and RBS are the most effective measures of noncredible cognitive complaints. RBS scores are most specifically associated with overreported memory complaints. These differences are reflected in the interpretive recommendations for the scales provided in Tables 6-4–6-8.

As shown in Table 6-11 and just discussed, scores on the MMPI-2-RF overreporting indicators can be invalidated by content nonresponsiveness. Specifically, nonresponding can artifactually lower scores on these measures, whereas random responding and fixed responding artifactually increase scores on F-r, Fp-r, Fs, FBS-r, and RBS. Genuine psychopathology can also raise scores to varying degrees on these measures. F-r is most sensitive to genuine psychopathology; hence the cutoff for concluding that a protocol is invalid owing to overreporting based on this scale is set at the highest possible T score: 120.

Figure 6-6 illustrates such a case. Scores of 53 on VRIN-r and 65T on TRIN-r rule out random and fixed responding as factors contributing to the 120 T score on F-r. Research reviewed in Chapter 4 indicates that psychopathology alone also cannot account for an F-r score this high, leaving a marked pattern of psychological symptom overreporting as the most likely explanation for this result. The protocol is therefore invalid, and scores on the Substantive Scales cannot be interpreted. By contrast, in the case depicted in Figure 6-7, the T score of 106 on F-r falls in a range that does occur in individuals with genuine, *severe* psychopathology. Therefore, determination of whether this score indicates overreporting is contingent on extratest information about the test taker. For an individual with no documented history or current evidence of psychopathology, it most likely indicates overreporting, and scores on the Substantive Scales should be interpreted with this understanding. In a test taker with a history or current corroborating evidence of severe psychopathology, a T score of 106 on F-r can reflect psychopathology rather than overreporting, particularly if, as in this case, none of the other overreporting indicators is elevated.

A lower cutoff (T score of 100) is used to identify invalid protocols owing to pervasive overreporting of psychopathology symptoms based on Fp-r because, by design, scores on this scale are less sensitive to psychopathology than are F-r scores. Figure 6-8 presents a case in which the test taker's Fp-r T score is 111. With a CNS score of 9, the first step in interpreting this Validity Scale profile requires inspection of the Response % findings, which indicate that the test taker responded to at least 90% of the items on all but the K-r Scale. Thus, random and fixed responding can be ruled out as potential sources for the high Fp-r score based on

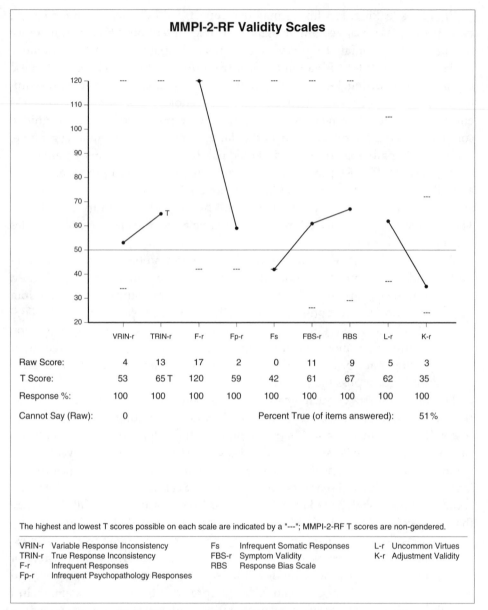

Figure 6-6. MMPI-2-RF Score Report Validity Scales profile showing a highly elevated F-r score reflecting overreporting.

respective VRIN-r and TRIN-r T scores of 48 and 57T. An Fp-r score this high is very uncommon even in individuals with genuine severe psychopathology who report credible symptoms. Therefore, this individual very likely intentionally overreported severe psychopathology symptoms, rendering scores on the Substantive Scales invalid and uninterpretable. The T score of 107 on Fs indicates that this test taker also presented with a very large number of somatic symptoms that are uncommon in individuals with substantial medical problems. Thus, there is also evidence of substantial somatic symptom overreporting in this case.

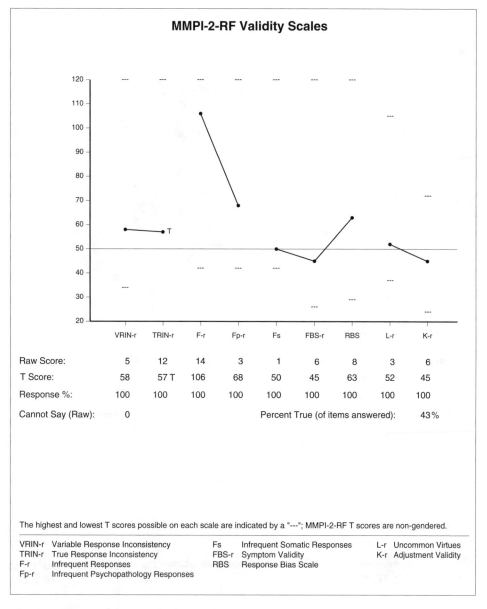

MMPI-2-RF Validity Scales

	VRIN-r	TRIN-r	F-r	Fp-r	Fs	FBS-r	RBS	L-r	K-r
Raw Score:	5	12	14	3	1	6	8	3	6
T Score:	58	57 T	106	68	50	45	63	52	45
Response %:	100	100	100	100	100	100	100	100	100

Cannot Say (Raw):   0   Percent True (of items answered):   43%

The highest and lowest T scores possible on each scale are indicated by a "---"; MMPI-2-RF T scores are non-gendered.

VRIN-r	Variable Response Inconsistency	Fs	Infrequent Somatic Responses	L-r	Uncommon Virtues
TRIN-r	True Response Inconsistency	FBS-r	Symptom Validity	K-r	Adjustment Validity
F-r	Infrequent Responses	RBS	Response Bias Scale		
Fp-r	Infrequent Psychopathology Responses				

Figure 6-7. MMPI-2-RF Score Report Validity Scales profile showing an elevated F-r scale possibly reflecting genuine psychopathology.

At first glance, the high L-r score (76) shown in Figure 6-8 may appear to contradict the possibility of overreporting because it is associated with underreporting. However, as discussed in the following section, the kind of underreporting associated with high L-r scores—denial of moral flaws and assertions of virtuous qualities—is not inconsistent with efforts to misportray oneself as experiencing severe psychopathology, somatic problems, or cognitive difficulties.[2] For example, an individual charged with a serious crime tested as part of an evaluation to determine criminal responsibility may attempt to appear severely disturbed psychologically,

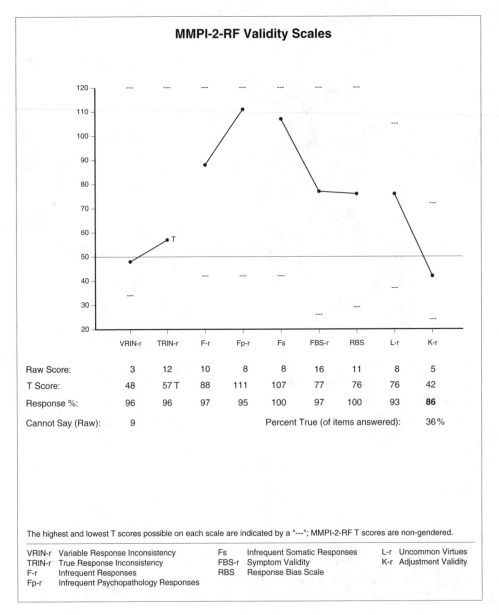

MMPI-2-RF Validity Scales

	VRIN-r	TRIN-r	F-r	Fp-r	Fs	FBS-r	RBS	L-r	K-r
Raw Score:	3	12	10	8	8	16	11	8	5
T Score:	48	57 T	88	111	107	77	76	76	42
Response %:	96	96	97	95	100	97	100	93	**86**

Cannot Say (Raw):   9   Percent True (of items answered):   36%

The highest and lowest T scores possible on each scale are indicated by a "---"; MMPI-2-RF T scores are non-gendered.

VRIN-r	Variable Response Inconsistency	Fs	Infrequent Somatic Responses	L-r	Uncommon Virtues
TRIN-r	True Response Inconsistency	FBS-r	Symptom Validity	K-r	Adjustment Validity
F-r	Infrequent Responses	RBS	Response Bias Scale		
Fp-r	Infrequent Psychopathology Responses				

Figure 6-8. MMPI-2-RF Score Report Validity Scales profile showing an elevated Fp-r score reflecting overreporting of severe psychopathology.

while naively denying common moral flaws. A Validity Scale profile such as the one provided in Figure 6-8, obtained in a case in which the test taker is externally motivated to overreport and there are other indications of noncredible symptom presentation (e.g., behavioral inconsistencies), could support the conclusion that the individual is malingering.

As noted in Table 6-11, Fs, FBS-r, and RBS scores can also be artifactually elevated by psychopathology. Somatoform Disorder and somatic delusions, both of which manifest in noncredible somatic symptom reporting, can contribute to elevated

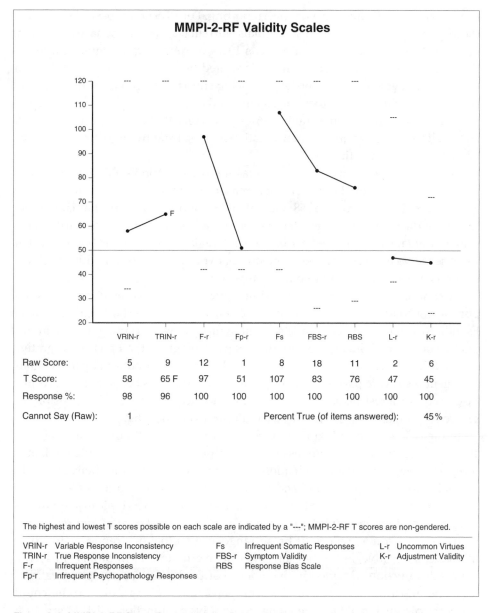

MMPI-2-RF Validity Scales

	VRIN-r	TRIN-r	F-r	Fp-r	Fs	FBS-r	RBS	L-r	K-r
Raw Score:	5	9	12	1	8	18	11	2	6
T Score:	58	65 F	97	51	107	83	76	47	45
Response %:	98	96	100	100	100	100	100	100	100

Cannot Say (Raw):   1   Percent True (of items answered):   45%

The highest and lowest T scores possible on each scale are indicated by a "---"; MMPI-2-RF T scores are non-gendered.

VRIN-r	Variable Response Inconsistency	Fs	Infrequent Somatic Responses	L-r	Uncommon Virtues
TRIN-r	True Response Inconsistency	FBS-r	Symptom Validity	K-r	Adjustment Validity
F-r	Infrequent Responses	RBS	Response Bias Scale		
Fp-r	Infrequent Psychopathology Responses				

Figure 6-9. MMPI-2-RF Score Report Validity Scales profile showing an elevated Fs score very likely indicating overreporting of somatic symptoms.

scores on Fs and FBS-r. Medical conditions can also elevate scores on these scales to some extent. However, as conveyed in the interpretive guidelines in Tables 6-6 and 6-7, test takers whose T scores reach or exceed 100 on Fs or FBS-r present, re-spectively, with a large number of uncommon responses or an unusual combination of responses that is atypical of individuals with substantial medical problems. For test takers with substantial medical problems, scores in the 80–99 range on these scales are possible but may still reflect symptom exaggeration. For test takers with no documented history or current findings of medical problems, scores in this range can indicate significant symptom overreporting. For RBS (Table 6-8), elevations in the 80–99 range can be found in individuals with substantial emotional dysfunction. However, if the score reaches or exceeds 100, overreporting of cognitive difficulties, specifically memory problems, is indicated by a very unusual combination of responses even for test takers experiencing substantial emotional dysfunction. Because Fs, FBS-r, and RBS focus on somatic and cognitive symptoms, the interpretive implications provided in Tables 6-6–6-8 for scores that exceed the upper cutoff (100) indicate a need to qualify interpretation of the substantive measures of somatic and cognitive dysfunction.

Figure 6-9 shows a case where a test taker scored 107 on Fs. Random and fixed responding can be ruled out as possible reasons for this score based on respective VRIN-r and TRIN-r scores of 58 and 65F. FBS-r and RBS are substantially lower than Fs, indicating that this test taker's symptom overreporting is primarily in the somatic domain. As discussed earlier, research reviewed in Chapter 4 indicates that F-r is sensitive to a broad range of symptom overreporting and, in this case, may similarly reflect somatic symptom overreporting.

By contrast, in the case reproduced in Figure 6-10, there is evidence of overreporting of somatic, cognitive, and psychological symptoms. The T score of 120 on Fs indicates an extreme pattern of somatic symptom overreporting, which, in this case, co-occurs with likely overreporting of psychological (F-r, Fp-r) and cognitive (FBS-r, RBS) difficulties. The T score of 94 on Fp-r may be produced by individuals with genuine severe psychopathology, but it may also reflect exaggeration. As just discussed, for a test taker without current evidence or a documented history of severe psychopathology, it very likely indicates overreporting.

In the case shown in Figure 6-11, the most prominent finding is a T score of 109 on RBS, which is strongly associated with noncredible memory complaints. It reflects a very unusual combination of responses even in individuals with substantial emotional dysfunction and indicates that the score on the COG Scale is invalid and uninterpretable in this case. The T score of 99 on Fs indicates significant somatic symptom overreporting as well. As in the case shown in Figure 6-9, the high score on F-r may reflect the broad range of symptom overreporting to which this scale is sensitive, but it may also indicate overreported symptoms of psychological dysfunction. Coupled with evidence of poor effort on symptom validity tests and an external incentive (e.g., compensation seeking), this profile could support a conclusion of malingered neurocognitive dysfunction (Slick, Sherman & Iverson, 1999).

Finally, it is important to note that a finding of overreporting, and even a diagnosis of malingering, is not evidence that a test taker is free of dysfunction. Psychopathology and overreporting are not mutually exclusive. Individuals with genuine disorders may overreport their symptoms or fabricate others for a variety of reasons. Therefore, "positive" findings on the MMPI-2-RF overreporting indicators do not, in themselves, rule out the possibility that the test taker is psychologically disordered. However, they do call into question the credibility of the test taker's self-reported symptoms.

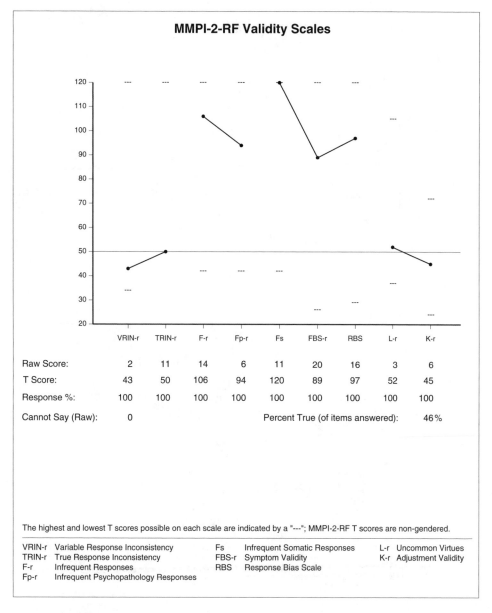

MMPI-2-RF Validity Scales

	VRIN-r	TRIN-r	F-r	Fp-r	Fs	FBS-r	RBS	L-r	K-r
Raw Score:	2	11	14	6	11	20	16	3	6
T Score:	43	50	106	94	120	89	97	52	45
Response %:	100	100	100	100	100	100	100	100	100

Cannot Say (Raw):   0   Percent True (of items answered):   46%

The highest and lowest T scores possible on each scale are indicated by a "---"; MMPI-2-RF T scores are non-gendered.

VRIN-r	Variable Response Inconsistency	Fs	Infrequent Somatic Responses
TRIN-r	True Response Inconsistency	FBS-r	Symptom Validity
F-r	Infrequent Responses	RBS	Response Bias Scale
Fp-r	Infrequent Psychopathology Responses		

L-r	Uncommon Virtues
K-r	Adjustment Validity

Figure 6-10. MMPI-2-RF Score Report Validity Scales profile showing scale elevations very likely reflecting overreporting of somatic, cognitive, and psychological symptoms.

Underreporting

Underreporting occurs when the test taker's self-presentation suggests a level of functioning that is better than would be indicated by a hypothetical objective assessment. As with the term *overreporting, underreporting* is preferred over such terms as *faking good* or *positive malingering,* which connote an intentionality that cannot be inferred from test data alone. Self-report measures of personality and

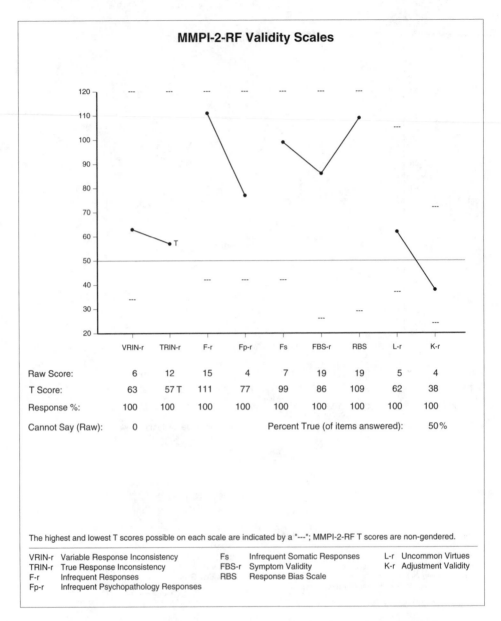

MMPI-2-RF Validity Scales

	VRIN-r	TRIN-r	F-r	Fp-r	Fs	FBS-r	RBS	L-r	K-r
Raw Score:	6	12	15	4	7	19	19	5	4
T Score:	63	57 T	111	77	99	86	109	62	38
Response %:	100	100	100	100	100	100	100	100	100

Cannot Say (Raw):   0   Percent True (of items answered):   50%

The highest and lowest T scores possible on each scale are indicated by a "---"; MMPI-2-RF T scores are non-gendered.

VRIN-r	Variable Response Inconsistency	Fs	Infrequent Somatic Responses	L-r	Uncommon Virtues
TRIN-r	True Response Inconsistency	FBS-r	Symptom Validity	K-r	Adjustment Validity
F-r	Infrequent Responses	RBS	Response Bias Scale		
Fp-r	Infrequent Psychopathology Responses				

Figure 6-11. MMPI-2-RF Score Report Validity Scales profile showing an elevated RBS score very likely reflecting exaggerated cognitive complaints.

psychopathology are inherently susceptible to intentional underreporting, which is most likely to occur when, given the assessment context, good adjustment is a highly desirable quality and the individual has a great deal at stake (e.g., child custody evaluations, preemployment assessments, release from involuntary commitment). However, underreporting can also result from lack of awareness of or insight into psychological dysfunction.

Just as for overreporting, differentiating intentional from unintentional under-reporting requires consideration of extratest data. For example, if, when responding to the MMPI-2-RF items, a test taker presents as extraordinarily well adjusted but is known to be experiencing considerable psychosocial difficulties, this increases the likelihood that the individual is *knowingly* underreporting. At the same time, as will be explained shortly, elevated scores on the two MMPI-2-RF underreporting indicators can, at least to some extent, reflect factors other than underreporting (e.g., being raised in a very traditional environment, being considerably better adjusted than average).

Regardless of whether the underreporting is intentional or unintentional or can be explained by other factors, elevated scores on the MMPI-2-RF underreporting scales indicate a need for caution in the interpretation of the Substantive Scales. Specifically, nonelevated and, in particular, low scores (i.e., a T score of 38 or lower) on the Substantive Scales are uninterpretable and cannot be relied upon to rule out problems when there are indications of underreporting. Elevated scores on the Substantive Scales are interpretable under these circumstances, but they may underestimate the problems associated with the elevations.

As shown in Table 6-11, a number of possible confounds need to be considered when interpreting scores on the underreporting indicators. As discussed earlier, nonresponding can artifactually lower scores on these scales. Moreover, because the items on L-r and K-r are predominantly keyed false, indiscriminant true responding can also artifactually lower scores on these scales. On the other hand, scores on these measures can be artifactually elevated by random and indiscriminate false responding. These confounds need to be considered by examination of CNS, Response %, VRIN-r, and TRIN-r.

If content nonresponsiveness is ruled out, extratest confounds need also to be considered for cases in which scores on L-r and K-r reach interpretable levels. As indicated in the interpretive recommendations for L-r in Table 6-9, scores in the 65–69 range on this scale indicate possible underreporting. However, a background stressing traditional values can also account for such scores. As the L-r score rises above 69, and, in particular, if it reaches 80 or above, the reason for the elevation being a traditional upbringing becomes increasingly less likely, and underreporting becomes increasingly more likely.

Such a case is shown in Figure 6-12. The test taker's T score of 81 on L-r cannot be attributed to random or fixed responding because scores on VRIN-r and TRIN-r are 63 and 57T, respectively. Thus, the high L-r score indicates that the test taker presented in an extremely positive light by denying minor faults and shortcomings that most people acknowledge. Any absence of elevation on the Substantive Scales is therefore uninterpretable, and elevated scores might underestimate problems assessed by these measures. As seen in Figure 6-13, this test taker produced clinically elevated scores on Cynicism (RC3) and Ideas of Persecution (RC6). These are interpretable findings. However, they may underestimate the levels of cynicism and persecutory thinking that characterize this test taker.

As just mentioned, better than average psychological adjustment can contribute to the score on K-r because the items on this scale, as keyed, denote good psychological adjustment. Thus, as reflected in the interpretive recommendations for this scale (Table 6-10), interpretation of K-r requires consideration of

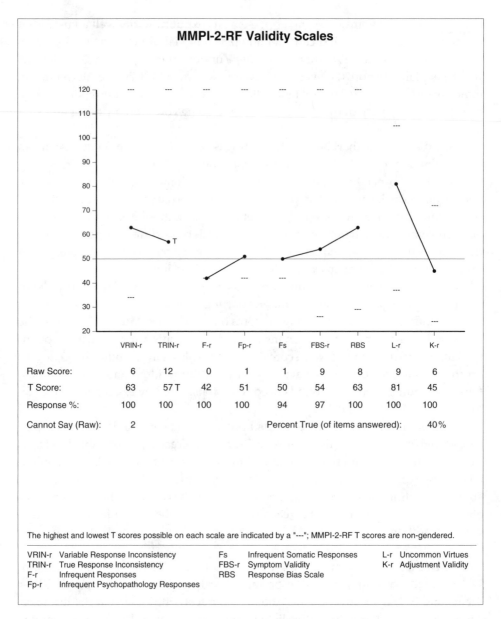

	VRIN-r	TRIN-r	F-r	Fp-r	Fs	FBS-r	RBS	L-r	K-r
Raw Score:	6	12	0	1	1	9	8	9	6
T Score:	63	57 T	42	51	50	54	63	81	45
Response %:	100	100	100	100	94	97	100	100	100

Cannot Say (Raw):   2   Percent True (of items answered):   40%

The highest and lowest T scores possible on each scale are indicated by a "---"; MMPI-2-RF T scores are non-gendered.

VRIN-r	Variable Response Inconsistency	Fs	Infrequent Somatic Responses	L-r	Uncommon Virtues
TRIN-r	True Response Inconsistency	FBS-r	Symptom Validity	K-r	Adjustment Validity
F-r	Infrequent Responses	RBS	Response Bias Scale		
Fp-r	Infrequent Psychopathology Responses				

Figure 6-12. MMPI-2-RF Score Report Validity Scales profile showing an elevated L-r score very likely reflecting underreporting.

extratest evidence of the test taker's psychological adjustment. K-r T scores in the 60–65 range are not uncommon in individuals who are psychologically well adjusted. Such persons are unlikely to be administered the MMPI-2-RF in clinical settings, but they may take the test in other circumstances such as preemployment screening of candidates for public safety positions or selection of candidates for special military assignments. As the K-r score increases beyond this level, and, in particular, if it reaches the highest possible T-score level of 72, the likelihood

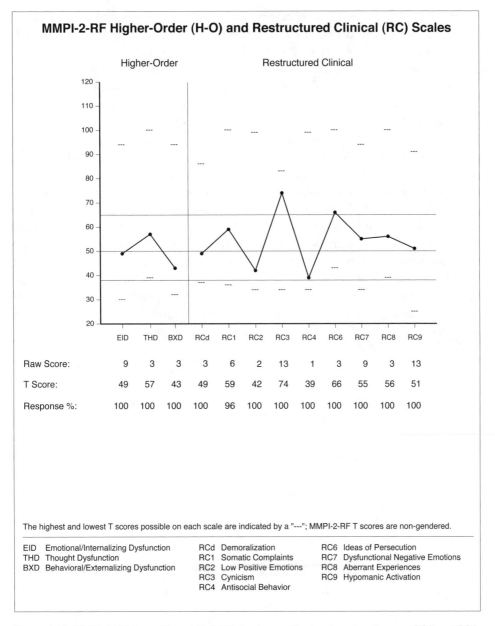

Figure 6-13. MMPI-2-RF Score Report H-O/RC Scales profile showing elevations on RC3 and RC6.

that good psychological adjustment accounts for this score is significantly diminished, and it is increasingly more likely an indication of underreporting.

Such a scenario is shown in Figure 6-14, when the test taker's K-r score reaches the highest possible level. Random and fixed responding can be ruled out as possible confounds based on respective VRIN-r and TRIN-r scores of 43 and 65F. Good psychological adjustment is very unlikely to account for a score this high on K-r. Therefore, this Validity Scale profile most likely reflects an effort by the test taker to portray herself or himself in an overly positive manner by claiming to be remarkably well adjusted. Unlike cases for which underreporting is indicated by a high score on L-r, in this case, it is very unlikely that any clinically significant elevations will be found on the Substantive Scales. However, this cannot be interpreted as indicating that the individual is free of psychopathology. In the unlikely event that an interpretable finding occurs on a Substantive Scale, it is likely to underestimate the magnitude of the problems assessed by that measure.

Finally, Figure 6-15 provides a case in which a test taker produced very high scores on both L-r and K-r. In fact, this individual responded in the keyed direction to all but 1 of the 28 items scored on these scales. Random and fixed responding can readily be ruled out because the test taker produced the lowest possible scores on both VRIN-r and TRIN-r.[3] Raw scores of zero on F-r, Fp-r, and Fs indicate that the test taker did not answer a single one of the 69 infrequent response items in the keyed direction. Taken together, this individual's Validity Scale scores indicate that he responded to the test items in a careful and deliberate manner, denied a very large number of minor faults that most people are willing to acknowledge, and presented an unrealistic picture of remarkably good psychological adjustment. Intentional underreporting is the most likely explanation for this extreme pattern of scores on the MMPI-2-RF Validity Scales.

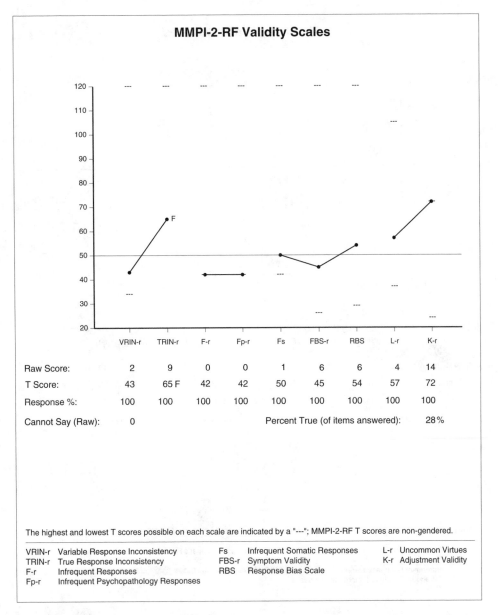

Figure 6-14. MMPI-2-RF Score Report Validity Scales profile showing an elevated K-r score very likely reflecting underreporting.

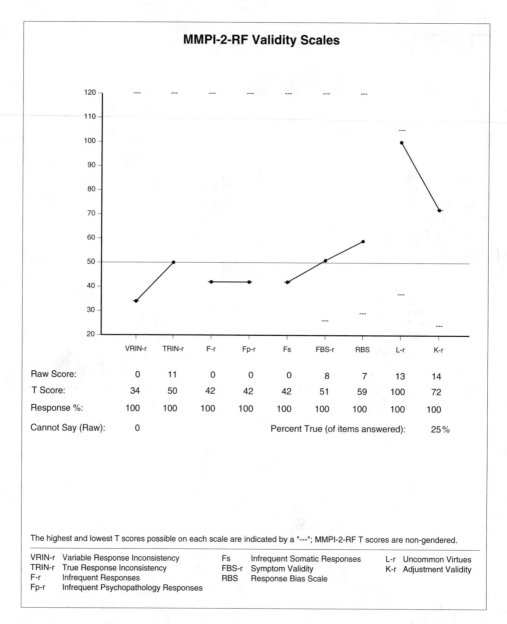

MMPI-2-RF Validity Scales

	VRIN-r	TRIN-r	F-r	Fp-r	Fs	FBS-r	RBS	L-r	K-r
Raw Score:	0	11	0	0	0	8	7	13	14
T Score:	34	50	42	42	42	51	59	100	72
Response %:	100	100	100	100	100	100	100	100	100

Cannot Say (Raw):   0   Percent True (of items answered):   25%

The highest and lowest T scores possible on each scale are indicated by a "---"; MMPI-2-RF T scores are non-gendered.

VRIN-r	Variable Response Inconsistency	Fs	Infrequent Somatic Responses	L-r	Uncommon Virtues
TRIN-r	True Response Inconsistency	FBS-r	Symptom Validity	K-r	Adjustment Validity
F-r	Infrequent Responses	RBS	Response Bias Scale		
Fp-r	Infrequent Psychopathology Responses				

Figure 6-15. MMPI-2-RF Score Report Validity Scales profile showing elevated scores on L-r and K-r very likely reflecting underreporting.

CHAPTER 7

Interpreting the MMPI-2-RF Substantive Scales

This chapter provides interpretive statements recommended for various levels of scores on the Substantive Scales of the MMPI-2-RF. Interpretation of scores on these scales should proceed only after careful consideration of the potential threats to the validity of the test protocol and with whatever caveats are indicated based on a review of scores on the Validity Scales. For example, as discussed in Chapter 6, low scores on the Substantive Scales should not be interpreted at face value if there are indications of underreporting on Uncommon Virtues (L-r) or Adjustment Validity (K-r). And as previously mentioned, the protocol is invalid and uninterpretable if there are indications of excessive inconsistent responding or marked overreporting.

The cutoffs provided in the interpretive tables included in this chapter are intended to function as heuristic guidelines rather than as rigid demarcation rules. They are designed to apply broadly to test results in mental health settings. Population differences, reflected in dissimilar MMPI-2-RF scale score means and standard deviations, may suggest the need to alter these interpretive ranges in specific settings. Comparison group data provided in the *MMPI-2-RF Technical Manual* and embedded in the Pearson scoring software can assist in making these judgments.[1] Use of comparison group data in MMPI-2-RF interpretation is illustrated with case studies in Chapter 9.

In the descriptive accounts in this chapter, the content of the items in a given MMPI-2-RF scale is defined from a measurement perspective as the content of the *responses* to these items *as keyed* for that scale. For example, Somatic Complaints (RC1) contains 11 true-keyed items regarding a variety of somatic concerns and 16 false-keyed items indicating a sense of physical well-being or the absence of physical difficulties. However, the statement that the RC1 items describe "a range of somatic complaints" is a general characterization of responses to all 27 items as keyed for RC1.

Interpretive guidelines for each of the 42 MMPI-2-RF Substantive Scales are provided in Tables 7-1–7-42, which are reproduced from the *MMPI-2-RF Manual for Administration, Scoring, and Interpretation*. The recommended interpretive statements in each table are organized into three sections labeled "Clinical Symptoms, Behavioral Tendencies, and Personality Characteristics," "Diagnostic Considerations," and "Treatment Considerations." The first section is further divided into content-based statements (generated on the basis of the item content for that scale), which appear under the heading "Test Responses," and statements based on the extratest correlates of the scales, which appear under the heading "Empirical Correlates." The latter are based on the findings reported in Appendix A of the *MMPI-2-RF Technical Manual* and the published literature reviewed in Chapters 2 and 3 of this book.

Rather than provide an exhaustive list of the empirical correlates, which, given the hierarchical structure of the test, would include a large number of redundant entries, the interpretive statements emphasize the distinctive correlates of each scale. Redundant correlates are usually attributed to the scale with which they are most highly correlated.[2] Some statements under "Diagnostic Considerations" are based on empirical data, whereas others are inferences. All the statements under "Treatment Considerations" are inferential, meaning that they reflect our[3] conclusions about the implications of MMPI-2-RF findings for treatment planning.

A majority of the Substantive Scales include both low scores and high scores that are interpretable as distinctive from average scores. Interpretation of low scores reflects the quasi-continuous nature of the MMPI-2-RF scales and the constructs they assess. Unless indicated otherwise, interpretive statements about distinctive low scores refer to T scores of 38 or lower (comparable in percentile terms to a T score of 65).

Unless otherwise specified, the interpretive statements about elevated scores listed in Tables 7-1–7-42 are intended to apply to T scores of 65 and higher, which corresponds to the 92nd percentile and higher (see Table 5-1). However, guidelines for the content-based statements are linked to at least two different specified levels of elevated scores. For the first level of elevation (usually in the T-score range 65–79), these statements reflect the general theme of the item content as keyed on a scale. At higher levels of elevation, interpretive statements reflect the specific content of items the test taker must answer in the keyed direction to obtain a score in the specified range. Similarly, if for a statement in the "Empirical Correlates," "Diagnostic Considerations," or "Treatment Considerations" sections, a T-score level above 65 is specified, it is indicated in parentheses following the statement (i.e., >75). In general, the higher the score on a scale, the more likely it is that the statements listed for it will apply, and the more severe will be the impairment reflected in those statements. Severity may be inferred in this manner owing to the quasi-continuous nature of the MMPI-2-RF scales.

The following interpretive recommendations for the Substantive Scales are organized into five sets of scales—Higher-Order (H-O), Restructured Clinical (RC), Specific Problems (SP), Interests, and Personality Psychopathology Five (PSY-5). A detailed description of the development, conceptualization, and psychometric properties of these scales can be found in Chapter 2 for the RC Scales and Chapter 3 for the rest. To summarize, the H-O Scales represent the broadest constructs; the RC Scales represent the more circumscribed, though generally multifaceted, mid-level constructs; and the SP and Interest Scales represent narrower-band constructs designed either to highlight facets of (but not necessarily represented by items from) the RC Scales or to measure features not directly targeted by the higher-level scales. The SP Scales are in turn subdivided into subsets on the basis of empirical (correlational) analyses and conceptual considerations. The PSY-5 Scales embody Harkness and McNulty's (1994) model of personality pathology and link the clinically oriented content of the MMPI-2-RF to the Five Factor Model of personality. The PSY-5 dimensions are clearly related to but also distinct from the hierarchical structure developed on the basis of the RC Scales.

HIGHER-ORDER SCALES

From factor analyses (described in Chapter 3), three H-O dimensions have clearly emerged: Emotional/Internalizing Dysfunction (EID), Thought Dysfunction (THD), and Behavioral/Externalizing Dysfunction (BXD), demarcating clinically important individual variations in the basic domains of affect, thought, and action. It may be helpful to view the role of these broad measures as analogous to the function of broad-band intelligence measures such as the Verbal Comprehension, Perceptual Reasoning, Working Memory, and Processing Speed scales of the Wechsler Adult Intelligence Scale–Fourth Edition (WAIS-IV; Wechsler, 2008) in cognitive assessments. On one hand, an individual's MMPI-2-RF EID, THD, and BXD scores will often provide meaningful indications of overall functioning in the three respective domains; on the other hand, as in the aptitude area, score levels within the average range on the H-O Scales may be the result of contrasting within-domain strengths and weaknesses, which may be revealed by narrower-band subdomain measures. In other words, the absence of elevation on an H-O Scale does not rule out all problems within that domain. For example, a test taker may produce an average score on the EID Scale while showing evidence of risk for a depressive disorder, as indicated by an elevated score on Low Positive Emotions (RC2). Finally, the relative elevation of scores on the H-O Scales can provide an indication of the prominence of the difficulties they assess when more than one exceeds an interpretable threshold.

Emotional/Internalizing Dysfunction (EID)

EID is a 41-item scale designed to assess a broad range of emotional and internalizing problems. The test taker's EID score provides an overall gauge of his or her emotional functioning. Low EID scores reflect a below-average level of emotional difficulties, whereas elevated scores indicate that the test taker reported a broad range of emotional and internalizing difficulties. Table 7-1 provides interpretive statements for different levels of EID. Information on specific manifestations of internalizing dysfunction can be obtained by consulting the tables providing interpretation of scores on the EID-associated RC, SP, and PSY-5 Scales, also listed in Table 7-1.

Thought Dysfunction (THD)

THD is a 26-item scale designed to assess a broad range of difficulties associated with disordered thinking. The test taker's score on THD provides an overall estimate of his or her level of reported thought dysfunction. Elevated scores indicate substantial difficulties associated with thought disturbance. Table 7-2 provides interpretive statements for different elevation levels. Information on specific manifestations of thought dysfunction can be obtained by consulting the tables providing interpretation of scores on the THD-related RC and PSY-5 Scales, also noted in Table 7-2.

Table 7-1. EID (Emotional/Internalizing Dysfunction) Interpretation

Clinical Symptoms, Behavioral Tendencies, and Personality Characteristics

Test Responses

T score < 39

His/Her responses indicate a better than average level of emotional adjustment

T score 65–79

His/Her responses indicate significant emotional distress

T score ≥ 80

His/Her responses indicate considerable emotional distress that is likely to be perceived as a crisis

Empirical Correlates

A broad range of symptoms and difficulties associated with demoralization, low positive emotions, and negative emotional experiences (e.g., low morale, depression, anxiety, feeling overwhelmed, helpless, pessimistic). Specific manifestations of emotional/internalizing dysfunction will be characterized by elevated scores on RCd, RC2, RC7, SUI, HLP, SFD, NFC, STW, AXY ANP, BRF, MSF, NEGE-r, and INTR-r.

Diagnostic Considerations

Evaluate for internalizing disorders

Treatment Considerations

Emotional difficulties may motivate him or her for treatment

Table 7-2. THD (Thought Dysfunction) Interpretation

Clinical Symptoms, Behavioral Tendencies, and Personality Characteristics

Test Responses

T score 65–79

His or her responses indicate significant thought dysfunction

T score ≥ 80

His or her responses indicate serious thought dysfunction

Empirical Correlates

A broad range of symptoms and difficulties associated with disordered thinking (e.g., paranoid and nonparanoid delusions, auditory and visual hallucinations, unrealistic thinking). Specific manifestations of thought dysfunction will be characterized by scores on RC6, RC8, and PSYC-r.

Diagnostic Considerations

Evaluate for disorders associated with thought dysfunction

Treatment Considerations

May require inpatient treatment for thought dysfunction

Need for antipsychotic medication should be evaluated

Table 7-3. BXD (Behavioral/Externalizing Dysfunction) Interpretation

Clinical Symptoms, Behavioral Tendencies, and Personality Characteristics

Test Responses

T score < 39

His or her responses indicate a higher-than-average level of behavioral constraint; he or she is unlikely to engage in externalizing, acting-out behavior

T score 65–79

His or her responses indicate significant externalizing, acting-out behavior, which is likely to have gotten him or her into difficulties

T score ≥ 80

His or her responses indicate considerable externalizing, acting-out behavior that is very likely to result in marked dysfunction and to have gotten him or her into difficulties

Empirical Correlates

A broad range of behaviors and difficulties associated with undercontrolled behavior (e.g., substance abuse, a history of criminal behavior, violent and abusive behavior, poor impulse control). Specific manifestations of behavioral/externalizing dysfunction will be reflected in elevated scores on RC4, RC9, JCP, SUB, AGG, ACT, AGGR-r, and DISC-r.

Diagnostic Considerations

Evaluate for externalizing disorders

Treatment Considerations

Unlikely to be internally motivated for treatment

At significant risk for treatment noncompliance

Inadequate self-control as a target for intervention

Behavioral/Externalizing Dysfunction (BXD)

BXD is a 23-item scale designed to assess a broad range of behavioral problems. The test taker's score on BXD provides an overall gauge of his or her proclivity for behavioral acting out. Low scores indicate that the test taker reported a higher-than-average level of behavioral constraint, whereas elevated scores indicate a broad range of externalizing, acting-out behaviors. Table 7-3 provides interpretive statements for this scale. Information on specific manifestations of externalizing dysfunction is provided in the tables containing interpretation of scores of the BXD-linked RC, SP, and PSY-5 Scales, also listed in Table 7-3.

RESTRUCTURED CLINICAL SCALES

Interpretive recommendations for the RC Scales are based on the empirical correlates reported in Appendix A of the *MMPI-2-RF Technical Manual* and the substantial body of research published since the introduction of the scales in 2003. These findings are summarized in Chapter 2, which provides detailed reviews of the constructs measured by the RC Scales and their psychometric properties.

For several of the RC Scales (Demoralization [RCd], Somatic Complaints [RC1],

Antisocial Behavior [RC4], Dysfunctional Negative Emotions [RC7], and Hypomanic Activation [RC9]), interpretation is facilitated by also examining the test taker's scores on the SP Scales that focus on a facet of an RC Scale or are empirically and conceptually linked to it. For each RC Scale, findings on its affiliated SP Scales (e.g., for RC4, Juvenile Conduct Problems [JCP] and Substance Abuse [SUB]) can help the interpreter identify the attributes that are linked to the RC Scale and should be emphasized or deemphasized in the interpretation. A detailed strategy for incorporating this information is described and illustrated in Chapter 8. In the following sections, the SP Scales associated with each RC Scale have been identified.

Most of the RC Scales (RCd, RC1, RC2, RC3, RC4, RC7, and RC9) include both low scores and high scores that are interpretable as distinctive from average scores. However, as noted earlier, whenever the Validity Scales indicate underreporting, interpretations of low scores should be qualified or avoided altogether, depending on the degree of underreporting.

Demoralization (RCd)

RCd is a 24-item scale called "Demoralization," representing a pervasive and affect-laden dimension of unhappiness and dissatisfaction with life. A low RCd score reflects avowal of a relatively high level of morale and life satisfaction. Individuals scoring high on Demoralization encounter problems in living that they experience as overwhelming, in the face of which they feel helpless and ineffective. A high level of demoralization is a common accompaniment of being a mental health or medical patient, of "patienthood." Elevated scores on the other RC Scales and on the SP and PSY-5 Scales can help to identify the types of psychological problems that contribute to demoralization. The SP Scales associated specifically with RCd—Suicidal/Death Ideation (SUI), Helplessness/Hopelessness (HLP), Self-Doubt (SFD), and Inefficacy (NFC)—highlight its salient manifestations.

Suicidal ideation is one of the empirical RCd correlates to be considered in any assessment in which the test taker generates an elevated score on this scale. Two SP Scales, SUI and HLP, provide particularly relevant additional information. A high SUI score provides the most direct evidence of suicidal ideation and requires immediate attention. However, when RCd is elevated but SUI is not, a high score on HLP should raise concerns about possible risk for self-harm that need to be addressed with a follow-up assessment. These and other interpretive statements for RCd are listed in Table 7-4.

Somatic Complaints (RC1)

RC1 consists of 27 items that describe a range of somatic complaints often associated with Somatoform Disorder and unexplained medical conditions. Low RC1 scores indicate a sense of relative somatic well-being. As is true for any self-report measures of somatoform problems, a moderate RC1 score may reflect contributions of genuine physical health problems. Interpretations of the test taker's score need to

Table 7-4. RCd (Demoralization) Interpretation

Clinical Symptoms, Behavioral Tendencies, and Personality Characteristics
Test Responses
T score < 39
Reports a higher-than-average level of morale and life satisfaction
T score 65–79
Reports:
Feeling sad and unhappy
Being dissatisfied with his or her current life circumstances
T score ≥ 80
Reports:
Experiencing significant emotional turmoil
Feeling overwhelmed
Being extremely unhappy, sad, and dissatisfied with his or her life
Empirical Correlates
At risk for suicidal ideation (if SUI or HLP ≥ 65)
Complains about depression or anxiety
Feels hopeless and pessimistic about the future
Does not cope well with stress
Has low self-esteem
Feels incapable of dealing with current life circumstances
Has difficulty concentrating
Is worry-prone and ruminative
Feels sad
Is pessimistic
Is insecure
Diagnostic Considerations
Evaluate for depression-related disorder
Treatment Considerations
Evaluate risk for self-harm (if SUI or HLP ≥ 65)
Emotional difficulties may motivate him or her for treatment
Relief of psychological distress as an initial target for intervention

take these contributions into careful consideration. Nevertheless, as the RC1 score increases, so does the likelihood that psychological factors play a significant role in the somatic symptoms reported by the individual.

Five SP Scales, Malaise (MLS), Gastrointestinal Complaints (GIC), Head Pain Complaints (HPC), Neurological Complaints (NUC), and Cognitive Complaints (COG), provide information about the particular kinds of somatic complaints reported by the test taker. Interpretive recommendations for RC1 are provided in Table 7-5.

Table 7-5. RC1 (Somatic Complaints) Interpretation

Clinical Symptoms, Behavioral Tendencies, and Personality Characteristics
Test Responses
T score < 39
Reports a sense of somatic well-being
T score 65–79
Reports multiple somatic complaints that may include head pain, neurological, and gastrointestinal symptoms
T score ≥ 80
Reports a diffuse pattern of somatic complaints involving different bodily systems that probably include head pain and neurological and gastrointestinal symptoms
Empirical Correlates
Is preoccupied with physical health concerns
Is prone to developing physical symptoms in response to stress
Has a psychological component to his or her somatic complaints
Complains of fatigue
Presents with multiple somatic complaints
Diagnostic Considerations
Evaluate for somatoform disorder (consider a conversion disorder if RC3 ≤ 39 and SHY ≤ 39)
Treatment Considerations
Is likely to reject psychological interpretations of somatic complaints

Low Positive Emotions (RC2)

RC2 is a 17-item scale designed to measure the lack of positive emotional experiences, which has been identified as a distinctive feature of Major Depression. Although demoralization is also commonly characteristic of individuals with a depressive disorder, it is not a distinctive characteristic of depression and, as noted earlier, co-occurs with many other conditions. A finding of low positive emotions, or anhedonia, is similarly not a pathognomonic sign of depression. As literature reviewed in Chapter 2 shows, it can also be a feature of Schizophrenia and Posttraumatic Stress Disorder.

Because all the items on this scale are keyed false, care should be taken when interpreting a high RC2 score to ensure that fixed false responding (measured by True Response Inconsistency [TRIN-r]) did not inflate the score. Low scores on RC2 indicate that the test taker reported a high level of psychological well-being and a wide range of emotionally positive experiences, provided, in this case, that fixed true responding (again, as measured by TRIN-r) did not spuriously lower the score. None of the SP Scales is associated directly with this scale. Interpretive statements for RC2 are listed in Table 7-6.

Table 7-6. RC2 (Low Positive Emotions) Interpretation

Clinical Symptoms, Behavioral Tendencies, and Personality Characteristics
Test Responses
T score < 39
Reports:
A high level of psychological well-being
A wide range of emotionally positive experiences
Feeling confident and energetic
T score ≥ 65
Reports:
A lack of positive emotional experiences
Significant anhedonia
Lack of interest
Empirical Correlates
T score < 39
Is optimistic
Is extraverted
Is socially engaged
T score ≥ 65
Is pessimistic
Is socially introverted
Is socially disengaged
Lacks energy
Displays vegetative symptoms of depression
Diagnostic Considerations
Evaluate for depression-related disorder
Evaluate for depression-related disorder, possibly major depression (If RC2 ≥ 80)
Treatment Considerations
Need for antidepressant medication should be evaluated
May require inpatient treatment for significant depression (RC2 ≥ 75)
Low positive emotionality may interfere with engagement in treatment
Anhedonia as a target for intervention

Cynicism (RC3)

RC3 consists of 15 items stating (as keyed) opinions conveying a highly negative view of human nature. By contrast, low scores on RC3 indicate that the test taker describes others as well intentioned and trustworthy. Individuals who produce elevated scores on this scale report a variety of cynical beliefs about other people's motivations. The content is non-self-referential; that is, the RC3 items, as keyed, do not claim that one is personally being singled out for mistreatment, as would be

Table 7-7. RC3 (Cynicism) Interpretation

Clinical Symptoms, Behavioral Tendencies, and Personality Characteristics
Test Responses
T score < 39
Describes others as well-intentioned and trustworthy and disavows cynical beliefs about them
Possibly overly trusting
T score ≥ 65
Reports:
Having cynical beliefs
Being distrustful of others
Believing others look out only for their own interests
Empirical Correlates
Is hostile toward and feels alienated from others
Is distrustful of others
Has negative interpersonal experiences
Diagnostic Considerations
Evaluate for personality disorders involving mistrust of and hostility toward others
Treatment Considerations
Cynicism may interfere with forming a therapeutic relationship
Lack of interpersonal trust as a target for intervention

indicated by an elevated score on RC6 (to be discussed shortly). Rather, the items assert that others look out only for their own interests and are not to be trusted. As detailed in Chapter 2, cynicism, as measured by RC3, has been identified as a significant psychological risk factor for cardiovascular disease. It is also likely to manifest in substantial interpersonal problems.

Although interpretation of scores on RC3 is not specifically related to any of the SP Scales, its content and correlates can be meaningfully integrated with information provided by the SP Scales that focus on interpersonal functioning: Interpersonal Passivity (IPP), Social Avoidance (SAV), Shyness (SHY), and Disaffiliativeness (DSF). Interpretive statements for RC3 are listed in Table 7-7.

Antisocial Behavior (RC4)

RC4 consists of 22 items that describe various antisocial behaviors and related family conflict. Low scores on RC4 indicate that the test taker reported a below-average level of past antisocial behavior, associated with a reduced risk for the various acting-out behaviors linked empirically with this scale. Because many of the items on the scale are worded in the past tense, individuals who produce elevated scores are most accurately described as reporting a history of antisocial behavior. Elevations on RC4 are associated with a wide range of empirical correlates reflecting rule breaking and irresponsible behavior. Specific interpretations of elevated

Table 7-8. RC4 (Antisocial Behavior) Interpretation

Clinical Symptoms, Behavioral Tendencies, and Personality Characteristics
Test Responses
T score < 39
Reports below-average level of past antisocial behavior
T score ≥ 65
Reports a significant history of antisocial behavior
Empirical Correlates
Has been involved with the criminal justice system
Fails to conform to societal norms and expectations
Has difficulties with individuals in positions of authority
Experiences conflictual interpersonal relationships
Is impulsive
Acts out when bored
Has antisocial characteristics
Has a history of juvenile delinquency
Engages in substance abuse
Has family problems
Is interpersonally aggressive
Diagnostic Considerations
Evaluate for antisocial personality disorder, substance use disorders, and other externalizing disorders
Treatment Considerations
Acting-out tendencies can result in treatment noncompliance and interfere with the development of a therapeutic relationship
Inadequate self-control as a target for intervention

RC4 scores are facilitated by considering scores on two SP Scales: Juvenile Conduct Problems (JCP) and Substance Abuse (SUB). Interpretive statements for RC4 are provided in Table 7-8.

Ideas of Persecution (RC6)

RC6 consists of 17 items designed to assess the extent to which the test taker holds persecutory beliefs. Most of these items, which, by definition, are "self-referential" in contrast to the items of RC3, reflect extreme beliefs (e.g., that one is being followed) and were very rarely endorsed in the MMPI-2-RF normative sample. Consequently, answering only three of the RC6 items in the keyed direction results in an elevated score. No SP Scales are linked directly to the interpretation of scores on RC6.

Because significant persecutory thinking may require immediate intervention, RC6 has been designated as one of seven MMPI-2-RF scales with critical content. When the scale is elevated, the RC6 items the test taker answered in the keyed direction are printed out in the MMPI-2-RF Score Report and Interpretive Report.

Table 7-9. RC6 (Ideas of Persecution) Interpretation

Clinical Symptoms, Behavioral Tendencies, and Personality Characteristics
Test Responses
Reports:
Significant persecutory ideation such as believing that others seek to harm him or her
Prominent persecutory ideation that likely rises to the level of paranoid delusions (RC6 ≥ 80)
Empirical Correlates
Experiences paranoid delusional thinking (RC6 ≥ 80)
Is suspicious of and alienated from others
Experiences interpersonal difficulties as a result of suspiciousness
Lacks insight
Blames others for his or her difficulties
Diagnostic Considerations
Evaluate for disorders involving persecutory ideation
Evaluate for disorders involving paranoid delusional thinking (RC6 ≥ 80)
Treatment Considerations
Persecutory ideation may interfere with forming a therapeutic relationship and treatment compliance
Persecutory ideation as a target for intervention
May require inpatient treatment for paranoid delusional thinking (RC6 ≥ 80)
Need for antipsychotic medication should be evaluated (RC6 ≥ 80)

This information can help the interpreter evaluate the extent and seriousness of the test taker's reported persecutory ideation. Interpretive statements for RC6 are outlined in Table 7-9.

Dysfunctional Negative Emotions (RC7)

RC7 is a 24-item scale designed to assess the extent to which the test taker reported various negative emotional experiences (e.g., anxiety, anger, and fear). Low RC7 scores indicate a below-average level of reported dysfunctional negative emotional experiences and a lower risk for such experiences and the difficulties empirically associated with elevated scores on this scale. High scores have been linked in the literature to an increased risk for anxiety-related psychopathology. Although consistent with theoretical expectations, scores on RCd and RC7 are substantially correlated, and the content and empirical correlates of the two scales and the interpretive statements for each (cf. Tables 7-4 and 7-10) are distinctive.

Specific interpretations of RC7 scores are facilitated by considering the test taker's results on the following SP Scales: Stress/Worry (STW), Anxiety (AXY), Anger Proneness (ANP), Behavior-Restricting Fears (BRF), and Multiple Specific Fears (MSF). Interpretive statements for RC7 are listed in Table 7-10.

Table 7-10. RC7 (Dysfunctional Negative Emotions) Interpretation

Clinical Symptoms, Behavioral Tendencies, and Personality Characteristics
Test Responses
T score < 39
Reports a below-average level of negative emotional experience
T score ≥ 65
Reports various negative emotional experiences including anxiety, anger, and fear
Empirical Correlates
Is inhibited behaviorally because of negative emotions
Experiences intrusive ideation
Is anger-prone
Is stress-reactive
Experiences problems with sleep, including nightmares
Worries excessively
Engages in obsessive rumination
Perceives others as overly critical
Is self-critical and guilt-prone
Diagnostic Considerations
Evaluate for anxiety-related disorders
Treatment Considerations
Emotional difficulties may motivate him or her for treatment
Dysfunctional negative emotions as targets for intervention
Need for anxiolytic medication should be evaluated (if RC7 ≥ 80)

Aberrant Experiences (RC8)

RC8 consists of 18 items that describe various unusual thought and perceptual experiences characteristic of disordered thinking. Elevated scores are associated empirically with symptoms of psychotic disorders, and highly elevated scores indicate the possibility of significantly disorganized thinking. No SP Scales contribute directly to the interpretation of scores on RC8.

Because the symptoms associated with elevated scores may require immediate intervention, RC8 has been included among the scales designated as having critical content. Accordingly, if the RC8 score is elevated, all items the test taker answered in the keyed direction are printed out in the MMPI-2-RF interpretive report and score report.

As is the case with all self-report measures of thought and sensory/perceptual processes, certain neurological disorders (e.g., temporal lobe epilepsy) can account for at least some of the experiences described by the RC8 items. Substance-induced psychotic symptoms will also result in some elevation on this scale. These possibilities underscore the need to bring as much extratest information as can be obtained

Table 7-11. RC8 (Aberrant Experiences) Interpretation

Clinical Symptoms, Behavioral Tendencies, and Personality Characteristics
Test Responses
T score 65–74
Reports various unusual thought and perceptual processes
T score ≥ 75
Reports a large number of unusual thoughts and perceptions
Empirical Correlates
Experiences thought disorganization
Engages in unrealistic thinking
Believes he or she has unusual sensory-perceptual abilities
His or her aberrant experiences may include somatic delusions (if RC1, HPC, or NUC ≥ 65)
His or her aberrant experiences may be substance-induced (if SUB ≥ 65)
Aberrant experiences may include auditory and/or visual hallucinations and non-persecutory delusions such as thought broadcasting and mind reading (if RC8 ≥ 80)
Reality testing may be significantly impaired (if RC8 ≥ 80)
Experiences significant impairment in occupational and interpersonal functioning (if RC8 ≥ 80)
Diagnostic Considerations
Evaluate for disorders manifesting psychotic symptoms
Evaluate for disorders manifesting psychotic symptoms, including schizophrenia, paranoid type (if RC6 ≥ 70)
Evaluate for personality disorders manifesting unusual thoughts and perceptions
Treatment Considerations
Impaired thinking may disrupt treatment
Assist him or her in gaining insight about his or her thought dysfunction
May require inpatient treatment for disorganized thinking (if RC8 ≥ 75)
Need for antipsychotic medication should be evaluated (if RC8 ≥ 75)
Significantly impaired thinking is likely to disrupt treatment (if RC8 ≥ 75)
May need to be stabilized if treatment is to be successfully implemented (if RC8 ≥ 75)
Psychotic symptoms as targets for intervention (if RC8 ≥ 75)

to the interpretation of RC8 results. Interpretive statements for RC8 are presented in Table 7-11.

Hypomanic Activation (RC9)

RC9 consists of 28 items describing a variety of emotions, cognitions, attitudes, and behaviors consistent with hypomanic activation. The specific item content includes thought racing, high energy, heightened mood and self-regard, excitement seeking, and aggression, all features associated with hypomanic states.

Low RC9 scores indicate that the test taker reported a below-average level of

Table 7-12. RC9 (Hypomanic Activation) Interpretation

Clinical Symptoms, Behavioral Tendencies, and Personality Characteristics
Test Responses
T score < 39
Reports a below-average level of activation and engagement with his or her environment
T score 65–74
Reports an above-average level of activation and engagement with his or her environment
T score ≥ 75
Reports a considerably above-average level of activation and engagement with his or her environment
Empirical Correlates
T score < 35
Has a very low energy level
Is disengaged from his or her environment
T score ≥ 65
Is restless and becomes bored
Is overactivated, as manifested in:
poor impulse control
aggression
mood instability
euphoria
excitability
sensation-seeking, risk-taking and other forms of undercontrolled behavior
Displays narcissistic personality features
May have a history of symptoms associated with manic or hypomanic episodes
Diagnostic Considerations
T score ≥ 65
Evaluate for narcissistic personality disorder
T score ≥ 75
Evaluate for:
cycling mood disorder
manic or hypomanic episode
schizoaffective disorder (if RC6 ≥ 70 or RC8 ≥ 70)
Treatment Considerations
T score ≥ 75
Excessive behavioral activation may interfere with treatment
Mood stabilization in initial stages of treatment as a target for intervention
May require inpatient treatment for hypomania
Need for mood-stabilizing medication should be evaluated

activation and engagement with his or her environment. The co-occurrence of a low RC9 score and an elevated RC2 score reflects a combination of pronounced anhedonia and behavioral disengagement that may signal a vegetative depressive state.

Interpretation of elevated RC9 scores can be facilitated by considering the test taker's results on two SP Scales specifically linked to RC9: Aggression (AGG) and Activation (ACT). Interpretive statements for RC9 are provided in Table 7-12.

SPECIFIC PROBLEMS SCALES

Most of the MMPI-2-RF SP Scales are intended to highlight important characteristics that are subsumed by or associated with one of the RC Scales but are not exclusively or directly targeted by that scale. However, it is important to note that the SP Scales are not limited to this auxiliary role and that their interpretive use does not require a particular score on an associated RC Scale. Data reported in the *MMPI-2-RF Technical Manual* indicate that the SP Scales are sufficiently valid to be interpreted as substantive measures in their own right.

On the basis of empirical analyses and conceptual considerations, the SP Scales have been organized into four subsets: Somatic/Cognitive, Internalizing, Externalizing, and Interpersonal.

Somatic/Cognitive Scales

Scores on the Somatic/Cognitive Scales should be interpreted in light of the test taker's results on three Validity Scales: Somatic Responses (Fs), Symptom Validity (FBS-r), and Response Bias Scale (RBS). As noted in Chapter 6, elevated scores on these measures indicate the possibility that the test taker overreported somatic (Fs, FBS-r) and cognitive (FBS-r, RBS) symptoms (see Tables 6-6–6-8). Elevations on these three scales do not indicate that the individual is knowingly overreporting. Such an inference requires extratest data indicative of intentionality and, in the case of malingering, an external incentive.

By contrast, in Somatoform Disorders, the patient genuinely experiences the distress and impairment associated with his or her complaints, even though the somatic symptoms he or she reports cannot be explained by a medical condition. Therefore, when the Fs, FBS-r, or RBS T score reaches or exceeds 100, the content-based statements for the Somatic/Cognitive Scales can be used to characterize the test taker's symptom presentation, but the (probabilistic) empirical correlates of these scales, particularly those reflecting actual physical and cognitive symptoms, should not be included in the interpretation.

Malaise (MLS)

MLS consists of eight items describing a generalized sense of poor health and physical debilitation. Its relation to the other three Somatic Scales (described next) is comparable to that of RCd to the eight other RC Scales; that is, the elevation on

Table 7-13. MLS (Malaise) Interpretation

Clinical Symptoms, Behavioral Tendencies, and Personality Characteristics

Test Responses

   T score < 39

      Reports a generalized sense of physical well-being

   T score 65–79

      Reports experiencing poor health and feeling weak or tired

   T score ≥ 80

      Reports a general sense of malaise manifested in poor health and feeling tired, weak, and incapacitated

Empirical Correlates

      Is preoccupied with poor health

      Likely to complain of:

      sleep disturbance

      fatigue

      low energy

      sexual dysfunction

Diagnostic Considerations

      If physical origin for malaise has been ruled out, evaluate for somatoform disorder

Treatment Considerations

      Malaise may impede his or her willingness or ability to engage in treatment

---

MLS provides an indication of the extent to which the test taker presented himself or herself as being physically incapacitated, while the remaining Somatic Scales indicate what types of somatic symptoms the test taker reported. In some instances, a test taker may produce an elevated score on MLS but not on RC1 or any of the other Somatic/Cognitive Scales. In such cases, he or she is likely to present with a vague, nonspecific preoccupation with poor physical health and fatigue. As is true for all the Somatic Scales, accurate interpretation of the MLS score is dependent on being adequately informed about the test taker's medical condition. It is particularly important to note that malaise, as defined and measured here, is a nonspecific manifestation of a broad range of acute and chronic medical conditions. Also noteworthy are findings that extremely high MLS scores are associated with noncredible symptom reporting in personal injury litigants. A low MLS score indicates that the test taker reported a generalized sense of physical well-being. Interpretive statements for scores on MLS are provided in Table 7-13.

Gastrointestinal Complaints (GIC)

GIC is composed of five items that describe various gastrointestinal problems, including poor appetite, nausea, vomiting, and recurring upset stomach. An elevated GIC score needs to be evaluated in light of extratest information, particularly whether any medical conditions have been verified that might account for at least some of

Table 7-14. GIC (Gastrointestinal Complaints) Interpretation

Clinical Symptoms, Behavioral Tendencies, and Personality Characteristics
Test Responses:
T score 65–89
Reports a number of gastrointestinal complaints
T score ≥ 90
Reports a large number of gastrointestinal complaints such as poor appetite, nausea, vomiting, and recurring upset stomach
Empirical Correlates:
Has a history of gastrointestinal problems
Is preoccupied with health concerns
Diagnostic Considerations
If physical origin for gastrointestinal complaints has been ruled out, evaluate for somatoform disorder
Treatment Considerations
Stress reduction for gastrointestinal complaints if stress-related

Table 7-15. HPC (Head Pain Complaints) Interpretation

Clinical Symptoms, Behavioral Tendencies, and Personality Characteristics
Test Responses
T score 65–79
Reports head pain
T score ≥ 80
Reports diffuse head and neck pain, recurring headaches, and developing head pain when upset
Empirical Correlates
Presents with multiple somatic complaints
Is prone to developing physical symptoms in response to stress
Is preoccupied with physical health problems
Complains about:
headaches
chronic pain
difficulty concentrating
Diagnostic Considerations
If physical origin for head pain complaints has been ruled out, evaluate for somatoform disorder
Treatment Considerations
Pain management for head pain complaints as a target for intervention

these symptoms. If this is ruled out, the symptoms may be stress related, suggesting that stress management might be considered in treatment planning. Interpretive recommendations for GIC are provided in Table 7-14.

Head Pain Complaints (HPC)

HPC includes six items that describe various complaints about head and neck pain. Elevated scores are associated with a preoccupation with pain-related difficulties as well as features of a Somatoform Disorder (e.g., presenting with a diffuse pattern of multiple somatic complaints and a tendency to develop physical symptoms in response to stress). As with all the Somatic Scales, interpretation of the HPC findings requires consideration of the individual's medical condition. If medical explanations of the complaints can be ruled out, pain management may be an appropriate treatment recommendation. These and other interpretive statements for HPC are presented in Table 7-15.

Neurological Complaints (NUC)

NUC consists of 10 items describing various problems that may be neurological in origin such as dizziness, numbness, weakness, and involuntary movement. Elevated scores need to be considered in light of the test taker's medical conditions. This may require a neuropsychological and/or neurological evaluation. If an underlying medical condition is ruled out, an elevated score on NUC, coupled with low scores on RC3 and SHY, may suggest the inference of a somatoform condition such as a Conversion Disorder. Interpretive recommendations for NUC are listed in Table 7-16.

Cognitive Complaints (COG)

COG consists of 10 items describing an assortment of cognitive difficulties, including memory problems, intellectual limitations, difficulty concentrating, and confusion. Elevated scores are empirically associated with concentration problems, complaints about memory, not coping well with stress, and low tolerance for frustration. Because elevated scores on FBS-r and RBS (see recommended levels and interpretive implications in Tables 6-7 and 6-8) are associated with an increased likelihood of noncredible reporting of cognitive difficulties, a test taker's COG score should be interpreted only after careful consideration of his or her score on these Validity Scales. In any event, COG scores reflect the extent to which a test taker presents with cognitive complaints. They do not predict, and should not be interpreted as measures of, actual cognitive functioning. Interpretive recommendations for COG are provided in Table 7-17.

Table 7-16. NUC (Neurological Complaints) Interpretation

Clinical Symptoms, Behavioral Tendencies, and Personality Characteristics
Test Responses
T score 65–91
Reports vague neurological complaints
T score ≥ 92
Reports a large number of vague neurological complaints (e.g., dizziness, loss of balance, numbness, weakness and paralysis, and loss of control over movement, including involuntary movement)
Empirical Correlates
Presents with multiple somatic complaints
Is preoccupied with physical health concerns
Is prone to developing physical symptoms in response to stress
Is likely to present with:
dizziness
coordination difficulties
sensory problems
Diagnostic Considerations
If physical origin for neurological complaints has been ruled out, evaluate for somatoform disorder (consider a conversion disorder if RC3 ≤ 39 and SHY ≤ 39)
Treatment Considerations
If physical origin for neurological complaints has been established, refer for medical and/or behavioral management

Table 7-17. COG (Cognitive Complaints) Interpretation

Clinical Symptoms, Behavioral Tendencies, and Personality Characteristics
Test Responses
T score 65–80
Reports a diffuse pattern of cognitive difficulties
T score ≥ 81
Reports a diffuse pattern of cognitive difficulties including memory problems, difficulties concentrating, intellectual limitations, and confusion
Empirical Correlates
Complains about memory problems
Has low tolerance for frustration
Experiences difficulties in concentration
Diagnostic Considerations
None
Treatment Considerations
Origin of cognitive complaints should be explored. This may require a neuropsychological evaluation.

Internalizing Scales

The nine Internalizing Scales measure aspects or inherent correlates of two RC Scales, Demoralization (RCd) and Dysfunctional Negative Emotions (RC7). Suicidal/Death Ideation (SUI), Helplessness/Hopelessness (HLP), Self-Doubt (SFD), and Inefficacy (NFC) assess various manifestations or correlates of RCd. Stress/Worry (STW), Anxiety (AXY), Anger Proneness (ANP), Behavior-Restricting Fears (BRF), and Multiple Specific Fears (MSF) measure facets of RC7. A strategy for incorporating findings on the Internalizing Scales when interpreting scores on RCd and RC7 is detailed and illustrated in Chapter 8.

As expected, the correlations between the scales within each subset are quite high. However, Appendix A of the *MMPI-2-RF Technical Manual* presents for each of these scales unique empirical correlates that are reflected in the interpretive recommendations that follow. As noted earlier, SP Scales are not merely aids to interpreting findings on other scales; they also serve as substantive measures. Low scores are interpretable for three of the Internalizing Scales: NFC, STW, and MSF.

Suicidal/Death Ideation (SUI)

SUI consists of five items that describe recent suicidal ideation or acts. Because endorsement of these items was rare in the MMPI-2-RF normative sample, a raw score of 1 on SUI is sufficient to produce an elevated score on the scale. As a result, the absence of elevation on SUI indicates that the test taker did not endorse any of the items that directly describe suicidal ideation. It does not indicate that the test taker is in fact free of suicidal ideation or intent. Correlate data reported in Appendix A of the *MMPI-2-RF Technical Manual* indicate that scores on SUI are strongly associated with recent suicidal ideation or attempts. Thus, an elevated score on this scale indicates the need for an immediate suicide risk assessment. SUI is one of the seven MMPI-2-RF scales identified as having critical content. Therefore, if the test taker's SUI score is elevated, the MMPI-2-RF Interpretive Report and Score Report print out all SUI items he or she answered in the keyed direction. Interpretive statements for SUI are presented in Table 7-18.

Helplessness/Hopelessness (HLP)

HLP is made up of five items describing beliefs that the individual is incapable of overcoming his or her problems and of making changes needed to reach his or her life goals. Elevated scores are associated with feeling that life is a strain and feeling hopeless, helpless, and overwhelmed; believing that one gets a raw deal from life; and lacking motivation for change. Since HLP is one of the scales designated as having critical content, items answered in the keyed direction are printed in the MMPI-2-RF Score Report and Interpretive Report whenever the test taker's HLP score is elevated. Interpretive statements for HLP are presented in Table 7-19.

Table 7-18. SUI (Suicide/Death Ideation) Interpretation

Clinical Symptoms, Behavioral Tendencies, and Personality Characteristics
Test Responses
T score 65–99
Reports a history of suicidal ideation and/or attempts
T score = 100
Reports current suicidal ideation and a history of suicidal ideation and attempts
Empirical Correlates
Is preoccupied with suicide and death
Is at risk for suicide attempt (this risk is exacerbated by poor impulse control if BXD or RC4 or RC9 or DISC-r ≥ 65 and/or by substance abuse if SUB ≥ 65)
May have recently attempted suicide
Helplessness and hopelessness
Diagnostic Considerations
None
Treatment Considerations
Risk for suicide should be assessed immediately

Table 7-19. HLP (Helplessness/Hopelessness) Interpretation

Clinical Symptoms, Behavioral Tendencies, and Personality Characteristics
Test Responses
T score 65–79
Reports feeling hopeless and pessimistic
T score ≥ 80
Reports believing he or she cannot change and overcome his or her problems and is incapable of reaching his or her life goals
Empirical Correlates
Feels hopeless and pessimistic
Feels overwhelmed and that life is a strain
Believes he or she cannot be helped
Believes he or she gets a raw deal from life
Lacks motivation for change
Diagnostic Considerations
None
Treatment Considerations
Loss of hope and feelings of despair as early targets for intervention

Self-Doubt (SFD)

SFD consists of four items that describe lack of confidence and feeling useless. Elevated scores are associated with poor self-esteem, feelings of inferiority, insecurity, and self-disparagement. These problems can be appropriate targets for intervention. Interpretive statements for SFD are provided in Table 7-20.

Inefficacy (NFC)

NFC includes nine items describing beliefs that one is incapable of making decisions and dealing effectively with major and minor crises. Low NFC scores indicate that the test taker described himself or herself as someone who wants to be in control and is self-reliant. Elevated scores indicate that faced with difficulties, the test taker is likely to be passive and lack self-reliance. High NFC scores are associated negatively with being power oriented. Interpretive statements for NFC are presented in Table 7-21.

Stress/Worry (STW)

STW includes seven items that describe experiences of stress and worry, including preoccupation with disappointments, difficulty with time pressure, and specific worries about misfortune and finances. A low STW score indicates a below average level of reported stress and worry and of proneness to manifest the stress- and worry-related characteristics just noted. Elevated scores are associated with being stress reactive, perceiving situations as stressful that others would not, being worry prone, and engaging in obsessive rumination. Interpretive statements for STW are provided in Table 7-22.

Anxiety (AXY)

AXY consists of five items describing experiences indicative of pervasive anxiety. Elevated AXY scores are correlated with significant anxiety and anxiety-related problems, intrusive ideation, sleep difficulties, and posttraumatic distress. Regarding the last correlate, an elevated AXY score does not in itself indicate exposure to trauma or its severity. However, among individuals who have been exposed to trauma, elevated AXY scores are associated substantially with symptoms of Posttraumatic Stress Disorder. Since AXY items were very rarely endorsed in the MMPI-2-RF normative sample, a raw AXY score of 2 corresponds to a T score with an interpretable elevation. Because the problems associated with elevated AXY scores may require immediate attention, the scale has been designated as having critical content. Therefore, if the test taker's AXY score is elevated, the items answered in the keyed direction are printed out in the MMPI-2-RF Score Report and Interpretive Report. Interpretive statements for AXY are provided in Table 7-23.

Table 7-20. SFD (Self-Doubt) Interpretation

Clinical Symptoms, Behavioral Tendencies, and Personality Characteristics

Test Responses

   T score 65–69

      Reports self-doubt

   T score ≥ 70

      Reports lacking confidence and feeling useless

Empirical Correlates

      Feels insecure and inferior

      Is self-disparaging

      Is prone to rumination

      Is intropunitive

      Presents with lack of confidence and feelings of uselessness

Diagnostic Considerations

   None

Treatment Considerations

   Low self-esteem and other manifestations of self-doubt as targets for intervention

Table 7-21. NFC (Inefficacy) Interpretation

Clinical Symptoms, Behavioral Tendencies, and Personality Characteristics

Test Responses

   T score < 39

      He or she did not endorse items indicating indecisiveness or ineffectualness

   T score 65–79

      Reports:

      Being passive, indecisive, and inefficacious

      Believing he or she is incapable of coping with current difficulties

   T score = 80

      Reports:

      Being very indecisive and inefficacious

      Believing he or she is incapable of making decisions and dealing effectively with crises

      Having difficulties when dealing with small, inconsequential matters

Empirical Correlates

   T score < 39

      He or she is likely to be self-reliant and power-oriented

   T score ≥ 65

      Is unlikely to be self-reliant

      Is passive

Diagnostic Considerations

   None

Treatment Considerations

   Indecisiveness may interfere with establishing treatment goals and progress in treatment

Table 7-22. STW (Stress/Worry) Interpretation

Clinical Symptoms, Behavioral Tendencies, and Personality Characteristics

Test Responses

T score < 39

Reports a below-average level of stress or worry

T score 65–79

Reports an above-average level of stress and worry

T score ≥ 80

Reports multiple problems involving experiences of stress and worry, including preoc-cupation with disappointments, difficulties with time pressure, and specific worries about misfortune and finances

Empirical Correlates

Is stress-reactive

Is worry-prone

Engages in obsessive rumination

Diagnostic Considerations

Evaluate for disorders involving excessive stress and worry such as obsessive–compulsive disorder

Treatment Considerations

Stress management and excessive worry and rumination as targets for intervention

Table 7-23. AXY (Anxiety) Interpretation

Clinical Symptoms, Behavioral Tendencies, and Personality Characteristics

Test Responses

T score 65–99

Reports feeling anxious

T score = 100

Reports feeling constantly anxious, often feeling that something dreadful is about to happen, being frightened by something every day, and having frequent nightmares

Empirical Correlates

Experiences:

Significant anxiety and anxiety-related problems

Intrusive ideation

Sleep difficulties, including nightmares

Posttraumatic distress

Diagnostic Considerations

Evaluate for anxiety-related disorders, including PTSD

Treatment Considerations

Need for anxiolytic medication should be evaluated (if AXY ≥ 80)

Anxiety as a target for intervention

Anger Proneness (ANP)

ANP consists of seven items describing anger and anger-related tendencies, including getting upset easily, being impatient with others, and becoming angered easily. Elevations on ANP are associated with anger problems such as temper tantrums and holding grudges. ANP content and correlates center on negative emotional experiences and expressions of anger rather than on aggressive acting out per se. The latter is more directly assessed by the Aggression (AGG) Scale. Interpretive statements for ANP are listed in Table 7-24.

Behavior-Restricting Fears (BRF)

BRF consists of nine items describing fears that significantly restrict the individual's normal activities inside and outside the home. It is associated empirically with agoraphobia and, more generally, with fearfulness. The behavior of individuals who produce high scores on this scale is likely to be significantly inhibited. An elevated BRF score indicates that behavior-restricting fears can be considered intervention targets. Interpretive statements for BRF are provided in Table 7-25.

Multiple Specific Fears (MSF)

MSF consists of nine items that describe seemingly distinct fears of various animals and acts of nature. In addition to being at risk for certain specific phobias, individuals who produce elevated scores on MSF are likely to be risk averse and harm avoidant. A low MSF score indicates that the test taker, having reported a lower-than-average number of fears, is less likely to have the characteristics associated empirically with this measure and may be quite comfortable in situations where she or he may be at risk for physical harm. Interpretive statements for MSF appear in Table 7-26.

Externalizing Scales

The four Externalizing Scales measure facets of two RC Scales, Antisocial Behavior (RC4) and Hypomanic Activation (RC9). The Juvenile Conduct Problems (JCP) and Substance Abuse (SUB) scales measure facets of RC4, whereas Aggression (AGG) and Activation (ACT) assess aspects of RC9. As is true of any SP Scale, the externalizing measures can help highlight the primary problems underlying elevated scores on the associated RC Scales, but they are also fully interpretable when the RC Scales in question are not elevated. For example, if a test taker produces a moderate elevation on RC4, an elevated score on JCP, but no elevation on SUB or the Family Problems (FML) Interpersonal Scale, interpretation of the elevated RC4 score would emphasize the features associated with a history of juvenile misconduct and deemphasize features related to substance abuse and family dysfunction. Even if the RC4 score falls within the normal range, elevated scores on JCP or SUB remain interpretable. For two of the Externalizing Scales, AGG and ACT, low scores are also interpretable.

Table 7-24. ANP (Anger-Proneness) Interpretation

Clinical Symptoms, Behavioral Tendencies, and Personality Characteristics
Test Responses
T score 65–79
Reports being anger prone
T score = 80
Reports getting upset easily, being impatient with others, becoming easily angered, and sometimes even being overcome by anger
Empirical Correlates
Has problems with:
anger
irritability
low tolerance for frustration
Holds grudges
Has temper tantrums
Is argumentative
Diagnostic Considerations
Evaluate for anger-related disorders
Treatment Considerations
Anger management as a target for intervention

Table 7-25. BRF (Behavior-Restricting Fears) Interpretation

Clinical Symptoms, Behavioral Tendencies, and Personality Characteristics
Test Responses
T score 65–89
Reports multiple fears that significantly restrict normal activity in and outside the home
T score ≥ 90
Reports multiple fears that significantly restrict normal activity in and outside the home, including fears of leaving home, open spaces, small spaces, the dark, dirt, sharp objects, and handling money
Empirical Correlates
Agoraphobia
Fearfulness
Diagnostic Considerations
Evaluate for anxiety disorders, particularly agoraphobia
Treatment Considerations
Behavior-restricting fears as targets for intervention

Table 7-26. MSF (Multiple Specific Fears) Interpretation

Clinical Symptoms, Behavioral Tendencies, and Personality Characteristics
Test Responses
T score < 39
Reports a lower-than-average number of specific fears
T score 65–77
Reports multiple specific fears of certain animals and acts of nature
T score = 78
Reports multiple specific fears such as blood, fire, thunder, water, natural disasters, spiders, mice, and other animals
Empirical Correlates
Risk averse
Harm avoidant
Diagnostic Considerations
Evaluate for specific phobias
Treatment Considerations
Specific fears as targets for intervention

To reiterate a point made earlier, if Validity Scale scores suggest that under-reporting is likely, nonelevated scores on the Substantive Scales, in particular the Externalizing Scales, cannot be interpreted as indicating that a test taker is unlikely to act out or experience other difficulties associated with these measures. Moreover, in cases in which the underreporting measures do not reach interpretable levels, if nonelevated scores on the Externalizing Scales contradict extratest evidence of problems (e.g., if an individual has a documented history of and ongoing problems associated with substance abuse but produces a nonelevated SUB score), in them-selves, these findings point to a circumscribed pattern of underreporting.

Juvenile Conduct Problems (JCP)

JCP consists of six items describing a juvenile history of undesirable school con-duct, stealing, and being negatively influenced by peers. Elevated JCP scores are associated with both juvenile delinquency and current acting out. If JCP is the only elevated behavioral dysfunction indicator (i.e., BXD, RC4, RC9, SUB, AGG, ACT, AGGR-r, and DISC-r are all within normal limits), the overall configuration may characterize a test taker who acknowledges a history of juvenile misconduct but no longer engages in acting-out behaviors. Interpretive statements for JCP appear in Table 7-27.

Substance Abuse (SUB)

SUB consists of seven items describing significant past or current substance abuse, with most of the item content focusing on alcohol abuse. Elevated scores are associated

Table 7-27. JCP (Juvenile Conduct Problems) Interpretation

Clinical Symptoms, Behavioral Tendencies, and Personality Characteristics
Test Responses
T score 65–79
Reports a history of problematic behavior at school
T score > 80
Reports a history of juvenile conduct problems such as problematic behavior at school, stealing, and being influenced negatively by peers
Empirical Correlates
Has a history of juvenile delinquency and criminal and antisocial behavior
Experiences conflictual interpersonal relationships
Engages in acting-out behavior
Has difficulties with individuals in positions of authority
Has difficulties trusting others
Diagnostic Considerations
Evaluate for externalizing disorders, particularly antisocial personality disorder
Treatment Considerations
None

with a substantially increased risk for substance abuse, including both alcohol and drugs, impaired functioning as a result of substance abuse, and a general sensation-seeking tendency. A nonelevated SUB score indicates denial if the test taker is known to be currently involved in substance abuse, another illustration of the importance of integrating extratest information in MMPI-2-RF interpretation. As just discussed, in this scenario, the nonelevated SUB score can itself be interpreted as evidence of underreporting, at least insofar as substance misuse is concerned. Because the problems associated with an elevated SUB score may require immediate attention, the scale has been identified as having critical content. Therefore, if the test taker's SUB score is elevated, the items answered in the keyed direction will be printed in the MMPI-2-RF Score Report and Interpretive Report. Interpretive statements for SUB are presented in Table 7-28.

Aggression (AGG)

AGG consists of nine items describing physically aggressive behavior. Although low AGG scores generally indicate a below-average level of aggressive behavior, this interpretation does not apply if the Validity Scales indicate underreporting. Individuals with elevated AGG scores are likely to have a history of violence and interpersonal abusiveness. Because problems associated with elevated AGG scores may require immediate attention, the scale has been identified as having critical content. Accordingly, if the test taker's AGG score is elevated, the MMPI-2-RF Score Report and Interpretive Report will print all AGG items that were answered in the keyed direction. Interpretive statements for AGG are listed in Table 7-29.

Table 7-28. SUB (Substance Abuse) Interpretation

Clinical Symptoms, Behavioral Tendencies, and Personality Characteristics
Test Responses
T score 65–79
Reports significant past and current substance abuse
T score ≥ 80
Reports:
A significant history of substance abuse
Current substance abuse
Frequent use of alcohol and drugs
Using alcohol to "relax and open up"
Empirical Correlates
Has a history of problematic use of alcohol or drugs
Has had legal problems as a result of substance abuse
Is sensation-seeking
Diagnostic Considerations
Evaluate for substance-use-related disorders
Treatment Considerations
Reduction or cessation of substance abuse as a target for intervention

Table 7-29. AGG (Aggression) Interpretation

Clinical Symptoms, Behavioral Tendencies, and Personality Characteristics
Test Responses
T score < 39
Reports a below-average level of aggressive behavior
T score 65–79
Reports engaging in physically aggressive, violent behavior and losing control
T score ≥ 80
Reports engaging in physically aggressive, violent behavior, including explosive behavior, physical altercations, and enjoying intimidating others
Empirical Correlates
Has a history of violent behavior toward others
Is abusive
Experiences anger-related problems
Diagnostic Considerations
Evaluate for disorders associated with interpersonal aggression
Treatment Considerations
Reduction in interpersonally aggressive behavior as a target for intervention

Activation (ACT)

ACT consists of eight items describing experiences of heightened excitation and energy level, uncontrollable mood swings, and lack of sleep. A low ACT score indicates that the test taker reported a below-average level of energy and activation. Elevated ACT scores are associated with a history of manic or hypomanic episodes and a current high level of activation. The possibility that some of the experiences described by the ACT items are substance induced should be considered when weighing the diagnostic and treatment implications of an elevated score. Interpretive statements for ACT appear in Table 7-30.

Interpersonal Scales

The content and correlates of most, possibly all, MMPI-2-RF Substantive Scales include aspects that describe or have implications for interpersonal functioning. For example, individuals with elevated scores on RC2 are likely to be socially disengaged, those with elevations on RC6 are likely to experience interpersonal difficulties as a consequence of their persecutory beliefs, and those with high SUB scores are likely to experience impairment in social functioning as a result of substance abuse. For the five SP Scales designated Interpersonal Scales—Family Problems (FML), Interpersonal Passivity (IPP), Social Avoidance (SAV), Shyness (SHY), and Disaffiliativeness (DSF)—interpersonal functioning is the primary focus. Four of the scales (FML, IPP, SAV, and SHY) have both high and low scores that are interpretable as nonaverage.

Family Problems (FML)

FML consists of 10 items describing negative family experiences, including quarrels, dislike of family members, feeling unappreciated, and feeling that family members cannot be counted on in times of need. A low FML score indicates that the test taker reported a comparatively conflict-free family environment. Elevated FML scores are associated with poor family relations: conflicts with and negative feelings about one's family members and blaming them for one's difficulties. Most of the FML items can apply to the test taker's current family and to his or her family of origin; a smaller number refer specifically (directly or indirectly) to the family of origin. It is not possible to determine based on the FML score alone whether the test taker's familial dysfunction is limited to family of origin, current family, or both. Interpretive statements for FML are provided in Table 7-31.

Interpersonal Passivity (IPP)

IPP is made up of 10 items keyed in a direction describing unassertive, passive, submissive behavior; failure to stand up for oneself; not having strong opinions; and not liking to be in charge. It is a good example of an MMPI-2-RF scale for which meaningful findings are associated bidirectionally with deviations from the

Table 7-30. ACT (Activation) Interpretation

Clinical Symptoms, Behavioral Tendencies, and Personality Characteristics
Test Responses
T score < 39
Reports a below-average level of energy and activation
T score 65–79
Reports episodes of heightened excitation and energy level
T score > 80
Reports episodes of heightened excitation and energy level, uncontrollable mood swings, and lack of sleep
Empirical Correlates
Experiencing excessive activation
Has a history of manic or hypomanic episodes (if ACT ≥ 80)
Diagnostic Considerations
Evaluate for manic or hypomanic episodes or other conditions associated with excessive energy and activation
Treatment Considerations
Need for mood-stabilizing medication should be evaluated
Excessive behavioral activation may interfere with treatment

Table 7-31. FML (Family Problems) Interpretation

Clinical Symptoms, Behavioral Tendencies, and Personality Characteristics
Test Responses
T score < 39
Reports a comparatively conflict-free past and current family environment
T score 65–79
Reports conflictual family relationships and lack of support from family members
T score ≥ 80
Reports conflictual family relationships and lack of support from family members. Negative family attitudes and experiences include frequent quarrels, dislike of family members, feeling unappreciated by family members, and feeling that family members cannot be counted on in time of need.
Empirical Correlates
Has family conflicts
Experiences poor family functioning
Has strong negative feelings about family members
Blames family members for his or her difficulties
Diagnostic Considerations
None
Treatment Considerations
Family problems as targets for intervention

Table 7-32. IPP (Interpersonal Passivity) Interpretation

Clinical Symptoms, Behavioral Tendencies, and Personality Characteristics

Test Responses

   T score < 39

      Describes him- or herself as:

      having strong opinions

      standing up for him- or herself

      being assertive and direct

      being able to lead others

   T score 65–79

      Reports being unassertive

   T score ≥ 80

      Reports:

      being unassertive and submissive

      not liking to be in charge

      failing to stand up for him- or herself

      being ready to give in to others

Empirical Correlates

   T score < 39

      Believes he or she has leadership capabilities but is likely to be viewed by others as domineering, self-centered, and possibly grandiose

   T score ≥ 65

      Is passive and submissive in interpersonal relationships

      Is overcontrolled

Diagnostic Considerations

   T score ≥ 65

      Evaluate for disorders characterized by passive-submissive behavior such as dependent personality disorder

   T score ≤ 38

      Evaluate for features associated with narcissistic personality disorder

Treatment Considerations

      Reducing passive, submissive behavior as a target for intervention norm. Low IPP scores indicate that the test taker sees himself or herself as having leadership capabilities and that he or she seeks to take charge of situations but is likely to be viewed by others as domineering, self-centered, and possibly grandiose. Elevated IPP scores are associated with passivity and with being submissive and behaviorally overcontrolled. High scorers prefer not to be in charge. Interpretive statements for IPP appear in Table 7-32.

Social Avoidance (SAV)

SAV consists of 10 items keyed to indicate that the respondent does not enjoy social events and avoids social situations. A low SAV score indicates the opposite: that the test taker is outgoing, is gregarious, and enjoys social situations. Elevated SAV scores are associated with social introversion and being emotionally restricted and with having difficulties forming close relationships. An elevated SAV score coupled with a nonelevated score on SHY is an indication that the test taker's social avoidance is linked not so much to social anxiety as to an avoidant personality style, particularly if in addition to SAV, SFD and NFC are elevated. Interpretive statements for SAV appear in Table 7-33.

Shyness (SHY)

SHY consists of seven items describing various manifestations of social anxiety, including being easily embarrassed and feeling uncomfortable around others. A low SHY score indicates relative absence of social anxiety, which is a normal-range personality characteristic, although it is associated with psychopathy and Conversion Disorder when combined with certain other qualities. Elevated SHY scores are associated with social introversion and inhibition, feeling anxious in social situations, and the possibility that the test taker may meet diagnostic criteria for Social Phobia. Interpretive statements for SHY are presented in Table 7-34.

Disaffiliativeness (DSF)

DSF consists of six items describing, if answered as keyed, a respondent who dislikes people and being around them, has never had a close relationship, and prefers being alone. Elevated DSF scores are associated with being asocial. When the DSF score is extremely high (a T score of 100), it may be one of the indications of Schizoid Personality Disorder. Interpretive statements for DSF are presented in Table 7-35.

INTEREST SCALES

The MMPI-2-RF Interest Scales were derived from Clinical Scale 5, Masculinity/Femininity, which was originally labeled the "Interest Scale." Research on various measures of masculinity and femininity has resulted in the identification of two relatively independent dimensions rather than a single bipolar construct. Consistent with these findings, analyses of Clinical Scale 5 have revealed the two relatively

Table 7-33. SAV (Social Avoidance) Interpretation

Clinical Symptoms, Behavioral Tendencies, and Personality Characteristics

Test Responses

T score < 39

Reports enjoying social situations and events

T score 65–79

Reports not enjoying social events and avoiding social situations

T score = 80

Reports not enjoying social events and avoiding social situations, including parties and other events where crowds are likely to gather

Empirical Correlates

T score < 39

Likely to be perceived as outgoing and gregarious

T score ≥ 65

Is introverted

Has difficulty forming close relationships

Is emotionally restricted

Diagnostic Considerations

T Score > 65

Evaluate for disorders associated with social avoidance such as avoidant personality disorder

Treatment Considerations

Difficulties associated with social avoidance as a target for intervention

Table 7-34. SHY (Shyness) Interpretation

Clinical Symptoms, Behavioral Tendencies, and Personality Characteristics

Test Responses

T score < 39

Reports little or no social anxiety

T score ≥ 65

Reports being shy, easily embarrassed, and uncomfortable around others

Empirical Correlates

Is socially introverted and inhibited

Is anxious and nervous in social situations

Is generally anxious

Diagnostic Considerations

Evaluate for social phobia

Treatment Considerations

Anxiety in social situations as a target for intervention

Table 7-35. DSF (Disaffiliativeness) Interpretation

Clinical Symptoms, Behavioral Tendencies, and Personality Characteristics
Test Responses
T score 65–79
Reports disliking people and being around them
T score 80–99
Reports disliking people and being around them, preferring to be alone
T score = 100
Reports disliking people and being around others, preferring to be alone, and never having had a close relationship
Empirical Correlates
Is asocial
Diagnostic Considerations
Evaluate for schizoid personality disorder (if DSF T score = 100)
Treatment Considerations
His or her aversive response to close relationships may make it difficult to form a therapeutic alliance and achieve progress in treatment

Table 7-36. AES (Aesthetic–Literary Interests) Interpretation

Clinical Symptoms, Behavioral Tendencies, and Personality Characteristics
Test Responses
T score < 39
Reports no interest in activities or occupations of an aesthetic or literary nature (e.g., writing, music, the theater)
T score ≥ 65
Reports an above-average interest in activities or occupations of an aesthetic or literary nature (e.g., writing, music, the theater)
Empirical Correlates
Is empathic
Is sentient
Diagnostic Considerations
None
Treatment Considerations
Lack of outside interests as a target for intervention (if T score on both AES and MEC < 39)

independent dimensions represented by the Aesthetic–Literary Interests (AES) and Mechanical–Physical Interests (MEC) scales.

Low scores on these two scales are interpretable. If scores on both AES and MEC are low, this is an indication that the test taker lacks outside interests and may be psychologically disengaged from his or her environment. This pattern is sometimes found in individuals experiencing significant problems with depression, which would be indicated by elevated scores on RCd and RC2.

Table 7-37. MEC (Mechanical–Physical Interests) Interpretation

Clinical Symptoms, Behavioral Tendencies, and Personality Characteristics
Test Responses
T score < 39
Reports no interest in activities or occupations of a mechanical or physical nature (e.g., fixing and building things, the outdoors, sports)
T score 65–77
Reports an above-average interest in activities or occupations of a mechanical or physical nature (e.g., fixing and building things, the outdoors, sports)
T score = 78
Reports a well-above-average interest in activities or occupations of a mechanical or physical nature (e.g., fixing and building things, the outdoors, sports)
Empirical Correlates
Is adventure-seeking
Is sensation-seeking
Diagnostic Considerations
None
Treatment Considerations
Lack of outside interests as a target for intervention (if T score on both AES and MEC < 39)

Aesthetic–Literary Interests (AES)

AES consists of seven items describing interests in activities or occupations of an aesthetic or literary nature such as writing, music, the theater, and the arts. A low AES score is an indication of no expressed interest in aesthetic and/or literary activities. Elevated scores are associated with empathy and sentience (i.e., being appreciative of and responsive to sensory experiences). Interpretive statements for AES appear in Table 7-36.

Mechanical–Physical Interests (MEC)

MEC consists of nine items describing an interest in activities or occupations of a mechanical or physical nature such as fixing and building things, the outdoors, and sports. A low MEC score is an indication of no expressed interest in mechanical and/or physical activities. An elevated MEC score indicates that the test taker is likely to be adventure- and sensation-seeking. Interpretive statements for MEC are presented in Table 7-37.

PERSONALITY PSYCHOPATHOLOGY FIVE SCALES

The MMPI-2-RF PSY-5 Scales are updated versions of five MMPI-2 scales embodying Harkness and McNulty's (1994) dimensional model of personality pathology. The conceptualization and analyses that yielded these revised scales are described in

Chapter 3. The PSY-5 Scales provide a temperament-oriented perspective on major dimensions of personality pathology linking the MMPI-2-RF to the Five Factor Model of personality and to dimensional perspectives on Axis II disorders. For all five scales, both low and high scores are interpretable.

Aggressiveness–Revised (AGGR-r)

AGGR-r consists of 18 items describing aggressively assertive behavior. Low AGGR-r scores indicate that the test taker is likely to be passive and submissive. Elevated scores are associated with instrumental aggressiveness (i.e., behavior designed to accomplish a desired goal, as opposed to being reactive).

AGGR-r is negatively correlated with the Agreeability dimension of the Five Factor Model of personality but focuses more strongly on dysfunctional manifestations. With respect to personality pathology, elevated AGGR-r scores are associated with features of *DSM-IV* Cluster B disorders, in particular with narcissistic and antisocial. Among the MMPI-2-RF scales, AGGR-r is most strongly (and negatively) correlated with IPP. Interpretive statements for AGGR-r appear in Table 7-38.

Psychoticism–Revised (PSYC-r)

PSYC-r consists of 26 items describing a variety of experiences associated with peculiarities of thought and perception. A low PSYC-r score reflects an absence of reported thought disturbance. Elevated scores are associated with unusual perceptual experiences and thoughts and with being alienated from others.

PSYC-r does not have a clear counterpart in the Five Factor Model of personality, although it has been linked by default to certain conceptions of the Openness dimension. With regard to personality pathology, elevated scores are associated with features of the *DSM-IV* Cluster A disorders, in particular with schizotypal and paranoid. Among the MMPI-2-RF scales, the highest correlation of PSYC-r is with THD. Interpretive statements for PSYC-r are provided in Table 7-39.

Disconstraint–Revised (DISC-r)

DISC-r consists of 20 items describing a variety of manifestations of disconstrained behavior. Low DISC-r scores indicate a relatively high level of behavioral constraint. Elevated scores are associated with poor impulse control, acting out, and sensation and excitement seeking.

DISC-r is a particularly effective measure of impulsive behavior in comparison with other MMPI-2-RF Externalizing Scales. Individuals who produce elevated DISC-r scores have significant difficulty reining in their impulses. How this manifests behaviorally will depend on the nature of the individual's impulses, indications of which may be found with other MMPI-2-RF measures. For example, an elevation on SUI coupled with a high DISC-r score indicates an increased risk that the test taker will act on her or his suicidal thoughts.

DISC-r is (negatively) correlated with the Conscientiousness dimension of the Five

Table 7-38. AGGR-r (Aggressiveness–Revised) Interpretation

Clinical Symptoms, Behavioral Tendencies, and Personality Characteristics

Test Responses

T score < 39

   Reports being interpersonally passive and submissive

T score ≥ 65

   Reports being interpersonally aggressive and assertive

Empirical Correlates

T score < 39

   Is passive and submissive in interpersonal relationships

T score ≥ 65

   Is overly assertive and socially dominant

   Engages in instrumentally aggressive behavior

   Believes he or she has leadership capabilities

   Is viewed by others as domineering

Diagnostic Considerations

   Evaluate for Cluster B personality disorders

Treatment Considerations

   Reduction of interpersonally aggressive behavior as a target for intervention

Table 7-39. PSYC-r (Psychoticism–Revised) Interpretation

Clinical Symptoms, Behavioral Tendencies, and Personality Characteristics

Test Responses

T score < 39

   Reports no experiences of thought disturbance

T score ≥ 65

   Reports various experiences associated with thought dysfunction

Empirical Correlates

T Score ≥ 65

   Experiences unusual thought processes and perceptual phenomena

   Is alienated from others

   Engages in unrealistic thinking

   Presents with impaired reality testing

Diagnostic Considerations

   Evaluate for Cluster A personality disorders

Treatment Considerations

   Thought dysfunction as a target for intervention

Table 7-40. DISC-r (Disconstraint–Revised) Interpretation

Clinical Symptoms, Behavioral Tendencies, and Personality Characteristics
Test Responses
T score < 39
Reports overly constrained behavior
T score ≥ 65
Reports various manifestations of disconstrained behavior
Empirical Correlates
Is behaviorally disconstrained
Engages in acting-out behaviors
Acts out impulsively
Is sensation- and excitement-seeking
Diagnostic Considerations
Evaluate for Cluster B personality disorders
Treatment Considerations
Unlikely to be internally motivated for treatment
Is at significant risk for treatment noncompliance
Inadequate impulse control as a target for intervention

Factor Model of personality, but with a stronger focus on dysfunctional behavior. Among the personality disorders, elevated DISC-r scores are associated primarily with features of *DSM-IV* Cluster B disorders, in particular with antisocial and borderline. Of the MMPI-2-RF scales, the highest DISC-r correlation is with BXD. Interpretive statements for DISC-r are presented in Table 7-40.

Negative Emotionality/Neuroticism–Revised (NEGE-r)

NEGE-r consists of 20 items describing a wide range of negative emotional experiences. Low NEGE-r scores indicate that the test taker reported not being prone to experiencing negative emotions. Elevated scores are associated with negative emotions, such as anxiety, insecurity, and worry, as well as with a general tendency to catastrophize and expect the worst to happen. NEGE-r is associated with the Neuroticism dimension of the Five Factor Model of personality. Among the personality disorders, elevated NEGE-r scores are associated with features of *DSM-IV* Cluster C disorders, in particular with dependent and obsessive–compulsive. Of the MMPI-2-RF scales, the highest NEGE-r correlation is with RC7. Interpretive statements for NEGE-r are provided in Table 7-41.

Introversion/Low Positive Emotionality–Revised (INTR-r)

INTR-r consists of 20 items describing a lack of positive emotional experiences and avoidance of social situations and interactions. Low INTR-r scores indicate that the test taker is disposed to being socially engaged and to experiencing a wide range

Table 7-41. NEGE-r (Negative Emotionality/Neuroticism–Revised) Interpretation

Clinical Symptoms, Behavioral Tendencies, and Personality Characteristics
Test Responses
T score < 39
Reports a below-average level of negative emotional experiences
T score ≥ 65
Reports various negative emotional experiences
Empirical Correlates
Experiences various negative emotions including:
anxiety
insecurity
worry
Is inhibited behaviorally because of negative emotions
Is self-critical and guilt-prone
Experiences intrusive ideation
Diagnostic Considerations
Evaluate for Cluster C personality disorders
Treatment Considerations
Emotional difficulties may motivate him or her for treatment
Need for anxiolytic medication should be evaluated
His or her focus on negative information as a target for intervention

of positive emotions. Elevated scores are associated with social introversion, anhedonia, restricted interests, and a pessimistic outlook.

INTR-r is associated (negatively) with the Extraversion dimension of the Five Factor Model of personality. Among the personality disorders, elevated INTR-r scores are associated with features of *DSM-IV* Cluster C disorders, in particular with avoidant. Of the MMPI-2-RF scales, the highest INTR-r correlation is with RC2. Interpretive statements for INTR-r are listed in Table 7-42.

Table 7-42. INTR-r (Introversion/Low Positive Emotions) Interpretation

Clinical Symptoms, Behavioral Tendencies, and Personality Characteristics
Test Responses
T score < 39
Reports feeling energetic and having many positive emotional experiences
T score ≥ 65
Reports:
a lack of positive emotional experiences
avoiding social situations
Empirical Correlates
Lacks positive emotional experiences
Experiences significant problems with anhedonia
Complains about depression
Lacks interests
Is pessimistic
Is socially introverted
Diagnostic Considerations
Evaluate for Cluster C personality disorders
Treatment Considerations
Need for antidepressant medication should be evaluated
Lack of positive emotions may interfere with engagement in therapy

CHAPTER 8

Interpreting the MMPI-2-RF: Recommended Framework and Process

This chapter describes and illustrates a recommended framework and process for MMPI-2-RF interpretation. Test users who follow the procedures spelled out in this chapter should produce reasonably similar interpretations of the same set of scores. This is a desirable outcome in any evaluation, and a necessary one in some settings (e.g., forensic), where discordant interpretations of the same protocol can raise significant questions about the credibility of the interpreter and the test. The chapter begins with a description of a recommended framework for organizing MMPI-2-RF findings and then describes a process for integrating the scale-by-scale interpretive statements provided in Chapters 6 and 7. Case examples are used to illustrate how this information can serve as a starting point for generating a narrative interpretation of the test results.

USING THE MMPI-2-RF INTERPRETATION WORKSHEET

Table 8-1 provides a recommended framework for organizing MMPI-2-RF findings and identifies the sources of information (the MMPI-2-RF scale scores) relevant to each of the domains assessed with the test. This framework is incorporated in the MMPI-2-RF interpretation worksheet, which is reproduced in Figure 8-1. By following the process described in this chapter, an MMPI-2-RF user can generate a worksheet that provides the same interpretive statements that would be found for a given protocol in an MMPI-2-RF interpretive report. Whether relying on the worksheet or the interpretive report, the process recommended in this chapter calls for the MMPI-2-RF user to generate her or his own interpretation of the test results by integrating test findings with extratest information in the context of the referral issues.

Because of the inherent limitations of self-report-based assessment, the first step in any interpretation is to appraise the validity of the test protocol. Therefore, the first part of the recommended framework for MMPI-2-RF interpretation presented in Table 8-1 is intended to facilitate consideration of scores on the Validity Scales. If the analysis of protocol validity indicates that interpretation of scores on the Substantive Scales is warranted, the Substantive Scales section of the framework presents the eight domains addressed: Somatic/Cognitive Dysfunction, Emotional Dysfunction, Thought Dysfunction, Behavioral Dysfunction, Interpersonal Functioning, Interests, Diagnostic Considerations, and Treatment Considerations. The placement of Somatic/Cognitive Dysfunction immediately following the protocol

Table 8-1. Recommended Framework and Sources of Information for MMPI-2-RF Interpretation

Domains	MMPI-2-RF sources
I. Protocol validity	
a. Content nonresponsiveness	CNS, VRIN-r, TRIN-r
b. Overreporting	F-r, Fp-r, Fs, FBS-r, RBS
c. Underreporting	L-r, K-r
II. Substantive Scale findings	
a. Somatic/cognitive dysfunction	RC1, MLS, GIC, HPC, NUC, COG
b. Emotional dysfunction	EID, RCd, RC2, RC7, SUI, HLP, SFD, NFC, STW, AXY, ANP, BRF, MSF, NEGE-r, INTR-r
c. Thought dysfunction	THD, RC6, RC8, PSYC-r
d. Behavioral dysfunction	BXD, RC4, RC9, JCP, SUB, AGG, ACT, AGGR-r, DISC-r
e. Interpersonal functioning	FML, RC3, IPP, SAV, SHY, DSF, INTR-r
f. Interests	AES, MEC
g. Diagnostic considerations	Most Substantive Scales
h. Treatment recommendations	All Substantive Scales

validity section reflects the need to consider the possible impact of somatoform psychopathology on MMPI-2-RF Substantive Scale scores, in effect providing a bridge between the Validity and Substantive Scales.

As illustrated later, when writing a narrative report of MMPI-2-RF findings, the first four domains can be addressed according to their relative prominence in the protocol. For example, when findings indicate that symptoms related to Emotional Dysfunction are likely to be the most prominent in a particular case, this topic would be addressed first, and scores on all the scales listed under this domain in Table 8-1 would be interpreted at this point. Typically, Interpersonal Functioning and Interests will be discussed in a report after the first four domains have been addressed.

The seventh and eighth domains in the Substantive Scale section of the framework deal with Diagnostic and Treatment Considerations, which are relevant when the MMPI-2-RF is administered in clinical settings. These sections may be replaced or augmented with other salient topics in nonclinical settings. For example, in personnel screening, possible risk factors associated with hiring a candidate (e.g., poor impulse control) can be identified; in correctional settings, factors associated with the potential for causing harm to self and others may be suggested for follow-up evaluation.

Use of the worksheet is discussed and illustrated in the following sections, beginning with the Validity Scales.

MMPI-2-RF® Interpretation Worksheet

Protocol Validity

Content Non-Responsiveness   CNS _____   VRIN-r _____   TRIN-r _____

_____

_____

_____

_____

_____

_____

Overreporting   F-r _____   Fp-r _____   Fs _____   FBS-r _____   RBS _____

_____

_____

_____

_____

_____

_____

_____

_____

Underreporting   L-r _____   K-r _____

_____

_____

_____

_____

_____

Figure 8-1. MMPI-2-RF interpretation worksheet.

Substantive Scale Interpretation

Somatic/Cognitive Dysfunction   RC1 ____   GIC ____   NUC ____

MLS ____   HPC ____   COG ____

_____

_____

_____

_____

_____

_____

_____

Emotional Dysfunction   EID ____   RCd ____   RC2 ____   RC7 ____

SUI ____   INT-r ____   STW ____

HLP ____   AXY ____

SFD ____   ANP ____

NFC ____   BRF ____

MSF ____

NEGE-r ____

_____

_____

_____

_____

_____

_____

_____

_____

_____

Figure 8-1. MMPI-2-RF interpretation worksheet, continued.

Thought Dysfunction   THD _____   RC6 _____   RC8 _____   PSYC-r _____

_____

_____

_____

_____

_____

_____

_____

Behavioral Dysfunction   BXD _____   RC4 _____   RC9 _____   AGGR-r_____

JCP _____   AGG _____   DISC-r _____

SUB _____   ACT _____

_____

_____

_____

_____

_____

_____

_____

_____

Interpersonal Functioning:

FML _____   RC3 _____   IPP _____   SAV _____   SHY _____   DSF _____

_____

_____

_____

_____

_____

_____

Figure 8-1. MMPI-2-RF interpretation worksheet, continued.

Interests: AES _____   MEC _____

_____

_____

_____

Diagnostic Considerations

_____

_____

_____

_____

_____

_____

_____

_____

_____

Treatment Considerations

_____

_____

_____

_____

_____

_____

_____

_____

_____

_____

_____

Figure 8-1. MMPI-2-RF interpretation worksheet, continued.

Validity Scale Interpretation

Figure 8-2 demonstrates use of the Validity Scale page of the worksheet with the profile provided in Figure 8-3. Scores for Cannot Say (CNS) and the nine Validity Scales are recorded on the worksheet first. Next, Tables 6-1–6-10 are consulted to generate the typed statements in Figure 8-2. For example, the first statement in the underreporting section, "Underreporting is reflected in the test taker presenting himself in an extremely positive light by denying many minor faults and short-comings that most people acknowledge," appears in Table 6-9 under the heading "Protocol Validity Concerns" for Uncommon Virtues (L-r) T scores greater than or equal to 80.

The completed worksheet can then serve as a starting point for generating a nar-rative report of the Validity Scale findings, which would combine the statements in Figure 8-2 with relevant extratest information. For example, if the individual who produced this Validity Scale profile was evaluated in the context of preemployment screening as a candidate for a public safety position, the following interpretation could be provided:

> Mr. X's scores on the MMPI-2-RF validity scales indicate that he responded to all the items and did so in a remarkably consistent manner. There is no evidence of overreporting. However, there is very substantial evidence of underreporting. Mr. X portrayed himself in an extremely positive light by de-nying minor faults and shortcomings that most people acknowledge. He also presented as being remarkably well adjusted. Owing to substantial findings of marked underreporting, the absence of problematic findings on the Substan-tive Scales cannot be relied on to rule out significant psychological dysfunction in Mr. X, which was the purpose of this evaluation. His test-taking approach raises significant concerns about Mr. X's cooperation with this assessment.

In this example, after reporting the test findings, the narrative discusses the impli-cations of an extremely guarded test-taking approach for evaluating a candidate for a public safety position.

Substantive Scale Interpretation

Use of the worksheet in the interpretation of MMPI-2-RF Substantive Scale scores is illustrated with the case of Mr. B, a 47-year-old married man who was admitted for inpatient treatment with complaints of depression and suicidal ideation. He had recently lost his job and was experiencing financial and marital difficulties. Mr. B's MMPI-2-RF Score Report is reproduced in Figure 8-4. As shown on page 2 of the report (the first page of Figure 8-4), Mr. B's Validity Scale scores were within normal limits and need not be considered in detail. His scores on the Substantive Scales are profiled on pages 3–6 of the report, and scores on all 51 scales are sum-marized on page 7 (the sixth page of Figure 8-4). These scores are transcribed to

MMPI-2-RF® Interpretation Worksheet

Protocol Validity

Content Non-Responsiveness   CNS 0   VRIN-r 34   TRIN-r 50

The test taker provided scorable responses to all 338 items.

There is evidence of remarkably consistent responding.

There is no evidence of content-inconsistent fixed responding.

Overreporting   F-r 42   Fp-r 42   Fs 42   FBS-r 51   RBS 59

There is no evidence of overreporting.

Underreporting   L-r 100   K-r 72

Underreporting is indicated by the test taker presenting himself in an extremely positive light by denying minor faults and shortcomings that most people acknowledge. Underreporting is also indicated by the test taker presenting himself as remarkably well adjusted. Any absence of elevation on the Substantive Scales should be interpreted with caution. Elevated scores in the Substantive Scales may underestimate the problems assessed by those scales.

Figure 8-2. MMPI-2-RF interpretation worksheet with completed Validity Scales page.

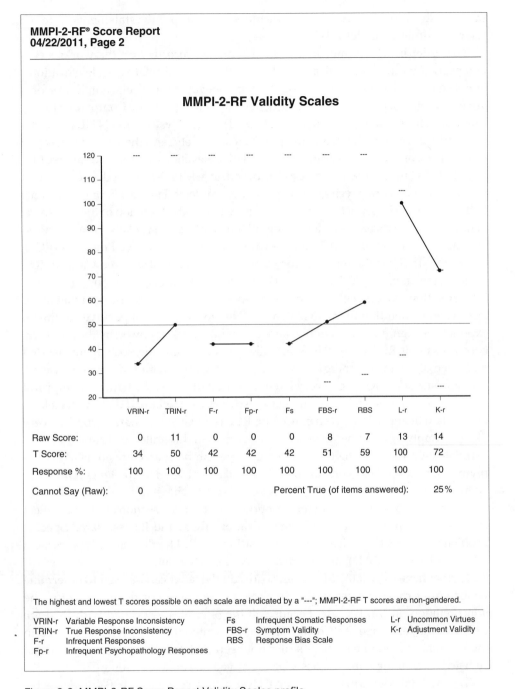

MMPI-2-RF® Score Report
04/22/2011, Page 2

MMPI-2-RF Validity Scales

	VRIN-r	TRIN-r	F-r	Fp-r	Fs	FBS-r	RBS	L-r	K-r
Raw Score:	0	11	0	0	0	8	7	13	14
T Score:	34	50	42	42	42	51	59	100	72
Response %:	100	100	100	100	100	100	100	100	100

Cannot Say (Raw):   0   Percent True (of items answered):   25%

The highest and lowest T scores possible on each scale are indicated by a "---"; MMPI-2-RF T scores are non-gendered.

VRIN-r	Variable Response Inconsistency	Fs	Infrequent Somatic Responses	L-r	Uncommon Virtues
TRIN-r	True Response Inconsistency	FBS-r	Symptom Validity	K-r	Adjustment Validity
F-r	Infrequent Responses	RBS	Response Bias Scale		
Fp-r	Infrequent Psychopathology Responses				

Figure 8-3. MMPI-2-RF Score Report Validity Scales profile.

the worksheet (see Figure 8-5); also included are interpretive statements from the relevant entries in Tables 7-1–7-42.

The order in which interpretive statements are recorded on the worksheet is determined by the hierarchical structure of the test and relative scale elevations. For each of the first four substantive domains, elevated (or, if relevant, low) scores are interpreted beginning with the broadest measures (Somatic Complaints [RC1], Emotional/Internalizing Dysfunction [EID], Thought Dysfunction [THD], and Behavioral/Externalizing Dysfunction [BXD], respectively) and then lower-level scale scores are incorporated according to their relative elevations across subdomains. RC1 is included here because it provides the broadest MMPI-2-RF-based assessment of possible somatoform psychopathology. For example, in Figure 8-5, the statements in the Emotional Dysfunction domain begin with an interpretation of the EID score: "His responses indicate considerable emotional distress that is likely to be perceived as a crisis." This is followed by an interpretation of Low Positive Emotions (RC2), on which Mr. B has the highest score among the three Restructured Clinical (RC) Scales in this domain (RCd, RC2, and Dysfunctional Negative Emotions [RC7]). The interpretation of RC2 begins with content-based statements reflecting what Mr. B said when responding to the RC2 items—"He reports a lack of positive emotional experiences, significant anhedonia, and lack of interest"—followed by the empirical correlates of his RC2 score: "He is very likely to be pessimistic, socially introverted and disengaged, to lack energy, and to display vegetative symptoms of depression." Probabilistic language (e.g., "very likely") is used to reflect the nature of empirical correlates (i.e., as the scale score increases, so does the likelihood that the correlates of a scale will apply in a given case). The RC2 correlates are characterized as very likely to apply to Mr. B because of his high score on this scale. As a rule of thumb, correlates for scales in the 65–79 T-score range can be characterized as likely applying to the test taker, whereas for T scores of 80 or higher, a greater certainty can be indicated by characterizing them as very likely to characterize the test taker.

The next set of statements in the Emotional Dysfunction section of the worksheet are based on Mr. B's scores on Demoralization (RCd) and its associated Specific Problems (SP) Scales: Suicidal/Death Ideation (SUI), Helplessness/Hopelessness (HLP), Self-Doubt (SFD), and Inefficacy (NFC). When interpreting scores on RC Scales that have associated SP Scales, scores on the latter can be used to determine which empirical correlates of the RC Scale to emphasize or deemphasize in the interpretation. In Mr. B's case, because all the SP Scales associated with RCd are elevated, the full range of RCd correlates is presented in the statements entered in the worksheet. Had one of these scales not been elevated, its correlates would not be listed, even if they are also associated with an elevated score on RCd.

The final statements in the Emotional Dysfunction section of Mr. B's worksheet— "He reports an above average level of stress and worry and is likely to be stress reactive and worry prone and to engage in obsessive rumination"—are based on his score on the Stress/Worry (STW) SP Scale. Recall that SP Scale scores can be interpreted even when the RC Scales with which they are associated (in this case, RC7) are not elevated.

The two PSY-5 Scales associated with emotional dysfunction are also elevated

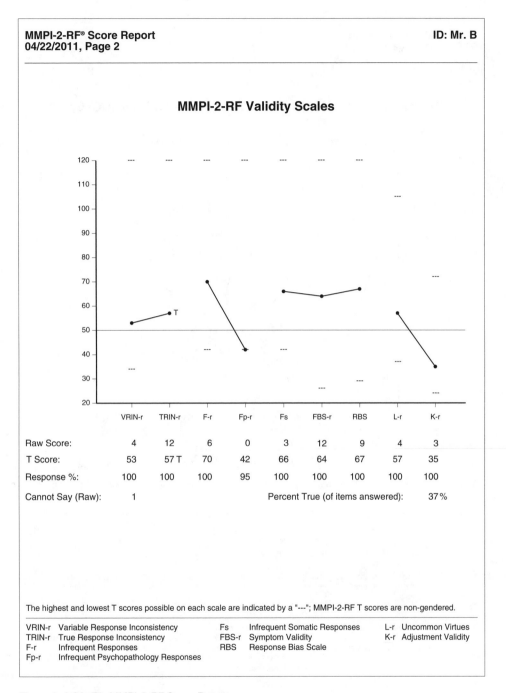

MMPI-2-RF Validity Scales

	VRIN-r	TRIN-r	F-r	Fp-r	Fs	FBS-r	RBS	L-r	K-r
Raw Score:	4	12	6	0	3	12	9	4	3
T Score:	53	57 T	70	42	66	64	67	57	35
Response %:	100	100	100	95	100	100	100	100	100

Cannot Say (Raw):   1   Percent True (of items answered):   37%

The highest and lowest T scores possible on each scale are indicated by a "---"; MMPI-2-RF T scores are non-gendered.

VRIN-r	Variable Response Inconsistency	Fs	Infrequent Somatic Responses
TRIN-r	True Response Inconsistency	FBS-r	Symptom Validity
F-r	Infrequent Responses	RBS	Response Bias Scale
Fp-r	Infrequent Psychopathology Responses		

L-r	Uncommon Virtues
K-r	Adjustment Validity

Figure 8-4. Mr. B's MMPI-2-RF Score Report.

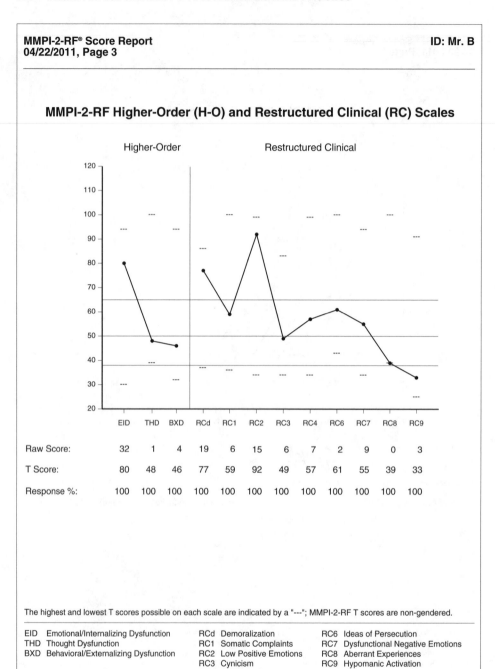

MMPI-2-RF® Score Report   **ID: Mr. B**
04/22/2011, Page 3

MMPI-2-RF Higher-Order (H-O) and Restructured Clinical (RC) Scales

Higher-Order   Restructured Clinical

	EID	THD	BXD	RCd	RC1	RC2	RC3	RC4	RC6	RC7	RC8	RC9
Raw Score:	32	1	4	19	6	15	6	7	2	9	0	3
T Score:	80	48	46	77	59	92	49	57	61	55	39	33
Response %:	100	100	100	100	100	100	100	100	100	100	100	100

The highest and lowest T scores possible on each scale are indicated by a "---"; MMPI-2-RF T scores are non-gendered.

EID Emotional/Internalizing Dysfunction	RCd Demoralization	RC6 Ideas of Persecution
THD Thought Dysfunction	RC1 Somatic Complaints	RC7 Dysfunctional Negative Emotions
BXD Behavioral/Externalizing Dysfunction	RC2 Low Positive Emotions	RC8 Aberrant Experiences
	RC3 Cynicism	RC9 Hypomanic Activation
	RC4 Antisocial Behavior	

Figure 8-4. Mr. B's MMPI-2-RF Score Report, continued.

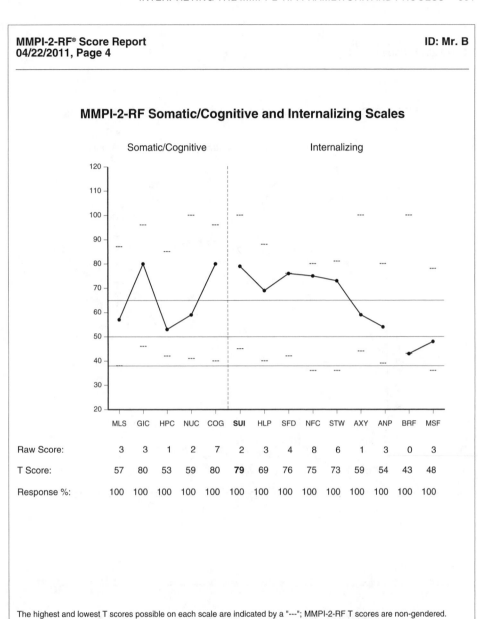

MMPI-2-RF Somatic/Cognitive and Internalizing Scales

Somatic/Cognitive

Internalizing

	MLS	GIC	HPC	NUC	COG	SUI	HLP	SFD	NFC	STW	AXY	ANP	BRF	MSF
Raw Score:	3	3	1	2	7	2	3	4	8	6	1	3	0	3
T Score:	57	80	53	59	80	79	69	76	75	73	59	54	43	48
Response %:	100	100	100	100	100	100	100	100	100	100	100	100	100	100

The highest and lowest T scores possible on each scale are indicated by a "---"; MMPI-2-RF T scores are non-gendered.

MLS	Malaise	SUI	Suicidal/Death Ideation	AXY	Anxiety
GIC	Gastrointestinal Complaints	HLP	Helplessness/Hopelessness	ANP	Anger Proneness
HPC	Head Pain Complaints	SFD	Self-Doubt	BRF	Behavior-Restricting Fears
NUC	Neurological Complaints	NFC	Inefficacy	MSF	Multiple Specific Fears
COG	Cognitive Complaints	STW	Stress/Worry		

Figure 8-4. Mr. B's MMPI-2-RF Score Report, continued.

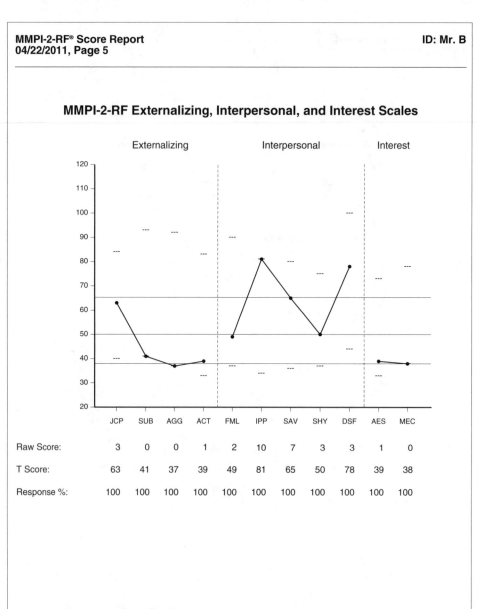

Figure 8-4. Mr. B's MMPI-2-RF Score Report, continued.

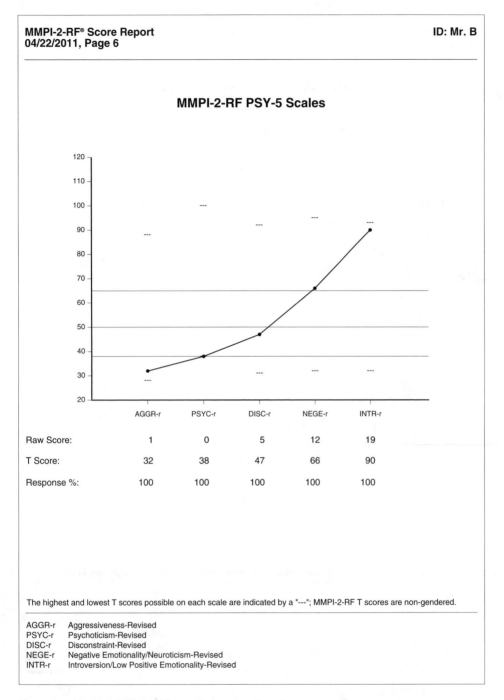

Figure 8-4. Mr. B's MMPI-2-RF Score Report, continued.

MMPI-2-RF® Score Report
04/22/2011, Page 7

ID: Mr. B

MMPI-2-RF T SCORES (BY DOMAIN)

PROTOCOL VALIDITY

Content Non-Responsiveness		
1	53	57 T
CNS	VRIN-r	TRIN-r

Over-Reporting					
70	42		66	64	67
F-r	Fp-r		Fs	FBS-r	RBS

Under-Reporting	
57	35
L-r	K-r

SUBSTANTIVE SCALES

Somatic/Cognitive Dysfunction

59	57	80	53	59	80
RC1	MLS	GIC	HPC	NUC	COG

Emotional Dysfunction

80		77	**79**	69	76	75
EID		RCd	**SUI**	HLP	SFD	NFC

		92	90
		RC2	INTR-r

		55	73	59	54	43	48	66
		RC7	STW	AXY	ANP	BRF	MSF	NEGE-r

Thought Dysfunction

48		61
THD		RC6

		39
		RC8

		38
		PSYC-r

Behavioral Dysfunction

46		57	63	41
BXD		RC4	JCP	SUB

		33	37	39	32	47
		RC9	AGG	ACT	AGGR-r	DISC-r

Interpersonal Functioning

49	49	81	65	50	78
FML	RC3	IPP	SAV	SHY	DSF

Interests

39	38
AES	MEC

Note. This information is provided to facilitate interpretation following the recommended structure for MMPI-2-RF interpretation in Chapter 5 of the *MMPI-2-RF Manual for Administration, Scoring, and Interpretation*, which provides details in the text and an outline in Table 5-1.

Figure 8-4. Mr. B's MMPI-2-RF Score Report, continued.

MMPI-2-RF® Interpretation Worksheet
Mr. B

Protocol Validity

Content Non-Responsiveness   CNS __1__   VRIN-r __53__   TRIN-r __57T__

There are no indications of non-responsiveness.

_____

_____

_____

_____

_____

_____

Overreporting   F-r __70__   Fp-r __42__   Fs __66__   FBS-r __64__   RBS ____

There are no indications of overreporting.

_____

_____

_____

_____

_____

_____

_____

_____

Underreporting   L-r __57__   K-r __35__

There are no indications of underreporting.

_____

_____

_____

_____

_____

Figure 8-5. Mr. B's MMPI-2-RF completed interpretation worksheet.

Substantive Scale Interpretation

Somatic/Cognitive Dysfunction   RC1 59   GIC 80   NUC 59

MLS 57   HPC 53   COG 80

He reports a large number of gastrointestinal complaints and likely has a history of gastrointestinal problems and is preoccupied with health concerns. He reports a diffuse pattern of cognitive difficulties including memory problems, difficulties concentrating, intellectual limitations, and confusion. He is likely to complain about memory problems, to have a low tolerance for frustration, and to experience difficulties in concentration.

Emotional Dysfunction   EID 80   RCd 77   RC2 92   RC7 55

SUI 79   INT-r 90   STW 73

HLP 69   AXY 59

SFD 76   ANP 54

NFC 75   BRF 43

MSF 48

NEGE-r 66

His responses indicate considerable emotional distress that is likely to be perceived as a crisis. He reports a lack of positive emotional experiences, significant anhedonia, and lack of interest. He is very likely to be pessimistic, to be socially introverted and disengaged, to lack energy, and to display vegetative depression. He reports being sad and unhappy, and being dissatisfied with his current life circumstances. He reports a history of suicidal ideation and/or attempts and is likely to be preoccupied with suicide or death, is at risk for a suicide attempt, and may have recently attempted suicide. He reports feeling hopeless and pessimistic and likely feels overwhelmed and that life is a strain, believes he cannot be helped, believes he gets a raw deal from life, and lacks motivation for change. He reports lacking confidence, and likely feels inferior and insecure, is self-disparaging, is prone to rumination, is intropunitive, and presents with lack of confidence and feelings of uselessness. He reports being passive, indecisive, and inefficacious and believes he is incapable of coping with his current difficulties. He is unlikely to be self-reliant. He reports an above average level of stress and worry and is likely to be stress-reactive and worry-prone and to engage in obsessive rumination.

Figure 8-5. Mr. B's MMPI-2-RF completed interpretation worksheet, continued.

Thought Dysfunction   THD 44   RC6 61   RC8 39   PSYC-r 38

There are no indications of thought dysfunction.

_____

_____

_____

_____

_____

_____

Behavioral Dysfunction   BXD 44   RC4 57   RC9 33   AGGR-r 32

JCP 63   AGG 37   DISC-r 47

SUB 41   ACT 39

He reports a below average level of activation and engagement with his environment and is

likely to have a very low energy level and be disengaged from his environment. He reports

a below average level of physically aggressive behavior and reports being interpersonally

passive and submissive.

_____

_____

_____

_____

Interpersonal Functioning:

FML 49   RC3 49   IPP 81   SAV 65   SHY 50   DSF 78

He reports being unassertive and submissive, not liking to be in charge, failing to stand up for

himself, and being ready to give in to others. He is likely to be passive and submissive in his

interpersonal relationships and to be over-controlled. He reports not enjoying social events

and avoiding social situations. He is likely to be introverted, have difficulty forming close

relationships, and be emotionally restricted. He reports disliking people and being around

them and is likely to be asocial.

Figure 8-5. Mr. B's MMPI-2-RF completed interpretation worksheet, continued.

Interests: AES 39   MEC   38

He reports no interest in activities or occupations of a mechanical or physical nature (e.g.,

fixing and building things, the outdoors, sports).

Diagnostic Considerations

If physical origin for gastrointestical complaints have been ruled out, evaluate for

Somatoform Disorder.

Internalizing Disorders.

Major Depression.

Cluster C Personality Disorder.

Disorders involving excessive stress and worry such as Obsessive–Compulsive Disorder.

Dependent Personality Disorder.

Treatment Considerations

Stress reduction for gastrointestinal complaints. Origin of cognitive complaints should

be explored. Emotional difficulties may motivate him for treatment. Evaluate need for

antidepressant medication. May require inpatient treatment for significant depression. Low

positive emotions may interefere with treatment. Anhedinia as a target for treatment. RISK

FOR SUICIDE SHOULD BE ASSESSED IMMEDIATELY. Loss of hope and feelings

of despair as early targets for intervention. Indecisiveness may interfere with establishing

treatment goals and progress in treatment. Stress management and excessive worry and

rumination as targets for intervention. Reducing passive-submissive behavior as a target

for intervention. His aversive response to relationships may make it difficult to form a

therapeutic alliance. Lack of outside interests as a target for intervention.

Figure 8-5. Mr. B's MMPI-2-RF completed interpretation worksheet, continued.

in Mr. B's case. The correlates of these scales overlap substantially with statements generated by the other measures and are, therefore, not repeated. Personality Disorder features are specifically associated with PSY-5 Scale elevations, as noted in the inclusion of Cluster C Personality Disorders in the Diagnostic Considerations section of the worksheet.

The remaining sections of Mr. B's worksheet illustrate other elements of the recommended process for interpreting MMPI-2-RF Substantive Scale scores. The highest-level measure in the Somatic/Cognitive Dysfunction domain, RC1, is not elevated. Therefore, the interpretive statements in this section are based on the two SP Scales on which Mr. B produced elevated scores: Gastrointestinal Complaints (GIC) and Cognitive Complaints (COG). Because none of the scales in the Thought Dysfunction domain is elevated, the statement "There are no indications of thought dysfunction" is entered in that part of the worksheet. Mr. B did not produce any elevated scores in the Behavioral Dysfunction domain.[1] However, his low scores on Hypomanic Activation (RC9), Aggression (AGG), and Aggressiveness–Revised (AGGR-r) are interpretable, and the relevant statements from the interpretive tables for these scales in Chapter 7 are recorded in this section of the worksheet. Scores on the Interpersonal Functioning scales are interpreted in the order they appear on the worksheet, which was determined on the basis of conceptual consideration of associations between the constructs assessed by these measures. Scores on the two Interest Scales are also interpreted in order of their appearance on the worksheet.

As noted earlier, the Diagnostic and Treatment Considerations sections of the worksheet are relevant primarily when the MMPI-2-RF is used in clinical assessments, as was the case with Mr. B. While interpreting the scales in the first six Substantive Scale subsections of the worksheet, the relevant diagnostic and treatment considerations can be recorded in these final two sections. For example, the first statements appearing under "Diagnostic Considerations" are provided in Table 7-14 for the diagnostic and treatment considerations for elevated GIC scores.

Once completed, the worksheet can be used to write a narrative interpretation of the test results. A typical narrative report would begin with a discussion of Validity Scale findings, followed by interpretation of the Substantive Scale scores. Special circumstances indicating a need to qualify interpretive statements listed on the worksheet would then be considered. For example, Mr. B had a known medical condition that could account for his gastrointestinal complaints. Therefore, his GIC score is not to be interpreted as indicating a possible Somatoform Disorder. Because he was already admitted to an inpatient facility, there is no need to mention a possible need for hospitalization to treat his severe depression.

As noted earlier, the order in which the first four substantive areas (Somatic/ Cognitive, Emotional, Thought, and Behavioral Dysfunction) are addressed in a narrative report can be based on the relative prominence of dysfunction in these domains. In Mr. B's case, Emotional Dysfunction is the most prominent finding and would therefore be addressed first, following discussion of the validity of his test protocol. A finding of possible risk for self-harm would in most circumstances be mentioned early in the report.

Following the process just described, a narrative report of Mr. B's MMPI-2-RF results would read as follows:

Mr. B. produced a valid and interpretable MMPI-2-RF protocol. His scores on the Substantive Scales are likely to provide an accurate portrayal of his psychological functioning, reflecting a cooperative approach to the evaluation.

Mr. B's responses indicate considerable emotional distress that is likely to be perceived as a crisis. He reports current suicidal ideation and is likely to be preoccupied with suicide and death. He is indeed at increased risk for attempting suicide. Mr. B also reports a marked lack of positive emotional experiences, significant anhedonia, and a lack of interests. He is very likely to be pessimistic, to lack energy, and to display vegetative symptoms of depression.

Mr. B reports feeling sad, unhappy, and hopeless and that he is dissatisfied with his current life circumstances. He is likely to feel that life is a strain, to believe that he cannot be helped, and to feel overwhelmed. He is also likely to believe that he gets a raw deal from life.[2] Mr. B reports harboring self-doubts, and he is likely to feel insecure. He is also likely to be self-disparaging, intropunitive, and prone to rumination. In addition, Mr. B is likely to express feelings of uselessness and lack of confidence. He also describes himself as passive, indecisive, and inefficacious, and he is unlikely to be self-reliant. Mr. B also reports an above average level of stress and worry and is likely to be stress-reactive and worry-prone and to engage in obsessive ruminations.

Mr. B reports below-average levels of activation and aggression. He is likely to have a very low energy level and to be disengaged from his environment.

Mr. B reports a number of gastrointestinal complaints that are consistent with his known medical condition.[3] He also reports a diffuse pattern of cognitive difficulties and is likely to complain about memory problems, to experience difficulties with concentration, and to have low tolerance for frustration.

Interpersonally, Mr. B describes himself as unassertive and submissive, willing to give in to others, not standing up for himself, and not liking to take charge. He is indeed very likely to be passive, submissive, and overcontrolled. He also reports not enjoying social situations and events, disliking people and being around them, and preferring to be alone. He is likely to be introverted, asocial, and emotionally restricted. His introversion is not associated with social anxiety.

Mr. B indicates no interest in activities or occupations of a mechanical or physical nature (e.g., fixing and building things, the outdoors, sports). He is unlikely to be adventure seeking.

Mr. B's test results indicate a number of possible diagnoses warranting further consideration. It is recommended that he be evaluated for depression-related disorders, possibly Major Depression. The possibility of disorders involving excessive stress and worry, such as Obsessive–Compulsive Disorder, should also be considered. The possibility of an Axis II Cluster C disorder, particularly Dependent Personality Disorder, should also be evaluated.

Mr. B's risk for self-harm should be evaluated immediately. The need for antidepressant medication should be assessed. The origin of Mr. B's cognitive complaints should be explored, which may require a neuropsychological evaluation.

Mr. B's test results point to potential process issues for consideration in treatment planning. On one hand, his emotional difficulties may motivate him to participate. On the other hand, Mr. B's indecisiveness may interfere with setting treatment goals and achieving treatment progress, and his aversive response to close relationships may make it difficult for him to form a therapeutic alliance.

Potential targets for intervention include Mr. B's depressive symptoms, loss of hope, feelings of despair, low self-esteem, excessive worrying and rumination, and passivity and social avoidance.

This report illustrates how a completed worksheet can be used to generate a narrative interpretation of the Substantive Scales. The process of writing a full MMPI-2-RF interpretation is demonstrated next.

CASE EXAMPLE: MR. I

The report is based on the case of Mr. I, whose results were used to illustrate the MMPI-2-RF Score Report and Interpretive Report in Chapter 5. Mr. I is a 36-year-old married man admitted for inpatient treatment after presenting with psychotic thinking and assaultive behavior. At intake, he described a recent pattern of decreased sleep and presented with bizarre delusional thinking, religious preoccupation, visual hallucinations, and tangential and circumstantial thinking. He had previously been diagnosed with Schizophrenia and Schizoaffective Disorder.

Mr. I's MMPI-2-RF Score Report is reproduced in Figure 8-6. The first step in the interpretation process is to enter Mr. I's MMPI-2-RF scores onto a worksheet. All the scores are on page 7 of the report. A worksheet containing Mr. I's scores and the recommended interpretive statements associated with them is presented in Figure 8-7.

Interpretation of Mr. I's MMPI-2-RF results begins with an examination of his Validity Scale scores. The CNS score of 17 indicates that Mr. I did not provide scorable responses to a fairly large number of items, necessitating examination of the Response % findings for all MMPI-2-RF scales. Mr. I provided less than 90% scorable responses to the items of four scales: Symptom Validity (FBS-r), Adjustment Validity (K-r), Cynicism (RC3), and Aesthetic–Literary Interests (AES). Of these, RC3 clearly stands out, with scorable responses to less than half of the items. For some reason, Mr. I was reluctant to respond to items designed to gauge cynical beliefs. Therefore, this topic cannot be assessed with his MMPI-2-RF results. Reasons for his reluctance can be explored in a follow-up interview. Mr. I's low score on AES is also uninterpretable owing to nonresponding.[4]

Although Mr. I responded to less than 90% of the items on two of the validity indicators, had he responded to all the unscorable items in the keyed direction, his scores on these scales would have fallen short of interpretable levels. Specifically,

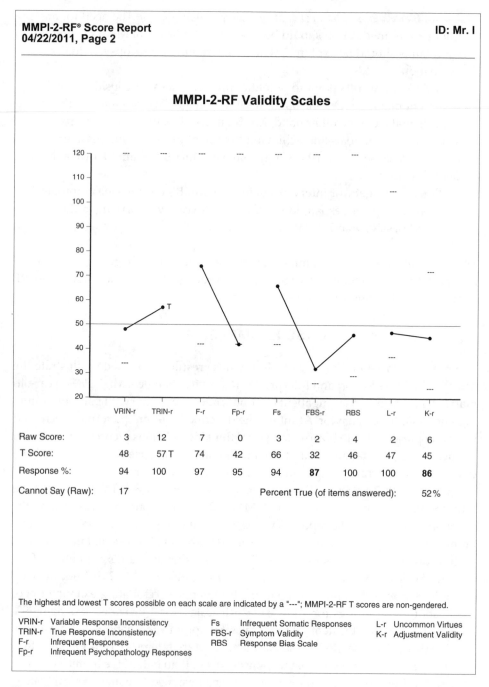

MMPI-2-RF® Score Report
04/22/2011, Page 2

ID: Mr. I

MMPI-2-RF Validity Scales

	VRIN-r	TRIN-r	F-r	Fp-r	Fs	FBS-r	RBS	L-r	K-r
Raw Score:	3	12	7	0	3	2	4	2	6
T Score:	48	57 T	74	42	66	32	46	47	45
Response %:	94	100	97	95	94	**87**	100	100	**86**

Cannot Say (Raw):   17   Percent True (of items answered):   52%

The highest and lowest T scores possible on each scale are indicated by a "---"; MMPI-2-RF T scores are non-gendered.

VRIN-r	Variable Response Inconsistency	Fs	Infrequent Somatic Responses	L-r	Uncommon Virtues
TRIN-r	True Response Inconsistency	FBS-r	Symptom Validity	K-r	Adjustment Validity
F-r	Infrequent Responses	RBS	Response Bias Scale		
Fp-r	Infrequent Psychopathology Responses				

Figure 8-6. Mr. I's MMPI-2-RF Score Report.

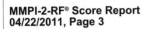

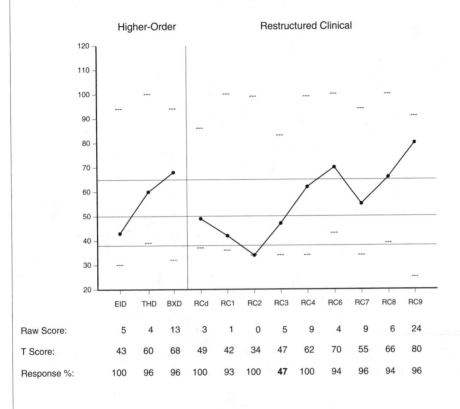

MMPI-2-RF Higher-Order (H-O) and Restructured Clinical (RC) Scales

	Higher-Order				Restructured Clinical							
	EID	THD	BXD	RCd	RC1	RC2	RC3	RC4	RC6	RC7	RC8	RC9
Raw Score:	5	4	13	3	1	0	5	9	4	9	6	24
T Score:	43	60	68	49	42	34	47	62	70	55	66	80
Response %:	100	96	96	100	93	100	47	100	94	96	94	96

The highest and lowest T scores possible on each scale are indicated by a "---"; MMPI-2-RF T scores are non-gendered.

EID Emotional/Internalizing Dysfunction	RCd Demoralization	RC6 Ideas of Persecution
THD Thought Dysfunction	RC1 Somatic Complaints	RC7 Dysfunctional Negative Emotions
BXD Behavioral/Externalizing Dysfunction	RC2 Low Positive Emotions	RC8 Aberrant Experiences
	RC3 Cynicism	RC9 Hypomanic Activation
	RC4 Antisocial Behavior	

Figure 8-6. Mr. I's MMPI-2-RF Score Report, continued.

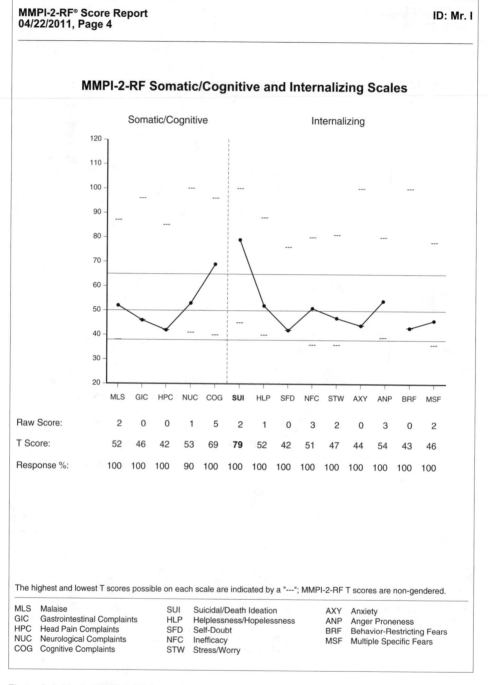

MMPI-2-RF® Score Report
04/22/2011, Page 4

ID: Mr. I

MMPI-2-RF Somatic/Cognitive and Internalizing Scales

Somatic/Cognitive   Internalizing

	MLS	GIC	HPC	NUC	COG	SUI	HLP	SFD	NFC	STW	AXY	ANP	BRF	MSF
Raw Score:	2	0	0	1	5	2	1	0	3	2	0	3	0	2
T Score:	52	46	42	53	69	79	52	42	51	47	44	54	43	46
Response %:	100	100	100	90	100	100	100	100	100	100	100	100	100	100

The highest and lowest T scores possible on each scale are indicated by a "---"; MMPI-2-RF T scores are non-gendered.

MLS	Malaise	SUI	Suicidal/Death Ideation	AXY	Anxiety
GIC	Gastrointestinal Complaints	HLP	Helplessness/Hopelessness	ANP	Anger Proneness
HPC	Head Pain Complaints	SFD	Self-Doubt	BRF	Behavior-Restricting Fears
NUC	Neurological Complaints	NFC	Inefficacy	MSF	Multiple Specific Fears
COG	Cognitive Complaints	STW	Stress/Worry		

Figure 8-6. Mr. I's MMPI-2-RF Score Report, continued.

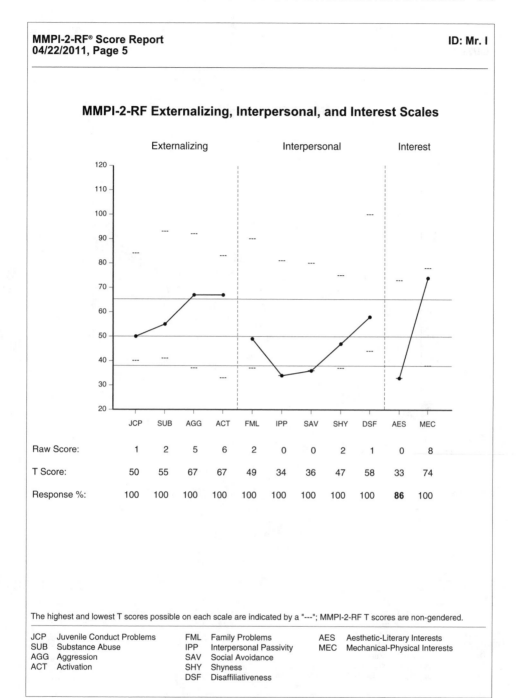

MMPI-2-RF Externalizing, Interpersonal, and Interest Scales

	Externalizing				Interpersonal					Interest	
	JCP	SUB	AGG	ACT	FML	IPP	SAV	SHY	DSF	AES	MEC
Raw Score:	1	2	5	6	2	0	0	2	1	0	8
T Score:	50	55	67	67	49	34	36	47	58	33	74
Response %:	100	100	100	100	100	100	100	100	100	86	100

The highest and lowest T scores possible on each scale are indicated by a "---"; MMPI-2-RF T scores are non-gendered.

JCP	Juvenile Conduct Problems	FML	Family Problems	AES	Aesthetic-Literary Interests
SUB	Substance Abuse	IPP	Interpersonal Passivity	MEC	Mechanical-Physical Interests
AGG	Aggression	SAV	Social Avoidance		
ACT	Activation	SHY	Shyness		
		DSF	Disaffiliativeness		

Figure 8-6. Mr. I's MMPI-2-RF Score Report, continued.

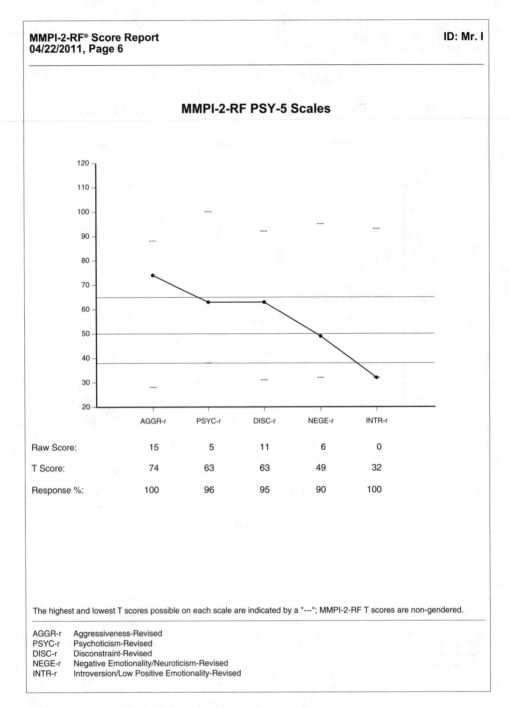

Figure 8-6. Mr. I's MMPI-2-RF Score Report, continued.

MMPI-2-RF T SCORES (BY DOMAIN)

PROTOCOL VALIDITY

Content Non-Responsiveness

17	48	57 T
CNS	VRIN-r	TRIN-r

Over-Reporting

74	42		66	32*	46
F-r	Fp-r		Fs	FBS-r	RBS

Under-Reporting

47	45*
L-r	K-r

SUBSTANTIVE SCALES

Somatic/Cognitive Dysfunction

42	52	46	42	53	69
RC1	MLS	GIC	HPC	NUC	COG

Emotional Dysfunction

43		49	**79**	52	42	51		
EID		RCd	**SUI**	HLP	SFD	NFC		
		34	32					
		RC2	INTR-r					
		55	47	44	54	43	46	49
		RC7	STW	AXY	ANP	BRF	MSF	NEGE-r

Thought Dysfunction

60		70
THD		RC6
		66
		RC8
		63
		PSYC-r

Behavioral Dysfunction

68		62	50	55		
BXD		RC4	JCP	SUB		
		80	67	67	74	63
		RC9	AGG	ACT	AGGR-r	DISC-r

Interpersonal Functioning

49	47*	34	36	47	58
FML	RC3	IPP	SAV	SHY	DSF

Interests

33*	74
AES	MEC

*The test taker provided scorable responses to less than 90% of the items scored on this scale. See the relevant profile page for the specific percentage.

Note. This information is provided to facilitate interpretation following the recommended structure for MMPI-2-RF interpretation in Chapter 5 of the *MMPI-2-RF Manual for Administration, Scoring, and Interpretation*, which provides details in the text and an outline in Table 5-1.

Figure 8-6. Mr. I's MMPI-2-RF Score Report, continued.

MMPI-2-RF® Interpretation Worksheet
Mr. I

Protocol Validity

Content Non-Responsiveness   CNS __17__   VRIN-r __48__   TRIN-r __57T__

Non-responding limits the interpretability of scores on FBS-r, K-r, RC3, and AES. Of these, only RC3 is impacted appreciably. Cynical beliefs cannot be assessed as a result of non-responding. There are no indications of inconsistent responding.

Overreporting   F-r __74__   Fp-r __42__   Fs __66__   FBS-r __32__   RBS __46__

There are no indications of overreporting.

Underreporting   L-r __47__   K-r __45__

There are no indications of underreporting.

Figure 8-7. Mr. I's completed MMPI-2-RF interpretation worksheet.

Substantive Scale Interpretation

Somatic/Cognitive Dysfunction   RC1 _42_   GIC _46_   NUC _53_

MLS _52_   HPC _42_   COG _69_

He reports a diffuse pattern of cognitive difficulties and is likely to complain of memory

problems, have low tolerance for frustration, and experience difficulties in concentration.

Emotional Dysfunction   EID _43_   RCd _49_   RC2 _34_   RC7 _55_

SUI _79_   INT-r _32_   STW _47_

HLP _52_   AXY _44_

SFD _42_   ANP _54_

NFC _51_   BRF _43_

MSF _46_

NEGE-r _49_

He reports a high level of psychological well-being, a wide range of emotionally positive

experiences, and feeling confident and energetic. He is likely to be optimistic, extraverted,

and socially engaged. He reports a history of suicidal ideation and/or attempts, is preoccupied

with suicide and death, and may have recently attempted suicide.

Figure 8-7. Mr. I's completed MMPI-2-RF interpretation worksheet, continued.

Thought Dysfunction   THD 60   RC6 70   RC8 66   PSYC-r 63

He reported persecutory ideation such as believing that others seek to harm him. He is likely suspicious and alienated from others and likely to experience interpersonal difficulties as a result of suspiciousness. He likely lacks insight and blames others for his difficulties. He reports various unusual thought and perceptual processes and likely experiences thought disorganization, engages in unrealistic thinking, and believes he has unusual sensory abilities.

Behavioral Dysfunction   BXD 68   RC4 62   RC9 80   AGGR-r 74
                                            JCP 50   AGG 67   DISC-r 63
                                            SUB 55   ACT 67

His responses indicate significant externalizing, acting-out behavior, which is likely to have gotten him into difficulties. He reports a considerably above average level of activation and engagement with his environment. He is likely restless and easily bored and overactivated as manifested in poor impulse control, aggression, mood instability, euphoria, excitability, sensation-seeking, risk-taking, and other forms of under-controlled behavior. He likely displays Narcissistic Personality features and may have a history associated with Hypomanic symptoms. He reports engaging in physically aggressive, violent behavior and losing control. He is likely to have a history of violent behavior toward others, be abusive, and experience anger-related problems. He reports episodes of hightened excitation and energy level.

Interpersonal Functioning:

         FML 49   RC3 47   IPP 34   SAV 36   SHY 47   DSF 58

He describes himself as having strong opinions, standing up for himself, being assertive and direct, and being able to lead others. Although he believes that he has strong leadership abilities, he is likely to be viewed by others as domineering, self-centered, and possibly grandiose. He reports enjoying social situations and social events and is likely to be outgoing and gregarious.

Figure 8-7. Mr. I's completed MMPI-2-RF interpretation worksheet, continued.

Interests: AES _33_   MEC _74_

He reports above-average interest in activities or occupations of a mechanical or physical

nature (e.g., fixing and building things, the outdoors, sports) and is likely to be adventure-

seeking and sensation-seeking.

Diagnostic Considerations

Externalizing Disorders, Cycling Mood Disorder, Manic or Hypomanic episodes,

Schizoaffective Disorder.

Disorders associated with interpersonal aggression.

Cluster B Disorder.

Disorders involving persecutory ideation, disorders manifesting psychotic symptoms,

including Schizophrenia, Paranoid Type.

Features of Narcissistic Personality Disorder.

Treatment Considerations

Unlikely to be internally motivated for treatment, a significant risk for treatment non-

compliance, inadequate self-control as a target for intervention. Excessive behavioral

activation may interfere with treatment. Mood stabilization in the initial stages of treatment

as a target for intervention, may require inpatient treatment for hypomania. Need for mood-

stabilizing medication should be evaluated. Reduction in interpersonally aggressive behavior

as a target for intervention. Persecutory ideation may interfere with forming a therapeutic

relationship and treatment compliance. Persecutory ideation as a target for intervention.

Impaired thinking may disrupt treatment. Needs assistance in gaining insight about his

thought dysfunction. RISK FOR SUICIDE SHOULD BE ASSESSED IMMEDIATELY.

Origin of cognitive complaints should be explored; this may require a neuropsychological

evaluation.

Figure 8-7. Mr. I's completed MMPI-2-RF interpretation worksheet, continued.

Mr. I did not provide scorable responses to four of the FBS-r items and two of the K-r items. Adding four and two raw-score points respectively to the actual raw scores he obtained on these scales would result in T scores of 45 on FBS-r and 52 on K-r. Thus, despite a relatively large number of unscorable responses, all Mr. I's Validity Scale scores are interpretable, and with the exception of being unable to interpret scores on RC3, they do not raise concerns about the validity of this protocol.

Substantive Scale entries on Mr. I's worksheet begin with statements associated with his only elevated score in the Somatic/Cognitive Dysfunction domain, COG. The Emotional Dysfunction domain entries reflect seemingly contradictory statements associated with a low score on RC2 and a high SUI score. This apparent contradiction is resolved in the narrative interpretation that follows by linking Mr. I's report of a wide range of positive emotional experiences with mood disorder symptoms that are in fact consistent with suicidal ideation. Statements in the Thought Dysfunction domain are associated with Mr. I's elevated scores on Ideas of Persecution (RC6) and Aberrant Experiences (RC8). An extensive list of interpretive statements appears in the Behavioral Dysfunction section of Mr. I's worksheet. They begin with statements associated with an elevated Behavioral/Externalizing Dysfunction (BXD) score. Of the two RC Scales in this domain, RC9 is elevated, and this score is interpreted next, along with elevated scores on Aggression (AGG), Activation (ACT), and Aggressiveness–Revised (AGGR-r). In the Interpersonal Functioning domain, low scores on Interpersonal Passivity (IPP) and Social Avoidance (SAV) are interpretable, as is an elevated Mechanical–Physical Interests (MEC) score in the Interests domain. As just discussed, Mr. I's low score on AES is uninterpretable owing to nonresponding.

The next step in interpreting Mr. I's MMPI-2-RF test results is to integrate in a narrative report the statements recorded on the worksheet with available information regarding Mr. I's background and referral. As always, the report begins with an analysis of protocol validity. Interpretation of Mr. I's Substantive Scale scores begins with the Externalizing domain, where his test results indicate that he is experiencing the greatest dysfunction. A narrative report following these procedures would read as follows:

> Mr. I did not provide scorable responses to a large number of items, in particular those designed to assess cynicism. As a result, it is not possible to assess his cynical beliefs. He did respond to a sufficient number of the Validity Scale items to provide interpretable findings. There were no indications of inconsistent responding, overreporting, or underreporting in this protocol. Therefore, scores on the Substantive Scales should provide an accurate indication of Mr. I's functioning.
>
> His responses indicate that Mr. I engages in significant externalizing, acting-out behavior, which is likely to have gotten him into difficulties. He reports a considerably above average-level of activation and engagement with his environment as well as a heightened energy and excitation level. He is very likely restless and easily bored. Mr. I is also very likely overactivated, as manifested in poor impulse control, aggression, mood instability, euphoria,

excitability, sensation seeking, risk taking, and other forms of undercontrolled behavior. He likely displays narcissistic personality features and may have a history associated with hypomanic symptoms. Mr. I reports engaging in physically aggressive, violent behavior and losing control. He is likely to have a history of violent behavior toward others, to be abusive, and to experience anger-related problems.

Mr. I's mood is congruent with his state of overactivation. He reports a high level of psychological well-being, a wide range of emotionally positive experiences, and feeling confident and energetic. He is likely to present as optimistic, extraverted, and socially engaged. On the other hand, he reports a history of suicidal ideation and/or attempts and is likely preoccupied with suicide and death and may have recently attempted suicide. These seemingly contradictory findings can be understood as manifestations of a cycling mood disorder.

Mr. I reports persecutory ideation such as believing that others seek to harm him. He is likely suspicious and alienated from others and is likely to experience interpersonal difficulties as a result of suspiciousness. He also likely lacks insight and blames others for his difficulties. Mr. I also reports various unusual thought and perceptual processes and likely experiences disorganized thinking. He is likely to engage in unrealistic thinking and to believe he has unusual sensory abilities.

Mr. I reports a diffuse pattern of cognitive difficulties. He is likely to complain of memory problems, to have low tolerance for frustration, and to experience difficulties in concentration.

Interpersonally, Mr. I describes himself as having strong opinions, standing up for himself, being assertive and direct, and being able to lead others. He believes he has strong leadership abilities, but he is likely to be viewed by others as domineering, self-centered, and possibly grandiose. He also reports enjoying social situations and social events and is likely to present as being outgoing and gregarious.

Mr. I reports above average interest in activities or occupations of a mechanical physical nature (e.g., fixing and building things, the outdoors, and sports) and is likely to be adventure seeking.

Diagnostically, Mr. I's MMPI-2-RF results raise several areas for further consideration. These include the possibility that he is presently experiencing a manic or hypomanic episode and that he has a mood cycling disorder and/or a psychotic disorder, including, possibly, Schizophrenia, Paranoid Type. In light of the combined hypomanic and thought dysfunction symptoms, Mr. I should be evaluated further to see whether he meets diagnostic criteria for Schizoaffective Disorder. Other diagnostic possibilities include a Cluster B disorder on Axis II. In particular, Narcissistic Personality Disorder is indicated for further evaluation.

Mr. I's MMPI-2-RF scores identify several areas for follow-up and intervention. *Risk for suicide should be assessed immediately.* Mood stabilization should be considered as an initial target for intervention, and Mr. I's need for mood-stabilizing medication should be evaluated. Other targets for intervention include reduction of aggressive behavior and persecutory ideation and assistance in gaining insight into his disordered thinking. The origin of Mr. I's cognitive complaints should be explored. This may require a neuropsychological evaluation. The possibility that Mr. I's cognitive complaints are linked to a thought disorder should also be explored.

Mr. I's results point to several potential impediments to successful treatment. He is unlikely to be internally motivated for treatment or change and is at high risk for treatment noncompliance. Excessive behavioral activation, persecutory ideation, and impaired thinking may interfere with his treatment.

After several days of observation on an inpatient basis, Mr. I was diagnosed with Schizoaffective Disorder and treated with antipsychotic and mood-stabilizing medication.

CONCLUSION

A recommended framework and process for interpreting scores on the MMPI-2-RF Validity and Substantive Scales were detailed and illustrated in this chapter. The case illustrations included were designed to demonstrate use of the MMPI-2-RF interpretation worksheet to organize findings and guide the writing of a narrative report of the test results. In a typical psychological evaluation, other sources of information (e.g., collateral contacts, other testing, and interview findings) are considered along with the MMPI-2-RF results to address specific referral questions. In many settings where the test is used, interpretation also involves consideration of comparison group data (described in Chapter 5). The case studies presented in the next chapter of this book illustrate these additional aspects of MMPI-2-RF interpretation.

CHAPTER 9

MMPI-2-RF Case Studies

In this chapter, MMPI-2-RF interpretation is illustrated with 10 cases representing various settings in which the test is used. Each case description begins with relevant background information, although some nonessential details have been changed to protect test takers' identities. Next, an MMPI-2-RF interpretation following the format described in Chapter 8 is provided for each case, followed by a discussion of how the test findings can assist in addressing specific referral questions. Relevant comparison group data are printed along with the test takers' scores for each of the cases. Some examples also illustrate use of item-level information, although the actual item content is redacted to protect the security of MMPI-2-RF items.

MS. G: OBSESSIVE–COMPULSIVE SYMPTOMS

Ms. G, a 35-year-old single woman, was self-referred for outpatient treatment at a community mental health center after losing her job owing to obsessive–compulsive behavior. She was preoccupied with worry that her apartment would catch fire or be burglarized and was repeatedly checking that her gas stove pilot light remained on, appliances were turned off, and the apartment door was locked. The intensity of her obsessive thoughts and compulsive checking behavior had been increasing for several months and was affecting her work, as she began to report late owing to her compulsive checking behavior. After repeated warnings, she was let go from her clerical position following continued late arrivals and reduced productivity.

Ms. G had no prior history of involvement with the mental health system. She came from an intact family and did not report any abuse history. She had been involved in a long-term romantic relationship that ended a few months before her seeking services. Prior to their separation, she had been residing with her boyfriend in a house that he owned, and this was the first time she had ever lived on her own.

At intake, Ms. G reported feeling anxious, depressed, embarrassed, and guilty over her job loss. She was diagnosed provisionally with Obsessive–Compulsive Disorder. Following her intake interview, an MMPI-2 was administered to assist with treatment planning. The MMPI-2-RF was scored later from this protocol and is reproduced in Figure 9-1. The outpatient community mental health center women comparison group was selected for inclusion with her results.

MMPI-2-RF Interpretation

Ms. G responded to all the MMPI-2-RF items, and her Validity Scale scores indicate that she did so in a relevant and consistent manner. There is no evidence of

Minnesota Multiphasic
Personality Inventory-2
Restructured Form®

Score Report

MMPI-2-RF®

Minnesota Multiphasic Personality Inventory-2-Restructured Form®

Yossef S. Ben-Porath, PhD, & Auke Tellegen, PhD

ID Number:	Ms. G
Age:	35
Gender:	Female
Marital Status:	Not reported
Years of Education:	Not reported
Date Assessed:	04/22/2011

PEARSON

⑫ *PsychCorp*

Figure 9-1. Ms. G's MMPI-2-RF Score Report.

MMPI-2-RF® Score Report
04/22/2011, Page 2

ID: Ms. G

MMPI-2-RF Validity Scales

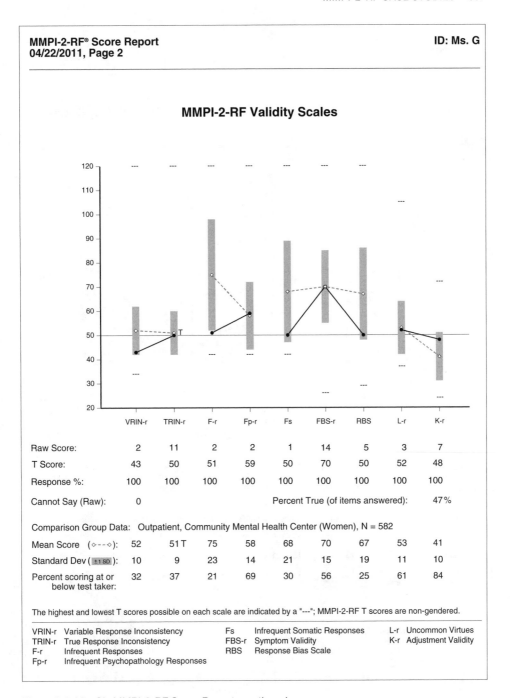

	VRIN-r	TRIN-r	F-r	Fp-r	Fs	FBS-r	RBS	L-r	K-r
Raw Score:	2	11	2	2	1	14	5	3	7
T Score:	43	50	51	59	50	70	50	52	48
Response %:	100	100	100	100	100	100	100	100	100

Cannot Say (Raw):   0   Percent True (of items answered):   47%

Comparison Group Data: Outpatient, Community Mental Health Center (Women), N = 582

Mean Score ($\diamond$--$\diamond$):	52	51 T	75	58	68	70	67	53	41
Standard Dev (±1 SD):	10	9	23	14	21	15	19	11	10
Percent scoring at or below test taker:	32	37	21	69	30	56	25	61	84

The highest and lowest T scores possible on each scale are indicated by a "---"; MMPI-2-RF T scores are non-gendered.

VRIN-r	Variable Response Inconsistency	Fs	Infrequent Somatic Responses	L-r	Uncommon Virtues
TRIN-r	True Response Inconsistency	FBS-r	Symptom Validity	K-r	Adjustment Validity
F-r	Infrequent Responses	RBS	Response Bias Scale		
Fp-r	Infrequent Psychopathology Responses				

Figure 9-1. Ms. G's MMPI-2-RF Score Report, continued.

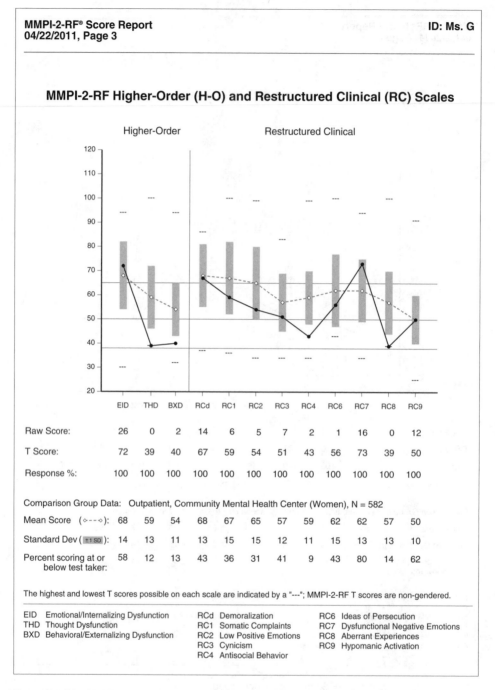

MMPI-2-RF Higher-Order (H-O) and Restructured Clinical (RC) Scales

Higher-Order   Restructured Clinical

	EID	THD	BXD	RCd	RC1	RC2	RC3	RC4	RC6	RC7	RC8	RC9
Raw Score:	26	0	2	14	6	5	7	2	1	16	0	12
T Score:	72	39	40	67	59	54	51	43	56	73	39	50
Response %:	100	100	100	100	100	100	100	100	100	100	100	100

Comparison Group Data: Outpatient, Community Mental Health Center (Women), N = 582

Mean Score (◇--◇):	68	59	54	68	67	65	57	59	62	62	57	50
Standard Dev (±1 SD):	14	13	11	13	15	15	12	11	15	13	13	10
Percent scoring at or below test taker:	58	12	13	43	36	31	41	9	43	80	14	62

The highest and lowest T scores possible on each scale are indicated by a "---"; MMPI-2-RF T scores are non-gendered.

EID Emotional/Internalizing Dysfunction	RCd Demoralization	RC6 Ideas of Persecution
THD Thought Dysfunction	RC1 Somatic Complaints	RC7 Dysfunctional Negative Emotions
BXD Behavioral/Externalizing Dysfunction	RC2 Low Positive Emotions	RC8 Aberrant Experiences
	RC3 Cynicism	RC9 Hypomanic Activation
	RC4 Antisocial Behavior	

Figure 9-1. Ms. G's MMPI-2-RF Score Report, continued.

MMPI-2-RF Somatic/Cognitive and Internalizing Scales

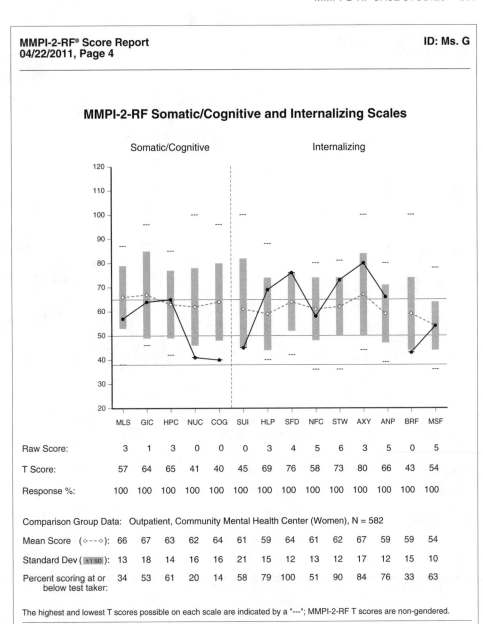

	MLS	GIC	HPC	NUC	COG	SUI	HLP	SFD	NFC	STW	AXY	ANP	BRF	MSF
Raw Score:	3	1	3	0	0	0	3	4	5	6	3	5	0	5
T Score:	57	64	65	41	40	45	69	76	58	73	80	66	43	54
Response %:	100	100	100	100	100	100	100	100	100	100	100	100	100	100

Comparison Group Data: Outpatient, Community Mental Health Center (Women), N = 582

Mean Score (◇--◇):	66	67	63	62	64	61	59	64	61	62	67	59	59	54
Standard Dev (±1 SD):	13	18	14	16	16	21	15	12	13	12	17	12	15	10
Percent scoring at or below test taker:	34	53	61	20	14	58	79	100	51	90	84	76	33	63

The highest and lowest T scores possible on each scale are indicated by a "---"; MMPI-2-RF T scores are non-gendered.

MLS	Malaise	SUI	Suicidal/Death Ideation	AXY	Anxiety
GIC	Gastrointestinal Complaints	HLP	Helplessness/Hopelessness	ANP	Anger Proneness
HPC	Head Pain Complaints	SFD	Self-Doubt	BRF	Behavior-Restricting Fears
NUC	Neurological Complaints	NFC	Inefficacy	MSF	Multiple Specific Fears
COG	Cognitive Complaints	STW	Stress/Worry		

Figure 9-1. Ms. G's MMPI-2-RF Score Report, continued.

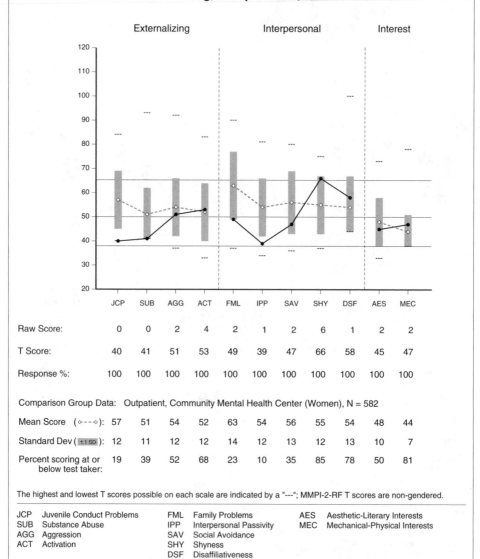

MMPI-2-RF Externalizing, Interpersonal, and Interest Scales

	Externalizing	Interpersonal	Interest

	JCP	SUB	AGG	ACT	FML	IPP	SAV	SHY	DSF	AES	MEC
Raw Score:	0	0	2	4	2	1	2	6	1	2	2
T Score:	40	41	51	53	49	39	47	66	58	45	47
Response %:	100	100	100	100	100	100	100	100	100	100	100

Comparison Group Data: Outpatient, Community Mental Health Center (Women), N = 582

	JCP	SUB	AGG	ACT	FML	IPP	SAV	SHY	DSF	AES	MEC
Mean Score (◇--◇):	57	51	54	52	63	54	56	55	54	48	44
Standard Dev (±1 SD):	12	11	12	12	14	12	13	12	13	10	7
Percent scoring at or below test taker:	19	39	52	68	23	10	35	85	78	50	81

The highest and lowest T scores possible on each scale are indicated by a "---"; MMPI-2-RF T scores are non-gendered.

JCP	Juvenile Conduct Problems	FML	Family Problems	AES	Aesthetic-Literary Interests
SUB	Substance Abuse	IPP	Interpersonal Passivity	MEC	Mechanical-Physical Interests
AGG	Aggression	SAV	Social Avoidance		
ACT	Activation	SHY	Shyness		
		DSF	Disaffiliativeness		

Figure 9-1. Ms. G's MMPI-2-RF Score Report, continued.

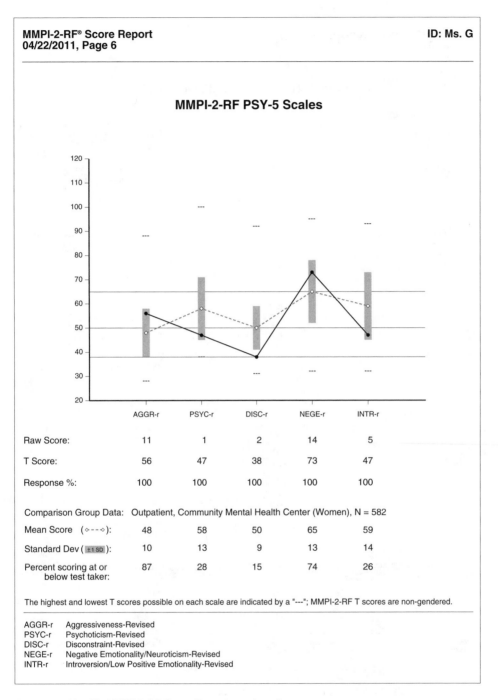

The highest and lowest T scores possible on each scale are indicated by a "---"; MMPI-2-RF T scores are non-gendered.

AGGR-r   Aggressiveness-Revised
PSYC-r   Psychoticism-Revised
DISC-r   Disconstraint-Revised
NEGE-r   Negative Emotionality/Neuroticism-Revised
INTR-r   Introversion/Low Positive Emotionality-Revised

Figure 9-1. Ms. G's MMPI-2-RF Score Report, continued.

MMPI-2-RF T SCORES (BY DOMAIN)

PROTOCOL VALIDITY

Content Non-Responsiveness

0	43	50
CNS	VRIN-r	TRIN-r

Over-Reporting

51	59		50	70	50
F-r	Fp-r		Fs	FBS-r	RBS

Under-Reporting

52	48
L-r	K-r

SUBSTANTIVE SCALES

Somatic/Cognitive Dysfunction

59	57	64	65	41	40
RC1	MLS	GIC	HPC	NUC	COG

Emotional Dysfunction

72
EID

67	45	69	76	58
RCd	SUI	HLP	SFD	NFC

54	47
RC2	INTR-r

73	73	80	66	43	54	73
RC7	STW	AXY	ANP	BRF	MSF	NEGE-r

Thought Dysfunction

39
THD

56
RC6

39
RC8

47
PSYC-r

Behavioral Dysfunction

40
BXD

43	40	41
RC4	JCP	SUB

50	51	53	56	38
RC9	AGG	ACT	AGGR-r	DISC-r

Interpersonal Functioning

49	51	39	47	66	58
FML	RC3	IPP	SAV	SHY	DSF

Interests

45	47
AES	MEC

Note. This information is provided to facilitate interpretation following the recommended structure for MMPI-2-RF interpretation in Chapter 5 of the *MMPI-2-RF Manual for Administration, Scoring, and Interpretation*, which provides details in the text and an outline in Table 5-1.

Figure 9-1. Ms. G's MMPI-2-RF Score Report, continued.

ITEM-LEVEL INFORMATION

Unscorable Responses

The test taker produced scorable responses to all the MMPI-2-RF items.

Critical Responses

Seven MMPI-2-RF scales--Suicidal/Death Ideation (SUI), Helplessness/Hopelessness (HLP), Anxiety (AXY), Ideas of Persecution (RC6), Aberrant Experiences (RC8), Substance Abuse (SUB), and Aggression (AGG)--have been designated by the test authors as having critical item content that may require immediate attention and follow-up. Items answered by the individual in the keyed direction (True or False) on a critical scale are listed below if her T score on that scale is 65 or higher. The percentage of the MMPI-2-RF normative sample (NS) and of the Outpatient, Community Mental Health Center (Women) comparison group (CG) that answered each item in the keyed direction are provided in parentheses following the item content.

Helplessness/Hopelessness (HLP, T Score = 69)

    135. Item content removed. (True; NS 24.2%, CG 50.2%)
    282. Item content removed. (False; NS 17.3%, CG 46.2%)
    336. Item content removed. (True; NS 38.0%, CG 36.1%)

Anxiety (AXY, T Score = 80)

    228. Item content removed. (True; NS 17.3%, CG 57.6%)
    275. Item content removed. (True; NS 5.0%, CG 34.5%)
    289. Item content removed. (True; NS 12.7%, CG 45.5%)

End of Report

Figure 9-1. Ms. G's MMPI-2-RF Score Report, continued.

overreporting or underreporting in her protocol. The resulting MMPI-2-RF scores should provide an accurate assessment of her psychological functioning.

Ms. G's responses indicate that she is experiencing significant psychological distress. She reports various negative emotional experiences, including anxiety and anger, which place her at risk for an anxiety-related disorder. She is likely to experience intrusive ideation and to be anger prone and stress reactive. She likely experiences sleep-related difficulties, including nightmares. She is prone to excessive worry and to engaging in obsessive rumination. Ms. G likely perceives others as being overly critical of her, while she is self-critical and guilt prone. She reports an above-average level of stress and worry. She is likely to experience anxiety and anxiety-related problems and, possibly, posttraumatic distress, and likely has problems with anger, irritability, and low tolerance for stress. Ms. G also likely holds grudges and has temper tantrums, and she is likely to be argumentative.

Ms. G also reports feeling sad and unhappy and being dissatisfied with her current life circumstances. She reports feeling hopeless and pessimistic and having self-doubts. She likely feels overwhelmed and that life is a strain, and she is likely to believe that she cannot be helped and that she gets a raw deal from life. Ms. G likely feels incapable of dealing with her current life circumstances. She may lack motivation for change and likely feels inferior and insecure. She is likely to be self-disparaging and intropunitive and to present as lacking in confidence and feeling useless. Ms. G's helplessness and hopelessness place her at risk for suicidal ideation. However, she denies any thoughts about suicide, recent suicide attempts, or preoccupation with death.

Ms. G reports head pain. If a physical origin of her head pain is ruled out, she is likely prone to developing physical symptoms in response to stress and to complain of headaches, chronic pain, and difficulty concentrating.

Ms. G reports that she is shy, easily embarrassed, and uncomfortable around others. She is likely to be socially introverted and inhibited, and she likely becomes anxious in social situations.

Ms. G's MMPI-2-RF results indicate the need to evaluate her for internalizing psychopathology, including an anxiety-related disorder, in particular for disorders involving excessive stress and worry such as Obsessive–Compulsive Disorder, Posttraumatic Stress Disorder (PTSD), as well as anger-related or depression-related disorders. Her scores also indicate a need to evaluate Ms. G for a possible Social Phobia and, if a physical origin for her head pain complaints is ruled out, a Somatoform Disorder. The possibility for an Axis II Cluster C disorder is also indicated for further evaluation.

Ms. G's test results indicate that her emotional difficulties may motivate her for treatment, and her feelings of loss of hope and despair should be considered as early intervention targets. Risk for self-harm should be evaluated in light of her level of hopelessness and helplessness. Dysfunctional negative emotions, including excessive stress and worry, anxiety, and anger, are indicated as possible treatment targets. Other potential treatment targets include feelings of depression, pain management for headaches if a physical origin is ruled out, low self-esteem, and anxiety in social situations. Her tendency to focus on negative information may also be a target for intervention.

Discussion

Ms. G's MMPI-2-RF results indicate that her problems lie within the Emotional/Internalizing domain. Comparison group results reported on page 3 of Figure 9-1 indicate that 58% of the 582 women who make up the outpatient community mental health center comparison group scored the same as or below Ms. G on the Emotional/Internalizing Dysfunction (EID) Scale. Thus, her clinically significant level of emotional dysfunction (as indicated by a T score of 72 on EID) is within the range found typically in women assessed at outpatient community mental health centers.

Ms. G's score on the Dysfunctional Negative Emotions (RC7) Scale stands out the most among the three RC Scales associated with EID (Demoralization [RCd], Low Positive Emotions [RC2], and RC7). It also stands out the most in reference to the comparison group, with 80% of the female outpatient community mental health center women scoring at or below Ms. G on this scale. Together, these findings indicate that anxiety-related psychopathology is the most prominent source of Ms. G's difficulties. Examination of scores on the Specific Problems Scales associated with RC7 indicates that stress and worry, anxiety, and anger are the most prominent negative emotions she is experiencing. Her score on the Stress/Worry (STW) Scale stands out the most in reference to the comparison group. Ms. G's score on this measure of ruminative thinking and stress reactivity is at or above those of 90% of members of the comparison group.

Ms. G's MMPI-2-RF results also indicate that she is experiencing a clinically significant level of demoralization, marked primarily by low self-esteem and a sense of helplessness and hopelessness. Her poor self-concept stands out the most in reference to the outpatient community mental health center comparison group, as indicated by the finding that 100% of the group members scored at or below Ms. G on the Self-Doubt (SFD) Scale. Although not as prominent, her clinically elevated score on the Helplessness/Hopelessness (HLP) Scale indicates a risk for suicidal ideation, which Ms. G denied in responding to the test items (as indicated by a raw score of zero on the Suicidal/Death Ideation [SUI] Scale).

It is quite possible that Ms. G's demoralization is a reaction to losing her job and other difficulties she has experienced as a result of her Anxiety Disorder. Nevertheless, it, too, will need to be addressed in planning for her treatment at the mental health center. Three other MMPI-2-RF findings identify other possible targets for intervention. Her clinically elevated score on the Head Pain Complaints (HPC) Scale indicates a need first to explore whether a physical origin of these complaints can be identified, and, if this is ruled out, the finding indicates possible somatoform psychopathology. Alternatively, Ms. G's somatic complaints may be related to excessive physiological arousal, an associated feature of some anxiety disorders. Ms. G's elevated score on the Shyness (SHY) Scale indicates that social anxiety, possibly rising to the level of a Social Phobia, needs also to be explored and, if verified, addressed in treatment. Finally, Ms. G's elevated score on the Personality

Psychopathology Five (PSY-5) Negative Emotionality/Neuroticism (NEGE-r) Scale indicates the possibility that some of her difficulties are more chronic in nature and may reflect manifestations of an Axis II Cluster C disorder.

Considered in light of Ms. G's presenting complaints, the MMPI-2-RF results are consistent with the intake clinician's preliminary diagnosis of Obsessive–Compulsive Disorder of moderate severity. Her test results also indicate the need to address Ms. G's demoralization and, in particular, her low self-esteem and sense of helplessness and hopelessness as well as significant interpersonal anxiety. Although her current level of emotional distress may motivate Ms. G to become engaged in treatment, the finding of a possible underlying Axis II disorder indicates that in the course of addressing her obsessive thinking and compulsive behaviors, the therapist may need to attend to more deeply seated interpersonal insecurities.

Ms. G attended weekly therapy sessions for approximately three months. The treating therapist identified Obsessive–Compulsive Disorder symptoms and low self-esteem as the initial targets for treatment and reported that Ms. G made steady progress in reducing the frequency and intensity of her obsessive thinking and compulsive behavior. The therapist reported that with the reduction in Obsessive–Compulsive Disorder symptoms, Ms. G's mood improved considerably, particularly after she was able to find a new job. However, this development also made it difficult for Ms. G to continue attending therapy sessions, and her treatment was discontinued by mutual agreement, although the therapist indicated in her discharge report that low self-esteem and a tendency to somaticize in response to stress should be addressed with a more insight-oriented approach should Ms. G return for treatment.

MR. P: A CHRONIC AND SEVERE DISORDER

Mr. P is a 49-year-old single male assessed at intake to an inpatient psychiatric unit of a community hospital. He had a long-standing diagnosis of Schizophrenia, Paranoid Type. He received this diagnosis in his late teenage years and resided with his parents most of his adult life. His father passed away when Mr. P was in his late 20s. He continued to reside with his mother, who was in her 70s at the time of the present hospitalization. Mr. P received case management services in the community and was periodically employed as an unskilled laborer under the auspices of the community mental health agency where he received his treatment.

Several weeks prior to his hospitalization, Mr. P became embroiled in a conflict with one of his coworkers, and his employment status was suspended as a consequence of a physical altercation between the two. Mr. P became very upset following his suspension and discontinued taking his medication. According to his mother, he began to show signs of deterioration, marked by preoccupation with beliefs that he was the victim of a government conspiracy to take his employment income and deprive him of disability benefits. Mr. P's mother contacted his case manager and informed her of his deterioration and specifically that he had threatened to retaliate against his supervisor and coworker. Although he did not have a history of violent acting out, his treating psychiatrist determined that there was a significant risk that Mr. P would act on his threats, and he was admitted on a three-day hold for inpatient assessment and treatment.

Mr. P was administered the MMPI-2-RF as part of this assessment. His test results are reproduced in Figure 9-2. The psychiatric inpatient community hospital men comparison group data were selected for use in this evaluation.

MMPI-2-RF Interpretation

Mr. P responded to all but two of the MMPI-2-RF items. The only scale affected by nonresponding was Multiple Specific Fears (MSF), for which only 89% of Mr. P's item responses were scorable. His Consistency Scale scores indicate that Mr. P responded relevantly to the test items. He provided a larger-than-average number of infrequent responses. However, this level of infrequent responding can occur in individuals with significant psychopathology like Mr. P, and it does not indicate overreporting in this case. There are no other indications of overreporting.

Possible underreporting is indicated by Mr. P's presenting himself in a positive light by denying some minor faults and shortcomings that most people acknowledge. Any absence of elevation on the Substantive Scales should, therefore, be interpreted with caution. Elevated scores on the Substantive Scales may underestimate the problems assessed by those scales.

Mr. P's responses indicate significant thought dysfunction. He reports prominent persecutory ideation that probably rises to the level of paranoid delusions, and he is indeed very likely to experience paranoid delusional thinking. He is also very likely to be suspicious and alienated from others and to experience interpersonal difficulties as a result of suspiciousness. Mr. P also very likely lacks insight, and he is very likely to blame others for his difficulties. In addition, Mr. P reports unusual thought and perceptual processes. He likely experiences thought disorganization, and he is likely to engage in unrealistic thinking and to believe that he has unusual sensory/perceptual abilities. His aberrant experiences may include somatic delusions.

Mr. P reports multiple somatic complaints that primarily comprise vague neurological symptoms. He is likely prone to developing physical symptoms in response to stress, and, in particular, he is likely to complain about dizziness, coordination difficulties, and sensory problems. As just noted, it is possible that Mr. P's somatic complaints are delusional in nature.

Mr. P reports feeling anxious, and he is likely to experience significant anxiety and anxiety-related problems, including intrusive ideation; sleep difficulties, including nightmares; and posttraumatic distress. He also reports fears that significantly restrict his normal activity inside and outside the home, and he is likely to experience general fearfulness.

Mr. P reports that he is interpersonally aggressive and assertive. He is likely to be overly assertive and socially dominant, to engage in instrumentally aggressive behavior, to believe that he has leadership abilities, and to be viewed by others as domineering. He reports having cynical beliefs, being distrustful of others, and believing that others look out only for their own interests. Mr. P is likely to be hostile toward and distrustful of others and to have negative interpersonal experiences.

Minnesota Multiphasic
Personality Inventory-2
Restructured Form®

Score Report

MMPI-2-RF®

Minnesota Multiphasic Personality Inventory-2-Restructured Form®

Yossef S. Ben-Porath, PhD, & Auke Tellegen, PhD

ID Number:	Mr. P
Age:	49
Gender:	Male
Marital Status:	Never Married
Years of Education:	11
Date Assessed:	04/22/2011

PEARSON   ⑫ *PsychCorp*

Figure 9-2. Mr. P's MMPI-2-RF Score Report.

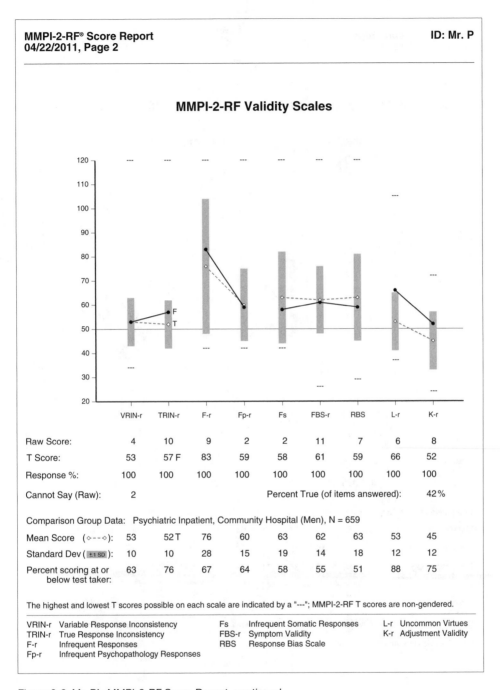

MMPI-2-RF Validity Scales

	VRIN-r	TRIN-r	F-r	Fp-r	Fs	FBS-r	RBS	L-r	K-r
Raw Score:	4	10	9	2	2	11	7	6	8
T Score:	53	57 F	83	59	58	61	59	66	52
Response %:	100	100	100	100	100	100	100	100	100

Cannot Say (Raw):   2   Percent True (of items answered):   42%

Comparison Group Data: Psychiatric Inpatient, Community Hospital (Men), N = 659

	VRIN-r	TRIN-r	F-r	Fp-r	Fs	FBS-r	RBS	L-r	K-r
Mean Score (◇--◇):	53	52 T	76	60	63	62	63	53	45
Standard Dev (±1 SD):	10	10	28	15	19	14	18	12	12
Percent scoring at or below test taker:	63	76	67	64	58	55	51	88	75

The highest and lowest T scores possible on each scale are indicated by a "---"; MMPI-2-RF T scores are non-gendered.

VRIN-r	Variable Response Inconsistency	Fs Infrequent Somatic Responses	L-r Uncommon Virtues
TRIN-r	True Response Inconsistency	FBS-r Symptom Validity	K-r Adjustment Validity
F-r	Infrequent Responses	RBS Response Bias Scale	
Fp-r	Infrequent Psychopathology Responses		

Figure 9-2. Mr. P's MMPI-2-RF Score Report, continued.

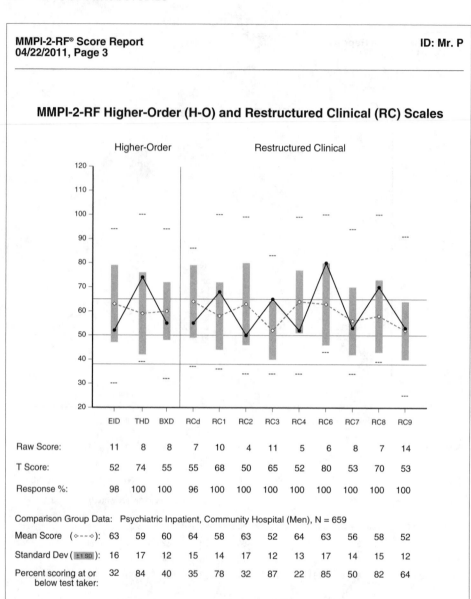

MMPI-2-RF® Score Report
04/22/2011, Page 3   ID: Mr. P

MMPI-2-RF Higher-Order (H-O) and Restructured Clinical (RC) Scales

Higher-Order   Restructured Clinical

	EID	THD	BXD	RCd	RC1	RC2	RC3	RC4	RC6	RC7	RC8	RC9
Raw Score:	11	8	8	7	10	4	11	5	6	8	7	14
T Score:	52	74	55	55	68	50	65	52	80	53	70	53
Response %:	98	100	100	96	100	100	100	100	100	100	100	100

Comparison Group Data: Psychiatric Inpatient, Community Hospital (Men), N = 659

	EID	THD	BXD	RCd	RC1	RC2	RC3	RC4	RC6	RC7	RC8	RC9
Mean Score (◇- - -◇):	63	59	60	64	58	63	52	64	63	56	58	52
Standard Dev (±1 SD):	16	17	12	15	14	17	12	13	17	14	15	12
Percent scoring at or below test taker:	32	84	40	35	78	32	87	22	85	50	82	64

The highest and lowest T scores possible on each scale are indicated by a "---"; MMPI-2-RF T scores are non-gendered.

EID Emotional/Internalizing Dysfunction	RCd Demoralization	RC6 Ideas of Persecution
THD Thought Dysfunction	RC1 Somatic Complaints	RC7 Dysfunctional Negative Emotions
BXD Behavioral/Externalizing Dysfunction	RC2 Low Positive Emotions	RC8 Aberrant Experiences
	RC3 Cynicism	RC9 Hypomanic Activation
	RC4 Antisocial Behavior	

Figure 9-2. Mr. P's MMPI-2-RF Score Report, continued.

MMPI-2-RF Somatic/Cognitive and Internalizing Scales

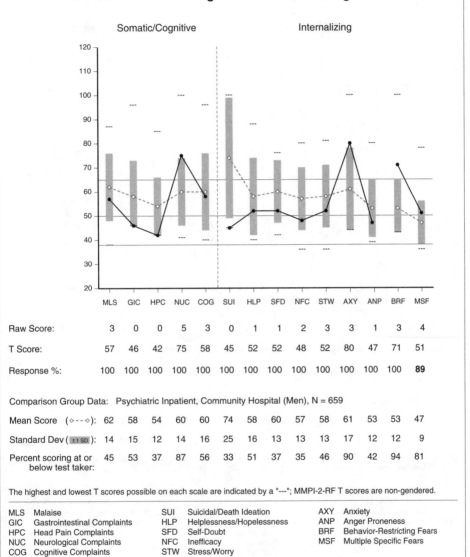

	MLS	GIC	HPC	NUC	COG	SUI	HLP	SFD	NFC	STW	AXY	ANP	BRF	MSF
Raw Score:	3	0	0	5	3	0	1	1	2	3	3	1	3	4
T Score:	57	46	42	75	58	45	52	52	48	52	80	47	71	51
Response %:	100	100	100	100	100	100	100	100	100	100	100	100	100	**89**

Comparison Group Data: Psychiatric Inpatient, Community Hospital (Men), N = 659

Mean Score (◇--◇):	62	58	54	60	60	74	58	60	57	58	61	53	53	47
Standard Dev (±1 SD):	14	15	12	14	16	25	16	13	13	13	17	12	12	9
Percent scoring at or below test taker:	45	53	37	87	56	33	51	37	35	46	90	42	94	81

The highest and lowest T scores possible on each scale are indicated by a "---"; MMPI-2-RF T scores are non-gendered.

MLS	Malaise	SUI	Suicidal/Death Ideation	AXY	Anxiety
GIC	Gastrointestinal Complaints	HLP	Helplessness/Hopelessness	ANP	Anger Proneness
HPC	Head Pain Complaints	SFD	Self-Doubt	BRF	Behavior-Restricting Fears
NUC	Neurological Complaints	NFC	Inefficacy	MSF	Multiple Specific Fears
COG	Cognitive Complaints	STW	Stress/Worry		

Figure 9-2. Mr. P's MMPI-2-RF Score Report, continued.

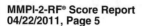

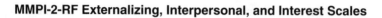

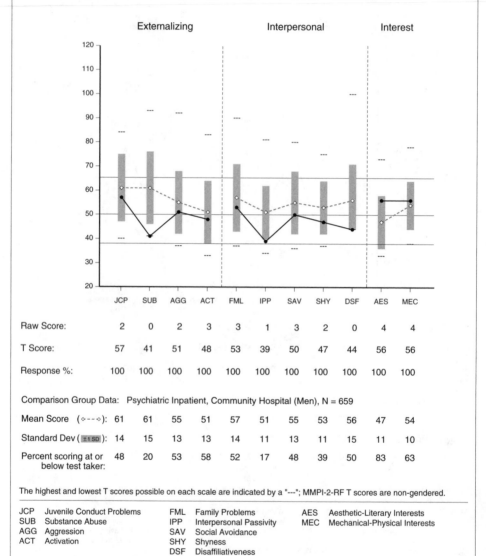

Figure 9-2. Mr. P's MMPI-2-RF Score Report, continued.

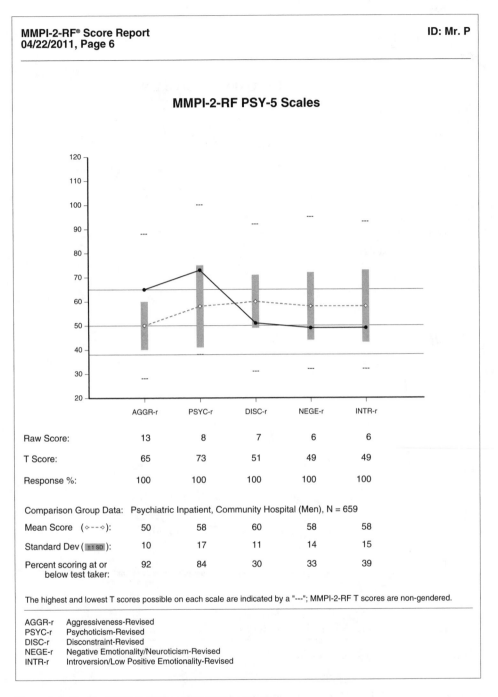

MMPI-2-RF PSY-5 Scales

	AGGR-r	PSYC-r	DISC-r	NEGE-r	INTR-r
Raw Score:	13	8	7	6	6
T Score:	65	73	51	49	49
Response %:	100	100	100	100	100

Comparison Group Data: Psychiatric Inpatient, Community Hospital (Men), N = 659

Mean Score (◇- - -◇):	50	58	60	58	58
Standard Dev (±1 SD):	10	17	11	14	15
Percent scoring at or below test taker:	92	84	30	33	39

The highest and lowest T scores possible on each scale are indicated by a "---"; MMPI-2-RF T scores are non-gendered.

AGGR-r   Aggressiveness-Revised
PSYC-r   Psychoticism-Revised
DISC-r   Disconstraint-Revised
NEGE-r   Negative Emotionality/Neuroticism-Revised
INTR-r   Introversion/Low Positive Emotionality-Revised

Figure 9-2. Mr. P's MMPI-2-RF Score Report, continued.

MMPI-2-RF T SCORES (BY DOMAIN)

PROTOCOL VALIDITY

Content Non-Responsiveness

2	53	57 F
CNS	VRIN-r	TRIN-r

Over-Reporting

83	59		58	61	59
F-r	Fp-r		Fs	FBS-r	RBS

Under-Reporting

66	52
L-r	K-r

SUBSTANTIVE SCALES

Somatic/Cognitive Dysfunction

68	57	46	42	75	58
RC1	MLS	GIC	HPC	NUC	COG

Emotional Dysfunction

52		55	45	52	52	48		
EID		RCd	SUI	HLP	SFD	NFC		

50	49
RC2	INTR-r

53	52	80	47	71	51*	49
RC7	STW	AXY	ANP	BRF	MSF	NEGE-r

Thought Dysfunction

74		80
THD		RC6

70
RC8

73
PSYC-r

Behavioral Dysfunction

55		52	57	41		
BXD		RC4	JCP	SUB		

53	51	48	65	51
RC9	AGG	ACT	AGGR-r	DISC-r

Interpersonal Functioning

53	65	39	50	47	44
FML	RC3	IPP	SAV	SHY	DSF

Interests

56	56
AES	MEC

*The test taker provided scorable responses to less than 90% of the items scored on this scale. See the relevant profile page for the specific percentage.

Note. This information is provided to facilitate interpretation following the recommended structure for MMPI-2-RF interpretation in Chapter 5 of the *MMPI-2-RF Manual for Administration, Scoring, and Interpretation*, which provides details in the text and an outline in Table 5-1.

Figure 9-2. Mr. P's MMPI-2-RF Score Report, continued.

ITEM-LEVEL INFORMATION

Unscorable Responses

Following is a list of items to which the test taker did not provide scorable responses. Unanswered or double answered (both True and False) items are unscorable. The scales on which the items appear are in parentheses following the item content.

   172. Item content removed. (EID, RCd)
   184. Item content removed. (MSF)

Critical Responses

Seven MMPI-2-RF scales--Suicidal/Death Ideation (SUI), Helplessness/Hopelessness (HLP), Anxiety (AXY), Ideas of Persecution (RC6), Aberrant Experiences (RC8), Substance Abuse (SUB), and Aggression (AGG)--have been designated by the test authors as having critical item content that may require immediate attention and follow-up. Items answered by the individual in the keyed direction (True or False) on a critical scale are listed below if his T score on that scale is 65 or higher. The percentage of the MMPI-2-RF normative sample (NS) and of the Psychiatric Inpatient, Community Hospital (Men) comparison group (CG) that answered each item in the keyed direction are provided in parentheses following the item content.

Anxiety (AXY, T Score = 80)

   79. Item content removed. (True; NS 6.2%, CG 27.2%)
  275. Item content removed. (True; NS 5.0%, CG 30.8%)
  289. Item content removed. (True; NS 12.7%, CG 22.5%)

Ideas of Persecution (RC6, T Score = 80)

  150. Item content removed. (True; NS 2.0%, CG 7.1%)
  194. Item content removed. (True; NS 17.1%, CG 43.6%)
  212. Item content removed. (False; NS 9.1%, CG 28.4%)
  233. Item content removed. (True; NS 5.5%, CG 29.7%)
  264. Item content removed. (True; NS 5.3%, CG 21.4%)
  310. Item content removed. (True; NS 3.0%, CG 16.5%)

Aberrant Experiences (RC8, T Score = 70)

   32. Item content removed. (True; NS 21.1%, CG 51.0%)
   85. Item content removed. (False; NS 17.1%, CG 35.2%)
  179. Item content removed. (True; NS 12.6%, CG 23.7%)
  199. Item content removed. (True; NS 12.1%, CG 20.6%)
  216. Item content removed. (True; NS 10.2%, CG 18.5%)
  240. Item content removed. (True; NS 8.8%, CG 23.2%)
  330. Item content removed. (True; NS 15.2%, CG 19.0%)

Figure 9-2. Mr. P's MMPI-2-RF Score Report, continued.

User-Designated Item-Level Information

The following item-level information is based on the report user's selection of additional scales, and/or of lower cutoffs for the critical scales from the previous section. Items answered by the test taker in the keyed direction (True or False) on a selected scale are listed below if his T score on that scale is at the user-designated cutoff score or higher. The percentage of the MMPI-2-RF normative sample (NS) and of the Psychiatric Inpatient, Community Hospital (Men) comparison group (CG) that answered each item in the keyed direction are provided in parentheses following the item content.

Somatic Complaints (RC1, T Score = 68)

   28. Item content removed. (False; NS 24.6%, CG 17.8%)
   69. Item content removed. (False; NS 9.5%, CG 19.7%)
113. Item content removed. (False; NS 11.0%, CG 25.8%)
162. Item content removed. (False; NS 12.8%, CG 23.7%)
174. Item content removed. (False; NS 7.5%, CG 37.8%)
227. Item content removed. (False; NS 7.8%, CG 20.5%)
242. Item content removed. (True; NS 9.9%, CG 16.2%)
254. Item content removed. (False; NS 28.6%, CG 40.7%)
290. Item content removed. (False; NS 19.2%, CG 27.8%)
313. Item content removed. (False; NS 15.4%, CG 31.6%)

Neurological Complaints (NUC, T Score = 75)

   69. Item content removed. (False; NS 9.5%, CG 19.7%)
113. Item content removed. (False; NS 11.0%, CG 25.8%)
162. Item content removed. (False; NS 12.8%, CG 23.7%)
227. Item content removed. (False; NS 7.8%, CG 20.5%)
313. Item content removed. (False; NS 15.4%, CG 31.6%)

End of Report

This and previous pages of this report contain trade secrets and are not to be released in response to requests under HIPAA (or any other data disclosure law that exempts trade secret information from release). Further, release in response to litigation discovery demands should be made only in accordance with your profession's ethical guidelines and under an appropriate protective order.

Figure 9-2. Mr. P's MMPI-2-RF Score Report, continued.

Mr. P's MMPI-2-RF results identify a number of diagnostic considerations. He should be evaluated for a possible thought disorder, particularly one involving paranoid delusional thinking, including Schizophrenia, Paranoid Type. If a physical origin for Mr. P's neurological complaints can be ruled out, a possible Somatoform Disorder or the possibility that he is experiencing somatic delusions should be considered. The possibility that Mr. P is also experiencing an anxiety disorder, particularly PTSD and agoraphobia, also needs to be considered. The possibility of an Axis II Cluster B disorder, particularly one involving mistrust of and hostility toward others, is also indicated for further consideration.

Mr. P's results raise the possibility that he may require inpatient treatment for thought dysfunction, and the need for antipsychotic medication should be evaluated. His persecutory ideation and cynicism may interfere with forming a therapeutic relationship and complying with treatment. A neurological and/or neuropsychological evaluation may be needed to clarify the nature and origin of Mr. P's vague neurological complaints. Anxiety and behavior-restricting fears should also be considered as targets for intervention.

Discussion

Mr. P's Validity Scale scores illustrate the utility of considering relevant comparison group data. As noted in the interpretation, his F-r T score (83) is considerably above average in reference to the general population normative sample. However, when compared with other male psychiatric inpatients, this score falls near the comparison group mean. In fact, as reported on page 2 of Figure 9-2, 67% of individuals in the comparison group scored at or below Mr. P's T score on F-r; thus one-third of the men in this group scored higher than Mr. P on this scale. By contrast, his L-r T score (66), although representing a lesser deviation from the general population norm than his score on F-r, is more uncommon when compared with other male psychiatric inpatients. Only 12% of the men in the inpatient comparison group scored higher than Mr. P on L-r. Consequently, underreporting, particularly as it pertains to immoral or undesirable behavior, is of greater concern than is overreporting in Mr. P's case. As indicated in the interpretation, this finding precludes relying on the absence of Substantive Scale elevations to rule out the presence of problems assessed by these scales, and it raises the possibility that elevated scores may underestimate Mr. P's dysfunction.

As would be expected with his history, Mr. P's scores on the Substantive Scales indicate that he is likely experiencing symptoms of a thought disorder marked by substantial persecutory ideation that manifests in paranoid delusional beliefs. As just discussed, his relatively high L-r score indicates that Mr. P's scores on the thought dysfunction measures may underestimate the severity of his symptoms.

Elevated scores on Somatic Complaints (RC1) and Neurological Complaints (NUC) were not expected given the absence of any history of somatic complaints by Mr. P. His Validity Scale scores did not identify any concerns about somatic symptom overreporting. To obtain additional information about the nature of Mr. P's somatic complaints, his MMPI-2-RF Score Report was reprinted with RC1 and

NUC selected for inclusion as user-designated item-level information (see Chapter 5 for a discussion of this reporting option). This information appears on page 9 of Figure 9-2. Examination of these item-level responses raised the possibility that most of Mr. P's complaints were related to extrapyramidal symptoms. Mr. P later confirmed that this was one of the reasons he had discontinued taking his medication, which was eventually adjusted in an effort to control these side-effects.

Elevations on the Anxiety (AXY) and Behavior-Restricting Fears (BRF) scales were also unexpected. Hospital staff concluded ultimately that Mr. P's reported problems in these areas were secondary to his exacerbated thought disorder. This conclusion is consistent with the absence of elevation on the Higher-Order or Restructured Clinical Scales associated with emotional dysfunction.

Of particular concern in this evaluation was whether Mr. P posed a threat (to himself or others) that would justify involuntary hospitalization. His T score (65) on the PSY-5 Aggressiveness (AGGR-r) Scale was the only clinically significant elevation he produced on any of the externalizing dysfunction indicators. However, as discussed earlier, Mr. P's elevated score on L-r precluded reliance on nonelevated Externalizing Scale scores to rule out the possibility that he would act on his paranoid delusional beliefs.

Mr. P was referred for a neuropsychological evaluation that ruled out the presence of any prominent neurocognitive dysfunction beyond what might be expected of an individual with a long-standing thought disorder. The attending psychiatrist adjusted Mr. P's medication, and he agreed to stay in the hospital for a week after his 72-hour hold expired. His acute paranoia subsided, and he was discharged back to his mother's home and to follow-up care in the community.

MS. L: AN ABUSIVE RELATIONSHIP ENDS

Ms. L is a 20-year-old single college student who presented at a college counseling clinic with complaints that she was experiencing academic difficulties following a breakup with her boyfriend. A professor in one of her classes recommended that she seek counseling at the clinic.

At intake, Ms. L reported that she had been involved in an abusive relationship with her boyfriend for over a year. They frequently wound up in arguments that culminated in physical altercations. These arguments were triggered by Ms. L's suspicions that her boyfriend was unfaithful to her. Although they did not require medical attention as a result of these altercations, Ms. L and her boyfriend would often have bruises that they had difficulty explaining to others. These altercations would typically occur when the two were intoxicated.

Ms. L indicated that her boyfriend ended their relationship three weeks prior to her coming to the clinic. She went on a two-week drinking binge following the breakup. During that time, she had sexual relationships with several men she had met at bars, where she was using forged identification. She also stopped attending classes and missed several exams. After a friend threatened to tell her parents about her activities, Ms. L stopped going to bars and started attending classes again. When discussing her failing grade in a class and attempting to explain the reason for her absence from an exam, Ms. L broke down and told her professor about the events just described. The professor recommended that she seek assistance at the university's counseling clinic.

Ms. L was administered the MMPI-2-RF as part of the standard intake assessment procedures at the college counseling clinic. Her results are reproduced in Figure 9-3. The college counseling clinic women comparison group was selected for inclusion with her results.

MMPI-2-RF Interpretation

Ms. L provided scorable responses to all but three of the MMPI-2-RF items. Examination of the Response % statistics reported in Figure 9-3 indicates that this resulted in less than 90% scorable responses to the items of the STW Scale (see page 4 of Figure 9-3), rendering Ms. L's nonelevated score on this scale uninterpretable. This is the only scale affected by her unscorable responses. Her scores on the Validity Scales indicate that Ms. L responded to the MMPI-2-RF items in a relevant and consistent manner, and there is no evidence of overreporting or underreporting in her protocol. With the exception of the STW Scale, Ms. L's MMPI-2-RF scores should provide an accurate indication of her psychological functioning.

Ms. L's responses indicate significant externalizing, acting-out behavior, which is likely to have gotten her into difficulties. She reports a significant history of antisocial behavior and is likely to fail to conform to social norms and expectations, to have difficulties with individuals in positions of authority, to experience conflictual interpersonal relationships, to be impulsive and act out when bored, and to have antisocial characteristics. She reports significant past and current substance abuse and is likely to have a history of problematic use of alcohol or drugs, to frequently use alcohol or drugs, and to use alcohol to loosen up.

Ms. L also reports an above-average level of activation and engagement with her environment and is likely restless and easily bored and overactivated, as manifested in poor impulse control, aggression, mood instability, euphoria, excitability, sensation seeking, risk taking, and other forms of undercontrolled behavior. She is likely to display narcissistic personality features. Ms. L does indeed report engaging in physically aggressive, violent behavior and losing control. She likely has a history of violent behavior toward others and is likely to be abusive and to experience anger-related problems.

Somewhat unexpectedly, Ms. L reports a high level of psychological well-being, including a wide range of emotionally positive experiences, and that she feels energetic. This report is, however, consistent with the just-noted possibility that she experiences mood swings and, occasionally, euphoria.

Ms. L reports significant persecutory ideation such as believing that others seek to harm her. Examination of her item-level responses indicates that her persecutory thoughts center on beliefs that she is being talked about by others who say negative things about her and that others are trying to influence her. She is likely suspicious of and alienated from others and may experience interpersonal difficulties as a result of her suspiciousness. Ms. L is also likely to lack insight and to blame others for her

Minnesota Multiphasic
Personality Inventory-2
Restructured Form®

Score Report

MMPI-2-RF®

Minnesota Multiphasic Personality Inventory-2-Restructured Form®

Yossef S. Ben-Porath, PhD, & Auke Tellegen, PhD

ID Number:	Ms. L
Age:	20
Gender:	Female
Marital Status:	Never Married
Years of Education:	15
Date Assessed:	04/22/2011

PEARSON   ⓦ *PsychCorp*

Figure 9-3. Ms. L's MMPI-2-RF Score Report.

MMPI-2-RF® Score Report   ID: Ms. L
04/22/2011, Page 2

MMPI-2-RF Validity Scales

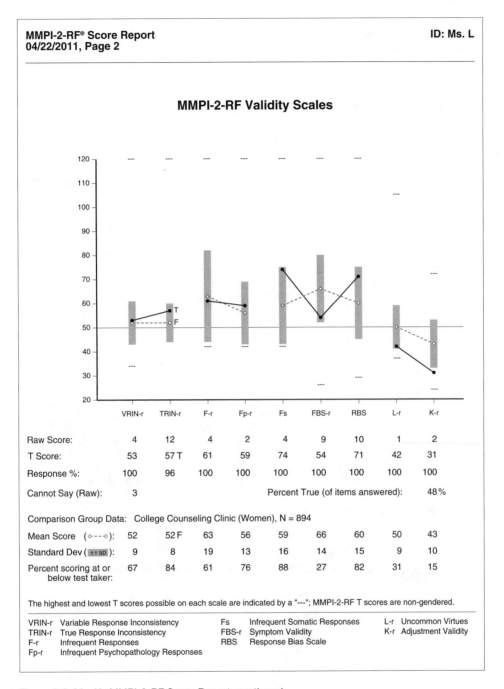

	VRIN-r	TRIN-r	F-r	Fp-r	Fs	FBS-r	RBS	L-r	K-r
Raw Score:	4	12	4	2	4	9	10	1	2
T Score:	53	57 T	61	59	74	54	71	42	31
Response %:	100	96	100	100	100	100	100	100	100

Cannot Say (Raw):   3   Percent True (of items answered):   48%

Comparison Group Data: College Counseling Clinic (Women), N = 894

	VRIN-r	TRIN-r	F-r	Fp-r	Fs	FBS-r	RBS	L-r	K-r
Mean Score (◇--◇):	52	52 F	63	56	59	66	60	50	43
Standard Dev (±1 SD):	9	8	19	13	16	14	15	9	10
Percent scoring at or below test taker:	67	84	61	76	88	27	82	31	15

The highest and lowest T scores possible on each scale are indicated by a "---"; MMPI-2-RF T scores are non-gendered.

VRIN-r	Variable Response Inconsistency	Fs	Infrequent Somatic Responses	L-r Uncommon Virtues
TRIN-r	True Response Inconsistency	FBS-r	Symptom Validity	K-r Adjustment Validity
F-r	Infrequent Responses	RBS	Response Bias Scale	
Fp-r	Infrequent Psychopathology Responses			

Figure 9-3. Ms. L's MMPI-2-RF Score Report, continued.

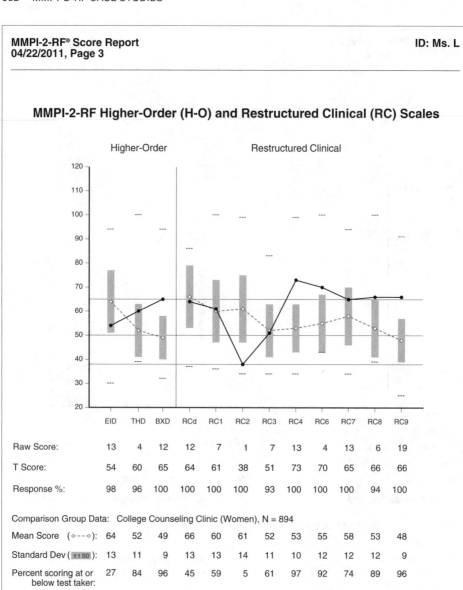

MMPI-2-RF Higher-Order (H-O) and Restructured Clinical (RC) Scales

Higher-Order

Restructured Clinical

	EID	THD	BXD	RCd	RC1	RC2	RC3	RC4	RC6	RC7	RC8	RC9
Raw Score:	13	4	12	12	7	1	7	13	4	13	6	19
T Score:	54	60	65	64	61	38	51	73	70	65	66	66
Response %:	98	96	100	100	100	100	93	100	100	100	94	100

Comparison Group Data: College Counseling Clinic (Women), N = 894

	EID	THD	BXD	RCd	RC1	RC2	RC3	RC4	RC6	RC7	RC8	RC9
Mean Score (◇- - -◇):	64	52	49	66	60	61	52	53	55	58	53	48
Standard Dev (±1 SD):	13	11	9	13	13	14	11	10	12	12	12	9
Percent scoring at or below test taker:	27	84	96	45	59	5	61	97	92	74	89	96

The highest and lowest T scores possible on each scale are indicated by a "---"; MMPI-2-RF T scores are non-gendered.

EID Emotional/Internalizing Dysfunction	RCd Demoralization	RC6 Ideas of Persecution
THD Thought Dysfunction	RC1 Somatic Complaints	RC7 Dysfunctional Negative Emotions
BXD Behavioral/Externalizing Dysfunction	RC2 Low Positive Emotions	RC8 Aberrant Experiences
	RC3 Cynicism	RC9 Hypomanic Activation
	RC4 Antisocial Behavior	

Figure 9-3. Ms. L's MMPI-2-RF Score Report, continued.

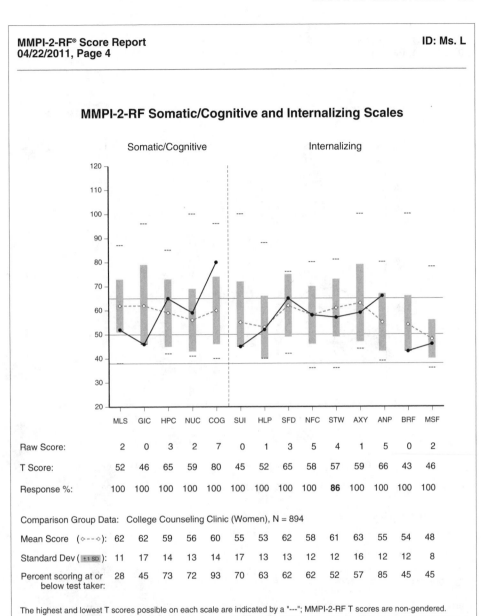

MMPI-2-RF Somatic/Cognitive and Internalizing Scales

	MLS	GIC	HPC	NUC	COG	SUI	HLP	SFD	NFC	STW	AXY	ANP	BRF	MSF
Raw Score:	2	0	3	2	7	0	1	3	5	4	1	5	0	2
T Score:	52	46	65	59	80	45	52	65	58	57	59	66	43	46
Response %:	100	100	100	100	100	100	100	100	100	**86**	100	100	100	100

Comparison Group Data: College Counseling Clinic (Women), N = 894

	MLS	GIC	HPC	NUC	COG	SUI	HLP	SFD	NFC	STW	AXY	ANP	BRF	MSF
Mean Score (◇---◇):	62	62	59	56	60	55	53	62	58	61	63	55	54	48
Standard Dev (±1 SD):	11	17	14	13	14	17	13	13	12	12	16	12	12	8
Percent scoring at or below test taker:	28	45	73	72	93	70	63	62	62	52	57	85	45	45

The highest and lowest T scores possible on each scale are indicated by a "---"; MMPI-2-RF T scores are non-gendered.

MLS	Malaise	SUI	Suicidal/Death Ideation	AXY	Anxiety
GIC	Gastrointestinal Complaints	HLP	Helplessness/Hopelessness	ANP	Anger Proneness
HPC	Head Pain Complaints	SFD	Self-Doubt	BRF	Behavior-Restricting Fears
NUC	Neurological Complaints	NFC	Inefficacy	MSF	Multiple Specific Fears
COG	Cognitive Complaints	STW	Stress/Worry		

Figure 9-3. Ms. L's MMPI-2-RF Score Report, continued.

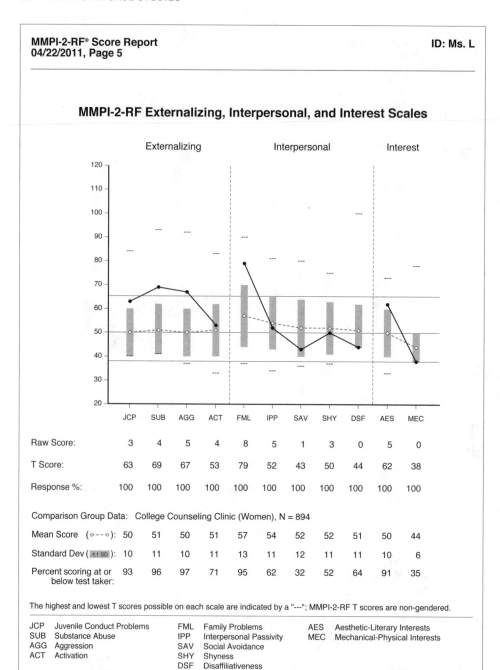

MMPI-2-RF Externalizing, Interpersonal, and Interest Scales

	Externalizing	Interpersonal	Interest

	JCP	SUB	AGG	ACT	FML	IPP	SAV	SHY	DSF	AES	MEC
Raw Score:	3	4	5	4	8	5	1	3	0	5	0
T Score:	63	69	67	53	79	52	43	50	44	62	38
Response %:	100	100	100	100	100	100	100	100	100	100	100

Comparison Group Data: College Counseling Clinic (Women), N = 894

	JCP	SUB	AGG	ACT	FML	IPP	SAV	SHY	DSF	AES	MEC
Mean Score (◇--◇):	50	51	50	51	57	54	52	52	51	50	44
Standard Dev (±1 SD):	10	11	10	11	13	11	12	11	11	10	6
Percent scoring at or below test taker:	93	96	97	71	95	62	32	52	64	91	35

The highest and lowest T scores possible on each scale are indicated by a "---"; MMPI-2-RF T scores are non-gendered.

JCP	Juvenile Conduct Problems	FML	Family Problems	AES	Aesthetic-Literary Interests
SUB	Substance Abuse	IPP	Interpersonal Passivity	MEC	Mechanical-Physical Interests
AGG	Aggression	SAV	Social Avoidance		
ACT	Activation	SHY	Shyness		
		DSF	Disaffiliativeness		

Figure 9-3. Ms. L's MMPI-2-RF Score Report, continued.

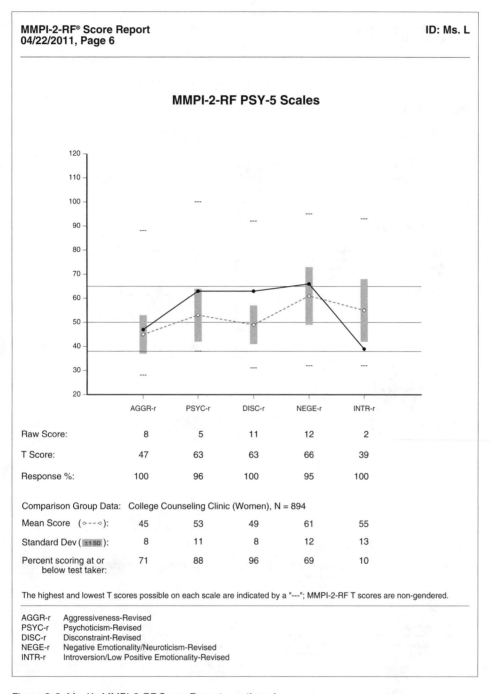

MMPI-2-RF PSY-5 Scales

	AGGR-r	PSYC-r	DISC-r	NEGE-r	INTR-r
Raw Score:	8	5	11	12	2
T Score:	47	63	63	66	39
Response %:	100	96	100	95	100

Comparison Group Data: College Counseling Clinic (Women), N = 894

	AGGR-r	PSYC-r	DISC-r	NEGE-r	INTR-r
Mean Score (◇--◇):	45	53	49	61	55
Standard Dev (±1 SD):	8	11	8	12	13
Percent scoring at or below test taker:	71	88	96	69	10

The highest and lowest T scores possible on each scale are indicated by a "---"; MMPI-2-RF T scores are non-gendered.

AGGR-r   Aggressiveness-Revised
PSYC-r   Psychoticism-Revised
DISC-r   Disconstraint-Revised
NEGE-r   Negative Emotionality/Neuroticism-Revised
INTR-r   Introversion/Low Positive Emotionality-Revised

Figure 9-3. Ms. L's MMPI-2-RF Score Report, continued.

MMPI-2-RF® Score Report
04/22/2011, Page 7

ID: Ms. L

MMPI-2-RF T SCORES (BY DOMAIN)

PROTOCOL VALIDITY

Content Non-Responsiveness	3	53	57 T		
	CNS	VRIN-r	TRIN-r		

Over-Reporting	61	59		74	54	71
	F-r	Fp-r		Fs	FBS-r	RBS

Under-Reporting	42	31
	L-r	K-r

SUBSTANTIVE SCALES

Somatic/Cognitive Dysfunction		61	52	46	65	59	80
		RC1	MLS	GIC	HPC	NUC	COG

Emotional Dysfunction	54	64	45	52	65	58		
	EID	RCd	SUI	HLP	SFD	NFC		
		38	39					
		RC2	INTR-r					
		65	57*	59	66	43	46	66
		RC7	STW	AXY	ANP	BRF	MSF	NEGE-r

Thought Dysfunction	60	70
	THD	RC6
		66
		RC8
		63
		PSYC-r

Behavioral Dysfunction	65	73	63	69		
	BXD	RC4	JCP	SUB		
		66	67	53	47	63
		RC9	AGG	ACT	AGGR-r	DISC-r

Interpersonal Functioning	79	51	52	43	50	44
	FML	RC3	IPP	SAV	SHY	DSF

Interests	62	38
	AES	MEC

*The test taker provided scorable responses to less than 90% of the items scored on this scale. See the relevant profile page for the specific percentage.

Note. This information is provided to facilitate interpretation following the recommended structure for MMPI-2-RF interpretation in Chapter 5 of the *MMPI-2-RF Manual for Administration, Scoring, and Interpretation*, which provides details in the text and an outline in Table 5-1.

Figure 9-3. Ms. L's MMPI-2-RF Score Report, continued.

ITEM-LEVEL INFORMATION

Unscorable Responses

Following is a list of items to which the test taker did not provide scorable responses. Unanswered or double answered (both True and False) items are unscorable. The scales on which the items appear are in parentheses following the item content.

    73. Item content removed. (TRIN-r, EID, STW, NEGE-r)
    85. Item content removed. (VRIN-r, THD, RC8, PSYC-r)
  238. Item content removed. (RC3)

Critical Responses

Seven MMPI-2-RF scales--Suicidal/Death Ideation (SUI), Helplessness/Hopelessness (HLP), Anxiety (AXY), Ideas of Persecution (RC6), Aberrant Experiences (RC8), Substance Abuse (SUB), and Aggression (AGG)--have been designated by the test authors as having critical item content that may require immediate attention and follow-up. Items answered by the individual in the keyed direction (True or False) on a critical scale are listed below if her T score on that scale is 65 or higher. The percentage of the MMPI-2-RF normative sample (NS) and of the College Counseling Clinic (Women) comparison group (CG) that answered each item in the keyed direction are provided in parentheses following the item content.

Ideas of Persecution (RC6, T Score = 70)

  194. Item content removed. (True; NS 17.1%, CG 36.0%)
  212. Item content removed. (False; NS 9.1%, CG 12.3%)
  233. Item content removed. (True; NS 5.5%, CG 15.0%)
  287. Item content removed. (True; NS 3.1%, CG 5.7%)

Aberrant Experiences (RC8, T Score = 66)

   32. Item content removed. (True; NS 21.1%, CG 29.6%)
  106. Item content removed. (True; NS 8.7%, CG 15.2%)
  159. Item content removed. (True; NS 6.0%, CG 13.4%)
  179. Item content removed. (True; NS 12.6%, CG 18.6%)
  199. Item content removed. (True; NS 12.1%, CG 14.1%)
  257. Item content removed. (True; NS 12.4%, CG 28.4%)

Substance Abuse (SUB, T Score = 69)

   49. Item content removed. (True; NS 29.6%, CG 32.9%)
  141. Item content removed. (True; NS 34.2%, CG 34.9%)
  237. Item content removed. (False; NS 27.4%, CG 38.9%)
  297. Item content removed. (True; NS 14.4%, CG 19.4%)

Aggression (AGG, T Score = 67)

   23. Item content removed. (True; NS 39.0%, CG 45.0%)
   26. Item content removed. (True; NS 19.9%, CG 16.3%)

Figure 9-3. Ms. L's MMPI-2-RF Score Report, continued.

MMPI-2-RF® Score Report
04/22/2011, Page 9

ID: Ms. L

---

84. Item content removed. (True; NS 12.1%, CG 15.7%)
316. Item content removed. (True; NS 45.1%, CG 27.1%)
337. Item content removed. (True; NS 50.2%, CG 60.4%)

End of Report

Figure 9-3. Ms. L's MMPI-2-RF Score Report, continued.

difficulties. She also reports unusual perceptual and thought processes. Examination of item-level data indicates that she describes having unusual experiences and blackouts that may be a product of substance abuse. The aberrant experiences she describes may indeed be substance induced.

Ms. L reports various negative emotions, the most prominent among them being anger. She likely has problems with anger and irritability and a low tolerance for frustration, and she is likely to hold grudges, to have temper tantrums, and to be argumentative. She also reports self-doubt and is likely to feel inferior and insecure and to be self-disparaging, prone to rumination, intropunitive, and lacking in confidence.

Ms. L reports a diffuse pattern of cognitive difficulties. She is likely to complain about memory problems and experience difficulties in concentration. She also reports head pain and is likely to complain about headaches and chronic pain. She may be prone to developing physical symptoms in response to stress.

Ms. L reports no interests in activities or occupations of a mechanical or physical nature (e.g., fixing and building things, the outdoors, sports). She reports an average level of aesthetic and literary interest.

Interpersonally, Ms. L reports conflictual family relationships and a lack of support from family members. She is indeed likely to have significant conflict with family members, to experience poor family functioning, to have strong negative feelings about members of her family, and to blame them for her difficulties.

Ms. L's test results indicate a number of possible diagnoses for follow-up evaluation. Externalizing disorders, including those involving substance abuse and antisocial behavior, are associated with Ms. L's MMPI-2-RF results. The possibility of Narcissistic Personality Disorder is also indicated for further evaluation. Disorders associated with interpersonal aggression and anger should also be evaluated. If a physical origin for Ms. L's head pain complaints is ruled out, the possibility that she has a Somatoform Disorder should also be considered. The origin of her cognitive complaints should be explored. This may require a neuropsychological evaluation.

The MMPI-2-RF results suggest the following process issues for consideration in treatment planning. Ms. L is unlikely to be internally motivated for treatment and is at significant risk for treatment noncompliance. Her acting-out tendencies may interfere with the development of a therapeutic relationship. Potential targets for intervention include undercontrolled behavior, particularly substance abuse, and interpersonal aggression. Other possible targets include anger management and family problems.

Discussion

Ms. L's MMPI-2-RF results indicate that she should be considered for a diagnosis of alcohol abuse on Axis I as well as an Axis II disorder. In particular, features of Antisocial and Narcissistic Personality disorders were indicated for further consideration. Her score on Hypomanic Activation (RC9) was not sufficiently high to warrant consideration of a possible cycling mood disorder; rather, in Ms. L's case, the elevated RC9 score most likely reflected proclivities toward aggressive interpersonal behavior. This was consistent with a significant elevation on the Specific Problems Scale Aggression (AGG) and a nonelevated score on the Activation (ACT) Scale. Although Ms. L did not ultimately meet diagnostic criteria for a specific personality disorder, she was diagnosed with a personality disorder with antisocial and narcissistic features as well as with alcohol abuse.

Underscoring the significance of Ms. L's externalizing behavior, examination of the comparison group data shows that she scored at or above the scores of 96% of the 894 women in the college counseling clinic comparison group on Behavioral/ Externalizing Dysfunction (BXD), RC9, Substance Abuse (SUB), and Disconstraint– Revised (DISC-r) and at or above 97% of these women on Antisocial Behavior (RC4) and AGG.

The interpersonal suspiciousness reflected in Ms. L's MMPI-2-RF results was thought by the assessing psychologist to play a significant role in her concerns about her boyfriend's fidelity, particularly during periods of intoxication. Substance misuse was also determined to account for her reported aberrant experiences. Ms. L's cognitive complaints were thought to be related to her reaction to the breakup and substance abuse. However, she was referred for a follow-up neuropsychological evaluation. Ms. L's dysfunctional negative emotions were found to center on anger and irritability.

Based in part on the MMPI-2-RF findings indicating significant externalizing psychopathology, the assessing psychologist recommended that Ms. L's treatment focus initially on reducing her substance misuse and establishing more productive ways for her to engage with others. Longer-term goals included exploration of Ms. L's conflictual family relationships and the role they played in her externalizing behaviors. In light of literature indicating that individuals with externalizing disorders are at increased risk for treatment noncompliance and premature termination, the assessing psychologist noted a guarded prognosis for Ms. L's success in treatment. Ms. L did, in fact, fail to keep her third therapy appointment and did not respond to efforts to reestablish contact.

MR. E: SUBSTANCE-INDUCED PSYCHOTIC SYMPTOMS

Mr. E, a 28-year-old single male, was admitted to a psychiatric inpatient unit of a community hospital after presenting with what were initially thought to be symptoms of a psychotic disorder. He had a recent history of a relationship breakup and an assault that led to his arrest. Mr. E had an extensive history of alcohol and drug abuse and had been involved in a number of unsuccessful substance-abuse treatment programs.

At intake, Mr. E was described as being intoxicated, having recently been on a crack cocaine binge. His thinking was characterized as being paranoid and suspicious, and he was described as showing evidence of ideas of reference. He was also noted to be engaging in obsessive thinking and to be religiously preoccupied.

Mr. E did not have a history of prior involvement with the mental health system, although, as just discussed, he had been previously involved in unsuccessful substance-abuse treatment programs. Enrollment in these programs followed episodes of alcohol and drug abuse that resulted in Mr. E's arrest and relatively minor assault-related charges. Successful completion of a substance-abuse treatment program was a condition of Mr. E being placed on community control. However, despite repeated failures, he was never sentenced to any lengthy periods of incarceration.

The present hospitalization followed Mr. E's arrest for an altercation at a bar. He had caused serious injuries to an individual whom he did not know after this person asked him to lower his voice. The victim was transported to a hospital for treatment of a head injury. The arresting officer noted that Mr. E was mumbling somewhat incoherently and appeared to be very preoccupied religiously. He was taken to a crisis stabilization unit, where staff concluded that he was intoxicated from consuming alcohol and crack cocaine, but he also appeared possibly to be acutely psychotic. Inpatient hospitalization for the purpose of detoxification and observation to assess for symptoms of a psychotic disorder was recommended, and Mr. E agreed to be admitted to a local community hospital.

As part of the intake evaluation process, Mr. E was administered the MMPI-2 the day following his admission, which was three days after his arrest. The protocol was subsequently converted to the MMPI-2-RF, and the results are reported in Figure 9-4, in which the inpatient community hospital comparison group data are plotted along with Mr. E's results.

MMPI-2-RF Interpretation

Mr. E responded to all the MMPI-2-RF items, and there were no indications of inconsistent responding. He provided a larger-than-average number of infrequent responses, but this level of infrequent responding can occur in individuals with significant psychopathology, like Mr. E, and it does not indicate overreporting in this case. Possible overreporting of somatic and/or cognitive symptoms is indicated by the assertion of a much larger-than-average number of somatic symptoms rarely described by individuals with genuine medical problems and by an unusual combination of responses that is associated with noncredible somatic and/or cognitive complaints. There is no evidence of underreporting in this protocol.

Mr. E's responses indicate significant externalizing, acting-out behavior, which is likely to have gotten him into difficulties. He reports a significant history of antisocial behavior and is likely to have been involved with the criminal justice system. He likely fails to conform to societal norms and expectations and likely has difficulties with individuals in positions of authority. He is also likely to experience conflictual interpersonal relationships, to act out when bored, and to have antisocial characteristics. Mr. E reports a history of problematic behavior at school and likely has a history of juvenile delinquency and involvement with the juvenile justice system. He also reports a significant history of substance abuse, current substance abuse, frequent use of alcohol and drugs, and using alcohol to relax and open up. He is very likely to have had legal problems as a result of substance abuse and to be sensation seeking. Mr. E also reports episodes of heightened excitation and energy level, and he is likely to experience excessive activation. He reports various manifestations of disconstrained behavior and is likely to have poor impulse control.

Minnesota Multiphasic
Personality Inventory-2
Restructured Form®

Score Report

MMPI-2-RF®

Minnesota Multiphasic Personality Inventory-2-Restructured Form®

Yossef S. Ben-Porath, PhD, & Auke Tellegen, PhD

ID Number:	Mr. E
Age:	28
Gender:	Male
Marital Status:	Not reported
Years of Education:	Not reported
Date Assessed:	04/22/2011

PEARSON   ⓌPsychCorp

Figure 9-4. Mr. E's MMPI-2-RF Score Report.

MMPI-2-RF® Score Report   ID: Mr. E
04/22/2011, Page 2

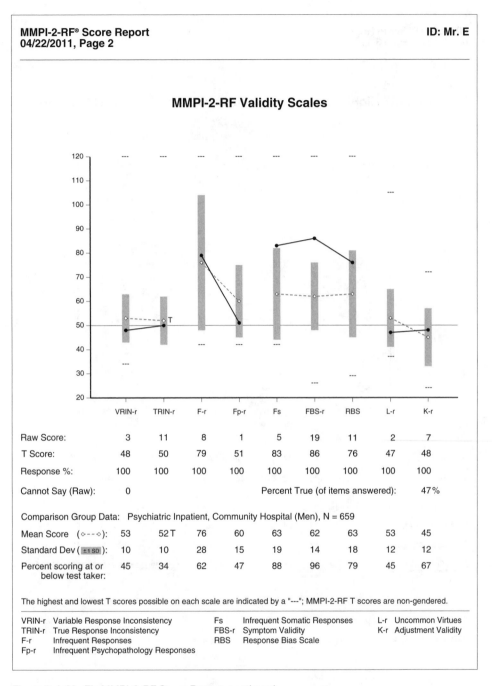

MMPI-2-RF Validity Scales

	VRIN-r	TRIN-r	F-r	Fp-r	Fs	FBS-r	RBS	L-r	K-r
Raw Score:	3	11	8	1	5	19	11	2	7
T Score:	48	50	79	51	83	86	76	47	48
Response %:	100	100	100	100	100	100	100	100	100

Cannot Say (Raw):   0   Percent True (of items answered):   47%

Comparison Group Data: Psychiatric Inpatient, Community Hospital (Men), N = 659

	VRIN-r	TRIN-r	F-r	Fp-r	Fs	FBS-r	RBS	L-r	K-r
Mean Score (◇--◇):	53	52 T	76	60	63	62	63	53	45
Standard Dev (±1 SD):	10	10	28	15	19	14	18	12	12
Percent scoring at or below test taker:	45	34	62	47	88	96	79	45	67

The highest and lowest T scores possible on each scale are indicated by a "---"; MMPI-2-RF T scores are non-gendered.

VRIN-r	Variable Response Inconsistency	Fs	Infrequent Somatic Responses	L-r	Uncommon Virtues
TRIN-r	True Response Inconsistency	FBS-r	Symptom Validity	K-r	Adjustment Validity
F-r	Infrequent Responses	RBS	Response Bias Scale		
Fp-r	Infrequent Psychopathology Responses				

Figure 9-4. Mr. E's MMPI-2-RF Score Report, continued.

MMPI-2-RF Higher-Order (H-O) and Restructured Clinical (RC) Scales

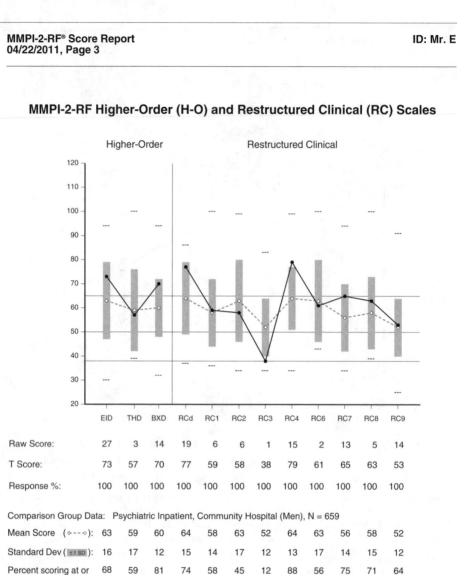

	EID	THD	BXD	RCd	RC1	RC2	RC3	RC4	RC6	RC7	RC8	RC9
Raw Score:	27	3	14	19	6	6	1	15	2	13	5	14
T Score:	73	57	70	77	59	58	38	79	61	65	63	53
Response %:	100	100	100	100	100	100	100	100	100	100	100	100

Comparison Group Data: Psychiatric Inpatient, Community Hospital (Men), N = 659

	EID	THD	BXD	RCd	RC1	RC2	RC3	RC4	RC6	RC7	RC8	RC9
Mean Score (◇---◇):	63	59	60	64	58	63	52	64	63	56	58	52
Standard Dev (±1 SD):	16	17	12	15	14	17	12	13	17	14	15	12
Percent scoring at or below test taker:	68	59	81	74	58	45	12	88	56	75	71	64

The highest and lowest T scores possible on each scale are indicated by a "---"; MMPI-2-RF T scores are non-gendered.

EID	Emotional/Internalizing Dysfunction	RCd	Demoralization	RC6	Ideas of Persecution
THD	Thought Dysfunction	RC1	Somatic Complaints	RC7	Dysfunctional Negative Emotions
BXD	Behavioral/Externalizing Dysfunction	RC2	Low Positive Emotions	RC8	Aberrant Experiences
		RC3	Cynicism	RC9	Hypomanic Activation
		RC4	Antisocial Behavior		

Figure 9-4. Mr. E's MMPI-2-RF Score Report, continued.

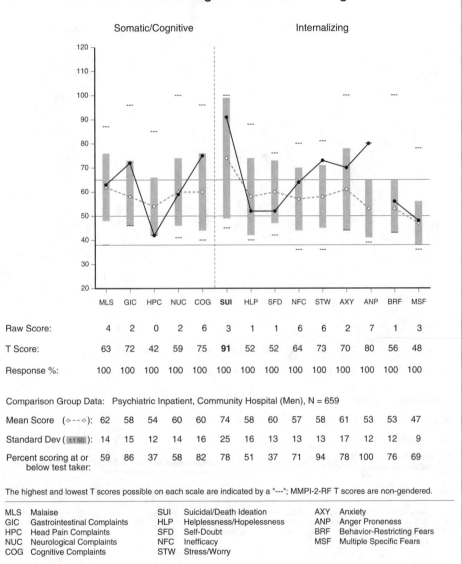

MMPI-2-RF Somatic/Cognitive and Internalizing Scales

Somatic/Cognitive   Internalizing

	MLS	GIC	HPC	NUC	COG	SUI	HLP	SFD	NFC	STW	AXY	ANP	BRF	MSF
Raw Score:	4	2	0	2	6	3	1	1	6	6	2	7	1	3
T Score:	63	72	42	59	75	91	52	52	64	73	70	80	56	48
Response %:	100	100	100	100	100	100	100	100	100	100	100	100	100	100

Comparison Group Data: Psychiatric Inpatient, Community Hospital (Men), N = 659

Mean Score (◇- -◇):	62	58	54	60	60	74	58	60	57	58	61	53	53	47
Standard Dev (±1 SD):	14	15	12	14	16	25	16	13	13	13	17	12	12	9
Percent scoring at or below test taker:	59	86	37	58	82	78	51	37	71	94	78	100	76	69

The highest and lowest T scores possible on each scale are indicated by a "---"; MMPI-2-RF T scores are non-gendered.

MLS	Malaise	SUI	Suicidal/Death Ideation	AXY	Anxiety
GIC	Gastrointestinal Complaints	HLP	Helplessness/Hopelessness	ANP	Anger Proneness
HPC	Head Pain Complaints	SFD	Self-Doubt	BRF	Behavior-Restricting Fears
NUC	Neurological Complaints	NFC	Inefficacy	MSF	Multiple Specific Fears
COG	Cognitive Complaints	STW	Stress/Worry		

Figure 9-4. Mr. E's MMPI-2-RF Score Report, continued.

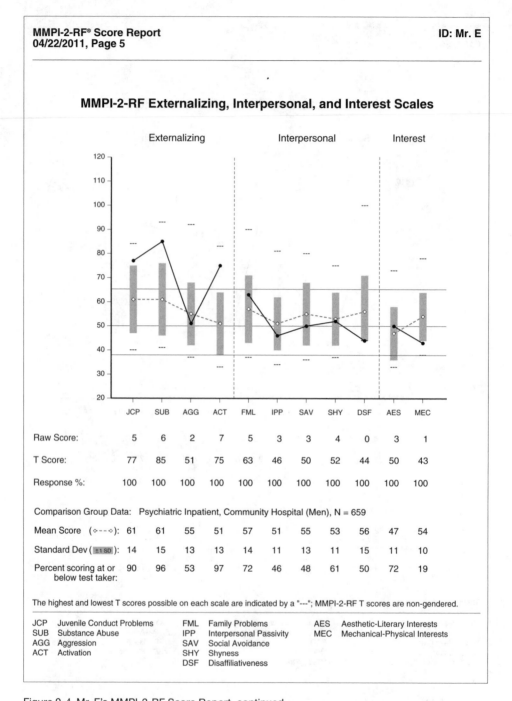

MMPI-2-RF® Score Report   **ID: Mr. E**
04/22/2011, Page 5

MMPI-2-RF Externalizing, Interpersonal, and Interest Scales

	JCP	SUB	AGG	ACT	FML	IPP	SAV	SHY	DSF	AES	MEC
Raw Score:	5	6	2	7	5	3	3	4	0	3	1
T Score:	77	85	51	75	63	46	50	52	44	50	43
Response %:	100	100	100	100	100	100	100	100	100	100	100

Comparison Group Data: Psychiatric Inpatient, Community Hospital (Men), N = 659

	JCP	SUB	AGG	ACT	FML	IPP	SAV	SHY	DSF	AES	MEC
Mean Score (◇--◇):	61	61	55	51	57	51	55	53	56	47	54
Standard Dev (±1 SD):	14	15	13	13	14	11	13	11	15	11	10
Percent scoring at or below test taker:	90	96	53	97	72	46	48	61	50	72	19

The highest and lowest T scores possible on each scale are indicated by a "---"; MMPI-2-RF T scores are non-gendered.

JCP	Juvenile Conduct Problems	FML	Family Problems	AES	Aesthetic-Literary Interests
SUB	Substance Abuse	IPP	Interpersonal Passivity	MEC	Mechanical-Physical Interests
AGG	Aggression	SAV	Social Avoidance		
ACT	Activation	SHY	Shyness		
		DSF	Disaffiliativeness		

Figure 9-4. Mr. E's MMPI-2-RF Score Report, continued.

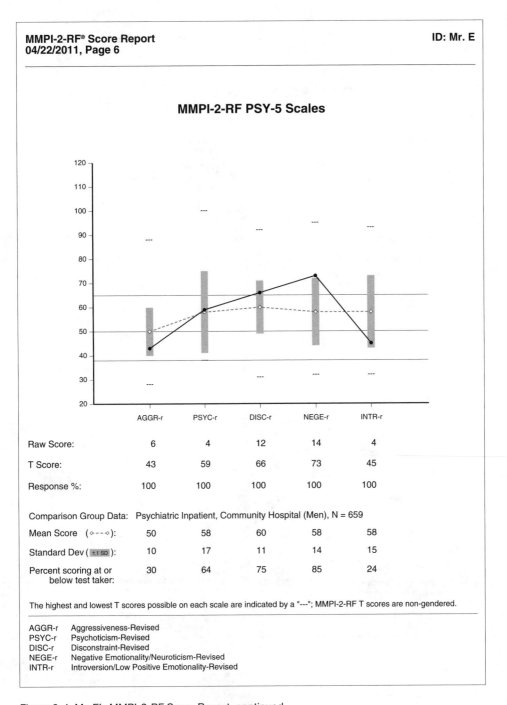

MMPI-2-RF PSY-5 Scales

	AGGR-r	PSYC-r	DISC-r	NEGE-r	INTR-r
Raw Score:	6	4	12	14	4
T Score:	43	59	66	73	45
Response %:	100	100	100	100	100

Comparison Group Data: Psychiatric Inpatient, Community Hospital (Men), N = 659

	AGGR-r	PSYC-r	DISC-r	NEGE-r	INTR-r
Mean Score (◇--◇):	50	58	60	58	58
Standard Dev (±1 SD):	10	17	11	14	15
Percent scoring at or below test taker:	30	64	75	85	24

The highest and lowest T scores possible on each scale are indicated by a "---"; MMPI-2-RF T scores are non-gendered.

AGGR-r	Aggressiveness-Revised
PSYC-r	Psychoticism-Revised
DISC-r	Disconstraint-Revised
NEGE-r	Negative Emotionality/Neuroticism-Revised
INTR-r	Introversion/Low Positive Emotionality-Revised

Figure 9-4. Mr. E's MMPI-2-RF Score Report, continued.

MMPI-2-RF T SCORES (BY DOMAIN)

PROTOCOL VALIDITY

Content Non-Responsiveness

0	48	50
CNS	VRIN-r	TRIN-r

Over-Reporting

79	51		83	86	76
F-r	Fp-r		Fs	FBS-r	RBS

Under-Reporting

47	48
L-r	K-r

SUBSTANTIVE SCALES

Somatic/Cognitive Dysfunction

59	63	72	42	59	75
RC1	MLS	GIC	HPC	NUC	COG

Emotional Dysfunction

73					
EID					

77	**91**	52	52	64		
RCd	**SUI**	HLP	SFD	NFC		

58	45
RC2	INTR-r

65	73	70	80	56	48	73
RC7	STW	AXY	ANP	BRF	MSF	NEGE-r

Thought Dysfunction

57
THD

61
RC6

63
RC8

59
PSYC-r

Behavioral Dysfunction

70
BXD

79	77	85
RC4	JCP	SUB

53	51	75	43	66
RC9	AGG	ACT	AGGR-r	DISC-r

Interpersonal Functioning

63	38	46	50	52	44
FML	RC3	IPP	SAV	SHY	DSF

Interests

50	43
AES	MEC

Note. This information is provided to facilitate interpretation following the recommended structure for MMPI-2-RF interpretation in Chapter 5 of the *MMPI-2-RF Manual for Administration, Scoring, and Interpretation*, which provides details in the text and an outline in Table 5-1.

Figure 9-4. Mr. E's MMPI-2-RF Score Report, continued.

ITEM-LEVEL INFORMATION

Unscorable Responses

The test taker produced scorable responses to all the MMPI-2-RF items.

Critical Responses

Seven MMPI-2-RF scales--Suicidal/Death Ideation (SUI), Helplessness/Hopelessness (HLP), Anxiety (AXY), Ideas of Persecution (RC6), Aberrant Experiences (RC8), Substance Abuse (SUB), and Aggression (AGG)--have been designated by the test authors as having critical item content that may require immediate attention and follow-up. Items answered by the individual in the keyed direction (True or False) on a critical scale are listed below if his T score on that scale is 65 or higher. The percentage of the MMPI-2-RF normative sample (NS) and of the Psychiatric Inpatient, Community Hospital (Men) comparison group (CG) that answered each item in the keyed direction are provided in parentheses following the item content.

Suicidal/Death Ideation (SUI, T Score = 91)

93. Item content removed. (True; NS 3.7%, CG 58.7%)
164. Item content removed. (True; NS 1.7%, CG 42.3%)
334. Item content removed. (True; NS 13.5%, CG 35.5%)

Anxiety (AXY, T Score = 70)

228. Item content removed. (True; NS 17.3%, CG 42.2%)
289. Item content removed. (True; NS 12.7%, CG 22.5%)

Substance Abuse (SUB, T Score = 85)

49. Item content removed. (True; NS 29.6%, CG 51.3%)
141. Item content removed. (True; NS 34.2%, CG 59.3%)
192. Item content removed. (True; NS 11.2%, CG 25.8%)
237. Item content removed. (False; NS 27.4%, CG 52.0%)
266. Item content removed. (True; NS 5.0%, CG 39.0%)
297. Item content removed. (True; NS 14.4%, CG 35.5%)

End of Report

Figure 9-4. Mr. E's MMPI-2-RF Score Report, continued.

Mr. E's responses also indicate considerable emotional distress. He reports feeling sad and unhappy and being dissatisfied with his current circumstances. He is at risk for suicidal ideation and does indeed report current suicidal ideation. He is likely to complain about depression or anxiety, to not cope well with stress, and to feel incapable of dealing with his current life circumstances. He is also likely to be ruminative, to feel sad, and to be pessimistic and insecure. Mr. E also reports various negative emotional experiences, including anxiety and anger, and he is likely to perceive others as overly critical. He reports getting upset easily, being impatient with others, becoming easily angered, and sometimes even being overcome with anger. Mr. E is indeed very likely to have problems with anger, irritability, and low tolerance for frustration; to hold grudges; to have temper tantrums; and to be argumentative. He also reports an above-average level of stress and worry and is likely to be stress reactive and worry prone and to engage in obsessive rumination. In addition, Mr. E reports feeling anxious and is likely to have significant anxiety and anxiety-related problems and to experience intrusive ideation; sleep difficulties, including nightmares; and posttraumatic distress.

Mr. E reports a number of gastrointestinal complaints and a diffuse pattern of cognitive difficulties. He is likely to complain about memory problems and may experience difficulties in concentration. However, as discussed earlier, scores on the Validity Scales raise the possibility that Mr. E's somatic and cognitive complaints are not credible.

Unexpectedly, Mr. E describes others as well intentioned and trustworthy, and he disavows holding cynical beliefs about people's motives.

Mr. E's MMPI-2-RF results identify a number of diagnostic considerations. He should be evaluated for externalizing disorders, particularly those involving substance abuse, antisocial behavior, and poor impulse control. Possible manic or hypomanic episodes or other conditions associated with excessive energy and activation should also be considered. Internalizing disorders, including those related to depression, anxiety, and anger, are also indicated for further evaluation. A possible Somatoform Disorder associated with gastrointestinal complaints should be evaluated as well.

Mr. E's scores also identify a number of areas for follow-up. He reports ongoing suicidal ideation, he is demoralized, and he is prone to impulsive acting out, placing him at significant risk for self-harm. The risk for a suicide attempt should be assessed immediately. Mr. E's current emotional state may motivate him temporarily for treatment, and relief of psychological distress can be an initial target for intervention. However, he is unlikely to remain internally motivated for treatment once the immediate crisis subsides, and he is at significant risk for treatment noncompliance. Inadequate self-control should be a longer-term target for intervention. Stress and anger management and excessive worry and rumination may also be appropriate targets for intervention. The origins of Mr. E's gastrointestinal and cognitive complaints should be explored. The latter may require a neuropsychological evaluation. The prognosis for any intervention initiated with Mr. E is guarded owing to his proclivity to act out and to his poor impulse control.

Discussion

As described earlier, Mr. E was manifesting what appeared to be psychotic symptoms and agitation on admission to the inpatient facility. A critical question under such circumstances is whether he would be able to provide meaningful self-report data for the evaluation. Examination of his Validity Scale scores indicates that Mr. E was in fact able to participate meaningfully in psychological testing. In particular, his scores on Variable Response Inconsistency (VRIN-r) and True Response Inconsistency (TRIN-r) indicate that Mr. E was able to understand and respond relevantly to the MMPI-2-RF items. Although his Infrequent Responses (F-r) T score (79) reached the lower threshold for raising the possibility of overreporting, the psychiatric inpatient community hospital men comparison group data included in Figure 9-4 show that his score on this scale is very near the mean for this group. His Infrequent Psychopathology Responses (Fp-r) T score (51) is actually below average for men assessed at psychiatric inpatient facilities. On the other hand, his Infrequent Somatic Responses (Fs) and Symptom Validity (FBS-r) T scores (83 and 86, respectively) fall outside the range found typically in male psychiatric inpatients, raising the possibility of overreporting in the Somatic and Cognitive domains. Overall, his Validity Scale scores do not raise concerns about the appropriateness of relying on his MMPI-2-RF results in addressing the primary referral question related to the origin of Mr. E's psychotic symptoms.

Examination of Mr. E's scores on the Higher-Order (H-O) and Restructured Clinical (RC) Scales (page 3 of Figure 9-4) did not identify likely symptoms of a primary thought disorder. In fact, Thought Dysfunction (THD) was the only nonelevated H-O Scale. Mr. E's MMPI-2-RF results pointed instead toward both externalizing and internalizing pathology being present in this case. On the basis of the test results, history, and observation, hospital staff concluded that Mr. E's religious preoccupation and ideas of reference were substance induced, that he met diagnostic criteria for Polysubstance Dependence and Antisocial Personality disorder, and that his emotional dysfunction was the result of his arrest and recognition that he was facing the possibility of receiving a lengthy prison sentence. Risk for self-harm was assessed and determined to be substantial, and appropriate precautions were taken. The excessive activation indicated by Mr. E's elevated Activation (ACT) Scale score was attributed to substance-induced agitation.

After a week of detoxification, Mr. E's substance-induced symptoms subsided, and he was discharged to the custody of law enforcement officials for processing of the charges against him.

MR. D: BARIATRIC SURGERY CANDIDATE

Mr. D is a 32-year-old separated man assessed at a medical facility as a candidate for bariatric surgery. He was morbidly obese, with a body mass index of 46, and had been diagnosed with a number of medical conditions that were attributed to his excessive weight. These conditions included hypertension, type 2 diabetes, sleep apnea, and other manifestations of abnormal pulmonary functioning.

Prior efforts at weight loss through diet and physical activity had been unsuccessful.

Mr. D and his wife of two years had separated three months prior to the evaluation. Mr. D reported that he had initiated the separation after discovering that his wife was e-mailing regularly with a former boyfriend and she refused his demand that she end the correspondence. The couple did not have any children, and Mr. D moved in with his brother, with whom he had resided prior to his marriage. Mr. D reported that he had not been in touch with his wife since he left their home and that after leaving, he had decided that he wanted to focus on "taking care of myself." Mr. D indicated that he had a good relationship with his brother and that other sources of social support included a close friend and his parents, who lived approximately 30 minutes away from him. He did not have any prior involvement with the mental health system or any known history of substance abuse or dependence.

Mr. D's physician recommended that he undergo bariatric surgery for weight loss and referred him to the medical facility where he was evaluated. The routine presurgical process followed at this facility included an assessment by a psychologist, who administered the MMPI-2-RF as part of the evaluation. The purpose of the assessment was to determine whether psychological factors might interfere with Mr. D's ability to comply with presurgical procedures and rigorous postsurgical behavioral guidelines.

Mr. D's MMPI-2-RF protocol is reproduced in Figure 9-5. The sample of male bariatric surgery candidates was selected as the relevant comparison group for this case.

MMPI-2-RF Interpretation

Mr. D provided scorable responses to all but two of the MMPI-2-RF items, and no scale was affected by excessive nonresponding. Although he provided more inconsistent responses than is typically found in male bariatric surgery candidates, the level of inconsistent responding reflected in Mr. D's Validity Scale scores is not cause for concern about the validity of his test results. There are no indications of overreporting in his protocol. Possible underreporting is indicated by Mr. D's presenting himself in a positive light by denying minor faults and shortcomings that most people acknowledge. This level of virtuous self-presentation may reflect a background stressing traditional values. However, any absence of elevation on the Substantive Scales should be interpreted with caution. Elevated scores on the Substantive Scales may underestimate the problems assessed by those scales.

Mr. D's responses indicate significant emotional distress. He reports a lack of positive emotional experiences, significant anhedonia, and lack of interest, and he is likely to be pessimistic, to lack energy, and to display vegetative symptoms of depression. He indeed reports a below-average level of energy and activation. Mr. D also reports feeling sad and unhappy and being dissatisfied with his current life circumstances. He is likely to complain about depression or anxiety, to not cope well with stress, and to feel sad and insecure. In particular, he reports being passive, indecisive, and inefficacious and believes that he is incapable of coping with his current difficulties. He is unlikely to be self-reliant and is likely to be passive in his

Minnesota Multiphasic
Personality Inventory-2
Restructured Form®

Score Report

MMPI-2-RF®

Minnesota Multiphasic Personality Inventory-2-Restructured Form®

Yossef S. Ben-Porath, PhD, & Auke Tellegen, PhD

ID Number:	Mr. D
Age:	32
Gender:	Male
Marital Status:	Separated
Years of Education:	12
Date Assessed:	04/22/2011

PEARSON

PsychCorp

Figure 9-5. Mr. D's MMPI-2-RF Score Report.

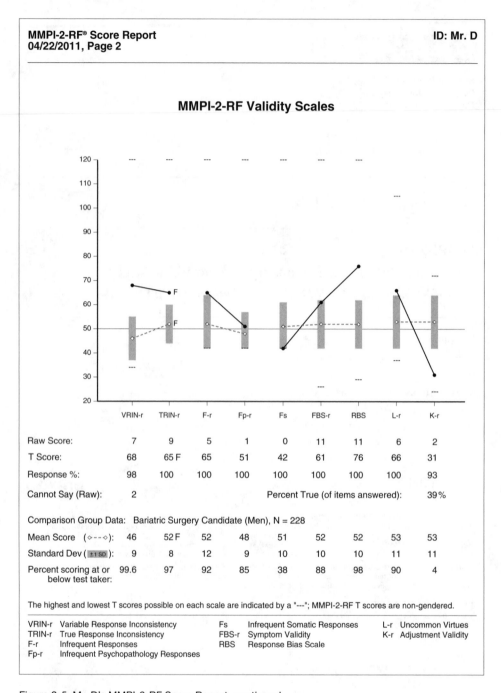

MMPI-2-RF® Score Report   ID: Mr. D
04/22/2011, Page 2

MMPI-2-RF Validity Scales

	VRIN-r	TRIN-r	F-r	Fp-r	Fs	FBS-r	RBS	L-r	K-r
Raw Score:	7	9	5	1	0	11	11	6	2
T Score:	68	65 F	65	51	42	61	76	66	31
Response %:	98	100	100	100	100	100	100	100	93

Cannot Say (Raw):   2   Percent True (of items answered):   39%

Comparison Group Data: Bariatric Surgery Candidate (Men), N = 228

Mean Score (◇---◇):	46	52 F	52	48	51	52	52	53	53
Standard Dev (±1 SD):	9	8	12	9	10	10	10	11	11
Percent scoring at or below test taker:	99.6	97	92	85	38	88	98	90	4

The highest and lowest T scores possible on each scale are indicated by a "---"; MMPI-2-RF T scores are non-gendered.

VRIN-r	Variable Response Inconsistency	Fs	Infrequent Somatic Responses
TRIN-r	True Response Inconsistency	FBS-r	Symptom Validity
F-r	Infrequent Responses	RBS	Response Bias Scale
Fp-r	Infrequent Psychopathology Responses		

L-r Uncommon Virtues
K-r Adjustment Validity

Figure 9-5. Mr. D's MMPI-2-RF Score Report, continued.

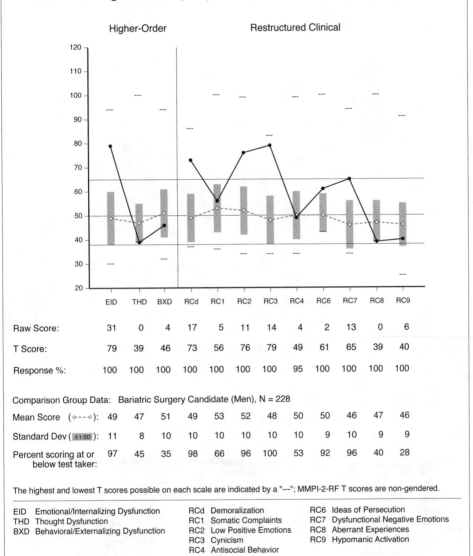

MMPI-2-RF Higher-Order (H-O) and Restructured Clinical (RC) Scales

Higher-Order   Restructured Clinical

	EID	THD	BXD	RCd	RC1	RC2	RC3	RC4	RC6	RC7	RC8	RC9
Raw Score:	31	0	4	17	5	11	14	4	2	13	0	6
T Score:	79	39	46	73	56	76	79	49	61	65	39	40
Response %:	100	100	100	100	100	100	100	95	100	100	100	100

Comparison Group Data: Bariatric Surgery Candidate (Men), N = 228

	EID	THD	BXD	RCd	RC1	RC2	RC3	RC4	RC6	RC7	RC8	RC9
Mean Score (◇---◇):	49	47	51	49	53	52	48	50	50	46	47	46
Standard Dev (±1 SD):	11	8	10	10	10	10	10	10	9	10	9	9
Percent scoring at or below test taker:	97	45	35	98	66	96	100	53	92	96	40	28

The highest and lowest T scores possible on each scale are indicated by a "---"; MMPI-2-RF T scores are non-gendered.

EID Emotional/Internalizing Dysfunction	RCd Demoralization	RC6 Ideas of Persecution
THD Thought Dysfunction	RC1 Somatic Complaints	RC7 Dysfunctional Negative Emotions
BXD Behavioral/Externalizing Dysfunction	RC2 Low Positive Emotions	RC8 Aberrant Experiences
	RC3 Cynicism	RC9 Hypomanic Activation
	RC4 Antisocial Behavior	

Figure 9-5. Mr. D's MMPI-2-RF Score Report, continued.

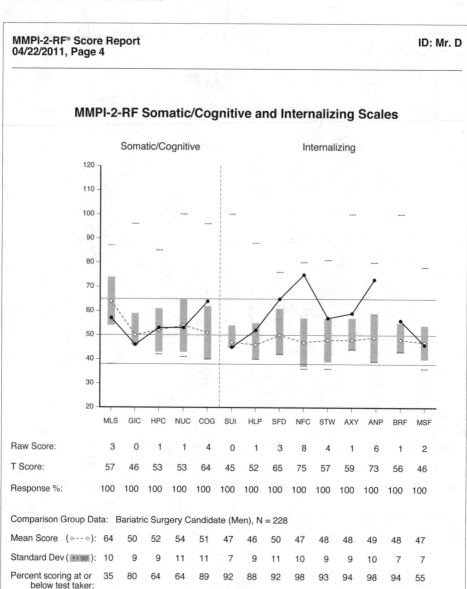

MMPI-2-RF® Score Report
04/22/2011, Page 4

ID: Mr. D

MMPI-2-RF Somatic/Cognitive and Internalizing Scales

Somatic/Cognitive   Internalizing

	MLS	GIC	HPC	NUC	COG	SUI	HLP	SFD	NFC	STW	AXY	ANP	BRF	MSF
Raw Score:	3	0	1	1	4	0	1	3	8	4	1	6	1	2
T Score:	57	46	53	53	64	45	52	65	75	57	59	73	56	46
Response %:	100	100	100	100	100	100	100	100	100	100	100	100	100	100

Comparison Group Data: Bariatric Surgery Candidate (Men), N = 228

	MLS	GIC	HPC	NUC	COG	SUI	HLP	SFD	NFC	STW	AXY	ANP	BRF	MSF
Mean Score (◇- - -◇):	64	50	52	54	51	47	46	50	47	48	48	49	48	47
Standard Dev (±1 SD):	10	9	9	11	11	7	9	11	10	9	9	10	7	7
Percent scoring at or below test taker:	35	80	64	64	89	92	88	92	98	93	94	98	94	55

The highest and lowest T scores possible on each scale are indicated by a "---"; MMPI-2-RF T scores are non-gendered.

MLS	Malaise	SUI	Suicidal/Death Ideation	AXY	Anxiety
GIC	Gastrointestinal Complaints	HLP	Helplessness/Hopelessness	ANP	Anger Proneness
HPC	Head Pain Complaints	SFD	Self-Doubt	BRF	Behavior-Restricting Fears
NUC	Neurological Complaints	NFC	Inefficacy	MSF	Multiple Specific Fears
COG	Cognitive Complaints	STW	Stress/Worry		

Figure 9-5. Mr. D's MMPI-2-RF Score Report, continued.

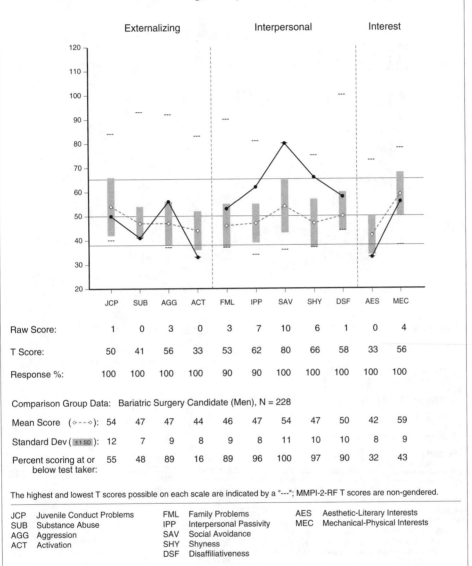

MMPI-2-RF Externalizing, Interpersonal, and Interest Scales

	Externalizing				Interpersonal					Interest	
	JCP	SUB	AGG	ACT	FML	IPP	SAV	SHY	DSF	AES	MEC
Raw Score:	1	0	3	0	3	7	10	6	1	0	4
T Score:	50	41	56	33	53	62	80	66	58	33	56
Response %:	100	100	100	100	90	90	100	100	100	100	100

Comparison Group Data: Bariatric Surgery Candidate (Men), N = 228

Mean Score (◇--◇):	54	47	47	44	46	47	54	47	50	42	59
Standard Dev (±1 SD):	12	7	9	8	9	8	11	10	10	8	9
Percent scoring at or below test taker:	55	48	89	16	89	96	100	97	90	32	43

The highest and lowest T scores possible on each scale are indicated by a "---"; MMPI-2-RF T scores are non-gendered.

JCP	Juvenile Conduct Problems	FML	Family Problems
SUB	Substance Abuse	IPP	Interpersonal Passivity
AGG	Aggression	SAV	Social Avoidance
ACT	Activation	SHY	Shyness
		DSF	Disaffiliativeness

AES	Aesthetic-Literary Interests
MEC	Mechanical-Physical Interests

Figure 9-5. Mr. D's MMPI-2-RF Score Report, continued.

MMPI-2-RF PSY-5 Scales

	AGGR-r	PSYC-r	DISC-r	NEGE-r	INTR-r
Raw Score:	5	1	2	13	15
T Score:	41	47	38	69	77
Response %:	100	100	100	100	100

Comparison Group Data: Bariatric Surgery Candidate (Men), N = 228

	AGGR-r	PSYC-r	DISC-r	NEGE-r	INTR-r
Mean Score (◇---◇):	52	47	53	47	54
Standard Dev (±1 SD):	9	9	9	10	11
Percent scoring at or below test taker:	12	64	7	97	97

The highest and lowest T scores possible on each scale are indicated by a "---"; MMPI-2-RF T scores are non-gendered.

AGGR-r	Aggressiveness-Revised
PSYC-r	Psychoticism-Revised
DISC-r	Disconstraint-Revised
NEGE-r	Negative Emotionality/Neuroticism-Revised
INTR-r	Introversion/Low Positive Emotionality-Revised

Figure 9-5. Mr. D's MMPI-2-RF Score Report, continued.

MMPI-2-RF T SCORES (BY DOMAIN)

PROTOCOL VALIDITY

Content Non-Responsiveness

2	68	65 F
CNS	VRIN-r	TRIN-r

Over-Reporting

65	51		42	61	76
F-r	Fp-r		Fs	FBS-r	RBS

Under-Reporting

66	31
L-r	K-r

SUBSTANTIVE SCALES

Somatic/Cognitive Dysfunction

56	57	46	53	53	64
RC1	MLS	GIC	HPC	NUC	COG

Emotional Dysfunction

79		73	45	52	65	75
EID		RCd	SUI	HLP	SFD	NFC

76	77
RC2	INTR-r

65	57	59	73	56	46	69
RC7	STW	AXY	ANP	BRF	MSF	NEGE-r

Thought Dysfunction

39		61
THD		RC6

39
RC8

47
PSYC-r

Behavioral Dysfunction

46		49	50	41
BXD		RC4	JCP	SUB

40	56	33	41	38
RC9	AGG	ACT	AGGR-r	DISC-r

Interpersonal Functioning

53	79	62	80	66	58
FML	RC3	IPP	SAV	SHY	DSF

Interests

33	56
AES	MEC

Note. This information is provided to facilitate interpretation following the recommended structure for MMPI-2-RF interpretation in Chapter 5 of the *MMPI-2-RF Manual for Administration, Scoring, and Interpretation*, which provides details in the text and an outline in Table 5-1.

Figure 9-5. Mr. D's MMPI-2-RF Score Report, continued.

ITEM-LEVEL INFORMATION

Unscorable Responses

Following is a list of items to which the test taker did not provide scorable responses. Unanswered or double answered (both True and False) items are unscorable. The scales on which the items appear are in parentheses following the item content.

> 60. Item content removed. (VRIN-r, IPP)
> 80. Item content removed. (K-r, RC4, FML)

Critical Responses

Seven MMPI-2-RF scales--Suicidal/Death Ideation (SUI), Helplessness/Hopelessness (HLP), Anxiety (AXY), Ideas of Persecution (RC6), Aberrant Experiences (RC8), Substance Abuse (SUB), and Aggression (AGG)--have been designated by the test authors as having critical item content that may require immediate attention and follow-up. Items answered by the individual in the keyed direction (True or False) on a critical scale are listed below if his T score on that scale is 65 or higher.

The test taker has not produced an elevated T score ($\geq$ 65) on any of these scales.

End of Report

Figure 9-5. Mr. D's MMPI-2-RF Score Report, continued.

behavior. He also reports self-doubt and is likely to feel inferior and insecure, to be self-disparaging, to be prone to rumination and being intropunitive, and to present with lack of confidence and feelings of uselessness. In addition, Mr. D reports experiencing various negative emotions, particularly anger. He likely has problems with anger and irritability and a low tolerance for frustration, and he is likely to hold grudges, to have temper tantrums, and to be argumentative.

Mr. D reports that he does not enjoy social events and that he avoids social situations, including parties and other events where crowds are likely to gather. He is very likely to be introverted, to have difficulty forming close relationships, and to be emotionally restricted. He also reports being shy, easily embarrassed, and uncomfortable around others, and he is likely to be socially inhibited, anxious, and nervous in social situations. In addition, Mr. D reports having cynical beliefs, being distrustful of others, and believing that others look out only for their own interests. He is very likely to be hostile toward and alienated from others and distrustful of them and to have negative interpersonal experiences.

Mr. D reports no interests in activities or occupations of an aesthetic or literary nature such as writing, music, or theater. He reports an average level of mechanical and physical interest.

His MMPI-2-RF results identify a number of diagnostic considerations for Mr. D. He should be evaluated for internalizing disorders, particularly Major Depression, as well as for anger-related disorders. A possible Social Phobia is also indicated for further evaluation. The MMPI-2-RF results also point to possible features of Axis II disorders. In particular, the possibility of a Cluster C disorder involving social avoidance and features of Cluster B disorders involving mistrust of and hostility toward others are indicated for further evaluation.

Mr. D's MMPI-2-RF results identify a number of treatment considerations. His need for antidepressant medication should be evaluated, and he may require inpatient treatment for depression. Anhedonia, psychological distress, low self-esteem, anger proneness, lack of interpersonal trust, difficulties associated with social avoidance, and social anxiety are identified as potential targets for intervention. The emotional distress he is experiencing may motivate Mr. D to seek help. However, his anhedonia and cynicism may interfere with his ability to establish a therapeutic relationship if he is referred for psychotherapy. Indecisiveness may interfere with establishing treatment goals and progress in treatment.

Discussion

As mentioned earlier, presurgical evaluations of bariatric surgery candidates are designed to identify potential impediments to successful outcomes for this radical medical intervention. These include active thought or mood disorders; substance abuse; impulsive, nonadherent behavioral tendencies; lack of motivation for improvement; and the absence of or inability to benefit from family or social support. In Mr. D's case, his L-r T score (66) raised concerns about possible underreporting. Available background information did not indicate that he was raised in a traditional home or environment. Moreover, as reflected in the comparison group data reported on page 2 of Figure 9-5, most male bariatric surgery candidates do not produce elevated scores on the MMPI-2-RF underreporting indicators, and only 10% scored higher than Mr. D on L-r. His somewhat guarded approach to the test has implications for the ability to rule out some of the relevant risk factors and raises concerns about Mr. D's level of cooperation with the evaluation. In particular, it is not possible to rule out externalizing behavioral tendencies as risk factors based on the absence of elevation on the MMPI-2-RF externalizing indicators.

Despite his guarded test-taking approach, Mr. D's MMPI-2-RF results do identify some problems that likely need to be addressed prior to surgery. Specifically, there are significant indications of a possible internalizing disorder, in particular, Major Depression. As seen on page 3 of Figure 9-5, 96% to 98% of the male bariatric surgery candidates in the comparison group scored at or below Mr. D's level on the H-O Emotional/Internalizing Dysfunction (EID) Scale and on the RC Low Positive Emotions (RC2) and Demoralization (RCd) scales. Mr. D's scores also indicate significant difficulty with making decisions; his score on the Specific Problems Inefficacy (NFC) Scale also falls at or above that of 98% of male bariatric surgery candidates. His indecisiveness could manifest in a last-minute withdrawal from surgery. Anger management problems are also identified in Mr. D's protocol. This, coupled with his low tolerance for frustration, may make it difficult for him to cope with the challenges of his inpatient stay and to interact appropriately with health care providers.

A second area of concern raised by Mr. D's MMPI-2-RF results pertains to his ability to receive and benefit from social support. His test results indicate that Mr. D is socially avoidant. In fact, 100% of the male bariatric surgery candidates scored at or below Mr. D's level on the Social Avoidance (SAV) Scale. He also feels awkward in the presence of others, and he harbors pronounced cynical beliefs about others and their motives. Mr. D's level of cynicism is also at or above that of all the men in the bariatric surgery candidate comparison group. These interpersonal characteristics may interfere with his ability to rely on family members or friends as sources of support during the stressful period leading up to and following surgery. They also raise concerns about his ability to participate productively in group activities offered to bariatric surgery patients at the facility where he was a surgical candidate.

Following up on the results of the evaluation, Mr. D was diagnosed with Major Depression and prescribed antidepressant medication. His depressive symptoms were found to predate his separation and were not deemed to be the result of this significant event in Mr. D's life. The presurgical assessment team recommended that he receive individual psychotherapy for at least three months and that this treatment focus on monitoring and alleviating his level of depression and improving his social skills to increase his ability to benefit from social support and participation in group activities. Surgery was performed six months after the evaluation, and at last report, Mr. D had steadily lost weight and was showing substantial improvement in his comorbid medical conditions six months following his surgery. His adherence to behavioral changes (diet, nutritional supplementation, and physical activity) was rated as good. However, Mr. D dropped out of the postsurgical support group he had been referred to, indicating that participation made him anxious and that he did not see any benefit from the two sessions he had attended. He did attend all postoperative appointments and continued to take non–sustained release antidepressant medication.

MS. B: SPINE SURGERY CANDIDATE

Ms. B, a 41-year-old married woman, was administered the MMPI-2-RF as part of a presurgical psychological screening prior to L4–5 fusion surgery intended to relieve back pain and improve her functional abilities. Ms. B reported that her pain-related difficulties began approximately three years prior to the evaluation, when she slipped and fell at work. She had already undergone two surgeries that she described as producing a poor outcome. Ms. B indicated that following her second surgery, she was in a wheelchair for two months. She wears a brace and uses crutches daily to assist with walking. Ms. B also reported that she spends most of her time at home and is fairly inactive, attempting to avoid pain.

Ms. B reported that she has never been involved with the mental health system. However, her personal physician prescribed antidepressant medication and an anxiolytic after she complained about depression and anxiety following her latest surgery. She was also using prescribed nonsteroidal anti-inflammatory drugs to alleviate pain. Ms. B denied any alcohol use but acknowledged smoking approximately one pack of cigarettes per day, although she had been told by the surgeon that she would need to stop smoking prior to surgery. She was receiving Social Security disability benefits and indicated that she hoped surgery would improve her condition and reduce her suffering, but she did not expect to return to work.

Ms. B had been married for 10 years and reported that she did not have children by choice. She indicated that her husband, who was employed, was very supportive, and she did not know what she would do without him.

Her personal physician referred Ms. B to a new surgeon to determine whether a third attempt at surgery might improve her condition. This surgeon referred all of his spine surgery candidates for a presurgical psychological screening to determine whether any psychological risk factors associated with negative outcomes were present. The MMPI-2-RF was administered as a routine component of the evaluation.

Ms. B's MMPI-2-RF results are reproduced in Figure 9-6. The spine surgery/spinal cord stimulator candidate women sample was selected as the relevant comparison group for this evaluation.

MMPI-2-RF Interpretation

Ms. B responded to all the MMPI-2-RF items. She provided relevant and consistent responses, and there is no evidence of overreporting in her protocol. There is evidence of significant underreporting. Specifically, Ms. B presented herself in a very positive light by denying minor faults and shortcomings that most people acknowledge. This level of virtuous self-presentation is uncommon but may, to some extent, reflect a background stressing traditional values. She also presented herself as psychologically well adjusted, which is inconsistent with her reported level of

Minnesota Multiphasic
Personality Inventory-2
Restructured Form®

Score Report

MMPI-2-RF®

Minnesota Multiphasic Personality Inventory-2-Restructured Form®

Yossef S. Ben-Porath, PhD, & Auke Tellegen, PhD

ID Number:	Ms. B
Age:	41
Gender:	Female
Marital Status:	Married
Years of Education:	12
Date Assessed:	04/22/2011

PEARSON

🅦*PsychCorp*

Figure 9-6. Ms. B's MMPI-2-RF Score Report.

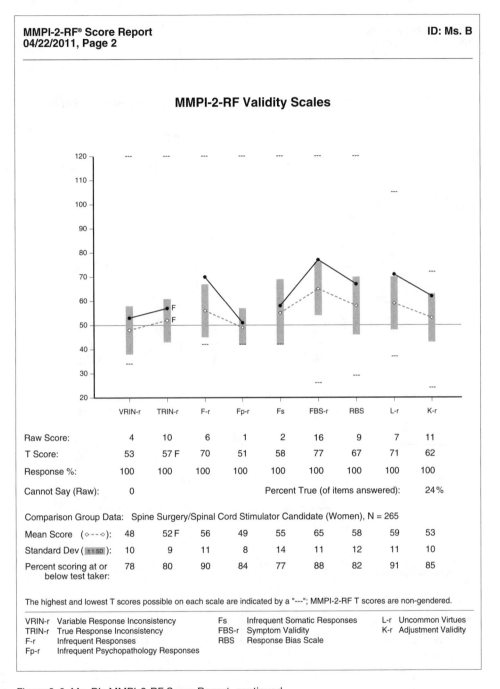

Figure 9-6. Ms. B's MMPI-2-RF Score Report, continued.

MMPI-2-RF Higher-Order (H-O) and Restructured Clinical (RC) Scales

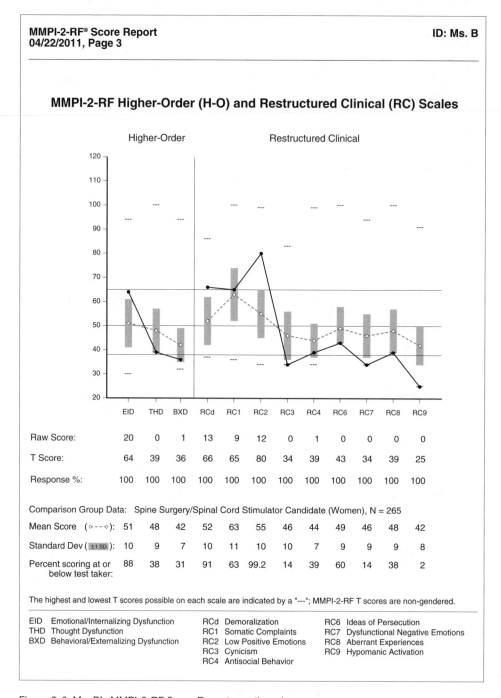

Higher-Order

Restructured Clinical

	EID	THD	BXD	RCd	RC1	RC2	RC3	RC4	RC6	RC7	RC8	RC9
Raw Score:	20	0	1	13	9	12	0	1	0	0	0	0
T Score:	64	39	36	66	65	80	34	39	43	34	39	25
Response %:	100	100	100	100	100	100	100	100	100	100	100	100

Comparison Group Data: Spine Surgery/Spinal Cord Stimulator Candidate (Women), N = 265

Mean Score (◇---◇):	51	48	42	52	63	55	46	44	49	46	48	42
Standard Dev (±1 SD):	10	9	7	10	11	10	10	7	9	9	9	8
Percent scoring at or below test taker:	88	38	31	91	63	99.2	14	39	60	14	38	2

The highest and lowest T scores possible on each scale are indicated by a "---"; MMPI-2-RF T scores are non-gendered.

EID Emotional/Internalizing Dysfunction	RCd Demoralization	RC6 Ideas of Persecution
THD Thought Dysfunction	RC1 Somatic Complaints	RC7 Dysfunctional Negative Emotions
BXD Behavioral/Externalizing Dysfunction	RC2 Low Positive Emotions	RC8 Aberrant Experiences
	RC3 Cynicism	RC9 Hypomanic Activation
	RC4 Antisocial Behavior	

Figure 9-6. Ms. B's MMPI-2-RF Score Report, continued.

MMPI-2-RF Somatic/Cognitive and Internalizing Scales

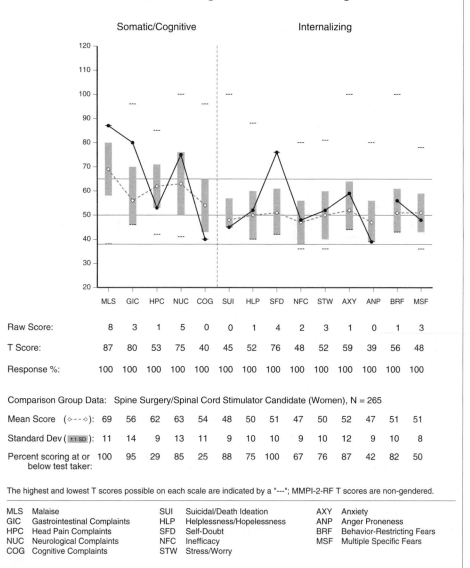

	MLS	GIC	HPC	NUC	COG	SUI	HLP	SFD	NFC	STW	AXY	ANP	BRF	MSF
Raw Score:	8	3	1	5	0	0	1	4	2	3	1	0	1	3
T Score:	87	80	53	75	40	45	52	76	48	52	59	39	56	48
Response %:	100	100	100	100	100	100	100	100	100	100	100	100	100	100

Comparison Group Data: Spine Surgery/Spinal Cord Stimulator Candidate (Women), N = 265

Mean Score (◇- - -◇):	69	56	62	63	54	48	50	51	47	50	52	47	51	51
Standard Dev (±1SD):	11	14	9	13	11	9	10	10	9	10	12	9	10	8
Percent scoring at or below test taker:	100	95	29	85	25	88	75	100	67	76	87	42	82	50

The highest and lowest T scores possible on each scale are indicated by a "---"; MMPI-2-RF T scores are non-gendered.

MLS	Malaise	SUI	Suicidal/Death Ideation	AXY	Anxiety
GIC	Gastrointestinal Complaints	HLP	Helplessness/Hopelessness	ANP	Anger Proneness
HPC	Head Pain Complaints	SFD	Self-Doubt	BRF	Behavior-Restricting Fears
NUC	Neurological Complaints	NFC	Inefficacy	MSF	Multiple Specific Fears
COG	Cognitive Complaints	STW	Stress/Worry		

Figure 9-6. Ms. B's MMPI-2-RF Score Report, continued.

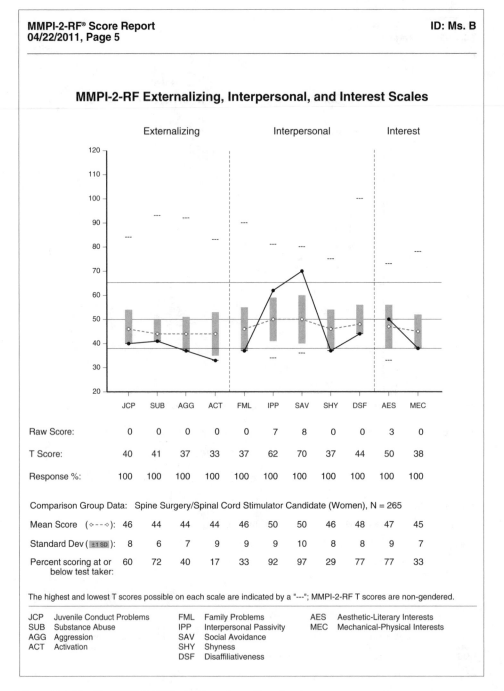

MMPI-2-RF Externalizing, Interpersonal, and Interest Scales

	Externalizing				Interpersonal					Interest	
	JCP	SUB	AGG	ACT	FML	IPP	SAV	SHY	DSF	AES	MEC
Raw Score:	0	0	0	0	0	7	8	0	0	3	0
T Score:	40	41	37	33	37	62	70	37	44	50	38
Response %:	100	100	100	100	100	100	100	100	100	100	100

Comparison Group Data: Spine Surgery/Spinal Cord Stimulator Candidate (Women), N = 265

Mean Score (◇---◇):	46	44	44	44	46	50	50	46	48	47	45
Standard Dev (±1 SD):	8	6	7	9	9	9	10	8	8	9	7
Percent scoring at or below test taker:	60	72	40	17	33	92	97	29	77	77	33

The highest and lowest T scores possible on each scale are indicated by a "---"; MMPI-2-RF T scores are non-gendered.

JCP	Juvenile Conduct Problems	FML	Family Problems	AES	Aesthetic-Literary Interests
SUB	Substance Abuse	IPP	Interpersonal Passivity	MEC	Mechanical-Physical Interests
AGG	Aggression	SAV	Social Avoidance		
ACT	Activation	SHY	Shyness		
		DSF	Disaffiliativeness		

Figure 9-6. Ms. B's MMPI-2-RF Score Report, continued.

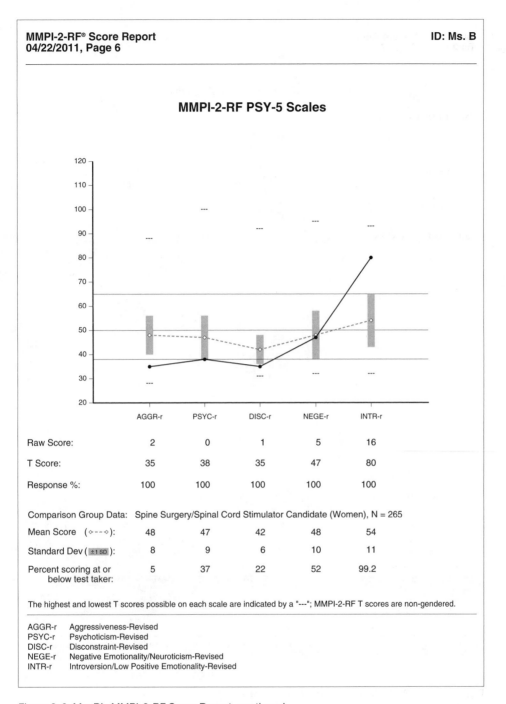

MMPI-2-RF PSY-5 Scales

	AGGR-r	PSYC-r	DISC-r	NEGE-r	INTR-r
Raw Score:	2	0	1	5	16
T Score:	35	38	35	47	80
Response %:	100	100	100	100	100

Comparison Group Data: Spine Surgery/Spinal Cord Stimulator Candidate (Women), N = 265

	AGGR-r	PSYC-r	DISC-r	NEGE-r	INTR-r
Mean Score (◇--◇):	48	47	42	48	54
Standard Dev (±1 SD):	8	9	6	10	11
Percent scoring at or below test taker:	5	37	22	52	99.2

The highest and lowest T scores possible on each scale are indicated by a "---"; MMPI-2-RF T scores are non-gendered.

AGGR-r   Aggressiveness-Revised
PSYC-r   Psychoticism-Revised
DISC-r   Disconstraint-Revised
NEGE-r   Negative Emotionality/Neuroticism-Revised
INTR-r   Introversion/Low Positive Emotionality-Revised

Figure 9-6. Ms. B's MMPI-2-RF Score Report, continued.

MMPI-2-RF T SCORES (BY DOMAIN)

PROTOCOL VALIDITY

Content Non-Responsiveness	0	53	57 F			
	CNS	VRIN-r	TRIN-r			
Over-Reporting	70	51		58	77	67
	F-r	Fp-r		Fs	FBS-r	RBS
Under-Reporting	71	62				
	L-r	K-r				

SUBSTANTIVE SCALES

Somatic/Cognitive Dysfunction		65	87	80	53	75	40
		RC1	MLS	GIC	HPC	NUC	COG
Emotional Dysfunction	64	66	45	52	76	48	
	EID	RCd	SUI	HLP	SFD	NFC	
		80	80				
		RC2	INTR-r				
		34	52	59	39	56	48	47
		RC7	STW	AXY	ANP	BRF	MSF	NEGE-r
Thought Dysfunction	39	43					
	THD	RC6					
		39					
		RC8					
		38					
		PSYC-r					
Behavioral Dysfunction	36	39	40	41			
	BXD	RC4	JCP	SUB			
		25	37	33	35	35	
		RC9	AGG	ACT	AGGR-r	DISC-r	
Interpersonal Functioning		37	34	62	70	37	44
		FML	RC3	IPP	SAV	SHY	DSF
Interests		50	38				
		AES	MEC				

Note. This information is provided to facilitate interpretation following the recommended structure for MMPI-2-RF interpretation in Chapter 5 of the *MMPI-2-RF Manual for Administration, Scoring, and Interpretation*, which provides details in the text and an outline in Table 5-1.

Figure 9-6. Ms. B's MMPI-2-RF Score Report, continued.

ITEM-LEVEL INFORMATION

Unscorable Responses

The test taker produced scorable responses to all the MMPI-2-RF items.

Critical Responses

Seven MMPI-2-RF scales--Suicidal/Death Ideation (SUI), Helplessness/Hopelessness (HLP), Anxiety (AXY), Ideas of Persecution (RC6), Aberrant Experiences (RC8), Substance Abuse (SUB), and Aggression (AGG)--have been designated by the test authors as having critical item content that may require immediate attention and follow-up. Items answered by the individual in the keyed direction (True or False) on a critical scale are listed below if her T score on that scale is 65 or higher.

The test taker has not produced an elevated T score (≥ 65) on any of these scales.

End of Report

Figure 9-6. Ms. B's MMPI-2-RF Score Report, continued.

debilitation and need for antidepressant and anxiolytic medication. These findings of underreporting indicate that the absence of elevation on the Substantive Scales of the MMPI-2-RF should be interpreted with caution, and elevated scores on these scales may underestimate the problems they are designed to assess.

Ms. B reports multiple somatic complaints that may include head pain and neurological and gastrointestinal symptoms. Her overall level of somatic complaints is typical of spine surgery candidates. However, she reported a general sense of malaise manifested in poor health and feeling tired, weak, and incapacitated that far exceeds that of most women in the relevant comparison group. She is very likely to be preoccupied with poor health and to complain of sleep disturbance, fatigue, low energy, and sexual dysfunction. She reports a number of gastrointestinal complaints and is likely to have a history of gastrointestinal problems. She also reports vague neurological symptoms and is likely prone to developing physical symptoms in response to stress. She is likely to present with dizziness, coordination difficulties, and sensory problems.

Ms. B also reports a lack of positive emotional experiences, significant anhedonia, and lack of interest. She is very likely to be pessimistic and socially disengaged and may display vegetative symptoms of depression. Relatedly, Ms. B also reports a below-average level of activation and engagement with her environment. In addition, she reports feeling sad and unhappy and being dissatisfied with her current life circumstances. She is likely to complain about depression and anxiety, to not cope well with stress, and to have low self-esteem. She does indeed report lacking confidence and feeling useless, and she is very likely to feel inferior and insecure, to be self-disparaging and prone to rumination, and to be intropunitive.

Ms. B reports that she does not enjoy social events and that she avoids social situations. She is likely to be introverted and to have difficulties forming close relationships. She is also likely to be emotionally restricted. On the other hand, she denies experiencing any anxiety in social situations. She describes others as well intentioned and trustworthy and disavows cynical beliefs about them. She may be overly trusting.

Ms. B reports having no interest in activities or occupations of a mechanical or physical nature such as fixing and building things, the outdoors, or sports. She reports an average level of aesthetic and literary interest.

Her MMPI-2-RF results identify a number of diagnostic considerations for Ms. B. Specifically, the possibility of a Somatoform Disorder, in particular of Conversion Disorder, is indicated for further evaluation. Ms. B's MMPI-2-RF results also indicate that she should be evaluated for a depression-related disorder and features of Avoidant Personality Disorder.

Ms. B's MMPI-2-RF results also identify several treatment considerations. A very substantial level of malaise may impede her willingness to engage in any recommended psychological treatment, and she is likely to reject psychological interpretations of her somatic complaints. Nonetheless, the emotional distress she is experiencing may initially motivate Ms. B to consider psychological intervention if she perceives it as necessary to proceed with surgery. Intervention targets can include depression, low self-esteem, and social avoidance. Her ongoing need for antidepressant medication should be evaluated.

Discussion

Ms. B's scores on the MMPI-2-RF Validity Scales raised concerns about underreporting. Her L-r T score (71) is quite uncommon in this population. As reflected in the comparison group data reported on page 2 of Figure 9-6, only 9% of female spine surgery candidates scored higher than Ms. B on this scale. She also reports a better-than-average level of psychological adjustment that is uncommon in spine surgery candidates and is inconsistent with her objective situation. These findings indicate that Ms. B attempted to minimize psychological and behavioral problems, perhaps out of concern that they might preclude her from receiving the surgery she was seeking. They also indicate that she may lack insight into the psychological aspects of her condition. With respect specifically to the validity of her MMPI-2-RF results, evidence of significant underreporting precludes the interpretation of nonelevated scores as indicating the absence of the problems they are designed to assess. In particular, Ms. B's low scores on indicators of externalizing dysfunction are uninterpretable.

Despite her effort to portray herself in an overly positive manner and claim above-average psychological adjustment, Ms. B's scores on the Substantive Scales do point to some significant psychological dysfunction. Specifically, although her general level of somatic complaints is consistent with what is typically reported by female spine surgery candidates, her self-reported malaise falls well beyond the expected range for this population. One hundred percent of the women in the relevant comparison group scored at or below Ms. B's T score on the Malaise (MLS) Scale (87). This finding indicates that Ms. B perceives herself as being extremely debilitated and likely does not expect her condition to improve. It is consistent with her report to the assessing psychologist that she does not expect ever to be able to return to work.

Her vague neurological complaints, coupled with a naive denial of faults in others and of experiencing any social anxiety, raise the possibility that Ms. B manifests symptoms of a Conversion Disorder. However, the diagnostic criteria for this condition indicate that if the primary source of the somatic complaints is pain, the more appropriate diagnosis may be a Pain Disorder.

The nature of Ms. B's gastrointestinal complaints should be investigated. In particular, the possibility that she is experiencing side-effects of the nonsteroidal anti-inflammatory drugs she has been prescribed should be investigated. Regardless of the specific diagnosis, Ms. B's MMPI-2-RF results indicate a substantial likelihood that her somatic complaints are at least in part somatoform in origin, raising concerns about the effectiveness of surgical intervention. She experiences greater pain than would be expected on the basis of identified physical pathology.

Ms. B's MMPI-2-RF results also raise the possibility that she is experiencing symptoms of Major Depression. However, her elevated Low Positive Emotions (RC2) score may be associated with her perceived extreme physical debilitation. The assessing psychologist considered a diagnosis of Major Depression but ruled it out and attributed Ms. B's anhedonia and self-reported depression to chronic pain.

The assessing psychologist recommended that surgery be delayed so that Ms. B could receive therapy to assist in setting reasonable expectations for surgery and to address her reported symptoms of depression. The psychologist also recommended that Ms. B's risk for developing an addiction to opiate-based analgesics be evaluated. These recommendations were not followed, and Ms. B underwent surgery shortly after the evaluation. Approximately one year after surgery, Ms. B reported that her pain had worsened and that she was now completely debilitated by it. She also indicated that surgery failed to meet even her minimal expectations and that she was extremely dissatisfied with the outcome. Ms. B also reported that she was extremely depressed and was now using opiate-based medication in unsuccessful efforts to reduce pain.

MS. X: A CASE OF FACTITIOUS DISORDER

Ms. X is a 47-year-old separated woman who underwent a forensic neuropsychological evaluation in connection with a personal injury lawsuit she had filed. The litigation involved a motor vehicle accident that occurred several months prior to the evaluation. According to Ms. X, she was cut off by another vehicle while driving, and, unable to avoid a collision, she broadsided the other car. She recalls striking her head against a window but was uncertain whether she lost consciousness. She was transported to a local hospital, where she remained hospitalized for several days. Ms. X was discharged with diagnoses of a severe neck sprain, a contusion resulting from restraint by her seatbelt, a bladder infection, torn ligaments in her left leg, and nerve damage in her left foot.

Medical records indicated that the attending paramedic who first evaluated Ms. X described her mental status as normal. At the hospital, her Glasgow Coma Scale score was 15/15. She is described in these records as presenting with a series of vaguely related symptoms and complaints that were investigated over the course of her hospitalization. Medical imaging studies did not reveal any abnormalities. Following discharge, after a series of complaints, Ms. X was deemed to be incapable of caring for her own basic needs and was found eligible to receive 24-hour assistance with basic living skills.

Ms. X reported having sustained another injury 10 years prior to the recent motor vehicle accident when she fell into a ditch. According to her report, a vertebral fracture was diagnosed and treated unsuccessfully several years after this accident. She reported that prior to the first accident, she had been employed as a paraprofessional, but she became disabled by the accident and had not worked since this event. A review of medical records indicated that a number of evaluators concluded that Ms. X's symptoms and complaints following the initial accident could not be explained medically.

Ms. X's main complaint at the time of the current evaluation involved speech problems. Specifically, she complained that her speech was slowed and dysfluent and that it required considerable effort for her to be able to speak. She also complained of diffuse pain with an unusual distribution, for which she was receiving very high doses of opiate-based medication. Ms. X claimed that since the accident, she had lost her ability to perform simple math and was experiencing significant memory problems. She also reported experiencing mood swings and sleep difficulties.

Ms. X was referred for an independent neuropsychological evaluation by attorneys for the insurance company that was handling her case. The evaluating neuropsychologist observed that she presented with very atypical stuttering speech and other pseudoneurologic symptoms. Effort tests were administered as part of the neuropsychological test battery, and the results indicated that Ms. X exerted adequate effort. Cognitive testing indicated intact functioning in most areas likely to be affected by a brain injury, with some problems most likely due to extensive medication use.

The MMPI-2-RF was administered as part of the independent neuropsychological evaluation. Ms. X's MMPI-2-RF results are provided in Figure 9-7. The forensic neuropsychological examination litigant/claimant women sample was used as the comparison group in this case.

MMPI-2-RF Interpretation[1]

Ms. X responded to all the MMPI-2-RF items. Her Validity Scale scores indicate that she responded relevantly and consistently to the test items. Possible overreporting of psychological dysfunction is indicated by Ms. X providing a larger than average number of infrequent responses. This level of infrequent responding may occur in individuals with genuine psychological difficulties who report credible symptoms. However, for individuals with no history or current corroborating evidence of dysfunction, it probably indicates overreporting. Possible overreporting of somatic symptoms is reflected in the assertion of a much larger than average number of somatic symptoms rarely described by individuals with genuine medical problems. Possible overreporting is also indicated by unusual combinations of responses that are associated with noncredible somatic and cognitive complaints and, in particular, complaints about memory. This level and type of infrequent responding may occur in individuals with substantial medical conditions who report credible symptoms, but it could also reflect exaggeration. There is no evidence of underreporting in this protocol.

Ms. X reports a diffuse pattern of somatic complaints involving different bodily systems. She is very likely to be preoccupied with physical health concerns, to be prone to developing physical symptoms in response to stress, to have a psychological component to her somatic complaints, and to complain of fatigue. She reports a general sense of malaise manifested in poor health and feeling tired, weak, and incapacitated. She is very likely to complain of sleep disturbance and sexual dysfunction. She also reports head pain and is likely to complain about headaches, chronic pain, and difficulty concentrating. In addition, Ms. X reports a large number of various vague neurological complaints (e.g., dizziness, loss of balance, numbness, weakness and paralysis, and loss of control over movement, including involuntary movement). She is also very likely to complain about various sensory problems. Ms. X also reports a diffuse pattern of cognitive difficulties, and she is very likely to complain about memory problems and concentration difficulties.

Ms. X's responses indicate significant emotional distress. She reports a lack of positive emotional experiences, significant anhedonia, and lack of interest. She is

**Minnesota Multiphasic
Personality Inventory-2
Restructured Form®**

Score Report

MMPI-2-RF®

Minnesota Multiphasic Personality Inventory-2-Restructured Form®

Yossef S. Ben-Porath, PhD, & Auke Tellegen, PhD

ID Number:	Ms. X
Age:	47
Gender:	Female
Marital Status:	Separated
Years of Education:	18
Date Assessed:	04/22/2011

PEARSON   Ⓦ *PsychCorp*

Figure 9-7. Ms. X's MMPI-2-RF Score Report.

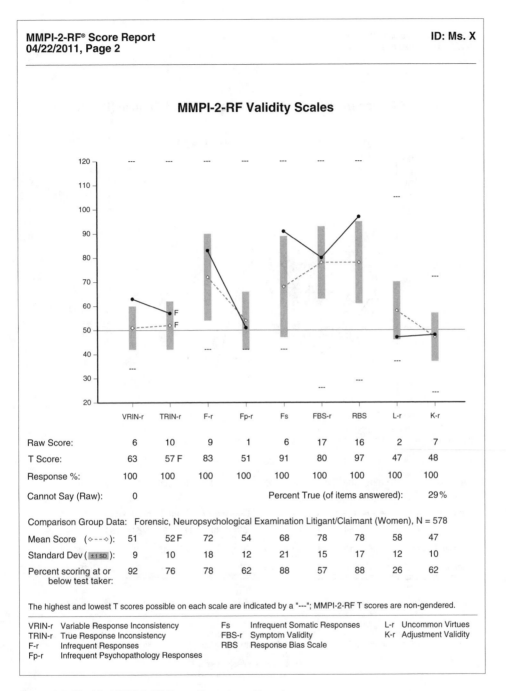

MMPI-2-RF Validity Scales

	VRIN-r	TRIN-r	F-r	Fp-r	Fs	FBS-r	RBS	L-r	K-r
Raw Score:	6	10	9	1	6	17	16	2	7
T Score:	63	57 F	83	51	91	80	97	47	48
Response %:	100	100	100	100	100	100	100	100	100

Cannot Say (Raw):   0   Percent True (of items answered):   29%

Comparison Group Data: Forensic, Neuropsychological Examination Litigant/Claimant (Women), N = 578

	VRIN-r	TRIN-r	F-r	Fp-r	Fs	FBS-r	RBS	L-r	K-r
Mean Score (◇--◇):	51	52 F	72	54	68	78	78	58	47
Standard Dev (±1 SD):	9	10	18	12	21	15	17	12	10
Percent scoring at or below test taker:	92	76	78	62	88	57	88	26	62

The highest and lowest T scores possible on each scale are indicated by a "---"; MMPI-2-RF T scores are non-gendered.

VRIN-r	Variable Response Inconsistency	Fs	Infrequent Somatic Responses	L-r	Uncommon Virtues
TRIN-r	True Response Inconsistency	FBS-r	Symptom Validity	K-r	Adjustment Validity
F-r	Infrequent Responses	RBS	Response Bias Scale		
Fp-r	Infrequent Psychopathology Responses				

Figure 9-7. Ms. X's MMPI-2-RF Score Report, continued.

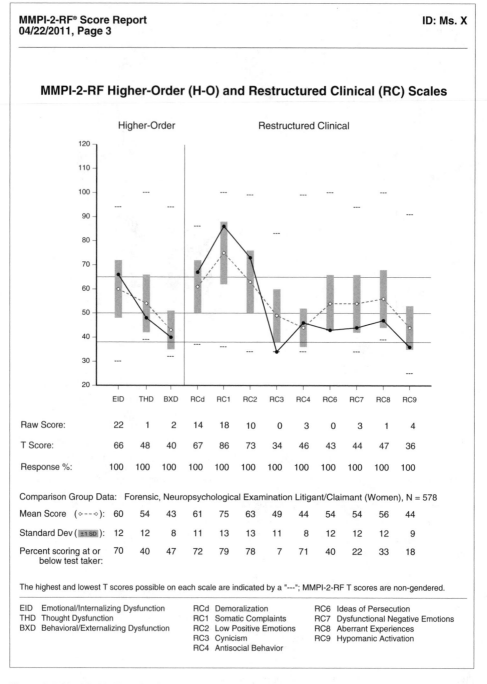

MMPI-2-RF Higher-Order (H-O) and Restructured Clinical (RC) Scales

Higher-Order   Restructured Clinical

	EID	THD	BXD	RCd	RC1	RC2	RC3	RC4	RC6	RC7	RC8	RC9
Raw Score:	22	1	2	14	18	10	0	3	0	3	1	4
T Score:	66	48	40	67	86	73	34	46	43	44	47	36
Response %:	100	100	100	100	100	100	100	100	100	100	100	100

Comparison Group Data: Forensic, Neuropsychological Examination Litigant/Claimant (Women), N = 578

Mean Score (◇- - -◇):	60	54	43	61	75	63	49	44	54	54	56	44
Standard Dev (±1 SD):	12	12	8	11	13	13	11	8	12	12	12	9
Percent scoring at or below test taker:	70	40	47	72	79	78	7	71	40	22	33	18

The highest and lowest T scores possible on each scale are indicated by a "---"; MMPI-2-RF T scores are non-gendered.

EID Emotional/Internalizing Dysfunction	RCd Demoralization	RC6 Ideas of Persecution
THD Thought Dysfunction	RC1 Somatic Complaints	RC7 Dysfunctional Negative Emotions
BXD Behavioral/Externalizing Dysfunction	RC2 Low Positive Emotions	RC8 Aberrant Experiences
	RC3 Cynicism	RC9 Hypomanic Activation
	RC4 Antisocial Behavior	

Figure 9-7. Ms. X's MMPI-2-RF Score Report, continued.

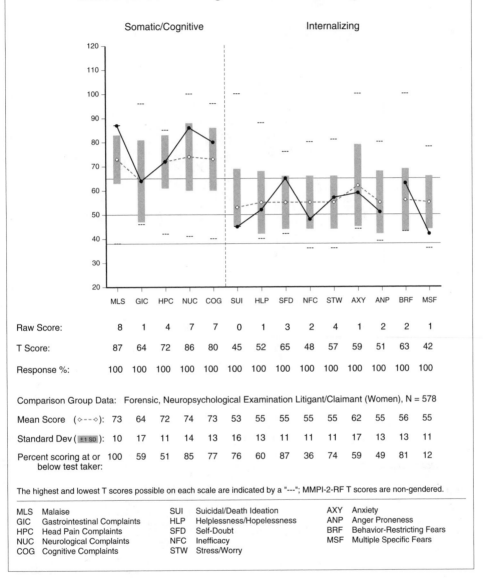

Figure 9-7. Ms. X's MMPI-2-RF Score Report, continued.

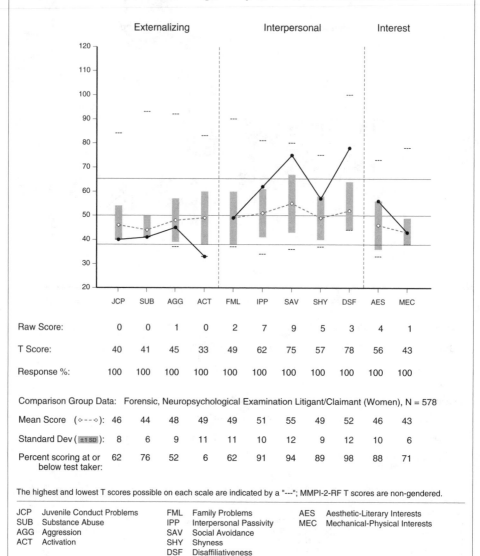

MMPI-2-RF Externalizing, Interpersonal, and Interest Scales

Externalizing   Interpersonal   Interest

	JCP	SUB	AGG	ACT	FML	IPP	SAV	SHY	DSF	AES	MEC
Raw Score:	0	0	1	0	2	7	9	5	3	4	1
T Score:	40	41	45	33	49	62	75	57	78	56	43
Response %:	100	100	100	100	100	100	100	100	100	100	100

Comparison Group Data: Forensic, Neuropsychological Examination Litigant/Claimant (Women), N = 578

	JCP	SUB	AGG	ACT	FML	IPP	SAV	SHY	DSF	AES	MEC
Mean Score (◇--◇):	46	44	48	49	49	51	55	49	52	46	43
Standard Dev (±1 SD):	8	6	9	11	11	10	12	9	12	10	6
Percent scoring at or below test taker:	62	76	52	6	62	91	94	89	98	88	71

The highest and lowest T scores possible on each scale are indicated by a "---"; MMPI-2-RF T scores are non-gendered.

JCP	Juvenile Conduct Problems	FML	Family Problems	AES	Aesthetic-Literary Interests
SUB	Substance Abuse	IPP	Interpersonal Passivity	MEC	Mechanical-Physical Interests
AGG	Aggression	SAV	Social Avoidance		
ACT	Activation	SHY	Shyness		
		DSF	Disaffiliativeness		

Figure 9-7. Ms. X's MMPI-2-RF Score Report, continued.

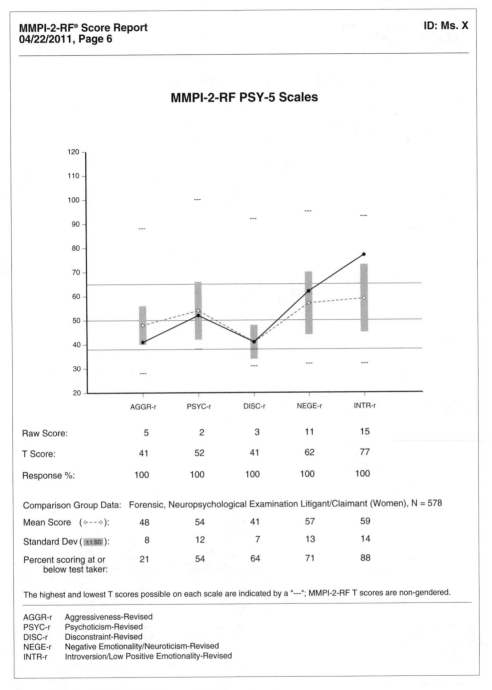

MMPI-2-RF PSY-5 Scales

	AGGR-r	PSYC-r	DISC-r	NEGE-r	INTR-r
Raw Score:	5	2	3	11	15
T Score:	41	52	41	62	77
Response %:	100	100	100	100	100

Comparison Group Data: Forensic, Neuropsychological Examination Litigant/Claimant (Women), N = 578

Mean Score (◇--◇):	48	54	41	57	59
Standard Dev (±1 SD):	8	12	7	13	14
Percent scoring at or below test taker:	21	54	64	71	88

The highest and lowest T scores possible on each scale are indicated by a "---"; MMPI-2-RF T scores are non-gendered.

AGGR-r	Aggressiveness-Revised
PSYC-r	Psychoticism-Revised
DISC-r	Disconstraint-Revised
NEGE-r	Negative Emotionality/Neuroticism-Revised
INTR-r	Introversion/Low Positive Emotionality-Revised

Figure 9-7. Ms. X's MMPI-2-RF Score Report, continued.

MMPI-2-RF® Score Report
04/22/2011, Page 7

ID: Ms. X

MMPI-2-RF T SCORES (BY DOMAIN)

PROTOCOL VALIDITY

Content Non-Responsiveness	0	63	57 F
	CNS	VRIN-r	TRIN-r

Over-Reporting	83	51		91	80	97
	F-r	Fp-r		Fs	FBS-r	RBS

Under-Reporting	47	48
	L-r	K-r

SUBSTANTIVE SCALES

Somatic/Cognitive Dysfunction	86	87	64	72	86	80
	RC1	MLS	GIC	HPC	NUC	COG

Emotional Dysfunction	66	67	45	52	65	48	
	EID	RCd	SUI	HLP	SFD	NFC	
		73	77				
		RC2	INTR-r				
		44	57	59	51	63	42	62
		RC7	STW	AXY	ANP	BRF	MSF	NEGE-r

Thought Dysfunction	48	43
	THD	RC6
		47
		RC8
		52
		PSYC-r

Behavioral Dysfunction	40	46	40	41		
	BXD	RC4	JCP	SUB		
		36	45	33	41	41
		RC9	AGG	ACT	AGGR-r	DISC-r

Interpersonal Functioning	49	34	62	75	57	78
	FML	RC3	IPP	SAV	SHY	DSF

Interests	56	43
	AES	MEC

Note. This information is provided to facilitate interpretation following the recommended structure for MMPI-2-RF interpretation in Chapter 5 of the *MMPI-2-RF Manual for Administration, Scoring, and Interpretation*, which provides details in the text and an outline in Table 5-1.

Figure 9-7. Ms. X's MMPI-2-RF Score Report, continued.

ITEM-LEVEL INFORMATION

Unscorable Responses

The test taker produced scorable responses to all the MMPI-2-RF items.

Critical Responses

Seven MMPI-2-RF scales--Suicidal/Death Ideation (SUI), Helplessness/Hopelessness (HLP), Anxiety (AXY), Ideas of Persecution (RC6), Aberrant Experiences (RC8), Substance Abuse (SUB), and Aggression (AGG)--have been designated by the test authors as having critical item content that may require immediate attention and follow-up. Items answered by the individual in the keyed direction (True or False) on a critical scale are listed below if her T score on that scale is 65 or higher.

The test taker has not produced an elevated T score (≥ 65) on any of these scales.

End of Report

Figure 9-7. Ms. X's MMPI-2-RF Score Report, continued.

likely to be pessimistic and may display vegetative signs of depression. Relatedly, she reports a below-average level of activation and engagement with her environment. Ms. X also reports feeling sad and unhappy and being dissatisfied with her current life circumstances, and she is likely to complain about depression or anxiety, to not cope well with stress, and to have low self-esteem. She indeed reports self-doubt and likely feels inferior and insecure, and she is likely to be self-disparaging, prone to rumination, and intropunitive. She likely presents with lack of confidence and feelings of uselessness.

Ms. X reports disliking people and being around them, and she is likely asocial. She also reports not enjoying social events and avoiding social situations, but not because people make her anxious. She is likely to be introverted, to have difficulty forming close relationships, and to be emotionally restricted. On the other hand, Ms. X describes others as well intentioned and trustworthy, and she disavows cynical beliefs about them. She may be overly trusting.

The MMPI-2-RF results identify a number of diagnostic considerations for Ms. X. Validity Scale scores raise the possibility that Ms. X overreported somatic, cognitive, and emotional symptoms. If this is corroborated by other findings, the possibility of intentional overreporting associated with malingering or a Factitious Disorder should be considered. She should also be evaluated for a Somatoform Disorder, and in particular, the possibility of a Conversion Disorder is indicated for further evaluation. The MMPI-2-RF results also raise the possibility that Ms. X has a depressive disorder, particularly Major Depression. An Axis II disorder, particularly one with features of Avoidant and Dependent Personality disorders, is also indicated for further consideration.

Discussion

A critical question when considering Ms. X's MMPI-2-RF results relates to the implications of her Validity Scale scores. Although they do not reach levels that indicate an invalid protocol, these scores indicate a significant possibility that she is overreporting. In a forensic case such as this, where an incentive to overreport exists, the possibility of malingering is raised. As mentioned earlier, records available to the evaluator identified a long-standing pattern of unexplained medical complaints and inconsistent symptom presentation that predated the motor vehicle accident but that was also linked to an event (the earlier accident) that triggered a disability claim. The examiner also noted a very unlikely set of complaints reported by Ms. X and pseudoneurologic symptoms she displayed during her interview for the present evaluation.

An alternative explanation for Ms. X's past and ongoing unexplained medical complaints could be a Somatoform Disorder. In light of the prominence of vague neurological symptoms, the possibility of a Conversion Disorder, in particular, would need to be considered. Ms. X's MMPI-2-RF results, particularly her highly elevated Neurological Complaints (NUC) T score (86) and her low score on Cynicism (RC3), are consistent with a possible Conversion Disorder. On the other hand, her extremely high T score on the Malaise (MLS) Scale (87), which falls well outside the range of scores found typically in this population (as shown on page 4 of Figure 9-7), is not consistent with a relative lack of concern about the nature or implications of the reported symptoms, an associated feature of Conversion Disorder.

Considering the long-standing and pervasive nature of her unexplained medical complaints and her willingness to incapacitate herself through surgical intervention and to risk real medical problems, the forensic neuropsychologist who conducted this evaluation concluded that neither malingering nor a Conversion Disorder best accounted for Ms. X's symptoms and presentation. Instead, the examiner concluded that Ms. X's feigning of a wide variety of symptoms was intended to get sympathy, attention, and support by assuming a sick role and thus was best viewed as a Factitious Disorder with combined psychological and physical signs and symptoms.

DSM-IV diagnostic criteria for Factitious Disorder require intentional feigning of physical signs and symptoms motivated by the desire to assume the sick role. They also require that external incentives (such as economic gain) be absent. The examiner concluded that in this case, the behavior justifying this diagnosis predated the accident at issue in litigation and had lasted long beyond the prior accident for which she was already receiving disability benefits. The examiner concluded that the earlier event initially triggered a Somatoform Disorder, which ultimately developed into a debilitating Factitious Disorder. Psychological symptoms, in particular anhedonia, as reflected by Ms. X's elevated RC2 score, were determined to be most likely attributable to heavy sedation resulting from possible abuse of opiate-based medication.

MS. R: A CASE OF POSTTRAUMATIC STRESS DISORDER

Ms. R is a 47-year-old separated woman who underwent a forensic evaluation in connection with a disability claim. She had been employed as a night-shift sales clerk at a convenience store for several months, when an individual brandishing a firearm approached her and demanded that she hand over all the cash in her register. Consistent with company policy, she did so, at which point, the robber demanded that she open the safe. Ms. R responded that she did not have a key to the safe and pointed to a sign to that effect posted in the store. The robber became enraged and threatened to kill her if she did not open the store safe. He pointed his pistol at her, cocked it, and appeared to prepare to fire. Ms. R attempted to flee, and the assailant struck her in the face and subdued her. He then locked her in a back room, threatening to come back and kill her if she called the police, and left. All these events were documented with the store's video surveillance system.

After waiting approximately five minutes, Ms. R called the store manager, who alerted the police. The investigating officer's report described Ms. R as "being in a daze" when he arrived at the scene. She had difficulty recounting what had transpired and describing her assailant. Paramedics were called, and Ms. R was transported to a local hospital, where she was given a sedative and her facial wounds were treated. A social worker spoke with her briefly and provided a referral to a local community mental health center for follow-up. Ms. R's manager told her to take the next night off and to return to work the following evening.

Ms. R reported that she slept most of the next 24 hours, and when the time came for her to prepare to go back to work, she became extremely upset and frightened. She called her manager to report that she could not return to the store. She had learned from the police that the robber had yet to be apprehended, and she was concerned that he would return to harm her, as he had indicated he would if the police were summoned. The manager instructed Ms. R to stay home that night and go to the community mental health center for an evaluation the next day.

Records forwarded by the community mental health center indicate that Ms. R presented the next day, as instructed. She was described by the intake clinician as extremely distraught, tearful, and frightened. She complained that she was "losing her mind" and was constantly reliving the robbery. Ms. R was diagnosed with an acute stress disorder, and arrangements were made for her to go on temporary disability for two weeks to give her an opportunity to receive treatment. She was seen twice a week for two weeks without much improvement, and after another two weeks of treatment, Ms. R was referred for an independent evaluation to determine whether she was eligible for further disability benefits. The assessing psychologist was also asked to recommend a course of treatment if Ms. R were found to have a psychological disability.

Ms. R's evaluation took place approximately six weeks after the robbery. The MMPI-2-RF was administered as part of a battery of tests. Additional testing included measures of cognitive functioning, effort, and emotional dysfunction. Ms. R was found to have exerted good effort throughout the evaluation. Cognitive testing indicated some impairment in attention and concentration, which was attributed to excessive psychological arousal. Other measures indicated a heightened level of emotional distress and anxiety.

Ms. R's MMPI-2-RF results are reproduced in Figure 9-8. The forensic disability claimant women comparison group data are printed along with her results.

MMPI-2-RF Interpretation

Ms. R responded to all the MMPI-2-RF items. Her Validity Scale scores indicate that she provided relevant and consistent responses. Possible overreporting is indicated by an unusual combination of responses that is associated with noncredible memory complaints. However, this combination of responses may occur in individuals with substantial emotional dysfunction, although it can also reflect exaggeration. There are no other indications of overreporting and no indications of underreporting in this protocol.

Ms. R's responses indicate significant emotional distress. She reports various negative emotional experiences, including anxiety and fear. She is likely to be inhibited behaviorally because of negative emotions, to experience intrusive ideation, and to perceive others as overly critical. She is also likely to be self-critical and guilt prone. Ms. R reports feeling anxious and is very likely to have significant anxiety and anxiety-related problems and to experience sleep difficulties and nightmares as well as posttraumatic distress. She reports multiple fears that significantly restrict normal activity inside and outside the home, and she is very likely to be quite fearful.

Minnesota Multiphasic
Personality Inventory-2
Restructured Form®

Score Report

MMPI-2-RF®
Minnesota Multiphasic Personality Inventory-2-Restructured Form®
Yossef S. Ben-Porath, PhD, & Auke Tellegen, PhD

ID Number:	Ms. R
Age:	45
Gender:	Female
Marital Status:	Separated
Years of Education:	10
Date Assessed:	04/22/2011

PEARSON

☯ *PsychCorp*

Figure 9-8. Ms. R's MMPI-2-RF Score Report.

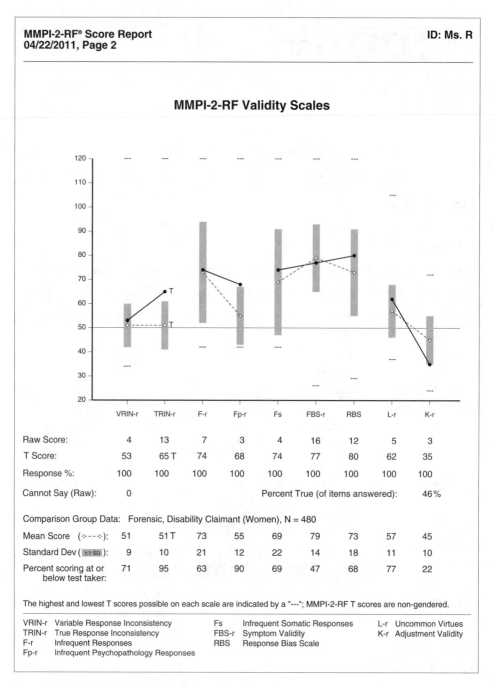

MMPI-2-RF® Score Report   ID: Ms. R
04/22/2011, Page 2

MMPI-2-RF Validity Scales

	VRIN-r	TRIN-r	F-r	Fp-r	Fs	FBS-r	RBS	L-r	K-r
Raw Score:	4	13	7	3	4	16	12	5	3
T Score:	53	65 T	74	68	74	77	80	62	35
Response %:	100	100	100	100	100	100	100	100	100

Cannot Say (Raw):   0   Percent True (of items answered):   46%

Comparison Group Data: Forensic, Disability Claimant (Women), N = 480

	VRIN-r	TRIN-r	F-r	Fp-r	Fs	FBS-r	RBS	L-r	K-r
Mean Score (◇---◇):	51	51 T	73	55	69	79	73	57	45
Standard Dev (±1 SD):	9	10	21	12	22	14	18	11	10
Percent scoring at or below test taker:	71	95	63	90	69	47	68	77	22

The highest and lowest T scores possible on each scale are indicated by a "---"; MMPI-2-RF T scores are non-gendered.

VRIN-r	Variable Response Inconsistency	Fs	Infrequent Somatic Responses	L-r Uncommon Virtues
TRIN-r	True Response Inconsistency	FBS-r	Symptom Validity	K-r Adjustment Validity
F-r	Infrequent Responses	RBS	Response Bias Scale	
Fp-r	Infrequent Psychopathology Responses			

Figure 9-8. Ms. R's MMPI-2-RF Score Report, continued.

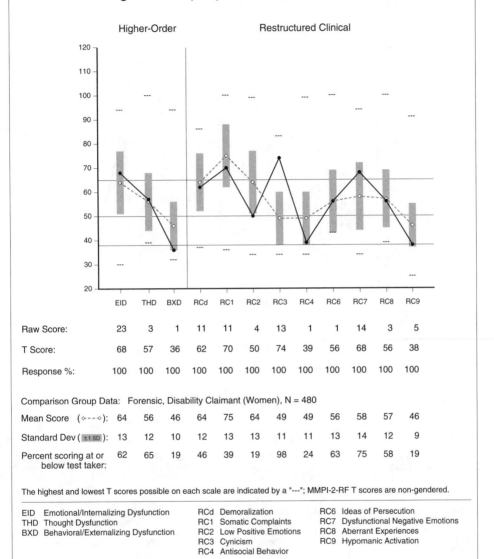

MMPI-2-RF Higher-Order (H-O) and Restructured Clinical (RC) Scales

Higher-Order   Restructured Clinical

	EID	THD	BXD	RCd	RC1	RC2	RC3	RC4	RC6	RC7	RC8	RC9
Raw Score:	23	3	1	11	11	4	13	1	1	14	3	5
T Score:	68	57	36	62	70	50	74	39	56	68	56	38
Response %:	100	100	100	100	100	100	100	100	100	100	100	100

Comparison Group Data: Forensic, Disability Claimant (Women), N = 480

	EID	THD	BXD	RCd	RC1	RC2	RC3	RC4	RC6	RC7	RC8	RC9
Mean Score (◇--◇):	64	56	46	64	75	64	49	49	56	58	57	46
Standard Dev (±1 SD):	13	12	10	12	13	13	11	11	13	14	12	9
Percent scoring at or below test taker:	62	65	19	46	39	19	98	24	63	75	58	19

The highest and lowest T scores possible on each scale are indicated by a "---"; MMPI-2-RF T scores are non-gendered.

EID Emotional/Internalizing Dysfunction	RCd Demoralization	RC6 Ideas of Persecution
THD Thought Dysfunction	RC1 Somatic Complaints	RC7 Dysfunctional Negative Emotions
BXD Behavioral/Externalizing Dysfunction	RC2 Low Positive Emotions	RC8 Aberrant Experiences
	RC3 Cynicism	RC9 Hypomanic Activation
	RC4 Antisocial Behavior	

Figure 9-8. Ms. R's MMPI-2-RF Score Report, continued.

MMPI-2-RF® Score Report   ID: Ms. R
04/22/2011, Page 4

MMPI-2-RF Somatic/Cognitive and Internalizing Scales

Somatic/Cognitive   Internalizing

	MLS	GIC	HPC	NUC	COG	SUI	HLP	SFD	NFC	STW	AXY	ANP	BRF	MSF
Raw Score:	5	0	5	2	6	0	0	2	5	7	4	2	5	6
T Score:	69	46	78	59	75	45	40	56	58	81	91	51	86	59
Response %:	100	100	100	100	100	100	100	100	100	100	100	100	100	100

Comparison Group Data: Forensic, Disability Claimant (Women), N = 480

	MLS	GIC	HPC	NUC	COG	SUI	HLP	SFD	NFC	STW	AXY	ANP	BRF	MSF
Mean Score (◇--◇):	75	67	71	71	68	57	58	60	57	58	66	55	57	53
Standard Dev (±1 SD):	9	18	11	14	15	19	14	12	13	12	18	12	14	10
Percent scoring at or below test taker:	30	33	75	25	69	67	25	55	60	100	94	46	98	83

The highest and lowest T scores possible on each scale are indicated by a "---"; MMPI-2-RF T scores are non-gendered.

MLS	Malaise	SUI	Suicidal/Death Ideation	AXY	Anxiety
GIC	Gastrointestinal Complaints	HLP	Helplessness/Hopelessness	ANP	Anger Proneness
HPC	Head Pain Complaints	SFD	Self-Doubt	BRF	Behavior-Restricting Fears
NUC	Neurological Complaints	NFC	Inefficacy	MSF	Multiple Specific Fears
COG	Cognitive Complaints	STW	Stress/Worry		

Figure 9-8. Ms. R's MMPI-2-RF Score Report, continued.

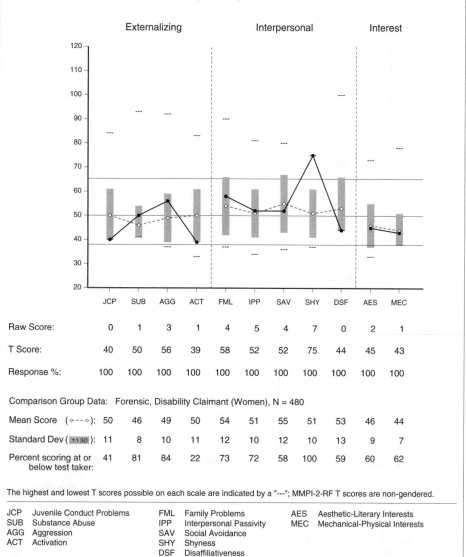

MMPI-2-RF Externalizing, Interpersonal, and Interest Scales

	JCP	SUB	AGG	ACT	FML	IPP	SAV	SHY	DSF	AES	MEC
Raw Score:	0	1	3	1	4	5	4	7	0	2	1
T Score:	40	50	56	39	58	52	52	75	44	45	43
Response %:	100	100	100	100	100	100	100	100	100	100	100

Comparison Group Data: Forensic, Disability Claimant (Women), N = 480

	JCP	SUB	AGG	ACT	FML	IPP	SAV	SHY	DSF	AES	MEC
Mean Score (◇--◇):	50	46	49	50	54	51	55	51	53	46	44
Standard Dev (+1 SD):	11	8	10	11	12	10	12	10	13	9	7
Percent scoring at or below test taker:	41	81	84	22	73	72	58	100	59	60	62

The highest and lowest T scores possible on each scale are indicated by a "---"; MMPI-2-RF T scores are non-gendered.

JCP	Juvenile Conduct Problems	FML	Family Problems	AES	Aesthetic-Literary Interests
SUB	Substance Abuse	IPP	Interpersonal Passivity	MEC	Mechanical-Physical Interests
AGG	Aggression	SAV	Social Avoidance		
ACT	Activation	SHY	Shyness		
		DSF	Disaffiliativeness		

Figure 9-8. Ms. R's MMPI-2-RF Score Report, continued.

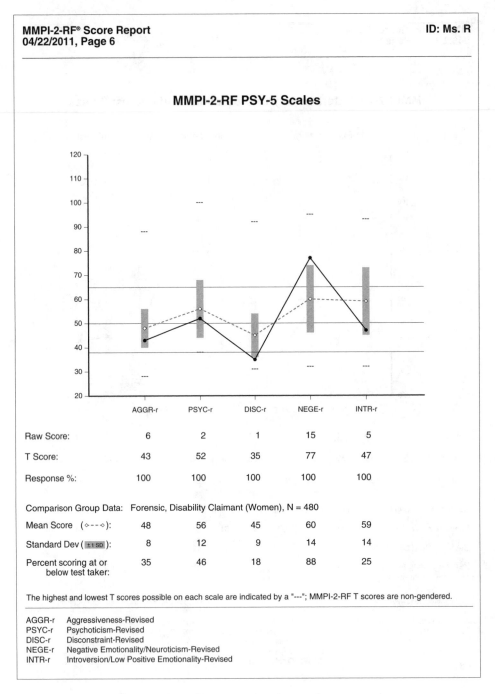

MMPI-2-RF PSY-5 Scales

	AGGR-r	PSYC-r	DISC-r	NEGE-r	INTR-r
Raw Score:	6	2	1	15	5
T Score:	43	52	35	77	47
Response %:	100	100	100	100	100

Comparison Group Data: Forensic, Disability Claimant (Women), N = 480

	AGGR-r	PSYC-r	DISC-r	NEGE-r	INTR-r
Mean Score (◇--◇):	48	56	45	60	59
Standard Dev (±1 SD):	8	12	9	14	14
Percent scoring at or below test taker:	35	46	18	88	25

The highest and lowest T scores possible on each scale are indicated by a "---"; MMPI-2-RF T scores are non-gendered.

AGGR-r   Aggressiveness-Revised
PSYC-r   Psychoticism-Revised
DISC-r   Disconstraint-Revised
NEGE-r   Negative Emotionality/Neuroticism-Revised
INTR-r   Introversion/Low Positive Emotionality-Revised

Figure 9-8. Ms. R's MMPI-2-RF Score Report, continued.

MMPI-2-RF T SCORES (BY DOMAIN)

PROTOCOL VALIDITY

Content Non-Responsiveness

0	53	65 T
CNS	VRIN-r	TRIN-r

Over-Reporting

74	68		74	77	80
F-r	Fp-r		Fs	FBS-r	RBS

Under-Reporting

62	35
L-r	K-r

SUBSTANTIVE SCALES

Somatic/Cognitive Dysfunction

70	69	46	78	59	75
RC1	MLS	GIC	HPC	NUC	COG

Emotional Dysfunction

68					
EID					

62	45	40	56	58
RCd	SUI	HLP	SFD	NFC

50	47
RC2	INTR-r

68	81	91	51	86	59	77
RC7	STW	AXY	ANP	BRF	MSF	NEGE-r

Thought Dysfunction

57
THD

56
RC6

56
RC8

52
PSYC-r

Behavioral Dysfunction

36
BXD

39	40	50
RC4	JCP	SUB

38	56	39	43	35
RC9	AGG	ACT	AGGR-r	DISC-r

Interpersonal Functioning

58	74	52	52	75	44
FML	RC3	IPP	SAV	SHY	DSF

Interests

45	43
AES	MEC

Note. This information is provided to facilitate interpretation following the recommended structure for MMPI-2-RF interpretation in Chapter 5 of the *MMPI-2-RF Manual for Administration, Scoring, and Interpretation*, which provides details in the text and an outline in Table 5-1.

Figure 9-8. Ms. R's MMPI-2-RF Score Report, continued.

ITEM-LEVEL INFORMATION

Unscorable Responses

The test taker produced scorable responses to all the MMPI-2-RF items.

Critical Responses

Seven MMPI-2-RF scales--Suicidal/Death Ideation (SUI), Helplessness/Hopelessness (HLP), Anxiety (AXY), Ideas of Persecution (RC6), Aberrant Experiences (RC8), Substance Abuse (SUB), and Aggression (AGG)--have been designated by the test authors as having critical item content that may require immediate attention and follow-up. Items answered by the individual in the keyed direction (True or False) on a critical scale are listed below if her T score on that scale is 65 or higher. The percentage of the MMPI-2-RF normative sample (NS) and of the Forensic, Disability Claimant (Women) comparison group (CG) that answered each item in the keyed direction are provided in parentheses following the item content.

Anxiety (AXY, T Score = 91)

   79. Item content removed. (True; NS 6.2%, CG 36.7%)
 146. Item content removed. (True; NS 1.8%, CG 17.5%)
 228. Item content removed. (True; NS 17.3%, CG 51.3%)
 289. Item content removed. (True; NS 12.7%, CG 44.8%)

End of Report

Figure 9-8. Ms. R's MMPI-2-RF Score Report, continued.

She also reports an above-average level of stress and worry and is very likely to be stress reactive and worry prone and to engage in obsessive rumination.

Ms. R reports multiple somatic complaints that include head pain and general concerns about her health. She is likely preoccupied with physical health concerns and prone to developing physical symptoms in response to stress. She likely has a psychological component to her somatic complaints and is likely to complain of fatigue. Specifically, Ms. R is likely to complain about headaches, chronic pain, and difficulty concentrating. She does indeed report a diffuse pattern of cognitive difficulties and is likely to complain about memory problems, to have low tolerance for frustration, and to experience difficulties in concentration. Ms. R also reports experiencing poor health and feeling weak or tired. She is likely to complain of fatigue, low energy, and sexual dysfunction.

Ms. R's responses also indicate a higher-than-average level of behavioral constraint. She is unlikely to engage in externalizing behavior.

Interpersonally, Ms. R reports being shy, easily embarrassed, and uncomfortable around others. She is likely to be introverted and inhibited and to become anxious and nervous in social situations. She also reports having cynical beliefs, being distrustful of others, and believing that others look out only for their own interests. Ms. R is likely hostile toward others and feels alienated. She is likely to be distrustful and to have negative interpersonal experiences.

Ms. R's MMPI-2-RF results identify a number of diagnostic considerations. She should be evaluated for an anxiety-related disorder, particularly PTSD, Obsessive–Compulsive Disorder, and Social Phobia. The possibility of a Somatoform Disorder is also indicated for further evaluation. She should also be evaluated for disorders involving mistrust of and hostility toward others. A possible Axis II disorder, particularly one with features of Cluster C disorders, is also raised by her test scores.

Treatment considerations identified by Ms. R's MMPI-2-RF findings include a possible need for anxiolytic medication and, if this has not already been done, a medical evaluation to rule out a physical origin for her head pain complaints. The origins of her cognitive complaints should also be explored, although, as indicated, they may be a product of emotional dysfunction. Potential intervention targets include anxiety, behavior-restricting fears, stress management and excessive worry, social anxiety, pain management, and lack of interpersonal trust. Her heightened level of anxiety may motivate Ms. R to initiate treatment; however, her malaise and cynical view of others may impede the formation of a therapeutic relationship.

Discussion

The possibility of overreporting needs always to be considered carefully in a disability evaluation. Ms. R's Validity Scale scores indicate a generally cooperative test-taking approach. A finding that indicates possible overreporting of memory complaints, an RBS T score of 80, falls in a range that, as indicated in the interpretation, can occur in individuals experiencing significant emotional dysfunction. In addition, her RBS score falls very near the mean for the female forensic disability claimant comparison group, and her effort testing did not raise concerns about suboptimal performance on cognitive measures. Finally, none of the other Validity Scales that would be expected to be elevated in a test taker who is overreporting PTSD symptoms, particularly F-r, is at a level that would indicate concerns about overreporting. These findings, coupled with Ms. R's well-documented trauma, indicate against overreporting in this case.

Ms. R's scores on the MMPI-2-RF Substantive Scales identify PTSD as a likely diagnosis. Elevations on Dysfunctional Negative Emotions (RC7) and Anxiety (AXY) are both associated empirically with increased risk for PTSD. This, coupled with a documented traumatic event that is sufficient to trigger this condition, led the examiner to diagnose Ms. R with acute PTSD and to attribute its acquisition to her work-related experience.

Ms. R's head pain complaints were attributed to residual effects of the facial injury she sustained rather than to a Somatoform Disorder. Her elevation on RC1 was understood in terms of the physiological arousal that often accompanies PTSD. Elevations on the Behavior-Restricting Fears (BRF) and Stress/Worry (STW) scales were also attributed to Ms. R's recent traumatic experience.

The examiner recommended that Ms. R be evaluated by a psychiatrist for possible anxiolytic medication and that she receive cognitive–behavioral therapy for PTSD. In light of her increased cynicism level, a note of caution was raised regarding Ms. R's readiness to form a therapeutic relationship. The examiner recommended that in the early stages, the therapist focus on establishing a trusting relationship with Ms. R.

Ms. R's temporary disability status was extended, and she began receiving therapy. Anxiolytic medication was prescribed, and Ms. R reported that her physiological arousal symptoms and nightmares subsided. An initial attempt to return to work after five weeks of treatment was unsuccessful, and Ms. R decided that she did not want to return to the same location. Her employer offered an alternative location at a larger store and a day shift rather than a night shift. Ms. R resumed full-time employment approximately six months following the robbery, although she continued to report residual reexperiencing and avoidance symptoms.

MR. M: NOT GUILTY BY REASON OF INSANITY

Mr. M, a 21-year-old single male, was evaluated pursuant to a court order in connection with a not guilty by reason of insanity plea. A patrol officer had observed Mr. M driving erratically, weaving in and out of traffic on a county highway. The officer followed the defendant in a marked police cruiser and eventually activated the vehicle's lights and siren. Rather than pulling over, Mr. M accelerated his driving speed, and a several-mile chase ensued. Other cruisers were called in, and Mr. M, who had pulled off the highway and was driving on back roads, was surrounded. He then drove straight at the patrol officer's vehicle and rammed it several times, managing to escape, and continued driving until his vehicle ran out of fuel. At that point, he was apprehended, arrested, and charged with aggravated assault of a police officer. He was taken to a hospital to clean up minor wounds, and from there, Mr. M was transported to the county jail.

In his report, the arresting officer wrote that Mr. M appeared to be terrified, repeatedly shouting, "Don't shoot me, don't kill me," even after he was already handcuffed and sitting in the back of a cruiser. Records forwarded by the hospital where Mr. M was treated for his wounds described him as initially agitated, paranoid, and incoherent. Hospital staff suspected that Mr. M may have been under the influence of drugs or alcohol; however, the results of a toxicology screen were negative. Mr. M was given a sedative, eventually calmed down, and was transported to the jail, where he was assessed by a mental health worker. The worker's notes indicated that Mr. M claimed that he had been chased by a gang that was hired to kill him. He was placed in the jail's mental health unit and evaluated later that day by a psychiatrist, who diagnosed Mr. M with "atypical psychosis" and recommended that he be observed for a few days to help determine an appropriate diagnosis and course of treatment.

At his arraignment, a court-appointed attorney entered pleas of not guilty and not guilty by reason of insanity on behalf of Mr. M, who was referred by the court for an evaluation of his mental condition at the time of the alleged offense. As part of the evaluation, interviews were conducted with Mr. M's parents, who reported that the defendant had graduated from high school two years prior to his arrest and had continued to reside with them. He was employed at a local grocery store and had been functioning normally until approximately four months prior to his arrest. His parents reported that Mr. M, an amateur musician, became "obsessed" with the idea that a nationally known musical group had stolen his material. He wrote to members of the group, posted about the "theft" online, and called local radio stations to "out the thieves." He began to isolate socially; broke up with his girlfriend, refusing to tell her or his family why he had done so; and spent most of the time he was not at work playing guitar in the basement of his parents' home. The parents went on to describe Mr. M as becoming increasingly preoccupied, frequently looking out at the street and telling them that the musical group had hired a local gang to "take him out."

When interviewed at the jail, Mr. M told a similar story and explained that he was driving home from work in the dark when he noticed that he was being followed. He believed that the vehicle following him was driven by gang members who had been hired to kill him and tried to "outrun them." When he saw the lights and heard the siren, he concluded that the gang had stolen a police cruiser, and he continued to try to escape. He explained that he was actually trying to drive home, which was indeed the direction he was heading when he ran out of fuel. When he found himself surrounded by several cruisers, he rammed the one that had been following him to try to get home. Interviews with Mr. M's manager at work and documents forwarded by his attorney corroborated information provided by Mr. M and his parents.

Mr. M was administered the MMPI-2 (which was subsequently converted to an MMPI-2-RF protocol) as part of his not guilty by reason of insanity evaluation. His MMPI-2-RF protocol is reproduced in Figure 9-9. Data for the male forensic, pretrial criminal defendant comparison group are reported along with Mr. M's test results.

**Minnesota Multiphasic
Personality Inventory-2
Restructured Form®**

Score Report

MMPI-2-RF®

Minnesota Multiphasic Personality Inventory-2-Restructured Form®

Yossef S. Ben-Porath, PhD, & Auke Tellegen, PhD

ID Number:	Mr. M
Age:	21
Gender:	Male
Marital Status:	Not reported
Years of Education:	Not reported
Date Assessed:	04/22/2011

PEARSON   Ⓦ*PsychCorp*

Figure 9-9. Mr. M's MMPI-2-RF Score Report.

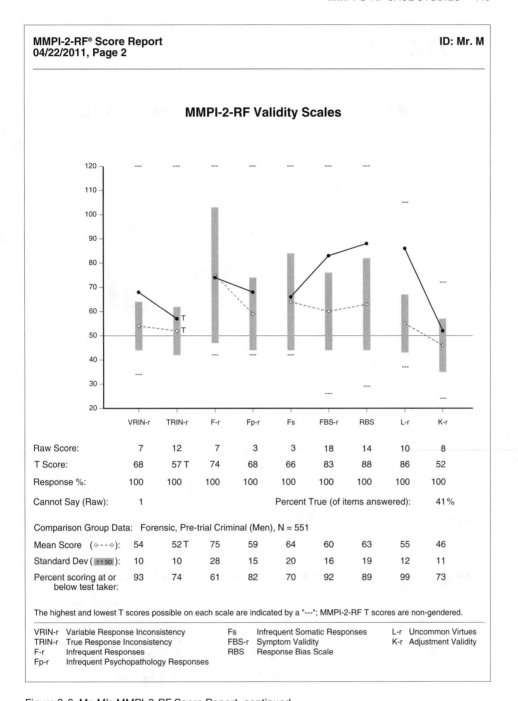

MMPI-2-RF Validity Scales

	VRIN-r	TRIN-r	F-r	Fp-r	Fs	FBS-r	RBS	L-r	K-r
Raw Score:	7	12	7	3	3	18	14	10	8
T Score:	68	57 T	74	68	66	83	88	86	52
Response %:	100	100	100	100	100	100	100	100	100

Cannot Say (Raw):   1   Percent True (of items answered):   41%

Comparison Group Data: Forensic, Pre-trial Criminal (Men), N = 551

	VRIN-r	TRIN-r	F-r	Fp-r	Fs	FBS-r	RBS	L-r	K-r
Mean Score (◇--◇):	54	52 T	75	59	64	60	63	55	46
Standard Dev (±1 SD):	10	10	28	15	20	16	19	12	11
Percent scoring at or below test taker:	93	74	61	82	70	92	89	99	73

The highest and lowest T scores possible on each scale are indicated by a "---"; MMPI-2-RF T scores are non-gendered.

VRIN-r	Variable Response Inconsistency	Fs	Infrequent Somatic Responses	L-r	Uncommon Virtues
TRIN-r	True Response Inconsistency	FBS-r	Symptom Validity	K-r	Adjustment Validity
F-r	Infrequent Responses	RBS	Response Bias Scale		
Fp-r	Infrequent Psychopathology Responses				

Figure 9-9. Mr. M's MMPI-2-RF Score Report, continued.

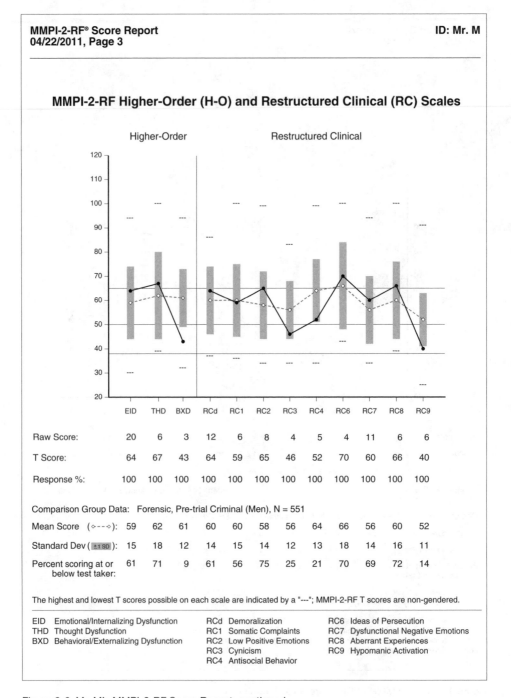

MMPI-2-RF Higher-Order (H-O) and Restructured Clinical (RC) Scales

Higher-Order   Restructured Clinical

	EID	THD	BXD	RCd	RC1	RC2	RC3	RC4	RC6	RC7	RC8	RC9
Raw Score:	20	6	3	12	6	8	4	5	4	11	6	6
T Score:	64	67	43	64	59	65	46	52	70	60	66	40
Response %:	100	100	100	100	100	100	100	100	100	100	100	100

Comparison Group Data: Forensic, Pre-trial Criminal (Men), N = 551

Mean Score (◇---◇):	59	62	61	60	60	58	56	64	66	56	60	52
Standard Dev (±1 SD):	15	18	12	14	15	14	12	13	18	14	16	11
Percent scoring at or below test taker:	61	71	9	61	56	75	25	21	70	69	72	14

The highest and lowest T scores possible on each scale are indicated by a "---"; MMPI-2-RF T scores are non-gendered.

EID Emotional/Internalizing Dysfunction	RCd Demoralization	RC6 Ideas of Persecution
THD Thought Dysfunction	RC1 Somatic Complaints	RC7 Dysfunctional Negative Emotions
BXD Behavioral/Externalizing Dysfunction	RC2 Low Positive Emotions	RC8 Aberrant Experiences
	RC3 Cynicism	RC9 Hypomanic Activation
	RC4 Antisocial Behavior	

Figure 9-9. Mr. M's MMPI-2-RF Score Report, continued.

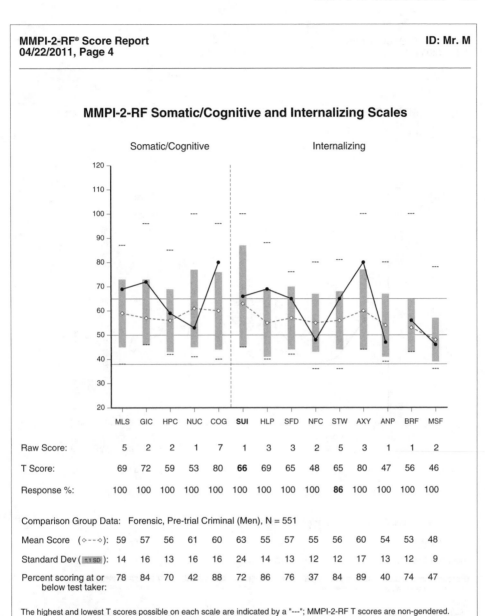

MMPI-2-RF Somatic/Cognitive and Internalizing Scales

Somatic/Cognitive   Internalizing

	MLS	GIC	HPC	NUC	COG	SUI	HLP	SFD	NFC	STW	AXY	ANP	BRF	MSF
Raw Score:	5	2	2	1	7	1	3	3	2	5	3	1	1	2
T Score:	69	72	59	53	80	66	69	65	48	65	80	47	56	46
Response %:	100	100	100	100	100	100	100	100	100	86	100	100	100	100

Comparison Group Data: Forensic, Pre-trial Criminal (Men), N = 551

	MLS	GIC	HPC	NUC	COG	SUI	HLP	SFD	NFC	STW	AXY	ANP	BRF	MSF
Mean Score (◇--◇):	59	57	56	61	60	63	55	57	55	56	60	54	53	48
Standard Dev (±1 SD):	14	16	13	16	16	24	14	13	12	12	17	13	12	9
Percent scoring at or below test taker:	78	84	70	42	88	72	86	76	37	84	89	40	74	47

The highest and lowest T scores possible on each scale are indicated by a "---"; MMPI-2-RF T scores are non-gendered.

MLS	Malaise	SUI	Suicidal/Death Ideation	AXY	Anxiety
GIC	Gastrointestinal Complaints	HLP	Helplessness/Hopelessness	ANP	Anger Proneness
HPC	Head Pain Complaints	SFD	Self-Doubt	BRF	Behavior-Restricting Fears
NUC	Neurological Complaints	NFC	Inefficacy	MSF	Multiple Specific Fears
COG	Cognitive Complaints	STW	Stress/Worry		

Figure 9-9. Mr. M's MMPI-2-RF Score Report, continued.

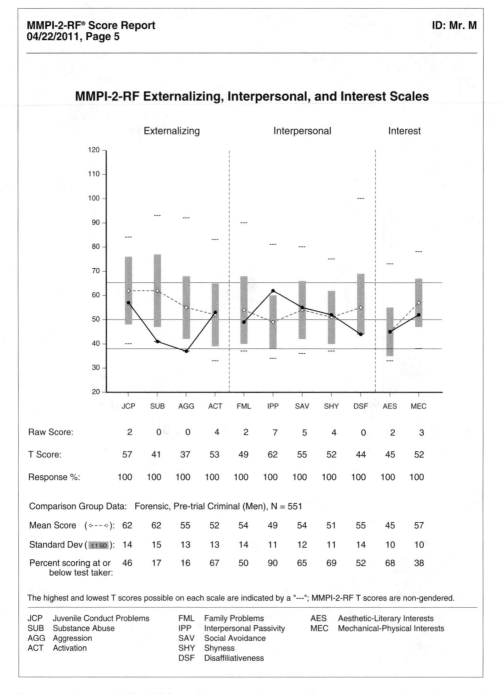

MMPI-2-RF Externalizing, Interpersonal, and Interest Scales

	JCP	SUB	AGG	ACT	FML	IPP	SAV	SHY	DSF	AES	MEC
Raw Score:	2	0	0	4	2	7	5	4	0	2	3
T Score:	57	41	37	53	49	62	55	52	44	45	52
Response %:	100	100	100	100	100	100	100	100	100	100	100

Comparison Group Data: Forensic, Pre-trial Criminal (Men), N = 551

	JCP	SUB	AGG	ACT	FML	IPP	SAV	SHY	DSF	AES	MEC
Mean Score (◇--◇):	62	62	55	52	54	49	54	51	55	45	57
Standard Dev (±1 SD):	14	15	13	13	14	11	12	11	14	10	10
Percent scoring at or below test taker:	46	17	16	67	50	90	65	69	52	68	38

The highest and lowest T scores possible on each scale are indicated by a "---"; MMPI-2-RF T scores are non-gendered.

JCP	Juvenile Conduct Problems	FML	Family Problems
SUB	Substance Abuse	IPP	Interpersonal Passivity
AGG	Aggression	SAV	Social Avoidance
ACT	Activation	SHY	Shyness
		DSF	Disaffiliativeness

AES   Aesthetic-Literary Interests
MEC   Mechanical-Physical Interests

Figure 9-9. Mr. M's MMPI-2-RF Score Report, continued.

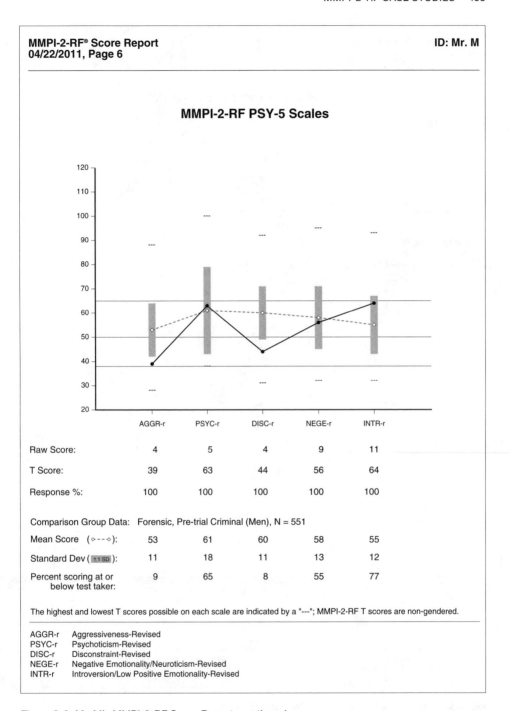

MMPI-2-RF PSY-5 Scales

	AGGR-r	PSYC-r	DISC-r	NEGE-r	INTR-r
Raw Score:	4	5	4	9	11
T Score:	39	63	44	56	64
Response %:	100	100	100	100	100

Comparison Group Data: Forensic, Pre-trial Criminal (Men), N = 551

	AGGR-r	PSYC-r	DISC-r	NEGE-r	INTR-r
Mean Score (◇--◇):	53	61	60	58	55
Standard Dev (±1 SD):	11	18	11	13	12
Percent scoring at or below test taker:	9	65	8	55	77

The highest and lowest T scores possible on each scale are indicated by a "---"; MMPI-2-RF T scores are non-gendered.

AGGR-r   Aggressiveness-Revised
PSYC-r   Psychoticism-Revised
DISC-r   Disconstraint-Revised
NEGE-r   Negative Emotionality/Neuroticism-Revised
INTR-r   Introversion/Low Positive Emotionality-Revised

Figure 9-9. Mr. M's MMPI-2-RF Score Report, continued.

MMPI-2-RF® Score Report
04/22/2011, Page 7

ID: Mr. M

MMPI-2-RF T SCORES (BY DOMAIN)

PROTOCOL VALIDITY

Content Non-Responsiveness		1	68	57 T		
		CNS	VRIN-r	TRIN-r		
Over-Reporting		74	68		66	83	88
		F-r	Fp-r		Fs	FBS-r	RBS
Under-Reporting		86	52				
		L-r	K-r				

SUBSTANTIVE SCALES

Somatic/Cognitive Dysfunction

59	69	72	59	53	80
RC1	MLS	GIC	HPC	NUC	COG

Emotional Dysfunction

64		64	**66**	69	65	48	
EID		RCd	**SUI**	HLP	SFD	NFC	
		65	64				
		RC2	INTR-r				
		60	65*	80	47	56	46	56
		RC7	STW	AXY	ANP	BRF	MSF	NEGE-r

Thought Dysfunction

67		70
THD		RC6
		66
		RC8
		63
		PSYC-r

Behavioral Dysfunction

43		52	57	41	
BXD		RC4	JCP	SUB	
		40	37	53	39	44
		RC9	AGG	ACT	AGGR-r	DISC-r

Interpersonal Functioning

49	46	62	55	52	44
FML	RC3	IPP	SAV	SHY	DSF

Interests

45	52
AES	MEC

*The test taker provided scorable responses to less than 90% of the items scored on this scale. See the relevant profile page for the specific percentage.

Note. This information is provided to facilitate interpretation following the recommended structure for MMPI-2-RF interpretation in Chapter 5 of the *MMPI-2-RF Manual for Administration, Scoring, and Interpretation*, which provides details in the text and an outline in Table 5-1.

Figure 9-9. Mr. M's MMPI-2-RF Score Report, continued.

ITEM-LEVEL INFORMATION

Unscorable Responses

Following is a list of items to which the test taker did not provide scorable responses. Unanswered or double answered (both True and False) items are unscorable. The scales on which the items appear are in parentheses following the item content.

224. Item content removed. (STW)

Critical Responses

Seven MMPI-2-RF scales--Suicidal/Death Ideation (SUI), Helplessness/Hopelessness (HLP), Anxiety (AXY), Ideas of Persecution (RC6), Aberrant Experiences (RC8), Substance Abuse (SUB), and Aggression (AGG)--have been designated by the test authors as having critical item content that may require immediate attention and follow-up. Items answered by the individual in the keyed direction (True or False) on a critical scale are listed below if his T score on that scale is 65 or higher. The percentage of the MMPI-2-RF normative sample (NS) and of the Forensic, Pre-trial Criminal (Men) comparison group (CG) that answered each item in the keyed direction are provided in parentheses following the item content.

Suicidal/Death Ideation (SUI, T Score = 66)
334. Item content removed. (True; NS 13.5%, CG 26.1%)

Helplessness/Hopelessness (HLP, T Score = 69)
169. Item content removed. (True; NS 4.3%, CG 26.0%)
214. Item content removed. (True; NS 10.4%, CG 24.3%)
336. Item content removed. (True; NS 38.0%, CG 27.4%)

Anxiety (AXY, T Score = 80)
228. Item content removed. (True; NS 17.3%, CG 31.8%)
275. Item content removed. (True; NS 5.0%, CG 28.1%)
289. Item content removed. (True; NS 12.7%, CG 26.1%)

Ideas of Persecution (RC6, T Score = 70)
110. Item content removed. (True; NS 9.9%, CG 36.3%)
168. Item content removed. (True; NS 2.8%, CG 7.6%)
287. Item content removed. (True; NS 3.1%, CG 16.7%)
310. Item content removed. (True; NS 3.0%, CG 18.3%)

Aberrant Experiences (RC8, T Score = 66)
32. Item content removed. (True; NS 21.1%, CG 57.4%)
159. Item content removed. (True; NS 6.0%, CG 33.8%)
179. Item content removed. (True; NS 12.6%, CG 26.9%)
199. Item content removed. (True; NS 12.1%, CG 23.8%)
257. Item content removed. (True; NS 12.4%, CG 32.1%)

Figure 9-9. Mr. M's MMPI-2-RF Score Report, continued.

MMPI-2-RF® Score Report   **ID: Mr. M**
04/22/2011, Page 9

---

311. Item content removed. (True; NS 32.4%, CG 32.3%)

End of Report

Figure 9-9. Mr. M's MMPI-2-RF Score Report, continued.

MMPI-2-RF Interpretation[2]

Mr. M responded to all but one MMPI-2-RF item that appears on the Stress/Worry (STW) Scale. As a result of his unscorable response to this item, the percentage of scorable responses to the STW Scale fell below 90% (see page 4 of Figure 9-9). Although he produced a clinically elevated score on this scale, this result may underestimate the magnitude of Mr. M's stress reactivity.

Mr. M's Validity Scale scores indicate that he responded consistently and relevantly to the test items, and there are no indications that he attempted to overreport psychopathology symptoms. He did provide an unusual combination of responses that is associated with noncredible reporting of somatic and cognitive complaints. However, this combination of responses can occur in individuals experiencing significant medical problems or psychological dysfunction.

Underreporting is indicated by Mr. M presenting himself in an extremely positive light by denying minor faults and shortcomings that most people acknowledge. This level of virtuous self-presentation is very uncommon even in individuals with a background stressing traditional values. Any absence of elevation on the Substantive Scales is uninterpretable. Elevated scores on the Substantive Scales may underestimate the problems assessed by those scales.

Mr. M's responses indicate significant thought dysfunction. He reports significant persecutory ideation such as believing that others seek to harm him. Mr. M is likely to be suspicious of and alienated from others and to experience interpersonal difficulties as a result of suspiciousness. He also likely lacks insight and blames others for his difficulties. In addition, Mr. M reports various unusual thought and perceptual processes. He is likely to experience thought disorganization, to engage in unrealistic thinking, and to believe that he has unusual sensory abilities.

Mr. M also reports a lack of positive emotional experiences, anhedonia, and lack of interest. He is likely to be pessimistic and to lack energy and may display vegetative signs of depression. Mr. M reports that he is preoccupied with death and feels hopeless and pessimistic. He likely feels overwhelmed and that life is a strain, and he believes that he cannot be helped and gets a raw deal from life. He may lack motivation for change. In addition, Mr. M reports self-doubt, and he likely feels inferior and insecure and is self-disparaging, prone to rumination and intropunitive, and presents with a lack of confidence and feelings of uselessness. Mr. M also reports feeling anxious and likely experiences significant anxiety; intrusive ideation; sleep difficulties, including nightmares; and posttraumatic distress. He also reports an above-average level of stress and worry and is likely stress reactive and worry prone.

Mr. M reports a diffuse pattern of cognitive difficulties. He very likely complains about memory problems, experiences difficulties in concentration, and has low tolerance for frustration. He also reports a number of gastrointestinal complaints and reports generally experiencing poor health and feeling weak and tired. Mr. M is likely preoccupied with poor health and is likely to complain of fatigue, low energy, and sexual dysfunction.

Mr. M's MMPI-2-RF results identify a number of diagnostic considerations. He should be evaluated for a thought disorder involving persecutory ideation and unusual sensory and perceptual processes and, possibly, psychotic symptoms. He should also be evaluated for a possible depressive disorder and anxiety-related psychopathology. If a physical origin for his somatic complaints is ruled out, a possible Somatoform Disorder should be considered as well. Clarification of the nature and origin of his cognitive complaints may require a neuropsychological evaluation.

Discussion

Mr. M's Validity Scale scores raise the two seemingly contradictory possibilities that he is both overreporting and underreporting. However, as discussed and illustrated in Chapter 6, it is possible for test takers to overreport some problems while trying to maintain a façade of having high moral values; that is, test takers can produce elevations on one or more of the overreporting indicators as well as on L-r. In Mr. M's case, his elevated FBS-r and RBS scores are near the lower threshold for raising concerns about noncredible somatic and cognitive complaints, at levels that can be found in individuals experiencing significant medical or psychological problems. Although Mr. M did not have any documented medical problems, as discussed next, the evaluator concluded that he was showing signs of an early-stage thought disorder, and his FBS-r and RBS scores were not viewed as indications of actual overreporting.

Mr. M's high L-r T score (86) indicates an effort to portray himself in a positive manner or, conversely, a reluctance to make negative statements about himself. As discussed in Chapters 4 and 6, it is possible for individuals with high L-r scores to produce clinically significant elevations on Substantive Scales, and this information is interpretable, although the resulting Substantive Scale scores may underestimate the test taker's level of dysfunction. To some extent, this could explain why Mr. M, who was manifesting early signs of a Schizophrenic Disorder, did not score higher than he did on the MMPI-2-RF thought dysfunction measures. In addition, nonelevated Substantive Scale scores cannot be interpreted as indicating the absence of the problems they are designed to assess. Consequently, Mr. M's nonelevated scores on measures of externalizing dysfunction cannot be relied on to rule out problems in this domain.

In addition to identifying possible symptoms of a thought disorder characterized by persecutory beliefs and disorganized thinking, Mr. M's Substantive Scale scores point to several other areas of concern. His elevated score on the Cognitive Complaints (COG) Scale was understood in this case to be associated with Mr. M's emerging thought disorder. Recall that, as described in Chapter 3, the COG items appear on the original Clinical Scale 8. In Mr. M's case, his COG score likely reflects the "I'm losing my mind" experience reported by some individuals who are in the early stages of developing a thought disorder. His self-reported anhedonia, sense of hopelessness, self-doubt, and anxiety were also deemed to be linked to an emerging thought disorder. The somatic complaints Mr. M reported prompted a recommendation for a follow-up medical evaluation.

The forensic examiner in this case diagnosed Mr. M with a Schizophreniform Disorder because his symptoms, at that point, had been present less than six months. The examiner also offered an opinion that Mr. M's action of ramming the police cruiser was committed without knowledge of its wrongfulness because his mental disorder led him to believe that his life was in danger. This opinion was supported by records that contained the information discussed earlier. The prosecution and defense stipulated to the examiner's written opinion, and Mr. M was found not guilty by reason of insanity. He was hospitalized for inpatient treatment and was later diagnosed with Schizophrenia, Paranoid Type.

MR. F: LAW ENFORCEMENT OFFICER CANDIDATE

Mr. F is a 22-year-old single male who was evaluated as a candidate for an entry-level law enforcement officer position with a medium-size urban police department. He had earned a two-year associate of arts degree in criminology, and this was the first position for which he had applied. After passing the department's initial screening process, he was given a conditional offer of employment and referred for medical and psychological evaluation.

Mr. F reported that he was raised in an intact family and denied any history of abuse. He described a good relationship with his parents and siblings and reported that he was not very active socially, although he did have one friend with whom he engaged in age-appropriate activities while growing up. He indicated that he had never been involved in a romantic relationship. Because of some early developmental delays, Mr. F repeated kindergarten and, as a result, did not graduate from high school until the age of 19. He did not have any academic difficulties or disciplinary problems but was not involved in any extracurricular activities. Mr. F worked at a number of part-time positions during his last two years of high school and in college. He initially denied having any conflicts with supervisors or coworkers or having ever been dismissed for cause from any these positions. Mr. F also denied any history of alcohol or drug use or ever requiring or receiving mental health services. In addition, he denied ever having been arrested or cited for any traffic violations.

Mr. F completed the MMPI-2-RF as part of a battery of tests administered by the psychologist who conducted his evaluation. Other measures included a brief intelligence test, a detailed psychosocial history, and a normal personality measure. The intelligence measure indicated that Mr. F functions in the average range. The primary findings from the psychosocial history questionnaire were just summarized, and the test of normal personality did not provide any remarkable findings.

Mr. F's MMPI-2-RF protocol is reproduced in Figure 9-10. The personnel screening, law enforcement officer comparison group data are included along with Mr. F's results.[3]

**Minnesota Multiphasic
Personality Inventory-2
Restructured Form®**

Score Report

MMPI-2-RF®

Minnesota Multiphasic Personality Inventory-2-Restructured Form®

Yossef S. Ben-Porath, PhD, & Auke Tellegen, PhD

ID Number:	Mr. F
Age:	22
Gender:	Male
Marital Status:	Not reported
Years of Education:	Not reported
Date Assessed:	04/22/2011

PEARSON   **PsychCorp**

Figure 9-10. Mr. F's MMPI-2-RF Score Report.

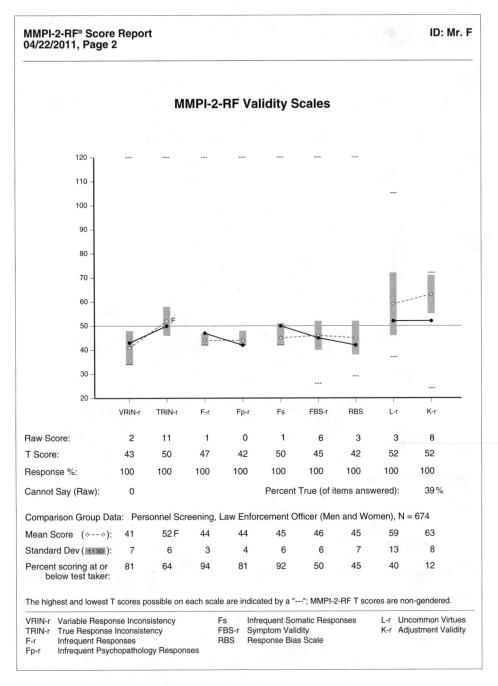

Figure 9-10. Mr. F's MMPI-2-RF Score Report, continued.

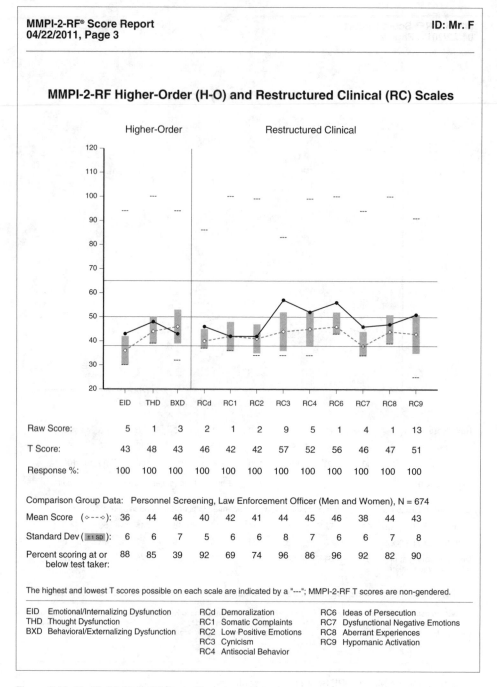

Figure 9-10. Mr. F's MMPI-2-RF Score Report, continued.

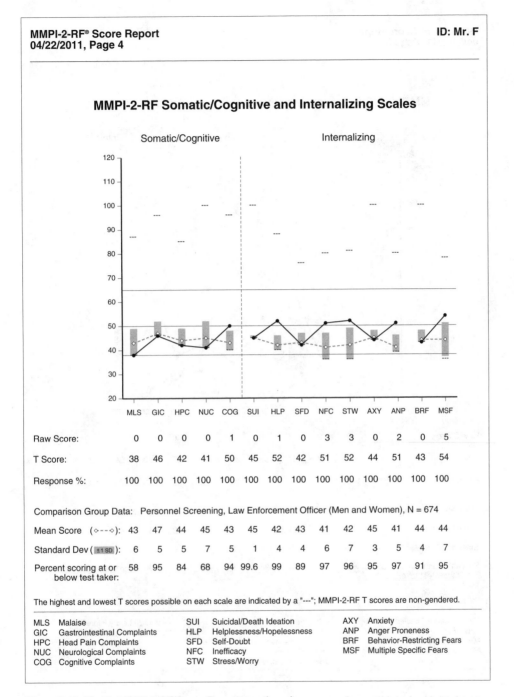

MMPI-2-RF Somatic/Cognitive and Internalizing Scales

	MLS	GIC	HPC	NUC	COG	SUI	HLP	SFD	NFC	STW	AXY	ANP	BRF	MSF
Raw Score:	0	0	0	0	1	0	1	0	3	3	0	2	0	5
T Score:	38	46	42	41	50	45	52	42	51	52	44	51	43	54
Response %:	100	100	100	100	100	100	100	100	100	100	100	100	100	100

Comparison Group Data: Personnel Screening, Law Enforcement Officer (Men and Women), N = 674

	MLS	GIC	HPC	NUC	COG	SUI	HLP	SFD	NFC	STW	AXY	ANP	BRF	MSF
Mean Score (◇--◇):	43	47	44	45	43	45	42	43	41	42	45	41	44	44
Standard Dev (±1 SD):	6	5	5	7	5	1	4	4	6	7	3	5	4	7
Percent scoring at or below test taker:	58	95	84	68	94	99.6	99	89	97	96	95	97	91	95

The highest and lowest T scores possible on each scale are indicated by a "---"; MMPI-2-RF T scores are non-gendered.

MLS	Malaise	SUI	Suicidal/Death Ideation	AXY	Anxiety
GIC	Gastrointestinal Complaints	HLP	Helplessness/Hopelessness	ANP	Anger Proneness
HPC	Head Pain Complaints	SFD	Self-Doubt	BRF	Behavior-Restricting Fears
NUC	Neurological Complaints	NFC	Inefficacy	MSF	Multiple Specific Fears
COG	Cognitive Complaints	STW	Stress/Worry		

Figure 9-10. Mr. F's MMPI-2-RF Score Report, continued.

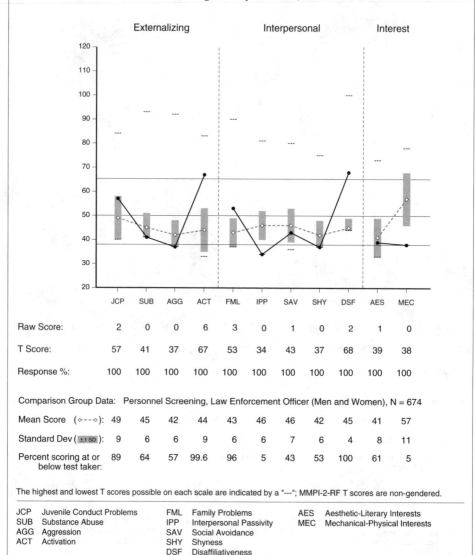

MMPI-2-RF Externalizing, Interpersonal, and Interest Scales

	Externalizing				Interpersonal				Interest	
	JCP	SUB	AGG	ACT	FML	IPP	SAV	SHY	DSF	AES	MEC
Raw Score:	2	0	0	6	3	0	1	0	2	1	0
T Score:	57	41	37	67	53	34	43	37	68	39	38
Response %:	100	100	100	100	100	100	100	100	100	100	100

Comparison Group Data: Personnel Screening, Law Enforcement Officer (Men and Women), N = 674

	JCP	SUB	AGG	ACT	FML	IPP	SAV	SHY	DSF	AES	MEC
Mean Score (◇---◇):	49	45	42	44	43	46	46	42	45	41	57
Standard Dev (±1 SD):	9	6	6	9	6	6	7	6	4	8	11
Percent scoring at or below test taker:	89	64	57	99.6	96	5	43	53	100	61	5

The highest and lowest T scores possible on each scale are indicated by a "---"; MMPI-2-RF T scores are non-gendered.

JCP	Juvenile Conduct Problems	FML	Family Problems	AES	Aesthetic-Literary Interests
SUB	Substance Abuse	IPP	Interpersonal Passivity	MEC	Mechanical-Physical Interests
AGG	Aggression	SAV	Social Avoidance		
ACT	Activation	SHY	Shyness		
		DSF	Disaffiliativeness		

Figure 9-10. Mr. F's MMPI-2-RF Score Report, continued.

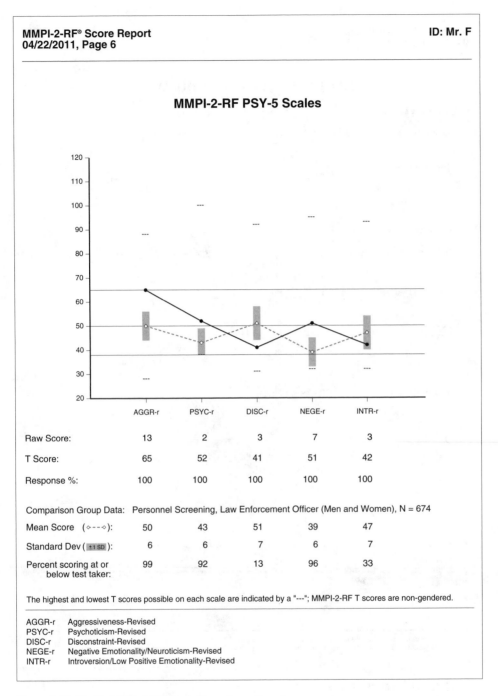

MMPI-2-RF PSY-5 Scales

	AGGR-r	PSYC-r	DISC-r	NEGE-r	INTR-r
Raw Score:	13	2	3	7	3
T Score:	65	52	41	51	42
Response %:	100	100	100	100	100

Comparison Group Data: Personnel Screening, Law Enforcement Officer (Men and Women), N = 674

	AGGR-r	PSYC-r	DISC-r	NEGE-r	INTR-r
Mean Score (◇- - -◇):	50	43	51	39	47
Standard Dev (±1 SD):	6	6	7	6	7
Percent scoring at or below test taker:	99	92	13	96	33

The highest and lowest T scores possible on each scale are indicated by a "---"; MMPI-2-RF T scores are non-gendered.

AGGR-r   Aggressiveness-Revised
PSYC-r   Psychoticism-Revised
DISC-r   Disconstraint-Revised
NEGE-r   Negative Emotionality/Neuroticism-Revised
INTR-r   Introversion/Low Positive Emotionality-Revised

Figure 9-10. Mr. F's MMPI-2-RF Score Report, continued.

MMPI-2-RF T SCORES (BY DOMAIN)

PROTOCOL VALIDITY

Content Non-Responsiveness

0	43	50
CNS	VRIN-r	TRIN-r

Over-Reporting

47	42		50	45	42
F-r	Fp-r		Fs	FBS-r	RBS

Under-Reporting

52	52
L-r	K-r

SUBSTANTIVE SCALES

Somatic/Cognitive Dysfunction

42	38	46	42	41	50
RC1	MLS	GIC	HPC	NUC	COG

Emotional Dysfunction

43						
EID						

46	45	52	42	51
RCd	SUI	HLP	SFD	NFC

42	42
RC2	INTR-r

46	52	44	51	43	54	51
RC7	STW	AXY	ANP	BRF	MSF	NEGE-r

Thought Dysfunction

48
THD

56
RC6

47
RC8

52
PSYC-r

Behavioral Dysfunction

43
BXD

52	57	41
RC4	JCP	SUB

51	37	67	65	41
RC9	AGG	ACT	AGGR-r	DISC-r

Interpersonal Functioning

53	57	34	43	37	68
FML	RC3	IPP	SAV	SHY	DSF

Interests

39	38
AES	MEC

Note. This information is provided to facilitate interpretation following the recommended structure for MMPI-2-RF interpretation in Chapter 5 of the *MMPI-2-RF Manual for Administration, Scoring, and Interpretation*, which provides details in the text and an outline in Table 5-1.

Figure 9-10. Mr. F's MMPI-2-RF Score Report, continued.

ITEM-LEVEL INFORMATION

Unscorable Responses

The test taker produced scorable responses to all the MMPI-2-RF items.

Critical Responses

Seven MMPI-2-RF scales--Suicidal/Death Ideation (SUI), Helplessness/Hopelessness (HLP), Anxiety (AXY), Ideas of Persecution (RC6), Aberrant Experiences (RC8), Substance Abuse (SUB), and Aggression (AGG)--have been designated by the test authors as having critical item content that may require immediate attention and follow-up. Items answered by the individual in the keyed direction (True or False) on a critical scale are listed below if his T score on that scale is 65 or higher.

The test taker has not produced an elevated T score (≥ 65) on any of these scales.

User-Designated Item-Level Information

The following item-level information is based on the report user's selection of additional scales, and/or of lower cutoffs for the critical scales from the previous section. Items answered by the test taker in the keyed direction (True or False) on a selected scale are listed below if his T score on that scale is at the user-designated cutoff score or higher. The percentage of the MMPI-2-RF normative sample (NS) and of the Personnel Screening, Law Enforcement Officer (Men and Women) comparison group (CG) that answered each item in the keyed direction are provided in parentheses following the item content.

Cynicism (RC3, T Score = 57)

    10. Item content removed. (True; NS 35.9%, CG 20.5%)
    36. Item content removed. (True; NS 58.3%, CG 45.0%)
    55. Item content removed. (True; NS 47.7%, CG 35.6%)
    87. Item content removed. (True; NS 39.7%, CG 29.8%)
    99. Item content removed. (True; NS 53.6%, CG 35.3%)
   171. Item content removed. (True; NS 51.5%, CG 31.0%)
   213. Item content removed. (True; NS 71.4%, CG 57.0%)
   260. Item content removed. (True; NS 36.2%, CG 19.7%)
   279. Item content removed. (True; NS 39.1%, CG 13.8%)

Ideas of Persecution (RC6, T Score = 56)

    34. Item content removed. (True; NS 10.6%, CG 10.1%)

Activation (ACT, T Score = 67)

    72. Item content removed. (True; NS 81.5%, CG 56.8%)
    81. Item content removed. (True; NS 12.1%, CG 6.1%)
  166. Item content removed. (True; NS 38.9%, CG 22.4%)
  207. Item content removed. (True; NS 66.9%, CG 44.2%)
  219. Item content removed. (True; NS 51.5%, CG 37.1%)
  285. Item content removed. (True; NS 21.9%, CG 8.2%)

Figure 9-10. Mr. F's MMPI-2-RF Score Report, continued.

MMPI-2-RF® Score Report   ID: Mr. F
04/22/2011, Page 9

Disaffiliativeness (DSF, T Score = 68)
   175. Item content removed. (True; NS 8.1%, CG 1.3%)
   291. Item content removed. (True; NS 10.7%, CG 1.5%)

Aggressiveness-Revised (AGGRr, T Score = 65)
   24. Item content removed. (False; NS 74.6%, CG 96.3%)
   39. Item content removed. (True; NS 51.0%, CG 39.5%)
   104. Item content removed. (True; NS 67.1%, CG 51.6%)
   147. Item content removed. (True; NS 75.2%, CG 87.8%)
   182. Item content removed. (True; NS 33.6%, CG 71.5%)
   197. Item content removed. (True; NS 62.5%, CG 79.8%)
   239. Item content removed. (True; NS 60.7%, CG 90.1%)
   256. Item content removed. (True; NS 65.7%, CG 31.2%)
   276. Item content removed. (True; NS 50.0%, CG 76.4%)
   302. Item content removed. (True; NS 67.9%, CG 87.8%)
   319. Item content removed. (False; NS 64.7%, CG 94.7%)
   321. Item content removed. (True; NS 31.3%, CG 26.1%)
   327. Item content removed. (True; NS 41.7%, CG 20.3%)

End of Report

Figure 9-10. Mr. F's MMPI-2-RF Score Report, continued.

MMPI-2-RF Interpretation[4]

Mr. F responded to all the MMPI-2-RF items, and his Validity Scale scores indicate that he responded in a consistent and relevant manner. There is no evidence of overreporting or underreporting in his protocol. In fact, his score on one of the underreporting measures was considerably lower than is typical of law enforcement candidates, an unusual finding that raises questions about why Mr. F would not attempt to portray himself in a more positive light, as do most individuals tested under similar circumstances.

There are no indications of substantial internalizing, thought, or externalizing dysfunction in Mr. F's MMPI-2-RF protocol. There are, however, a number of anomalous and potentially problematic findings.

Mr. F reports episodes of heightened excitation and energy level. He likely experiences excessive activation. His level of self-reported activation is clinically significant and also much greater than what is reported typically by law enforcement candidates. He also describes himself as having strong opinions, standing up for himself, being assertive and direct, and being able to lead others. Although some of these may be desirable attributes in a law enforcement officer, his level of self-reported directness far exceeds what is typically reported by individuals tested for police officer positions. Only 5% of law enforcement candidates describe a similar level of directness. He is likely to be viewed by others as domineering, self-centered, and possibly grandiose. Mr. F does indeed report that he is interpersonally aggressive, more so than do 98% of law enforcement candidates. He is likely to be overly assertive and socially dominant, to engage in instrumentally aggressive behavior, and to believe that he has leadership capabilities.

Mr. F also reports that he dislikes people and being around them, an extremely rare finding in law enforcement candidates. Relatedly, he reports a much larger number of cynical beliefs and attitudes than do most law enforcement candidates, suggesting that he tends to be hostile toward and alienated from others. On the other hand, he reports experiencing little or no social anxiety. Mr. F also reports having no mechanical or physical interests, which is also quite rare in law enforcement candidates.

Discussion

Mr. F's case illustrates the importance and potential utility of using the law enforcement candidate comparison group data when assessing candidates for police officer positions. Because of the considerable amount of screening that occurs before a candidate is tendered a conditional offer of employment and referred for a psychological evaluation, as well as the inherent motivation to "look good," clinically elevated MMPI-2-RF scores are relatively uncommon in this population. Indeed, Mr. F did not produce clinically elevated scores on the H-O or RC Scales, although his scores on Activation (ACT), Interpersonal Passivity (IPP), Shyness (SHY), and Aggressiveness–Revised (AGGR-r) did reach interpretable levels (see Chapter 7).

Consideration of the comparison group data, and, in particular, information about the percentage of individuals in the group who scored at or below the test taker's score, allows for the identification of anomalous findings for this population, including those that would not be particularly noteworthy in other settings. For example, in most settings and types of assessments, Mr. F's T score on K-r (52) can be viewed positively as an indication that he was open and cooperative with the testing. However, as seen on page 2 of Figure 9-10 (and just discussed in the interpretation), this is a very unusual finding for an individual assessed in the context of a preemployment evaluation of a law enforcement candidate. Only 12% of the individuals in the comparison group scored as low as or lower than Mr. F on K-r. As noted in the interpretation, this raises a question about why Mr. F did not make more of an effort to appear better adjusted than average when responding to the MMPI-2-RF items.

Comparison group data can also assist in emphasizing the significance of clinically elevated scores. For example, as seen on page 5 of Figure 9-10, 99.6% of members of the law enforcement candidate comparison group scored at or below Mr. F's T score (67) on ACT. This is an extremely rare finding in law enforcement candidates.

The low occurrence of clinically elevated scores for law enforcement candidates also has implications for use of MMPI-2-RF item-level information. Because law enforcement candidates do not typically generate clinically elevated scores on the seven scales designated as having critical content, scores on these scales are rarely high enough to trigger a list of Critical Responses for this population. As seen on page 8 of Figure 9-10, Mr. F indeed did not produce clinically elevated scores on any of the scales designated as having critical content.

Mr. F's case illustrates the potential utility of MMPI-2-RF users' ability to generate customized lists of item-level responses. As described in Chapter 5, it is possible to print or reprint an MMPI-2-RF report with a user-designated selection of additional scales and alternative cutoffs.[5] In this case, item-level responses were generated for RC3 and Ideas of Persecution (RC6), scales on which Mr. F scored below 65, but at levels that are quite uncommon in this population and that have been found empirically to be associated with negative outcomes in law enforcement candidates. In the case of RC3, examination of Mr. F's item-level responses reflected a large number of cynical beliefs, and this was incorporated in the interpretation. These item-level responses also served as prompts for inquiries during his interview. In the case of RC6, the one item Mr. F answered in the keyed direction pertains to beliefs in ghosts and spirits. This is of less concern than would be a statement of a more blatantly persecutory belief. On page 9 of Figure 9-10, user-designated item-level information is provided for the three scales on which Mr. F did generate clinically elevated scores, and this information can also be used to prompt questions during the interview phase of the evaluation.

Guided by the information provided by the MMPI-2-RF, the examiner focused the interview, in particular, on Mr. F's interpersonal style and relationships. Mr. F initially tried to deny or minimize the implications of some of his responses to the MMPI-2-RF items. However, when asked to explain his responses to several RC3 items, he became angry, told the examiner that he was wasting his time, and suggested that the examiner move on to other, more important issues. When asked about his leadership skills, Mr. F responded that he views himself as a natural born leader and recounted that some of his supervisors in past positions were jealous of his superior leadership skills and intellect. When asked about statements to the effect that he was happiest when alone, Mr. F replied that he is often bored by others with whom he interacts, which is why he does not have any friends.

On the basis of the information just described, Mr. F received a negative recommendation regarding his suitability for an entry-level law enforcement officer position.

CHAPTER 10

Summary and Initial Appraisals
of the MMPI-2-RF

As a member of the Restandardization Committee that developed the MMPI-2, Auke Tellegen proposed that the revision include a major, long-overdue update of the Clinical Scales. However, the committee made a strategic decision not to update the then 40-plus-year-old measures to preserve continuity between the original and revised versions of the test. Undoubtedly, this decision facilitated a rapid transition from the MMPI to the MMPI-2. However, it left at the core of the test a set of scales with significant psychometric limitations. A range of indirect fixes to work around these limitations had been developed over the years, including a transition to code type–based interpretation and the use of numerous subscales and supplementary measures. Seeking to address these limitations directly, and, at the same time, to modernize the now 50-year-old Clinical Scales, Tellegen, in the early 1990s, began a program of research that produced first the Restructured Clinical (RC) Scales and then the MMPI-2-RF.

Applying an exploratory, empirically guided scale construction approach, Tellegen identified nine major distinctive components of the eight original Clinical Scales, excluding Scales 5 and 0, and developed the RC Scales to assess these constructs. Tellegen and I spent several years studying the new measures, examining their psychometric properties with a broad range of samples and extratest criterion data. We also explored with multiple case reviews the potential contributions of the scales to MMPI-2 interpretation. The development and psychometric properties of the Restructured Scales were reported in a monograph that also provided recommendations for integrating RC Scale findings into MMPI-2 interpretation and illustrated this process with a series of case studies (Tellegen, Ben-Porath, McNulty, Arbisi, Graham & Kaemmer, 2003). In the concluding section of the monograph, we anticipated that through further scale development efforts, "it may be possible to eventually capture the full range of core attributes represented by the large body of MMPI-2 constructs with a set of new scales more transparent and effective than those currently available" (Tellegen et al., 2003, p. 86). Thus our goal for the MMPI-2-RF was to produce a comprehensive set of measures representing the clinically significant substance of the entire MMPI-2 item pool in a psychometrically adequate manner. The test was published in 2008, some 15 years after Tellegen first began exploring a psychometric restructuring of the Clinical Scales.

Because, with the exception of some of the Validity Scales, MMPI-2-RF interpretation cannot rely on empirical findings with the MMPI-2, we report extensive psychometric data in the *Technical Manual* for the test. These include reliability and standard errors of measurement findings in clinical and nonclinical settings, extensive internal and external correlate data, and descriptive statistics for the MMPI-2-RF scales for a broad range of samples representing populations and settings in which the test can be used. These data, along with findings reported in journal articles, can also be used to appraise the MMPI-2-RF. An unprecedented quantity and quality of psychometric data are available for this purpose because existing MMPI-2 data sets can be used to study the new and revised scales. This substantial benefit of using existing MMPI-2 items to construct and norm the revised inventory came at the cost of being unable to modify existing items that can undoubtedly be improved or to add new ones to strengthen existing scales and allow for the development of others.

A critical question about the MMPI-2-RF is whether we succeeded in representing the clinically significant substance of the entire MMPI-2 item pool. As detailed in the chapters chronicling the development of the test, Tellegen and I made a concerted effort to do so and sought input from experts about this question along the way. Nevertheless, it is quite conceivable that we missed important constructs and that further developments in the field will identify new ones worthy of assessment with the MMPI-2-RF. As has been the case throughout the history of the MMPI instruments—undoubtedly a critical contributor to its longevity—research and development efforts will continue, and new scales and procedures for integrating information from existing scales will be added to the inventory.

A review of initial appraisals of the MMPI-2-RF concludes this volume.

APPRAISALS OF THE MMPI-2-RF

Appraisals of the MMPI, MMPI-2, and RC Scales discussed in Chapters 1 and 2 included consideration of use patterns, research, and commentary. No systematic surveys of MMPI-2-RF use patterns have been conducted as of this writing; it is probably too soon following its publication for one to be done. However, as reviewed in Chapters 2, 3, and 4, a sizable literature on various elements of the MMPI-2-RF has been produced within this relatively short time. Two factors contribute to this productivity: restriction of the MMPI-2-RF to the existing MMPI-2 item pool, allowing for MMPI-2-RF studies to be conducted with existing MMPI-2 data sets, and the earlier (2003) publication of the RC Scales,[1] on which a sizable literature accumulated before publication of the MMPI-2-RF. The scope and implications of this research base are discussed later when considering a commentator's appraisal of the validation of the MMPI-2-RF scales.

Authors of two of the major MMPI-2 textbooks (Graham, 2011; Greene, 2011) include appraisals of the MMPI-2-RF in updated editions of their books. After listing advantages and disadvantages of the revised inventory, both authors provide detailed guidelines for its use and interpretation. The advantages they see in the new version include brevity, ease of interpretation, and links to the contemporary literature on personality and psychopathology. Both cite the loss of information from Clinical Scale code types as a primary disadvantage for the MMPI-2-RF. However, Graham (2011) notes that "one could argue that code types evolved largely as a way to deal with the heterogeneity of the Clinical Scales and are not necessary because of the homogeneity of the RC Scales and other MMPI-2-RF scales" (p. 414). This issue is discussed in detail in Chapter 2 of this book.

Both authors also note the absence of certain supplementary MMPI-2 measures as disadvantages. Graham (2011) specifically mentions the MacAndrew Alcoholism Scale–Revised (MAC-R; MacAndrew, 1965) and the Hostility Scale (Ho; Cook & Medley, 1954) in this regard (p. 414). A third scale, Ego Strength (Es; Barron, 1953), is discussed in terms of its positive focus on psychological resources (p. 414). Examination of Table 3-16 of the *MMPI-2-RF Technical Manual* (Tellegen & Ben-Porath, 2008/2011) reveals that MAC-R is most closely associated with the Higher Order Behavioral Externalizing Dysfunction (BXD) Scale of the MMPI-2-RF. As discussed in Chapter 2, Cynicism (RC3) measures the cynical hostility component of Ho, which was implicated in increased risk for coronary artery disease. Es is a more heterogeneous scale that does not have a direct parallel in the MMPI-2-RF. However, interpretive recommendations provided in the *MMPI-2-RF Manual for Administration, Scoring, and Interpretation* (Ben-Porath & Tellegen, 2008/2011) identify positive features associated with low scores on several MMPI-2-RF scales that are relevant to this issue.

Greene (2011) adds a third disadvantage:

> The "MMPI-2" in MMPI-2-RF is a misnomer because the only relationship to the MMPI-2 is its use of a subset of the MMPI-2 item pool, its normative group, and similar validity scales. The MMPI-2-RF should not be conceptualized as a revised or restructured form of the MMPI-2, but as a *new* self-report inventory that chose to select its items from the MMPI-2 item pool and use its normative group. (p. 22)

Chapters 1–4 of this book detail the procedures followed in restructuring the MMPI-2 and the conceptual and psychometric reasons for doing so. Calling this instrument anything but a restructured version of the MMPI-2 would, in fact, be misleading.

Greene (2011) goes on to advise that "clinicians who use the MMPI-2-RF should realize that they have forsaken the MMPI-2 and its 70 years of clinical and research history, and they are learning a new inventory" (p. 22). Nonetheless, he provides detailed recommendations on how to use the MMPI-2-RF, which span roughly one-fourth of his book and include several case studies.

A third author (Butcher, 2011) provides an exclusively negative appraisal of the MMPI-2-RF and recommends against its use. Much of Butcher's appraisal consists of the repetition of criticisms of the RC Scales discussed in detail in Chapter 2. Butcher (2011) does not attend to the substance of responses to these critiques but lists a number of new concerns about the MMPI-2-RF. Pointing out the relatively low reliabilities for some Specific Problems Scales, he indicates that they "need to be studied further to determine if they provide consistent and valid predictions" (p. 191). In fact, external correlate data reported in Appendix A of the *Technical Manual* address this need and provide evidence of the validity of these measures. The implications of low reliability estimates and the need to consider them in the context of standard error of measurement statistics are discussed in the reliability section of the *Technical Manual*.

Under the heading "Insufficient Validation," Butcher (2011) asserts that "the majority of the scales incorporated in the MMPI-2-RF are insufficiently validated to provide the practitioner with confidence in assessment" (p. 189). In fact, extensive external correlate data documenting the validity of MMPI-2-RF scale scores were collected in outpatient and inpatient mental health facilities, medical centers, criminal and civil forensic evaluations, and a nonclinical setting. Criterion data used in these analyses include reports by intake staff and therapists, systematic file reviews, and other self-report measures. All told, Appendix A of the *Technical Manual* reports well over 50,000 validity coefficients. A comparable set of validation data has not been compiled in one source and integrated into interpretive recommendations for any other version of the MMPI.

Butcher (2011) expresses concern about "Information Loss from the MMPI-2 in the Construction of the MMPI-2-RF" (p. 191) and cites as particularly problematic the loss of items related to "work adjustment" and "treatment resistance and attitudes toward mental health treatment" (p. 193). The items alluded to here are scored on two of the MMPI-2 Content Scales (Butcher, Graham, Williams & Ben-Porath, 1990): Work Interference (WRK) and Negative Treatment Indicators (TRT). Examination of Table 3-16 of the *MMPI-2-RF Technical Manual* reveals that both these scales are oversaturated with demoralization variance. The distinctive features of the scales are assessed in the MMPI-2-RF with the Inefficacy (NFC) and Helplessness/Hopelessness (HLP) Scales, respectively. Butcher asserts that "information on potential problems in treatment planning or resilience for dealing with problems is not available to practitioners on the MMPI-2-RF" (p. 193). However, treatment considerations are included in the interpretive recommendations for most of the MMPI-2-RF Substantive Scales.

Finally, under the heading "Confusion Resulting from Two Forms of the MMPI-2 Producing Highly Different Interpretations," Butcher (2011) remarks that "it is likely that the interpretations and conclusions drawn from the MMPI-2-RF will differ substantially from an MMPI-2 interpretation" (p. 190). This is an empirical question that has not been studied systematically in the context of the full MMPI-2-RF. Sellbom, Ben-Porath, McNulty, Arbisi, and Graham (2006) addressed this question with respect to the Clinical and the RC Scales. They concluded that the two sets of scales are, in fact, largely congruent. If a Clinical Scale was elevated, in the vast majority of cases, its restructured counterpart was elevated as well, and vice versa. In the relatively uncommon cases when they were incongruent, the RC Scale scores were likely to be more consistent with extratest findings.

CONCLUSION

Initial appraisals of the MMPI-2-RF by two of the leading MMPI-2 textbook authors led them to include in the most recent editions of their books the revised test and detailed interpretive recommendations for its use. A third author, who has opposed efforts to modernize the MMPI-2, weighed in against the revised inventory. As has been the case throughout the history of the MMPI, research will highlight strengths and weaknesses of this new version of the instrument and point to ways in which it can be developed further to improve the assessment of personality and psychopathology.

Notes

2. Transitioning to the MMPI-2-RF

1   This was a problem of considerable concern to Hathaway (A. Tellegen, personal communication 1998).
2   An explanation for how such items wound up on a psychopathy measure is provided in the following section.
3   Clinical Scales 5 and 0 were included in this step (and Steps 3–4) to ensure that the resulting RC Scales would be distinct from the core components of those scales as well. However, because the Restructured Scales were intended to assess core components of psychopathology, RC Scales were not derived for Scales 5 and 0, which were set aside for further scale development intended to cover the full range of constructs represented by the MMPI-2 item pool (see Chapter 3).
4   A detailed description of the PSY-5 model and its MMPI-2-RF measures is provided in Chapter 3.

3. Completing Development of the MMPI-2-RF: The Substantive Scales

1   First person plural references are to MMPI-2-RF coauthors Auke Tellegen and Yossef Ben-Porath.
2   A third relevant line of investigation began with Allport's quest to develop a lexically founded personological taxonomy—the direct antecedent to the ubiquitous Five Factor Model (FFM) of personality. Because the FFM has been linked primarily to the assessment of personality disorders (REF), this literature is considered in detail later in this chapter in the section on the set of MMPI-2-RF scales known as the Personality Psychopathology Five (PSY-5), which were developed to provide a dimensional approach to the assessment of Axis II symptomatology.
3   Tellegen and Waller (2008) indicate that the Positive Emotionality higher-order factor can be bifurcated into agentic Positive Emotionality and communal Positive Emotionality, the former emphasizing positive emotional responsiveness and effectance and the latter combining positive emotions with interpersonal connectedness.
4   Although the authors of some early MMPI factor-analytic studies referred to a "psychotic" factor, examination of the reported factor structures indicates that this label was based on the high loading of Clinical Scale 8 on a factor that is also

associated strongly with Clinical Scale 7 and that has typically been identified as related to internalizing disorders.

5 The acronyms for the MMPI-2-RF PSY-5 Scales include an "-r," identifying the scales as revised.

4. Completing Development of the MMPI-2-RF: The Validity Scales

1 The reading level required to complete the MMPI-2-RF is discussed in detail in Chapter 5.

2 The scale was subsequently relabeled "Cannot Say," with CNS used commonly as the abbreviation.

3 However, in the article cited, Meehl (1946) actually uses a cutoff T score of 70 on CNS, which, as just mentioned, corresponded to a raw score over 100 on this scale.

4 Because a full label for K is not mentioned in the original writings describing its development, none of the subsequently proposed labels (e.g., "Correction," "Defensiveness") is used here.

5 As a graduate student at the University of Minnesota at the time, I had the good fortune of assisting Tellegen in the selection of items for and the construction of the VRIN and TRIN Scales.

6 Paul Arbisi was a staff psychologist on a VA psychiatric inpatient unit at the time we began the work needed to develop F_p. His observation of the inordinate number of cases of test takers with severe psychopathology who produced technically invalid MMPI-2 protocols prompted us to explore the origin of this phenomenon and develop F_p as a solution.

7 Originally named the "Fake Bad Scale" (hence FBS), the label of the scale was changed to "Symptom Validity" shortly after its addition to the Validity Scale profile. The change was designed to address concerns about the potential prejudicial impact of the original label in forensic evaluations (for details, please see Ben-Porath, Greve et al., 2009). The original acronym, FBS, was kept to link the scale with the extensive research literature available to guide and support its interpretation.

8 As in Chapter 3, first-person plural references are to MMPI-2-RF coauthors Auke Tellegen and Yossef Ben-Porath.

9 A nonscorable response to either item is treated as a nonscorable response to that item pair.

10 Although we noted in the *MMPI-2-RF Technical Manual* that Bagby and Marshall (2004) linked the two-factor structure they obtained to the constructs of Impression Management and Self-Deception, as discussed later, we do not believe that these labels accurately characterize the underreporting mechanisms assessed by the two scales.

5. Administering and Scoring the MMPI-2-RF

1 The administration, response-recording, and scoring materials and software described in this chapter are available from Pearson Assessments (http://psychcorp.pearsonassessments.com/).

2   Information on approved translations of the MMPI-2-RF can be obtained from the University of Minnesota Press at http://www.upress.umn.edu/tests/.

3   Additional, setting-specific reports are in development.

4   Test authors Auke Tellegen and me.

5   Additional standard comparison groups are added to the software as they become available.

6   Although Mr. I's T score on F-r (74) falls two points below the comparison group mean (76), in the final row of scores under F-r, we see that 58% of the comparison group scores at or below 74. This reflects the positively skewed distribution of scores that characterizes most MMPI-2-RF scales and produces a median score that is lower than the mean.

6. Interpreting the MMPI-2-RF Validity Scales

1   Recall that VRIN-r and TRIN-r are scored on the test taker's responses to pairs of items.

2   This would not be true of K-r, on which high scores reflect assertions of good psychological adjustment that would be inconsistent with overreporting.

3   Recall that 50 is the lowest possible TRIN-r score.

7. Interpreting the MMPI-2-RF Substantive Scales

1   See Chapter 5 for information on how to access comparison group data.

2   Some redundancy does occur across different levels of the hierarchical structure of the test. For example, anger-related problems are identified as empirical correlates of both the Dysfunctional Negative Emotions (RC7) and Anger Proneness (ANP) scales. A strategy for integrating information from higher- and lower-level scales is discussed and illustrated in Chapter 8.

3   "Our" refers to test authors Auke Tellegen and Yossef Ben-Porath.

8. Interpreting the MMPI-2-RF: Recommended Framework and Process

1   Mr. B's JCP score approaches a clinically significant elevation. For an individual in his late 40s who shows no other indications of externalizing behavioral tendencies, this is not a remarkable finding. For a young man in his late teens or early 20s, the behaviors reflected in a moderately elevated JCP score would be more recent and, therefore, potentially more salient.

2   A correlate having to do with lacking motivation for change is not included here because of other indications that emotional distress may motivate Mr. B for treatment (at least initially).

3   As noted earlier, absent extratest information about Mr. B's medical condition, this would probably be interpreted here as an indicator of somatoform psychopathology.

4   An interpretation of Mr. I's CNS score would typically also entail examination

of the content of the 17 items Mr. I left unanswered. To protect the security of the MMPI-2-RF items, this part of the interpretation is not illustrated here.

9. MMPI-2-RF Case Studies

1 Treatment considerations are not listed in this interpretation because they were not the focus of this forensic evaluation.
2 Treatment considerations are not listed here because they were not the focus of this insanity evaluation.
3 Like all the personnel screening comparison groups, the law enforcement candidate group is a combined-gender sample made up of an equal number of male and female law enforcement candidates. Combined-gender samples are used in personnel screening to comply with federal prohibitions on use of gender-based norms in employment-related evaluations.
4 Because diagnoses and treatment recommendations are not typically made in these assessments, the MMPI-2-RF interpretation does not include diagnostic and treatment considerations.
5 Actual item responses are redacted from Figure 9-10 to protect the security of MMPI-2-RF items.

10. Summary and Initial Appraisals of the MMPI-2-RF

1 A detailed discussion of appraisals of the RC Scales, much of which would also apply to use of the MMPI-2-RF, is presented at the end of Chapter 2.

References

Aaronson, A. L., Dent, O. B., & Kline, C. D. (1996). Cross-validation of MMPI and MMPI-2 predictor scales. *Journal of Clinical Psychology, 52,* 311–315.

Achenbach, T. M. (1966). The classification of children's psychiatric symptoms: A factor-analytic study. *Psychological Monographs, 80,* 1–37.

Achenbach, T. M., & Edelbrock, C. S. (1978). The classification of child psychopathology: A review and analysis of empirical efforts. *Psychological Bulletin, 85,* 1275–1301.

Adams, D. K., & Horn, J. L. (1965). Non-overlapping keys for the MMPI Scales. *Journal of Consulting Psychology, 29,* 284.

Adler, T. (1990, April). Does the "new" MMPI beat the "classic"? *APA Monitor,* pp. 18–19.

AERA, APA & NCME (1999). *Standards for educational and psychological testing.* Washington, DC: AERA, APA, and NCME.

Allard, G., & Faust, D. (2000). Errors in scoring objective personality tests. *Assessment, 7*(2), 119–131.

Allen, L., Conder, R. L., Green, P., & Cox, D. R. (1997). *CARB' 97 manual for the computerized assessment of response bias.* Durham, NC: CogniSyst.

Almada, S. J., Zonderman, A. B., Shekelle, R. B., Dyer, A. R., Daviglus, M. L., Costa, P. T., et al. (1991). Neuroticism and cynicism and risk of death in middle-aged men: The Western Electric Study. *Psychosomatic Medicine, 53,* 165–175.

American Psychiatric Association (1980). *Diagnostic and statistical manual of mental disorders* (3rd ed.) (*DSM-III*). Washington, DC: American Psychiatric Association.

American Psychiatric Association (1987). *Diagnostic and statistical manual of mental disorders* (3rd ed., rev.) (*DSM-III-R*). Washington, DC: American Psychiatric Association.

American Psychiatric Association (1994). *Diagnostic and statistical manual of mental disorders* (4th ed.) (*DSM-IV*). Washington, DC: American Psychiatric Association.

American Psychiatric Association (2000). *Diagnostic and statistical manual of mental disorders* (4th ed., text rev.) (*DSM-IV-TR*). Washington, DC: American Psychiatric Association.

Angst, J., Adolfsson, R., Benazzi, F., Gamma, A., Hantouche, E., Meyer, T. D., et al. (2005). The HCL-32: Towards a self-assessment tool for hypomanic symptoms in outpatients. *Journal of Affective Disorders, 88,* 217–233.

Aragona, M., Tarsitani, L., De Nitto, S., & Inghilleri, M. (2008). *DSM-IV-TR* "pain disorder associated with psychological factors" as a nonhysterical form of somatization. *Pain Research and Management, 13,* 13–18.

Arbisi, P. A., & Ben-Porath, Y. S. (1995). An MMPI-2 infrequent response scale for use with psychopathological populations: The Infrequency-Psychopathology Scale, F(p). *Psychological Assessment, 7,* 424–431.

Arbisi, P. A., Ben-Porath, Y. S., & McNulty, J. L. (2003). Refinement of the MMPI-2 F(p) Scale is not necessary: A response to Gass and Luis. *Assessment, 10,* 123–128.

Arbisi, P. A., Polusny, M. A., Erbes, C. R., Thuras, P., & Reddy, M. K. (2011). The Minnesota Multiphasic Personality Inventory 2 Restructured Form in National Guard soldiers screening positive for Posttraumatic Stress Disorder and mild traumatic brain injury. *Psychological Assessment, 23,* 203–214.

Arbisi, P. A., Sellbom, M., & Ben-Porath, Y. S. (2008). Empirical correlates of the MMPI-2 Restructured Clinical (RC) Scales in psychiatric inpatients. *Journal of Personality Assessment, 90,* 122–128.

Archer, R. P., Buffington-Vollum, J. K., Stredny, R. V., & Handel, R. W. (2006). A survey of psychological test use patterns among forensic psychologists. *Journal of Personality Assessment, 87,* 84–94.

Archer, R. P., Handel, R. W., & Couvadelli, B. (2004). An evaluation of the incremental validity of the MMPI-2 Superlative (S) Scale in an inpatient psychiatric sample. *Assessment, 11,* 102–108.

Baer, R. A., & Miller, J. (2002). Underreporting of psychopathology on the MMPI-2: A meta-analytic review. *Psychological Assessment, 41,* 16–26.

Baer, R. A., Wetter, M. W., Nichols, D., Greene, R., & Berry, D. T. R. (1995). Sensitivity of MMPI-2 Validity Scales to underreporting of symptoms. *Psychological Assessment, 7,* 419–423.

Bagby, R. M., & Marshall, M. B. (2004). Assessing underreporting response bias on the MMPI-2. *Assessment, 11,* 115–126.

Bagby, R. M., Marshall, M. B., & Bacchiochi, J. R. (2005). The validity and clinical utility of the MMPI-2 Malingering Depression Scale. *Journal of Personality Assessment, 85,* 304–311.

Bagby, R. M., Nicholson, R. A., Bacchiochi, J. R., Ryder, A. G., & Bury, A. S. (2002). The predictive capacity of the MMPI-2 and PAI Validity Scales and indexes to detect coached and uncoached feigning. *Journal of Personality Assessment, 78,* 69–86.

Bagby, R. M., Nicholson, R. A., Buis, T., Radovanovic, H., & Fidler, B. J. (1999). Defensive responding on the MMPI-2 in family custody and access evaluations. *Psychological Assessment, 11,* 24–28.

Bagby, R. M., Rogers, R., Nicholson, R. A., Buis, T., Seeman, M. V., & Rector, N. A. (1997). Effectiveness of the MMPI-2 validity indicators in the detection of defensive responding in clinical and nonclinical samples. *Psychological Assessment, 9,* 406–413.

Bagby, R. M., Ryder, A. G., Ben Dat, D., Bacchiochi, J., & Parker, J. D. A. (2002). Validation of the dimensional factor structure of the Personality Psychopathology Five in clinical and nonclinical samples. *Journal of Personality Disorders, 16,* 304–316.

Bagby, R. M., Sellbom, M., Costa, P. T., & Widiger, T. A. (2008). Predicting *Diagnostic and Statistical Manual of Mental Disorders–IV* personality disorders with the Five-Factor Model of personality and the Personality Psychopathology Five. *Personality and Mental Health, 2*(2), 55–69.

Bandura, A. (1994). Social cognitive theory of mass communication. In J. Bryant & D. Zillmann (Eds.), *Media effects: Advances in theory and research* (pp. 61–90). Hillsdale, NJ: Lawrence Erlbaum Associates.

Bandura, A. (2001). Social cognitive theory: An agentic perspective. *Annual Review of Psychology, 52,* 1–26.

Barber-Rioja, V., Zottoli, T. M., Kucharski, L. T., & Duncan, S. (2009). The utility of the MMPI- 2 criminal offender Infrequency (Fc) Scale in the detection of malingering in criminal defendants. *International Journal of Forensic Mental Health, 8,* 16–24.

Barefoot, J. C., Dahlstrom, W. G., & Williams, R. B. (1983). Hostility, CHD incidence, and total mortality: A 25-yr follow-up study of 255 physicians. *Psychosomatic Medicine, 45,* 59–63.

Barefoot, J. C., Dodge, K. A., Peterson, B. L., Dahlstrom, W. G., & Williams, R. B. (1989). The Cook–Medley Hostility Scale: Item content and ability to predict survival. *Psychosomatic Medicine, 51,* 46–57.

Barefoot, J. C., Larsen, S., von der Leith, L., & Schroll, M. (1995). Hostility, incidence of acute myocardial infarction, and mortality in a sample of older Danish men and women. *American Journal of Epidemiology, 142,* 477–484.

Barlow, K., Grenyer, B., & Ilkiw-Lavalle, O. (2000). Prevalence and precipitants of aggression in psychiatric inpatient units. *Australian and New Zealand Journal of Psychiatry, 34,* 967–974.

Barron, F. (1953). An ego-strength scale which predicts response to psychotherapy. *Journal of Consulting Psychology, 17,* 327–333.

Barsky, A. J., Orav, E. J., & Bates, D. W. (2005). Somatization increases medical utilization and costs independent of psychiatric and medical comorbidity. *Archives of General Psychiatry, 62,* 903–910.

Barthlow, D. L., Graham, J. R., Ben-Porath, Y. S., Tellegen, A., & McNulty, J. L. (2002). The appropriateness of the MMPI-2 K correction. *Assessment, 9*, 219–229.

Baucom, D. H. (1976). Independent masculinity and femininity scales on the California psychological inventory. *Journal of Consulting and Clinical Psychology, 44*, 876.

Beck, A. T., Weissman, A., Lester, D., & Trexler, L. (1974). The measurement of pessimism: The Hopelessness Scale. *Journal of Consulting and Clinical Psychology, 42*, 861–865.

Bem, S. (1974). The measurement of psychological androgyny. *Journal of Consulting and Clinical Psychology, 42*, 155–162.

Benazzi, F. (2004). Factor structure of recalled *DSM–IV* hypomanic symptoms of Bipolar II Disorder. *Comprehensive Psychiatry, 45*, 441–446.

Benning, S. D., Patrick, C. J., Hicks, B. M., Blonigen, D. M., & Krueger, R. F. (2003). Factor structure of the psychopathic personality inventory: Validity and implications for clinical assessment. *Psychological Assessment, 15*, 340–350.

Ben-Porath, Y. S. (2003). Introducing the MMPI-2 Restructured Clinical (RC) Scales. *SPA Exchange, 15*, 16–17, 23.

Ben-Porath, Y. S., & Butcher, J. N. (1989a). The comparability of MMPI and MMPI-2 scales and profiles. *Psychological Assessment: A Journal of Consulting and Clinical Psychology, 1*, 345–347.

Ben-Porath, Y. S., & Butcher, J. N. (1989b). The psychometric stability of rewritten MMPI items. *Journal of Personality Assessment, 53*, 645–653.

Ben-Porath, Y. S., & Butcher, J. N. (1991). The historical development of personality assessment. In C. E. Walker (Ed.), *Clinical psychology: Historical and research roots* (pp. 121–156). New York: Plenum.

Ben-Porath, Y. S., Butcher, J. N., & Graham, J. R. (1991). Contribution of the MMPI-2 Content Scales to the differential diagnosis of psychopathology. *Psychological Assessment: A Journal of Consulting and Clinical Psychology, 3*, 634–640.

Ben-Porath, Y. S., & Forbey, J. D. (2003). *Non-gendered norms for the MMPI-2.* Minneapolis: University of Minnesota Press.

Ben-Porath, Y. S., Graham, J. R., & Tellegen, A. (2009). *The MMPI-2 Symptom Validity (FBS) Scale: Development, research findings, and interpretive recommendations.* Minneapolis: University of Minnesota Press.

Ben-Porath, Y. S., Greve, K. W., Bianchini, K. J., & Kaufmann, P. M. (2009). The MMPI-2 Symptom Validity Scale (FBS) is an empirically-validated measure of over-reporting in personal injury litigants and claimants: Reply to Butcher et al. (2008). *Psychological Injury and the Law, 1*, 62–85.

Ben-Porath, Y. S., & Sherwood, N. E. (1993). *The MMPI-2 Content Component Scales: Development, psychometric characteristics, and clinical applications.* Minneapolis: University of Minnesota Press.

Ben-Porath, Y. S., & Tellegen, A. (2008/2011). *MMPI-2-RF (Minnesota Multiphasic Personality Inventory–2 Restructured Form) manual for administration, scoring, and interpretation.* Minneapolis: University of Minnesota Press.

Ben-Porath, Y. S., & Tellegen, A. (2011). *MMPI-2-RF: User's guide for reports* (2nd ed.). Minneapolis: University of Minnesota Press.

Bernreuter, R. J. (1933). Theory and construction of the personality inventory. *Journal of Social Psychology, 4*, 387–405.

Bernstein, D., Arntz, A., & Travaglini, L. (2009). Schizoid and Avoidant Personality disorders. In T. Millon (Ed.), *Oxford textbook of psychopathology* (2nd ed., pp. 586–601). New York: Oxford University Press.

Berry, D. T. R., Wetter, M. W., Baer, R. A., Widiger, T. A., Sumpter, J. C., Reynolds, S. K., et al. (1991). Detection of random responding on the MMPI-2: Utility of F, Back F, and VRIN scales. *Psychological Assessment, 3*, 418–423.

Bhar, S. S., Ghahramanlou-Holloway, M., Brown, G. K., & Beck, A. T. (2008). Self-esteem and suicide ideation in psychiatric outpatients. *Suicide and Life Threatening Behavior, 38*, 511–516.

Bianchini, K. J., Greve, K. W., & Glynn, G. (2005). Review article: On the diagnosis of malingered pain-related disability: Lessons from cognitive malingering research. *The Spine Journal, 5,* 404–417.

Bigos, S., Battie, M., Spengler, D., Fisher, L., Fordyce, W., Hansson, T., et al. (1991). A prospective study of work perceptions and psychosocial factors affecting the report of back injury. *Spine, 16,* 1–6.

Binder, R. L., & McNeil, D. E. (1988). Effects of diagnosis and context on dangerousness. *American Journal of Psychiatry, 145,* 728–732.

Binford, A., & Liljequist, L. (2008). Behavioral correlates of selected MMPI-2 Clinical, Content, and Restructured Clinical Scales. *Journal of Personality Assessment, 60,* 608–614.

Blais, M. A. (2010). The common structure of normal personality and psychopathology: Preliminary exploration in a non-patient sample. *Journal of Personality and Individual Differences, 48,* 322–326.

Blanchard, J. L., Horan, W. P., & Brown, S. A. (2001). Diagnostic differences in social anhedonia: A longitudinal study of Schizophrenia and Major Depressive Disorder. *Journal of Abnormal Psychology, 110,* 363–371.

Block, J. (1965). *The challenge of response sets: Unconfounding meaning, acquiescence, and social desirability in the MMPI.* East Norwalk, CT: Appleton-Century-Crofts.

Blonigen, D. M., Carlson, M. D., Hicks, B. M., Krueger, R. F., & Iacono, W. G. (2008). Stability and change in personality traits from late adolescence to early adulthood: A longitudinal twin study. *Journal of Personality, 76,* 229–266.

Blonigen, D. M., Carlson, S. R., Krueger, R. F., & Patrick, C. J. (2003). A twin study of self-reported psychopathic personality traits. *Personality and Individual Differences, 35,* 179–197.

Blonigen, D. M., Hicks, B. M., Krueger, R. F., Patrick, C. J., & Iacono, W. G. (2005). Psychopathic personality traits: Heritability and genetic overlap with internalizing and externalizing psychopathology. *Psychological Medicine: A Journal of Research in Psychiatry and the Allied Sciences, 35,* 637–648.

Boccaccini, M. T., & Brodsky, L. (1999). Diagnostic test usage by forensic psychologists in emotional injury cases. *Professional Psychology: Research and Practice, 30,* 253–259.

Bolinskey, P. K., Trumbetta, S. L., Hanson, D. R., & Gottesman, I. I. (2010). Predicting adult psychopathology from adolescent MMPIs: Some victories. *Personality and Individual Differences, 49,* 324–330.

Bornstein, R. F. (2005). Context-specific deficits and strengths. *The Dependent Patient.* 57–72.

Boyle, S. H., Mortensen, L., Gronbaek, M., & Barefoot, J. C. (2008). Hostility, drinking pattern and mortality. *Addiction, 103,* 54–59.

Boyle, S. H., Williams, R. B., Mark, D. B., Brummett, B. H., Siegler, I. C., Helms, M. J., et al. (2004). Hostility as a predictor of survival in patients with coronary artery disease. *Psychosomatic Medicine, 66,* 629–632.

Briere, J. (2001). *Detailed Assessment of Posttraumatic Stress (DAPS).* Odessa, FL: Psychological Assessment Resources.

Broadbent, D. E., Cooper, P. F., Fitzgerald, P., & Parkers, K. R. (1982). The cognitive failure questionnaire and its correlates. *British General of Clinical Psychology, 21,* 1–16.

Brown, S. A. (2008). The reality of persecutory beliefs: Base rate information for clinicians. *Ethical Human Psychology and Psychiatry: An International Journal of Critical Inquiry, 10,* 163–178.

Brown, T. A., Chorpita, B. F., & Barlow, D. H. (1998). Structural relationships among dimensions of the *DSM–IV* anxiety and mood disorders and dimensions of negative affect, positive affect, and autonomic arousal. *Journal of Abnormal Psychology, 107,* 179–192.

Buckley, P. F., Miller, B. J., Lehrer, D. S., & Castle, D. J. (2009). Psychiatric comorbidities and Schizophrenia. *Schizophrenia Bulletin, 35,* 383–402.

Buechley, R., & Ball, H. (1952). A new test of "validity" for the group MMPI. *Journal of Clinical Psychology, 16,* 299–301.

Bunde, J., & Suls, J. (2006). A quantitative analysis of the relationship between the Cook–Medley

Hostility Scale and traditional coronary artery disease risk factors. *Health Psychology, 25,* 493–500.

Burchett, D. L., & Ben-Porath, Y. S. (2010). The impact of overreporting on MMPI-2-RF substantive scale score validity. *Assessment, 17,* 497–516.

Burke, J. D., Loeber, R., & Lahey, B. B. (2007). Adolescent Conduct Disorder and interpersonal callousness as predictors of psychopathy in young adults. *Journal of Clinical Child and Adolescent Psychology, 36,* 334–346.

Buss, A. H., & Perry, M. (1992). The Aggression Questionnaire. *Journal of Personality and Social Psychology, 63,* 452–459.

Butcher, J. N. (1972a). *Objective personality assessment: Changing perspectives.* Oxford, England: Academic Press.

Butcher, J. N. (1972b). Personality assessment: Problems and perspectives. In J. N. Butcher (Ed.), *Objective personality assessment: Changing perspectives* (pp. 1–20). New York: Academic Press.

Butcher, J. N. (1985). Personality assessment in industry: Theoretical issues and illustrations. In H. J. Bernardin (Ed.), *Personality assessment in organizations* (pp. 277–310). New York: Praeger.

Butcher, J. N. (2011). *MMPI-2: A beginner's guide* (3rd ed.). Washington, DC: American Psychological Association.

Butcher, J. N., Aldwin, C. L., Levenson, M. R., Ben-Porath, Y. S., Spiro, A., & Bosse, R. (1991). Personality and aging: A study of the MMPI-2 aging elderly men. *Psychology of Aging, 6,* 361–370.

Butcher, J. N., Arbisi, P. A., Atlis, M. M., & McNulty, J. L. (2003). The construct validity of the Lees-Haley Fake-Bad Scale (FBS): Does this scale measure somatic malingering and feigned emotional distress? *Archives of Clinical Neuropsychology, 18,* 473–485.

Butcher, J. N., Dahlstrom, W. G., Graham, J. R., Tellegen, A. & Kaemmer, B. (1989). *Manual for the restandardized Minnesota Multiphasic Personality Inventory: MMPI-2.* Minneapolis: University of Minnesota Press.

Butcher, J. N., Gass, C. S., Cumella, E., Kally, Z., & Williams, C. L. (2008). Potential for bias in MMPI-2 assessments using the Fake Bad Scale (FBS). *Psychological Injury and Law, 1,* 191–209.

Butcher, J. N., Graham, J. R., Ben-Porath, Y. S., Tellegen, A., Dahlstrom, W. G., & Kaemmer, B. (2001). *MMPI-2: Manual for administration and scoring* (Rev. ed.). Minneapolis: University of Minnesota Press.

Butcher, J. N., Graham, J. R., Dahlstrom, W. G., & Bowman, E. (1990). The MMPI-2 with college students. *Journal of Personality Assessment, 54,* 1–15.

Butcher, J. N., Graham, J. R., Williams, C. L., & Ben-Porath, Y. S. (1990). *Development and use of the MMPI-2 Content Scales.* Minneapolis: University of Minnesota Press.

Butcher, J. N., Hamilton, C. K., Rouse, S. V., & Cumella, E. J. (2006). The deconstruction of the Hy Scale of MMPI-2: Failure of RC3 in measuring somatic symptom expression. *Journal of Personality Assessment, 87,* 186–192.

Butcher, J. N., & Han, K. (1995). Development of an MMPI-2 scale to assess the presentation of self in a superlative manner: The S Scale. In J. N. Butcher & C. D. Spielberger (Eds.), *Advances in personality assessment* (Vol. 10, pp. 25–50). Hillsdale, NJ: Lawrence Erlbaum Associates.

Butcher, J. N., Jeffrey, T., Cayton, T. G., Colligan, S., DeVore, J., & Minnegawa, R. (1990). A study of active duty military personnel with the MMPI-2. *Military Psychology, 2,* 47–61.

Butcher, J. N., Williams, C. L., Graham, J. R., Archer, R., Tellegen, A., Ben-Porath, Y. S., et al. (1992). *MMPI-A manual for administration, scoring, and interpretation.* Minneapolis: University of Minnesota Press.

Cady, V. M. (1923). The estimation of juvenile incorrigibility. *Juvenile Delinquency Monographs, 2.*

Caldwell, A. B. (1969). *MMPI critical items.* Unpublished manuscript.

Caldwell, A. B. (2006). Maximal measurement or meaningful measurement: The interpretive challenges of the MMPI-2 Restructured Clinical (RC) Scales. *Journal of Personality Assessment, 87,* 193–201.

Camara, W. J., Nathan, J. S., & Puente, A. E. (2000). Psychological test usage: Implications in professional psychology. *Professional Psychology: Research and Practice, 31,* 141–154.

Campbell, D. P. (1972). The practical problems of revising an established psychological test. In J. N. Butcher (Ed.), *Objective personality assessment: Changing perspectives* (pp. 117–130). Oxford, England: Academic Press.

Carver, C. S., & White, T. L. (1994). Behavioral inhibition, behavioral activation, and affective responses to impending reward and punishment: The BIS/BAS scales, *Journal of Personality and Social Psychology, 67,* 319–333.

Cassidy, F., Ahearn, E. P., & Carroll, B. J. (2002). Symptom profile consistency in recurrent manic episodes. *Comprehensive Psychiatry, 43,* 179–181.

Cassidy, F., Forest, K., Murry, E., & Carroll, B. J. (1998). A factor analysis of the signs and symptoms of mania. *Archives of General Psychiatry, 55,* 27–32.

Castro, Y., Gordon, K. H., Brown, J. S., Anestis, J. C., & Joiner, T. E. (2008). Examination of racial differences on the MMPI-2 Clinical and Restructured Clinical Scales in an outpatient sample. *Assessment, 15,* 277–286.

Cattell, R. B. (1965). *The scientific analysis of personality.* Oxford, England: Penguin Books.

Cattell, R. B. (Ed.). (1966). *Handbook of multivariate experimental psychology.* Chicago: Rand McNally.

Cattell, R. B., Eber, H. W., & Tatsuoka, M. (1970). *Handbook for the Sixteen Personality Factor question-naire.* Champaign, IL: Institute of Personality and Ability Testing.

Chapman, L. J., & Chapman, J. P. (1980). Scales for rating psychotic and psychotic-like experiences as continua. *Schizophrenia Bulletin, 6,* 476–489.

Chapman, L. J., Chapman, J. P., & Raulin, M. L. (1976). Scales for physical and social anhedonia. *Journal of Abnormal Psychology, 85,* 374–382.

Chapman, L. J., Chapman, J. P., & Raulin, M. L. (1978). Body-image aberration in Schizophrenia. *Journal of Abnormal Psychology, 87,* 399–407.

Clark, L. A. (1993). *Manual for the Schedule for Nonadaptive and Adaptive Personality (SNAP).* Minneapolis: University of Minnesota Press.

Clark, L. A., & Watson, D. (1991). Tripartite model of anxiety and depression: Psychometric evidence and taxonomic implications. *Journal of Abnormal Psychology, 100,* 316–336.

Clark, M. E. (1996). MMPI-2 negative treatment indicators Content and Content Component Scales: Clinical correlates and outcome prediction for men with chronic pain. *Psychological Assessment, 8,* 32–38.

Clarke, D. M., & Kissane, D. W. (2002). Demoralization: Its phenomenology and importance. *Australian and New Zealand Journal of Psychiatry, 6,* 733–742.

Cleckley, H. (1941). *The mask of sanity: An attempt to reinterpret the so-called psychopathic personality.* Oxford, England: Mosby.

Cofer, C. N., Chance, J. E., & Judson, A. J. (1949). A study of malingering on the MMPI. *Journal of Psychology, 27,* 491–499.

Colligan, R. C., Osborne, D., Swenson, W. M., & Offord, K. P. (1983). *The MMPI: A contemporary normative study.* New York: Praeger.

Combs, D. R., & Mueser, K. T. (2007). Schizophrenia. In M. Hersen, S. Turner, & D. Beidel (Eds.), *Adult psychopathology and diagnosis* (5th ed., pp. 234–285). New York: John Wiley.

Constantinople, A. (1973). Masculinity–femininity: An exception to a famous dictum? *Psychological Bulletin, 80,* 389–407.

Cook, W. W., & Medley, D. M. (1954). Proposed hostility and Pharisaic-virtue scales for the MMPI. *Journal of Applied Psychology, 38,* 414–418.

Cooke, D. J., & Michie, C. (2001). Refining the construct of psychopath: Towards a hierarchical model. *Psychological Assessment, 13,* 171–188.

Cooke, D. J., Michie, C., & Hart, S. D. (2006). Facets of clinical psychopathy: Toward clearer measurement. In C. J. Patrick (Ed.), *Handbook of psychopathy* (pp. 91–106). New York: Guilford Press.

Cooke, D. J., Michie, C., Hart, S. D., & Clark, D. A. (2004). Reconstructing psychopathy: Clarifying the significance of antisocial and socially deviant behavior in the diagnosis of Psychopathic Personality Disorder. *Journal of Personality Disorders, 18*, 337–357.

Cooke, D. J., Michie, C., Hart, S. D., & Clark, D. (2005). Searching for the pan-cultural core of Psychopathic Personality Disorder. *Personality and Individual Differences, 39*, 283–295.

Costa, P. T., Jr., & McCrae, R. R. (1985). *The NEO personality inventory manual.* Odessa, FL: Psychological Assessment Resources.

Costa, P. T., & McCrae, R. R. (1992). *NEO PI-R professional manual.* Odessa, FL: Psychological Assessment Resources.

Costa, P. T., Zonderman, A. B., McCrae, R. R., & Williams, R. B. (1986). Cynicism and paranoid alienation in the Cook and Medley HO Scale. *Psychosomatic Medicine, 48*, 283–285.

Cronbach, L. J., & Meehl, P. E. (1955). Construct validity in psychological tests. *Psychological Bulletin, 52*, 281–302.

Cuadra, C. A. (1953). *A psychometric investigation of control factors in psychological adjustment.* Unpublished doctoral dissertation, University of California, Berkeley.

Dahlstrom, W. G. (1972). Wither the MMPI? In J. N. Butcher (Ed.), *Objective personality assessment: Changing perspectives* (pp. 85–115). New York: Academic Press.

Dahlstrom, W. G. (1992). The growth in acceptance of the MMPI. *Professional Psychology: Research and Practice, 23*, 345–348.

Dahlstrom, W. G., Archer, R. P., Hopkins, D. G., Jackson, E., & Dahlstrom, L. E. (1994). *Assessing the readability of the Minnesota Multiphasic Personality Inventory Instruments: The MMPI, MMPI-2, MMPI-A.* Minneapolis: University of Minnesota Press.

Dahlstrom, W. G., & Welsh, G. S. (1960). *An MMPI handbook: A guide to use in clinical practice and research.* Minneapolis: University of Minnesota Press.

Dahlstrom, W. G., Welsh, G. S., & Dahlstrom, L. E. (1972). *An MMPI handbook: Vol. I. Clinical interpretation* (Rev. ed.). Minneapolis: University of Minnesota Press.

Dahlstrom, W. G., Welsh, G. S., & Dahlstrom, L. E. (1975). *An MMPI handbook: Vol. II. Research applications.* Minneapolis: University of Minnesota Press.

Dalsgaard, S., Mortensen, P. B., Frydenberg, M., & Thomsen, P. H. (2002). Conduct problems, gender and adult psychiatric outcome of children with Attention-Deficit Hyperactivity Disorder. *British Journal of Psychiatry, 181*, 416–421.

de Figuiredo, J. M. (1993). Depression and demoralization: Phenomenological differences and research perspectives. *Comprehensive Psychiatry, 34*, 308–311.

Delis, D. C., & Wetter, S. R. (2007). Cogniform Disorder and cogniform condition: Proposed diagnoses for excessive cognitive symptoms. *Archives of Clinical Neuropsychology, 22*, 589–604.

Derogatis, L. R. (1994). *Symptom Checklist-90-R: Administration, scoring, and procedures manual.* Minneapolis, MN: NCS Pearson.

Detrick, P., Chibnall, J. T., & Rosso, M. (2001). Minnesota Multiphasic Personality Inventory–2 in police officer selection: Normative data and relation to the Inwald Personality Inventory. *Professional Psychology: Research and Practice, 32*, 484–490.

Dick, D. M. (2007). Identification of genes influencing a spectrum of externalizing psychopathology. *Current Directions in Psychological Science, 16*, 331–335.

Dimsdale, J. P., & Creed, F. (2009). The proposed diagnosis of somatic symptom disorders in *DSM–V* to replace Somatoform Disorders in *DSM–IV* — a preliminary report. *Journal of Psychosomatic Disorders, 66*, 473–476.

Dionysus, K. E., Denney, R. L., & Halfaker, D. A. (2011). Detecting negative response bias with the Fake Bad Scale, Response Bias Scale, Henry–Heilbronner Index of the Minnesota Multiphasic Personality Inventory–2. *Archives of Clinical Neuropsychology, 26*, 81–88.

Dohrenwend, B. P., Shrout, P. E., Egri, G., & Mendelsohn, F. S. (1980). Nonspecific psychological distress and other dimensions of psychopathology. *Archives of General Psychiatry, 37*, 1229–1236.

Downey, C. A., & Chang, E. C. (2007). Perfectionism and symptoms of eating disturbances in female college students: Considering the role of negative affect and body dissatisfaction. *Eating Behaviors, 8,* 497–503.

Dragon, W. R., Ben-Porath, Y. S., & Handel, R. W. (2011). Examining the impact of unscorable item responses on the validity and interpretability of MMPI-2 Restructured Clinical (RC) Scale scores. *Assessment.* Retrieved from http://asm.sagepub.com/content/early/recent

Duits, A., Munnecom, T., van Heugten, C., & van Oostenbrugge, R. J. (2008). Cognitive complaints in the early phase after stroke are not indicative of cognitive impairment. *Journal of Neurology, Neurosurgery and Psychiatry, 79,* 143–146.

Dunkley, D. M., & Grilo, C. M. (2007). Self-criticism, low self-esteem, depressive symptoms, and over-evaluation of shape and weight in Binge Eating Disorder patients. *Behaviour Research and Therapy, 45,* 139–149.

Eckblad, M., & Chapman, L. J. (1983). Magical ideation as an indicator of Schizotypy. *Journal of Consulting and Clinical Psychology, 51,* 215–225.

Eckblad, M., & Chapman, L. J. (1986). Development and validation of a scale for hypomanic personality. *Journal of Abnormal Psychology, 95,* 214–222.

Eckhardt, C. I., Norlander, B., & Deffenbacher, J. L. (2004). The assessment of anger and hostility: A critical review. *Aggression and Violent Behavior: A Review Journal, 9,* 17–43.

Edwards, A. L. (1957). Social desirability and probability of endorsement of items in the interpersonal check list. *Journal of Abnormal and Social Psychology, 55,* 394–396.

Edwards, A. L. (1963). A factor analysis of experimental social desirability and response set scales. *Journal of Applied Psychology, 47,* 308–316.

Edwards, A. L. (1964). Social desirability and performance on the MMPI. *Psychometrika, 29,* 295–308.

Egger, J. I. M., Delsing, P. A. M., & De Mey, H. R. A. (2003). Differential diagnosis using the MMPI-2: Goldberg's index revisited. *European Psychiatry, 18,* 409–411.

Egger, J. I. M., De Mey, H. R. A., Derksen, J. J. L., & van der Staak, C. P. F. (2003). Cross-cultural replication of the five-factor model and comparison of the NEO-PI-R and MMPI-2 PSY-5 scales in a Dutch psychiatric sample. *Psychological Assessment, 15,* 81–88.

Egland, B., Erickson, M., Butcher, J. N., & Ben-Porath, Y. S. (1991). MMPI-2 profiles of women at risk for child abuse. *Journal of Personality Assessment, 57,* 254–263.

Elliot, T. R., & Gramling, S. E. (1990). Personal assertiveness and the effects of social support among college students. *Journal of Counseling Psychology, 37,* 427–436.

Englert, D. R., Weed, N. C., & Watson, G. S. (2000). Convergent, discriminant, and internal properties of the Minnesota Multiphasic Personality Inventory (2nd ed.) Low Self-Esteem Content Scale. *Measurement and Evaluation in Counseling and Development, 33,* 42–49.

Evans, L., Cowlishaw, S., & Hopwood, M. (2009). Family functioning predicting outcomes for veterans in treatment for Posttraumatic Stress Disorder. *Journal of Family Psychology, 23,* 531–539.

Eysenck, H. J. (1953). *The structure of human personality.* New York: John Wiley.

Eysenck, H. J. (1977). *Crime and personality.* London: Routledge & Kegan Paul.

Eysenck, H. J., & Eysenck, S. B. G. (1964). *Manual of the Eysenck Personality Inventory.* London: University London Press.

Eysenck, H. J., & Eysenck, S. B. G. (1975). *Eysenck Personality Questionnaire.* San Diego, CA: Educational and Industrial Testing Service.

Fairbank, J. A., McCaffrey, R. J., & Keane, T. M. (1985). Psychometric detection of fabricated symptoms of Posttraumatic Stress Disorder. *American Journal of Psychiatry, 42,* 501–503.

Fava, G. A., Freyberger, H. J., Bech, P., Christodoulou, G., Sensky, T., Theorell, T., et al. (1995). Diagnostic criteria for use in psychosomatic research. *Psychotherapy and Psychosomatics, 63,* 1–8.

Fazel, S., Langstrom, N., Hjern, A., Grann, M., & Lichtenstein, P. (2009). Schizophrenia, substance abuse, and violent crime. *Journal of the American Medical Association, 301,* 2016–2023.

Fenig, S., & Levav, I. (1991). Demoralization and social supports among Holocaust survivors. *Journal of Nervous and Mental Disease, 179,* 167–172.

Ferrier-Auerbach, A. G., Kehle, S. M., Erbes, C. R., Arbisi, P. A., Thuras, P., & Polusny, M. A. (2009). Predictors of alcohol use prior to deployment in National Guard soldiers. *Addictive Behaviors, 34,* 625–631.

Finney, J. C. (1968). Correction for unwanted variance. *Psychological Reports, 23,* 1231–1235.

Forbes, D., Elhai, J. D., Miller, M. W., & Creamer, M. (2010). Internalizing and externalizing classes in Posttraumatic Stress Disorder: A latent class analysis. *Journal of Traumatic Stress, 23,* 340–349.

Forbey, J. D., & Ben-Porath, Y. S. (2007). A comparison of the MMPI-2 RC Scales and Clinical Scales in a substance abuse treatment sample. *Psychological Services, 4,* 46–58.

Forbey, J. D., & Ben-Porath, Y. S. (2008). Empirical correlates of the MMPI-2 Restructured Clinical (RC) Scales in a nonclinical setting. *Journal of Personality Assessment, 90,* 136–141.

Forbey, J. D., Ben-Porath, Y. S., & Gartland, D. (2009). Validation of the MMPI-2 Computerized Adaptive version (MMPI-2-CA) in a correctional intake facility. *Psychological Services, 6,* 279–292.

Forbey, J. D., Lee, T. T. C., & Handel, R. W. (2010). Correlates of the MMPI-2-RF in a college setting. *Psychological Assessment, 22,* 734–744.

Fordyce, W. E. (1998). Environmental issues in disability status. *Canadian Journal of Rehabilitation, 11,* 170–171.

Fordyce, W. E., Bigos, S., Battie, M., & Fisher, L. (1992). MMPI Scale 3 as a predictor of back pain report: What does it tell us? *Clinical Journal of Pain, 8,* 222–226.

Frank, J. D. (1974). Psychotherapy: The restoration of morale. *American Journal of Psychiatry, 131,* 271–274.

Frank, J. D. (1985). Further thoughts on the anti-demoralization hypothesis of psychotherapeutic effectiveness. *Integrative Psychiatry, 3,* 17–20.

Frank, J. D., & Frank, J. B. (1996). Demoralization and unexplained illness in two cohorts of American soldiers overseas. *Journal of Nervous and Mental Disease, 184,* 445–446.

Freeman, D. (2007). Suspicious minds: The psychology of persecutory delusions. *Clinical Psychology Review, 27,* 425–457.

Freeman, D., & Garety, A. (2000). Comments on the content of persecutory delusions: Does the definition need clarification? *British Journal of Clinical Psychology, 39,* 407–414.

Freeman, D., Gittins, M., Pugh, K., Antley, A., Slater, M., & Dunn, G. (2008). What makes one person paranoid and another persona anxious? The differential prediction of social anxiety and persecutory ideation in an experimental situation. *Psychological Medicine, 38,* 1121–1132.

Freeman, D., Pugh, K., Green, C., Valmaggia, L., Dunn, G., & Garety, P. (2007). A measure of state persecutory ideation for experimental studies. *Journal of Nervous and Mental Disease, 195,* 781–784.

Friedman, M., & Rosenman, R. H. (1959). Association of specific overt behavior pattern with blood and cardiovascular findings. *Journal of the American Medical Association, 169,* 1286–1296.

Friedman, M., Rosenman, R. H., Carroll, V., & Tat, R. J. (1958). Changes in the serum cholesterol and blood clotting time in men subjected to cyclic variation of occupational stress. *Circulation, 17,* 852–861.

Galton, F. (1888). Co-relations and their measurement. *Proceedings of the Royal Society, London Series, 45,* 135–145.

Gard, D. E., Gard, M. G., Kring, A. M., & John, O. P. (2006). Anticipatory and consummatory components of the experience of pleasure: A scale development study. *Journal of Research in Personality, 40,* 1086–1102.

Gard, D. E., Kring, A. M., Gard, M. G., Horan, W. P., & Green, M. F. (2007). Anhedonia in Schizophrenia: Distinctions between anticipatory and consummatory pleasure. *Schizophrenia Research, 93,* 253–260.

Gass, C. S., & Luis, C. A. (2001). MMPI-2 Scale F(p) and feigning: Scale refinement. *Assessment, 8,* 425–429.

Gatchel, R. J., Polatin, P. B., & Kinney, R. K. (1995). Predicting outcome of chronic back pain using clinical predictors of psychopathology: A prospective analysis. *Health Psychology, 14,* 415–420.

Gendreau, P., Goggin, C., & Smith, P. (2002). Is the PCL-R really the "unparalleled" measure of offender risk? A lesson in knowledge cumulation. *Criminal Justice and Behavior, 29,* 397–426.

Gervais, R. O., Ben-Porath, Y. S., & Wygant, D. B. (2009). Empirical correlates and interpretation of the MMPI-2-RF Cognitive Complaints Scale. *Clinical Neuropsychologist, 23,* 996–1015.

Gervais, R. O., Ben-Porath, Y. S., Wygant, D. B., & Green, P. (2007). Development and validation of a Response Bias Scale (RBS) for the MMPI-2. *Assessment, 14,* 196–208.

Gervais, R. O., Ben-Porath, Y. S., Wygant, D. B., & Sellbom, M. (2010). Incremental validity of the MMPI-2-RF over-reporting scales and RBS in assessing the veracity of memory complaints. *Archives of Clinical Neuropsychology, 25,* 274–284.

Gilberstadt, H., & Duker, J. (1965). *A handbook for clinical and actuarial MMPI interpretation.* Philadelphia: Saunders.

Glassmire, D. M., Stolberg, R. A., Greene, R. L., & Bongar, B. (2001). The utility of MMPI-2 suicide items for assessing suicidal potential: Development of a suicidal potential scale. *Assessment, 8,* 281–290.

Goldberg, L. R. (1965). Diagnosticians vs. diagnostic signs: The diagnosis of psychosis versus neurosis for the MMPI. *Psychological Monographs, 79.*

Goldberg, L. R. (1968). *The diagnosis of psychosis and neurosis from the MMPI.* Paper presented at the Third Annual Symposium on Use of the MMPI, Minneapolis, MN.

Goldberg, L. R. (1969). The search for configural relationships in personality assessment: The diagnosis of psychosis vs. neurosis from the MMPI. *Multivariate Behavioral Research, 4,* 523–536.

Goldberg, L. R. (1971). A historical survey of personality scales and inventories. In P. McReynolds (Ed.), *Advances in psychological assessment* (Vol. 2, pp. 293–336). Palo Alto, CA: Science and Behavior Books.

Good, M. I. (1978). Primary Affective Disorder, aggression, and criminality: A review and clinical study. *Archives of General Psychiatry, 35,* 954–960.

Gough, H. G. (1946). Diagnostic patterns on the MMPI. *Journal of Clinical Psychology, 2,* 23–37.

Gough, H. G. (1947). Simulated patterns on the Minnesota Multiphasic Personality Inventory. *Journal of Abnormal and Social Psychology, 42,* 215–255.

Gough, H. G. (1948). A new dimension of status: I. Development of a personality scale. *American Sociology Review, 13,* 401–409.

Gough, H. G. (1951). Studies of social intolerance: I. Psychological and sociological correlates of anti-Semitism. *Journal of Social Psychology, 33,* 237–246.

Gough, H. G. (1957). *Manual for the California Psychological Inventory.* Palo Alto, CA: Consulting Psychologists Press.

Gough, H. G., McClosky, H., & Meehl, P. E. (1951). A personality scale for dominance. *Journal of Abnormal and Social Psychology, 46,* 360–366.

Graham, J. R. (1977). *The MMPI: A practical guide.* Baltimore, MD: Waverly Press.

Graham, J. R. (2006). *MMPI-2: Assessing personality and psychopathology* (4th ed.). New York: Oxford University Press.

Graham, J. R. (2011). *MMPI-2: Assessing personality and psychopathology* (5th ed.). New York: Oxford University Press.

Graham, J. R., Ben-Porath, Y. S., & McNulty, J. L. (1996). *MMPI-2 correlates for outpatient mental health settings.* Minneapolis: University of Minnesota Press.

Graham, J. R., & Butcher, J. N. (1988). *Differentiating Schizophrenia and major affective disorders with the revised form of the MMPI.* Paper presented at the 23rd annual symposium on Recent Developments in the Use of the MMPI, St. Petersburg Beach, FL.

Graham, J. R., Timbrook, R. E., Ben-Porath, Y. S., & Butcher, J. N. (1991). Congruence between

MMPI and MMPI-2: Separating fact from artifact. *Journal of Personality Assessment, 57,* 205–215.

Grassi, L., Rossi, E., Sabato, S., Cruciani, G., & Zambelli, M. (2004). Diagnostic criteria for psycho-somatic research and psychosocial variables in breast cancer patients. *Psychosomatics: Journal of Consultation Liaison Psychiatry, 45,* 483–491.

Gray, J. A. (1970). The psychophysiological basis of introversion–extraversion. *Behaviour Research and Therapy, 8,* 249–266.

Grayson, H. M. (1951). *A psychological admissions testing program and manual.* Los Angeles, CA: Veterans Administration Center, Neuropsychiatric Hospital.

Green, C., Garety, P. A., Freeman, D., Fowler, D., Bebbington., P., Dunn, G., et al. (2006). Content and affect in persecutory delusions. *British Journal of Clinical Psychology, 45,* 561–577.

Green, D. P., Goldman, S. L., & Salovey, P. (1993). Measurement error masks bipolarity in affect ratings. *Journal of Personality and Social Psychology, 64,* 1029–1041.

Green, P. (2004). *Memory Complaints Inventory.* Edmonton, AL, Canada: Green's.

Green, P., Allen, L., & Astner, K. (1996). *Manual for Computerised Word Memory Test.* Durham, NC: CogniSyst.

Greene, R. L. (1978). An empirically derived MMPI carelessness scale. *Journal of Clinical Psychology, 34,* 407–410.

Greene, R. L. (1980). *The MMPI: An interpretive manual.* New York: Grune & Stratton.

Greene, R. L. (2011). *The MMPI-2/MMPI-2-RF: An interpretive manual* (3rd ed.). Boston: Pearson.

Greene, R. L., Weed, N. C., Butcher, J. N., Arredondo, R., & Davis, H. G. (1992). A cross validation of the MMPI-2 substance abuse scales. *Journal of Personality Assessment, 58,* 405–410.

Greiffenstein, M. F., Baker, W. J., Axelrod, B., Peck, E. A., & Gervais, R. (2004). The Fake Bad Scale and MMPI-2 F-family in detection of implausible psychological trauma claims. *Clinical Neuropsychologist, 18,* 573–590.

Greiffenstein, M. F., Fox, D., & Lees-Haley, P. R. (2007). The MMPI-2 Fake Bad Scale in detection of noncredible brain injury claims. In K. Boone (Ed.), *Assessment of feigned cognitive impairment: A neuropsychological perspective* (pp. 210–235). New York: Guilford Press.

Greve, K. W., & Bianchini, K. J. (2004). Response to Butcher et al., The construct validity of the Lees-Haley Fake-Bad Scale. *Archives of Clinical Neuropsychology, 19,* 337–339.

Greve, K. W., Bianchini, K. J., Love, J. M., Brennan, A., & Heinly, M. T. (2006). Sensitivity and specificity of MMPI-2 Validity Scales and indicators to malingered neurocognitive dysfunction in traumatic brain injury. *Clinical Neuropsychologist, 20,* 491–512.

Grunebaum, M . F., Galfalvy, H. C., Nichols, C. M., Caldeira, N. A., Sher, L., Dervic, K., et al. (2006). Aggression and substance abuse in Bipolar Disorder. *Bipolar Disorders, 8,* 496–502.

Guilford, J. P. (1939). *General psychology.* New York: Van Nostrand.

Guilford, J. P. (1959). *Personality.* New York: McGraw-Hill.

Guilford, J. P. (1977). *Way beyond the IQ.* New York: Creative Education Foundation.

Gutkovich, Z., Rosenthal, R. N., Galynker, I., Muran, C., Batchelder, S., & Itskhoki, E. (1999). Depression and demoralization among Russian-Jewish immigrants in primary care. *Psychosomatics: Journal of Consultation Liaison Psychiatry, 40,* 117–125.

Haertzen, C. A., & Hill, H. E. (1963). Assessing subjective effects of drugs: An index of carelessness and confusion for use with the Addiction Research Center Inventory (ARCI). *Journal of Clinical Psychology, 19,* 407–412.

Halevy, A., Moos, R. H., & Soloman, G. F. (1965). A relationship between blood serotonin concentrations and behavior in psychiatric patients. *Journal of Psychiatric Research, 3,* 1–10.

Han, K., Weed, N. C., Calhoun, R. F., & Butcher, J. N. (1995). Psychometric characteristics of the MMPI-2 Cook–Medley Hostility Scale. *Journal of Personality Assessment, 65,* 567–585.

Handel, R. W., & Archer, R. P. (2008). An investigation of the psychometric properties of the MMPI-2 Restructured Clinical (RC) Scales with mental health inpatients. *Journal of Personality Assessment, 90,* 239–249.

Handel, R. W., Arnau, R. C., Archer, R. P., & Dandy, K. L. (2006). An evaluation of the MMPI-2 and MMPI-A true response inconsistency (TRIN) scales. *Assessment, 13*, 98–106.

Handel, R. W., Ben-Porath, Y. S., Tellegen, A., & Archer, R. P. (2007). *Psychometric functioning of the MMPI-2-RF VRIN-r and TRIN-r scales with varying degrees of randomness, acquiescence, and nonacquiescence.* Paper presented at the 42nd annual symposium on Recent Developments in the Use of the MMPI-2/MMPI-A, Fort Lauderdale, FL.

Handel, R. W., Ben-Porath, Y. S., Tellegen, A., & Archer, R. P. (2010). Psychometric Functioning of the MMPI-2-RF VRIN-r and TRIN-r scales with varying degrees of randomness, acquiescence, and counter-acquiescence. *Psychological Assessment, 22*, 87–95.

Hanvik, L. J. (1951). MMPI profiles in patients with low-back pain. *Journal of Consulting Psychology, 15*, 350–353.

Hare, R. D. (1991). *The revised psychopathy checklist.* Toronto, ON, Canada: Multi-Health Systems.

Hare, R. D. (2003). *Hare Psychopathy Checklist–Revised (PCL-R), Technical manual* (2nd ed.). North Tonawanda, NY: Multi-Health Systems.

Hare, R. D., & Neumann, C. S. (2006). The PCL-R assessment of psychopathy: Development, structural properties, and new directions. In C. Patrick (Ed.), *Handbook of psychopathy* (pp. 58–90). New York: Guilford Press.

Harkness, A. R. (1992). Fundamental topics in the personality disorders: Candidate trait dimensions from lower regions of the hierarchy. *Psychological Assessment, 4*, 251–259.

Harkness, A. R., & McNulty, J. L. (1994). The Personality Psychopathology Five (PSY-5): Issues from the pages of a diagnostic manual instead of a dictionary. In S. Strack & M. Lorr (Eds.), *Differentiating normal and abnormal personality* (pp. 291–315). New York: Springer.

Harkness, A. R., & McNulty, J. L. (2007). *Restructured versions of the MMPI-2 Personality Psychopathology Five (PSY-5) Scales.* Paper presented at the meeting of the American Psychological Association, San Francisco, CA.

Harkness, A. R., McNulty, J. L., & Ben-Porath, Y. S. (1995). The Personality Psychopathology Five (PSY-5): Constructs and MMPI-2 scales. *Psychological Assessment, 7*, 104–114.

Harkness, A. R., McNulty, J. L., Ben-Porath, Y. S., & Graham, J. R. (2002). *MMPI-2 Personality Psychopathology Five (PSY-5) Scales: Gaining an overview for case conceptualization and treatment planning.* Minneapolis: University of Minnesota Press.

Harp, J. P., Jasinski, L. J., Shandera-Ochsner, A. L., Mason, L. H., & Berry, D. T. R. (2011). Detection of malingered ADHD using the MMPI-2-RF. *Psychological Injury and Law, 4*, 32–43.

Harris, R., & Lingoes, J. (1955). *Subscales for the Minnesota Multiphasic Personality Inventory.* Unpublished manuscript.

Hart, S., Cox, D., & Hare, R. (1995). *The Hare PCL: SV Psychopathy Checklist: Screening version.* North Tonawanda, NY: Multi-Health Systems.

Hartshorne, H., May, M. A., & Shuttleworth, F. K. (1930). *Studies in the nature of character: Vol. 3. Studies in the organization of character.* New York: Macmillan.

Hathaway, S. R. (1947). A coding system for MMPI profiles. *Journal of Consulting Psychology, 11*, 334–337.

Hathaway, S. R. (1956). Scale 5 (Masculinity–Femininity), Scale 6 (Paranoia) and Scale 8 (Schizophrenia). In G. S. Welsh & W. G. Dahlstrom (Eds.), *Basic readings on the MMPI in psychology and medicine* (pp. 104–111). Minneapolis: University of Minnesota Press.

Hathaway, S. R. (1960). Foreword. In W. G. Dahlstrom & G. S. Welsh (Eds.), *An MMPI handbook: A guide to use in clinical practice and research* (pp. vii–xi). Minneapolis: University of Minnesota Press.

Hathaway, S. R. (1972a). Foreword. In W. G. Dahlstrom, G. S. Welsh, & L. E. Dahlstrom (Eds.), *An MMPI handbook: Vol. 1. Clinical interpretation* (pp. xiii–iv). Minneapolis: University of Minnesota Press.

Hathaway, S. R. (1972b). Where have we gone wrong? The mystery of the missing progress. In

J. N. Butcher (Ed.), *Objective personality assessment: Changing perspectives* (pp. 21–43). Oxford, England: Academic Press.

Hathaway, S. R., & Briggs, P. F. (1957). Some normative data on new MMPI scales. *Journal of Clinical Psychology, 13,* 364–368.

Hathaway, S. R., & McKinley, J. C. (1940). A multiphasic personality schedule (Minnesota): I. Construction of the schedule. *Journal of Psychology, 10,* 249–254.

Hathaway, S. R., & McKinley, J. C. (1942). A multiphasic personality schedule (Minnesota): III. The measurement of symptomatic depression. *Journal of Psychology, 14,* 73–84.

Hathaway, S. R., & McKinley, J. C. (1943). *The Minnesota Multiphasic Personality Inventory.* Minneapolis: University of Minnesota Press.

Hathaway, S. R., & McKinley, J. C. (1946). *Supplementary manual for the Minnesota Multiphasic Personality Inventory. Part I. The K scale and its use.* New York: Psychological Corp.

Hathaway, S. R., & McKinley, J. C. (1951). *Manual for the Minnesota Multiple Personality Inventory.* New York: Psychological Corporation.

Hathaway, S. R., & McKinley, H. C. (1967). *Minnesota Multiphasic Personality Inventory Manual—Revised.* New York: Psychological Corporation.

Hawk, G. L., & Cornell, D. G. (1989). MMPI profiles of malingerers diagnosed in pretrial forensic evaluations. *Journal of Clinical Psychology, 45,* 673–678.

Heilbrun, A. B. J. (1961). Male and female personality correlates of early termination in counseling. *Journal of Counseling Psychology, 8,* 31–36.

Heiser, N. A., Turner, S. M., Beidel, D. C., & Roberson-Nay, R. (2009). Differentiating social phobia from shyness. *Journal of Anxiety Disorders, 23,* 469–476.

Helmes, E., & Reddon, J. R. (1993). A perspective on developments in assessing psychopathology: A critical review of the MMPI and MMPI-2. *Psychological Bulletin, 113,* 453–471.

Hemphill, J. F., Hare, R. D., & Wong, S. (1998). Psychopathy and recidivism: A review. *Legal and Criminological Psychology, 3*(Part 1), 139–170.

Henry, G. K., Heilbronner, R. L., Mittenberg, W., Enders, C., & Stanczal, S. R. (2008). Comparison of the Lees-Haley Fake Bad Scale, Henry–Heilbronner Index, and Restructured Clinical Scale 1 in identifying noncredible symptom reporting. *Clinical Neuropsychologist, 22,* 919–929.

Heymans, G., & Wiersma, E. (1906). Beitrage zur spezillen psychologie auf grund einer massenunterschung. *Zeitschrift fur Psychologie, 43,* 81–127.

Hickman, M. J., Piquero, N. L., & Piquero, A. R. (2004). The validity of Niederhoffer's cynicism scale. *Journal of Criminal Justice, 32,* 1–13.

Hicks, B. M., DiRago, A. C., Iacono, W. G., & McGue, M. (2009). Gene–environment interplay in internalizing disorders: Consistent findings across six environmental risk factors. *Journal of Child Psychology and Psychiatry, 50,* 1309–1317.

Hicks, B. M., Markon, K. E., Patrick, C. J., Krueger, R. F., & Newman, J. P. (2004). Identifying psychopathy subtypes on the basis of personality structure. *Psychological Assessment, 16,* 276–288.

Hirschel, D., Hutchison, I. W., & Shaw, M. (2010). The interrelationship between substance abuse and the likelihood of arrest, conviction, and re-offending in cases of intimate partner violence. *Journal of Family Violence, 25,* 81–90.

Hjemboe, S., Almagor, M., & Butcher, J. N. (1992). Empirical assessment of marital distress: The Marital Distress Scale (MDS) for the MMPI-2. In C. D. Spielberger & J. N. Butcher (Eds.), *Advances in personality assessment* (Vol. 9, pp. 141–152). Hillsdale, NJ: Lawrence Erlbaum Associates.

Hoch, A., & Amsden, G. S. (1913). A guide to the descriptive study of the personality. With special reference to the taking of anamneses of cases with psychoses. *Review of Neurology and Psychiatry, 11,* 577–587.

Hoelzle, J. B., & Meyer, G. J. (2009). The invariant component structure of the Personality Assessment Inventory (PAI) full scales. *Journal of Personality Assessment, 91,* 175–186.

Hofmann, S. G., Richey, J. A., Sawyer, A., Ansaani, A., & Rief, W. (2009). Social Anxiety Disorder and the *DSM–V*. In D. McKay, J. S. Abramowitz, S. Taylor, & G. J. G. Asmundson (Eds.), *Current perspectives on the anxiety disorders: Implications for DSM–V and beyond* (pp. 411–429). New York: Springer.

Horan, W. P., Kring, A. M., & Blanchard, J. J. (2006). Anhedonia in Schizophrenia: A review of assessment strategies. *Schizophrenia Bulletin, 32,* 259–273.

Horan, W. P., Reise, S. P., Subotnik, K. L., Ventura, J., & Nuechterlein, K. H. (2008). The validity of Psychosis Proneness Scales as vulnerability indicators in recent-onset Schizophrenia patients. *Schizophrenia Research, 100,* 224–236.

Horst, P. (1941). The role of predictor variables which are independent of the criterion. *Social Science Research Bulletin, 48,* 431–436.

Hughes, M. E., Alloy, L. B., & Cogswell, A. (2008). Repetitive thought in psychopathology: The relation of rumination and worry to depression and anxiety symptoms. *Journal of Cognitive Psychotherapy: An International Quarterly, 22,* 273–291.

Humm, D. G., & Wadsworth, G. W. (1935). The Humm–Wadsworth temperament scale. *American Journal of Psychiatry, 92,* 163–200.

Hunt, H. F. (1948). The effect of deliberate deception on Minnesota Multiphasic Personality Inventory performance. *Journal of Consulting Psychology, 12,* 396–402.

Ingram, P. B., Kelso, K. M., & McCord, D. M. (2011). Empirical correlates and expanded interpretation of the MMPI-2-RF Restructured Clinical Scale 3 (Cynicism). *Assessment, 18,* 95–101.

Inwald, R. (1992). *Inwald Personality Inventory technical manual* (Rev. ed.). New York: Hilson Research.

Jackson, D. N. (1970). A sequential system for personality scale development. In C. D. Spielberger (Ed.), *Current practices in clinical and community psychology* (Vol. 2, pp. 60–96). New York: Academic Press.

Jackson, D. N. (1971). The dynamics of structured personality tests. *Psychological Review, 78,* 229–248.

Jackson, D. N. (1989). *Basic Personality Inventory.* London, ON, Canada: Sigma Assessment Systems.

Jackson, D. N., Fraboni, M., & Helmes, E. (1997). MMPI-2 Content Scales: How much content do they measure? *Assessment, 4,* 111–117.

Jackson, D. N., & Messick, S. (1962). Response styles on the MMPI: Comparison of clinical and normal samples. *Journal of Abnormal and Social Psychology, 65,* 285–299.

Jaffee, S. R., Belsky, J., Harrington, H., Caspi, A., & Moffitt, T. E. (2006). When parents have a history of Conduct Disorder: How is the caregiving environment affected? *Journal of Abnormal Psychology, 115,* 309–319.

James, L., & Taylor, J. (2008). Revisiting the structure of mental disorder: Borderline Personality Disorder and the internalizing/externalizing spectra. *British Journal of Clinical Psychology, 47,* 361–380.

Janca, A., Burke, J. D., Jr., Isaac, M., Burke, K. C., Costa e Silva, J. A., Acuda, S. W., et al. (1995). The World Health Organization Somatoform Disorders schedule: A preliminary report on design and reliability. *European Psychiatry, 10,* 373–378.

Joiner, T. E., Walker, R. L., Pettit, J. W., Perez, M., & Cukrowicz, K. C. (2005). Evidence-based assessment of depression in adults. *Psychological Assessment, 17,* 267–277.

Judge, T. A., Erez, A., Bono, J. E., & Thoresen, C. J. (2002). Discriminant and incremental validity of four personality traits: Are measures of self-esteem, neuroticism, locus of control, and generalized self-efficacy indicators of a common core construct? *Journal of Personality and Social Psychology, 83,* 693–710.

Kashdan, T. B., Elhai, J. D., & Frueh, B. C. (2006). Anhedonia and emotional numbing in combat veterans with PTSD. *Behaviour Research and Therapy, 44,* 457–467.

Kashdan, T. B., Uswatte, G., Steger, M. F., & Julian, T. (2006). Fragile self-esteem and affective instability in Posttraumatic Stress Disorder. *Behaviour Research and Therapy, 44,* 1609–1619.

Kaslow, N. J., Thompson, M. P., Brooks, A. E., & Twomey, H. B. (2000). Ratings of family functioning of suicidal and nonsuicidal African American women. *Journal of Family Psychology, 14*, 585–599.

Kassebaum, G. G., Couch, A. S., & Slater, P. E. (1959). The factorial dimensions of the MMPI. *Journal of Consulting Psychology, 23*, 226–236.

Katz, M. M., & Lyerly, S. B. (1963). Methods for measuring adjustment and social behavior in the community. *Psychological Reports, 13*, 503–535.

Keane, T. M., Malloy, P. F., & Fairbank, J. A. (1984). Empirical development of an MMPI subscale for the assessment of combat-related posttraumatic stress disorder. *Journal of Consulting and Clinical Psychology, 52*(5), 888–891.

Keane, T. M., Taylor, K. L., & Penk, W. E. (1997). Differentiating Posttraumatic Stress Disorder (PTSD) from Major Depression (MDD) and Generalized Anxiety Disorder (GAD). *Journal of Anxiety Disorders, 11*, 317–328.

Keller, L. S., & Butcher, J. N. (1991). *Use of the MMPI-2 with chronic pain patients.* Minneapolis: University of Minnesota Press.

Klein, D. F. (1974). Endogenomorphic depression: A conceptual and terminological revision. *Archives of General Psychiatry, 31*, 447–454.

Klonsky, E. D., Oltmanns, T. F., Turkheimer, E., & Fiedler, E. (2000). Recollections of conflict with parents and family support in the personality disorders. *Journal of Personality Disorders, 14*, 311–322.

Knop, J., Penick, E. C., Nickel, E. J., Mortensen, E. L., Sullivan, M. A., Murtaza, S., et al. (2009). Childhood ADHD and Conduct Disorder as independent predictors of male alcohol dependence at age 40. *Journal of Studies on Alcohol and Drugs, 70*, 169–177.

Koss, M. P., & Butcher, J. N. (1973). A comparison of psychiatric patients' self-report with other sources of clinical information. *Journal of Research in Personality, 7*, 225–236.

Koss, M. P., Butcher, J. N., & Hoffman, N. G. (1976). The MMPI critical items: How well do they work? *Journal of Consulting and Clinical Psychology, 44*, 921–928.

Kraepelin, E. (1921). Ueber Entwurtzelung. *Zeitschrift fur die Gesamte Neurologie und Psychiatrie, 63*, 1–8.

Kramer, M. D., Krueger, R. F., & Hicks, B. M. (2008). The role of internalizing and externalizing liability factors in accounting for gender differences in the prevalence of common psychopathological syndromes. *Psychological Medicine: A Journal of Research in Psychiatry and the Allied Sciences, 38*, 51–61.

Kring, A. M., & Germans, M. K. (2000). Anhedonia. In A. E. Kazdin (Ed.), *Encyclopedia of psychology* (Vol. 1, pp. 174–175). Washington, DC: American Psychological Association.

Kroll, J. (2003). Posttraumatic symptoms and the complexity of responses to trauma. *Journal of the American Medical Association, 290*, 667–670.

Kroll, J., & McDonald, C. (2003). A diverse refugee population requires complex solutions. *Psychiatric Times, 20*(10). Retrieved from http://www.psychiatrictimes.com/display/article/10168/48371

Krueger, R. F., Chentsova-Dutton, Y. E., Markon, K. E., Goldberg, D., & Ormel, J. (2003). A cross-cultural study of the structure of comorbidity among common psychopathological syndromes in the general health care setting. *Journal of Abnormal Psychology, 112*, 437–447.

Krueger, R. F., Hicks, B. M., Patrick, C. J., Carlson, S. R., Iacono, W. G., & McGue, M. (2002). Etiologic connections among substance dependence, antisocial behavior and personality: Modeling the externalizing spectrum. *Journal of Abnormal Psychology, 111*, 411–424.

Krueger, R. F., & Markon, K. E. (2006). Reinterpreting comorbidity: A model-based approach to understanding and classifying psychopathology. *Annual Review of Clinical Psychology, 2*, 111–133.

Krueger, R. F., Markon, K. E., Patrick, C. J., Benning, S. D., & Kramer, M. D. (2007). Linking antisocial behavior, substance use, and personality: An integrative quantitative model of the adult externalizing spectrum. *Journal of Abnormal Psychology, 116*, 645–666.

Krueger, R. F., Markon, K. E., Patrick, C. J., & Iacono, W. G. (2005). Externalizing psychopathology in adulthood: A dimensional-spectrum conceptualization and its implications for *DSM–V*. *Journal of Abnormal Psychology, 114,* 537–550.

Kwapil, T. R., Miller, M. B., Zinser, M. C., Chapman, L. J., Chapman, J., & Eckblad, M. (2000). A longitudinal study of high scorers on the Hypomanic Personality Scale. *Journal of Abnormal Psychology, 109,* 222–226.

Lachar, D., & Wrobel, T. A. (1979). Validating clinicians' hunches: Construction of a new MMPI critical item set. *Journal of Consulting and Clinical Psychology, 47,* 277–284.

Lally, S. J. (2003). What tests are acceptable for use in forensic evaluations? A survey of experts. *Professional Psychology: Research and Practice, 34,* 491–498.

Lamberty, G. (2008). *Understanding somatization in the practice of clinical neuropsychology.* New York: Oxford University Press.

Landis, C., & Katz, S. E. (1934). The validity of certain questions which purport to measure neurotic tendencies. *Journal of Applied Psychology, 18,* 343–356.

Landis, C., Zubin, J., & Katz, S. E. (1935). Empirical validation of three personality adjustment inventories. *Journal of Educational Psychology, 26,* 321–330.

Lange, R. T., Sullivan, K. A., & Scott, C. (2010). Comparison of MMPI-2 and PAI validity indicators to detect feigned depression and PTSD symptom reporting. *Psychiatry Research, 176,* 229–235.

Larrabee, G. J. (2007). *Assessment of malingered neuropsychological deficits.* New York: Oxford University Press.

Lee, S., & Swanson-Crockett, M. (1994). Effect of assertiveness training on levels of stress and assertiveness experienced by nurses in Taiwan, Republic of China. *Issues in Mental Health Nursing, 15,* 419–432.

Lees-Haley, P. R. (1984). Detecting the psychological malingerer. *American Journal of Forensic Psychology, 2,* 165–169.

Lees-Haley, P. R. (1989). Malingering Post-traumatic Stress Disorder on the MMPI. *Forensic Reports, 2,* 89–91.

Lees-Haley, P. R. (1992). Efficacy of MMPI-2 Validity Scales and MCMI-II modifier scales for detecting spurious PTSD claims: F, F–K, Fake Bad Scale, Ego Strength, Subtle–Obvious subscales, DIS, and DEB. *Journal of Clinical Psychology, 48,* 681–689.

Lees-Haley, P. R., English, L. T., & Glenn, W. J. (1991). A fake bad scale on the MMPI-2 for personal injury claimants. *Psychological Reports, 68,* 203–210.

Lees-Haley, P. R., & Fox, D. D. (2004). Commentary on Butcher, Arbisi, Atlis, and McNulty (2003) on the Fake Bad Scale. *Archives of Clinical Neuropsychology, 19,* 333–336.

Lees-Haley, P. R., Smith, H. H., Williams, C. W., & Dunn, J. T. (1995). Forensic neuropsychological test usage: An empirical survey. *Archives of Clinical Neuropsychology, 11,* 45–51.

Leistico, A. R., Salekin, R. T., DeCoster, J., & Rogers, R. (2008). A large-scale meta-analysis relating the Hare measures of psychopathy to antisocial conduct. *Law and Human Behavior, 32,* 28–45.

Lepore, S. J. (1995). Cynicism, social support, and cardiovascular reactivity. *Health Psychology, 14,* 210–216.

Levenson, M. R., Kiehl, K. A., & Fitzpatrick, C. M. (1995). Assessing psychopathic attributes in a noninstitutionalized population. *Journal of Personality and Social Psychology, 68,* 151–158.

Lewinsohn, P. M., Pettit, J. W., Joiner, T., & Seeley, J. R. (2003). The symptomatic expression of Major Depressive Disorder in adolescents and young adults. *Journal of Abnormal Psychology, 112,* 244–252.

Lewis, A. (1970). Paranoia and paranoid: A historical perspective. *Psychological Medicine: A Journal of Research in Psychiatry and the Allied Sciences, 1,* 2–12.

Lightsey, O. R., Burke, M., Ervin, A., Henderson, D., & Lee, C. (2006). Generalized self efficacy, self-esteem, and negative effect. *Canadian Journal of Behavioural Science, 38,* 72–80.

Lilienfeld, S. O., & Andrews, P. (1996). Development and preliminary validation of a self-report measure of psychopathic personality traits in noncriminal populations. *Journal of Personality Assessment, 66,* 488–524.

Lim, J., & Butcher, J. N. (1996). Detection of faking on the MMPI-2: Differentiating among faking-bad, denial, and claiming extreme virtue. *Journal of Personality Assessment, 67,* 1–25.

Locke, D. E. C., Kirlin, K. A., Thomas, M. L., Osborne, D., Hurst, D. F., Drazkowsi, J. F., et al. (2010). The Minnesota Multiphasic Personality Inventory–Restructured Form in the epilepsy monitoring unit. *Epilepsy and Behavior, 17,* 252–258.

Loevinger, J. (1957). Objective tests as instruments of psychological theory. *Psychological Reports, 3,* 635–694.

Loevinger, J. (1972). Some limitations of objective personality tests. In J. N. Butcher (Ed.), *Objective personality assessment: Changing perspectives* (pp. 45–58). Oxford, England: Academic Press.

Lord, F. M., & Novick, M. R. (1968). *Statistical theories of mental test scores.* Reading, MA: Addison-Wesley.

Lubin, B., Wallis, R. R., & Paine, C. (1971). Patterns of psychological test usage in the United States: 1935–1969. *Professional Psychology, 2,* 70–74.

Lukoff, D., Nuechterlein, K., & Ventura, J. (1986). Manual for the Expanded Brief Psychiatric Rating Scale. *Schizophrenia Bulletin, 12,* 578–602.

Lykken, D. T. (1957). A study of anxiety in the sociopathic personality. *Journal of Abnormal and Social Psychology, 55,* 6–10.

Lykken, D. T. (1995). *The antisocial personalities.* Hillsdale, NJ: Lawrence Erlbaum Associates.

Lykken, D. T. (2006). Psychopathic personality: The scope of the problem. In C. J. Patrick (Ed.), *Handbook of psychopathy* (pp. 3–13). New York: Guilford Press.

Lynum, L. I., Wilberg, T., & Karterud, S. (2008). Self-esteem in patients with Borderline and Avoidant Personality disorders. *Scandinavian Journal of Psychology, 49,* 469–77.

MacAndrew, C. (1965). The differentiation of male alcoholic out-patients from nonalcoholic psychiatric patients by means of the MMPI. *Quarterly Journal of the Studies on Alcohol, 26,* 238–246.

MacCorquodale, K., & Meehl, P. E. (1948). On a distinction between hypothetical constructs and intervening variables. *Psychological Review, 55,* 95–107.

Maher, B. A. (1974). Delusional thinking and perceptual disorder. *Journal of Individual Psychology, 30,* 98–113.

Maller, J. B. (1932). *Character sketches.* New York: Teachers College, Columbia University.

Mangelli, L., Fava, G. A., Grandi, S., Grassi, L., Ottolini, F., & Porcelli, P. (2005). Assessing demoralization and depression in the setting of medical disease. *Journal of Clinical Psychiatry, 66,* 391–394.

Manschreck, T. C. (1979). The assessment of paranoid features. *Comprehensive Psychiatry, 20,* 370–377.

Marion, B. E., Sellbom, M., & Bagby, R. M. (2011). The detection of feigned psychiatric disorders using the MMPI-2-RF overreporting Validity Scales: An analog investigation. *Psychological Injury and Law, 4,* 1–12.

Markey, M. A., & Vander Wal, J. S. (2007). The role of emotional intelligence and negative affect in bulimic symptomatology. *Comprehensive Psychiatry, 48,* 458–464.

Markon, K. E., Krueger, R. F., & Watson, D. (2005). Delineating the structure of normal and abnormal personality: An integrative hierarchical approach. *Journal of Personality and Social Psychology, 88,* 139–157.

Marks, P. A., & Seeman, W. (1963). *The actuarial description of abnormal personality: An atlas for use with the MMPI.* Baltimore: Williams & Wilkins.

Marshall, G. N., Miles, J. N. V., & Stewart, S. H. (2010). Anxiety sensitivity and PTSD symptom severity are reciprocally related: Evidence from a longitudinal study of physical trauma survivors. *Journal of Abnormal Psychology, 119,* 143–150.

Maslach, C., & Goldberg, J. (1998). Prevention of burnout: New perspectives. *Applied and Preventive Psychology, 7,* 63–74.

Maslach, C., & Jackson, S. E. (1981). The measurement of experienced burnout. *Journal of Occupational Behavior, 2,* 99–113.

Maslach, C., Schaufeli, W. B., & Leiter, M. P. (2001). Job burnout. *Annual Review of Psychology, 52,* 397–422.

Mathews, K. A., Glass, D. C., Rosenman, R. H., & Bortner, R. W. (1977). Competitive drive, pattern a, and coronary heart disease: A further analysis of some data from the Western Collaborative Group Study. *Journal of Chronic Disease, 30,* 489–498.

McCord, D. M., & Drerup, L. C. (2011). Relative practical utility of the Minnesota Multiphasic Personality Inventory–2 Restructured Clinical Scales versus the Clinical Scales in a chronic pain patient sample. *Journal of Clinical and Experimental Neuropsychology, 33,* 140–146.

McDevitt-Murphy, M. E., Weathers, F. W., Flood, A. M., Eakin, D. E., & Benson, T. A. (2007). The utility of the PAI and the MMPI-2 for discriminating PTSD, depression, and social phobia in trauma-exposed college students. *Assessment, 14,* 181–195.

McKay, R., Langdon, R., & Coltheart, M. (2006). The Persecutory Ideation Questionnaire. *Journal of Nervous and Mental Disease, 194,* 628–631.

McKenna, T., & Butcher, J. N. (1987). *Continuity of the MMPI with alcoholics.* Paper presented at the 22nd annual symposium on Recent Developments in the Use of the MMPI, Seattle, WA.

McKinley, J. C., & Hathaway, S. R. (1940). A multiphasic personality schedule (Minnesota): II. A differential study of hypochondriasis. *Journal of Psychology, 10,* 255–268.

McKinley, J. C., & Hathaway, S. R. (1942). A multiphasic personality schedule (Minnesota): IV. Psychasthenia. *Journal of Applied Psychology, 26,* 614–624.

McKinley, J. C., & Hathaway, R. (1943). The identification and measurement of the psychoneuroses in medical practice. *Journal of the American Medical Association, 122,* 161–167.

McKinley, J. C., & Hathaway, S. R. (1944). A multiphasic personality schedule (Minnesota): V. Hysteria, hypomania, and psychopathic deviate. *Journal of Applied Psychology, 28,* 153–174.

McKinley, J. C., Hathaway, S. R., & Meehl, P. E. (1948). The MMPI: VI. The K scale. *Journal of Consulting Psychology, 12,* 20–31.

McLean, C., & Anderson, E. R. (2009). Brave men and timid women? A review of the gender differences in fear and anxiety. *Clinical Psychology Review, 29,* 496–505.

McLellan, A. T., Luborsky, L., O'Brien, C. P., & Woody, G. E. (1980). An improved diagnostic instrument for substance abuse patients, the Addiction Severity Index. *Journal of Nervous and Mental Diseases, 168,* 26–33.

McMillan, D., Gilbody, S., Beresford, E., & Neilly, L. (2007). Can we predict suicide and nonfatal self-harm with the Beck Hopelessness Scale? A meta-analysis. *Psychological Medicine, 37,* 769–778.

McNeil, D. E., Binder, R. L., & Greenfield, T. K. (1988). Predictors of violence in civilly committed acute psychiatric patients. *American Journal of Psychiatry, 145,* 965–970.

McNulty, J. L., Ben Porath, Y. S., & Graham, J. R. (1998). An empirical examination of the correlates of well-defined and not defined MMPI-2 code types. *Journal of Personality Assessment, 71,* 393–410.

Meehl, P. E. (1945a). The dynamics of "structured" personality tests. *Journal of Clinical Psychology, 1,* 296–303.

Meehl, P. E. (1945b). An investigation of a general normality or control factor in personality testing. *Psychological Monographs, 59*(4; Whole no. 274).

Meehl, P. E. (1946). Profile analysis of the MMPI in differential diagnosis. *Journal of Applied Psychology, 30,* 517–524.

Meehl, P. E. (1954). *Clinical versus statistical prediction: A theoretical analysis and a review of the evidence.* Minneapolis: University of Minnesota Press.

Meehl, P. E. (1956). Wanted—a good cookbook. *American Psychologist, 11,* 263–272.

Meehl, P. E. (1962). Schizotaxia, Schizotypy, Schizophrenia. *American Psychologist, 17,* 827–838.

Meehl, P. E. (1972). Reactions, reflections, projections. In J. N. Butcher (Ed.), *Objective personality assessment: Changing perspectives* (pp. 131–189). Oxford, England: Academic Press.

Meehl, P. E. (1975). Hedonic capacity: Some conjectures. *Bulletin of the Menninger Clinic, 39*, 295–307.

Meehl, P. E. (1978). Theoretical risks and tabular asterisks: Sir Karl, Sir Ronald, and the slow progress of soft psychology. *Journal of Consulting and Clinical Psychology, 46*, 806–834.

Meehl, P. E. (1987). "Hedonic capacity" ten years later: Some clarifications. In D. C. Clark & J. Fawcett (Eds.), *Anhedonia and affect deficit states* (pp. 47–50). New York: PMA.

Meehl, P. E. (2001). Primary and secondary hypohedonia. *Journal of Abnormal Psychology, 110*, 188–193.

Meehl, P. E., & Dahlstrom, W. G. (1960). Objective configural rules for discriminating psychotic from neurotic MMPI profiles. *Journal of Consulting Psychology, 24*, 375–387.

Meehl, P. E., & Hathaway, S. R. (1946). The K factor as a suppressor variable in the MPI. *Journal of Applied Psychology, 30*, 525–564.

Mendonca-de-Souza, A. C. F., Souza, G. G. L., Vieira, A., Fischer, N., Souza, W. F., Rumjanek, V. M., et al. (2007). Negative affect as a predisposing factor for cortisol release after an acute stress—the impact of unpleasant priming. *Stress: The International Journal on the Biology of Stress, 10*, 362–367.

Meyer, T. D., & Hautzinger, M. (2003). Screening for Bipolar Disorders using the Hypomanic Personality Scale. *Journal of Affective Disorders, 75*, 149–154.

Meyer, T. D., & Hoffman, B. U. (2005). Assessing the dysregulation of the behavioral activation system: The hypomanic personality scale and the BIS-BAS scales. *Journal of Personality Assessment, 85*, 318–324.

Michaelis, B. H., Goldberg, J. F., Davis, G. P., Singer, T. M., Garno, J. L., & Wenze, S. J. (2004). Dimensions of impulsivity and aggression associated with suicide attempts among bipolar patients: A preliminary study. *Suicide and Life-Threatening Behavior, 34*, 172–186.

Miller, M. W., Fogler, J. M., Wolf, E. J., Kaloupek, D. G., & Keane, T. M. (2008). The internalizing and externalizing structure of psychiatric comorbidity in combat veterans. *Journal of Traumatic Stress, 21*, 58–65.

Miller, M. W., Greif, J. L., & Smith, A. A. (2003). Multidimensional Personality Questionnaire profiles of veterans with traumatic combat exposure: Externalizing and internalizing subtypes. *Psychological Assessment, 15*, 205–215.

Miller, M. W., Kaloupek, D. G., Dillon, A. L., & Keane, T. M. (2004). Externalizing and internalizing subtypes of combat-related PTSD: A replication and extension using the PSY-5 scales. *Journal of Abnormal Psychology, 113*, 636–645.

Miller, M. W., Vogt, D. S., Mozley, S. L., Kaloupek, D. G., & Keane, T. M. (2006). PTSD and substance-related problems: The mediating roles of disconstraint and negative emotionality. *Abnormal Psychology, 115*, 369–379.

Miller, M. W., Wolf, E. J., Harrington, K. M., Brown, T. A., Kaloupek, D. G., & Keane, T. M. (2010). An evaluation of competing models for the structure of PTSD symptoms using external measures of comorbidity. *Journal of Traumatic Stress, 23*, 631–638.

Millon, T. (1981). *Disorders of personality.* Hoboken, NJ: John Wiley.

Mineka, S., Watson, D., & Clark, L. A. (1998). Comorbidity of anxiety and unipolar mood disorders. *Annual Review of Psychology, 49*, 377–412.

Miranda, R., Fontes, M., & Marroquin, B. (2008). Cognitive content-specificity in future expectancies: Role of hopelessness and intolerance of uncertainty in depression and GAD symptoms. *Behaviour Research and Therapy, 46*, 1151–1159.

Monnot, M. J., Quirk, S. W., Hoerger, M., & Brewer, L. (2009). Racial bias in personality assessment: Using the MMPI-2 to predict psychiatric diagnoses of African American and Caucasian chemical dependency patients. *Psychological Assessment, 21*, 137–151.

Moran, P. (1999). The epidemiology of Antisocial Personality Disorder. *Social Psychiatry and Psychiatric Epidemiology, 34*, 231–242.

Morey, L. C. (1991). *Personality Assessment Inventory professional manual.* Odessa, FL: Psychological Assessment Resources.

Morey, L. C. (2007). *Personality Assessment Inventory professional manual* (2nd ed.). Odessa, FL: Psychological Assessment Resources.

Morey, L. C., Warner, M. B., & Hopwood, C. J. (2007). *The Personality Assessment Inventory*. In A. Goldstein (Ed.), *Forensic psychology: Advanced Topics for forensic mental experts and attorneys* (pp. 97–126). Hoboken, NJ: John Wiley.

Myrtek, M. (2007). Type A behavior and hostility as independent risk factors for coronary heart disease. In J. Jordan, B. Barde, & A. M. Zeiher (Eds.), *Contributions toward evidence-based psychocardiology: A systematic review of the literature* (pp. 159–183). Washington, DC: American Psychological Association.

Najt, P., Perez, J., Sanches, M., Peluso, M. A. M., Glahn, D., & Soares, J. C. (2007). Impulsivity and Bipolar Disorder. *European Neuropsychopharmacology, 17,* 313–320.

Neiss, M. B., Stevenson, J., Legrand, L. N., Iacono, W. G., & Sedikides, C. (2009). Self-esteem, negative emotionality, and depression as a common temperamental core: A study of mid-adolescent twin girls. *Journal of Personality, 77,* 327–346.

Nelson, N., Hoelzle, J., Sweet, J., Arbisi, P., & Demakis, G. (2010). Updated meta-analysis of the MMPI-2 Symptom Validity Scale (FBS): Verified utility in forensic practice. *Clinical Neuropsychologist, 24,* 701–724.

Nelson, N. W., Sweet, J. J., & Demakis, G. J. (2006). Meta-analysis of the MMPI-2 Fake Bad Scale: Utility in forensic practice. *Clinical Neuropsychologist, 20,* 39–58.

Nelson, N. W., Sweet, J. J., & Heilbronner, R. L. (2007). Examination of the new MMPI-2 Response Bias Scale (Gervais): Relationship with MMPI-2 Validity Scales. *Journal of Clinical and Experimental Neuropsychology, 29,* 67–72.

Nichols, D. S. (2006). The trials of separating bath water from baby: A review and critique of the MMPI-2 Restructured Clinical Scales. *Journal of Personality Assessment, 87,* 121–138.

Niederhoffer, A. (1967). *Behind the shield: The police in urban society.* New York: Doubleday.

Nierenberg, A. A., Ghaemi, S. N., Clancy-Colecchi, K., Rosenbaum, J. F., & Maurizio, F. (1996). Cynicism, hostility, and suicidal ideation in depressed outpatients. *Journal of Nervous and Mental Disease, 184,* 607–610.

Norman, W. (1972). Psychometric considerations for a revision of the MMPI. In J. N. Butcher (Ed.), *Objective personality assessment: Changing perspectives* (pp. 59–83). New York: Academic Press.

Novaco, R. W. (1994). *Novaco Anger Scale and Provocation Inventory (NAS-PI).* Los Angeles, CA: Western Psychological Services.

Novaco, R. W., & Taylor, J. L. (2004). Assessment of anger and aggression among male offenders with developmental disabilities. *Psychological Assessment, 16,* 42–50.

Nunnally, J. C. (1967). *Psychometric theory.* New York: McGraw-Hill.

O'Connor, B. P. (2002). The search for dimensional structure differences between normality and abnormality: A statistical review of published data on personality and psychopathology. *Journal of Personality and Social Psychology, 83,* 962–982.

Orth, U., Robins, R. W., Trzesniewski, K. H., Maes, J., & Schmitt, M. (2009). Low self-esteem is a risk factor for depressive symptoms from young adulthood to old age. *Journal of Abnormal Psychology, 118,* 472–478.

Osberg, T. M., Haseley, E. N., & Kamas, M. M. (2008). The MMPI-2 Clinical Scales and Restructured Clinical (RC) Scales: Comparative psychometric properties and relative diagnostic efficiency in young adults. *Journal of Personality Assessment, 90,* 81–92.

Osberg, T. M., & Poland, D. L. (2002). Comparative accuracy of the MMPI-2 and the MMPI-A in the diagnosis of psychopathology in 18-year-olds. *Psychological Assessment, 14,* 164–169.

Papakostas, G. I., Crawford, C. M., Scalia, M. J., & Fava, M. (2007). Timing of clinical improvement and symptom resolution in the treatment of Major Depressive Disorder: A replication of findings with the use of a double-blind, placebo-controlled trial of *Hypericum perforatum* versus fluoxetine. *Neuropsychobiology, 56,* 132–137.

Pardis, A. D., Reinherz, H. Z., Giaconia, R. M., Beardslee, W. R., Ward, K. E., & Fitzmaurice, G. M. (2009). The long-term impact of family arguments and physical violence on adult functioning at age 30. *Journal of the American Academy of Child and Adolescent Psychiatry, 48,* 291–299.

Parwatikar, S. D., Holcomb, W. R., & Menninger, K. A. (1985). The detection of malingered amnesia in accused murderers. *Bulletin of the American Academy of Psychiatry and the Law, 13,* 97–103.

Patrick, C. J. (2007). Affective processes in psychopathy. In J. Rottenberg & S. L. Johnson (Eds.), *Emotion and psychopathology: Bridging affective and clinical science* (pp. 215–239). Washington, DC: American Psychological Association.

Patrick, C. J., Curtin, J. J., & Tellegen, A. (2002). "Development and validation of a brief form of the Multidimensional Personality Questionnaire": Correction to Patrick et al. (2002). *Psychological Assessment, 14,* 262.

Patrick, C. J., Fowles, D. C., & Krueger, R. F. (2009). Triarchic conceptualization of psychopathy: Development origins of disinhibition, boldness, and meanness. *Development and Psychopathology, 21,* 913–938.

Paulhus, D. L. (1984). Two-component models of socially desirable responding. *Journal of Personality and Social Psychology, 46,* 598–609.

Pearson, K., & Filon, L. (1898). Mathematical contributions to the theory of evolution, iv. On the probable errors of frequency constants and on the influence of random selection on variation and correlation. *Philosophical Transactions, Series A, 191,* 229–311.

Pedersen, S. S., Denollet, J., Erdman, R. A. M., Serruys, P. W., & van Domburg, R. T. (2009). Co-occurrence of diabetes and hopelessness predicts adverse prognosis following percutaneous coronary intervention. *Journal of Behavioral Medicine, 32,* 294–301.

Perkins, P. S., Klump, K. L., Iacono, W. G., & McGue, M. (2005). Personality traits in women with anorexia nervosa: Evidence for a treatment-seeking bias? *International Journal of Eating Disorders, 37,* 32–37.

Peterson, C. D., & Dahlstrom, W. G. (1992). The derivation of gender-role scales GM and GF for MMPI-2 and their relationship to Scale 5 (Mf). *Journal of Personality Assessment, 59,* 486–499.

Petroskey, L., Ben-Porath, Y. S., & Stafford, K. P. (2003). Correlates of the Minnesota Multiphasic Personality Inventory–2 (MMPI-2) Personality Psychopathology Five (PSY-5) scales in a forensic assessment setting. *Assessment, 10,* 393–399.

Pilowsky, D. J., Wickramartine, P., Nomura, Y., & Weissman, M. M. (2006). Family discord, parental depression, and psychopathology in offspring: 20-year follow-up. *Journal of the American Academy of Child and Adolescent Psychiatry, 45,* 452–460.

Pollack, D. R., & Grainey, T. F. (1984). A comparison of MMPI profiles for state and private disability insurance applicants. *Journal of Personality Assessment, 48,* 121–125.

Poole, E. D., & Regoli, R. M. (1979). Police professionalism and cynicism. *Criminal Justice and Behavior, 6,* 201–206.

Pope, K. S., Butcher, J. N., & Seelen, J. (1993). *MMPI, MMPI-2, & MMPI-A in court: A practical guide for expert witnesses and attorneys.* Washington, DC: American Psychological Association.

Posternak, M. A., & Zimmerman, M. (2002). Anger and aggression in psychiatric outpatients. *Journal of Clinical Psychiatry, 63,* 665–672.

Priebe, S., Fakhoury, W. K., & Henningsen, P. (2008). Functional incapacity and physical and psychological symptoms: How they interconnect in chronic fatigue syndrome. *Psychopathology, 41,* 339–345.

Rado, S. (1956). *Psychoanalysis of behavior; collected papers.* Oxford, England: Grune & Stratton.

Rafanelli, C., Roncuzzi, R., Milaneschi, Y., Tomba, E., Colistro, M. C., Pancaldi, L. G., et al. (2005). Stressful life events, depression and demoralization as risk factors for acute coronary heart disease. *Psychotherapy and Psychosomatics, 74,* 179–184.

Rafky, D. M., Lawley, T., & Ingram, R. (1976). Are police recruits cynical? *Journal of Police Science and Administration, 4,* 352–360.

Regoli, B., Crank, J. P., & Rivera, G. F. (1990). The construction and implementation of an alternative measure of police cynicism. *Criminal Justice and Behavior, 17,* 395–409.

Regoli, R. (1977). *Police in America.* Washington, DC: University Press of America.

Reid, R. C., & Carpenter, N. (2009). Exploring relationships of psychopathology in hypersexual patients using the MMPI-2. *Journal of Sex and Marital Therapy, 35,* 294–310.

Reiss, S., & McNally, R. (1985). Expectancy model of fear. In S. Reiss & R. R. Bootzin (Eds.), *Theoretical issues in behavior therapy* (pp. 107–121). New York: Academic Press.

Restifo, K., Harkavy-Friedman, J. M., & Shrout, P. E. (2009). Suicidal behavior in Schizophrenia: A test of the demoralization hypothesis. *Journal of Nervous and Mental Disease, 197,* 147–153.

Richardsen, A. M., Burke, R. J., & Martinussen, M. (2006). Work and health outcomes among police officers: The mediating role of police cynicism and engagement. *International Journal of Stress Management, 13,* 555–574.

Rogers, R., Bagby, R. M., & Dickens, S. E. (1992). *Structured Interview of Reported Symptoms professional manual.* Odessa, FL: Psychological Assessment Resources.

Rogers, R., Gillard, N. D., Berry, D. T. R., & Granacher, R. P. (2011). Effectiveness of the MMPI-2-RF Validity Scales for feigned mental disorders and cognitive impairment: A known-groups study. *Journal of Psychopathology and Behavioral Assessment.* Advance online publication. doi:10.1007/s10862-011-9222-0

Rogers, R., Sewell, K. W., Harrison, K. S., & Jordan, M. J. (2006). The MMPI-2 Restructured Clinical Scales: A paradigmatic shift in scale development. *Journal of Personality Assessment, 87,* 139–147.

Rogers, R., Sewell, K. W., Martin, M. A., & Vitacco, M. J. (2003). Detection of feigned mental disorders: A meta-analysis of the MMPI-2 and malingering. *Assessment, 10,* 160–177.

Rome, H. P., Swenson, W. M., Mataya, P., McCarthy, C. E., Pearson, J. S., Keating, F. R., et al. (1962). Symposium on automation techniques in personality assessment. *Proceedings of the Staff Meetings of the Mayo Clinic, 37,* 61–82.

Rosenman, R. H., Brand, R. J., Jenkins, C. D., Friedman, M., Strauss, R., & Wurum, M. (1975). Coronary heart disease in the Western Collaborative Group Study: Final follow-up experience of 8 1/2 years. *Journal of the American Medical Association, 233,* 872–877.

Rosenman, R. H., Friedman, M., Strauss, R., Wurm, M., Kositchek, R., Hahn, W., et al. (1964). A predictive study of coronary heart disease. *Journal of the American Medical Association, 189,* 15–22.

Rouse, S. V. (2007). Using reliability generalization methods to explore measurement error: An illustration using the MMPI-2 PSY-5 scales. *Journal of Personality Assessment, 88,* 264–275.

Rouse, S. V., Butcher, J. N., & Miller, K. B. (1999). Assessment of substance abuse in psychotherapy clients: The effectiveness of the MMPI-2 substance abuse scales. *Psychological Assessment, 11,* 101–107.

Rouse, S. V., Finger, M. S., & Butcher, J. N. (1999). Advances in clinical personality measurement: An item response theory analysis of the MMPI-2 PSY-5 scales. *Journal of Personality Assessment, 72,* 282–307.

Ruch, F. L. (1942). A technique for detecting attempts to fake performance on the self-inventory type of personality test. In Q. McNemar & M. A. Merrill (Eds.), *Studies in personality* (pp. 229–234). New York: McGraw-Hill.

Ruiz, M. A., & Edens, J. F. (2008). Recovery and replication of internalizing and externalizing dimensions within the Personality Assessment Inventory. *Journal of Personality Assessment, 90,* 585–592.

Sacks, S., Cleland, C. M., Melnick, G., Flynn, P. M., Knight, K., Friedmann, P. D., et al. (2009). Violence associated with co-occurring substance use and mental health problems: Evidence from CJDATS. *Behavioral Sciences and the Law, 27,* 51–69.

Sammut, S., Bethus, I., Goodall, G., & Muscat, R. (2002). Antidepressant reversal of interferon-a–induced anhedonia. *Physiology and Behavior, 75,* 765–772.

Santor, D. A., & Coyne, J. C. (2001). Evaluating the continuity of symptomatology between depressed and nondepressed individuals. *Journal of Abnormal Psychology, 110,* 216–225.

Sawrie, S. M., Kabat, M. H., Dietz, C. B., Greene, R. L., Arrendondo, R., & Mann, A. W. (1996). Internal structure of the MMPI-2 Addiction Potential Scale in alcoholic and psychiatric inpatients. *Journal of Personality Assessment, 66,* 177–193.

Scarpa, A., & Raine, A. (1997). Psychophysiology of anger and violent behavior. *Psychiatric Clinics of North America, 20,* 375–394.

Schinka, J. A., & Borum, R. (1993). Readability of adult psychopathology inventories. *Psychological Assessment, 5,* 384–386.

Schinka, J. A., & Lalone, L. (1997). MMPI-2 norms: Comparisons with a census-matched subsample. *Psychological Assessment, 9,* 307–311.

Schlaepfer, T. E., Cohen, M. X., Frick, C., Kosel, M., Brodesser, D., Axmacher, N., et al. (2008). Deep brain stimulation to reward circuitry alleviates anhedonia in refractory major depression. *Neuropsychopharmacology, 33,* 368–377.

Schmidt, H. O. (1945). Test profiles as a diagnostic aid: The Minnesota Multiphasic Inventory. *Journal of Applied Psychology, 29,* 115–131.

Schneider, K. (1959). *Clinical psychopathology* (5th ed.). Oxford, England: Grune & Stratton.

Schretlen, D., & Arkowitz, H. (1990). A psychological test battery to detect prison inmates who fake insanity or mental retardation. *Behavioral Sciences and the Law, 8,* 75–84.

Segarra, P., Ross, S. R., Pastor, M. C., Montanes, S., Poy, R., & Molto, J. (2007). MMPI-2 predictors of Gray's two-factor reinforcement sensitivity theory. *Personality and Individual Differences, 43,* 437–448.

Sellbom, M. (in press). Elaborating on the construct validity of the Levenson Self-Report Psychopathy Scale in incarcerated and non-incarcerated samples. *Law and Human Behavior.*

Sellbom, M., & Bagby, R. M. (2008). Validity of the MMPI-2-RF (Restructured Form) L-r and K-r scales in detecting underreporting in clinical and nonclinical samples. *Psychological Assessment, 20,* 370–376.

Sellbom, M., & Bagby, R. M. (2010). Detection of overreported psychopathology with the MMPI-2 RF form Validity Scales. *Psychological Assessment, 22,* 757–767.

Sellbom, M., & Ben-Porath, Y. S. (2005). Mapping the MMPI-2 Restructured Clinical Scales onto normal personality traits: Evidence of construct validity. *Journal of Personality Assessment, 85,* 179–187.

Sellbom, M., Ben-Porath, Y. S., & Bagby, R. M. (2008a). On the hierarchical structure of mood and anxiety disorders: Confirmatory evidence and elaboration of a model of temperament markers. *Journal of Abnormal Psychology, 117,* 576–590.

Sellbom, M., Ben-Porath, Y. S., & Bagby, R. M. (2008b). Personality and psychopathology: Mapping the MMPI-2 Restructured Clinical (RC) Scales onto the Five Factor Model of personality. *Journal of Personality Disorders, 22,* 291–312.

Sellbom, M., Ben-Porath, Y. S., Baum, L. J., Erez, E., & Gregory, C. (2008). Predictive validity of the MMPI-2 Restructured Clinical (RC) Scales in a batterers' intervention program. *Journal of Personality Assessment, 90,* 129–135.

Sellbom, M., Ben Porath, Y. S., & Graham, J. R. (2006). Correlates of the MMPI-2 Restructured Clinical (RC) Scales in a college counseling setting. *Journal of Personality Assessment, 86,* 89–99.

Sellbom, M., Ben-Porath, Y. S., Lilienfeld, S. O., Patrick, C. J., & Graham, J. R. (2005). Assessing psychopathic personality traits with the MMPI-2. *Journal of Personality Assessment, 85,* 334–343.

Sellbom, M., Ben-Porath, Y. S., & Stafford, K. P. (2007). A comparison of MMPI-2 measures of psychopathic deviance in a forensic setting. *Psychological Assessment, 19,* 430–436.

Sellbom, M., Fischler, G. L., & Ben-Porath, Y. S. (2007). Identifying MMPI-2 predictors of police officer integrity and misconduct. *Criminal Justice and Behavior, 34,* 985–1004.

Sellbom, M., Graham, J. R., & Schenk, P. W. (2006). Incremental validity of the MMPI-2 Restructured Clinical (RC) Scales in a private practice sample. *Journal of Personality Assessment, 86,* 196–205.

Sellbom, M., Toomey, J. A., Wygant, D. B., Kucharski, L. T., & Duncan, S. (2010). Utility of the MMPI-2-RF (Restructured Form) Validity Scales in detecting malingering in a criminal forensic setting: A known-groups design. *Psychological Assessment, 22,* 22–31.

Selzer, M. L. (1971). The Michigan Alcoholism Screening Test: The quest for a new diagnostic instrument. *American Journal of Psychiatry, 127,* 1653–1658.

Shaevel, B., & Archer, R. P. (1996). Effects of MMPI-2 and MMPI-A norms on T-score elevations for 18-year-olds. *Journal of Personality Assessment, 67,* 72–78.

Sharland, M. J., & Gfeller, D. (2007). A survey of neuropsychologists' beliefs and practices with respect to the assessment of effort. *Archives of Clinical Neuropsychology, 22,* 213–223.

Sharpe, J. P., & Desai, S. (2001). The revised NEO Personality Inventory and the MMPI-2 Psychopathology Five in the prediction of aggression. *Personality and Individual Differences, 31,* 505–518.

Simms, L. J., Casillas, A., Clark, L .A., Watson, D., & Doebbeling, B. I. (2005). Psychometric evaluation of the Restructured Clinical Scales of the MMPI-2. *Psychological Assessment, 17,* 345–358.

Simon, R., Goddard, R., & Patton, W. (2002). Hand-scoring error rates in psychological testing. *Assessment, 9,* 292–300.

Singer, M. S. H., Singer, A. E., & Burns, D. (1984). Police cynicism in New Zealand: A comparison between police officers and recruits. *Police Studies, 7,* 77–83.

Skinner, B. F. (1983). *A matter of consequences.* New York: Knopf.

Skinner, H. A., & Jackson, D. N. (1978). A model of psychopathology based on an integration of MMPI actuarial systems. *Journal of Consulting and Clinical Psychology, 46,* 231–238.

Slick, D. J., Sherman, E. M. S., & Iverson, G. L. (1999). Diagnostic criteria for malingered neurocognitive dysfunction: Proposed standards for clinical practice and research. *Clinical Neuropsychologist, 13,* 545–561.

Slutske, W. S., Eisen, S., Xian, H., True, W. R., Lyons, M. J., Goldberg, J., et al. (2001). A twin study of the association between pathological gambling and Antisocial Personality Disorder. *Journal of Abnormal Psychology, 110,* 297–308.

Smart, C. M., Nelson, N. W., Sweet, J. J., Bryant, F. B., Berry, D. T. R., Granacher, R. P., et al. (2008). Use of MMPI-2 to identify cognitive effort: A hierarchically optimal classification tree analysis. *Journal of the International Neuropsychological Society, 14,* 842–852.

Smith, E. E. (1959). Defensiveness, insight, and the K scale. *Journal of Consulting Psychology, 23,* 275–277.

Snibe, J. R., Peterson, P. J., & Sosner, B. (1980). Study of psychological characteristics of a workers compensation sample using the MMPI and Millon Clinical Multiaxial Inventory. *Psychological Reports, 47,* 959–966.

Song, Y. H., Terao, T., & Nakamura, J. (2007). Type A behaviour pattern is associated with cynicism and low self-acceptance in medical students. *Stress and Health: Journal of the International Society for the Investigation of Stress, 23,* 323–329.

Souza, W. F., Figueira, I., Mendlowicz, M. V., Volchan, E., Mendonca-de-Souza, A. C., Duarte, A. F. A., et al. (2008). Negative affect predicts posttraumatic stress symptoms in Brazilian volunteer United Nations peacekeepers in Haiti. *Journal of Nervous and Mental Disease, 196,* 852–855.

Spanier, G. B. (1976). Measuring dyadic adjustment: New scales for assessing the quality of marriage and similar dyads. *Journal of Marriage and the Family, 38,* 15–28.

Spence, J. T., Helmreich, R., & Stapp, J. (1975). Ratings of self and peers on sex role attributes and their relation to self-esteem and conceptions of masculinity and femininity. *Journal of Personality and Social Psychology, 32,* 29–39.

Spielberger, C. D., Jacobs, G., Russell, S., & Crane, R. S. (1983). Assessment of anger: The State–Trait Anger Scale. *Advances in Personality Assessment, 2,* 161–189.

Spitzer, R. L., Endicott, J., & Robins, E. (1978). Research diagnostic criteria: Rationale and reliability. *Archives of General Psychiatry, 35,* 773–782.

Stein, L. A. R., Graham, J. R., Ben-Porath, Y. S., & McNulty, J. L. (1999). Using the MMPI-2 to detect substance abuse in an outpatient mental health setting. *Psychological Assessment, 11,* 94–100.

Stenner, A. J., Horabin, I., Smith, D. R., & Smith, M. (1988, June). Most comprehension tests do measure reading comprehension: A response to McLean and Goldstein. *Phi Delta Kappan,* pp. 765–769.

Stern, S. L., Dhanda, R., & Hazuda, H. P. (2009). Helplessness predicts the development of hypertension in older Mexican and European Americans. *Journal of Psychosomatic Research, 67,* 333–337.

Stones, M. J., Clyburn, L. D., Gibson, M. C., & Woodbury, M. G. (2006). Predicting diagnosed depression and anti-depressant treatment in institutionalized older adults by symptom profiles: A closer look at anhedonia and dysphoria. *Canadian Journal on Aging, 25,* 153–159.

Strada, E. A. (2009). Grief, demoralization, and depression: Diagnostic challenges and treatment modalities. *Primary Psychiatry, 16,* 49–55.

Strong, E. K. (1938). *Manual for vocational interest blank for men.* Palo Alto, CA: Stanford University Press.

Strupp, H. H. (1973). Specific versus nonspecific factors in psychotherapy and the problem of control. In H. H. Strupp (Ed.), *Psychotherapy: Clinical, research, and theoretical issues* (pp. 103–212). Lanham, MD: Jason Aronson.

Stulemeijer, M., Vos, P., Bleijenberg, G., & van der Werf, S. (2007). Cognitive complaints after mild traumatic brain injury: Things are not always what they seem. *Journal of Psychosomatic Research, 63,* 637–645.

Sundberg, N. D. (1961). The practice of psychological testing in clinical services in the United States. *American Psychologist, 16,* 79–83.

Svanum, S., McGrew, J., & Ehrmann, L. (1994). Validity of the substance abuse scales of the MMPI-2 in a college student sample. *Journal of Personality Assessment, 62,* 427–439.

Swanson, S. C., Templer, D. I., Thomas-Dobson, S., Cannon, W. G., Streiner, D. L., Reynolds, R. M., et al. (1995). Development of a three-scale MMPI: The MMPI-TRI. *Journal of Clinical Psychology, 51,* 361–374.

Swenson, W. M., Pearson, J. D., & Osborne, D. (1973). *An MMPI source book: Basic item, scale, and pattern data on 50,000 medical patients.* Minneapolis: University of Minnesota Press.

Taft, C. T., Monson, C. M., Schumm, J. A., Watkins, L., Panuzio, J., & Resick, P. A. (2009). Posttraumatic Stress Disorder symptoms, relationship adjustment, and relationship aggression in a sample of female flood victims. *Journal of Family Violence, 24,* 389–396.

Tandon, R., & Jibson, M. D. (2003). Suicidal behavior in Schizophrenia: Diagnosis, neurobiology, and treatment implications. *Current Opinion in Psychiatry, 16,* 193–197.

Taylor, C. T., Laposa, J. M., & Alden, L. E. (2004). Is Avoidant Personality Disorder more than just social avoidance? *Journal of Personality Disorders, 18,* 573–597.

Tellegen, A. (1982). *Brief manual of the Multidimensional Personality Questionnaire.* Unpublished manuscript.

Tellegen, A. (1985). Structures of mood and personality and their relevance to assessing anxiety, with an emphasis on self-report. In A. H. Tuna & J. D. Maser (Eds.), *Anxiety and the anxiety disorders* (pp. 681–706). Hillsdale, NJ: Lawrence Erlbaum Associates.

Tellegen, A. (1988). The analysis of consistency in personality assessment. *Journal of Personality, 56,* 621–663.

Tellegen, A. (1995/2003). *Multidimensional Personality Questionnaire–276 (MPQ-276) test booklet.* Minneapolis: University of Minnesota Press.

Tellegen, A., & Ben-Porath, Y. S. (1992). The new uniform T-scores for the MMPI-2: Rationale, derivation, and appraisal. *Psychological Assessment, 4,* 145–155.

Tellegen, A., & Ben-Porath, Y. S. (1993). Code-type comparability of the MMPI and MMPI-2: Analysis of recent findings and criticisms. *Journal of Personality Assessment, 61,* 489–500.

Tellegen, A., & Ben-Porath, Y. S. (2005, April). *Restructured MMPI-2 Scales: A progress report on further developments.* Paper presented at the 40th annual symposium on Recent Research with the MMPI-2/MMPI-A, Fort Lauderdale, FL.

Tellegen, A., & Ben-Porath, Y. S. (2008/2011). *MMPI-2-RF (Minnesota Multiphasic Personality Inventory–2 Restructured Form) technical manual.* Minneapolis: University of Minnesota Press.

Tellegen, A., Ben-Porath, Y. S., McNulty, J. L., Arbisi, P. A., Graham, J. R., & Kaemmer, B. (2003). *The MMPI-2 Restructured Clinical Scales: Development, validation, and interpretation.* Minneapolis: University of Minnesota Press.

Tellegen, A., Ben-Porath, Y. S., Sellbom, M., Arbisi, P. A., McNulty, J. L., & Graham, J. R. (2006). Further evidence on the validity of the MMPI-2 Restructured Clinical (RC) Scales: Addressing questions raised by Rogers, Sewell, Harrison, and Jordan and Nichols. *Journal of Personality Assessment, 87,* 148–171.

Tellegen, A., Butcher, J. N., & Hoeglund, T. (1993). *Are unisex norms for the MMPI-2 needed? Would they work?* Paper presented at the 28th annual symposium on Recent Developments in the Use of the MMPI/MMPI-2/MMPI-A, St. Petersburg, FL.

Tellegen, A., Lykken, D. T., Bouchard, T. J., Wilcox, K. J., Segal, N. L., & Rich, S. (1988). Personality similarity in twins reared apart and together. *Journal of Personality and Social Psychology, 54,* 1031–1039.

Tellegen, A., & Waller, N. G. (2008). Exploring personality through test construction: Development of the Multidimensional Personality Questionnaire. In S. R. Briggs & J. M. Cheek (Eds.), *Personality measures: Development and evaluation* (pp. 261–292). Greenwich, CN: JAI Press.

Tellegen, A., Watson, D., & Clark, L. A. (1999a). Further support for a hierarchical model of affect: Reply to Green and Salovey. *Psychological Science, 10,* 307–309.

Tellegen, A., Watson, D., & Clark, L. A. (1999b). On the dimensional and hierarchical structure of affect. *Psychological Science, 10,* 297–303.

Terman, L., & Miles, C. C. (1936). *Sex and personality: Studies in masculinity and femininity.* New York: McGraw-Hill.

Thomas, M. L., & Locke, D. E. C. (2010). Psychometric properties of the MMPI-2-RF Somatic Complaints (RC1) Scale. *Psychological Assessment, 22,* 492–503.

Thomas, M. L., & Youngjohn, J. R. (2010). Let's not get hysterical: Comparing the MMPI-2 Validity, Clinical, and RC Scales in TBI litigants tested for effort. *Clinical Neuropsychologist, 23,* 1067–1084.

Timbrook, R. E., Graham, J. R., Keiller, S. W., & Watts, D. (1993). Comparison of the Wiener–Harmon Subtle–Obvious scales and the standard Validity Scales in detecting valid and invalid MMPI-2 profiles. *Psychological Assessment, 5,* 53–61.

Tolin, D. F., Steenkamp, M. M., Marx, B. P., & Litz, B. T. (2010). Detecting symptom exaggeration in combat veterans using the MMPI-2 symptom Validity Scales: A mixed group validation. *Psychological Assessment, 22,* 729–736.

Tombaugh, T. N. (1997). The Test of Memory Malingering (TOMM): Normative data from cognitively intact and cognitively impaired individuals. *Psychological Assessment, 9,* 260–268.

Trimble, M. (2004). *Somatoform Disorders: A medicolegal guide.* New York: Cambridge University Press.

Trull, T. J., Useda, J. D., Costa, P. T., & McCrae, R. R. (1995). Comparison of the MMPI-2 Personality Psychopathology Five (PSY-5), the NEO-PI, and NEO-PI-R. *Psychological Assessment, 7,* 508–516.

Tuohy, A., & McVey, C. (2008). Subscales measuring symptoms of non-specific depression, anhedonia, and anxiety in the Edinburgh Postnatal Depression Scale. *British Journal of Clinical Psychology, 47,* 153–169.

Tweed, D. L., Shern, D. L., & Ciarlo, J. A. (1988). Disability, dependency, and demoralization. *Rehabilitation Psychology, 33,* 143–154.

Vaidyanathan, U., Patrick, C., & Cuthbert, B. (2009). Linking dimensional models of internalizing psychopathology to neurobiological systems: Affect-modulated startle as an indicator of fear and distress disorders and affiliated traits. *Psychological Bulletin, 135,* 909–942.

Valtonen, H. M., Suominen, K., Haukka, J., Mantere, O., Arvilommi, P., Leppämäki, S., et al. (2009). Hopelessness across phases of Bipolar I or II Disorder: A prospective study. *Journal of Affective Disorders, 115,* 11–17.

Valtonen, H. M., Suominen, K., Haukka, J., Mantere, O., Leppämäki, S., Arvilommi, P., et al. (2008). Differences in incidence of suicide attempts during phases of Bipolar I and II Disorders. *Bipolar Disorders, 10,* 588–596.

Velissaris, S. L., Wilson, S. J., Newton, M. R., Berkovic, S. F., & Saling, M. M. (2009). Cognitive complaints after a first seizure in adulthood: Influence of psychological adjustment. *Epilepsia, 50,* 1012–1021.

Vendrig, A. A. (1999). Prognostic factors and treatment-related changes associated with return to work in the multimodal treatment of chronic back pain. *Journal of Behavioral Medicine, 22,* 217–232.

Vendrig, A. A., Derksen, J. J. L., & de Mey, H. R. (1999). Utility of selected MMPI-2 scales in the outcome prediction for patients with chronic back pain. *Psychological Assessment, 11,* 381–385.

Vendrig, A. A., Derksen, J. J. L., & de Mey, H. R. (2000). MMPI-2 Personality Psychopathology Five (PSY-5) and prediction of treatment outcome for patients with chronic back pain. *Journal of Personality Assessment, 74,* 423–438.

Viding, E., James R., Blair, R., Moffitt, T. E., & Plomin, R. (2005). Evidence for substantial genetic risk for psychopathy in 7-year-olds. *Journal of Child Psychology and Psychiatry, 46,* 592–597.

Viken, R. J., & Rose, R. J. (2007). Genetic variation and covariation in the original and Restructured Clinical Scales of the MMPI. *Journal of Abnormal Psychology, 116,* 842–847.

Waldman, I. D., & Slutske, S. (2000). Antisocial behavior and alcoholism: A behavioral genetic perspective on comorbidity. *Clinical Psychology Review, 20,* 255–287.

Walker, E. F., Bollini, A., Hochman, K., Kestler, L., & Mittal, V. A. (2007). Schizophrenia. In J. E. Maddox & B. A. Winstead (Eds.), *Psychopathology: Foundations for a contemporary understanding* (2nd ed.). New York: Lawrence Erlbaum Associates.

Walters, G. D. (2003). Predicting institutional adjustment and recidivism with the psychopathy checklist factor scores: A meta-analysis. *Law and Human Behavior, 27,* 541–558.

Walters, G. D., & Heilbrun, K. (2009). Violence risk assessment and facet 4 of the psychopathy checklist: Predicting institutional and community aggression in two forensic samples. *Assessment, 17,* 1–10.

Walters, G. D., Knight, R. A., Grann, M., & Dahle, K. (2008). Incremental validity of the Psychopathy Checklist facet scores: Predicting release outcome in six samples. *Journal of Abnormal Psychology, 117,* 396–405.

Walters, G. D., White, T. W., & Greene, R. L. (1988). Use of the MMPI to identify malingering and exaggeration of psychiatric symptomatology in male prison inmates. *Journal of Consulting and Clinical Psychology, 56,* 111–117.

Wasyliw, O. E., Grossman, L. S., Haywood, T. W., & Cavanaugh, J. L. (1988). The detection of malingering in criminal forensic groups: MMPI Validity Scales. *Journal of Personality Assessment, 52,* 321–333.

Watanabe, N., Hasegawa, K., & Yoshinaga, Y. (1995). Suicide in later life in Japan: Urban and rural differences. *International Psychogeriatrics, 7,* 253–261.

Watkins, E., Moulds, M., & Mackintosh, B. (2005). Comparisons between rumination and worry in a non-clinical population. *Behaviour Research and Therapy, 43,* 1577–1585.

Watson, D. (2005). Rethinking the mood and anxiety disorders: A quantitative hierarchical model for *DSM-V*. *Journal of Abnormal Psychology, 114,* 522–536.

Watson, D., & Clark, L. A. (1984). Negative affectivity: The disposition to experience aversive emotional states. *Psychological Bulletin, 96,* 465–490.

Watson, D., Clark, L. A., & Tellegen, A. (1988). Development and validation of brief measures of positive and negative affect: The PANAS scales. *Journal of Personality and Social Psychology, 54,* 1063–1070.

Watson, D., & Tellegen, A. (1985). Toward a consensual structure of mood. *Psychological Bulletin, 98,* 219–235.

Watson, D., Wiese, D., Vaidya, J., & Tellegen, A. (1999). The two general activation systems of affect: Structural findings, evolutionary considerations, and psychobiological evidence. *Journal of Personality and Social Psychology, 76,* 820–838.

Watson, L. C., Quilty, L. C., & Bagby, R. M. (2010). Differentiating Bipolar Disorder from Major Depressive Disorder using the MMPI-2-RF: A receiver operating characteristics (ROC) analysis. *Journal of Psychopathology and Behavioral Assessment, 33,* 368–374.

Webb, J. T., Levitt, E. E., & Rojdev, R. (1993). *After three years: A comparison of the clinical use of the MMPI and MMPI-2.* Paper presented at the 53rd annual meeting of the Society for Personality Assessment, San Francisco, CA.

Wechsler, D. (2008). *Wechsler Adult Intelligence Scale–fourth edition.* San Antonio, TX: Pearson.

Weed, N. C., Ben-Porath, Y. S., & Butcher, J. N. (1990). Failure of the MMPI Wiener and Harmon subtle scales as measures of personality and as validity indicators. *Psychological Assessment: A Journal of Consulting and Clinical Psychology, 2,* 281–285.

Weed, N. C., Butcher, J. N., McKenna, T., & Ben-Porath, Y. S. (1992). New measures for assessing alcohol and drug abuse with the MMPI-2: The APS and AAS. *Journal of Personality Assessment, 58,* 389–404.

Wells, F. L. (1914). The systematic observation of the personality in its relation to the hygiene of mind. *Psychological Review, 21,* 295–333.

Welsh, G. S. (1948). An extension of Hathaway's MMPI profile coding system. *Journal of Consulting Psychology, 12,* 343–344.

Welsh, G. S. (1956). Factor dimensions A and R. In G. S. Welsh & W. G. Dahlstrom (Eds.), *Basic readings on the MMPI in psychology and medicine* (pp. 264–281). Minneapolis: University of Minnesota Press.

Welsh, G. S., & Dahlstrom, W. G. (Eds.). (1956). *Basic readings on the MMPI in psychology and medicine.* Minneapolis: University of Minnesota Press.

Wenzel, A., Brown, G. K., & Beck, A. T. (2009). *Cognitive therapy for suicidal patients: Scientific and clinical applications.* Washington, DC: APA Books.

Whitney, K. A., Davis, J. J., Shepard, P. H., & Herman, S. M. (2008). Utility of the Response Bias Scale (RBS) and other MMPI-2 Validity Scales in predicting TOMM performance. *Archives of Clinical Neuropsychology, 23,* 777–786.

Why, Y. P., & Johnston, D. W. (2008). Cynicism, anger and cardiovascular reactivity during anger recall and human–computer interaction. *International Journal of Psychophysiology, 68,* 219–227.

Widiger, T. A., & Costa, P. T. (2002). Five Factor Model personality disorder research. In P. T. Costa & T. A. Widiger (Eds.), *Personality disorders and the Five Factor Model of personality* (2nd ed., pp. 59–87). Washington, DC: American Psychological Association.

Wiener, D. N. (1948). Subtle and obvious keys for the MMPI. *Journal of Consulting Psychology, 12,* 164–170.

Wiener, D. N. (1952). Personality characteristics of selected disability groups. *Genetic Psychology Monographs, 45,* 175–255.

Wiener, D. N., & Harmon, L. R. (1946). Subtle and obvious keys for the MMPI: Their development. *VA Advisement Bulletin, 16.*

Wiggins, J. S. (1959). Interrelationships among MMPI measures of dissimulation under standard and social desirability instructions. *Journal of Consulting Psychology, 23,* 419–427.

Wiggins, J. S. (1966). Substantive dimensions of self-report in the MMPI item pool. *Psychological Monographs, 80.*

Wiggins, J. S. (1968). Personality structure. *Annual Review of Psychology, 19,* 293–350.

Wiggins, J. S. (1990). Foreword. In J. N. Butcher, J. R. Graham, C. L. Williams, & Y. S. Ben-Porath (Eds.), *Development and use of the MMPI-2 Content Scales* (pp. vii–ix). Minneapolis: University of Minnesota Press.

Williams, C. B., Galanter, M., Dermatis, H., & Schwartz, V. (2008). The importance of hopelessness among university students seeking psychiatric counseling. *Psychiatric Quarterly, 79,* 311–319.

Williams, H. L. (1952). The development of a caudality scale for the MMPI. *Journal of Clinical Psychology, 8,* 293–297.

Williams, J. E., & Weed, N. C. (2004). Review of computer-based test interpretation software for the MMPI-2. *Journal of Personality Assessment, 83,* 78–83.

Williams, R. B., Jr., Haney, T. L., Lee, K. L., Hong-Kong, Y., Blumenthal, J. A., & Whalen, R. E. (1980). Type A behavior, hostility, and coronary atherosclerosis. *Psychosomatic Medicine, 42,* 539–549.

Wilt, G. M., & Bannon, D. (1976). Cynicism or realism: A critique of Niederhoffer's research into police attitudes. *Journal of Police Science and Administration, 4,* 38–45.

Wingate, L., Joiner, T., Walker, R., Rudd, M. D., & Jobes, D. (2004). Empirically informed approaches to topics in suicide risk assessment. *Behavioral Sciences and the Law, 22,* 1–15.

Wittenborn, J. R. (1951). Symptom patterns in a group of mental hospital patients. *Journal of Consulting Psychology, 15,* 290–302.

Wolf, E. J., Miller, M. W., Orazem, R. J., Weierich, M. R., Castillo, D. T., Milford, J., et al. (2008). The MMPI-2 Restructured Clinical Scales in the assessment of Posttraumatic Stress Disorder and comorbid disorders. *Psychological Assessment, 20,* 327–340.

Woodworth, R. S. (1920). *Personal data sheet.* Chicago: Stoelting.

World Health Organization (1992). *The ICD–10 classification of mental and behavioural disorders: Clinical descriptions and diagnostic guidelines.* Geneva, Switzerland: World Health Organization.

Wu, C. (2009). Factor analysis of the general self-efficacy scale and its relationship with individualism/collectivism among twenty-five countries: Application of multilevel confirmatory factor analysis. *Personality and Individual Differences, 46,* 699–703.

Wygant, D. B., Anderson, J. L., Sellbom, M., Rapier, J. L., Algeier, L. M., & Granacher, R. P. (2011). Association of MMPI-2 Restructured Form (MMPI-2-RF) Validity Scales with structured malingering criteria. *Psychological Injury and Law, 4,* 13–23.

Wygant, D. B., Ben-Porath, Y. S., & Arbisi, P. A. (2004). *Development and initial validation of a scale to detect infrequent somatic complaints.* Poster presented at the 39th annual symposium on Recent Developments of the MMPI-2/MMPI-A, Minneapolis, MN.

Wygant, D. B., Ben-Porath, Y. S., Arbisi, P. A., Berry, D. T. R., Freeman, D. B., & Heilbronner, R. L. (2009). Examination of the MMPI-2 Restructured Form (MMPI-2-RF) Validity Scales in civil forensic settings: Findings from simulation and known group samples. *Archives of Clinical Neuropsychology, 27,* 671–680.

Wygant, D. B., Boutacoff, L. I., Arbisi, P. A., Ben-Porath, Y. S., Kelly, P. H., & Rupp, W. M. (2007). Examination of the MMPI-2 Restructured Clinical (RC) Scales in a sample of bariatric surgery candidates. *Journal of Clinical Psychology in Medical Settings, 14,* 197–205.

Wygant, D. B., Sellbom, M., Ben-Porath, Y. S., Stafford, K. P., Freeman, D. B., & Heilbronner, R. I. (2007). The relation between symptom validity testing and MMPI-2 scores as a function of forensic evaluation context. *Archives of Clinical Neuropsychology, 22,* 488–499.

Wygant, D. B., Sellbom, M., Gervais, R. O., Ben-Porath, Y. S., Stafford, K. P., Freeman, D. B., et al. (2010). Further validation of the MMPI-2 and MMPI-2-RF response bias scale: Findings from disability and criminal forensic settings. *Psychological Assessment, 22,* 745–756.

Wygant, D. B., Sellbom, M., Graham, J. R., & Schenk, P. W. (2006). Incremental validity of the MMPI- 2 Personality Psychopathology Five (PSY-5) Scales in assessing self-reported personality disorder criteria. *Assessment, 13,* 178–186.

Ying, Y., & Akutsu, D. (1997). Psychological adjustment of Southeast Asian refugees: The contribution of sense of coherence. *Journal of Community Psychology, 25,* 125–139.

Youngjohn, J. R., Wershba, R., Stevenson, M., Sturgeon, J., & Thomas, M. L. (2011). Independent validation of the MMPI-2-RF somatic/cognitive and Validity Scales in TBI litigants tested for effort. *Clinical Neuropsychologist, 25,* 463–476.

Index of Subjects

A (A). *See* Anxiety (AXY) Scale

AAS. *See* Addiction Acknowledgment (AAS) Scale

Aberrant Experiences (RC8) Scale, 65, 102, 103, 105, 167, 204, 205, 352; conceptualizing, 84–86; described, 289–290; empirical findings with, 86–87; interpretation of, 290, 290 (table); scores, 87, 289

Abnormality, 34, 97, 100, 401

Absorption Scale, 87

Abusive relationships, 378–379, 389–390

ACM. *See* Cook–Medley Ho Scale

Acquiescence, 14, 135, 259

Activation (ACT) Scale, 118, 119, 120, 203, 205, 232, 292, 302, 304, 352, 379, 390, 401, 469; described, 307; interpretation of, 307, 308 (table); T score on, 470

Addiction Acknowledgment Scale (AAS), 26, 27, 118

Addiction Potential Scale (APS), 26, 27

Addiction Research Center Inventory, 151

Addiction Severity Index (ASI), 117

Additional Validity Indicators (Butcher, Dahlstrom, Graham, Tellegen, and Kaemmer), 148

ADHD. *See* Attention-Deficit Hyperactivity Disorder (ADHD)

Adjustment Scale (Katz and Lyerly), 21

Adjustment Validity (K-r) Scale, 192, 214, 259, 271–272, 274, 277, 341, 352, 470, 481n2; described, 165, 252; interpretation of, 253 (table); K and, 166; scores, 171, 173, 272, 273; underreporting and, 165

Administration: modalities, 175, 179, 180; standard, 179, 180–181

Aesthetic–Literary Interests (AES), Scale, 123–124, 214, 341, 352; described, 313; interpretation of, 312 (table), 313; MEC and, 125; scores, 125, 313

AGG. *See* Aggression (AGG) Scale

Aggression, 81, 100, 105, 352; instrumental, 314; interpersonal, 118, 389–390; physical, 118, 119, 130, 378, 379; verbal, 130; violence and, 114

Aggression (AGG) Scale, 118, 119–120, 203, 204, 205, 292, 302, 304, 339, 352, 390; described, 305; interpretation of, 305, 306 (table)

Aggressiveness–Revised (AGGR-r) Scale, 129, 203, 304, 339, 352, 378, 469; described, 314; interpretation, 314, 315 (table); scores, 130, 214, 314

AGGR-r. *See* Aggressiveness–Revised (AGGR-r) Scale

Agoraphobia, 62, 81, 114, 117, 302, 377

Alcohol abuse, 74, 100, 130, 379, 389, 390, 391, 413, 447, 459

Alienation, 69, 70, 72, 78

American Psychiatric Association (APA), 110, 136, 232

Anger, 42, 104, 288, 389; disorders, 411; excessive, 364; expressions of, 302; low, 74; management, 400, 412

Anger Proneness (ANP) Scale, 114, 115, 288, 297, 411, 481n2; described, 302; interpretation of, 302, 303 (table); scores, 117, 302

Anhedonia, 49, 53, 65, 84, 284, 292, 328, 340, 402, 411, 422, 423, 425, 457, 458; clinical, 61; depression and, 54, 64; empirical literature on, 64; Hypohedonia and, 61–62; Major Depression and, 63; physical/social, 63; PTSD and, 64; Schizophrenia and, 63, 64

Annotation of interpretive report, 232–233

ANP. *See* Anger Proneness (ANP) Scale

Antidepressant medications, 62, 63, 64, 65, 104, 112, 131, 411, 412, 413, 422

Antipsychotic medications, 86, 105, 354, 377

Antisocial behavior, 42, 49, 75, 96, 100, 107, 119, 120, 129, 286, 379, 390; alternative path model and, 73; conceptualizing, 70–72; empirical findings on, 72–73; four-factor model and, 72; preinjury, 157; psychopathy and, 72

Antisocial Behavior (RC4) Scale, 70–75, 96, 102, 103, 107, 117, 120, 282, 302, 304, 390; described, 286–287; empirical findings with, 73–75; interpretation of, 287, 287 (table); item pool, 71; scores, 74–75, 286, 287; substance abuse and, 75

Antisocial Personality Disorder (ASPD) Scale, 73, 75, 105, 106, 117, 119, 389, 401; criteria for, 70–71

Anxiety, 40, 42, 48, 55, 62, 83, 99, 100, 104, 105, 123, 288, 299, 400, 402, 413, 422, 434, 436, 457, 458; assessment of, 45; disorders, 60, 93, 112, 113, 114, 364, 365, 367, 377, 445; experiencing, 364; measures of, 80; symptomatic, 56

Anxiety (A) Scale (Welsh), 32, 80, 99

Anxiety (AXY) Scale, 65, 114, 115, 116–117, 204, 288, 297, 378; described, 299; interpretation of, 299, 301 (table)

Anxiolytic medication, 289 (table), 446

APA. See American Psychiatric Association (APA)

APA (American Psychological Association) Monitor, 27

APD. See Avoidant Personality Disorder (APD)

APS. See Addiction Potential (APS) Scale

Army Special Training Program, 141, 143, 145

ASI. See Addiction Severity Index (ASI)

ASPD. See Antisocial Personality Disorder (ASPD) Scale

Attention-Deficit Hyperactivity Disorder (ADHD), 117, 169

Attention difficulties, 85, 263

Authority Problems (Pd2), 42

Avoidance, 91, 116, 446. See also Social Avoidance (SAV) Scale

Avoidant and Dependent Personality, 434

Avoidant Personality Disorder (APD), 113, 121, 122, 422

Axis I disorders, 78, 126, 389

Axis II disorders, 36, 81, 126, 127, 314, 340, 353, 364, 366, 377, 389, 411, 434, 445

AXY. See Anxiety (AXY) Scale

Back F (F_B) Scale, 24, 25, 148, 154, 159, 162; described, 150

Bariatric surgery, 55, 64, 67, 74, 75, 78, 83, 207 (table), 401–402, 404 (fig.), 405 (fig.), 406 (fig.) 407 (fig.), 408 (fig.), 411–413

BAS. See Behavioral Activation System (BAS)

Basic Personality Inventory (BPI), 31

Basic Readings (Welsh and Dahlstrom), 3

Beck Hopelessness Scale (BHS), 112, 115

Behavior: acting-out, 72, 101, 286, 304, 352, 379, 391; aggressive, 70, 74, 205, 354, 367, 469; changes in, 412; control of, 74; disorganized, 84; feminine, 125; genetics, 15; problems with, 3, 45, 70, 100, 103, 104, 106, 116, 125, 231, 266, 281, 379, 389, 423; sexual, 71; verbal, 2; violent, 74, 353, 379. See also Antisocial behavior

Behavioral Activation, 79, 90, 118

Behavioral Activation System (BAS), 82, 128

Behavioral Dysfunction, 101, 102, 229, 319, 339, 352

Behavioral/Externalizing Dysfunction (BXD) Scale, 102, 103, 183, 203, 230, 279, 290, 304, 316, 328, 352, 475; described, 105–106, 281; interpretation of, 281, 281 (table); scores, 281

Behavioral Inhibition System (BIS), 79, 82, 118, 128

Behavioral medicine, 56, 65–68

Behavior-Restricting Fears (BRF) Scale, 114, 115, 203, 288, 297, 377, 378, 446; described, 302; interpretation, 302, 303 (table); scores, 117, 302

Bernreuter Personality inventory (BPI), 138

Bernreuter Psychoneurotic Inventory, 1

BHS. See Beck Hopelessness Scale (BHS)

Bias: evaluative, 31; negative response, 136, 163; positive response, 136; predictive, 95; reasoning, 76. See also Response Bias Scale (RBS)

Bipolar Disorder, 88, 89–90, 91, 112, 118, 120

BIS. See Behavioral Inhibition System (BIS)

Blame, 47; externalization, 69, 74, 78

Bootstrapping, 12, 13, 30

Borderline Personality Disorder, 101, 113, 118

Boston Normative Aging Study, 22

BPI. See Basic Personality Inventory (BPI); Bernreuter Personality inventory (BPI)

BPRS. See Brief Psychiatric Rating Scale (BPRS)

Brain injury, 110, 425

BRF. See Behavior-Restricting Fears (BRF) Scale

Brief Psychiatric Rating Scale (BPRS), 86

Briquet's syndrome, 57

Bulimia Nervosa, 82

Burnout: misconduct and, 69; multidimensional theory of, 68

Buss Perry Aggression Questionnaire, 118, 119

BXD. See Behavioral/Externalizing Dysfunction (BXD) Scale

California Psychological Inventory (CPI), 99, 124

Cannot Say (CNS) score, 25, 148, 156, 159, 160, 192, 218, 254, 255, 256, 257, 271, 325, 341, 480n2, 480n3, 481–482n4; described, 138–139, 148–149, 241; interpretation of, 242 (table); raw score, 139; scores, 147, 149, 263

CARB. *See* Computerized Assessment of Response Bias (CARB)

Cardiovascular disease, 65, 112

Carefree Nonplanfullness, 74

Carelessness (Ca), 151

Carelessness (CS) Scale, 151

Case studies, 100, 208, 355–471

CG. *See* Comparison group (CG)

Character Sketches, 138

CHD. *See* Coronary heart disease (CHD)

Chronic and severe disorder, 366–367, 377–378

Chronic Fatigue Syndrome, 109

Chronic pain, 59, 364, 389, 423, 445

Chronic Somatic Symptom Disorder, 57, 58, 110

Civil Rights Act (1991), 182

Clinical Scale 2. *See* Depression (D) Scale

Clinical Scale 3. *See* Hysteria (Hy) Scale

Clinical Scale 4. *See* Psychopathic deviate (Pd) Scale

Clinical Scale 5. *See* Masculinity/Femininity (Mf) Scale

Clinical Scale 6. *See* Paranoia (Pa) Scale

Clinical Scale 7. *See* Psychasthenia (Pt) Scale

Clinical Scale 8. *See* Schizophrenia (Sc) Scale

Clinical Scale 9. *See* Hypomania (Ma) Scale

Clinical Scale 0. *See* Social Introversion (Si) Scale

Clinical Scales, 1, 3, 5, 6, 8, 18, 19, 22, 24, 26,33, 34, 51, 91, 92, 93, 94, 96, 97, 99, 100, 107; changes to, 36, 44, 45; code types, 28, 36, 102, 106, 474; construction of, 12–13, 16, 30, 46, 47; core components of, 48–50; correlations between, 40, 47; criticism of, 15; distributions of, 23; heterogeneity of, 13, 19, 35, 40–41, 43, 474–475; intercorrelations of, 39–40, 45, 53; interpretation of, 7, 16–17; IPI and, 146; item overlap of, 13, 19, 35, 40, 159; K-corrected profiles and, 146; methodology and, 43; original, 95; problems with, 12, 13, 15–18, 21, 35, 36, 37, 39; random variance/psychometric noise to, 41; response styles and, 14; restructuring, xiii, 11, 37, 39–43, 44, 473;

retaining, 29, 30, 36; scores, 4, 23, 25, 41; solutions/pre-restructured, 42–43; Somatoform Disorders and, 109; subtle items and, 41; validity of, 146

Cluster A disorders, 78, 314

Cluster B disorders, 314, 316, 353, 377, 411

Cluster C disorders, 316, 317, 339, 340, 364, 366, 411, 445

CNS. *See* Cannot Say (CNS) score

Code types, 4–5, 14, 25, 30, 33, 34, 42, 43, 102, 103, 106, 474; clinical scales and, 36; described, 28–29; empirical correlates of, 21; interpretation of, 19; transition to, 473

Cognitive Complaints (COG) Scale, 110–111, 232, 248, 250, 268, 283, 339, 352, 458; described, 295; interpretation of, 295, 296 (fig.)

Cognitive difficulties, 21, 85, 110, 231, 265, 295, 353, 354, 389, 400, 445, 457, 458; noncredible, 263; overreporting of, 170–171, 192; substantive measures of, 268

Cognitive Failures Questionnaire, 111

Cognitive symptoms, 158, 163, 170, 246, 248, 263, 292; overreporting of, 268, 391, 434

Common factor, defining/capturing, 45–48

Comorbidity, 93, 94, 101; phenotypic, 84, 106

Comparison group (CG), 214, 218; standard, 206, 207–208 (table)

Computerized Assessment of Response Bias (CARB), 163

Conceptual problems, 26, 35, 86, 241

Conduct Disorder, 101, 117

Confounds, 255 (table)

Consistency Scales, 151, 367. *See also* True Response Inconsistency (TRIN) Scale; Variable Response Inconsistency (VRIN) Scale

Constraint, 98, 99, 101

Content Component Scales, 26, 107, 109

Content Nonresponsiveness, 219, 254

Content Scales, 7–8, 22, 23, 26, 30, 36, 150, 189, 476; described, 24; discriminant properties of, 31; validity of, 34

Conversion Disorder, 56, 57, 58, 295, 310, 422, 423, 434, 435

Cook–Medley Ho Scale, 27, 65, 66, 68, 70, 130, 475; ACM, 67

Core components of scales, identifying, 48–50

Coronary heart disease (CHD), 65, 66, 67–68, 70, 475

Correction (K) Scale, 12, 25; development of, 143, 144, 145, 146, 147, 148, 149, 150, 153, 156, 157, 159, 162, 164, 165, 173, 252; K-r and, 166

CPI. *See* California Psychological Inventory (CPI)

Criminal Behavior, 73

Critical content, 204, 287, 289

Critical Item Lists, described, 7

Critical Responses, 206, 240; described, 204–205

Cutoffs, 153, 214, 263; alternative, 205, 206; interpretive, 150, 171

Cynicism (RC3) Scale, 27, 49, 67, 87, 96, 102, 106, 114, 171, 204, 271, 282, 295, 341, 377, 400, 411, 434, 445, 470, 475; in behavioral medicine, 65–68; conceptualizing, 65; described, 285–286; empirical findings on, 65–70; interpretation of, 286, 286 (table); police misconduct and, 68–69; scores, 69–70, 352

DAST. *See* Drug Abuse Screening Test (DAST)

DCPR. *See Diagnostic Criteria for Psychosomatic Research (DCPR)*

Delusional Disorder, 59

Delusions, 59, 76, 78, 84, 85

Demoralization, 40, 45–46, 60, 77, 84, 97, 113, 114, 123, 284, 366; capturing, 47–48; components of, 48, 49, 50; conceptualizing, 53, 55; depression and, 53, 54; excessive, 107; helplessness/hopelessness in, 54; markers of, 48, 51; measured, 81; Neurotic Depression and, 62; phenotypic, 61; psychological problems and, 54; suicidality and, 54

Demoralization (RCd) Scale, 51, 52–56, 65, 80, 95, 96, 102, 103, 106, 107, 112, 115, 281, 288, 297, 312, 328, 365, 412; described, 47, 282; empirical findings with, 53–54, 55–56; interpretation of, 283 (table); validity of, 56

Dependent Personality Disorder, 121, 340

Depression, 16, 42, 48, 55, 56, 62, 79, 80, 87, 100, 104, 105, 111, 116, 120, 263, 284, 339, 364, 400, 413, 422; anhedonia and, 54, 64; demoralization and, 53, 54, 112; literature on, 54; markers of, 64; measures of, 80, 130–131; pathognomonic, 61; problems with, 312, 325; psychomotor changes of, 54; psychotic, 16; risk factor for, 60; Schizophrenia and, 65; self-esteem and, 113; self-reported, 423; vegetative symptoms of, 402, 424, 434. *See also* Anhedonia: depression and; Endogenomorphic Depression; Major Depression; Manic Depression; Neurotic Depression; Nonspecific Depression;

Postnatal Depression; Somatic Depression

Depression (D) Scale, 40, 42, 48–49, 60–61, 80; restructured version of, 51, 52

Depressive Disorder, 62, 104, 112, 145, 344, 458

Despondency, 105, 110, 341

Detoxification, 391, 401

Developmental delays, 459

Developmental theory, 15

Diabetes, 401

Diagnostic Considerations, 222 (fig.), 278, 319, 320, 339, 400; described, 229–230

Diagnostic Criteria for Psychosomatic Research (DCPR), 54

Dimensional measures, feasibility of, 103

Disaffiliativeness (DSF) Scale, 121, 122, 286, 307; correlates of, 123; described, 310; interpretation of, 310, 312 (table); scores, 123, 310; suicide attempts and, 123

Disconstraint (DISC), 127, 128

Disconstraint–Revised (DISC-r) Scale, 129, 183, 304, 390; described, 314, 316; interpretation of, 316, 316 (table); scores, 130, 314

Disinhibition, 72, 73, 91

Disordered thinking, 39, 101, 289, 458

"Does the 'New' MMPI Beat the 'Classic'?" (Adler), 27

Drug abuse, 100, 130, 379, 390, 391, 447, 459

Drug Abuse Screening Test (DAST), 118, 119

DSF. *See* Disaffiliativeness (DSF) Scale

DSM-III (APA), 19, 30, 53

DSM-III-R (APA), 126

DSM-IV (APA), 54, 56, 58, 59, 72, 88, 110, 113, 114, 115, 121, 136, 314, 316, 317, 435; ASPD and, 70–71; Conversion Disorder and, 57; Hypomanic episode and, 89

DSM-5 (APA), 57, 58, 81

Dyadic Adjustment Scale (Spanier), 21

"Dynamics of 'Structured' Personality Tests, The" (Meehl), 2

Dysfunctional Negative Emotions (RC7) Scale, 51, 65, 102, 103, 107, 113, 115, 282, 297, 328, 364, 365, 446, 481n2; conceptualizing, 79–81; described, 288; empirical findings with, 81–82, 83–84; interpretation of, 288, 289 (table); PTSD and, 83; scores, 288

Dysphoria, 53, 61, 65, 89, 104, 105, 116

Dysthymia, 56, 81

Eating disorders, 82, 113

Eccentric Perceptions Scale, 87

Edwards Social Desirability (Esd) Scale, 31

Ego strength, 13, 14, 80, 475
EID. *See* Emotional/Internalizing Dysfunction (EID) Scale
Emotional distress, 77, 340, 366, 400, 402, 425–426, 436
Emotional dysfunction, 39, 101, 102, 229, 231, 319, 320, 328, 339, 352, 436, 445; substantial, 249, 268
Emotional/Internalizing Dysfunction (EID) Scale, 102, 103, 104–105, 106, 230, 328, 365, 412; described, 279; interpretation, 280 (table)
Empirical correlates, 131, 218–219, 232, 278
"Empiricists Manifesto, The" (Wiggins), described, 8
Endnotes, 226 (fig.), 233
Endogenomorphic Depression, 61
Epilepsy, 59, 94, 289
Esd Scale. *See* Edwards Social Desirability (Esd) Scale
Euphoria, 352, 379
Excitability, 353, 379
Externalizing Scales, 117–120, 187 (fig.), 197 (fig.), 203, 212 (fig.), 237 (fig.), 314, 345 (fig.), 360 (fig.), 372 (fig.), 378, 384 (fig.), 396 (fig.), 407 (fig.), 418 (fig.), 430 (fig.), 441 (fig.), 452 (fig.), 464 (fig.); constructs of, 117–118; described, 302, 304
Externalizing Specific Problems Scales, 117, 118, 119, 332 (fig.)
Extraversion, 98, 99, 102, 126, 127, 317
Eysenck Personality Inventory (EPI), 99
Eysenck Personality Questionnaire (EPQ), 99

F Scale. *See* Infrequency (F) Scale
Factitious Disorder, 59, 136, 261, 343; case of, 424–425, 434–435; by Proxy, 58
"Fake bad," 136, 141, 142, 143, 145, 149, 155, 480n7
"Fake good," 136, 143, 145, 149, 269
Familial dysfunction, 122, 271, 307; personality disorder and, 120–121
Family problems, 17, 42, 257, 389; suicide attempts and, 121
Family Problems (FML) Scale, 120, 121, 122, 302; described, 307; interpretation of, 307, 308 (table)
Fatigue, 110, 422, 445, 457
F_B Scale. *See* Back F (F_B) Scale
FBS Scale. *See* Symptom Validity (FBS) Scale
FBS-r Scale. *See* Symptom Validity (FBS-r) Scale, revised
Fear, 81, 114, 288

Fears Content Scale, scores on, 34
Feelings of Future subscale (Beck Hopelessness Scale). 115
Femininity, tendency toward, 124, 125
FFM. *See* Five Factor Model (FFM)
Fifth Annual Symposium on Recent Developments in the Use of the MMPI, xiii, 11
Five Factor Model (FFM), 36, 55, 73, 91, 128, 278, 314, 316, 479n2
Fixed responding, 134, 151, 162, 167, 252, 273, 274; described, 135–136, 259
Flesch–Kincaid reading level index, 177–178, 179
FML Scale. *See* Family Problems (FML) Scale
Forensic evaluations, 176, 480n7, 482n1
49–94 code type, 42, 102, 103, 106
Four-factor model, antisocial behavior and, 72
Fp-r Scale. *See* Infrequent Psychopathology Responses (Fp-r) Scale
F_p Scale. *See* Infrequency Psychopathology (F_p) Scale
F-r Scale. *See* Infrequent Responses (F-r) Scale
Frustration, 125; low tolerance for, 389, 400
Fs Scale. *See* Infrequent Somatic Responses (Fs) Scale
Functional Neurological/Conversion Disorder, 58
Fundamental States, 88

GAD. *See* Generalized Anxiety Disorder (GAD)
Galton–Pearson correlational technique, 98
Gastrointestinal Complaints (GIC) Scale, 109, 110, 111, 247, 248, 283, 340, 400, 457; described, 293, 295; interpretation of, 294 (table), 295; scores, 293, 339
Gastrointestinal symptoms, 58, 110, 422
Gender Role–Feminine (GF) Scale, 25, 182
Gender Role–Masculine (GM) Scale, 24–25, 182
Gender roles, 23, 49, 101, 125, 183
Gender Role Scales, 124
General Distress Factor, 81
Generalized Anxiety Disorder (GAD), 56, 59, 62, 81, 113, 114
General Maladjustment, 40, 80
GIC. *See* Gastrointestinal Complaints (GIC) Scale
Glasgow Coma Scale, 424
Guilford–Zimmerman Temperament Survey, 99

Hallucinations, 78, 84, 86

Happiness/Unhappiness, 47, 53, 55, 80

Harmavoidance, 91

Harris–Lingoes subscales, 7, 26, 42, 43, 109, 110, 140, 309

Headaches, 364, 389, 445

Head pain, 389, 422, 445

Head Pain Complaints (HPC) Scale, 109, 111, 247, 248, 283; described, 295; interpretation of, 294 (table), 295

Helplessness, 364; demoralization and, 55, 56, 112, 115, 297

Helplessness/Hopelessness (HLP) Scale, 14, 112, 115, 204, 282, 328, 365; described, 297; interpretation of, 297, 298 (table)

Heterogeneity, of Clinical Scales, 13, 19, 35, 40–41, 43

Higher-Order (H-O) Scales, 97, 98–106, 108, 109, 129, 185 (fig.), 192, 195 (fig.), 203, 210 (fig.), 235 (fig.), 273 (fig.), 278, 330 (fig.), 343 (fig.), 358 (fig.), 370 (fig.), 378, 382 (fig.), 394 (fig.), 401, 405 (fig.), 416 (fig.), 428 (fig.), 439 (fig.), 450 (fig.), 462 (fig.); comparison group findings on, 214; described, 279; development of, 102–106; normal personality model for, 104; psychometric findings with, 103–104

HLP Scale. See Helplessness/Hopelessness (HLP) Scale

Homicidal ideation, 119

Hopelessness, 55, 56, 64, 112, 113, 115, 364, 458

Ho Scale. See Hostility (Ho) Scale

H-O Scales. See Higher-Order (H-O) Scales

Hostile Affect, 67

Hostility (Ho) Scale. See Cook–Medley Ho Scale

HPC. See Head Pain Complaints (HPC) Scale

Hs Scale. See Hypochondriasis (Hs) Scale

Humm–Wadsworth Temperament Scales, 1, 138

Hypertension, 112, 401

Hypochondriasis (Hs) Scale, 4, 5, 46, 48, 49; restructured version of, 51

Hypohedonia, anhedonia and, 61–62

Hypomania, 353, 400

Hypomania Checklist (HCL-32), 90

Hypomania (Ma) Scale, 17, 42, 146; demoralization and, 49; restructured version of 152

Hypomanic Activation (RC9) Scale, 39, 49, 51, 87–91, 102, 103, 117, 118, 120, 171, 203, 205, 232, 282, 302, 304, 307, 352, 389–390;

conceptualizing, 87–89; described, 290, 292; empirical findings on, 89–90, 90–91; interpretation of, 290, 291 (table); T score on, 214

Hypomanic Personality Scale (HYP), 118

Hysteria, 2, 56, 57

Hysteria (Hy) Scale, 40, 106, 109; and demoralization, 49; restructured version of, 52

Ideas of Persecution (RC6) Scale, 76–79, 85, 102, 103, 167, 171, 204, 205, 271, 286, 307, 352, 470; conceptualizing, 75–77; described, 287–288; empirical findings on, 77–78; interpretation of, 79, 288, 288 (table); psychotic symptoms and, 78; scores, 78, 287

Impulse control, 320, 352, 379, 400

Impulsiveness, 42, 70, 72, 74, 91, 411

Impulsive Nonconformity, 74, 85

Inconsistency Scales (MPQ), 24, 152, 161, 165, 166, 167

Inconsistent responses, 151, 219. See also True Response Inconsistency (TRIN) Scale; Variable Response Inconsistency (VRIN) Scale

Inefficacy (NFC) Scale, 112, 113, 115, 116, 282, 297, 310, 328, 412, 476; described, 299; interpretation of, 299, 300 (table); scores, 299

Infrequency (F) Scale, 148, 150, 151, 154, 156, 157, 159, 162, 166, 248; described, 140–142; development of, 24, 25, 124, 147; interpretation of, 153; "objectionable" items in, 149; overreporting and, 144

Infrequency Psychopathology (F_p) Scale, 25, 37, 148, 156, 159, 163, 166, 480n6; described, 153–155, 162

Infrequent Psychopathology Responses (Fp-r) Scale, 164, 166, 168, 192, 214, 218, 240, 255, 259, 268, 274; described, 162–163, 246; FR and, 169–170; interpretation of, 247 (table); scores, 258, 263, 264; T scores, 401

Infrequent Responses (F-r) Scale, 155, 163, 164, 166, 168, 192, 214, 218, 240, 255, 258, 259, 263, 268, 274, 391, 401, 446, 481n6; described, 162, 244, 246; Fp-r and, 169–170; interpretation of, 245 (table), 246; selecting items for, 162; T scores, 377

Infrequent Somatic Responses (Fs) Scale, 162, 192, 401; described, 163, 246–247; interpretation of, 248 (table)

Insecurity, 42, 55, 299, 457

Interest Scales, 97, 187 (fig.), 189, 197 (fig.), 203, 212 (fig.), 229, 237 (fig.), 310, 313, 332 (fig.), 339, 345 (fig.), 360 (fig.), 372 (fig.), 384 (fig.), 396 (fig.), 407 (fig.), 418 (fig.), 430 (fig.), 441 (fig.), 452 (fig.), 464 (fig.); construct validity of, 126; development of, 106. *See also* Aesthetic–Literary Interests (AES) Scale; Mechanical–Physical Interests (MEC) Scale

Internalizing Scales, 100, 101, 102, 111–117, 186 (fig.), 196 (fig.), 203, 211 (fig.), 236 (fig.), 292, 331 (fig.), 344 (fig.), 359 (fig.), 371 (fig.), 383 (fig.), 395 (fig.), 406 (fig.), 417 (fig.), 429 (fig.), 440 (fig.), 451 (fig.), 463 (fig.); constructs of, 111–115; described, 297

Interpersonal difficulties, 50, 78, 231, 292, 367, 411, 457

Interpersonal Disorders, 230

Interpersonal Dysfunction, 319

Interpersonal Functioning, 229, 307, 320, 339, 352

Interpersonal Passivity (IPP) Scale, 121, 122–123, 214, 286, 352, 469; described, 307, 310; interpretation of, 309 (table), 310; scores, 123, 310

Interpersonal relationships, 119, 129, 379, 391, 470

Interpersonal Scales, 120–125, 187 (fig.), 197 (fig.), 203, 212 (fig.), 237 (fig.), 307, 332 (fig.), 345 (fig.), 360 (fig.), 372 (fig.), 384 (fig.), 396 (fig.), 407 (fig.), 418 (fig.), 430 (fig.), 441 (fig.), 452 (fig.), 464 (fig.); constructs of, 120–122; described, 307; interpretation of, 307

Interpretation, 14–15, 149, 157, 159, 214, 218, 241, 281; automated, 219; code-type, 12; compromising, 254; computer-generated, 218, 219, 277, 319; configural, 19; data, 203; framework/process for, 319, 320 (table); guidelines, 174; narrative, 319; process, 203; scale-level, 12, 18; scoring and, 9; substantive, 131

Interpretation Worksheet, 319–320, 321–324 (fig.), 322, 326 (fig.), 328, 335–338 (fig.), 339–341, 354

Intropunitive, 340, 389, 411, 422, 434, 457

Introversion/Low Positive Emotionality (INTR) Scale, 127

Introversion/Low Positive Emotionality–Revised (INTR-r) Scale, 130–131, 214; described, 316–317; interpretation of, 317, 317 (table), 318 (table)

INTR-r Scale. *See* Introversion/Low Positive Emotionality–Revised (INTR-r) Scale

INTR Scale. *See* Introversion/Low Positive Emotionality (INTR) Scale

Intrusive ideation, 299, 367, 400, 457

Inwald Personality Inventory (IPI), 146

IPP Scale. *See* Interpersonal Passivity (IPP) Scale

IQ scores, 105, 116

Irritability, 88, 89, 117, 389, 400

IRT. *See* Item Response Theory (IRT)

Item-Level Information, 192, 200–202 (fig.), 215–217 (fig.), 223–225 (fig.), 229, 233, 239 (fig.), 363 (fig.), 375–376 (fig.), 387–388 (fig.), 399 (fig.), 410 (fig.), 421 (fig.), 433 (fig.), 444 (fig.), 455–456 (fig.), 467–468 (fig.); described, 203–206, 232; user-designated, 205–206, 232, 240

Item pools, xiii, 1, 5, 51, 71, 128, 155, 164, 178, 473, 474, 479n3; constraints of, 108; readability of, 177; security of, 355

Item Response Theory (IRT), 60, 127

JCP Scale. *See* Juvenile Conduct Problems (JCP) Scale

Journal of Personality Assessment, 95

Juvenile Conduct Disorder, 71

Juvenile Conduct Problems (JCP) Scale, 117, 119, 282, 287, 302, 481n1; described, 304; interpretation of, 304, 305 (table)

Juvenile delinquency, 73, 130, 304, 391

Juvenile misconduct, 70, 71, 75, 117, 304

K Correction, 12, 35; described, 142–147, 149; scores, 145, 156, 173

K-r Scale. *See* Adjustment Validity (K-r) Scale

K Scale. *See* Correction (K) Scale

Keying, 5, 277; balanced, 32; criterion, 17–18, 35; unbalanced, 31

Known-groups, 144, 158, 167

Kraepelinian nosology, 1, 2, 3, 4–5, 10, 11, 13, 14, 15, 16, 19, 29–30, 35, 58, 91, 92

Lack of Ego Mastery Cognitive, 110

Lack of Ego Mastery Conative, 110

Lassitude/Malaise, 309

Leadership skills, 353, 469, 471

Levinson Self-Report Psychopathy Scale, 74

Lie (L) Scale, 25, 139–140, 143, 144, 145, 147, 148, 149, 150, 153, 156, 157, 159, 162–163, 164, 165, 173; L-r and, 166

Likert-scale response formats, 134, 135, 136, 178, 179

Loss of Motivation subscale (Beck Hopelessness Scale), 115

Low Positive Emotions (RC2) Scale, 60–65, 79, 80, 81, 85, 91, 102, 103, 167, 171, 214, 279, 282, 292, 307, 312, 317, 352, 365, 412, 423, 435; conceptualizing, 60–62; described, 284; elevations on, 65; empirical findings with, 62–65; interpretation of, 284, 285 (table); scores, 284, 328

L-r Scale. *See* Uncommon Virtues (L-r) Scale

L Scale. *See* Lie (L) Scale

MacAndrew Alcoholism Scale–Revised (MAC-R), 26, 118, 475

Magical Ideation, 78, 85, 86, 105, 130

Magical Ideation (MIS) Scale, 85, 86, 87

Major Depression, 56, 62, 68, 81, 86, 90, 114, 120, 168, 284, 340, 411, 412, 423, 434; anhedonia and, 63; diagnostic criteria for, 54

Malaise (MLS) Scale, 109, 110–111, 247, 248, 283, 423, 434; described, 292–293; interpretation of, 293, 293 (table)

Malingering, 133, 141, 143, 157, 169, 170, 172, 261, 262, 266, 268, 434, 435; detecting, 173–174; positive, 136, 269

Mania, 87; melancholia and, 88

Manic Depression, 2, 89

Manic-Depressive Insanity, 87

Manic states, 87, 89, 91, 307, 353, 400

Manual for Administration, Scoring, and Interpretation (Ben-Porath and Tellegen), xiv, 96, 167, 171, 175, 182, 190, 218, 241, 257, 277, 475

Marital Distress Scale (MDS), 26

Masculinity, tendency toward, 124, 125

Masculinity/Femininity (Mf) Scale, 4, 52, 106, 123, 182, 189, 473, 479n3, 124, 310; demoralization and, 49

Maslach Burnout Inventory, 68, 69

MAST. *See* Michigan Alcoholism Screening Test (MAST)

Mayo Clinic, 163, 218

Measurement, errors, 40, 104

Mechanical–Physical Interests (MEC) Scale, 124, 125, 312, 352; described, 313; interpretation of, 313, 313 (table); scores, 125, 313

Medical Symptom Validity Test, 170

Melancholia, 87, 88

Memory Complaints Inventory (MCI), overreporting and, 169

Memory problems, 85, 171, 249, 263, 268, 295,

445. *See also* Response Bias (RBS) Scale

Mental disorders, 57, 61, 101, 114, 458

Mental health, 34, 104, 117, 355

Michigan Alcoholism Screening Test (MAST), 118, 119

Minnesota Multiphasic Personality Schedule, 133

Minnesota Teacher Attitude Inventory, 66

MIS. *See* Magical Ideation (MIS) Scale

MLS Scale. *See* Malaise (MLS) Scale

MMPI: appraisal of, 3, 9–18, 27, 92, 474; construction of, 2, 3–4; described, 1–9; empirical approach to, 14–15; eulogizing, 10–11; higher order structure of, 99; interpretation of, 5, 6–7; psychometric soundness of, 29; readability of, 177; revision of, 4, 9–18, 19–20, 21; transition from, 473

MMPI-2: appraisal of, 25, 27–29, 31, 92, 474; development of, 19–36, 97, 158–159, 473, 477; items of, 107–108; normative shifts of, 33; publication of, 2, 25; readability of, 177

MMPI-2 booklet, 22, 24, 33, 177

MMPI-2 Manual, 107, 177; described, 25–27; Validity Scales and, 150

MMPI-2 Manual, revised (2001), Validity Scales and, 153–156

MMPI-2 Research Symposium, 108

MMPI-2-RF Interpretive Report, 191, 218–219, 220–228 (fig.)

MMPI-2-RF Score Report, 193–202 (fig.), 329–334 (fig.), 356–363 (fig.), 368–376 (fig.), 380–388 (fig.), 392–399 (fig.), 403–410 (fig.), 414–421 (fig.), 426–433 (fig.), 437–444 (fig.), 448–456 (fig.), 460–468 (fig.)

MMPI-2-RF Technical Manual (Tellegen and Ben-Porath), xiv, 33, 59, 98, 103, 108, 110, 120, 126, 161, 165, 183, 206, 218, 277, 281, 292, 297, 475, 476, 480n10; PSY-5 Scales and, 129; psychometric data in, 473; validation data in, 166

MMPI-2-RF User's Guide for Reports (Ben-Porath and Tellegen), 176, 191, 206, 218

MMPI-A Manual (Butcher), 175

MMPI-AX, 21, 22, 33

MMPI Handbook (Dahlstrom, Welsh, and Dahlstrom), 5, 10, 139, 173

Mood, 44, 47, 53, 79, 93; disorders, 93, 352, 353, 379, 411; literature, 80; model, 80; stabilization, 353–354

Mp. *See* Positive Malingering (Mp) Scale

MPQ. *See* Multidimensional Personality Questionnaire (MPQ)

M Scale, development of, 124

MSF Scale. *See* Multiple Specific Fears (MSF) Scale

Multidimensional Personality Questionnaire (MPQ), 151; and demoralization, 44; and H-O Scales, 99,103–104, 105, 106; and Inconsistency Scales, 24, 151–152; and RC2 Scale, 64; and RC7 Scale, 79, 81–83; and RC8 Scale, 87; and RC9 Scale, 91

Multiple Fears, 107

Multiple Specific Fears (MSF) Scale, 114, 115, 183, 203, 288, 297, 367; described, 302; interpretation of, 302, 304 (table)

NA. *See* Negative Affect (NA)

Narcissism, 42, 90, 353, 390

Narcissistic Personality Disorder, 353, 389

National Computer Systems, 20

Negative Affect (NA), 47, 48, 62, 79, 80, 82

Negative Affectivity, 80, 81, 84

Negative Appraisals, 93

Negative Emotionality (NEM), 48, 49, 51, 79, 83, 84, 99, 100, 105, 112, 113, 114, 126; demoralization and, 80; MPQ-based, 82; variance in, 81

Negative Emotionality/Neuroticism (NEGE) Scale, 81, 82, 98, 102, 126, 128, 129, 366

Negative Emotionality/Neuroticism–Revised (NEGE-r) Scale, 129, 130; described, 316

Negative emotions, 81, 288, 302, 316, 390, 411

Negative Temperament, 83

Negative Treatment Indicators (TRT) Scale, 24, 476

NEGE Scale. *See* Negative Emotionality/ Neuroticism (NEGE) Scale

NEGE-r Scale. *See* Negative Emotionality/ Neuroticism–Revised (NEGE-r) Scale

NEM. *See* Negative Emotionality (NEM)

NEO Personality Inventory (NEO-PI), 128

NEO Personality Inventory–Revised (NEO-PI-R), 55, 64, 100, 128

Neurocognitive dysfunction, 170, 378

Neurological complaints, 377, 423, 425

Neurological Complaints (NUC) Scale, 109, 110, 111, 247, 248, 283, 378; described, 295; interpretation of, 295, 296 (table); scores, 295, 377, 434

Neurological dysfunction, 111, 114

Neurological evaluation, 295, 377

Neurological symptoms, 58, 367, 422

Neuropsychological evaluations, 158, 170, 295, 341, 354, 377, 378, 389, 390, 400, 424, 425, 458

Neuropsychology, 163, 248

Neurosis, psychosis and, 102

Neurotic Depression, 61, 62

Neuroticism, 80, 98, 99, 126

NFC. *See* Inefficacy (NFC) Scale

Nightmares, 114, 367, 400, 446, 457

Non-Content-Based Invalid Responding Measures, 160–162, 167–172

Nonresponding, 134, 135, 138, 252; described, 134, 254–257; impact of, 156, 160

Nonresponsiveness. *See* Content Nonresponsiveness

Nonspecific Depression, 62

Nonsteroidal anti-inflammatory drugs, 413, 423

Normal personality, 97, 99, 100–101, 104

Normative samples (NS), 20, 21, 23, 24, 28, 75, 150, 154, 155, 162, 164, 181–183, 204, 206, 214, 287, 377; demographics of, 22; nongendered, 182

Norms, 4, 33–34, 176, 180; concerns about, 28; gendered, 181, 182, 183, 206, 482n3; group-specific, 181; new, 22–23; nongendered, 181, 182, 183; test, 36

Nosology. *See* Kraepelinian nosology

Not guilty by reason of insanity, 446–447, 457–459

NUC Scale. *See* Neurological Complaints (NUC) Scale

Obsessive-compulsive, 316, 355, 364–366

Obsessive-Compulsive Disorder, 62, 316, 340, 355, 364–366, 445

Obvious/subtle subscales. *See* Wiener–Harmon Subtle and Obvious subscales

Olfactory hallucinations, 86

Opiate-based medications, 424, 435

Outcomes, 108–109, 319, 413

Overactivation, 90, 353

Overcontrolled/Internalizing Syndromes, 100

Overreporting, 144, 145, 147, 151, 153, 154, 155, 157, 163, 168–171, 192, 219, 230, 247, 248, 252–253, 256, 269, 292, 367, 377, 391, 413, 425, 434, 445, 446, 457, 469; assessing, 246; concerns about, 233, 240, 243; described, 136–137, 260–268; indicators, 162, 164, 168, 169, 170, 172–173, 254, 258, 259; intentional, 136, 141, 159, 262; marked, 277; possibility of, 259, 265; symptom, 162, 166, 246, 261, 263, 268; underreporting and, 270–271, 458; unintentional, 136–137, 142, 156, 159, 261

PA. *See* Positive Affect (PA)

PAI. *See* Personality Assessment Inventory (PAI)

Pain, 58, 110, 263, 364

Pain Disorder, 57, 58, 109, 423

PANAS. *See* Positive and Negative Affect Schedule (PANAS)

Panic Disorder, 57, 62

Paranoia, 378, 390, 447

Paranoia (Pa) Scale, 75–79, 102; demoralization and, 49; restructured version of, 51, 52

Paranoid subscale of Ho Scale, 68

PAS. *See* Perceptual Aberration (PAS) Scale

Passivity, 85, 121, 122, 341

PCL-R. *See* Psychopathy Checklist–Revised (PCL-R)

PCL-SV, 74, 96

Pd2. *See* Authority Problems (Pd2)

Pd5. *See* Self-Alienation (Pd5) subscale

Pd Scale. *See* Psychopathic deviate (Pd) Scale

Pearson Assessments, 20, 480n1

Pearson scoring, 277

Pearson software, 176, 190, 191, 205, 240; custom comparison groups and, 218; interface with, 206

PEM. *See* Positive Emotionality (PEM)

Perceptual Aberration, 78, 85, 86, 105, 130

Perceptual Aberration (PAS) Scale, 85, 86, 87

Perceptual processes, 389, 458

Perceptual Reasoning, 279

Peritraumatic Distress, 116

Persecutory beliefs, 32, 78, 79, 458, 470

Persecutory ideation, 76, 77, 78–79, 271, 353, 354, 377, 379, 458

Persecutory Ideation Questionnaire (PIQ), 77

Personal Data Sheet, 98, 138

Personality, xiii, 1, 44, 47, 48, 53, 80, 90, 91, 93, 106, 474; adult, 98; assessing, 20, 31, 36, 477; characteristics, 103; clinical assessments of, 3; inventories, 55, 64, 99, 100; measures of, 9, 18, 27, 133; pathology, 129, 313; studying, 9, 10, 36, 92; test development, 15

Personality Assessment Inventory (PAI), 100, 101, 170, 177

Personality Disorder, 81, 90, 120–121, 339, 479n2

Personality Psychopathology-Five (PSY-5) Scales, 81, 82, 97, 108, 126–131, 188 (fig.), 189, 198 (fig.), 203, 213 (fig.), 238 (fig.), 278, 279, 281, 282, 328, 333 (fig.), 339, 346 (fig.), 361 (fig.), 365–366, 373 (fig.), 385

(fig.), 397 (fig.), 408 (fig.), 419 (fig.), 431 (fig.), 442 (fig.), 453 (fig.), 465 (fig.), 479n2, 479n4; acronyms for, 480n5; BIS-BAS and, 128; described, 26, 313–314, 316–317; psychometric findings with, 129–131; rationales/objectives/development, 126–127

Physical anhedonia, 85

PIQ. *See* Persecutory Ideation Questionnaire (PIQ)

Pleasantness/Unpleasantness (PU), 47, 53, 55, 80

Polysubstance Dependence, 401

Positive Affect (PA), 47, 48, 79, 80

Positive and Negative Affect Schedule (PANAS), 81, 82

Positive Emotionality (PEM), 48, 64, 79, 98, 99, 100, 102, 105, 123, 126, 127, 479n3; demoralization and, 80

Positive Malingering (Mp) Scale, 164

Postnatal Depression, 62

Post-Traumatic Impairment, 116

Posttraumatic Stress Disorder (PTSD), 23, 55, 56, 59, 63, 65, 81, 82, 84, 93, 101, 105, 113, 114, 116, 117, 118, 128, 157, 168, 170, 284, 299, 364, 367, 377, 435–436, 445–446, 457; anhedonia and, 64; familial relationships and, 121; RC7 and, 83; scale, 25; treatment for, 75

Primary Thought Disorder, 87

Primary versus Secondary Function, 98, 99

Protocol Validity, 156, 159, 174, 219, 220 (fig.), 229, 239 (fig.), 241, 255 (table), 325; threats to, 133–138, 142, 172–173

Pseudoneurologic symptoms, 110, 425, 434

"Pseudo-subtle" subscales, 41

PSY-5 Scales. *See* Personality Psychopathology-Five (PSY-5) Scales

Psychasthenia (Pt) Scale, 39, 40, 48, 80, 84, 101, 102, 146, 480n4; demoralization and, 49; restructured version of, 51

Psychiatric problems, 45, 46, 101, 145, 166, 171

Psychological adjustment, 148, 157, 165, 271, 273, 274, 481n2

Psychological Corporation, 19

Psychological dysfunction, 46, 56, 84, 121, 246, 325, 364, 411, 423, 457; overreporting symptoms of, 268; underreporting, 270

Psychological functioning, 37, 137, 284, 340, 364, 379

Psychometric approach, 1, 2, 7, 8, 13, 16, 18, 19, 30, 41, 43, 84, 85, 97, 117 118, 133

Psychomotor acceleration, 89

Psychomotor agitation, 89

Psychomotor retardation, 84

Psychoneurosis, 101, 145

Psychopathic deviate (Pd) Scale, 17, 30, 40, 41, 42, 43, 46; demoralization and, 49; restructured version of, 51

Psychopathic Personality Inventory (PPI), 74

Psychopathology, xiii, 1, 2, 11–12, 29, 34, 44, 45, 46, 47, 48, 49, 71, 73, 79, 80, 82, 84, 91, 92, 93, 94, 95, 96, 102, 106, 109, 152, 155, 163, 172, 183, 254, 266, 270, 274, 310, 364, 367, 390, 391, 474, 479n3, 480n6, 481n3; adult, 98; anxiety-related, 288, 365, 458; assessment of, 20, 31, 36, 40, 53, 477; classification of, 16, 19; common structure of, 100–101; concealment of, 173–174; domain, 101, 126; feigning, 170; genuine, 154, 246, 263; internalizing/externalizing, 103; measures of, 10, 18, 27, 31, 35, 74–75, 133; overreporting, 192; preexisting, 157; primary, 178; research in, 9, 36; severe, 142, 156, 157, 246, 263, 265, 268; significant, 244; somatoform, 59, 320, 328, 365; symptoms, 263, 457

Psychopathy, 42, 75, 83–84, 91, 101, 479n2; antisocial behavior and, 72; ASPD and, 71; factors, 71–72, 73; PPI-assessed, 74

Psychopathy Checklist–Revised (PCL-R), 71, 72, 74, 75, 82, 96

Psychosis, 85, 86, 87, 89, 101, 105, 145, 263; atypical, 447; neurosis and, 102

Psychotherapy, 45, 46, 53, 231, 411

Psychotic disorders, 16, 17, 86, 101, 141, 173, 176, 289, 341, 390, 391

Psychoticism (PSYC) Scale, 99, 126, 128, 129

Psychoticism–Revised (PSYC-r) Scale, 129, 130; described, 314; interpretation, 314, 315 (table)

Psychotic symptoms, 78, 130, 246, 458; substance-induced, 289, 390–391, 400–401

Psychotropic medications, 104

PSYC-r Scale. See Psychoticism–Revised (PSYC-r) Scale

PSYC Scale. See Psychoticism (PSYC) Scale

PTSD. See Posttraumatic Stress Disorder (PTSD)

PU. See Pleasantness/Unpleasantness (PU)

Random responding, 151, 154, 162, 167, 252, 255, 256, 259, 271, 273, 274; described, 134–135, 257–258; intentional, 134, 257; quasi-, 47; unintentional, 134–135, 142, 257

Raw scores, 4, 23, 32, 34, 139, 141, 149, 151, 153, 157, 189, 192, 208, 218, 243, 255, 297; calculating, 181; distribution of, 183; standard scores and, 181

RBS. See Response Bias (RBS) Scale

RC1 Scale. See Somatic Complaints (RC1) Scale

RC2 Scale. See Low Positive Emotions (RC2) Scale

RC3 Scale. See Cynicism (RC3) Scale

RC4 Scale. See Antisocial Behavior (RC4) Scale

RC6 Scale. See Ideas of Persecution (RC6) Scale

RC7 Scale. See Dysfunctional Negative Emotions (RC7) Scale

RC8 Scale. See Aberrant Experiences (RC8) Scale

RC9 Scale. See Hypomanic Activation (RC9) Scale

RCd Scale. See Demoralization (RCd) Scale

RC Scales. See Restructured Clinical (RC) Scales

Reading, 252; level, 177–179; limitations, 18; proficiencies, 177; responses, 257; skills, 241; test takers and, 178

Relationship Liability, 73

Reports, 229; computer-generated, 191–192, 203–206, 208, 214, 218–219, 229–233, 240

Repression (R), 99

Responding, 150; content-based, 133, 136, 162–165; invalid, 133–134, 136, 160–162, 162–165, 167–172; keyed, 277; non-content-based, 133–134, 135, 160–162, 167–172; recording, 135, 175, 179, 480n1; stereotypic, 135. See also Fixed responding; Random responding

Response % statistics, 160, 172, 254, 257, 263, 271, 341, 379

Response Bias (RBS) Scale, 162, 166, 168, 169, 171, 192, 214, 246, 249, 255, 259, 263, 266, 268, 292, 295, 445, 458; described, 163–164; interpretation of, 250 (table); as MMPI-2 measure, 170

Response styles, 30, 43, 135, 181

Restandardization Committee, 21, 23, 25, 28, 29, 44, 148, 473; Clinical Scales and, 39; makeup of, 20; test norms and, 36

Restandardization Project, 1, 21, 22, 52, 107, 148; goals of, 20, 23

Restructured Clinical (RC) Scales, xiii, 1, 37, 97, 98, 109, 131, 185 (fig.), 473, 474, 475, 476, 479n3; appraisals of, 92–96, 482n1;

comparison group findings on, 214; convergent validities of, 92; delineating constructs of, 52–92; development of, 1, 43–52; and externalizing scales, 302–312; homogeneity of, 475; and H-O Scales, 102, 103; and Interest Scales, 123, 125; and Internalizing Scales, 297–302; interpretation of, 273 (fig.), 278, 279, 281–292, 382 (fig.), 394 (fig.), 401, 405 (fig.), 416 (fig.),428 (fig.), 439 (fig.), 450 (fig.), 462 (fig.), 469; and Interpretation Worksheet, 325, 328, 330 (fig.), 343 (fig.), 352, 358 (fig.); introduction of, 97; and PSY-5 Scales, 129; psychopathology and, 95; score report for, 192, 195 (fig.), 203, 204, 210 (fig.), 214, 235 (fig.); scores on, 83–84, 93, 171; and shortcomings of Clinical Scales, 39–43; and Specific Problems Scales, 106, 107, 112; and underreporting, 171; and Uniform T scores, 189; and unscorable responses, 167. *See individual scales*
Revision, 19–36; methods of, 21–22; participants in, 21–22
Rumination, 113, 341, 389, 411, 422, 434, 457; obsessive, 299, 340, 400, 445

SAV Scale. *See* Social Avoidance (SAV) Scale
Scale 1. *See* Hypochondriasis (Hs) Scale
Scale 2. *See* Depression (D) Scale
Scale 3. *See* Hysteria (Hy) Scale
Scale 4. *See* Psychopathic deviate (Pd) Scale
Scale 5. *See* Masculinity/Femininity (Mf) Scale
Scale 6. *See* Paranoia (Pa) Scale
Scale 7. *See* Psychasthenia (Pt) Scale
Scale 8. *See* Schizophrenia (Sc) Scale
Scale 9. *See* Hypomania (Ma) Scale
Scale 0. *See* Social Introversion (Si) Scale
Scale length, scale reliability and, 33
Schedule for Nonadaptive and Adaptive Personality (SNAP), 55, 64, 87
Schizoaffective Disorder, 341, 353, 354
Schizoid Personality Disorder, 121, 122, 310
Schizophrenia, 2, 54, 78, 84, 85, 86, 89, 100, 105, 118, 141, 142, 144, 145, 168, 171, 284, 341; anhedonia and, 61, 63, 64; depression and, 65; Paranoid Type, 353, 366, 377, 458
Schizophrenia (Sc) Scale, 39, 40, 101, 102, 110, 146, 480n4; demoralization and, 49; restructured version of, 51, 52
Schizophreniform Disorder, 459
Schizotypal Personality Disorder, 87
Schizotypy, 61, 314

Scorable responses, 160, 203, 233, 255, 256, 257, 341, 379, 457
Scoring: algorithms, 191; computerized, 190–191, 203, 254; configural, 18, 19; errors, 141, 147, 191; hand, 190–191, 203, 257; interpretation and, 9; procedures, 75; software for, 183, 191, 240
Seed Scales, 15, 50–51, 95, 106, 107, 108, 123
Seizures, 59, 94, 110
Self-Alienation (Pd5) subscale, 43
Self-concept, 136, 137, 365
Self-disparaging, 116, 299, 340, 411, 457
Self-doubt, 113, 114, 116, 340, 364, 389, 457, 458
Self-Doubt (SFD) Scale, 112, 115, 282, 297, 310, 328, 365; described, 299; interpretation of, 299, 300 (table); scores, 116, 299
Self-esteem, 47, 55, 56, 61, 116, 299, 422, 434; depression and, 113; low, 113, 120, 341, 364, 365, 366, 411; self-efficacy and, 113
Self-harm, 112, 282, 339, 400, 401; risk for, 341, 364
Self-presentation, 3, 252, 259, 269, 402, 413
Self-report, 45, 53, 100, 135, 269–270, 401, 475; activation, 469; criteria, 31; inventories, 1, 44, 98, 137, 178; measures, 6, 46, 47, 112, 113, 138, 178, 282, 289; skewed, 136–137; subjective, 136
SEM. *See* Standard errors of measurement (SEM)
Sensation seeking, 91, 305, 353, 379
Sensory problems, 111, 367, 422, 457, 458
SES. *See* Socioeconomic status
Sexual dysfunction, 110–111, 422, 425, 445, 457
SFD Scale. *See* Self-Doubt (SFD) Scale
Shyness (SHY) Scale, 115, 121, 122, 286, 295, 307, 365, 469; described, 310; interpretation of, 310, 311 (table); scores, 123, 310
68–86 code type, 102, 103, 106
Sleep difficulties, 59, 110, 299, 367, 400, 401, 422, 425, 457
SNAP. *See* Schedule for Nonadaptive and Adaptive Personality (SNAP)
Social anhedonia, 63, 85
Social anxiety, 77, 310, 365, 411, 469
Social Anxiety Disorder, 121
Social Avoidance (SAV) Scale, 112, 122, 214, 286, 307, 341, 352, 411, 412, 422; described, 310; interpretation of, 310, 311 (table); scores, 123, 310

Social desirability, 13, 14, 30–31, 95, 135

Social Desirability (Sd) Scale, 164

Social Deviance, 74

Social fears, 115, 123

Social Introversion (Si) Scale, 4, 52, 62, 106, 189, 473, 479n3; demoralization and, 50

Social Phobia, 62, 81, 115, 121, 310, 364, 365, 411, 445

Social Potency, 90, 123, 130

Social situations, 122, 310, 411, 434

Social support, 70, 402, 411, 412

Socioeconomic status: and CHD, 68; of norms, 28

Sociopaths, 17, 71, 101

Somatic/Cognitive Dysfunction, 229, 232, 292, 319–320, 339, 352

Somatic/Cognitive Scales, 186 (fig.), 196 (fig.), 203, 211 (fig.), 236 (fig.), 293, 331 (fig.), 339, 344 (fig.), 359 (fig.), 371 (fig.), 383 (fig.), 395 (fig.), 406 (fig.), 417 (fig.), 429 (fig.), 440 (fig.), 451 (fig.), 463 (fig.); constructs of, 109–111; described, 292

Somatic complaints, 60, 70, 110, 111, 231, 246, 263, 422, 423, 445, 457, 458; overreporting, 170–171, 192; psychological component of, 425

Somatic Complaints (RC1) Scale, 70, 102, 106, 109, 111, 167, 171, 247, 248, 277, 281, 293, 328, 339; conceptualizing, 56–58; described, 282–283; empirical findings on, 58–59; interpretation of, 283, 284 (table); psychometric properties of, 94; scores, 59, 60, 282, 283, 377

Somatic delusions, 60, 173, 247, 266, 367

Somatic Depression, 111

Somatic Responses (Fs) Scale, 162, 163, 164, 166, 168, 169, 170, 173, 214, 248–249, 255, 259, 263, 266, 267, 268, 274, 292

Somatic Scales, 110, 247, 248, 292, 293, 295

Somatic Symptom Disorders, 57, 58

Somatic symptoms, 59, 110, 163, 170, 246, 264, 283; overreporting, 168, 171, 264, 268, 343, 377, 391; reporting, 249, 266

Somatization, 57, 58, 59, 60, 94, 100, 101, 104, 106, 110

Somatoform Disorders, 9, 56, 57, 58, 59, 60, 110, 111, 137, 173, 247, 261, 266, 282, 292, 295, 339, 364, 377, 389, 400, 422, 423, 434, 435, 446, 458; Clinical Scales and, 109

SP. See Specific Problems (SP) Scales

Spearman–Brown formula, 33

Specific Problems (SP) Scales, 58, 97, 106–126, 203, 278, 279, 281, 283, 286, 287, 288, 289,

292, 292–293, 295, 297, 299, 302, 304–305, 307, 310, 312–313, 328, 365, 412, 475; development of, 107–108; organization of, 109–125

S Scale. See Superlative Self-Presentation (S) Scale

Standard deviations, 4, 183, 208, 214, 218

Standard errors of measurement (SEM), 115, 119, 122, 125, 129, 165, 166

Standard instructions, 168, 175, 180

Standard scores, 22; derivation of, 175, 183; raw scores and, 181

Standards for Educational and Psychological Testing, 180, 232

State Social Paranoia Scale, 77

Stereotypes, 125, 135, 136, 259

Stress, 56, 81, 364, 400, 445; reactive, 299, 457

Stress/Worry (STW) Scale, 113, 288, 297, 328; described, 299; interpretation of, 299, 301 (table); scale, 114, 115, 116, 365, 379, 446, 457

Strong Engagement/Disengagement (SD), 47

Strong Vocational Interest Blank (SVIB), 3,124

Structured Clinical Interview, 59

Structured Interview of Reported Symptoms (SIRS), 169

Structure of Personality, search for, 98–100

STW Scale. See Stress/Worry (STW) Scale

Subjective Distress, 101

SUB Scale. See Substance Abuse (SUB) Scale

Substance abuse, 42, 64, 69, 70, 72, 73, 91, 104, 105, 106, 119, 120, 304, 307, 379, 389, 391, 402, 411; assessing, 118; risk for, 305; symptoms, 401; treatment for, 22, 74, 75, 78, 117, 129, 130, 390

Substance Abuse (SUB) Scale, 117, 118, 119, 204, 282, 287, 290, 302, 307; described, 304–305; interpretation of, 305, 306 (table)

Substance Use Disorders, 73

Subtle/obvious subscales. See Wiener–Harmon Subtle and Obvious subscales

Suicidal/Death Ideation (SUI) Scale, 112, 115, 203, 204, 205, 256–257, 282, 328, 352, 365; described, 297; interpretation of, 297, 298 (table); scores, 214, 297

Suicidal ideation, 55, 56, 100, 107, 112, 115, 116, 123, 130, 131, 219, 325, 400

Suicide, 64, 71, 106; risk for, 54, 112, 205, 214, 231, 353

Suicide attempts, 55, 56, 105, 112, 115, 123, 218, 340, 353, 364; family problems and, 121

Superlative Self-Presentation (S) Scale, 26,

148, 153, 157, 159, 164, 165; described, 155–156

Supplementary Manual for the MMPI (Hathaway and McKinley), 146

Supplementary Scales, 5, 20, 23, 150, 182, 189; described, 26–27

Symptomatology, 61, 94, 121

Symptom Checklist 90–Revised, Somatization Scale of, 59

Symptoms, 45; overreporting, 162, 166, 246, 261, 263, 267, 268

Symptom Validity (FBS) Scale, 162, 163, 166; described, 157–159; development of, 148

Symptom Validity (FBS-r) Scale, revised, 164, 166, 168, 169, 171, 192, 214, 246, 250, 263, 266, 267, 268, 292, 295, 341, 352, 458; described, 163, 247–248; interpretation of, 249 (table); scores, 170, 249; T scores, 401

Symptom validity tests (SVTs), 169

Syndromes, assessment of, 95

TBI. *See* Traumatic brain injury (TBI)

Test of Memory Malingering (TOMM), 164, 170

Test–retest correlations, 16, 110, 119, 125

Test–Retest (TR) Scale, 150, 152

Tests: achievement, 257; administering, 178, 179, 180–181; cognitive, 158, 425, 436; gendered, 183; intelligence, 459; physical disabilities and, 176; privacy with, 176; projective, 3; psychological, 9, 18, 27, 219; reading ability, 178; results, 133, 154, 319

Test takers, 22, 34, 137, 183, 206, 252, 257, 267; age of, 175–176; assessibility of, 176–179; overreporting by, 263; psychological adjustment of, 272; reading and, 177, 178; supervising, 180–181; uncooperative/ defensive, 134, 242; validity indicators and, 180

THD. *See* Thought Dysfunction (THD) Scale

Thought Disorders, 87, 230, 231, 261, 367, 457, 458

Thought Dysfunction (THD) Scale, 84, 101–102, 103, 106, 229, 314, 319, 328, 339, 352, 401, 469; described, 105, 279; interpretation of, 280 (table)

Three-factor model, 72–73

TOMM. *See* Test of Memory Malingering (TOMM)

TR. *See* Test–Retest (TR) Scale

Traumatic brain injury (TBI), 94, 169

Treatment Considerations, 222–223 (fig.), 278, 319, 320, 482n1, 482n2; described, 230–231

Treatment planning, 180, 231, 278, 341, 354

TRIN-r Scale. *See* True Response Inconsistency (TRIN-r) Scale, revised

TRIN Scale. *See* True Response Inconsistency (TRIN) Scale

TRT Scale. *See* Negative Treatment Indicators (TRT) Scale

True–false, 134, 151, 178, 179, 180, 242, 259

True Response Inconsistency (TRIN) Scale, 24, 25, 37, 148, 150–153, 156, 159, 161, 166, 480n5; VRIN and, 151, 152–153, 154, 160

True Response Inconsistency (TRIN-r) Scale, revised, 165, 166, 167, 172, 190, 192, 214, 218, 240, 255, 259, 263, 264, 268, 271, 274, 284, 401, 481n1, 481n3; constructing, 160; criteria for, 160–161; described, 243–244; interpretation of, 244 (table); scores, 273; variance, 161–162; VRIN-r and, 160–162

T scores, 4, 6, 17, 23, 78, 104, 110, 115, 119, 122, 125, 129, 142, 146, 147, 148, 149, 150, 154, 157, 165, 167, 178, 204, 206, 208, 214, 218, 240, 242, 243, 244, 246–250, 252, 255, 257, 258, 259, 263, 264, 267, 268, 271, 272–273; converting to, 181; cutoff for, 205; deflated, 28; distribution of, 183, 189; by domain, 199 (fig.), 203, 334 (fig.), 347 (fig.), 362 (fig.), 374 (fig.), 386 (fig.), 398 (fig.), 409 (fig.), 420 (fig.), 432–433 (fig.), 443 (fig.), 454 (fig.), 466 (fig.); examination of, 138, 139–140; gendered, 182; high, 43; interpretation of, 35; linear, 28, 183, 189, 192; original, 34. *See also* Uniform T scores

27–72 code type, 102, 103, 106

Type A Behavior, 20, 24, 66, 68

Type B Behavior, 66

Uncommon Virtues (L-r) Scale, 192, 214, 259, 271, 274, 277, 325, 378, 412, 423, 458; described, 164, 250–251; interpretation of, 251 (table); L Scale and, 166; scores, 171, 173, 251, 265; T scores, 377, 411, 458

Underreporting, 136, 144, 145, 157, 165, 166, 171–172, 173, 174, 192, 219, 251, 252, 253, 269–274, 282, 325, 377, 379, 391, 411, 422, 423, 425, 457, 469; circumscribed pattern of, 304; concerns about, 243; described, 137; indicators of, 164, 171, 258, 259, 273, 412; intentional, 137, 159, 270, 271, 274; K and, 147; measure of, 143; meta-analysis of, 172; overreporting and, 270–271, 458; possibility of, 259, 265; unintentional, 137, 159, 271

Uniform T scores, 28, 189, 192, 203; deriving,

190 (fig.); function of, 34; percentile equivalents of, 191 (fig.)

University of Minnesota Hospital, 3, 20

University of Minnesota Press, 20, 25, 153, 158–159

Unscorable Responses, 167, 219, 255, 257; described, 204, 233, 240

Validity Scales, 3, 5, 20, 22–26, 31, 34, 37, 131, 137–139, 147, 148, 151, 153, 156, 159–174, 178, 180, 184 (fig.), 189, 192, 194 (fig.), 209 (fig.), 214, 219, 229, 230, 233, 234 (fig.), 240, 256 (fig.), 257, 258 (fig.), 260 (fig.), 261 (fig.), 262 (fig.), 264 (fig.), 265 (fig.), 266 (fig.), 267 (fig.), 269 (fig.), 270 (fig.), 272 (fig.), 275 (fig.), 276 (fig.), 277, 282, 292, 304, 319, 320, 327 (fig.), 329 (fig.), 340, 341, 342 (fig.), 354, 355, 357 (fig.), 369 (fig.), 379, 381 (fig.), 393 (fig.), 400, 402, 404 (fig.), 415 (fig.), 423, 425, 427 (fig.), 438 (fig.), 446, 449 (fig.), 461 (fig.), 473, 475, 480n7; adding, 97–98; construction of, 13–14; described, 8–9, 24, 148–159; findings with, 252–274; interpretation of, 241–244, 246–252, 325; *MMPI-2 Manuals* and, 150, 153–156; PAI, 170; profiles, 25–26, 156–157, 273–274; protocol validity and, 133; Protocol Validity/Confounds and, 255 (table); psychometric findings with, 165–172; scores on, 341, 352, 377, 401, 434, 445, 457, 458, 469

Variable Response Inconsistency (VRIN) Scale, 24, 25, 37, 148, 150–153, 159, 166, 480n5; interpretive recommendations for, 156; scale, 480n5; TRIN and, 151, 152–153, 154, 160

Variable Response Inconsistency (VRIN-r)

Scale, revised, 165, 166, 167, 172, 178, 190, 192, 218, 240, 254, 255, 258, 259, 263, 264, 268, 271, 274, 401, 481n1; constructing, 160; criteria for, 160–161; described, 242–243; interpretation of, 243 (table); scores, 214, 257, 273; TRIN-r and, 160–162; T score on, 214

Verbal Comprehension, 279

Violence, 74, 105, 353, 366, 379; aggression and, 114; domestic, 90, 119; interpersonal, 118

VRIN-r Scale. *See* Variable Response Inconsistency (VRIN-r) Scale, revised

VRIN Scale. *See* Variable Response Inconsistency (VRIN) Scale

WAIS-V. *See* Wechsler Adult Intelligence Scale–Fourth Edition (WAIS-IV)

Wechsler Adult Intelligence Scale–Fourth Edition (WAIS-IV), 279

Welsh Factor Scales, 6–7

Western Collaborative Group Study (WCGS), 66

"Where Have We Gone Wrong? The Mystery of the Missing Progress" (Hathaway), 11

Wiener–Harmon Subtle and Obvious subscales, 6, 25, 41

Wiggins Content Scales, 7–8, 36

WMT. *See* Word Memory Test (WMT)

Woodworth Psychoneurotic Inventory, 138

Word Memory Test (WMT), 163, 170

Working Memory, 279

Work Interference (WRK) Scale, 476

Worry, 445; excessive, 341, 364, 400; obsessive, 105; proneness to, 457; rumination and, 113

WRK. *See* Work Interference (WRK) Scale

Index of Names

Arbisi, Paul, 108, 476, 480n6; AXY scores and, 116–117; Clinical Scales and, 39; demoralization and, 55; FBS and, 158; F_p Scale and, 25, 148, 153, 154, 155, 162; Fp-r Scale and, 162; F-r Scale and, 162; F Scale and, 162; Fs Scale and, 163; Personality Psychopathology Five Scales and, 128; RC1 and, 59; RC2 and, 64; RC4 and, 73, 74; RC6 and, 77, 78; RC7 and, 83; RC8 and, 86; RC9 and, 90; Restructured Clinical Scales and, 1, 87, 189, 473; social desirability and, 31; Somatic Symptom Domain and, 163, 168

Archer, R. P., 59, 175; Inconsistency Scales and, 93, 153, 166, 167; MMPI-2 and, 27; RC1 and, 59; RC2 and, 64; RC3 and, 69; RC4 and, 74; RC6 and, 77, 78; RC7 and, 83; RC8 and, 86; RC9 and, 90; RCd and, 55, 56; reading level and, 177; Superlative Self-Presentation Scale and, 156; T scores and, 175

Bagby, R. M.: Bipolar Disorder and Major Depression and, 120; F_p Scale and, 155; F-r Scale and, 162; overreporting and, 168, 169; Personality Psychopathology Five Scales and, 127, 128; RC2 and, 62, 64; RC3 and, 69; RC4 and, 74; RC6 and, 102; RC7 and, 81; RC8 and, 102; RC9 and, 90, 91; RCd and, 55, 56–62; Superlative Self-Presentation Scale and, 156; underreporting and, 164, 171–172; validity indicators and, 180

Ball, H.: F scores and, 151; TR Scale and, 150

Bandura, A., 113

Barlow, K.: Bipolar Disorder and, 89; Depressive Disorder and, 62

Barron, F., 475

Beck, A. T.: self-esteem and, 113; suicide and, 112

Ben-Porath, Yossef: AAS and, 26; administration by booklet and computer, 179; appraisals of RF and, 475, 476; COG and, 111; Content Component scales and, 26; demoralization and, 56, 62; Externalizing Specific Problems Scales and, 119; FBS and, 148, 158, 159; FML Scale and, 122; F_p Scale and, 148, 153, 154, 155, 162; Fp-r Scale and, 162; F-r Scale and, 162; Fs Scale and, 163; Galton–Pearson correlational technique, 98; H-O Scales and, 102, 104; Inconsistency Scales and, 160, 166, 167, 186; Interest Scales and, 125; Internalizing Specific Problems Scales and, 115; Interpersonal Scales, and, 122; K correction and, 146; MMPI-2 items, revised, and, 22; nongendered norms and, 182–183; normative data and, 182; overreporting and, 168, 169; Personality Psychopathology Five Scales and, 26, 127, 128, 129; RC1 and, 60; RC2 and, 74; RC3 and, 70; RC4 and, 74; RC6 and, 78; RC7 and, 84; RC8 and, 86, 87; RC9 and, 90, 91; reading level and, 177; Response Bias Scale and, 162; Restructured Clinical Scales and, 16, 102, 473; score report and, 191–218; social desirability and, 31; Somatic/Cognitive Scales, 110, 163; standard scores and, 183, 189–190; subtle items, and, 41; SUI and, 115; test–retest coefficients and, 122; unscorable item responses and, 167; validity of protocol and, 133

Bernreuter, R. J.: Psychoneurotic Inventory, 1

Berry, D. T. R., 153; ADHD and, 169; Fp-r and, 169; F-r and, 169; overreporting and, 168; S and, 156

Bianchini, K. J., 170; FBS and, 158

Blanchard, J. L.: anhedonia and, 63; Schizophrenia and, 63

Block, J.: response style and, 9, 14, 31, 136

Briquet, Paul, 56, 57

Brown, S. A., 64, 77, 94; Depressive Disorder and, 62; Schizophrenia and, 63; self-esteem and, 113; suicide and, 112

Buechley, R.: F Scale scores and, 151; TR Scale and, 150

Burchett, D. L., 168; overreporting and, 168; RC1 and, 69; RC3 and, 69; RC4 and, 74; RC9 and, 90; RCd and, 55

Burke, J. D., 69; Conduct Disorder and, 117; self-esteem/self-efficacy and, 113

Butcher, James, 98; AAS and, 26, 118; Content Scales and, 23, 24, 25, 31, 189; critical items and, 7; FBS and, 158; interest scales and, 123; IRT and, 127; item pool and, 1, 7; Lexile values and, 177; L Scale and, 149; MAC Scale and, 26–27; malingering and, 174; MDS and, 26; MMPI-A and, 175; MMPI-2 and, 20–25; MMPI-2-RF, appraisal of, 475–476; nongendered norms and, 182; Personality Psychopathology Five Scales and, 127; RC3 and, 96; reading level and, 177; Restructured Clinical Scales and, 96, 123; revision of original MMPI and, 19, 20, 21, 22; SES of MMPI-2 norms and, 28; subtle items, and, 41; Superlative Self-Presentation Scale and, 26, 148, 155–156, 164; Uniform T scores and, 189; Validity Scales and, 148, 150, 153

Caldwell, A.: critical item list, 7

Cattell, R. B.: dimensional simplification approach of, 44; 16PF and, 43, 99, 127

Chapman, Jean, 78, 91; anhedonia and, 63; HYP and, 118; psychosis-proneness scales and, 86; schizotypy and, 85

Chapman, Loren, 78, 91; anhedonia and, 63; HYP and, 118; psychosis-proneness scales and, 86; schizotypy and, 85

Charcot, Jean-Martin, 56

Clark, L. A.: FFM by, 73; NA and, 80, 81, 82; Negative Temperament and, 83; PCL-R and, 73; RC7 and, 83; RCd and, 5; SNAP and, 87

Clark, M. E.: Content Component Scales and, 26

Clarke, D. M.: anhedonia and, 53; demoralization and, 54

Cleckley, H.: psychopathy and, 71, 126

Combs, D. R.: RC8 and, 84, 85

Constantinople, A., 124; Interest Scales and, 125

Cook, W. W.: Ho (Cook–Medley) Scale and, 27, 65, 66, 67, 68, 70, 475

Cooke, D. J.: antisocial behavior and, 72; FFM by, 73; PCL-R and, 72, 73; three-factor model and, 72–73

Cronbach, L. J., 9

Cumella, E.: FBS and, 158; RC3 and, 96

Dahlstrom, L. E.: L Scale score and, 140; reading level and, 177; Validity Scales and, 139, 148

Dahlstrom, W. Grant, 9; F Scale score and, 142; Gender Role Scales and, 124; Ho Scale and, 167; item pool and, 178; K correction and, 146; L Scale score and, 140; malingering and, 173; MMPI-2 and, 1, 3, 10, 19, 20, 21; reading level and, 177; TR index and, 151; T scores and, 147; Validity Scales and, 139, 148

Dionysus, K. E.: RBS and, 170

Dohrenwend, B. P., 46, 53

Duker, J.: code types and, 5

Eckblad, M., 78, 91; HYP and, 118; MIS and, 85

Edwards, A. L., 9, 14, 31, 93

Elhai, J. D.: anhedonia and, 63; RC7 and, 83

Erbes, C. R., 128; AXY scores and, 117

Eysenck, H. J., 99, 126

Forbey, J. D., 74, 78, 87, 90, 91, 183; COG and, 111; nongendered norms and, 182; normative data and, 182; RC1 and, 59; RC2 and, 64; RC3 and, 69; RC7 and, 83; RCd and, 55

Fordyce, W., 109

Frank, Jerome: demoralization and, 45, 46, 47, 53, 54, 55, 56, 61

Freeman, D. B.: overreporting and, 168; paranoia and, 77; persecutory delusions and, 76, 77

Freud, Sigmund, 56, 79

Galton, Francis, 98

Gard, D. E.: RC2 and, 64–65; Temporal Experience of Pleasure Scale and, 63

Gard, M. G.: Temporal Experience of Pleasure Scale and, 63

Garety, P. A.: paranoia and, 76, 77

Gass, L., 158, 162

Gervais, R.O., 158; COG and, 111; overreporting and, 169; RBS and, 162, 163, 170

Gilberstadt, H.: code types and, 5

Goldberg, L. R: configural scoring and, 9, 18, 19; MMPI and, 11; Personality Data Sheet, 98

Gottesman, Irving: on MMPI–MMPI-2 debate, 27; RC4 and, 75

Gough, H. G., 4, 5, 173; CPI and, 99, 124

Graham, John, 108; CNS and, 139; code

types and, 29, 42; Content Scales and, 23, 24, 25; FBS and, 159; item pool and, 1; K Correction and, 146; MAC-R and, 475; malingering and, 173; MMPI-2-RF, appraisal of, 476; Personality Psychopathology Five Scales and, 26, 127, 128; RC1 and, 59; RC2 and, 64; RC4 and, 74; RC7 and, 83; RC8 and, 86; RC9 and, 90; RCd and, 55; revision of original MMPI and, 21, 22, 23; social desirability and, 31; T scores and, 28; Validity Scales and, 148

Gray, J. A.: Behavioral Activation and, 79; BIS and, 79, 82, 83, 84, 128

Grayson, H. M.: critical item lists and, 7

Green, C., 63, 77

Green, D. P.: Pleasant/Unpleasant two-factor mood model and, 80

Green, P.: MCI and, 169; MSTV and, 170; RBS and, 162, 163; WMT and, 170

Greene, R. L., 26, 139, 173; K correction and, 146; MMPI-2-RF, appraisal of, 475; suicide and, 112

Han, K.: Superlative Self-Presentation Scale and, 148, 155, 156

Handel, R. W., 93, 153, 156; COG and, 111; data sets by, 166; psychopathology and, 27; random/fixed responding and, 167; RC1 and, 59; RC2 and, 64; RC3 and, 69; RC4 and, 74; RC6 and, 78; RC7 and, 83; RC8 and, 86; RC9 and, 90; RCd and, 55, 56; unscorable item responses and, 167

Hare, R. D.: antisocial behavior and, 72; four-factor model by, 72; PCL-R and, 96; PCL-SV and, 74, 96; psychopathy/ASPD and, 71

Harkness, A. R.: Personality Psychopathology Five Scales, 26, 81, 126, 127, 129, 278, 315

Harmon, L. R., 6, 25

Harris, R.: Harris–Lingoes subscales, 7

Hart, S. D.: antisocial behavior and, 72; FFM by, 73; PCL-R and, 73; PCL-SV and, 74

Hartshorne, H., 139

Hathaway, Starke, xiii, 19, 91; Clinical Scales and, 3, 35, 41, 145; content-based groupings and, 13; F-r Scale and, 162; F Scale and, 140, 141, 153, 244; demoralization and, 47; faking study and, 143, 173; gender differences and, 181; Interest Scales and, 124; item pool and, 1, 125; K Correction and, 142, 145, 146, 147; on known groups, 144; K Scale

and, 142, 143, 145, 146, 148; L Scale score and, 139, 140, 143, 149; L_6 items and, 144; MMPI, appraisals of, 4, 10–11, 30, 177; nongendered norms and, 181; nonresponding and, 160; on objective personality tests, 18; overreporting and, 141, 156; protocol validity and, 142; Question (CNS) Score and, 138; reading level, and 177; T scores and, 138, 140, 142; test–retest reliability and, 16; underreporting and, 164; Validity Scale Scores and, 137–142, 143–148

Heilbronner, R. L.: overreporting and, 168; RBS and, 170; RC1 scores and, 60

Helmes, E.: Clinical Scales, criticisms of, 29–36, 37, 92–93

Heymans, G., 98, 99, 102

Hippocrates, 56, 76

Hoeglund, T.: nongendered norms and, 182; RC Scales and, 123

Horan, W. P.: anhedonia and, 63; psychosis-proneness scales and, 86; Schizophrenia and, 63

Humm, D. G.: Humm–Wadsworth Temperament Scale, 1

Iacono, W. G., 72, 81, 101; dysfunctional negative emotions and, 82; self-esteem and, 113

Jackson, Douglas, 9, 101, 136; bootstrapping and, 13; BPI and, 31; Clinical Scales, criticisms of, 11, 13–15, 19, 21, 29, 30, 37, 41–44, 45, 51, 92, 93, 95; code types and, 14; on criterion keying, 18; Maslach Burnout Inventory and, 68; reading level and, 177

Janet, Piere, 56

Joiner, T. E., 94; demoralization and, 62; suicide and, 112

Kaemmer, Beverly, 1, 20, 25, 39, 97, 148, 176, 177, 189

Kahlbaum, Karl: on paranoia, 76

Katz, M. M.: Adjustment Scale and, 21

Keane, T. M., 64, 82, 101, 174; Personality Psychopathology Five Scales and, 128; PTSD and, 25, 114

Kissane, D. W.: anhedonia and, 53; demoralization and, 54

Klein, D. F.: depression and, 61–63

Koss, M.: critical item list, 7

Kraepelin, E., 2, 84, 87, 88, 89, 90

Kring, A. M.: anhedonia and, 61, 63; Temporal Experience of Pleasure Scale and, 63

Krueger, R. F., 100–101; disinhibitory personality traits and, 73; NEM and, 81–82; PCL-R and, 82; on triarchic conceptualization, 72

Lachar, D.: critical item list, 7

Lamberty, G., 57, 137; somatoform conditions and, 58; unexplained paralyses and, 60; wandering uterus and, 56

Lee, S., 66; assertiveness training and, 121; COG and, 111; self-esteem/self-efficacy and, 113

Lees-Haley, P. R., 27; FBS and, 148, 157–158, 174

Lepore, S. J.: cynicism and, 68, 70

Lilienfeld, S., 74

Lingoes, J.: Harris–Lingoes subscales, 7

Locke, D. E. C.: NUC and, 111; RC1 and, 59–60, 94, 111

Loevinger, Jane, 43, 51, 53; Clinical Scales, criticisms of, 15, 19, 29, 30, 35, 37, 92, 93; revising original MMPI and, 11–12, 13, 21

Lyerly, S. B.: adjustment scale and, 21

Lykken, D. T.: on antisocial personalities, 71; psychopathy and, 71

MacAndrew, C., 475

Maher, B. A.: paranoia and, 76; persecutory delusions and, 76

Marks, P., 7

McCord, D. M.: RC Scales and, 94; RC2 and, 64; RC3 and, 69; RCd and, 55

McKinley, J. C., 91, 183; Clinical Scales and, 3, 12, 35, 41; criterion keying and, 47; F-r Scale and, 162, 244; F Scale and, 140, 141, 153, 244; gendered norms and, 181; Interest Scales and, 124; item pool and, 1, 8, 125; K Correction and, 145, 146; K Scale and, 14, 148; L Scale score and, 139, 140, 149; MMPI, development of, 3–4, 177; nonresponding and, 160; on objective personality tests, 18; Question Score and, 138; scale construction method of, 2; T scores and, 138, 140, 142; underreporting and, 173; Validity Score and, 137, 138, 140, 147

McNulty, J. L., 1, 25, 27, 34, 39, 42; FBS and, 158; F_p Scale and, 162; K correction and, 146; Personality Psychopathology Five Scales and, 26, 81, 126, 127, 129, 278, 315;

Restructured Clinical Scales and, 97, 476; social desirability and, 31

Medley, D. M.: Ho (Cook–Medley) Scale and, 27, 65, 66, 67, 68, 70, 475

Meehl, Paul, 9, 45; anhedonia and, 61–62; Clinical Scales and, 35, 36, 37, 43, 92, 93, 145; code types and, 4–5; construct validity and, 15; criterion keying and, 17; 92; demoralization and, 93; faking study and, 143, 173; F Scale score and, 141, 154, 156; Hypohedonia and, 61–62; interpretation and, 18; on known groups, 144; Kraepelinian nosology and, 30, 92; K Scale and, 142, 143, 145, 146, 148; on L Scale, 143; L_6 items and, 144; methodological considerations and, 43; neurosis/psychosis and, 102; overreporting and, 141, 156; projective testing and, 3; protocol validity, threats to, 137, 139, 142, 165, 173; psychopathology domains and, 101–102; revision of original MMPI and, 11, 14–19, 21, 29, 36, 43, 44, 92; on Scale 4, 17; schizotypy and, 85; self-report personality inventories and, 2–3; taxonomic variables and, 16; test–retest reliability and, 16; thought dysfunction and, 101; underreporting and, 143, 164, 165, 173; unscorable responses and, 139; Validity Scales and, 3, 8, 141–147

Messick, S.: Clinical Scales and, 31, 135; psychopathology and, 9; response styles and, 14, 136

Michie, C.: antisocial behavior and, 72; FFM by, 73; PCL-R and, 73; three-factor model and, 72–73

Miller, J.: underreporting and, 164, 172

Miller, M. W.: PSY-5 Scales and, 128; PTSD and, 82; RC7 and, 83

Monnot, M. J.: RC Scales and, 94; RC2 and, 64; RC4 and, 75; RC6 and, 78; RC7 and, 83; RC8 and, 86

Mueser, K. T.: RC8 and, 84, 85

Neumann, C. S.: antisocial behavior and, 72; psychopathy/ASPD and, 71

Nichols, D. S.: RC Scales and, 95

Norman, Warren: Clinical Scales, criticisms of, 12–13, 16, 19, 29, 30, 37, 51, 92

Patrick, C. J., 101; antisocial behavior and, 73; depression and, 40; on disinhibition, 72; PCL-R and, 82; RC4 and, 74; on triarchic conceptualization, 72

Pearson, Karl, 98
Polusny, M. A.: AXY scores and, 116–117; DISC/NEGE and, 128

Quilty, L. C., 120; RC9 and, 90

Reddon, J. R.: Clinical Scales, criticisms of, 29–36, 37, 92, 93
Regoli, B., 69
Regoli, R. M., 69
Ribot, T. H.: anhedonia and, 61
Rogers, R., 169; F_p Scale and, 155; Restructured Clinical Scales and, 95
Rose, R. J.: on RC Scales, 94
Rouse, S. V., 27, 96; IRT and, 127

Schlenger, W. E.: PTSD scale, 25
Schmidt, H. O., 4
Seeman, W., 7
Sellbom, M., 170, 476; demoralization and, 56, 62, 81; MPQ and, 55; overreporting and, 168, 169; RC1 and, 59, 60; RC2 and, 64; RC3 and, 69, 70; RC4 and, 74, 75, 96; RC6 and, 102; RC7 and, 83, 84; RC8 and, 86, 102; RC9 and, 90, 91; social desirability and, 31; underreporting and, 171–172
Sewell, K. W.: F_p Scale and, 155; Restructured Clinical Scales and, 95
Sherwood, N.: Content Component Scales, 26
Simms, L. J., 59, 91, 94; RC8 scores and, 87
Skinner, H. A., 101
Spielberger, C., 114
Strada, E. A.: on anhedonia, 54
Strong, E. K.: Vocational Interest Blank and, 3, 124
Sydenham, Thomas, 56

Tellegen, Auke, 20, 249; AES/MEC scores and, 125; Clinical Scales and, xiii, 37, 39–41, 43, 46, 48–50, 93, 95, 473; demoralization and, 45–48, 51; Externalizing Specific Problems Scales and, 117–120; FBS-r Scale and, 249; FML Scale and, 122; Fs Scale and, 249; Higher-Order Scales and, 98–105, 126; Inconsistency Scales (VRIN and TRIN) and, 24, 151–152, 160–162, 167; Interest Scales and, 106–109, 123–125; Internalizing Specific Problems Scales and, 111–117; Interpersonal Scales and, 120–123; K correction and, 146; MMPI-2 and, 1, 20, 25, 33; 34; MPQ and, 24, 44, 81, 83, 99, 127, 151; NA (Negative Affect, relabeled Negative Activation) and, 47–62, 79, 80,

81, 82; NEM (Negative Emotionality) and, 48, 51, 79, 81, 82, 83, 84, 99, 100, 102, 105, 112, 113, 114, 126; nongendered norms and, 182; Personality Psychopathology Five Scales and, 126–131; PA (Positive Affect, relabeled Positive Activation) and, 47–48, 62, 79, 80, 81, 126; PEM (Positive Emotionality) and, 105, 123, 127, 479n3; random/fixed responding, 167; RC1 and, 59–60; RC2 and, 60–65; RC3 and, 65–70; RC4 and, 70–75; RC6 and, 75–79; RC7 and, 79–84; RC8 and, 84–87; RC9 and, 87–91; RCd and, 53–56, 96; reading level and, 177; Restructured Clinical Scales and, xiii, 37, 39, 43–52, 60, 78, 87, 91, 92, 93, 94, 95, 102, 123, 473; Score report and, 191–218; Seed Scales and, 50–51, 106; SEM and, 115; social desirability and, 31; Somatic/Cognitive Scales and, 109–111; Specific Problems Scales and, 106–109; SUI and, 115; syndromal fidelity and, 95; test–retest coefficients and, 122; Uniform T Scores and, 23, 34, 183–190; Validity Scales and, 148
Thomas, M. L.: 60; overreporting and, 169; TBI and, 94
Timbrook, R. E., 25

Viken, R. J.: on RC Scales, 94

Wadsworth, G. W.: Humm–Wadsworth Temperament Scale, 1
Walker, E. F.: Schizophrenia and, 85
Walker, R. L.: demoralization and, 62; suicide and, 112
Waller, N. G.: MPQ and, 44, 99; Positive Emotionality and, 479n3
Watson, D., 84, 100; NA Scale and, 80, 81, 82; RC7 and, 79; RCd and, 55; two-factor structure and, 47, 80
Watson, L. C., 120; RC9 and, 90
Weed, N. C., 218; AAS and, 26; subtle items and, 41
Welsh, G. S.: A Scale and, 7, 36, 80, 99; development of MMPI and, 3; K Correction and, 146; L Scale score and, 140; malingering and, 173; MMPI research and appraisals of, 9, 10; R Scale and, 7, 36; T scores and, 147; unscorable responses and, 139
Wiener, D. N., 6, 25, 41
Wiersma, E., 98, 99, 102
Wiggins, J. S.: Content Scales and, 7, 8, 24;

EPI and, 99; Social Desirability Scale and, 164

Williams, C. L., 22, 23, 24, 476

Williams, J. E., 218

Williams, R. B., 66, 67

Wolf, E. J.: PTSD and, 75, 101; RC1 and, 59; RC2 and, 64; RC7 and, 83; RCd and, 55 and Restructured Clinical Scales, 93–94

Wrobel, N.: critical item list, 7

Wygant, D. B.: bariatric surgery candidates and, 78, COG and, 111; Fs Scale and, 163; overreporting and, 60, 168, 169; Personality Psychopathology Five Scales and, 128; RC7 and maladaptive eating behavior, 83; Validity Scales and malingering, 170

Youngjohn, J. R., 94, 169

Yossef S. Ben-Porath is professor of psychology at Kent State University. He received his doctoral training at the University of Minnesota and has been involved extensively in MMPI research for the past twenty-six years. He is a codeveloper of the MMPI-2-RF and a coauthor of test manuals and numerous books, book chapters, and articles on the MMPI. He serves as codirector of the MMPI Workshops and Symposia series and is a member of the editorial board of several psychology journals. His clinical practice involves consulting for agencies that screen candidates for public safety positions and conducting criminal court forensic psychological evaluations.